THE NEXT QUEST FOR THE HISTORICAL JESUS

THE
NEXT QUEST

FOR THE

HISTORICAL
JESUS

EDITED BY

JAMES CROSSLEY AND CHRIS KEITH

WILLIAM B. EERDMANS PUBLISHING COMPANY
GRAND RAPIDS, MICHIGAN

Wm. B. Eerdmans Publishing Co.
4035 Park East Court SE, Grand Rapids, Michigan 49546
www.eerdmans.com

Book design by Lydia Hall

Printed in the United States of America

30 29 28 27 26 25 24   1 2 3 4 5 6 7

ISBN 978-0-8028-8270-7

Library of Congress Cataloging-in-Publication Data

A catalog record for this book is available from the Library of Congress.

For Maurice Casey and Larry Hurtado

CONTENTS

PREFACE

James Crossley

This volume grew out of a series of discussions between the editors (see the introduction) and at virtual (July 11, 2022) and hybrid (July 15–16, 2022) conferences, the latter held in Bedford, UK. We are grateful for the support and sponsorship from the Centre for the Critical Study of Apocalyptic and Millenarian Movements (CenSAMM) at the Panacea Charitable Trust, the Enoch Seminar, and Eerdmans for helping make this possible. We are especially grateful to Joshua Scott for his remarkable work on live streaming and recording the events thereby making these discussions more widely accessible.

The introduction should give a sense of the unifying features of what we call the "Next Quest" for the historical Jesus. Certainly, different approaches to the quest remain, and the intellectual trajectories represented here can be traced back through any of the big names from the previous generations. But as the new grows out of the old, traditional approaches to studying the historical Jesus still exist alongside the more innovative approaches that have developed from them. To anticipate the introduction, what unifies the participants in this volume is a willingness to push beyond the well-worn debates and incorporate new or previously overlooked emphases.

In this spirit, the contributions collected in this volume function as blunt interventions that stress understudied ideas, themes, or approaches. While we have gone for a level of consistency in presentation and style, we have allowed some scope for flexibility. Where the subject matter is familiar in historical Jesus studies, we have not typically included extensive bibliography. (Is another epic footnote on who thinks what concerning Jesus and the kingdom of God *really* needed?) By the same token, we also accept that some of the contributors have been working on research that is unfamiliar to those in or around historical Jesus studies. And so, while there will be more bibliographical detail in certain chapters, we nevertheless hope that the contributions remain accessible to both an academic audience and those with a wider interest in this perennially popular subject.

There are plenty of issues we have not addressed in this volume. But we contend that this does not have to be seen as a weakness. One of the driving ideas behind this collection was to provoke others not directly involved in the Next Quest project to develop new approaches or revitalize old ones. As such, we hope this volume functions as a wider invitation for all interested scholars to push for something different in historical Jesus studies.

Unsurprisingly, any edited volume and accompanying project will reflect the agendas of the editors and organizers. This volume is no different, but (and I write strictly in a personal capacity here) it is regrettable that Chris Keith was not able to publish more in it as we intended because of circumstances not of his own choosing. Nevertheless, in addition to his editorial duties, Chris's influence on several chapters in this volume will be obvious to anyone familiar with the subject area. His work on memory and literacy alongside his debunking of the so-called criteria of authenticity has undeniably opened up possibilities for new emphases to emerge relating to the historical Jesus.

ABBREVIATIONS

ANCIENT SOURCES

Old Testament Apocrypha and Pseudepigrapha

2 Bar.	2 Baruch
1 En.	1 Enoch
4 Ezra	4 Ezra
LAB	Liber antiquitatum biblicarum (Pseudo-Philo)
LAE	Life of Adam and Eve
Liv. Pro.	Lives of the Prophets
2 Macc	2 Maccabees
4 Macc	4 Maccabees
Pss. Sol.	Psalms of Solomon
Sib. Or.	Sibylline Oracles
Sir	Sirach
T. Ab.	Testament of Abraham
T. Benj.	Testament of Benjamin
T. Dan	Testament of Dan
T. Mos.	Testament of Moses
Tob	Tobit

Dead Sea Scrolls

1QapGen	Genesis Apocryphon (1Q20)
1QHᵃ	Thanksgiving Hymns
1QM	War Scroll

Greco-Roman Sources

Aem.	Plutarch, *Aemilius Paullus*
Aeth.	Heliodorus, *Aethiopica*
Alex.	Plutarch, *Alexander*
Ann.	Tacitus, *Annales*
Cim.	Plutarch, *Cimon*
Claud.	Suetonius, *Divus Claudius*
Cohib. ira.	Plutarch, *De cohibenda ira*
De arte	Hippocrates, *De arte*
Demon.	Lucian, *Demonax*
Descr.	Pausanias, *Graeciae descriptio*
Eloc.	Demetrius, *De elocutione*
Ep.	Seneca, *Epistulae morales*
Epid.	Hippocrates, *Epidemiae*
Epig.	Martial, *Epigrammata*
Fam.	Cicero, *Epistulae ad familiares*
Geogr.	Strabo, *Geographica*
Hist. rom.	Dio Cassius, *Historia romana*
Inst.	Quintilian, *Institutio oratoria*
Metam.	Apuleius, *Metamorphoses*
Mir.	Phlegon of Tralles, *Mirabilia*
Morb.	Hippocrates, *Morb.*
Mul.	Hippocrates, *Mul.*
Od.	Homer, *Odyssey*
Or.	Dio Chrysostom, *Orationes*
Phar.	Lucan, *Pharsalia*
Sol.	Plutarch, *Solon*
Sp.	Martial, *Liber spectaculorum*
Steril.	Hippocrates, *De sterilitate*
Tib.	Suetonius, *Tiberius*
Vesp.	Suetonius, *Vespasianus*
Vict.	Hippocrates, *De victu*

Virt. prof.	Plutarch, *Quomodo quis suos in virtute sentiat profectus*
Vit. phil.	Diogenes Laertius, *Vitae philosophorum*

Early Jewish, Rabbinic, and Christian Sources

A.J.	Josephus, *Antiquitates judaicae*
An.	Tertullian, *De anima*
Apoc. Pet.	Revelation of Peter
1 Apol.	Justin, *1 Apologia*
2 Apol.	Justin, *2 Apologia*
b.	Babylonian Talmud
Ber.	Berakot
B.J.	Josephus, *Bellum judaicum*
B. Qam.	Baba Qamma
C. Ap.	Josephus, *Contra Apionem*
Cels.	Origen, *Contra Celsum*
Comm. Jo.	Origen, *Commentarii in evangelium Joannis*
Conf.	Augustine, *Confessionum libri XIII*
Decal.	Philo, *De decalogo*
Deo	Philo, *De Deo*
Dial.	Justin, *Dialogus cum Tryphone*
Doctr. chr.	Augustine, *De doctrina christiana*
Ep.	Augustine, *Epistulae*
Ep. Apos.	Epistle to the Apostles
Exp. Gal.	Augustine, *Expositio in epistulam ad Galatas*
Faust.	Augustine, *Contra Faustum Manichaeum*
Gen. Rab.	Genesis Rabbah
Gos. Pet.	Gospel of Peter
Gos. Thom.	Gospel of Thomas
Haer.	Irenaeus, *Adversus haereses*
Herm. Mand.	Shepherd of Hermas, Mandate(s)
Herm. Vis.	Shepherd of Hermas, Vision(s)
Hist. eccl.	Eusebius, *Historia ecclesiastica*
Hom. Luc.	Origen, *Homiliae in Lucam*
Hypoth.	Philo, *Hypothetica*
Lam. Rab.	Lamentations Rabbah
Legat.	Philo, *Legatio ad Gaium*
Lev. Rab.	Leviticus Rabbah
Marc.	Tertullian, *Adversus Marcionem*

Mos.	Philo, *De vita Mosis*
NHC	Nag Hammadi Corpus
Opif.	Philo, *De opificio mundi*
Pan.	Epiphanius, *Panarion*
Pelag.	Jerome, *Adversus Pelagianos dialogi III*
Princ.	Origen, *De principiis*
Prob.	Philo, *Quod omnis probus liber sit*
Ps.-Clem. *Hom.*	Pseudo-Clementine *Homilies*
Ps.-Clem. *Rec.*	Pseudo-Clementine *Recognitions*
QE	Philo, *Quaestiones et solutiones in Exodum*
Retract.	Augustine, *Retractationum libri II*
Šabb.	Šabbat
Somn.	Philo, *De somniis*
Spec.	Philo, *De specialibus*
Strom.	Clement of Alexandria, *Stromateis*
Tg. Isa.	Targum Isaiah
Tg. Neb.	Targum of the Prophets
Tg. Obad.	Targum Obadiah
Tg. Zech.	Targum Zechariah
Virt.	Philo, *De virtutibus*
Vita	Josephus, *Vita*
y.	Jerusalem Talmud

Secondary Sources

ABRL	Anchor Bible Reference Library
AGJU	Arbeiten zur Geschichte des antiken Judentums und des Urchristentums
AJEC	Ancient Judaism and Early Christianity
AJP	*American Journal of Philology*
AJSR	*Association for Jewish Studies Review*
ANF	*The Ante-Nicene Fathers.* Edited by Alexander Roberts and James Donaldson. 1885–1887. 10 vols. Repr., Peabody, MA: Hendrickson, 1994
ANRW	*Aufstieg und Niedergang der römischen Welt: Geschichte und Kultur Roms im Spiegel der neueren Forschung.* Part 2, *Principat.* Edited by Hildegard Temporini and Wolfgang Haase. Berlin: de Gruyter, 1972–
ASSB	Anders Runesson, Donald D. Binder, and Birger Olsson. *The Ancient Synagogue: From Its Origins to 200 CE: A Source Book.* AJEC 72. Leiden: Brill, 2008

AYBRL	Anchor Yale Bible Reference Library
BBB	Bonner biblische Beiträge
BCT	*Bible and Critical Theory*
BDF	Blass, Friedrich, Albert Debrunner, and Robert W. Funk. *A Greek Grammar of the New Testament and Other Early Christian Literature.* Chicago: University of Chicago Press, 1961
BECNT	Baker Exegetical Commentary on the New Testament
BibInt	*Biblical Interpretation*
BIS	Biblical Interpretation Series
BJRL	*Bulletin of the John Rylands University Library of Manchester*
BJS	Brown Judaic Studies
BMSEC	Baylor-Mohr Siebeck Studies in Early Christianity
BSR	*Bulletin for the Study of Religion*
BTB	*Biblical Theology Bulletin*
BZNW	Beihefte zur Zeitschrift für die neutestamentliche Wissenschaft
CBQ	*Catholic Biblical Quarterly*
CBR	*Currents in Biblical Research*
CEJL	Commentaries on Early Jewish Literature
ChLA	*Chartae latinae antiquiores: Fascimilie Edition of the Latin Charters.* Edited by A. Brucker and R. Marichal. 49 vols. Olten-Zurich: Graf, 1954–1998
CIJ	*Corpus Inscriptionum Judaicarum.* Edited by Jean-Baptiste Frey. 2 vols. Rome: Pontifical Biblical Institute, 1936–1952
CJ	*Classical Journal*
ClAnt	*Classical Antiquity*
ConBNT	Coniectanea Neotestamentica or Coniectanea Biblica: New Testament Series
ConBOT	Coniectanea Biblica: Old Testament Series
CPG	*Clavis Patrum Graecorum.* Edited by Maurice Geerard. 5 vols. Turnhout: Brepols, 1974–1987
CQ	*Church Quarterly*
DSD	*Dead Sea Discoveries*
EC	*Early Christianity*
EJL	Early Judaism and Its Literature
ETL	*Ephemerides Theologicae Lovanienses*
FGH	*Die Fragmente der griechischen Historiker.* Edited by Felix Jacoby. Leiden: Brill, 1954–1964
GR	*Greece and Rome*
GRA	*Greco-Roman Associations: Texts, Translations, and Commentary.*

	Edited by John S. Kloppenborg and Richard S. Ascough. 3 vols. BZNW 181, 204, 246. Berlin: de Gruyter, 2011, 2014, 2020
HistTh	History and Theory
HSM	Harvard Semitic Monographs
HTR	Harvard Theological Review
HTS	Harvard Theological Studies
HvTSt	Hervormde teologiese studies
IC	Inscriptiones Creticae. Edited by Margherita Guarducci. 4 vols. Rome: Libreria dello Stato, 1935–1950
JAJ	Journal of Ancient Judaism
JAJSup	Journal of Ancient Judaism Supplement Series
JANES	Journal of the Ancient Near Eastern Society
JBL	Journal of Biblical Literature
JBR	Journal of Bible and Religion
JECH	Journal of Early Christian History
JEH	Journal of Ecclesiastical History
JESHO	Journal of the Economic and Social History of the Orient
JHS	Journal of Hellenic Studies
JR	Journal of Religion
JSHJ	Journal for the Study of the Historical Jesus
JSJSup	Journal for the Study of Judaism Supplement Series
JSNT	Journal for the Study of the New Testament
JSOTSup	Journal for the Study of the Old Testament Supplement Series
JSSR	Journal for the Scientific Study of Religion
JTS	Journal of Theological Studies
LDAB	Leuven Database of Ancient Books
LHBOTS	The Library of Hebrew Bible/Old Testament Studies
MTSR	Method and Theory in the Study of Religion
Neot	Neotestamentica
NHMS	Nag Hammadi and Manichean Studies
NovTSup	Supplements to Novum Testamentum
NTAbh	Neutestamentliche Abhandlungen
NTS	New Testament Studies
OBO	Orbis Biblicus et Orientalis
PEQ	Palestine Exploration Quarterly
PG	Patrologia Graeca [= Patrologiae Cursus Completus: Series Graeca]. Edited by Jacques-Paul Migne. 162 vols. Paris, 1857–1886
PRSt	Perspectives in Religious Studies
R&T	Religion and Theology

RBS	Resources for Biblical Study
RC	*Religion Compass*
RelS	*Religious Studies*
RHR	*Revue de l'histoire des religions*
SB	*Sammelbuch griechischer Urkunden aus Aegypten.* Edited by Friedrich Preisigke et al. Vols. 1–21. Wiesbaden: Harrassowitz, 1915–2002
SBAB	Stuttgarter biblische Aufsatzbände
SBLDS	Society of Biblical Literature Dissertation Series
SBT	Studies in Biblical Theology
SC	Sources chrétiennes
SEÅ	*Svensk exegetisk årsbok*
SemeiaSt	Semeia Studies
SJT	*Scottish Journal of Theology*
SMSR	*Studi e materiali di storia delle religioni*
SR	*Studies in Religion*
StPatr	Studia Patristica
SUNT	Studien zur Umwelt des Neuen Testaments
TAPA	*Transactions of the American Philological Association*
TAPS	Transactions of the American Philosophical Society
TBN	Themes in Biblical Narrative
TENTS	Texts and Editions for New Testament Study
TJT	*Toronto Journal of Theology*
TSAJ	Texte und Studien zum antiken Judentum
WBC	Word Biblical Commentary
WMANT	Wissenschaftliche Monographien zum Alten und Neuen Testament
WUNT	Wissenschaftliche Untersuchungen zum Neuen Testament
ZNW	*Zeitschrift für die neutestamentliche Wissenschaft und die Kunde der älteren Kirche*
ZPE	*Zeitschrift für Papyrologie und Epigraphik*

THE NEXT QUEST

James Crossley

The "Next Quest" for the historical Jesus was a term coined by Chris Keith in 2021.[1] It came out of a series of discussions we both had about our different disillusionments with the mainstream quest and the repetition of questions and methods in major books on Jesus. But however disillusioned we were, we were not pessimistic about the future, not least because of the generational changes in the make-up of the field that have taken place since the peak of the popularity of historical Jesus studies in the 1980s and 1990s. Put crudely, the big names of yesteryear no longer dominate the study of New Testament and Christian origins, and a new and more diverse generation is coming to the fore. Thus, what we mean by "Next Quest" is not so much to add another number to add to the quests—the precise numbering of quests is a dubious enterprise anyway[2]—but to see what we can now do that has different emphases from what came before. The Next Quest is

---

1. I am grateful for the feedback of Chris Keith on this introduction. It is regrettable that this could not have been a cowritten piece for reasons outside of Chris's control (see the preface), but I hope readers will appreciate the Keithean influences contained herein.

2. See, e.g., Clive Marsh, "Quests of the Historical Jesus in New Historicist Perspective," *Bib-Int* 5 (1997): 403–37; Dale C. Allison Jr., *Resurrecting Jesus: The Earliest Christian Tradition and Its Interpreters* (London: Continuum, 2005), 1–26; Fernando Bermejo-Rubio, "The Fiction of the 'Three Quests': An Argument for Dismantling a Dubious Historiographical Paradigm," *JSHJ* 7 (2009): 211–53; Maurice Casey, *Jesus of Nazareth: An Independent Historian's Account of His Life and Teachings* (London: T&T Clark, 2010), 1–59.

also, then, an invitation for this greater diversity of voices to engage with the quest for the historical Jesus.

FOUNDATIONS

On the rubble of some failed enterprises, we can build something new in historical Jesus studies. It is helpful, then, to look at both old and new foundations. It is now especially clear that the era of the hard version of the criteria of authenticity is over, which generated only occasionally useful tools showing what sort of ideas about Jesus were present in the years before the gospels.[3] Instead, to frame the question in the style of Keith (see his chapter), the Next Quest should move beyond searching for an uninterpreted reality "behind" the texts and hypothesize the historical Jesus by means of the material, cultural, and historical processes by which images of Jesus were produced and transmitted. What this further means is that the Next Quest works from the ancient portrayals of Jesus to reconstruct imaginatively a historical Jesus whose reception history leads to those portrayals (see Moxnes's chapter), which will, of course, have to take seriously the importance of, and agendas associated with, the written text(s) (see, in different ways, the chapters by Bond, Rodríguez, and Walsh).

Nevertheless, we can still stress the importance of reconstructing the social world and themes associated with Jesus that were most likely present around the 20s and 30s in Galilee and Judea without always knowing what actually applies to the historical Jesus. Such early ideas and themes do not necessarily have to form a coherent belief system (though they may) and we may end up with some degree of chaos in stressing competing or contradictory ideas about Jesus that look early and were associated with his part of the world. Are we ultimately going to be in touch with the historical Jesus? We may never know, but reconstructing ideas present in Galilee and Judea around the time of Jesus tells us something about the social world of the historical Jesus and thus something about Jesus himself. To take an obvious example: We may never know what Jesus's precise upbringing was like, but we can still look in detail at what it was like for children to be brought up in a place like rural Galilee (see Goodacre's chapter) or the effects that building projects nearby in Sepphoris and Tiberias might have had on their world. Hopefully, some of the thematic approaches taken up in this project lead us away from, to some extent, the competing and restrictive straightjackets or labels for

---

3. Chris Keith and Anthony Le Donne, eds., *Jesus, Criteria, and the Demise of Authenticity* (London: T&T Clark, 2012); James Crossley, *Jesus and the Chaos of History: Redirecting the Life of the Historical Jesus* (Oxford: Oxford University Press, 2015), 35–63.

Jesus (Cynic, prophet, etc). In the case of reconstructing the social world of Jesus, some of these generalizations will not be dependent on a given portrait. To take an example from the end of Jesus's life: If Jesus was perceived as a masculinized, feminized, or minoritized victim at his crucifixion, then that is not dependent on whether he was killed as an apocalyptic prophet, social critic, revolutionary leader, or for being in the wrong place at the wrong time. Nevertheless, the ways in which crucifixion was constructed and understood remain something we can establish about Jesus's death.

If the criteria have crumbled and been replaced, then the other foundation that is in the process of being flattened is the duplicitous rhetoric of "Jewishness," such as in claims that Jesus was "very Jewish" yet opposed high-profile aspects of Judaism.[4] If the era of Judaism as a convenient scholarly construct or foil for making Jesus better than or subtly different from Judaism is not over, then it should be. And that is before we even ask what scholars actually mean by the confusing rhetoric of *very* Jewish and, by implication, *moderately* Jewish, *a touch* Jewish, *unbelievably* Jewish, *not particularly* Jewish, and so on (or, if you prefer, "Judean," "Galilean," or "Israelite"). Rather than tagging "very Jewish" onto reconstructions as a loaded rhetorical flourish or a way of accusing more philosophical or Cynic Jesuses as somehow being "not Jewish" or even borderline fascist, the Next Quest should simply assume Jesus was, without qualification, Jewish.[5] We are not playing the game of measuring which Jew was more Jewish than others, or who was or was not a legitimate Jew, perhaps most bizarrely seen in the case of Christian scholars making such bold decisions on behalf of Judaism. We are analyzing if (or how and why) ancient actors presented themselves in such terms, and if (or how and why) they were perceived in such terms (on which, see Reinhartz's chapter).

History of Scholarship and Reception History

If we know what we are rejecting and what we are building upon, then the next question is the central one: What might such a wide-open Next Quest look like?

Let us take the most obvious instances of potential for innovation in historical Jesus studies: *the social history of scholarship* and the *reception history of the*

---

4. For a summary of the critique, see James Crossley, "A 'Very Jewish' Jesus: Perpetuating the Myth of Superiority," *JSHJ* 11 (2013): 109–29.

5. William Arnal, *The Symbolic Jesus: Historical Scholarship, Judaism and the Construction of Contemporary Identity* (London: Equinox, 2005), 17; John S. Kloppenborg, "As One Unknown, Without a Name? Co-opting the Apocalyptic Jesus," in *Apocalypticism, Anti-Semitism and the Historical Jesus: Subtexts in Criticism*, ed. John S. Kloppenborg and John W. Marshall (London: T&T Clark, 2005), 2 n. 3; Crossley, "'Very Jewish' Jesus."

historical Jesus. By *social history of scholarship*, I mean using scholarship as the object of study as part of a modern history of ideas that we locate in modern cultural and historical contexts. By *reception history*, I mean an overlapping concept, namely the uses of ideas relating to the quest and the history of constructions of the so-called human Jesus typically shorn of the supernatural. The data involved in reception history may often function beyond the familiar scholarly quests, but both projects participate in a similar cultural game about who Jesus "really" was. Such reception history may also involve ethnographic work or exploring contemporary uses of Jesus scholarship, such as the research Rebekka King has done looking at liberal church groups using the work of Marcus Borg and John Dominic Crossan.[6] But an embrace of reception history under the banner of the quest should also involve looking at the expansive histories of interpretation of passages we analyze—in the spirit of John Kloppenborg's work on the tenants in the vineyard[7]—both to see the inherited cultural baggage we do not usually perceive and to provide insights beyond strictly academic influences into how we have come to select and interpret the passages we use.

Why are *social history of scholarship* and *reception history* the most obvious areas for innovation? For a start, just think about the endless Jesus tropes covered in cinema, novels, plays, and other artistic media, or the ubiquity of the idea of the tolerant benign Jesus versus a manipulative intolerant church. Or think how many passages need the extensive type of treatment given by Kloppenborg to the history of interpretation of the tenants in the vineyard. Or think about how more fieldwork on uses of scholarship in the public domain is needed beyond liberal church groups in North America, as studied by King. In terms of the social history of scholarship, we might note that plenty of scholarly work has been done (and often overlooked in mainstream scholarship) on Jesus studies in the context of, for instance, the Enlightenment, nineteenth-century bourgeois nationalism, colonialism, Nazism, Fordist capitalism (see Massey's chapter), the Cold War, European and American Orientalism, feminism, neoliberalism, postmodernity, and the War on Terror, as well as biographical examinations of individual scholars such as Schweitzer and Vermes.[8] All these areas can still be expanded with more data and more analysis.

6. Rebekka King, "The Author, the Atheist, and the Academic Study of Religion: Bourdieu and the Reception of Biblical Criticism by Progressive Christians," *Bulletin for the Study of Religion* 41 (2012): 14–20.

7. John S. Kloppenborg, *The Tenants in the Vineyard: Ideology, Economics, and Agrarian Conflict in Jewish Palestine*, WUNT 195 (Tübingen: Mohr Siebeck, 2006).

8. Among many, see, e.g., Elisabeth Schüssler Fiorenza, *Jesus and the Politics of Interpretation* (New York: Continuum, 2000); Shawn Kelley, *Racializing Jesus: Race, Ideology and the Formation*

But there is a huge amount of material that has not yet attracted analysis from historical Jesus scholarship: the archives (letters, newspapers, pamphlets, etc.) containing material (scholarly and popular) relating to the historical Jesus have barely been touched, let alone exhausted. Once again, think about how much more archival material can be revealed from around the world in a range of cultural settings where the micro can help explain the macro. For instance, if there is anything to the argument about historical Jesus scholarship emerging as part of a colonial enterprise, then there will be plenty more archival and related work to do on the role of ideas about the historical Jesus in the modern colonial encounter, building on the work of R. S. Sugirtharajah (for instance).[9] The social history of historical Jesus scholarship, reception histories of gospel passages, and the reception history of popular quests will provide a vast amount of new material for doctoral and postdoctoral research projects for a long time yet (for now, see the chapters by Taylor, Fredriksen, Crossley, and Massey).

RECONSTRUCTING JESUS

But is there anything new that can be written about the earliest perceptions of Jesus? After all, we do not have any significant new data, at least not about Jesus himself. For a start, we can shift the emphases in the questions we ask of the data. Certainly, we could ask yet again whether the data reveals that Jesus thought himself the messiah, whether christological titles go back to Jesus, whether he revised restoration theology, and so on. But we could alternatively ask: What does this earliest material say about human phenomena we see commonly discussed in

---

of Modern Biblical Scholarship (London: Routledge, 2002); Peter Head, "The Nazi Quest for an Aryan Jesus," *JSHJ* 2 (2004): 55–89; Arnal, *Symbolic Jesus*; Amy-Jill Levine, *The Misunderstood Jew: The Church and the Scandal of the Jewish Jesus* (San Francisco: HarperCollins, 2006); Ward Blanton, *Displacing Christian Origins: Philosophy, Secularity, and the New Testament* (Chicago: Chicago University Press, 2007); Susannah Heschel, *The Aryan Jesus: Christian Theologians and the Bible in Nazi Germany* (Princeton: Princeton University Press, 2008); James Crossley, *Jesus in an Age of Terror: Scholarly Projects for a New American Century* (London: Equinox, 2008); Crossley, *Jesus in an Age of Neoliberalism: Quests, Scholarship, and Ideology* (London: Equinox, 2012); Halvor Moxnes, *Jesus and the Rise of Nationalism: A New Quest for the Nineteenth Century Historical Jesus* (London: I. B. Tauris, 2012); Robert J. Myles, "The Fetish for a Subversive Jesus," *JSHJ* 14 (2016): 52–70; Hilde Brekke Møller, *The Vermes Quest: The Significance of Geza Vermes for Jesus Research* (London: T&T Clark, 2017); Sarah E. Rollens and Anthony Le Donne, "The Historical Jesus," in *The Cambridge Companion to the New Testament*, ed. Patrick Gray (Cambridge: Cambridge University Press, 2021), 50–72.

9. E.g., R. S. Sugirtharajah, *Asian Biblical Hermeneutics and Postcolonialism: Contesting the Interpretations* (Sheffield: Sheffield Academic Press, 1998).

JAMES CROSSLEY

(say) religious studies or the humanities more generally, topics like mythmaking, violence, and trauma (see the chapters by Shedd and Young)? And what could historical Jesus studies offer in return?

Alternatively, we could engage the more traditional (as well as the less traditional) questions in relation to economics and class and view the ways in which ideas about Jesus were embedded in their everyday social and material world (see the chapter by Peters) or view class as a driver of historical change. Despite all the gospel passages on the rich and the poor and the punishment of the rich, some of the most prominent lives of Jesus have not taken class seriously—we are more likely to see extensive discussion on a redefined covenant than on economic relations. A revised understanding of class should also come with the following warning in case of misinterpretation: *this alternative should not involve a romanticizing of Jesus as a modern-day revolutionary or as a middle-class theologian.* Rather, this revised emphasis should take seriously class and land redistribution in Galilee during Jesus's life, as well as engage with comparative studies of material relations and social unrest in premodern agrarian or peasant societies (see Myles's chapter). We might go one step further and then see how all this helps us explain why a rural movement emerged when and where it did, why it survived and spread in urban settings, or why the process at least was presented—and accepted—in such a way in ancient sources (on which see, in different ways, the chapters by Walsh and Ferda). Here we might find particularly useful complementary work on ancient social networks, scribalism, cultural credibility, and the unpredictable power of crowds—some of these ideas that will be taken up in chapters from this volume (e.g., those by Rollens, Kloppenborg, Ferda, and Johnson). By foregrounding the work done on understanding Jesus as part of a wider network of human relations and as a product of the material interests of agrarian Galileans, we can finally overhaul the overwhelming stress on Jesus as a "Great Man" who almost single-handedly changed human history and acted with supreme agency.

Historical Jesus studies has lagged behind much of the recent critical work in the study of Christian origins, but the expertise is all there to bring it up to date. Important well-known work has been done in Christian origins and related areas on slavery, race, ethnicity, gender, sexuality, and disability, to name a few topics (see, e.g., chapters by Henning, Levine, Smith, Park, and Petrey). In anticipation of the common gossipy criticism that these topics reflect fashionable ideas that we impose on the ancient evidence, we might respond by arguing that fashions always come and go (or get absorbed) in the field, and we all ask questions out of interest and impose them on the evidence, whether it is about the messiah or about gender. Besides, it is hardly the case that questions of (say) the body or slavery are absent from ancient data any more than questions of temple or return from exile are (see, e.g., in different ways, the chapters by Petrey, Smith, and Young).

Indeed, it is remarkable that the topic of enslavement does not feature prominently in many major books on the historical Jesus. Enslavement and the institution of slavery were found across the ancient world and appear in the New Testament as both assumed facets of reality and fundamental metaphors for Christ devotion. Notable scholarship on slavery in early Christianity has been developing for some time, albeit outside the realm of historical Jesus studies.[10] Roland Boer and Christina Petterson even see slavery as integral to understanding the ancient mode of production generally and Christian origins specifically.[11] The Next Quest for the historical Jesus should utilize these innovative studies of ancient slavery to understand more about its different forms in the Roman Empire and how local Galilean and Judean audiences would have understood such references. Indeed, we should take seriously the idea that slavery was a part of the transmission of material about Jesus (along the lines of Candida Moss's work), just as we should take seriously that the whole institution of slavery and the enslaved labor involved was an assumed part of the household networks perpetuating the earliest ideas about Jesus, the survival of a movement in his name, and their vision of the world.[12] There are few topics in historical Jesus studies that need more ongoing scholarly investigation or foregrounding than slavery (see Smith's chapter).

And it is not just concerning questions of slavery where the quest for the historical Jesus has been left behind. We might think of some major issues in the study of early Judaism and Christian origins (e.g., questions of race and ethnicity) that should be embraced by more historical Jesus studies (see Park's chapter). Race and ethnicity have hardly been absent topics, but it does not take long to find claims that Jesus was different from other Jews based on generalizations about Judaism and ethnicity rather than an understanding of differing views in early Judaism.[13] While questions of the Jesus movement's construction of their ethnicity and perceptions by outsiders are hardly invalid, more work can be done

10. E.g., Jennifer A. Glancy, *Slavery in Early Christianity* (Oxford: Oxford University Press, 2002); Matthew V. Johnson, James A. Noel, and Demetrius K. Williams, eds., *Onesimus Our Brother: Reading Religion, Race, and Culture in Philemon* (Minneapolis: Fortress Press, 2012); Marianne Bjelland Kartzow, *The Slave Metaphor and Gendered Enslavement in Early Christian Discourse: Double Trouble Embodied* (London: Routledge, 2018); Ronald Charles, *The Silencing of Slaves in Early Jewish and Christian Texts* (London: Routledge, 2020).

11. Roland Boer and Christina Petterson, *Time of Troubles: A New Economic Framework for Early Christianity* (Minneapolis: Fortress, 2017).

12. Cf. Candida R. Moss, "Fashioning Mark: Early Christian Discussions about the Scribe and Status of the Second Gospel," *NTS* 67 (2021): 181–204; Moss, "Between the Lines: Looking for the Contributions of Enslaved Literate Laborers in a Second-Century Text," *Studies in Late Antiquity* 5.3 (2021): 432–52; Candida R. Moss, "The Secretary: Enslaved Workers, Stenography, and the Production of Early Christian Literature," *JTS* 74.1 (2023): 20–56.

13. For discussion, see, e.g., Crossley, *Jesus in an Age of Terror*, 173–94.

on the use of ancient slurs and how Romans categorized different peoples in the Empire, including when they executed and humiliated them. Following Wongi Park's work on Matthew, we should not miss the ethnoracial and minoritizing dimensions to the Roman charge "the King of the Jews."[14] We might develop Park's suggestions with reference to earlier ideas about Jesus and argue that this is a presentation of Jesus seen as an absurdity from the perspective of Roman power, and so this Jesus needed to be put in his place in an assertion of Roman superiority over Jewish or ethnic Judean inferiority. If this event did not happen, then we must still ask: From where does this idea arise and why? And then we can make further connections: How were ideas of ethnicity a product of changing material circumstances as mentioned above?

Likewise, we can make complementary arguments about issues of gender and sexuality. On the issue of slurs and counter slurs, we might think about how Roman punishment and violence could be cast in terms of gender and domination and how reactions associated with the Jesus movement were a product of changing material circumstances in Galilee and Judea. The passion and crucifixion could have been perceived, quite possibly at the same time, as Jesus emasculated or Jesus as someone who could take extensive beatings like a man, so to speak. Again, we can borrow and develop work from other areas of the study of Christian origins and related areas and see what they can do for historical Jesus studies.[15] Much of the existing research may involve post-Jesus and later constructions of righteous deaths, martyrdom, and masculinity, but the issues they raise are valid for the earliest material about Jesus the martyr, such as martyrdom as a manly act, as a form of emasculation, as aligned or in competition with Roman acts of violent masculinity, or as enhancing group identity, as well as butch martyrdom as a reaction to changing economic circumstances in Galilee and Judea (see also Barber's chapter).[16]

There is still much that could be done by building on the extensive scholarship on ancient constructions of gender and sexuality, including how such ideas were

14. Wongi Park, *The Politics of Race and Ethnicity in Matthew's Passion Narrative* (New York: Palgrave Macmillan, 2019).

15. E.g., works such as Stephen D. Moore and Janice Capel Anderson, "Taking It Like a Man: Masculinity in 4 Maccabees," *JBL* 117 (1998): 249–73; Colleen M. Conway, *Behold the Man: Jesus and Greco-Roman Masculinity* (Oxford: Oxford University Press, 2008); L. Stephanie Cobb, *Dying to Be Men: Gender and Language in Early Christian Martyr Texts* (New York: Columbia University Press, 2008); Candida Moss, *The Myth of Persecution: How Early Christians Invented a Story of Martyrdom* (New York: HarperOne, 2013); Paul Middleton, ed., *The Wiley Blackwell Companion to Christian Martyrdom* (Hoboken: Wiley & Sons, 2020).

16. So, now, James Crossley and Robert J. Myles, *Jesus: A Life in Class Conflict* (Winchester: Zero, 2023), 178–253.

used by and to describe the Jesus movement and how stereotypical expectations concerning roles within households and wider Galilean society help us understand the Jesus movement. Around twenty years ago, Moxnes wrote a book on issues of sexuality, gender, and economic relations in the Jesus movement.[17] Why not further Moxnes's agenda and provoke as much debate on the issues he raised as there has been, for instance, on whether Jesus thought he was the messiah or thought he was calling for Israel to return from exile, whether he was a Cynic-like provocateur or an eschatological prophet, and so on? One function of the Next Quest project is, then, to foreground existing work in such areas. To take one example from this volume: Imagine how a concept as ubiquitous as militarism might impact historical Jesus studies if it were to be regularly incorporated into standard works in light of Christopher Zeichmann's research (see Zeichmann's chapter). Or imagine how the standard chapters, sections, or paragraphs from the major historical Jesus books from a previous generation now look in light of Amy-Jill Levine's extensive work on Jesus and gender, not least her challenge to the anachronistic trope of Jesus being nicer to women than other Jews were (see Levine's chapter).

Anticipating Criticisms

One of the obvious changes faced by the Next Quest is that this is a quest that cannot escape social media and criticisms made there by scholars and those apparently outraged nonstop. Having experienced the remarks of some scholars already, let us try to counter them so the debate can move on to substantial issues.

We should start by noting a reasonable criticism of the quest as a scholarly enterprise, namely along the lines of "we can't do historical Jesus study because the data won't allow a reasonable biographical picture." This may well be true for some of the quest as conventionally understood, but as we have seen, our hope is that we can reconstruct more about the world of Jesus and the earliest ideas surrounding and about Jesus, which will hopefully shift the debate away from the often futile idea of proving (or disproving) that this or that passage goes back to the historical Jesus.

One familiar criticism that has come from what we might call the radical liberal North American–led wing of the outgoing establishment is along the lines of "we can't do historical Jesus study; it's too tied up with discourse and agendas." The response to this should be obvious: So is everything else, whether literary-

17. Halvor Moxnes, *Putting Jesus in His Place: A Radical Vision of Household and Kingdom* (Louisville: Westminster John Knox, 2003).

ideological readings of John's Gospel, reconstructing Q, or metacritical approaches to scholarship. The earliest perceptions about Jesus should get no special immunity from historical analysis (see Whitlock's chapter), whether radical liberal theorists or theological protectionists like it or not, and there is a case that we overlook lives from below in favor of elites lives if we abandon the quest (see Meggitt's chapter). Indeed, as Whitlock shows in his chapter, this avoidance of the historical Jesus itself contributes to the preservation of his special cultural aura.

Another criticism goes something like "some scholar has already written a book or article on a given topic and so what the Next Quest is doing is nothing new." We might reply that if we have a historic body of research into Jesus and books by some of the most famous scholars of their time that have looked in huge detail at discipleship, future kingdom, present kingdom, and eyewitnesses, then we can likewise spend more time and support more work on ancient, premodern, and agrarian ideas of class conflict, historical change, ritual, movements that survive, movements that do not, violence, death, fame, aura, trauma, ethnicity, gender, sexuality, disability, and enslavement, and how they intersect with the earliest ideas about and perceptions of Jesus.

Has some of this work been done before? Yes, and even famously so in certain cases! But we do not necessarily stop doing research because someone from the past has offered a learned discussion of, for instance, the body, and then think that is the final word. As we said of Moxnes, we should be building on older ideas, critiquing them, developing them, uncovering more contextual data, applying up-to-date cross-disciplinary approaches, *and making them mainstream,* just as people did with messianism, apocalypticism, and Cynic philosophy. We may never find more new data about Jesus himself, but analysis of comparable data is an ongoing project and, when applied to the earliest ideas about Jesus, will sharpen our preexisting knowledge, just as new archival work will expand the history of Jesus scholarship as a serious history of ideas, far away from the misleading three-quest paradigm. But it will also expand what we can say about the social processes underpinning the emergence of the Jesus movement, so we can explain how it took off when and where it did and its continuation and survival (see also Johnson's chapter).

Something New Under the Sun

Looking over a selection of the table of contents for some of the major historical Jesus books published over the past forty to fifty years is instructive. Here we find headings for sections, chapters, and subdivisions such as the following:[18]

18. Taken from (and hardly unique to) E. P. Sanders, *Jesus and Judaism* (London: SCM, 1985);

Judaism as a Religion
Miracles
The Coming of the Kingdom
The Kingdom: Israel, Gentiles, and Individuals
Jesus's View of His Role in God's Plan
Jesus and the Temple
New Temple and Restoration in Jewish Literature
The Sayings
Jesus and the Gentiles
The Kingdom of God: God Coming in Power to Rule
Other Sayings about a Present Kingdom
Miracles and Modern Minds
The Relationship between Present and Future in the Preaching of Jesus
Jesus as Healer: The Miracles of Jesus
Jesus as Poet: The Parables of Jesus
Jesus as Teacher: The Ethics of Jesus
Praxis of a Prophet
Stories of the Kingdom: Invitation, Welcome, Challenge, and Summons
Introduction: Kingdom, Symbol, Controversy
Jesus and the Nations
Jesus and the Kingdom of God
Apocalyptic Imagination and a Values' Revolution
Jesus and the Temple
Jesus the Apocalyptic Prophet
The Apocalyptic Teachings of Jesus
Proverbs and Parable
Jesus and the Kingdom of God
John the Baptist, Call and Ministry
The Kingdom of God

Anyone familiar with historical Jesus studies will know that these are recogniz-able categorizations of the material and that such examples could be multiplied. Repetition does not mean these were or are unreasonable topics to discuss. Nor

---

Sanders, *The Historical Figure of Jesus* (London: Penguin, 1993); Geza Vermes, *The Religion of Jesus the Jew* (London: SCM, 1993); N. T. Wright, *Jesus and the Victory of God*, vol. 2 of *Christian Origins and the Question of God* (Minneapolis: Fortress, 1996); Gerd Theissen and Annette Merz, *The Historical Jesus: A Comprehensive Guide* (Minneapolis: Fortress, 1998); Bart Ehrman, *Jesus: Apocalyptic Prophet of the New Millennium* (Oxford: Oxford University Press, 1999); Sean Freyne, *Jesus: A Jewish Galilean* (London: T&T Clark, 2004).

is this a criticism of the quality of the books. Nevertheless, these are *not* books that will tell us much about the proposed issues raised here that might constitute the Next Quest. And we know about other familiar recurring topics in previous quests. The history of scholarship—where it is included—might tell a familiar tale from Reimarus onward, often whizzing through and generalizing about the entire nineteenth century. For the bulk of a conventional historical Jesus book, we thus encounter familiar themes on kingdom, ethics, and Israel. Some prominent scholarship of the past generation even admits they were lacking in important areas of discussion. E. P. Sanders, for instance, has repeated his claim that details on economic conditions were beyond the scope of his work aside from where they might relate to the temple, priesthood, and taxation in relation to "religious dues."[19] How did we get to the stage when this became normative?

It might be countered that someone as prominent as (say) Crossan *did* cover in detail some of the topics raised here—and there would be some validity to this criticism. However, this does not tell the whole story. The previous generation had a golden opportunity to redirect the quest. Rather than repeatedly engage with Crossan on Jesus and Cynicism and his idiosyncratic use of reconstruction of sources and criteria, critical scholarship could have instead focused on the sociohistorical contextualization of Jesus, how socioeconomic changes help explain the emergence of a movement in Galilee, and how certain social processes helped it survive after Jesus's death. However, the mainstream scholarly reception of Crossan focused not on the socioeconomic reasons for why a movement emerged when and where it did and why it survived but instead, expectedly and arguably encouraged by Crossan himself, on the surface-level events, the controversies over his use of criteria, and whether his liberal, Cynic-like Jesus was the right kind of Jesus or not.[20]

To repeat, this is not to savage past scholarship entirely or diminish the wealth of scholarship that has been produced by learned people. Indeed, and to repeat further, the Next Quest should still sharpen and develop older, well-worn ideas. As Wayne Te Kaawa shows in his chapter, there is more to say on a topic as familiar as Jesus's genealogy through a comparison with Māori *whakapapa*. Apocalypticism may have received much scholarly attention already, but again more cross-cultural work could provide further insights.[21] For instance, premodern apocalypticism as a vehicle for discontent and imagining a replacement of a world gone awry

19. Sanders, *Jesus and Judaism*, 120, 159.
20. Crossley, *Jesus and the Chaos of History*, 13–19.
21. Along the lines of what was proposed in, e.g., Dale C. Allison Jr., *Jesus of Nazareth: Millenarian Prophet* (Philadelphia: Fortress, 1998).

with a new idealized hierarchy to replace the old could provide numerous points of comparison. To take different examples, more engagement with peasant or agrarian studies and related areas might lead us away from fantasies about entrepreneurial disciples having relatively successful fishing businesses or the existence of brokerless libertarian peasant communities and toward more useful comparative arguments about the prestige of the fisher in fishing societies or how peasant hierarchies function.[22] We have additional examples in this volume of how updating of older scholarship can be done. We might think of Meghan Henning locating the healing stories in ancient theo-medical discourses, Anders Runesson rethinking of the role of synagogues, Matthew Thiessen rereading of assumptions about purity, or Giovanni Bazzana's anthropological approach to understanding the spirit world in the Gospel tradition. Indeed, Justin Meggitt even shows how comparative material can still tell us more about something as heavily discussed as the resurrection.

Moving Forward

Yet it remains that many traditional topics have been done to death at the expense of alternatives. We began by mentioning the significance of generational changes and we can return to this point. The people now running seminars and sections at the Society for Biblical Literature, writing major books, or editing leading journals have somewhat different agendas than those of their famed predecessors even from ten or fifteen years ago. It is now time for a generation of more diverse historical Jesus scholars to take advantage of these changes and push for a range of different readings of the early material.

The micro-specialisms in biblical studies and related areas may certainly be a problem that will not disappear ("this over-specialized, bloated, micro-technical, myopic field-in-itself," to use William Arnal's memorable turn of phrase).[23] However, we can also use this as a strength by bringing together experts with diverse areas of expertise, including those representing areas that were not brought to the fore in mainstream scholarship of a previous generation. Against the Jesus Seminar's emphasis on voting and Meier's famed unpapal conclave still designed to get to the individual portrait of Jesus, a better and increasingly standard model

---

22. Work moving in this direction includes, e.g., Robert J. Myles, "Fishing for Entrepreneurs in the Sea of Galilee? Unmasking Neoliberal Interpretation in Biblical Interpretation," in *Class Struggle in the New Testament*, ed. Robert J. Myles (Lanham, MD: Lexington/Fortress Academic, 2019), 115–38; Crossley and Myles, *Jesus*, 74–126, 154–77.

23. William Arnal, "What Branches Grow Out of This Stony Rubbish? Christian Origins and the Study of Religion," *SR* 39 (2010): 551.

of collaborative academic work is promoting and learning from different experts. Such a wide range of ideas is largely beyond the grasp of any one individual in today's academic environment and especially so for those working on the popular subject matter of Jesus. The Next Quest for the historical Jesus will need people working on (among many areas) varied modern archival materials through those extensively read on peasant societies to those clued up on trauma studies, all of whom can be brought together so we make connections, see bigger pictures, and understand more about the earliest perceptions of Jesus and the history of interpretation. Everything is now in place to do things differently.

1

REBUILDING THE FOUNDATIONS

1

Reception History

Halvor Moxnes

In a short amount of time, reception history has become a fully recognized part of biblical studies. The area now has a journal (*Journal of the Bible and Its Reception*), a large encyclopedia (*Encyclopedia of the Bible and Its Reception*), and a commentary series where historical criticism is combined with reception history (*Blackwell's Bible Commentaries*). This shows how integrated reception history has become in historical-critical studies. In his introduction to the Next Quest for the historical Jesus, James Crossley brings historical-critical scholarship and reception history explicitly together. This raises the question of what reception history contributes to the Next Quest for the historical Jesus.

First it is important to introduce briefly the study of reception history.[1] The discipline was inspired by Hans-Georg Gadamer's work, *Wahrheit und Methode*, where he used the term *Wirkungsgeschichte* to refer to the way biblical texts shaped culture.[2] However, Gadamer asserted that the reader is not a passive recipient of the text but plays an active part in constructing its meaning. It was Gadamer's student, Hans Robert Jauss, who coined the term "reception history."[3]

1. Christine E. Joynes, "Changing Horizons: Reflections on a Decade at Oxford University's Centre for Reception History of the Bible," *JBR* 1.1 (2014): 161–71.
2. Hans-Georg Gadamer, *Wahrheit und Methode: Grundzüge einer philosophischen Hermeneutik* (Tübingen: Mohr, 1960).
3. H. R. Jauss, *Toward an Aesthetic of Reception*, trans. T. Bahti (Minneapolis: University of Minnesota Press, 1982).

He developed Gadamer's perspective into a method that could be adopted. Jauss describes the relation between the text and the reader as a relationship between "the producing subject" and the "consuming subject." The "consuming subject" points to the active role of the reader, who has an engagement with the text, which is necessary to create the meaning of the text.

With his large commentary on Matthew, Ulrich Luz explored the reception history of the Gospel and became a pioneer in the reception history of the New Testament.[4] Prior to Luz, the terminology used within early studies on reception history was not consistent. In his commentary, however, Luz distinguishes between "history of interpretation" and "reception history."[5] Luz understands history of interpretation as exegetical exposition in commentaries, which we may compare to the history of scholarship of Jesus. In contrast, Luz identifies reception history as *Wirkungsgeschichte* (the term used by Gadamer), which includes different media such as hymns and art. If we use the perspective of Hans Robert Jauss on reception history, these distinctions between the history of interpretation and reception history are not easy to maintain.

A reception history of Jesus is more than a description of Jesus through history; it includes an interaction between a picture of Jesus and the recipients. Any vision of who Jesus was and what he proclaimed bears the marks of our attitude to our own world, our ways of making sense of our communities and ourselves. Engagements with Jesus in literature, art, and film represent reception history in that they must make sense of Jesus in the world of the recipients. Studying the reception history of Jesus requires that we explore the presuppositions underlying the understanding of individuals, societies, and worldviews. Therefore, reception history of Jesus is a contextual study of Jesus, and Jesus is at the same time a lens for understanding a culture and for identifying the main issues in a society.

RECEPTION HISTORY IN THE NEXT QUEST

Since reception history as a separate approach was established after the introduction of the so-called Third Quest for the Historical Jesus, we need to reflect on the role of reception history in this Next Quest. In the introduction to this volume, Crossley several times refers to the relevance of reception history. The first goal for the Next Quest is to account for how early followers of Jesus conceptualized Jesus, that is, how they portrayed him. These portrayals were created through reception history. As Crossley states in his introduction: "the Next Quest works

---

4. Ulrich Luz, *Matthew: A Commentary*, Hermeneia, 3 vols. (Minneapolis: Fortress, 2007–2016).
5. Luz, *Matthew*, 1:65.

from the ancient portrayals of Jesus to reconstruct imaginatively a historical Jesus whose reception history leads to those portrayals."

This implies that there cannot be a reconstruction of the historical Jesus *apart* from the ancient portrayals of Jesus. Especially if we extend the period of reception into our own time, this position represents a significant departure from traditional ways of doing historical Jesus studies. These earlier studies jumped directly to the historical Jesus from their present situations, bypassing two thousand years of history. This left a hiatus between the historical Jesus and the present Jesus. In contrast, a reception history approach places the quest for Jesus in a historical continuity. First, receptions provide a broader context for the portrayal of Jesus. Second, they generate many different questions that can be addressed to the study of the historical Jesus. Finally, they make us aware of both the cultural presuppositions of earlier contributors to historical Jesus research and (implicitly) our own presuppositions as Jesus scholars. Thus, the portrayals of Jesus in reception history contribute to the study of the historical Jesus.

THE ROLE OF SCHOLARLY IMAGINATION

In their invitations to contributors to this volume, Crossley and Keith presented an argument for a new way to conceptualize a historical-critical method. As part of the new approach, they introduce the term "imagination." It must be important since Crossley and Keith emphasized the role of imagination as many as three times in their invitation. In one instance, they asked contributors "to imaginatively reconstruct a historical Jesus," and in another instance they stated: "We will accomplish this goal by hypothesizing what could have happened in the past by means of critical usage of the scholarly imagination." Finally, in their last point concerning historical methods they requested contributors to foreground "the role of the imagination in historical reconstruction." These ideas about imagination are taken up further in Keith's chapter in this volume.

Let us try to unpack these statements and put them in the context of the ongoing discussion of historiography. In a previous essay, Chris Keith discusses two competing models for the study of the historical Jesus.[6] The major difference between them is their treatment of the narrative frameworks of the Gospels. The first model, which for a long time has dominated the discussion, is based on form criticism and attempts to isolate words of Jesus or statements about him from the narrative framework of the gospels. This focus on "objective criteria," which

6. Chris Keith, "The Narratives of the Gospels and the Historical Jesus: Current Debates, Prior Debates, and the Goal of Historical Jesus Research," *JSNT* 38.4 (2016): 426–55.

attempts to go behind traditions of Jesus to gain access to the historical Jesus, does not leave much space for imagination.

The other model that Keith proposes, and which the Next Quest builds upon, starts from the narrative structure of the gospels, which in effect reveals how the gospel writers viewed Jesus. Starting from these interpretations, scholars may posit hypotheses about the historical Jesus without claiming to reach an objective fact. Keith speaks of "re-presenting the past via a scholarly narration of historical possibilities and plausibility."[7] Jens Schröter was one of the first to develop this perspective based on debates among historians. He emphasized that critical source study must be combined with historical imagination: "For the methodological foundation of the concept of history the insight into the not-to-be-separated processes of critical source study and historical imagination is indispensable, because only in this way can history come into being from sources in a methodologically considered manner."[8]

Both Keith and Schröter are aware of the discussions about imagination among historians.[9] Historians recognize that they engage in imagination in a general sense: "Simply defined, imagination is the power or the capacity of humans to form internal images of objects and situations."[10] However, there are different understandings of imagination. David Staley has a preference for what he calls a *mimetic* imagination: "History is a discipline that is enacted in imagination (in the mimetic sense). By this, I mean that historians assemble evidence from the past, these fragments of what was. In reading and otherwise interpreting these sources, the historians create a mental image."[11]

Imagination in this mimetic sense is different from *creative* imagination, which is characteristic of literature and fantasy where figures and events are made up. During the period of Romanticism, this creative imagination received positive attention, especially as it was expressed in art and literature. History, however, which in earlier periods was close to the genre of literature, moved closer to science in the nineteenth century.[12] Historians became increasingly skeptical of creative imagination; it was considered an excess. Toward the end of the twentieth century,

---

7. Keith, "Narratives of the Gospels," 444.

8. Jens Schröter, *From Jesus to the New Testament: Early Christian Theology and the Origin of the New Testament Canon*, trans. Wayne Coppins, BMSEC (Waco, TX: Baylor University Press, 2013), 14.

9. David J. Staley, *Historical Imagination* (London: Routledge, 2021).

10. Ann Pendleton-Jullian and John Seely Brown, *Design Unbound: Designing for Emergence in a White Water World* (Cambridge: MIT Press, 2018), 2:85.

11. Staley, *Historical Imagination*, 4.

12. Joyce Appleby, Lynn Hunt, and Margaret Jacob, *Telling the Truth about History* (New York: Norton, 1994), 52–90.

in an opposite movement, postmodernism challenged the dominance of objective and scientific history. However, this did not lead to many efforts to write fictional history or to align history with literature. Sarah Maza seems to strike a balance: "Agreement reigns in principle that historians are bound by facts and obey a strict embargo on invention. But the historian's task also consists in assembling scattered sources and connecting the dots between them and superior historical work involves the ability to imagine the past and recreate it in vivid language."[13] Maza recommends historians "recreate" rather than "invent" history; thus, she refers to mimetic imagination and not creative imagination. Her approach seems to correspond to the way Schröter speaks of imagination, when he says that the processes of critical source study and historical imagination cannot be separated.

Moreover, in their invitation to this volume's contributors, Crossley and Keith spoke of "critical usage of the scholarly imagination." They conclude by stating that their goal is to foreground "the role of imagination in historical reconstruction." This is not creative imagination, free from the constraints of observations and sources; rather it is an imagination that draws on a broader set of sources and methods. They stress a "foregrounding of the roles of historical imagination of the scholar and the varied receptions of the historical Jesus in the scholarly quest purposefully opens the quest for the historical Jesus to themes and methodologies that did not feature in prior quests." The themes they have suggested for the Next Quest indicate the assemblage of "scattered sources," including themes from modern life situations and politics. Thus, the Next Quest will create an interdisciplinary and broader context for constructing a historical Jesus.

History of Scholarship as Reception History

Crossley and Keith encourage us to combine readings of the "history of scholarship" and "the reception history of Jesus which emphasizes wider historical and cultural issues." So, what is the relationship between the "history of scholarship" and "reception history"? We can get a better grasp of the function of reception history if we view it together with memory studies.

In an earlier essay, Keith gives a poignant summary of the primary task of social memory theory; it is "to conceptualize and explain the various manners in which cultures (and individuals as culture-members) appropriate the past in light of, in terms of, and on behalf of the present."[14] In *The Reception of Jesus in the*

---

13. Sarah Maza, *Thinking about History* (Chicago: University of Chicago Press, 2017), 225.

14. Chris Keith, "Memory and Authenticity: Jesus Tradition and What Really Happened," *ZNW* 102 (2011): 168.

First Three Centuries, Keith and his colleagues point out two important features that reception history and memory studies share. First, both dismiss historical positivism, that is, the idea that "historians can attain an objective view of the actual past." The second shared feature is a focus on the sources not in an attempt to reconstruct the historical Jesus behind them, but to understand "how and why they came to portray the past in the manners that they did."[15] This broadens the task of the historian to include reception history.

I suggest that the main contribution that reception history can make consists in the *questions* it may address to historical scholarship on Jesus. The first question concerns how aware we are of our presuppositions when we as scholars study the historical Jesus. It is relatively easy to detect the presuppositions of earlier authors behind their historical portraits of Jesus, for instance ideas of nationalism behind nineteenth-century portrayals of Jesus.[16] It is more difficult to unmask our own presuppositions. However, these observations should raise our awareness. In a cover endorsement on my *Jesus and the Rise of Nationalism*, the systematic theologian Werner G. Jeanrond says: "Any vision of who Jesus was and what he proclaimed bears too the marks of our attitude to our own world, of our ways of making sense of ourselves, of our communities, and of our universe."

Keith and his colleagues have primarily dealt with the reception of Jesus in the first three centuries. My focus here is on later, but parallel, stages of the process. However, I think their questions concerning how scholars came to conceptualize Jesus in the ways they did are relevant also for modern scholars as well. Just as one could study how and why ancient sources portrayed Jesus, it is possible to explore how and why modern scholars portrayed Jesus the way they did.

In her presidential address to the Society of Biblical Literature in 1987 entitled "The Ethics of Biblical Scholarship," Elisabeth Schüssler Fiorenza challenged the notion of objective scholarship and demanded greater ethical self-awareness from her (male) colleagues.[17] She followed up this challenge in many later works, including her *Jesus and the Politics of Interpretation*.[18] Some scholars have taken up this challenge and included in studies of receptions an evaluation of their own presuppositions. Prefacing a special issue of the *Journal of the Bible and Its Recep-*

---

15. Chris Keith, Helen K. Bond, Christine Jacobi, and Jens Schröter, eds., *The Reception of Jesus in the First Three Centuries* (London: T&T Clark, 2020), 3:xxii–xxiii.

16. Halvor Moxnes, *Jesus and the Rise of Nationalism: A New Quest for the Nineteenth-Century Historical Jesus* (London: I. B. Tauris, 2012).

17. Elisabeth Schüssler Fiorenza, "The Ethics of Biblical Interpretation: Decentering Biblical Scholarship," *JBL* 107 (1988): 3–17.

18. Elisabeth Schüssler Fiorenza, *Jesus and the Politics of Interpretation* (New York: Continuum, 2000).

tion containing essays on biblical reception and the construction of masculinities, Peter-Ben Smit, Ovidiu Creangă, and Adriaan van Klinken identify two things we can learn from studying reception history. First, studying reception history breaks down the difference between experts and "ordinary" people. Second, it leads to self-awareness: "Studying biblical reception not only relativizes the difference between academic and 'vernacular' or 'ordinary' communities of interpretation, it also leads to an awareness of one's own contextuality and embeddedness in relationships that influence one's scholarship."[19]

This awareness of one's own presuppositions leads to a second group of questions that reception history addresses to the Next Quest for the historical Jesus. They concern the wider historical and cultural issues that make up our context and that influence the way we construct Jesus and his environment. An example that shows the impact of these new issues is Shawn Kelley's *Racializing Jesus*, which brought up the issue of race as a perspective on the history of biblical scholarship.[20] With the subtitle *Race, Ideology and the Formation of Modern Biblical Scholarship*, Kelley places biblical studies in a social and political context, of which we had not previously been aware.

To expand the context for the historical Jesus, Crossley and Keith suggest themes like "gender and sexuality," "race and ethnicity," and "whiteness." These themes will expand our insight into ancient societies, but more than that, they are perspectives that determine our own positions, identities, and ways of thinking. The introduction of these and other themes are now in the process of changing biblical studies and Jesus studies as well. These issues commonly result from interdisciplinary approaches that first appeared in disciplines like literature, anthropology, and history. Thus, compared to traditional historical Jesus studies, interdisciplinary approaches have brought in new material and provide perspectives that reflect contemporary culture.

WRITING A BIOGRAPHY OF JESUS

Reception history may initiate many questions addressed to the Next Quest for the historical Jesus. I will start with this central question: How did scholars understand Jesus as a human being? I will divide the main question into two subques-

19. Peter-Ben Smit, Ovidiu Creangă, and Adriaan van Klinken, "The Reception of the Bible in the Construction of Masculinities in Jewish and Christian Con/Texts," *JBR* 2 (2015): 142.

20. Shawn Kelley, *Racializing Jesus: Race, Ideology and the Formation of Modern Biblical Scholarship* (London and New York: Routledge, 2002).

tions. The first concerns the presuppositions in understanding a biography. The second raises the question of what we understand by the term "man."

In *The Reception of Jesus in the First Three Centuries*, Chris Keith and his colleagues discuss the various genres that early Christian texts use when portraying Jesus. In line with most recent scholarship, they found that the gospels are best understood as biographies.[21] However, how do scholars understand the meaning of biography? Are they aware of the presuppositions, in terms of anthropology and sociology of the individual, behind biographies? Modern Jesus scholars rarely ask these questions. They appear to take the meaning of biography for common knowledge without discussing the issue. E. P. Sanders's introduction to his *The Historical Figure of Jesus* is a case in point: "I shall discuss Jesus the human being— and I shall search for evidence and propose explanations just as does any historian when writing about history."[22] As a result, scholars miss important discussions about what it means to use the genre of biography to write about Jesus.

It was not always this way. For nineteenth-century Jesus scholars, presentations of Jesus in the form of biography represented a new approach. Therefore, they engaged in discussions on the genre of biography and its implications for the way they presented the historical Jesus.[23] One of the first was Friedrich Schleiermacher in his lectures early in the nineteenth century. Before he started his lectures, he told his students that there were some "preliminary matters" they must deal with: "The first will be that we must agree on what we actually mean by biography for that is what we wish to provide for the person of Christ."[24]

Schleiermacher's lectures introduced a controversial issue. His and other early studies of the historical Jesus broke with the image of a divine Christ and presented the life of Jesus as a biography of a human being.[25] Therefore, the question of what it meant to use biography as a model for Jesus led to further questions. For instance, should they portray a person as an individual or as part of a wider community? Was it possible within a human biography to speak of Jesus as a unique person?[26] The historian John Breuilly sums up the underlying presuppositions of biographies in the nineteeth century: "In this genre the individual came to be presented as a morally autonomous subject capable of shaping himself (rarely herself) and the world."[27]

21. Richard A. Burridge, *What Are the Gospels? A Comparison with Graeco-Roman Biography* (Cambridge: Cambridge University Press, 1992).

22. E. P. Sanders, *The Historical Figure of Jesus* (London: Penguin, 1993), 2.

23. Moxnes, *Jesus and the Rise of Nationalism*, 23–31.

24. Friedrich Schleiermacher, *The Life of Jesus*, ed. J. C. Verheyden (Philadelphia: Fortress, 1975), 3.

25. Moxnes, *Jesus and the Rise of Nationalism*, 17–38.

26. Schleiermacher, *Life of Jesus*, 12–15.

27. John Breuilly, "Nationalism and the History of Ideas," *Proceedings of the British Academy* 105 (Oxford: Oxford University Press, 2000): 200.

The issue of shaping oneself and one's relation to the world points to issues that concerned Schleiermacher when he discussed whether it was possible to speak of Jesus as a special or unique person.[28] It was a widely shared idea in nineteenth-century Europe that heroic individuals shaped history.[29] Most popular was the idea of the Great Man and his influence upon history. Schleiermacher's Jesus seems to fall into this category. However, in his lectures on the life of Jesus, Schleiermacher does not use the terminology of the Great Man. Instead, he speaks of "the individual and the common life," and says that there is a reciprocal relationship between them. An individual may have a "directing influence" upon the common life, but on the other hand he is also part of and shares the life of the common people.[30]

Schleiermacher's example is the legendary king of Prussia, Frederick the Great (1712–1786), whom he praised in several memorial lectures. In these lectures, Schleiermacher employed the terminology of the Great Man. However, he modified the superiority of the king and emphasized the interdependence between the king and people.[31] In this way, Schleiermacher could express a criticism of the currently reigning king of Prussia, the autocratic Frederick Wilhelm III. Furthermore, he could also use his discussion of biography to present Jesus and his relations with people as a contrast to the divine Christ, who was elevated above people. Schleiermacher's presentation of Jesus placed him in a historical context, but the historical discussion blended with reception into a contemporary context.

JESUS AS A UNIQUE INDIVIDUAL

The question of whether Jesus was a unique individual is still a relevant question in contemporary studies of the historical Jesus. Since historical Jesus studies for so long have been a Western hegemony, the individualism traditionally associated with biography has been generally accepted without questioning. Since historical Jesus scholars have not discussed their presuppositions regarding biography, they have almost automatically used individualism as a paradigm for presentations of Jesus.

In this context, we realize the importance of the invitation from Crossley and Keith. Here they challenge the idea of Jesus as the Great Man who changed history and put up the social group as an alternative: "We stress historical methods that go beyond certitude and beyond viewing the individual as the prime mover of

28. Schleiermacher, *Life of Jesus*, 11–14.

29. Thomas Carlyle, *On Heroes, Hero-Worship, and the Heroic in History*, ed. Carl Niemeyer (Lincoln: University of Nebraska Press, 1966).

30. Schleiermacher, *Life of Jesus*, 12–13.

31. Friedrich Schleiermacher, "Über den Begriff des grossen Manne. Am 24 Januar 1826," in *Werke: Auswahl in vier Bänden* (Leipzig: Eckhardt, 1910), 1:520–31.

historical change, foregrounding alternative understandings of historical change, social-scientific approaches to Jesus's society, and the role of the imagination in historical reconstruction." When they want to foreground "alternative under-standings of historical change," they join a long tradition among sociologists and historians who have criticized a focus on the unique individual and instead emphasized collaborative efforts and social structures.[32] Thus, Crossley and Keith force open a discussion of the presuppositions behind the portrayal of Jesus as a unique individual.

This is an important signal of why a Next Quest for the historical Jesus is needed. There have been some earlier attempts to see Jesus not as an individual leader figure but as engaged in a movement with a more collective leadership, such as those of Elisabeth Schüssler Fiorenza, Bruce Malina, and Richard Horsley.[33] However, Crossley and Keith now have lifted up this question as a priority issue of a Next Quest, which indicates a major shift in understanding the early Christian movement.

JESUS THE MAN

The issue of biography raises the question of how we understand Jesus as an individual. However, what does it mean to say that Jesus was a man? The feminist movement has created an awareness of the construction of gender. Thus, "man" can no longer be understood in a gender-neutral meaning as a human being. Our societies have become irrevocably gendered and the meaning of "man" cannot be taken for granted; the term must be defined and discussed. Masculinity studies were introduced to New Testament studies about twenty years ago.[34] It became obvious that both "woman" and "man" were socially constructed and contested categories.[35]

32. Halvor Moxnes, "Was Jesus a Charismatic Leader? The Use of Social Models in the History of the Jesus Movement," in *"Lampada per i miei passi è la tua parola, luce sul mio cammino" (Sal 119,105): Studi offerti a Marcello Del Verme in occasione del suo 75° compleanno*, ed. P. Giustiniani and F. del Pizzo (Bornato in Franciacorta: Sardini, 2017), 51–72.

33. Halvor Moxnes, "From Unique Personality to Charismatic Movement: 100 Years of Shifting Paradigms in Historical Jesus Research," in *Religion in Late Modernity: Essays in Honor of Pål Repstad*, ed. Inger Furseth and Paul Leer-Salvesen (Trondheim: Tapir, 2007), 187–200.

34. Stephen D. Moore and Janice Capel Anderson, "Taking It Like a Man: Masculinity in 4 Maccabees," *JBL* 117 (1998): 249–73.

35. Halvor Moxnes, "The Contextuality of Constructing Histories of Jesus: Modern and Ancient Masculinities," in *Jesus, quo vadis? Entwicklungen und Perspektiven der aktuellen Jesusforschung*, ed. Eckhart David Schmidt, Biblisch-Theologische Studien 177 (Göttingen: Vandenhoeck & Ruprecht, 2018), 93–114.

Colleen Conway's *Behold the Man: Jesus and Greco-Roman Masculinities* is an influential contribution to understanding the term "man" in early Christian texts.[36] It is a historical study, but Conway draws a link between history and the present: "By examining the influence of ancient gender ideologies in the Greco-Roman period, we might become ever more conscious of the multiple ways contemporary gender ideologies function in our lives."[37] However, I will contend that there is not only an influence from antiquity to modern conceptions of gender, but also the other way round. In fact, Conway's presentation of Jesus's masculinity is built on modern conceptions of masculinity. Thus, Conway's presentation of the masculinity of Jesus is both a historical reconstruction and a result of reception history.

Conway has chosen a modern concept for her presentation of Roman masculinities, namely, hegemonic masculinity. This is a theoretical approach based on social hierarchy, with a strong man as the model for masculinities based on patriarchial dominance.[38] Socially, this type of masculinity is popular and accepted among many Christian groups in the United States.

I have suggested that other theoretical forms of masculinities may be more socially acceptable and theoretically more relevant for interpreting the gospel narratives.[39] This has included the theory of masculinities developed in Nordic historical studies of masculinities in egalitarian societies.[40] Between men on the same level, conflicts are not expressed in terms of hierarchies but with contrasts between "manliness" and "unmanliness." Moreover, different from a focus on relations between men and women, this form of masculinity is based on men-to-men relations, that is, in terms of homosociality.[41] I suggest that this form of masculinity is more appropriate to make sense of the relationship between Jesus and his disciples in the gospels. Jesus is calling young men to follow him and leave the patriarchal household and their father (Mark 1:16–20). The new household that Jesus establishes is one without a father (10:28–30); the relations between men are expressed with the term "brothers" (3:35).

36. Colleen Conway, *Behold the Man: Jesus and Greco-Roman Masculinities* (Oxford: Oxford University Press, 2008).

37. Conway, *Behold the Man*, 6.

38. R. W. Connell and J. W. Messerschmidt, "Hegemonic Masculinity. Rethinking the Concept," *Gender and Society* 19 (2005): 829–59.

39. Moxnes, "Contextuality," 106–7.

40. J. Lorentzen and C. Ekenstam, eds., *Män i Norden. Manlighet och modernitet 1840–1940* (Hedemora: Gidlund. 2006).

41. John Tosh, *Manliness and Masculinities in Nineteenth-Century Britain* (Harlow: Longman, 2005).

THE CHALLENGE OF A TRANSGENDER JESUS

The receptions of Jesus take many forms, including literature, art, plays, and music. These various expressions are based on the claim that Jesus as Christ identified with all of humanity. This claim is reflected in artistic presentations of Jesus in all parts of the world, with people of all colors and from all ethnic groups. This diversity with regard to color and ethnicity in presentations of Jesus is generally accepted. However, a diversity in presentations of gender is more contested. The American feminist theologian Rosemary Radford Ruether questioned the role of a male Jesus in salvation: "Can a male savior redeem and save wo/men?"[42] This question went to the core of feminist criticism of male-dominated theology of salvation. The question revealed that this theology was based on the presupposition that "man" was a universal concept. Instead, feminist criticism claimed that it was gendered and privileged the masculine. A reception of the figure of Jesus as a feminine sculpture, Christa, by the British artist Edwina Sandys created much controversy when it was briefly displayed in the Cathedral of St. John the Divine in New York in 1984. Thirty years later the same cathedral welcomed an exhibition titled "The Christa Project—Manifesting Divine Bodies." This new exhibition displayed the original Christa sculpture together with works by twenty-one other artists.

Presentations of a transgender Jesus are the most recent examples of a controversial identification with Jesus. The most widespread example is the play *The Gospel according to Jesus, Queen of Heaven* by the trans woman Jo Clifford.[43] The play was first performed in a small theater in Glasgow in 2009 to much controversy and to the condemnation by the Roman Catholic bishop of Glasgow. The play has since been translated into many languages and played in many countries, especially Brazil. Among all other nations, Brazil has the highest number of murdered transgender and queer people; clearly, then, the trans and queer population of Brazil experiences massive hatred.[44] The play has been performed in theaters all over the country and has become a symbol of resistance against LGBTQ oppression. Hatred and aggression against transgender people is on the rise in many countries and provides the context for the performances of *The Gospel according to Jesus*.

The play was performed in Norwegian in September 2022 in a context that reflects the ambiguity of the situation for transgender people in Norway. After a

42. Rosemary Radford Ruether, "Can Christology Be Liberated from Patriarchy?," in *Reconstructing the Christ Symbol*, ed. M. Stevens (New York: Paulist, 1993), 7–29.

43. Jo Clifford, *The Gospel according to Jesus, Queen of Heaven*, ed. James T. Harding, Annabel Cooper, and Duncan Lockerbie, 10th anniversary ed. (Edinburgh: Stewed Rhubarb, 2019).

44. Ester Pinheiro, "Brazil Continues to Be the Country with the Largest Number of Trans People Killed," *Brasil de Fato*, January 24, 2022, https://www.brasildefato.com.br/2022/01/23/brazil-continues-to-be-the-country-with-the-largest-number-of-trans-people-killed.

period with aggressive criticism especially of transwomen in Norwegian social media, a terrorist mass shooting killed two people and wounded twenty-one others outside a gay bar in Oslo the night before the big Pride parade on June 25. On the other hand, the play was part of the celebration of the Year of Queer Culture by the Church of Norway (Lutheran), and it was performed in several churches or church-related venues. Against criticism from conservative groups, Solveig Fiske, the bishop in the diocese where the premiere was performed, supported the performance on the basis that the incarnation of Christ made it possible for everybody to identify with Christ.

I consider the play a respectful reading of the gospels by a lay woman, not a theologian. As a child, Jo Clifford was brought up to ask when she faced spiritual doubt: "What would Jesus do?" This is still her question: "Well, what would Jesus do if Jesus came back to earth now and was me, a trans woman? What would she do and what would she say? That was the origin of the play."

It is Clifford's experiences as a trans woman that throws new and unexpected light on familiar words of Jesus:[45]

> For to be us, to embody this so-called shame and this disgrace,
> Is a privilege
> And it is an honour.
> For the last shall be first,
> and the first last.

Clifford turns the commonly accepted condemnation of trans people upside down by reminding us of some uncomfortable words of Jesus:

> And remember, all of you:
> I never said beware of the homosexual and the transgendered and
>   the queer
> Because our lives are unnatural
> Or because we are depraved in our desires.
> I never said that.
> I said beware of the self-righteous and the hypocrite.

A retelling of stories about Jesus and of his parables made up the center section of the play. The stories are well known, but the figures are placed in situations that a trans woman would recognize. Take the story of the Samaritan woman:

---

45. Extract used from *The Gospel according to Jesus Queen of Heaven* by Jo Clifford, by permission of Alan Brodie Representation Ltd., www.alanbrodie.com.

she had that battered look that women have
When they've been battling hostility and rejection all their lives.

Well-known sayings of Jesus like the beatitudes receive a rewriting. In Clifford's play, the beatitudes transgress divisions of people into fixed categories; they appear to include the spectators in positive as well as in negative positions. What can this example of reception history—Jesus as a trans woman—contribute to the scholarly study of the historical Jesus? I will not suggest that the historical Jesus was a trans person. However, the eunuch saying in Matt 19:12 is an overlooked saying by Jesus that has been hidden under masses of hypermasculine interpretations. It may reflect accusations against Jesus and his followers that they were breaking with male roles in a dramatic way.[46]

Moreover, the transgender identification of Jesus in this play, by breaking the binaries of opposites, opens up new alternative interpretations of Jesus's sayings. In *Putting Jesus in His Place*, I have suggested that Jesus's sayings and his acts should be understood as queer, that is, as "a questioning of settled or fixed categories of identity, not accepting the given orders or structures of the places that people inhabit."[47] I was hesitant to use "queer" to refer to the sexuality of Jesus. However, I think that the now classic book by Robert Goss, *Jesus Acted Up: A Gay and Lesbian Manifesto* shows the possibilities of including sexuality in the historical context.[48] Moreover, the book combines astute historical readings with a reception in the lives of gay and lesbian people in the twentieth century.[49]

RECEPTION HISTORY AS CREATIVE IMAGINATION

Returning to the question wherewith we started—the relationship between historical scholarship of Jesus and different receptions of Jesus—I suggest that it can be understood in light of the difference between mimetic imagination and creative imagination. Historical scholarship is based on observations and sources along with the controlled use of mimetic imagination. Reception history builds on the same narrative stories of Jesus, but with a much freer use of imagination without strict controls. Reception history reflects the possibilities of creative imagination and not just the plausibilities.

46. Halvor Moxnes, *Putting Jesus in His Place: A Radical Vision of Household and Kingdom* (Louisville: Westminster John Knox, 2003), 72–90.
47. Moxnes, *Putting Jesus in His Place*, 5.
48. Robert Goss, *Jesus Acted Up: A Gay and Lesbian Manifesto* (San Francisco: Harper, 1993).
49. Halvor Moxnes, *Memories of Jesus. A Journey through Time* (Eugene, OR: Wipf & Stock, 2021), 193–96.

So, what can reception history contribute to the historical scholarship of Jesus? I have suggested that reception history might generate questions for historical scholarship. Take the play with Jesus as a trans woman. While the figure is historically implausible, it still questions the way we have read Jesus within a context of normality where, for instance, asceticism, eunuchs, single women, and slaves are relegated to the margins. The various genres of reception also affect its impact. A prevailing model of interpretation of Jesus and the law is that he accepted and supported traditional Jewish sexual morals. This conclusion is based on an exegesis of literary sources. A reception in the form of a play with living characters creates a different experience; it makes it possible to imagine the challenges involved in Jesus's encounters with various people, including both sinners and scribes.

Finally, the study of reception history makes us aware of the cultural presuppositions of earlier portrayals of Jesus and our own implicit presuppositions as contemporary Jesus scholars. As noted earlier, Smit, Creangă, and van Klinken have pointed out that scholars have the same presuppositions and prejudices as everybody else. This became clear in my own study of imaginations of nationalism that provided the context for the lives of Jesus produced by nineteenth-century European scholars. Not only that, but the same presuppositions and prejudices toward gender, race, and color manifested in our everyday lives are likewise active when we write scholarly studies of the historical Jesus.

Thus, when Crossley and Keith link historical reconstructions of Jesus and reception history closely together, it is with good reason. To study the reception history of Jesus brings us to a common ground of cultural presuppositions shared by scholars and the general population. These presuppositions also shape historical reconstructions. Therefore, it is impossible to make a firm distinction between the search for the historical meaning of a text and its contemporary reception. The goal of the Next Quest in this matter must be to increase our awareness of our contextuality and cultural embeddedness.

2

Rewriting the History of Scholarship

Brandon Massey

The Next Quest for the historical Jesus must account for the social, political, and cultural contexts of scholarship, describing the ways in which historical Jesus scholarship has influenced or been influenced by these contexts.

The Three Quests Model of the history of the Quest for the historical Jesus (henceforth, the Quest) is no longer viable. While previous histories of the Quest have typically separated this history into three, though sometimes four or even six, divisions (Old Quest, No Quest, Third Quest, and now, the Next Quest), recent histories of the Quest have shown this model to be a "failed construct."[1] The well-documented shortcomings of this paradigm, however, have not prevented its continued use. The Next Quest will abandon the Three Quests Model and instead adopt a social history of the Quest for the historical Jesus.

Recent histories of the discipline of sociology in the United States provide an example of the type of intellectual history the Next Quest will pursue. George Steinmetz traces the twentieth-century history of US sociology, utilizing what he

---

1. Fernando Bermejo-Rubio, "Theses on the Nature of *Leben-Jesu-Forschung*: A Proposal for a Paradigm Shift in Understanding the Quest," *JSHJ* 17 (2009): 9; Bermejo-Rubio, "The Fiction of the 'Three Quests': An Argument for Dismantling a Dubious Historical Paradigm," *JSHJ* 7 (2009): 211–53; Stanley E. Porter, *The Criteria of Authenticity in Historical Jesus Research: Previous Discussions and New Proposals* (Sheffield: Sheffield Academic Press, 2000), 28–62; Dale C. Allison Jr., "Secularizing Jesus," in *Resurrecting Jesus: The Earliest Christian Tradition and Its Interpreters* (London: T&T Clark, 2005), 1–26.

labels a social-epochal model, which "sheds light on the sources of the more wide-spread and implicit ideas shared by all of the actors in a settled scientific field."[2] This approach helpfully distinguishes between internal and external influences on a field of study.[3] Internal influences include a discipline's subfields, university systems, and the relation between the researcher and his or her object of study.[4] For historical Jesus research this would include various methodological approaches (form criticism, redaction criticism, criteria of authenticity, social memory approach, etc.), the differences between German, British, and American university systems, and the relationship between an individual scholar's theology and the gospel texts. External influences are all other sociocultural factors that impact the discipline, such as industrial capitalism, neoliberalism, social and political movements, and other macrosocial factors.[5] Traditionally, histories of the Quest have emphasized internal influences while rarely acknowledging or exploring external influences on the discipline. The Next Quest will seek to incorporate the insights of traditional histories of the Quest (while acknowledging and improving upon their methodological shortcomings) and explore new ground as this history is expanded and external influences are brought to bear on the internal influences to write a comprehensive social history of the Quest.

This brief chapter cannot, of course, fully rewrite the history of scholarship. My hope, however, is that the examples of a new social history of the Quest explored below can be a small start to asking new questions and exploring new connections between the Quest and the social, political, and cultural contexts in which it has taken place. This chapter will explore three ways in which a social history of the quest for the historical Jesus may be pursued. First, I will attempt to understand the form critics and post-Bultmannians within developments in twentieth-century industrial capitalism. Second, I will examine the ways traditional histories of the Quest have maligned works that fall outside traditional historical-critical methodologies, focusing on the work of Howard Thurman. Finally, I will briefly look at the relevance of the Zealot hypothesis for mid-twentieth-century politics and reactions to S. G. F. Brandon's work, focusing on the politics of (German) translation and reactions to the use of Brandon's work in Black theology.

2. George Steinmetz, "Scientific Authority and the Transition to Post-Fordism: The Plausibility of Positivism in U.S. Sociology since 1945," in *The Politics of Method in the Human Sciences: Positivism and Its Epistemological Other*, ed. George Steinmetz (Durham: Duke University Press, 2005), 291.

3. Steinmetz, "Scientific Authority," 288.

4. Steinmetz, "Scientific Authority," 288.

5. Steinmetz, "Scientific Authority," 288.

The Mode of Production and the Production of Historical Jesus Scholarship

In his work on the history of American higher education, Richard Ohmann argued that in order to understand twentieth-century scholarship, we must consider the class interests of scholars.[6] Following Antonio Gramsci, Ohmann argued that the function of the professorate in the twentieth century was to train the professional-managerial class, thus reproducing social relationships. In his essay "The Intellectuals," Gramsci stressed that intellectuals do not operate apart from class structures and serve a mediating function within class relations.[7] The relationship between intellectuals and production is not direct but is mediated between society and the superstructure at two levels—civil society and the state. In Gramsci's view, the intellectuals are the dominant group's deputies and, although they seek the appearance of independence of thought, they (unconsciously) reproduce the values and norms of the dominant group.[8] Despite claims of objectivity and appeals to timeless truths in the biblical text, historical Jesus scholars are not exempt and, as I show below, reproduce the values and norms of the dominant group through reconstructions of Jesus that align with larger economic and political trends. Additionally, the theological aspect of historical Jesus scholarship should not go unnoticed, as some strands of Jesus research reproduce theological conclusions that support the status quo in the name of unbiased historical research.

Ohmann observed three phases of development within the history of twentieth-century scholarship, which he tied firmly to developments within the history of capitalism. While the Three Quests Model must be rejected as inadequate, it is striking that the developments within Ohmann's model roughly align with traditional histories of the Quest. As the Next Quest moves beyond the Three Quests Model, it will situate historical Jesus scholarship within developments in capitalism and the ways in which scholars unconsciously (and sometimes consciously) reproduce the social relationships and logic of capitalism.[9]

The first phase outlined by Ohmann began around 1900 with the formation of a new middle class, which was necessary for the preservation of industrial or

6. Richard Ohmann, *Politics of Knowledge: The Commercialization of the University, the Professions, and Print Culture* (Middletown: Wesleyan University Press, 2003).

7. Antonio Gramsci, "The Intellectuals," in *Selections from the Prison Notebooks*, ed. and trans. Quintin Hoare and Geoffrey Nowell Smith (New York: International Publishers, 1971), 6.

8. Gramsci, "Intellectuals," 10–12.

9. Cf. Steven J. Friesen, "The Blessings of Hegemony: Poverty, Paul's Assemblies, and the Class Interests of the Professorate," in *The Bible in the Public Square*, ed. Cynthia Briggs Kitteredge, Ellen Bradshaw Aitken, and Jonathan A. Draper (Minneapolis: Fortress, 2008), 126–28, who reads the history of Pauline scholarship on poverty through Ohmann's framework.

Fordist capitalism. On January 5, 1914, Henry Ford announced that the Ford Motor Company was doubling its workers' wage to five dollars per day, a date that is the symbolic starting point of the economic and social system later known as Fordism.[10] This system was designed to produce "standardized, low-cost goods and afford its workers decent enough wages to buy them."[11] The use of these standardized parts on the assembly line, combined with the technological innovations of the period, allowed Ford's production of the Model T to flourish, and his philosophies and methods were exported around the world as economies sought to improve efficiency and output. The standardization of component parts, the division of labor, and rationalization of the housing industry were well underway in Germany as early as 1910.[12]

By the mid-1910s, Ford's philosophies had been exported around the world as economies sought to improve efficiency and output and were the foundation of post–World War II industrial reconstruction that led to a long economic boom that lasted until the early 1970s.[13] This economic context provides a setting within which the development of form criticism may be placed. Fordist principles were not limited to the production of consumer goods but applied to all areas of life. As David Harvey observes, Fordism was "less a mere system of mass production and more a total way of life."[14] The Fordist stress on efficiency and functionality contributed to the modernist aesthetic. The new consumer society required new public spaces that were built with mass-produced parts by unskilled laborers.[15] In his encyclopedic volume, Siegfried Gideon documents the ways in which mechanization was overtaking every aspect of life, including farming, furniture, transportation, cleaning, and even the bathroom.[16] Behind these various developments was the "grammar of rationalization":

10. For an overview of Fordism, see Simon Clarke, "What in F---'s Name is Fordism?," in *Fordism and Flexibility: Divisions and Change*, ed. Nigel Gilbert, Roger Burrows, and Anna Pollert (London: Macmillan, 1994), 13–30; David Harvey, *The Condition of Postmodernity: An Enquiry into the Origins of Cultural Change* (Cambridge: Blackwell, 1989), 125–40; Antonio Gramsci, "Americanism and Fordism," in *Selections from the Prison Notebooks*, 279–318.

11. Victoria de Grazia, *Irresistible Empire: America's Advance through 20th-Century Europe* (Cambridge: Harvard University Press, 2005), 4.

12. Christoph Bernhardt and Elsa Vonau, "Zwischen Fordsismus und Sozialreform: Rationalisierungsstrategien im deutschen und französischen Wohnungsbau 1900–1933," *Zeithistorische Forschungen* 6.2 (2009): 232.

13. Harvey, *Condition*, 129.

14. Harvey, *Condition*, 135.

15. David Gartman, *From Autos to Architecture: Fordism and Architectural Aesthetics in the Twentieth Century* (New York: Princeton Architectural Press, 2009), 12.

16. Siegfried Gideon, *Mechanization Takes Command: A Contribution to Anonymous History* (New York: Norton, 1948).

This grammar is based on the idea of decontextualization and of disassembling and recombining: Isolating complex processes from their context, breaking them down into their individual components, then combining them again to form a new structure. That which is superficial can be discarded; that which is mixed can be separated. The process, laden with significance, with meaning and morality, with traditions and arbitrariness, can be melted down to the pure scaffolding of relations—as translucent as crystal and as unsurprising as double-entry bookkeeping. This grammar, as everybody knows, provided for the victory of capitalism, step by step conquering science, technology and economy, judicial systems and management, the arts and philosophy.[17]

This "grammar of rationalization" that provided the victory for capitalism in all realms of society, including biblical studies, formed a context that aided in giving form criticism's conception of Jesus tradition its explanatory power, and the rationalization of nearly every component of life in the twentieth century provided a context where this underlying logic seemed obvious. The form-critical conception of Jesus tradition—the breakdown of the Markan framework into its individual units, the emphasis on pure forms, the deskilling of the labor of ancient tradents and authors—followed this grammar.

Jesus Tradition and the Grammar of Rationalization

The influence of the dominant mode of production of the Quest is often hidden and requires social historians to investigate individual scholars' biographies, political and social movements of different eras, and the effects of economic developments on everyday life. These threads converged in the creation of the *Evangelisch-Sozialer Kongress* (Evangelical Social Congress), which revealed the theological, social, and economic commitments of several prominent New Testament scholars.[18] The Congress was established in 1890 to oppose the Marxist Social Democrat party and develop a Protestant ethic that supported industrial capitalism.[19] Initially, efforts of the Congress were led by Georg Stöcker and Adolf

---

17. Hasso Spode, "Fordism, Mass Tourism and the Third Reich: The 'Strength through Joy' Seaside Resort as an Index Fossil," *Journal of Social History* 38.1 (2004): 129.

18. For a history of the Congress, see Harry Liebersohn, *Religion and Industrial Society: The Protestant Social Congress in Wilhelmine Germany*, Transactions of the American Philosophical Society 76.6 (Philadelphia: American Philosophical Society, 1986); Gottfried Kretschmar, *Der Evangelisch-Soziale Kongreß: Der deutsche Protestantismus und die soziale Frage* (Stuttgart: Evangelisches Verlagswerk, 1972).

19. Steven J. Friesen, "Poverty in Pauline Studies: Beyond the So-Called New Consensus," *JSNT* 23.3 (2004): 327.

von Harnack. Though Stöcker left in 1896, Harnack continued to preside over the efforts of the Congress from 1903 to 1911. Notable members of the Congress included Johannes Weiss (one of Bultmann's primary teachers), Adolf Deissmann (Dibelius's and Schmidt's teacher), and Ernst Troeltsch. In 1896 Friedrich Naumann and other right-leaning members split from the Congress to form the *Nationalsoczialer Verein* (National-Social Association), a party committed to combating Marxism with German nationalism and a Protestant work ethic, and believed that the bourgeoisie and working class must unite rather than engage in Marxist class struggle to create a strong and unified German Empire.[20] As a student, Martin Dibelius was active in National-Social Association alongside other New Testament scholars including Johannes Weiss and Wilhelm Bousset, and he later participated in the German propaganda group *Deutsche Institut für außenpolitische Forschung*, culminating in the publication of a book on British Christianity that supported National Socialist views on Britian.[21]

One example of the relation of industrial capitalism and the form critics is the ways in which the latter present the labor of ancient tradents within the process of oral tradition and the composition of the written gospels. At the end of the nineteenth century, a large percentage of laborers were skilled craftsmen who exerted control over the production process. In contrast, industrial capitalism relied on laborers with little to no traditional skills who worked long hours at a mundane task and had no control over their work. Under industrial capitalism, there were two types of minds: the creative minds of Henry Ford, Frederick Taylor, and other rational managers; and the minds of laboring men and women who were only capable of mundane tasks and who exerted no influence on the products they created.

Form criticism developed out of a scholarly tradition that commonly characterized ancient peoples as uneducated and unskilled. Hermann Gunkel stated, "Uncultivated peoples do not write history. They do not have the capacity to reproduce their experiences objectively, and they have no interest in passing on to posterity an accurate account of the events of their time."[22] The form critics likewise characterized the anonymous tradents of Jesus tradition as "unliterary," "uneducated," "unlettered," or "illiterate."[23] These descriptors of the early Pales-

20. On the *Nationalsozialer Verein* and New Testament scholarship, Albrecht Gerber, *Deissmann the Philologist*, BZNW 171 (Berlin: de Gruyter, 2010), 222–25.

21. Martin Dibelius, *Britisches Christentum und britische Weltmacht*, Schriften des deutschen Instituts für außenpolitische Forschung 36 (Berlin: Junker und Dünnhaupt, 1940).

22. Hermann Gunkel, *The Stories of Genesis: A Translation of the Third Edition of the Introduction to Hermann Gunkel's Commentary on the Book of Genesis*, trans. John J. Scullion, ed. William R. Scott (Vallejo: BIBAL, 1994), 1.

23. Dibelius's statement is indicative of form criticism's descriptions of the early Palestinian

tinian community represent both the anti-Semitism of the era and the negative depictions of the working class within industrialism.

The deskilling of the gospel production process did not end with the anonymous tradents but extended to the evangelists themselves. The evangelist did not assert his own personality onto the framework of the Jesus tradition, for authorial intent belonged to literature proper. Rather, according to Dibelius, the gospels were "unliterary writings" and the evangelists were "principally collectors, vehicles of tradition, editors" whose chief task was simply "handing down, grouping, and working over the material which has come to them."[24] For Bultmann, the evangelists had no literary ability and simply connected units with a simple *kai* or the intensified *euthys*, with place connections stating that Jesus went out of one scene and into the following one, or with temporal sequences in order to construct a gospel.[25] Thus, all the labor that went into handling the Jesus tradition and the production of the gospels was considered unskilled, and it was the job of modern scholars, those with "creative minds," to deconstruct the ancient process.

The connection between form criticism and industrial capitalism requires further examination, including understanding the breakdown of the Markan framework in relation to new forms of labor processes and the concept of pure literary forms within an era of production reliant on standardized parts. I do not want to suggest that the form critics formed their scholarly ideas on the factory floor; rather, their ideas should be understood not only in the history of biblical studies, but also in the context of rationalization of all areas of life.

POSTWAR FORDISM AND THE POST-BULTMANNIANS

The historian Eric Hobsbawm describes the three decades (1947–1973) following the Second World War as the "Golden Age" of the twentieth century.[26] In the wake of the devastation of the War, the industrialized world recovered through rapid economic, social, and cultural transformation through the spread of Fordist

---

church: "The company of unlettered people which expected the end of the world any day had neither the capacity nor the inclination for the production of books." See Martin Dibelius, *From Tradition to Gospel*, trans. B. Wolff (New York: Scribner's Sons, 1934), 9.

24. Dibelius, *From Tradition*, 3–4; Dibelius, "Jesus in Contemporary German Theology," *JR* 11.2 (1931): 182–83.

25. Rudolf Bultmann, *History of the Synoptic Tradition*, trans. John Marsh, 2nd rev. ed. (Oxford: Blackwell, 1968), 338–50.

26. Eric Hobsbawm, *The Age of Extremes: A History of the World, 1914–1991* (New York: Vintage, 1994), 8–9.

principles.[27] Postwar Fordism was not merely a system of mass production but a total way of life that manifested itself in mass consumption, modern aesthetics of functionality and efficiency, internationalization, and, in the Quest, a revitalized hope in the search for the authentic Jesus behind the gospels. In his social history of Jesus scholarship, Dieter Georgi concluded that the explosion of the so-called New Quest occurred in part because of its expression of the socioeconomic forces of the time, including the end of the New Deal and the rise of the middle class in the United States and Germany after World War II.[28]

Georgi, however, offered little evidence for these observations beyond a few brief comments. My intention is to build upon Georgi's observations and situate the post-Bultmannians within Western developments in postwar Fordism.[29] Although the post-Bultmannian movement began with a small circle of scholars in Germany, it should not be limited to German scholars. It included the Scottish scholar John Macquarrie and the American scholars James Robinson, R. H. Fuller, Schubert Ogden, and Van Austin Harvey.[30] This international participation led John Cobb to claim, "Post-Bultmannianism is more likely than any other theological movement to be a shared experience of the German and English-speaking theological communities."[31] The internationalism of this movement was possible, in part, because of the economic and social developments following the Second World War. I want to briefly make two observations that situate the post-Bultmannians within postwar Fordism.

27. Harvey, *Condition*, 129–37; Nicola Pizzolato, *Challenging Global Capitalism: Labor, Migration, Radical Struggle and Urban Change in Detroit and Turin* (New York: Palgrave Macmillan, 2013), 33–36.

28. Dieter Georgi, "The Interest in the Life of Jesus Theology as a Paradigm for the Social History of Biblical Criticism," *HTR* 85.1 (1992): 79–83. Similarly, Elizabeth Schüssler Fiorenza, *Jesus and the Politics of Interpretation* (New York: Continuum, 2000), 43.

29. In an effort to move beyond the Three Quests Model, I do not refer to the New Quest but to the post-Bultmannians. This change in terminology allows greater specificity and does not place all historical Jesus scholarship of this period within the "New Quest."

30. John Macquarrie, *The Scope of Demythologizing: Bultmann and His Critics* (London: SCM, 1960); James Robinson, *A New Quest for the Historical Jesus*, SBT 25 (London: SCM, 1959); Robinson, *The Problem of History in Mark*, SBT 21 (London: SCM, 1957); R. H. Fuller, *The Mission and Achievement of Jesus: An Examination of the Presuppositions of New Testament Theology*, SBT 12 (London: SCM, 1954); Schubert M. Ogden, *Christ without Myth: A Study Based on the Theology of Rudolf Bultmann* (New York: Harper & Bros., 1961); Van A. Harvey and Schubert Ogden, "How New Is the 'New Quest of the Historical Jesus'?," in *The Historical Jesus and the Kerygmatic Christ: Essays on the New Quest of the Historical Jesus*, ed. Carl W. Braaten and Roy A. Harrisville (New York: Abingdon, 1964), 197–242.

31. John B. Cobb Jr., "The Post-Bultmannian Trend," *JBR* 30.1 (1962): 3. Cf. James M. Robinson, "The Recent Debate on the 'New Quest,'" *JBR* 30.3 (1962): 198–208.

Prior to World War I, German historiography was largely optimistic, but Germany's defeat during the war, along with the humiliating sanctions and reparations imposed by the Treaty of Versailles, exacerbated doubts about the possibility of objective knowledge of the past.[32] In the aftermath of World War II, there was a notable break within German historiographical traditions as historians grappled with the multifaceted devastation of war that included a loss of traditions, the breaking of historical consciousness, coming to grips with the Nazi era, and accounting for the radical socioeconomic transformations of the late nineteenth and early twentieth centuries under industrial capitalism.[33] This larger conversation provides a context for the differences between Bultmann and the post-Bultmannians that has been unexplored in previous scholarship.[34]

Bultmann's reflections on philosophy and the historical method marked a substantial change in New Testament scholarly approaches to historical method.[35] Heinrich Ott praised Bultmann for rejecting and overcoming positivism in historical Jesus research and instead stressed Bultmann's "decisive contribution"—historical events are only historical when combined with their meaning and significance.[36] The Bultmannian combination of form criticism and existential

32. Georg G. Iggers, *The German Conception of History: The National Tradition of Historical Thought from Herder to the Present*, rev. ed (Middletown: Wesleyan University Press, 1983), 240; Karl Heussi, *Die Krisis des Historismus* (Tübingen: Mohr, 1932). Ernst Käsemann, *On Being a Disciple of the Crucified Nazarene: Unpublished Lectures and Sermons*, ed. Rudolf Landau, trans. Roy A. Harrisville (Grand Rapids: Eerdmans, 2010), xvii, wrote about the humiliation of Versailles and its influence in political and church affairs.

33. Iggers, *German Conception of History*, 12–13, 245–52.

34. Anthony Le Donne, "The Rise of the Quest for an Authentic Jesus: An Introduction to the Crumbling Foundations of Jesus Research," in *Jesus, Criteria, and the Demise of Authenticity*, ed. Chris Keith and Anthony Le Donne (London: T&T Clark, 2012), 6–7, briefly sketched the development of the criteria against developments in German philosophy but later focused attention on the American context. However, the German context is more important for the development of these ideas in historical Jesus scholarship while the American context is more important for their reception. Alexander J. M. Wedderburn, *Jesus and the Historians*, WUNT 269 (Tübingen: Mohr Siebeck, 2010), 81–89, concerned himself with the existentialist interpretation of history, discussed below, but not these broader questions; Van A. Harvey, *The Historian and the Believer: The Morality of Historical Knowledge and Christian Belief, with a New Introduction by the Author* (Urbana: University of Illinois Press, 1996), 164–68, rightly observed the "New Quest's" dissatisfaction with dialectical theology and Bultmann's perceived skepticism but did not set these debates within broader discussions of historiographical method after World War II.

35. Rudolf Bultmann, "The Problem of Hermeneutics," in *New Testament and Mythology and Other Basic Writings*, trans. and ed. Schubert M. Ogden (Philadelphia, Fortress, 1984), 69–93; Bultmann, "Is Exegesis without Presuppositions Possible?," in *New Testament and Mythology*, 154–63.

36. Heinrich Ott, "Rudolf Bultmann's Philosophy of History," in *The Theology of Rudolf Bultmann*, ed. Charles W. Kegley (New York: Harper & Row, 1966), 56–57.

interpretation proved to be influential to post-Bultmannians in Germany, Britain, and the United States. One significant methodological change, however, was a turn back to positivistic attempts to anchor the kerygmatic Christ to the historical Jesus.

The turn to positivism within the post-Bultmannians manifested itself in several ways throughout their writings. The most explicit way the post-Bultmannians embraced positivism is their assumption that the historical-critical method can conclusively establish facts about the life of Jesus through the application of the criteria of authenticity.[37] The question, then, is how to understand the positivistic turn in the post-Bultmannians within the developments of Fordism. As stated earlier, Fordism was not simply a method of production but also a way of organizing society around systems of mass production and consumption. As Steinmetz has shown, post–World War II Fordism produced an environment that welcomed positivist developments across a variety of disciplines; historical Jesus studies were no exception.

The theological dimension of the turn toward positivism should not go unnoticed, for the question concerning the continuity between the historical Jesus and the kerygma is primarily theological and only secondarily historical. The reaction against the historical and theological implications of Bultmann's program were certainly the guiding forces behind the post-Bultmannian attempts to establish continuity between Jesus and the kerygma. A secondary, and largely unconscious, factor of the post-Bultmannian developments is the Fordist reconstruction of society that provided stability, security, and continuity. Postwar economic policies sought to diminish economic upheavals through the rise in individual wages and the welfare state, thus reducing the financial turmoil for individuals, especially those earning middle and above wages, and allowing them to envision social practices that could be reliably predicted through the application of general laws.[38] Halvor Moxnes describes the master narrative of the post-Bultmannian quest as one of "continuity between the historical Jesus and the resurrected Christ of the church, a narrative within which the present church could inscribe itself."[39] The theology of the post-Bultmannians required continuity between the historical Jesus and the kerygmatic Christ so that they, as modern Christians, could also stand

---

37. Schüssler Fiorenza, *Jesus and the Politics of Interpretation*, 38.

38. Steinmetz, "Scientific Authority," 299–301.

39. Halvor Moxnes, "The Historical Jesus: From Master Narrative to Cultural Context," *BTB* 28.4 (1998): 138. Similarly, Schüssler Fiorenza, *Jesus and the Politics of Interpretation*, 42: "As master narratives of Western cultures, Historical-Jesus discourses are always implicated in and collude with the production and maintenance of systems of knowledge that foster either exploitation and oppression or contribute to a praxis and vision of emancipation and liberation."

in continuity with the early church. As Georgi observed, these developments are not coincidental, and the post-Bultmannian emphasis on historical and theological continuity makes sense in a world designed to restore stability and continuity after the devastation of World War II.

THE NEXT QUEST AND ECONOMIC CONTEXT

As the previous discussion indicates, the economic, political, and social contexts of the Quest for the historical Jesus provide new avenues for the Next Quest to explore. Despite insistence on independence of thought, the mode of production and the social structures that arise from it influence scholarship on the historical Jesus. The designation of "No Quest" for the form-critical era must be abandoned and this influential era understood within the major shifts taking place within capitalism. Following this, the post-Bultmannians should be understood both in their relation to Bultmann's program and within major postwar economic developments in historiography, politics, and culture. The Fordist era began to dissolve in the early 1970s and a consideration of the relationship between historical Jesus scholarship and post-Fordism or neoliberalism has already been undertaken by James Crossley.[40] As we begin to transition to whatever comes after neoliberalism (far right nationalism? reforms from the political center? the progressive left?), the Next Quest for the historical Jesus must be cognizant of the ways in which it is influenced by these political, economic, and social changes.

THE REVOLUTIONARY JESUS

The Next Quest must not only connect scholarship to the developments in capitalism, it also must understand the role historical Jesus scholarship has played in both animating countercultural revolutionary movements and its role in subduing revolutionary momentum (see also Crossley's chapter on "Chartism and Forgotten Quests"). I want to examine the ways in which historical Jesus scholarship influenced or responded to the civil rights movement in America. The civil rights movement sought to abolish racial segregation and discrimination and establish equal rights for African Americans. Martin Luther King Jr. called for nonviolent resistance and civil disobedience to highlight the injustices African Americans dealt with every day. One significant influence on King was the work of Howard Thurman and his nonviolent Jesus in *Jesus and the Disinherited*, a work that has

---

40. James G. Crossley, *Jesus in an Age of Neoliberalism: Quests, Scholarship and Ideology* (New York: Routledge, 2012).

been ignored in previous histories of the Quest. After discussing Thurman's work and reception, I will turn to S. G. F. Brandon's work on the Zealots and the politics at work in the translation of German works on the Zealots and the racism of Ernst Bammel as he critiqued the use of Brandon's hypothesis in Black theology. These examples reveal the racist roots of much historical Jesus scholarship and how supposedly objective and neutral scholarship was used to subvert movements that struggled for the rights of the marginalized.

THE HISTORICAL JESUS AND THE CIVIL RIGHTS MOVEMENT IN AMERICA

It is no secret that histories of the Quest for the historical Jesus have been overwhelmingly centered on white male scholars of European origins. Thus, it is not surprising that there are no references to Howard Thurman's 1949 book *Jesus and the Disinherited* in any of the "major" histories of historical Jesus scholarship.[41] The most attention Thurman's historical Jesus has received in these traditional publications has been a special issue of *Journal for the Study of the Historical Jesus* celebrating the seventieth anniversary of *Jesus and the Disinherited*. In his editorial foreword, Esau McCauley observes that one reason for Thurman's marginalization is that while other (white) Jesus scholars claimed to be neutral, Thurman was decidedly vocal on contemporary issues, especially the treatment of African Americans.[42] As we will see in the next section, scholars regularly use the appearance of neutrality to side with oppressors against the marginalized of society.

Thurman's *Jesus and the Disinherited* was intentionally outside of the traditional historical-critical scholarship characteristic of his era. In fact, according to Abraham Smith, Thurman questioned the value of historical-critical scholarship in his attempt to reconstruct the life of Jesus.[43] Thurman emphasized understanding "Jesus in his experience with God focused in a deep prayer life" and sought to expound the religion *of* Jesus, not religion *about* Jesus.[44] While he did not rigidly apply the historical-critical method to Jesus's life, Thurman did use historical-critical research to place Jesus within his first-century Jewish environment. Thurman's declaration of Jesus's Jewishness in 1949 stands in stark contrast to most historical Jesus scholarship of the era, which attempted to distance Jesus from Judaism. Thurman began with "the simple historical fact that Jesus was a Jew" and

41. Howard Thurman, *Jesus and the Disinherited* (New York: Abingdon-Cokesbury, 1949).
42. Esau McCauley, "Guest Editor's Foreword," *JSHJ* 17.3 (2019): 174.
43. Abraham Smith, "'Low in the Well': A Mystic's Creative Message of Hope in *Jesus and the Disinherited*," *JSHJ* 17.3 (2019): 191–92.
44. Thurman, quoted in Smith, "Low in the Well," 191.

notably "a poor Jew."[45] In his reconstruction of first-century Palestine, Thurman highlighted the fact that as a poor Jew, Jesus was a member of a minority group controlled by an occupying empire, Rome, and this position placed Jesus in the great mass of people throughout history—the poor and oppressed or, in Thurman's terms, those "with their backs against the wall."[46] According to Thurman, Jesus responded to the oppression of Rome with nonviolent resistance, which ultimately led to his death.

It is from this picture of the historical Jesus and his religious practices that Thurman develops his theological and political program of nonviolent resistance. There is, of course, much more to be said of Thurman's work, but I want to turn briefly to its reception, Thurman's influence, and the ways in which the Next Quest may begin to rewrite the history of scholarship and give scholars like Thurman their proper due (see also Mitzi Smith's chapter). As Smith, McCauley, and Thomas Slater have shown, Thurman was ignored for many reasons, including his rejection of the tenets of historical criticism, the fact that he was Black and taught at a historically Black university, and his unconcealed concern to write for the disinherited.[47] The Next Quest must deal with the embedded whiteness in the discipline, not only in matters relating to reconstructing Christian origins but also in the ways whiteness has dominated the intellectual history of the Quest (see Park's chapter). Thurman's influence on Martin Luther King Jr. and other civil rights leaders should not be understated—there is a legend that King carried a copy of Thurman's *Jesus and the Disinherited* in his coat pocket throughout the Montgomery bus boycott.[48] It is not an overstatement to say that Thurman's work on Jesus is more culturally and socially significant than Rudolf Bultmann's *Jesus and the Word*. The Next Quest will take these contributions seriously alongside more traditional historical-critical works and understand their presentation of Jesus and their reception history within the social-political contexts.

JESUS AND THE POLITICS OF TRANSLATION

While scholars like Thurman posed a nonviolent Jesus as an example in the face of oppression, others presented a militant or revolutionary Jesus consistent with

45. Thurman, *Jesus*, 5–7.
46. Thurman, *Jesus*, 1.
47. Thomas B. Slater, "Thurman, Johnson, Hendricks and the Third Quest," in *Afrocentric Interpretations of Jesus and the Gospel Traditions: Things Black Scholars See That White Scholars Overlook*, ed. Thomas B. Slater (Lewiston: Mellen, 2015), 37–55.
48. Paul Harvey, *Howard Thurman and the Disinherited: A Religious Biography* (Grand Rapids: Eerdmans, 2020), 5.

the ethos of the 1960s. In his 1967 book, *Jesus and the Zealots*, S. G. F. Brandon argued that Jesus, though not a Zealot himself, held similar views about Jewish independence from Rome and his mission was not incompatible with the Zealots.[49] According to Brandon, whatever else the phrase "kingdom of God" meant to the historical Jesus, it certainly "looked forward to the achievement of an apocalyptic situation that necessarily involved the elimination of Roman government in Judea."[50] In Brandon's reconstruction, Jesus was a revolutionary who was not afraid to resist the Romans through violence and, after his demonstration in the temple, was crucified for sedition as a would-be messiah who failed in his attempt to restore the kingdom of Israel. In this section, I want to look at the reception of Brandon's work and the ways in which Martin Hengel's books were translated to counter Brandon's revolutionary Jesus and, in effect, subdue social movements that found inspiration in this portrait of Jesus.

In contrast to Brandon's picture of the historical Jesus, Martin Hengel denied that Jesus was a revolutionary.[51] In his view, Jesus radically opposed the "apocalyptic Jewish 'theology of revolution'" with "agape: the way of nonviolent protest and willingness to suffer."[52] For Hengel, the kingdom Jesus sought to establish was of a spiritual, not political, nature and "true freedom from the powers begins with an inner freedom."[53]

The introductions of the English translations of Hengel's work expose motives beyond neutral scholarly understandings of Jesus and his political environment. The translators thought Hengel's work spoke to the issues of the day and called for readers to follow the example of the nonviolent Jesus Hengel presented as the answer to the period's social concerns (without the civil disobedience of someone like Thurman). Robin Scroggs situated Hengel's work as an answer to both European Marxist-Christian dialogue and George McGovern's 1968 US presidential campaign.[54] The core policy positions of the McGovern campaign included immediate withdrawal from the Vietnam War, granting amnesty to draft dodgers, a significant decrease in military spending and increase in social welfare, completing the promises of the civil rights movement, and enacting environmental

49. S. G. F. Brandon, *Jesus and the Zealots: A Study of the Political Factor in Primitive Christianity* (New York: Scribner's Sons, 1967).

50. Brandon, *Jesus and the Zealots*, 344.

51. Martin Hengel, *Was Jesus a Revolutionist?*, trans. William Klassen (Philadelphia: Fortress, 1971), 29.

52. Respectively, Martin Hengel, *Victory over Violence and Was Jesus a Revolutionist?*, trans. David E. Green (Minneapolis: Augsburg Fortress, 2003), 2; Hengel, *Was Jesus a Revolutionist?*, 32.

53. Hengel, *Was Jesus a Revolutionist?*, 34.

54. Hengel, *Victory over Violence*, x–xi.

protections.[55] McGovern lost in a landslide to Richard Nixon. Similarly, John Reuman noted the importance of Brandon's work to the student protests in France, Black power movements in America, and liberation theology and the significance of Hengel's refutation of the Zealot hypothesis. For both Scroggs and Reuman, Hengel's presentation of Jesus's relationship to the Zealot party was not only correct but had significant implications for the ways Christians engaged social movements, as it limited advocating for changes in material conditions and emphasized the inner disposition of the individual. The Next Quest will take seriously the politics of translation, question why certain books are selected for translation and others are not, and interrogate the intentions of the editors and translators.

Jesus and the Politics of Our Day

C. F. D. Moule and Ernst Bammel gathered a group of scholars together in the early 1970s to offer a "sober investigation of the evidence relating to Jesus's attitude to authority, both Jewish and Roman."[56] The contributors to this sober investigation included Walter Grundmann, a Nazi New Testament scholar called upon here three decades after World War II and whose anti-Semitic and pro-Nazi writings were well known within the guild. My aim here, however, does not involve Grundmann but instead Bammel's lengthy chapter on the political interpretation of Jesus.[57] In particular, I will focus on the eighth and final section of Bammel's chapter that deals with the political Jesus in Black theology, which reveals the whiteness of the discipline and the ways in which the voices of people of color have been marginalized in the history of research.

Bammel begins this section by observing that in the 1960s, "the view that Jesus was a revolutionary spread like a prairie fire over the five continents."[58] Instead of asking why this may be the case and investigating the social unrest that was pervasive throughout this period, Bammel instead laments the "arbitrarily selected citations from the works of German theologians" and lambasts attempts to modernize Jesus.[59] When he turns to the work of James Cone, Bammel writes:

55. Thomas J. Knock, *The Rise of a Prairie Statesman: The Life and Times of George McGovern* (Princeton: Princeton University Press, 2016), 391–406; Gary Warren Hart, *Right from the Start: A Chronicle of the McGovern Campaign* (New York: Quadrangle, 1973).

56. C. F. D. Moule and Ernst Bammel, eds., *Jesus and the Politics of His Day* (Cambridge: Cambridge University Press, 1983), xi.

57. Ernst Bammel, "The Revolution Theory from Reimarus to Brandon," in *Jesus and the Politics of His Day*, 11–68.

58. Bammel, "Revolution Theory," 57.

59. Bammel, "Revolution Theory," 57.

The black man himself is inclined to single out certain elements in the Bible and re-interpret them in the light of his own expectation. This can be done in a committed way and in a more detached manner which only makes use of the traditional material. Characteristic for the latter is the motto: 'seek ye first the political kingdom and all the rest will be added to you.' Basically it is lack of objective interest in Jesus and early Christianity that becomes manifest in this way.[60]

With these remarks, Bammel clearly states that, in his view, Black interpretation lacks objectivity while white European historical criticism provides an objective means of understanding Jesus. Bammell argues that Colin Morris's work, written from the perspective of a British missionary to Africa, uses Brandon's thesis to encourage violent tactics in Zambian liberation movements.[61] According to Bammel, it was through white authors like Morris that the idea of violence, a departure from the mere presentation of a revolutionary Jesus and a turn to the use of violence, was presented to the "black man."[62] According to Bammel, Morris's work had no real effect and was dismissed "by the sophisticated negroes of North America."[63] Bammel continues his critique of Black theology's use of the revolutionary Jesus along these lines, and later turns to a similar critique of Latin American liberation theology, though with less overt racism.

In her recent work, Angela Parker has questioned the historical-critical method, calling objectivity "one of the systemic evils of academic biblical studies" and argues for engaging with "the real lived experiences of a multiplicity of identities."[64] As David Horrell observes, the historical-critical method arose in Europe when colonialism was at its peak and "an ideology of religious and racial superiority" became embedded in the discipline.[65] Bammel's critique of Cone, Morris, and others reveals the ways in which whiteness is unmarked and any deviation from this perspective is considered Other and even dangerous. While

---

60. Bammel, "Revolution Theory," 58.

61. Colin Morris, *Unyoung, Uncoloured, Unpoor* (London: Epworth, 1969). For Morris's life and work as a missionary, Doris Marley Laird, "Colin Morris: Modern Missionary" (PhD diss., Florida State University, 1980). S. G. F. Brandon, "Jesus and the Zealots: The Aftermath," *BJRL* 54.1 (1971): 50, expressed surprise that his work was used by political radicals.

62. Bammel, "Revolution Theory," 59.

63. Bammel, "Revolution Theory," 60.

64. Angela N. Parker, *If God Still Breathes, Why Can't I? Black Lives Matter and Biblical Authority* (Grand Rapids: Eerdmans, 2021), 19, 52–53.

65. David G. Horrell, *Ethnicity and Inclusion: Religion, Race, and Whiteness in Constructions of Jewish and Christian Identities* (Grand Rapids: Eerdmans, 2020), 325.

critiquing portraits of Jesus used to advocate for violent resistance, Bammel failed
to realize the violence inherent in his own approach that owed much to European
colonialism.

CONCLUSION

In conclusion, there is no such thing as an objective approach to the historical
Jesus and as the Next Quest abandons the "Three Quest Model" of intellectual
history, it will be alert to the ways the Quest has been undertaken in its social-
epochal contexts. I have sketched three examples of this type of social history
of the Quest—the changes within the mode of production and developments
in historical Jesus scholarship, Howard Thurman and the historical Jesus in the
American civil rights movement, and the reception of the Zealot hypothesis—but
there are many ways and vantage points from which this social history can be
written, such as class conflict, gender, race, empire, theology, archival evidence,
and biography, among others. Within this social history of the Quest there must be
space for intellectual histories of method, which have dominated prior histories,
but we cannot continue as if the historical situation and material circumstances
of a scholar play no role in their scholarship. Ideas cannot be separated from the
material conditions in which they arose. The Next Quest will take these issues
seriously and produce a history of the Quest that accounts for the social, political,
and cultural contexts of historical Jesus scholarship.

3

Beyond the Jewish Jesus Debate

Adele Reinhartz

The Next Quest for the historical Jesus must do three things when it comes to the topic of Jesus's Jewishness: (1) take it as a given that Jesus was a Jewish man who participated in Jewish life in the same ways as did the Jews among whom he grew up and among whom he lived; (2) avoid *evaluating* Jesus's Jewishness ("very Jewish," "not too Jewish," etc.) and in doing so also avoid essentializing and homogenizing what constituted Jewishness in the first century;[1] and (3) focus attention on how Jesus's Jewishness was constructed by his biographers, starting with the gospel writers and including participants in the successive quests for the historical Jesus.

For most scholars, historical Jesus research involves the attempt to determine what Jesus, as a historical individual living in the first third of the first century CE, did and said during his lifetime. I confess, however, that I have not been at all preoccupied by such questions. As a non-Christian, neither the Jesus of history nor the Christ of faith has been pertinent to my own personal and spiritual life. Furthermore, as a historian, I am a minimalist. I see little reliable evidence for addressing historical questions pertaining to the life of Jesus, the authorship and audiences of the gospels, the establishment of the communities that loosely comprised the Jesus movement, or most other topics that seem so important to many of my fellow New Testament scholars. The absence of evidence compromises the

1. For details about and analysis of such misguided evaluations, see James G. Crossley, "A 'Very Jewish' Jesus: Perpetuating the Myth of Superiority," *JSHJ* 11.2 (2013): 109–29.

methodology by pushing scholars to employ a circular methodology: constructing historical hypotheses based on their readings of the gospels and then using those same hypotheses as lenses through which to explicate the gospels themselves.

Concerning the historical Jesus, I would suggest that we are on solid ground with regard to six points: (1) he was born in the Galilee (2) sometime right before or right after what we refer to as the turn of the eras; (3) he was baptized by John; (4) he gathered a following, and (5) he was crucified on the order of Pontius Pilate. Finally, (6) we can say with certainty that Jesus was a Jewish man. Birth and death are common to all human beings; it seems unlikely that Jesus's followers would have fabricated stories about his baptism and crucifixion, both of which they try to explain or explain away, and had he not gathered some sort of following there would have been no Jesus movement.

The matter of gender I leave to other contributors to this volume (see the chapters by Petrey and Levine). My focus is on Jesus's Jewishness and, in particular, how the canonical gospels, as the earliest written attempts to depict the historical Jesus, present Jesus's Jewishness. Future research on this topic should consider each gospel individually. For present purposes, however, I will take a composite view on the grounds that, for the better part of the last two millennia, this is how the canonical gospels have been read by Christians, and it is as a harmonized group that they have influenced both popular and scholarly notions about the historical Jesus.[2]

I begin with a brief look at what the gospels convey about Jesus's Jewishness. The purpose is not to "demonstrate" that Jesus was Jewish—this point is the default and needs no demonstration—but rather to set the stage for the main part of the chapter, in which I outline what I see as the three main factors that complicate the gospels' portrayal of Jesus's Jewishness. Finally, I will reflect on how one might go beyond the Jewish Jesus debate in the Next Quest for the historical Jesus.

THE GOSPELS' JEWISH JESUS

The Gospels of Matthew and Luke establish Jesus's Jewishness at the outset: although his father was apparently God, Jesus's mother was a Jewish Galilean. By the rules of matrilineal descent that were already well established at the time, the Jewishness of Jesus's mother establishes her son's Jewish identity.[3] The Gospel of Mark

2. Marion A. Taylor, *Women in the Story of Jesus: The Gospels through the Eyes of Nineteenth-Century Female Biblical Interpreters* (Grand Rapids: Eerdmans, 2016), 4.

3. Shaye J. D. Cohen, "The Origins of the Matrilineal Principle in Rabbinic Law," *AJSR* 10.1 (1985): 19–53.

does not portray Jesus's mother in any detail. John places her at a Jewish wedding in Cana, at which preparations had been made for the Jewish ritual handwashing required prior to a festive meal. On the genealogical principle, as understood in the first century, therefore, Jesus was undeniably Jewish. Matthew's genealogy underscores this point by situating Jesus in the line of Abraham, who was commonly, and probably nonhistorically, considered the patriarch of the Jewish people.

A person with a Jewish mother is a Jew, full stop.[4] This is true whether or not that person observes Jewish law and practice, reads the Jewish Scriptures, associates with other Jews, keeps the dietary or purity laws, or does anything else associated with Jewish identity.[5] Jewish identity is not a qualitative identity but an absolute one. Observing more or fewer laws and practices, engaging intensely or not at all with fellow Jews, does not make one more or less Jewish.

Nevertheless, Jews enact or express their Jewishness in different ways. In the first century, as in the present, the ways they did so depended on numerous factors including their individual, communal, geographical, and social locations. Various elements of Jewish practice, including Sabbath observance, pilgrimage, kashrut, and purity practices such as ritual handwashing, were discussed and contested.

The gospels collectively portray Jesus as a Jewish man who was concerned about the Sabbath, traveled to Jerusalem for the pilgrimage festivals, and dined with other Jews (e.g., Matt 12:1–8; Mark 2:15; Luke 7:36; John 2:13). They also suggest that he situated himself within the Jewish community, perhaps with little or no concern for outsiders. This stance is evident in the exchange between the Markan Jesus and the Syro-Phoenician woman in Mark 7:25–30, in which a woman identified by the narrator as a "gentile, of Syrophoenician origin" (Mark 7:26 NRSV) asks Jesus to cast a demon out of her daughter. Jesus responds rather rudely: "Let the children be fed first, for it is not fair to take the children's food and throw it

4. The same is true of people who become Jewish through conversion. On conversion in Second Temple Judaism, see Seth Schwartz, "Conversion to Judaism in the Second Temple Period: A Functionalist Approach," in *Studies in Josephus and the Varieties of Ancient Judaism: Louis H. Feldman Jubilee Volume*, ed. Shaye J. D. Cohen and Joshua J. Schwartz, AJEC 67 (Leiden: Brill, 2007), 223–36; Matthew Thiessen, *Contesting Conversion: Genealogy, Circumcision, and Identity in Ancient Judaism and Christianity* (Oxford: Oxford University Press, 2011); Shaye J. D. Cohen, "Crossing the Boundary and Becoming a Jew," *HTR* 82.1 (1989): 13–33.

5. The situation is more complicated with regard to male circumcision but even in this regard, aside from the ultra-orthodox, uncircumcised men born of a Jewish mother are considered Jewish. For the range of opinions, see David Golinkin, "What Is the Halakhic Status of an Uncircumcised Jew?," *Responsa in a Moment* 9.3, February 2015, https://schechter.edu/what-is-the-halakhic-status-of-an-uncircumcised-jew-responsa-in-a-moment-volume-9-issue-no-3-february-2015/. See also Shaye J. D. Cohen, "Judaism without Circumcision and 'Judaism' without 'Circumcision' in Ignatius," *HTR* 95.4 (2002): 395–415.

to the dogs" (Mark 7:27 NRSV). Presumably Jews are the children, and gentiles are the dogs. The woman's clever answer—"even the dogs under the table eat the children's crumbs" (7:28 NRSV)—persuades Jesus to act on her behalf. The gospels also present Jesus as involved with Jewish Scripture. Luke 4:17 has Jesus reading from Isaiah in the synagogue. Matthew has Jesus engaging in halakhic discourse in Matthew 5; John has Jesus using protorabbinic modes of interpretation in exegeting the manna passages in John 6.[6]

The gospels paint a consistent, if composite, picture of a man who is ethnically and genealogically Jewish, who observes the Jewish Sabbath and festivals, and who is knowledgeable about and engaged with Jewish Scriptures and modes of Jewish scriptural interpretation. Aside from Jesus's genealogical identity, we cannot know for sure whether the more specific reports of Jesus's words and deeds represent the man himself or the imagination of the evangelists. The important point for our purposes is that *the gospels depict Jesus as unquestionably Jewish.*

Whether the gospels situated Jesus within one of the specific Jewish groups known to us from Second Temple period or first-century sources, including the gospels themselves, is more difficult to determine. Although Jewish lifestyle choices could be individual or idiosyncratic, more often they conformed more or less to those common to the formal and informal social and kinship groups with which people affiliated. Different groups and communities had different practices, and even different calendars, leading them to celebrate the festivals on different dates.[7] There were likely many more groups than the ones for which we have specific literary or archaeological evidence.

In several books, Barbara Thiering has offered a portrait of Jesus as an Essene, though to my knowledge few scholars give this portrait much credence.[8] Hyam Maccoby has identified Jesus as a Pharisee.[9] This identification is not impossible, given that Jesus's ruling on divorce, as reported by the Synoptics and Paul, coin-

---

6. For detailed discussion of John's use of midrashic exegetical methods and comparisons to Philo, see Peder Borgen, *Bread from Heaven; an Exegetical Study of the Concept of Manna in the Gospel of John and the Writings of Philo* (Leiden: Brill, 1965); Borgen, *The Gospel of John: More Light from Philo, Paul and Archaeology: The Scriptures, Tradition, Exposition, Settings, Meaning,* NovTSupp 154 (Leiden: Brill, 2014). For discussion of scriptural interpretation as a source of conflict between Jesus and other scriptural teachers, see Chris Keith, *Jesus against the Scribal Elite: The Origins of the Conflict* (Grand Rapids: Baker Academic, 2014), 131–47.

7. On calendric differences, see Roger T. Beckwith, *Calendar and Chronology, Jewish and Christian: Biblical, Intertestamental and Patristic Studies* (Leiden: Brill, 2001).

8. B. E. Thiering, *Jesus and the Riddle of the Dead Sea Scrolls: Unlocking the Secrets of His Life Story* (Toronto: Doubleday Canada, 1992).

9. Hyam Maccoby, *Jesus the Pharisee* (London: SCM, 2003). See also Harvey Falk, *Jesus the Pharisee: A New Look at the Jewishness of Jesus* (New York: Paulist, 1985); Jens Schröter, "How

cides with that of the house of Shammai, a Pharisaic group. There are hints of a group focused on John the Baptizer; the gospel references to Jesus's baptism could imply that he was a member of this group.[10] But the evidence is too slim to allow for a definitive conclusion. Perhaps the best one can do is appeal to the category of common Judaism, described by E. P. Sanders as including circumcision, the temple, purity, sacrifices, tithes, worship of the God of Israel, and other features.[11] The gospels collectively refer to Jesus as engaging with most of these practices or ideas, enough to suggest that they viewed Jesus as "doing Jewish" in much the same way as those around him did. Even the so-called Sabbath controversies do not show Jesus as ignoring the Sabbath so much as following an understanding of Sabbath practice that differed from his interlocutors, as these are presented by the evangelists.

THE GOSPELS' UN-JEWISH JESUS

Although the gospels' Jesus cannot be pinned down to one specific group, he is not only Jewish but also knowledgeable about Jewish Scripture, scriptural interpretation, and observance, and he is engaged with his fellow Jews. And yet, from the late first century until the mid-twentieth century, most Christian exegetes, theologians, historians, and storytellers have attempted to dissociate Jesus from Jewishness. This ambivalence about the Jewish Jesus is evident even in the very same gospels that overtly construct Jesus as a Jewish man.

I attribute this ambivalence to three main factors: (1) the belief in Jesus's uniqueness; (2) the broadening of the Jesus movement to the gentiles; and (3) the narrative imperative inherent in the setting down of the gospel accounts. To view Jesus as an ordinary Jew who lived like other Galilean Jews flew in the face of these christological, demographic, and narrative requirements. If Jesus was a Jew like other early first-century Galilean Jews, in what ways can he be said to be unique, a claim that seems fundamental to the gospels' Christology? If Jesus belonged squarely within a Jewish milieu, how could the church justify outreach to the gentiles? And if Jesus was just a normal Jew, how could the evangelists write a story in which he was eventually executed on the orders of the Roman governor of Judea?

Close Were Jesus and the Pharisees?," in *The Pharisees*, ed. Joseph Sievers and Amy-Jill Levine (Grand Rapids: Eerdmans, 2021), 220–39.

10. Daniel S. Dapaah, *The Relationship between John the Baptist and Jesus of Nazareth: A Critical Study* (Lanham, MD: University Press of America, 2005).

11. E. P. Sanders, *Judaism: Practice and Belief, 63 BCE–66 CE*, rev. ed. (London: SCM, 1992).

THE UNIQUE JESUS

Implicit in the gospels is the question about what it was about Jesus, a Jewish Galilean, that stimulated his followers to establish a movement centered around the belief that he was the messiah and Son of God. Surely he must have been unique in important and identifiable ways; otherwise how are we to explain the following that he had in his lifetime and after his death?

It is not at all unusual for an individual at the center of a given belief system to be retrospectively awarded special qualities, such as miraculous powers, as well as accorded unusual beginnings in their conception, birth, or infancy. The infancy narratives in Matthew and Luke describe Jesus as the product of a unique union between the God of Israel and a human woman; similarly unusual, if not quite as extraordinary, stories are told about other ancient leaders such as Moses and the Buddha.

Beyond his unusual beginnings, the gospels' Jesus has special, if not unique, powers to heal and to cast out demons. In the gospel accounts, the acts that demonstrate these powers are greeted with wonder, incredulity, and, in some cases, negative judgment (e.g., Mark 1:22, 27). When Jesus forgives the sins of the paralytic, the scribes accuse him of blasphemy: "Why does this fellow speak in this way? It is blasphemy! Who can forgive sins but God alone?" (2:7 NRSV). The people in the synagogue who hear him teach are surprised, and not in a good way, that this man, "the carpenter, the son of Mary and brother of James and Joses and Judas and Simon" who was there with his sisters (6:3 NRSV), had wisdom and power (6:2). Jesus's uniqueness is also hinted at by God, who in Mark 1:11 and again in 9:7 refers to Jesus as God's beloved son. Of course, a Jew who lives his life in the ways that other Galilean Jews did could still be special in all the ways that Jesus was, according to the gospels' portrayals. Nevertheless, these comments by members of the audience within the narrative draw attention away from what Jesus shares with other Jews to what makes him different: his birth and his powers, to be sure, but most of all, the voice of God claiming him as God's Son.

The Gospel of John, probably written down several decades later than Mark, is more explicit in attributing uniqueness to Jesus. In the Prologue, John 1:18 refers to Jesus as *monogenēs theos*, God's "only-begotten" or "unique" son. Later John has the man born blind exclaim after Jesus has restored his sight: "Never since the world began has it been heard that anyone opened the eyes of a person born blind" (9:32 NRSV). John places great emphasis on Jesus's identity as God's son, which eclipses his human identity. That Jesus's christological identity separates him from other Jews is evident in John 8:41–44. In this infamous passage the Jews to whom Jesus is speaking declare that they "have one father, God himself." Jesus counters: "If God were your Father, you would love me, for I came from God, and now I am here. I did not come on my own, but he sent me" (8:42 NRSV). Far from being the children of God, Jesus insists, the Jews have the devil as their father (8:44).

These and other aspects of the gospels' descriptions of Jesus, and of the varied responses to his activities, take Jesus out of the lineup of ordinary Jews to posit a unique identity consisting of traits and powers associated with the divine. This emphasis undergirded the christological and soteriological claims that were foundational for the Jesus movement and, later, Christianity.

THE UNIVERSAL JESUS

The Letters of Paul testify that by the latter half of the first century the Jesus movement already included gentile groups and churches. To what extent the gospels reflect this demographic development is a matter of debate. But the tension involved in proclaiming this Jewish man relevant for "the nations" can be detected in all four canonical gospels as they try to answer the question: How can a man who is firmly situated in a Galilean Jewish context be made to appeal to non-Jews, including gentiles and Samaritans?

The Gospels of Mark, Luke, and John, as well as Acts, gesture toward the incoming of the gentiles. In Mark 7:28, as noted above, the Syro-Phoenician woman chastises Jesus for looking out only for Jews when she reminds Jesus that "even the dogs under the table eat the children's crumbs." At the very end of Matthew's Gospel, Jesus, now risen, tells the disciples, "Go therefore and make disciples of all nations, baptizing them in the name of the Father and of the Son and of the Holy Spirit" (28:19 NRSV). Luke-Acts posits a chronology whereby the good word went out first to the Jews and then to the gentiles, though some, such as Jeffrey Siker, have argued that the Gospel of Luke too envisions the church's spread to gentiles.[12] Luke's genealogy traces Jesus's ancestors through Joseph back through Adam and then God (3:38), making essentially the same point.

The Gospel of John also hints at knowledge of, or even participation in, the gentile mission.[13] At the end of the extended shepherd and sheep analogy, Jesus says: "I have other sheep that do not belong to this fold. I must bring them also, and they will listen to my voice. So there will be one flock, one shepherd" (10:16 NRSV). Although one can debate the identity of these "other sheep," they are most readily understood as gentiles.

12. Jeffrey S. Siker, "'First to the Gentiles': A Literary Analysis of Luke 4:16–30," *JBL* 111.1 (1992): 73.

13. This possibility was raised by Raymond Edward Brown, *The Community of the Beloved Disciple* (New York: Paulist, 1979), 55. For extended discussion, see Adele Reinhartz, *Cast Out of the Covenant: Jews and Anti-Judaism in the Gospel of John* (Lanham, MD: Lexington/Fortress Academic, 2018), 135–45.

John 12 provides a more explicit reference to gentile believers, assigning their incoming to the period after Jesus's death. John 12:20–26 refers to some Greeks who came to worship at the Passover festival. These Greeks are likely to be gentiles rather than Greek-speaking Jews.[14] They approach Philip with a request to see Jesus. Philip tells Andrew, and together they both tell Jesus about the request. Jesus responds cryptically: "The hour has come for the Son of Man to be glorified. Very truly, I tell you, unless a grain of wheat falls into the earth and dies, it remains just a single grain; but if it dies, it bears much fruit" (12:23–24 NRSV).

This declaration marks a turning point. Until this point in John's Gospel, Jesus has insisted that his hour has not yet come (2:4; 7:30; 8:20). But, with the coming of the first gentiles, the hour has finally arrived. The hour of glorification is also the hour of his death, a death that is necessary in order for his mission truly to bear fruit. This complex of ideas suggests that the Greeks who wish to see Jesus are themselves the fruit that will flourish on account of his (impending) death.[15]

Here the Greeks are anxious to do what the Jews, in their blindness, refuse to do, which is truly to see Jesus for who he is: the Son of God. In John 12:37, the narrator summarizes the first twelve chapters of the gospel: "Although he had performed so many signs in their presence, they [the Jews] did not believe in him" (NRSV). The choice had been put before them so many times, and as recently as 12:36: "While you have the light, believe in the light, so that you may become children of light" (NRSV). Their refusal of the light was not a failure of God, Jesus, or the proclamation, but rather a fulfillment of Isaiah's prophetic words. God "has blinded their eyes and hardened their heart, so that they might not look with their eyes, and understand with their heart and turn" (John 12:40 NRSV; cf. Isa 6:10).

Most telling, perhaps, is John's use of the identity label *Ioudaios* (plural *Ioudaioi*) which scholars translate as "Jew(s)."[16] As many scholars have documented, John uses this term seventy times. Although some of the references are in a neutral or descriptive context, as when John refers to a specific practice or a festival of the

---

14. This point has been demonstrated persuasively by Mary Coloe, who looks carefully at the prophetic quotations and allusions in John 12 to situate this brief narrative in an eschatological context in which all nations will acknowledge the sovereignty of Israel's God. Mary L. Coloe, "Gentiles in the Gospel of John: Narrative Possibilities—John 12:12–43," in *Attitudes to Gentiles in Ancient Judaism and Early Christianity*, ed. David C. Sim and James S. McLaren (London: Bloomsbury, 2013), 209–23.

15. Raymond Edward Brown, *The Gospel according to John*, AB 29–29A (Garden City, NY: Doubleday, 1966), 1:466.

16. On the appropriate translation of *Ioudaioi*, see Adele Reinhartz, "The Vanishing Jews of Antiquity," *Marginalia Review of Books*, June 24, 2014, http://marginalia.lareviewofbooks.org /vanishing-jews-antiquity-adele-reinhartz/.

Jews, most express hostility, as in 10:31 when *hoi Ioudaioi* take up stones again to stone Jesus. In many other verses, the context implies hostility toward Jews, as in 8:44. The term *hoi Ioudaioi* does not appear in the verse, but vv. 31 and 52 establish *hoi Ioudaioi* as the addressees.

John 4:9 is often cited as the exception to this pattern. Here Jesus is identified as a Jew by the Samaritan woman, who marvels: "'How is it that you, a Jew [*Ioudaios*], ask a drink of me, a woman of Samaria?' (Jews do not share things in common with Samaritans)" (NRSV). Jesus does not respond to the identification; he neither rejects it nor accepts it. Rather, he sets out to broaden her understanding of his identity: "If you knew the gift of God and who it is that is saying to you, 'Give me a drink,' you would have asked him, and he would have given you living water" (v. 10 NRSV). By the end of the passage, he has revealed his messianic identity. In response to the woman's statement, "I know that Messiah is coming" (v. 25 NRSV), Jesus confesses: "I am he, the one who is speaking to you" (v. 26 NRSV).

This is not to say that John denies the Jewishness of Jesus or of the disciples, who are also never referred to as *Ioudaioi*. Rather, this usage is related to John's redefinition of *Ioudaioi* primarily as the opponents of Jesus. Included also are Jews who sit on the fence (e.g., 7:12 NRSV: "While some were saying, 'He is a good man,' others were saying, 'No, he is deceiving the crowd'"). There are also some *Ioudaioi* who believe in Jesus after seeing a sign (11:45). Their belief, however, does not seem to have impressed the narrator all that much, as suggested in 2:23–25: "When he was in Jerusalem during the Passover festival, many believed in his name because they saw the signs that he was doing. But Jesus on his part would not entrust himself to them, because he knew all people and needed no one to testify about anyone, for he himself knew what was in everyone" (NRSV).

The titulus, identifying Jesus as King of the Jews, may also go against this pattern, but it should be noted that it is rejected by the Jewish leaders, thus maintaining John's general definition of the *Ioudaioi* as Jesus's opponents: "Then the chief priests of the Jews said to Pilate, 'Do not write, "The King of the Jews," but, "This man said, I am King of the Jews"'" (John 19:21 NRSV). Pilate does not take the bait, proclaiming: "What I have written I have written" (19:22 NRSV).

In theory, Jesus's Jewishness should not preclude a role that reaches beyond the Jewish community in Galilee and Judea. In practice, however, the universal and the particular came to be seen as mutually exclusive, perhaps already in John's time, as his rhetorical use of the label *Ioudaioi* for Jesus's enemies implies. For Jesus to be credible as the savior of the world, his affiliation with a specific, that is, Jewish, corner of that world had to be loosened.

If the gospels only loosen Jesus's connection with Jewishness, later Christian writings cut the cord altogether. In his comments on John 3:22 ("And He went away again beyond Jordan into the place where John was baptizing; and there He abode"), Cyril of Alexandria explained: "Leaving Jerusalem, the Saviour seeks a refuge in a place possessing springs of water, that He might signify obscurely as in a type how He would leave Judaea and go over to the Church of the Gentiles which possesses the fountains of Baptism . . . truly He went across from the synagogue of the Jews unto the Gentiles" (*Commentary on John* 7).[17]

Fast forwarding 1,500 years to the work of Ernst Renan, it becomes clear that not much has changed. According to Renan, Jesus may have been born Jewish but he came to reject and despise "the ancient Jewish religion."

> One idea, at least, which Jesus carried away from Jerusalem, and which hence-forth appeared to be rooted in his mind, was that there was no union possible between him and the ancient Jewish religion. The abolition of the sacrifices, which had caused him so much disgust, the suppression of an impious and haughty priesthood, and, in a general sense, the abrogation of the Law, appeared to him an absolute necessity! From this moment he is no longer a Jewish reformer, but it is as a destroyer of Judaism that he poses. Some advocates of the Messianic notions had already admitted that the Messiah would bring a new law, which should be common to all people. The Essenes, who were scarcely Jews, appear also to have been indifferent to the temple and to the Mosaic observances. But these were only isolated or unavowed instances of boldness. Jesus was the first who dared to say that from his time, or rather from that of John, the Law was abolished.[18]

The theological and institutional need for Jesus to be the unique and universal savior, messiah, and Son of God creates tension with the incontrovertible fact of his Jewishness. Although it is not impossible to imagine ways to configure these various points without dichotomizing them, I would argue that such nuances, while not beyond the evangelists' capabilities, were contrary to their overall theological and rhetorical interests. These would have included the need to present Jesus in ways that would appeal to communities that may well have been of gentile origin, or at least would have known about the gentile churches.

17. Translation from Thomas Randall, trans., *S. John 9–21*, vol. 2 of *Commentary on the Gospel according to S. John*, Library of the Fathers of the Holy Catholic Church 48 (London: Smith, 1885).

18. Joseph Ernest Renan, *The History of the Origins of Christianity: Book I. Life of Jesus* (London: Matthieson and Co., 1896), 129.

THE NARRATED JESUS

Additional pressure was exerted, however, by the narrative genre itself. Then as now, a narrative generally required that the events comprising its plot be linked through cause and effect. If the evangelists, like modern scholars, knew for a fact that Jesus was a Galilean Jew and they knew for a fact that Jesus was crucified by the order of the Roman governor, their challenge was to shape a narrative that made the latter fact plausible in light of the former fact.[19]

The gospel writers do so by narrating a series of escalating confrontations between Jesus and those whom they portray as Jewish leaders—Pharisees, chief priests, and scribes.[20] This plot thread develops in parallel to a second thread, which narrates Jesus's ever-increasing following. These two threads come together in the passion narratives, when Jesus's popularity among the crowds and the Jewish leaders' hatred and distrust converge as the factors that persuade a reluctant Pilate to order Jesus's execution. Think, for example, of Matthew's account of Pilate's concern to avoid a riot (27:24) and John's description of Caiaphas's rationale for hounding Jesus to death (11:49–52), and the ways in which the Jewish leaders and the Jewish crowds clamor for Jesus's death in all Four Gospels.

Of course, one cannot rule out the possibility that these narrative threads and their convergence simply "tell it like it is." One might argue, for example, that the overall similarities among the four canonical accounts of Jesus's passion constitute evidence for the historicity or, better, the facticity, of the events as described. Although the Four Gospels vary with respect to some of the details, they all portray some level of animosity between Jesus and other Jews, they all assign responsibility to the high priests and other leaders, albeit in different ways and to different degrees, and they all portray the crowds—presumably composed of Jews who, like Jesus, are in Jerusalem for the Passover—as shouting for Barabbas to be released and Jesus to be crucified (Matt 27:21; Mark 15:11; Luke 23:18; John 18:40).

Nevertheless, the transition between Jesus's conviction for blasphemy in the trial before the Jewish high priest, and his crucifixion as "King of the Jews" as

---

19. I have argued elsewhere for the similarities between historiography, including the gospels themselves as biographies, and historical fiction when it comes to telling the life of Jesus. See Adele Reinhartz, *Caiaphas the High Priest* (Columbia: University of South Carolina Press, 2011), 4–6. See also R. G. Collingwood, *The Idea of History* (Oxford: Clarendon, 1946); William H. Dray, *History as Re-Enactment: R. G. Collingwood's Idea of History* (Oxford: Clarendon, 1995); Ivan Jablonka, *History Is a Contemporary Literature: Manifesto for the Social Sciences* (Ithaca: Cornell University Press, 2018).

20. See Keith, *Jesus against the Scribal Elite.*

ordered by the Roman governor remains awkward. Crucifixion was normally reserved for acts of treason, a charge that may be hinted at by the titulus. Although biblical law states that a blasphemer should be put to death (Lev 24:13–16), the passion account suggests that the high priest either could not or would not carry out the sentence. The Fourth Gospel acknowledges this problem directly. When Pilate asks the Jewish leaders about the accusation they bring against Jesus (John 18:29), they sidestep the question: "If this man were not a criminal, we would not have handed him over to you" (18:30 NRSV). Pilate then tries to wash his hands of the affair, as he does in Matt 27:24, by placing the onus back onto them: "Take him yourselves and judge him according to your law." But the Jews insist: "We are not permitted to put anyone to death" (John 18:31 NRSV).

Familiarity with the gospels might make it difficult to recognize that the plot structures of the passion account fall short of the plausible cause-and-effect sequence for which historical narratives, including historical fiction, strive. What is technically a confrontation between Jesus and Pilate—one in which the latter orders the execution of the former—is transformed into a conflict between Jesus and the Jewish leadership. This transformation is needed in order to make sense of how a Roman governor came to pronounce the death sentence on a Galilean teacher and healer. Contrary to the text written on the titulus, Jesus did not proclaim himself to be the King of the Jews, at least, not according to his earliest biographers. Nor did he engage in activities that could be construed as treason. Constructing a conflict between Jesus and Jews who were powerful enough to exert pressure on Pilate resolves the cause-and-effect disconnect. Doing so, however, also requires distancing Jesus from other Jews, placing him over against rather than within the Jewish milieu to which he seemingly belongs.

Next Steps for the Next Quest

The Next Quest for the historical Jesus must shift its focus away from evaluating just how Jewish Jesus really was and toward the factors that have led to the ambivalent portrayal of Jesus's Jewishness in the gospels, which are the only sources for the historical Jesus. This approach is unlikely to satisfy those who view the goal of such a quest to be a highly specific and utterly factual account of what Jesus said and did during his lifetime. The Next Quest, however, is not that kind of quest. The reflections I have presented here suggest that to explore Jesus's Jewishness means to take into account the complexity, variety, and nuances of Jewish identity and practice in the Galilee and Judea in the early first century CE. To overcome the supersessionism and anti-Judaism that are embedded in historical Jesus writing and research means examining the ideological, theological, political, and social factors that have shaped these narratives, from the first century to the present.

A shift in perspective would lead us away from a search for facts and toward Jesus's broader context and the questions of how and why the historical Jesus came to be seen in particular ways, for example, as someone with a transcultural universal salvific mission that caused him to reject important elements of his tradition, such as Sabbath and purity laws, and brought him into such serious conflict with Jewish leaders that they did their utmost to get rid of him. Viewing Jesus as a Galilean Jew who lived the same sort of Jewish lifestyle as did other Galilean Jews will help us to pay more than lip service to his Jewish identity. Considering the gospels' ambivalent portraits of Jesus's Jewishness may help us to disentangle our views of the Jewish Jesus from the theological and narrative considerations that may have led the gospel writers to distance Jesus from Jewishness while also depicting him as fully Jewish.

4

BIOGRAPHY

Helen K. Bond

The Next Quest for the Historical Jesus must account for the *biographical na-ture of the Gospels*. At the heart of any kind of historical reconstruction is an appreciation of our sources—not just who wrote them and when (fundamental though these questions are), but, more crucially, what kind of literature we're dealing with: letters, eye-witness reports, theological tracts, legal material, po-etry, and so on. Some of these, we might assume, are more likely to provide us with reliable factual material than others. We might expect a letter, particularly from an observer, to be more useful than a poetic homily in terms of describing historical events, for example. All of this is equally true in any reconstruction of the historical Jesus. Besides a few scraps of information in the Pauline Letters and Josephus's *Testimonium Flavianum* (*A.J.* 18.63–64), we are largely dependent for our information on the canonical gospels. But what kind of literature are they? Were they written with a view to furnishing us with what we might think of as "historical facts," or for other reasons? And how did the first audiences interpret them?

In the following brief essay, I shall first consider the gospels as ancient biogra-phies, looking at what this important "discovery" can tell us about the historical reliability of their contents. Next, I'll turn my attention to a number of biograph-ical features within the gospels—sources and selectivity, *chreiai* (anecdotes) as literary compositions, style and structure—highlighting the difficulties that each of these poses to the historian.

STUDYING JESUS IN AN AGE OF SHIFTING GENRES

Until the close of the nineteenth century, it was widely assumed that the gospels were examples of ancient biography or *bioi*. The rise of form criticism at the beginning of the twentieth century, however, focused scholarly attention on the long period of oral transmission prior to the gospels. Now the evangelists were regarded as collectors and compilers of tradition, their work largely reduced to stitching one short paragraph to another like "beads on a string." Such examples of *Kleinliteratur* or *Urliteratur* (as Adolf Deissmann and Franz Overbeck had labeled them) didn't belong to any particular literary genre and had no real parallels in an ancient literary landscape. The gospels were widely assumed to be sui generis—a unique literary output for a unique body of material. What interested scholars wasn't an appreciation of the evangelists' literary abilities (or lack thereof), but rather an analysis of the processes of oral transmission on the building blocks of tradition. Once these were understood, it was assumed, later accretions could be stripped away to reveal the historical kernels at the heart of the tradition.[1] Variants of this approach inform the work of many historical Jesus scholars, from pioneers of the "New Quest" such as Joachim Jeremias, Günther Bornkamm, and Norman Perrin, through to representatives of the "Third Quest," including John Dominic Crossan, J. P. Meier, and the Jesus Seminar.[2]

Much, however, has changed in gospel study over recent years. Redaction critics stressed the role of the evangelists as authors, carefully altering inherited traditions so that they spoke more clearly to the pastoral or apologetic concerns of their communities. No longer were they seen as compilers and editors, but gifted theologians and writers. More recently still, narrative critics have highlighted the literary achievements of the evangelists, including their attention to character, plot and irony; the use of recurring themes and vocabulary; and their careful use of scriptural motifs. Whatever earlier sources and traditions they used—whether oral or written—have clearly been thoroughly reworked in the interests of specific literary aims. Rather curiously, perhaps, narrative critics spend very little time on the question of genre. Where the topic is discussed at all, it's simply assumed that the gospels are "stories" (*diēgēma* in Greek). These "stories" have most in common with the ancient novels in that—like fictional narratives—they create their own narrative world, supplying all that a reader needs in order to be able

---

1. For a fuller study, see my *The First Biography of Jesus: Genre and Method in Mark* (Grand Rapids: Eerdmans, 2020), esp. 15–25.

2. A number of challenges to this approach can be found in Chris Keith and Anthony LeDonne, eds., *Jesus, Criteria, and the Demise of Authenticity* (London: T&T Clark, 2012).

to interpret them. That's not to say that all narrative critics treat the gospels as fictional—in fact, the reverse is more likely to be true (narrative criticism avoids some of the awkward questions raised by historical criticism). But it does mean that questions of historicity tend to have little place in the work of narrative critics. Thus, those who attend most closely to the literary nature of the gospels are largely absent from discussions around their historical reliability. It's perhaps for this reason that some of the more sophisticated reconstructions of the historical Jesus in recent years—Ed Sanders's "big picture"; Dale Allison's "remembered gist"; or Jimmy Dunn's "oral traditioning"—display little real interest in the gospels as pieces of literature.

One significant development in gospel study, however, has brought historical and literary questions together. Since the early 1990s, a scholarly consensus has concluded (once again) that the gospels represent examples of ancient biography or *bioi*.[3] Fortunately, this new development has coincided with the rediscovery of *bioi* amongst classicists, leading to a surge of useful studies. No longer are biographers seen as "failed historians," but are now regarded as sophisticated authors in their own right with their own interests and concerns.[4] Comparison with classical *bioi* can greatly enhance our appreciation of the gospels and the role they would have played amongst the first Christ-following communities.

Genre in the ancient world was extremely flexible, but a recognizably biographical tradition seems to have emerged around the Hellenistic age. The life that was to have the most impact on Greek biography was that of Socrates, with Xenophon's *Memorabilia* serving as something of a model for later writers. The prominence of Socrates ensured that "the philosopher" would be a frequent subject, with well-known figures such as Plato, Pythagoras and Diogenes the Cynic all receiving several treatments in the Hellenistic and Roman periods. Good examples include Philo's mid-first-century *Life of Moses*, Lucian on his teacher *Demonax* in the early second century, Philostratus's third-century account of the *Life of Apol-*

---

3. Central here was the work of Richard Burridge, *What Are the Gospels? A Comparison with Graeco-Roman Biography* (Cambridge: Cambridge University Press, 1992) and David Aune, *The New Testament in Its Literary Environment* (Philadephia: Westminster, 1987).

4. See for example Mark J. Edwards and Simon Swain, eds., *Portraits: Biographical Representation in the Greek and Latin Literature of the Roman Empire* (Oxford: Clarendon, 1997); Tomas Hägg, *The Art of Biography in Antiquity* (Cambridge: Cambridge University Press, 2012); Rhiannon Ash, Judith Mossman, and Francis B. Titchener, eds., *Fame and Infamy: Essays for Christopher Pelling on Characterization in Greek and Roman Biography* (Oxford: Oxford University Press, 2015); Koen De Temmerman and Kristoffel Demoen, eds., *Writing Biography in Greece and Rome: Narrative Technique and Fictionalization* (Cambridge: Cambridge University Press, 2016); Koen De Temmerman, ed., *The Oxford Handbook of Ancient Biography* (Oxford: Oxford University Press, 2020).

lonius of Tyana, and Diogenes Laertius's broadly contemporary *Lives of Eminent Philosophers*. Latin biography (*vitae*) developed in the late republican period and tended to focus on public figures: emperors, statesmen, and generals. Biographical treatments grew naturally from the Roman interest in the *cursus honorum* (the course of a man's military and political posts) and the funeral oration.[5] By the first century, the magnetic pull of the *princeps* meant that even history tended to focus on an individual, blurring the distinction between history and biography. Despite the popularity of Latin *vitae*, however, it is the Greek biographies of philosophers that offer the closest parallels to the gospels.

Greek biography took many different forms. Some were heavily didactic, while others aimed at being more entertaining. Most took their place somewhere between history and encomium, though they might easily incorporate elements of other genres (tragedy, comedy, poetry, and so on). Despite their variety, however, they all have two things in common: (1) the desire to commemorate a great life (or occasionally to record a dissolute one); and (2) a hope that their audience would learn from it. It is this second, moralistic aspect of ancient biography that most sets it apart from its modern counterparts. Imitation (or *mimēsis*) was at the heart of the Greek education system, and students were expected not only to imitate great works from the past but also to emulate the behavior of great men. Short stories illustrating virtues and vices (*exempla* in Latin; *paradeigmata* in Greek) were common not only in oratory, but also in the works of philosophers (e.g., Seneca, *Ep.* 6.5) and historians (Tacitus, *Ann.* 3.65). In a sense, biography was *exempla* writ large: a person's life was laid out for others to imitate, as Plutarch clearly notes: "I began the writing of my *Lives* for the sake of others, but I find that I am continuing the work and delighting in it now for my own sake also, using history as a mirror and endeavouring in a manner to fashion and adorn my life in conformity with the virtues therein depicted" (*Aem.* 1 [Perrin, LCL]). The aim was not so much to encourage readers to imitate the heroes' specific deeds but rather the virtues that they displayed—loyalty, piety, courage, self-control, moderation, and so on.

A biography of a philosopher or teacher established a meaningful relationship between the living and the dead. In effect, it brought the philosopher back to life, introducing him to a new audience who might revere his memory and choose to model their lives on his. And while the content of his teaching was important, it was primarily his character that mattered, along with the display

---

5. Examples here include Cornelius Nepos's encyclopaedic *On Famous Men* (though only the section on generals survives); Suetonius's *Lives of the Caesars*; and Tacitus's *Agricola*. Nepos's work may well have been the inspiration for Plutarch's *Parallel Lives*, which was written in Greek but tended to focus on more typically Roman subjects.

of virtues for would-be followers to emulate. This was as important in a Jewish context as a Greco-Roman one, as indicated by numerous passages in both Philo (*Mos.* 1.158–159; see also 1.29) and the biographically driven history of the first half of Josephus's *Antiquities* (*A.J.* 1.14–15, 6.342, 8.418–420, 17.60). There was always a tension between the biographical subject as a unique, historical individual and the need to present his life as a paradigm for others. Often this led to an avoidance of the idiosyncratic and the flattening of character, so that the hero was little more than an embodiment of certain virtues. Ancient audiences, however, do not seem to have been too worried by this. Philo, for example, presents Moses as "the perfect man" (*Mos.* 1.1) who was "loved by God as few others" (2.67) and was even "named God and King of the whole nation" (*theos kai basileus*; 1.158), while at the same time calling on others to imitate his way of life.

The question that concerns the present essay, of course, is, how factual was ancient biography? And was historical accuracy even a concern within a genre devoted largely to moral instruction?

BIOGRAPHY AND HISTORICAL ACCURACY

We might well suspect that the moralizing purpose of most biographies led to a degree of distortion and idealization. At the very least, the biographer had to be selective, choosing from all available sources only those sayings and events that suited the portrait he wished to present. Lucian makes this clear in the closing lines of his *Demonax*, noting that "these are a very few things out of many which I might have mentioned, but they will suffice to give my readers a notion of the sort of man he was" (*Demon.* 67 [Harmon, LCL]). Plutarch also knew that real lives are not composed solely of virtue or vice, but admits in one of his exemplary lives that he strove to make the most of his subject's positive attributes while quietly dropping those that detracted (*Cim.* 2.4–5).[6] For most biographers, the tendency to caricature, exaggerate, and idealize must have been difficult to resist. Some (such as Suetonius or Plutarch) had at least an interest in historical research and reliability, while others (such as Xenophon in his *Cyropaedia* or Philostratus in the *Life of Apollonius*) were happy to draw on what was clearly legendary material.[7]

6. For a thoughtful discussion of history in Mark's Gospel, including the historian's inability to reconstruct Jesus without recourse to poetry, philosophy, and theology, see C. Clifton Black, *Mark's Gospel: History, Theology, Interpretation* (Grand Rapids: Eerdmans, 2023), 189–210.

7. On this, see the detailed discussion by Craig S. Keener, *Christobiography: Memories, History, and the Reliability of the Gospels* (Grand Rapids: Eerdmans, 2019). While he is very much aware of the bias and literary techniques common to *bioi* (see 121–50, 303–27), Keener's comparison of Suetonius and Plutarch with Tacitus concludes that biography is reasonably historical and

Even the most careful of biographers, however, allowed a degree of latitude, as demonstrated by Christopher Pelling's investigations of historical accuracy in Plutarch.[8] He finds that Plutarch was happy to use a story even when its accuracy had been disproved on chronological grounds, such as Solon's meeting with Croesus (*Sol.* 27.1). The biographer is far less critical in his use of sources if a particular story suits his purposes, such as accounts of the extravagance of Antony or his infatuation with Cleopatra. He adds circumstantial detail and bends the truth, either to highlight a certain character trait (for example Antony's passivity) or to improve the flow of his narrative (for example Caesar's trips to Greece and Rome are tidied up). Finally, the same events are recounted rather differently in different lives (for example Antony's behaviour at Philippi as narrated in *Antony* and *Brutus*). Pelling concludes:

> So what do we conclude about Plutarch's attitude to the truth? He does not always behave as we would, certainly; he tidies and improves, and in some cases he must have known he was being historically inaccurate. But the process has limits, and the untruthful tidying and improving is never very extensive. The big changes, the substantial improvements tend to come where he could generally claim—"yes, it must have been like that."[9]

There are limits to Plutarch's "creative reconstruction": he enhances a subject's role in a particular event, but only so far as it might help to draw out his character, and not to such an extent that it falsifies the central thrust of the life. Where there are gaps in his sources, particularly in relation to childhood, he generally feels no

---

contains "at least a core of genuine historical information" (497). In contrast, J. Bradley Chance compares the gospels with the *Ninus Romance*, Xenophon's *Cyropaedia*, Philostratus's *Life of Apollonius*, and the *Alexander Romance*, concluding that each of these works exhibits a high level of fiction and at times what appears to be a complete lack of concern for historical fact; see "Fiction in Ancient Biography: An Approach to a Sensitive Issue in Gospel Interpretation," *Perspectives in Religious Studies* 18 (1991): 125–42. Keener discounts these works on the grounds that they are novels rather than *bioi* and were all written long after the central character's death (*Christobiography*, 42–52), though it seems to me that the flexible borders of *bioi* mean that we cannot be too hard and fast in terms of what is allowed to be part of the genre and what is not.

8. C. B. R. Pelling, "Truth and Fiction in Plutarch's *Lives*," in *Antonine Literature*, ed. D. A. Russell (Oxford: Oxford University Press, 1990), 19–52; also, Pelling, *Life of Antony* (Cambridge: Cambridge University Press, 1988) in various places.

9. Pelling, "Truth and Fiction," 41; for similar sentiments, see also Pelling, *Life of Antony*, 35. As Pelling observes, Plutarch is more interested in history in certain lives (e.g., *Caesar*) than others (e.g., *Antony*); see "Truth and Fiction," 29.

need to fill them for the sake of completeness.[10] His central aim is not to mislead his readers, but to present the hero's character in the clearest possible terms.[11]

Similar findings characterize a recent collection of essays edited by Koen De Temmerman and Kristoffel Demoen on the topic of "fictionalization" in ancient biography. In the opening chapter, De Temmerman notes that the border between history and fiction tends to be blurred in most types of literature, but that biography is particularly prone to slip into fiction. This is partly due to the genre's encomiastic aims, but it is also because "biography is almost always having to conjecture, interpret and reconstruct actions, private moments, motivations and attitudes."[12] De Temmerman rightly argues that we need to move beyond any easy opposition between "truth" and "fiction." Biographies take their place along a spectrum with the lives of the poets and Xenophon's *Cyropoedia* at one end, and Plutarch and Suetonius at the other; some take historical accuracy more seriously, but none are free from some degree of fictionalization. Indeed, the process of constructing a narrative always lends a certain element of fiction to the account, even when authors include elaborate claims to diligent research. This expresses itself in a range of areas, from invented speeches to fictive accounts of birth and childhood, and from intertextual allusions to other characters to imagined details at the hero's death.

All of this should hardly surprise us: exactly the same challenges and constraints face even the most diligent of modern biographers. We are familiar in the modern world with the "research biography" in which the author/scholar has spent a great deal of time researching the minutiae of his or her chosen subject. We expect these often-lengthy tomes to be "factual" and "historically accurate." In fact, it would seriously diminish the biography's standing if reviewers could easily point to inaccuracies. And yet even here there are limitations. Much depends on the way material is put together, including the juxtapositions, links, or breaks that the biographer imposes on her material. Imputing a subject's inner feelings and motives is perhaps the most difficult of all. As Hilary Spurling, prize-winning biographer of Ivy Compton Burnett, Henri Matisse, and others, notes: "in order to convey . . . factual material, the biographer will generally, and I think inevitably, be forced to stoop to fiction. . . . Any reconstruction which is not to be purely external, and therefore superficial, must be quite largely made up. What you are

---

10. C. B. R. Pelling, "Childhood and Personality in Greek Biography," in *Characterization and Individuality in Greek Literature*, ed. C. B. R. Pelling (Oxford: Clarendon, 1990), 213–44.

11. For a similar assessment of Cornelius Nepos, see Molly M. Pryzwansky, "Cornelius Nepos: Key Issues and Critical Approaches," *CJ* 105 (2009): 97–108, esp. 99–100.

12. Koen De Temmerman, "Ancient Biography and Formalities of Fiction," in De Temmerman and Demoen, *Writing Biography*, 3–25, esp. 4.

doing, after all, is creating a character."[13] Even modern biography, then, however scrupulously researched, is not simply the transmission of certain well-researched facts; it too requires an imaginative element which turns words on a page into a living person.

Matters are made no easier by appeal to eyewitnesses. Many ancient biographers knew their subjects personally. Cornelius Nepos was on friendly terms with Atticus, Tacitus had a good relationship with his father-in-law, and Lucian had spent his formative years with his teacher, Demonax. Yet even here we see the same relaxed attitude to historical truth. Despite his close personal connection to Agricola, Tacitus was ready to bend historical facts in the interests of both him and his relative, highlighting his father-in-law's abilities and making his own political points.[14] And Lucian so thoroughly casts his teacher in his own image that some scholars would doubt his very existence.[15] In a rather immodest request that his friend Lucceius write a glowing account of his own consulship, Cicero suggests that he might "waive the laws of history" and allow his personal affection full reign in composing his account (*Fam.* 5.12.3).[16] Firsthand acquaintance clearly gave the biographer an excellent source of stories and information on which to draw, but it was only to be expected that the resulting life would be marked by the biographer's own interests and agenda, not to mention a frequently one-sided emphasis on the hero's exemplary virtues.[17]

All this means that while biography was closely related in many ways to history, and often took "historical" subjects as its focus, we need to be careful about assuming that biographers were interested in history for its own sake. Their purpose

13. Hilary Spurling, "Neither Morbid Nor Ordinary," in *The Troubled Face of Biography*, ed. Eric Homberger and John Charmley (London: Macmillan, 1988), 113–22, here 116. Similar sentiments are expressed by Victoria Glendinning, "Lies and Silences," 49–62 in the same volume. So also Hilary Mantel in her Radio 4 Reith Lectures entitled "Resurrection: the Art and Craft," *BBC Radio 4*, 2017, https://www.bbc.co.uk/programmes/b08vkm52.

14. On the historical value of the Agricola, see Dylan Sailor, "The Agricola," in *A Companion to Tacitus*, ed. Victoria E. Pagán (Chichester: Wiley-Blackwell, 2012), 23–44, esp. 39–41.

15. So, for example Diskin Clay, "Lucian of Samosata: Four Philosophical Lives (Nigrinus, Demonax, Peregrinus, Alexander Pseudomantis)," *ANRW* 36.5:3406–50, esp. 3425–29.

16. See also Arnaldo Momigliano, *The Development of Greek Biography* (Cambridge: Harvard University Press, 1971), 55–56.

17. Interestingly, eyewitness testimony is often regarded by modern biographers as problematic. Ann Thwaite writes: "Among the mass of available evidence, it is usually the survivors' memories I find least valuable, especially when someone has been dead fifty years or so. The people that remember them have repeated their memories so often that, like the words in the children's game Chinese Whispers, they bear little real meaning." See Thwaite, "Writing Lives" in Homberger and Charmley, *Troubled Face*, 17.

was not to provide an accurate list of all that their subject did and said, but to lay bare the essence of the man, to re-create a living character—to expose his "soul" as Plutarch put it (*Alex.* 1.3). As Plutarch realized, this often involved the minutiae of life, and where precise facts were no longer available, the biographer had to rely on conjecture, interpretation, and imaginative reconstruction. All of this is summarized well by Tomas Hägg in his exhaustive treatment of ancient *bioi*:

> Ancient life-writers did not encounter among their contemporaries the same demands for documentary truth as their modern colleagues do, nor did for that matter ancient historiographers.... Conversations are allowed to be fictitious, and insight is readily granted into the acting characters' feelings, thoughts, and motives, as long as some kind of verisimilitude is maintained. The establishment of any form of higher truth—be it poetic, psychological, philosophical, or religious—overrules demands for the truth of facts.[18]

Where does all of this leave the gospels? Are their efforts closer to the more "historical" accounts of Suetonius and Plutarch (with all the caveats noted above), or to Philostratus's more "legendary" *Life of Apollonius of Tyana* and the anonymous and often fanciful *Life of Aesop*?

The Gospels and Historical Material

As an initial observation, we might argue that the evangelists—like all biographers—were only as accurate as their sources. In an age of internet search engines, it's difficult to appreciate just how impossible it would have been to check facts in antiquity, even when eyewitnesses were still around. The differing dates of the crucifixion in the Synoptic and Johannine traditions illustrate how even the most important details may have been lost at an early stage.[19] Over the four decades prior to Mark, stories were likely to have been expanded, reshaped, invented, or forgotten; meditations on Scripture became part of the tradition; and material originally belonging to other preachers (such as John the Baptist or early Christian missionaries and prophets) may well have been ascribed to Jesus. It's beyond question that the evangelists inherited a range of material, both oral and written, though it's impossible now to extract it from its present literary context. The evangelists may have sometimes had several accounts to choose from, as

---

18. Hägg, *Art of Biography*, 3–4.

19. See my study, "Dating the Death of Jesus: Memory and the Religious Imagination," *NTS* 59 (2013): 461–75.

was often the case with Diogenes Laertius. In *Vit. phil.* 6.2.76–77, for example, Diogenes Laertius lists three competing accounts of the death of Diogenes the Cynic. While Diogenes Laertius chose to relate all the options, however, the evangelists (like most biographers) would have simply chosen whichever best suited their purposes. The Synoptic Gospels show how later authors were happy to edit Mark, and if John also knew Mark (as a growing number of scholars now claim), then the level of creativity may in fact be quite striking.[20]

And yet our discussion so far would urge even more caution. Although Jesus was a historical person, the gospels were written to strengthen faith in believers and to present him as God's Son and Anointed One, and even God incarnate. Those who gathered to hear them read out sought to deepen their sense of shared identity as Christ followers in an often-hostile Roman world and found in Jesus's life and self-denying character a model for their own discipleship. Like all biographers, the evangelists were clearly selective (John says as much in 20:30); only stories that fit their portrait of Jesus were included, and those that didn't—whether because they represented a hostile point of view or because they were simply different—were quietly forgotten. Later I shall analyse the evangelists' ordering of events to see how they conform to biographical conventions. First, though, I shall explore the building block of the Synoptic Gospels—the *chreia* or anecdote.

CHREIAI

Like many ancient Greek biographies, the gospels are "episodic" narratives, created from a series of small units (frequently known as *pericopae*, or paragraphs), often with little to connect one to another. Ancient grammarians referred to these short stories as *chreia* (*chreiai* in the plural). Ronald Hock defines the *chreia* as "a saying or action that is expressed concisely, attributed to a character, and regarded as useful for living."[21] After mastering basic composition, students were taught ways to adapt and elaborate *chreiai* as they moved up the educational system. The short stories were particularly associated with philosophers, neatly capturing their characteristic teaching or behavior and could be anything from the tersest of accounts to something more detailed and expansive.

Anecdotes were—and still are—indispensable to biographers. The problem, however, as Richard Saller points out, is that by their very nature anecdotes

20. See the contributions in Eve-Marie Becker, Helen K. Bond, and Catrin H. Williams, eds., *John's Transformation of Mark* (London: T&T Clark, 2021).

21. Hock, introduction to *The Chreia and Ancient Rhetoric: The Progymnasmata*, ed. Ronald F. Hock and Edward N. O'Neil (Atlanta: Scholars Press, 1986), 1:26.

were frequently of indeterminate origin, spread about by gossips or storytellers, or pressed into the service of orators or moralists as *exempla*.[22] Anecdotes are typically fluid, even when written down, and while the main point may retain a certain stability, other elements such as setting, incidental characters, and even the identity of the main protagonist are subject to almost infinite variety. None of this was of any great concern to the biographer: what mattered was that the anecdote exposed something of the subject's character, often in a concise and pithy manner. There are correspondences here with the modern concept of the "apocryphal story" which, irrespective of whether it actually happened, perfectly captures something of a person's nature. We are generally quite happy to repeat such stories, even in obituaries and memorial services, even if we are unsure as to their authenticity. Questions of historical accuracy—both now and in antiquity—are secondary to the anecdote's ability to say something profoundly true about the subject's character (e.g., Plutarch's "soul").

We might well suspect that something similar is happening with the anecdotes found in the gospels. And while it is possible that some came down in tradition (collections of *chreiai* were not uncommon), the vast majority must have been penned by Mark and the other evangelists themselves (how else could the style and length be so uniform?).[23] *Thus the many chreiai in the Gospels are not primarily repositories of oral tradition, but fundamentally literary creations, crafted to take their place in a larger biographical work.*

Many of Mark's *chreiai* may have links with actual events, but they have doubtless been shaped to illustrate specific aspects of Jesus's character, abilities, or way of life. As the form critics observed, some end with a pithy saying, others involve controversy, while others recount miraculous occurrences. There is most likely some historical fact at the core of these stories, though extracting it from its present literary context would be next to impossible. Other *chreiai* may have no historical roots at all. Examples might be the so-called nature miracles, such as the accounts of Jesus feeding the multitude (appearing first in Mark 6:32–44). As the early Christ followers compared Jesus to great figures like Elisha and Moses, it would not have been a great leap to move from a belief in a Jesus who *could* supply sustenance once again to a story in which he actually *did* so. We might expect the story to draw on both the account of Elisha in 2 Kgs 4:42–44 and the manna in the wilderness (Exod 16:1–36; Num 11:1–9) with elements of the Eucharist thrown in too. The resulting account might be apocryphal to us (in that it didn't actually take place), but it would be told and retold within the gospel context because it

22. Richard Saller, "Anecdotes as Historical Evidence for the Principate," *GR* 27 (1980): 69–83.
23. See, for example, Plutarch, *Cohib. ira.* 457d–e; *Virt. prof.* 78f; Seneca, *Ep.* 33.7–8.

72

perfectly captured a number of important things that followers wanted to say about Jesus and his relationship to both God and the story of Israel. In a similar vein, Philo flattered Augustus with the claim that he could calm storms and cure pestilence (*Legat.* 144–145); it would not be a huge move to create stories to illustrate those beliefs. Soon after Mark wrote, stories told of Vespasian's abilities to restore sight and limbs (Tacitus, *Hist.* 4.81–82; Suetonius, *Vesp.* 7.2; Dio Cassius, *Hist. rom.* 65.8), and Martial and other poets told how nature itself recognized the divinity of the Flavian emperors (*Sp.* 17; 30.1–4; *Epig.* 1.6; 8.21).[24] The late first century was a world where such stories were frequently associated with great men. What mattered wasn't their basis in historical fact, but what they said about the character and abilities of the subject.

STYLE AND STRUCTURE IN THE GOSPELS

As early as the church fathers, the evangelists' style was seen as inelegant and lacking in rhetorical flourishes, with Mark's Gospel coming under particular criticism.[25] It is certainly true that his writing is paratactic (he strings clauses together with *kai*), full of historic presents, and with a preference for periphrastic tenses in lieu of more elegant subordinate clauses. Some have claimed to detect a "residual orality" to his work, meaning that oral material left its mark in a number of stylistic features—the author's love of hyperbole and exaggeration, themes and variations on themes, repetitions, groups of three, concentric structures and chiasms, inclusios, echoes, and summaries, among others.[26] This is often used to bolster the idea that Mark and his fellow evangelists were only one step removed from oral traditions, and to distance their compositions from anything more literate. An alternative way to look at this evidence, however, is to assume that *Mark wrote in a colloquial style because he intended his work to be read out to a largely uneducated audience.* Quintilian advises students that they may need to adapt material for

24. Eric Eve, "Spit in Your Eye: The Blind Man of Bethsaida and the Blind Man of Alexandria," *NTS* 54 (2008): 1–17; Ulrike Riemer, "Miracle Stories and Their Narrative Intent in the Context of the Ruler Cult of Classical Antiquity," in *Wonders Never Cease: The Purpose of Narrating Miracle Stories in the New Testament and Its Religious Environment*, ed. Michael Labahn and B. Jan Lietaert Peerbolte, LNTS 288 (London: T&T Clark, 2006), 32–47.

25. On the embarrassment of the church fathers toward Christian writings, see N. W. Lund, *Chiasmus in the New Testament: A Study in Formgeschichte* (Chapel Hill: University of North Carolina Press, 1942), 4–7.

26. See, for example, Paul J. Achtemeier, "Omne Verbum Sonat: The New Testament and the Oral Environment of Late Western Antiquity," *JBL* 109 (1990): 3–27; and Kelly R. Iverson, "Orality and the Gospels: A Survey of Recent Research," *CBR* 8 (2009): 71–106.

people with little education (*Inst.* 3.8) and the grammatical handbooks advise *prepon* (or *aptum*), a "propriety" or "appropriateness" that considers both the content of communication and the audience.[27] A straightforward and engaging style was likely to have been appreciated by many early Christ followers.

All the canonical gospels take their structure from Mark, who was criticized by Papias for his lack of "order" (*taxis*).[28] Once again, Papias's comments have tended to cast a shadow over Mark's literary efforts and to bolster the form-critical view of the evangelists as little more than compilers of tradition. However, Richard Bauckham rightly points out that Papias is making a *chronological* comparison here with John's Gospel, hoping to stave off any awkward comparisons with a gospel often at variance with Mark's (and which was of course attributed to an eyewitness).[29] In fact, Mark's structure works perfectly well as an ancient biography. The work has a broadly geographical arrangement with Galilean material first, followed by an extended journey framed by stories of giving sight to blind men (8:22–10:52), and concluding with Jerusalem material. Within this structure is a topical arrangement, with a clustering of *chreiai* on related topics: conflict stories (2:1–3:6), parables (4:1–34), miracles (4:35–5:43), a cycle of gentile stories (7:1–8:10), material on discipleship (8:22–10:45), more conflict stories (11:27–12:37), and apocalyptic material (13:1–37). This is a much more careful structure than most Greek *bioi*, many of which are little more than a collection of short stories and witty sayings (Lucian's *Demonax* for example has little to connect episodes, and Diogenes Laertius's arrangements seem entirely random). The advantage of this kind of clustering is that it makes it easy for a listening audience to take away the main themes: that Jesus bettered his opponents in debate, that he told parables, worked miracles, and so on. Even if a listener doesn't catch every story, the overall account—reinforced by regular summaries—is clear.

The disadvantage of this structure for the historian is also easy to appreciate. It's often assumed that Jesus's ministry lasted less than one year in the Synoptic Gospels. The dominance of the Passover at Jesus's last visit to Jerusalem gives the impression that his ministry started some time earlier and culminated at

27. See the useful discussion in Alexander Damm, *Ancient Rhetoric and the Synoptic Problem: Clarifying Markan Priority*, BETL 252 (Leuven: Peeters, 2013), xix–xxx. Demetrius's advice to adopt a plain unadorned style may also be relevant here, even if he was writing for students who had already completed the *progymnasmata* (*Eloc.* 4.191).

28. Papias's critique is preserved now in Eusebius, *Hist. eccl.* 3.39.15.

29. Richard Bauckham, *Jesus and the Eyewitnesses: The Gospels as Eyewitness Testimony* (Grand Rapids: Eerdmans, 2006), 217–21. See the older studies of F. H. Colson, "Τάξει in Papias (The Gospels and Rhetorical Schools)," *JTS* 14 (1912): 62–69; M. Black, "The Use of Rhetorical Terminology in Papias on Mark and Matthew," *JSNT* 37 (1989): 31–41.

the feast, but this is never stated. In fact, Mark's arrangement tells us nothing about the length of Jesus's ministry—*it is simply not designed to be chronological.* Mark's arrangement forced him to put all the Jerusalem material at the end, from whatever period of Jesus's ministry it derived (if in fact he knew where it came from). The precise setting of much material must have been uncertain. Luke, for example, includes Jesus's visit to Martha and Mary in the earlier Galilean material (Luke 10:38–42), while John is quite clear that the sisters lived outside Jerusalem in Bethany (John 11:1–2). We might be tempted to believe John here, seduced by his fuller account of the sisters and their brother Lazarus, but how can we tell the difference between history and biographical art? Only John gives us any indication of the length to Jesus's ministry: the frequent visits of Jesus to Jerusalem in the gospel, which mark out roughly two and a half years, may reflect John's theology but may be no less historical for that.

Only at the end, in the final three chapters, is Synoptic material related chronologically. The change here is not a signal that Mark was drawing on an early source (as the form critics imagined) but is a standard biographical convention.[30] While anecdotes attributed to a philosopher or teacher could be recounted in almost any order, the events of his death needed to be told consecutively for them to make any sense. Thus Suetonius, who organises his imperial *Lives* with an antiquarian's topical interest, always recounts their deaths in sequential manner (as do Lucian, Diogenes Laertius, and others). The Markan passion narrative, with its greater circumstantial detail and stronger sense of cause and effect may give the impression of containing reliable historical material, yet we should exercise caution. The artificially parallel Jewish and Roman trial scenes, along with the constant comparisons between Jesus and others (e.g., the disciples in Gethsemane, Peter in the courtyard, the emperor in the soldiers' mockery), the use of Peter and Judas as examples of reprehensible behavior, and the veiled echoes of the imperial triumph that dance around the crucifixion scene all warn us to be on our guard.[31] Doubtless Jesus was crucified on the orders of Pontius Pilate, but how much more of the narrative has a basis in historical fact is impossible to say.

Conclusion

In the end, appreciation of genre alone cannot give us an exact measure of the evangelists' level of historical reliability. All we can say for sure is that biography

30. See for example, Martin Dibelius, *From Tradition to Gospel*, trans. B. L. Woolf. (New York: Scribner's Sons, 1934), 43, 178–217.

31. For a fuller discussion of all of these features, see my *First Biography*, 186–89, 231–46.

allowed a wide scope from the broadly historical to the almost completely fictional. Given this broad scope, the present chapter has urged historians to use the gospels with extreme caution: the bite-size anecdotes of the Synoptics are not necessarily pieces of oral tradition but may derive almost entirely from the evangelists themselves (predominately Mark); even what are often identified as "oral features" may similarly be part of this narrative art. The Synoptics have no interest in the length of Jesus's ministry, and the chronological arrangement of the passion narrative does not imply a new source at this point. Above all, the gospels are literary creations, ancient biographies written to present the life of Jesus to new generations. They undoubtedly contain some level of historical accuracy, but it is virtually impossible at this distance to isolate historical event from theological coloring. Going forward, the Next Quest for the historical Jesus will have to take the biographical and literary nature of our sources more seriously and not expect more historical information from them than they are able to give.

5

Ancient Media

Rafael Rodríguez

The Next Quest for the historical Jesus must account for the irreducibility of the early Jesus tradition to only one medium: the handwritten text. Questions of pre- and nonwritten Jesus tradition lay at the heart of the form-critical research agenda that developed a hundred years ago and led—in many ways directly—to an explosion of historical Jesus research from 1953 to 2012.[1] A century later, however, the presumptions and principles enabling form-critical historiography have been largely discredited.[2] Many form-critical concepts may remain relevant, including the formative role of the community in shaping the tradition, the influence of

---

I am grateful to Christopher W. Skinner, Heather M. Gorman, and Judith C. S. Redman for their help with and comments on an earlier draft of this paper.

1. Famously, if not quite accurately, post-Schweitzerian Jesus scholarship is often reputed to have begun in 1953 with Ernst Käsemann's lecture, *Das Problem des historischen Jesus*, published in English as "The Problem of the Historical Jesus," in *Essays on New Testament Themes*, trans. W. J. Montague, SBT 42 (London: SCM, 1964), 15–47. Though historical Jesus scholarship continues even today, the energy and quantity of its output have declined precipitously in the twenty-first century, attributable at least in part to the exposure of the criteriological method's weaknesses in Chris Keith and Anthony Le Donne, eds., *Jesus, Criteria, and the Demise of Authenticity* (London: T&T Clark, 2012).

2. Among many trenchant critiques, see Birger Gerhardsson, *Memory and Manuscript: Oral Tradition and Written Transmission in Rabbinic Judaism and Early Christianity* [1961] with *Tradition and Transmission in Early Christianity* [1964] (Grand Rapids: Eerdmans, 1998); Morna D. Hooker, "Christology and Methodology," *NTS* 17 (1971): 480–87; Hooker, "On Using the Wrong Tool," *Theology* 75 (1972): 570–81; Erhard T. Guttgemans, *Candid Questions concerning Gospel*

contemporary events and debates on the shape of the tradition, and the utility of the tradition for the community's present. How those concepts contribute to historical reconstruction, however, is hotly debated.[3] The remainder of this essay offers a programmatic proposal for how historical Jesus scholarship ought to account for the Jesus tradition in early Christian memory and media.

Toward a Post-Form-Critical Historiography

The first task facing historians of Jesus in the second quarter of the twenty-first century is to develop a post-form-critical historiography. Toward that end, I offer three broad observations. First, while the form critics highlighted the ability of tradents to create new images of Jesus, they took inadequate account of the *reception* of those images among Jesus's followers. Within the broad range of possible images of Jesus in the first century, novel interpretations of Jesus required some connection with previous images to gain currency among audiences. The author of Hebrews, for example, transforms Jesus into a priestly figure (Heb 4:14–10:39),

---

Form Criticism: A Methodological Sketch of the Fundamental Problematics of Form and Redaction Criticism, trans. William G. Doty (Pittsburgh: Wipf & Stock, 1979); Samuel Byrskog, "A Century with the Sitz im Leben: From Form-Critical Setting to Gospel Community and Beyond," *ZNW* 98 (2007): 1–27; Christopher Tuckett, "Form Criticism," in *Jesus in Memory: Traditions in Oral and Scribal Perspectives*, ed. Werner H. Kelber and Samuel Byrskog (Waco, TX: Baylor University Press, 2009), 21–38; Arland J. Hultgren, "Form Criticism and Jesus Research," in *Handbook for the Study of the Historical Jesus*, ed. Tom Holmén and Stanley E. Porter (Leiden: Brill, 2011), 1:649–71; Grant R. Osborne, "Tradition Criticism and Jesus Research," in Holmén and Porter, *Handbook*, 1:673–93; Dale C. Allison Jr., "It Don't Come Easy: A History of Disillusionment," in Keith and Le Donne, *Demise of Authenticity*, 186–99; Chris Keith, "The Indebtedness of the Criteria Approach to Form Criticism and Recent Attempts to Rehabilitate the Search for an Authentic Jesus," in Keith and Le Donne, *Demise of Authenticity*, 25–48; Ruben Zimmermann, *Puzzling the Parables of Jesus: Methods and Interpretation* (Minneapolis: Fortress, 2015).

3. Paul Foster, "Memory, Orality, and the Fourth Gospel: Three Dead-Ends in Historical Jesus Research," *JSHJ* 10 (2012): 191–227, distorts contemporary memory studies in the direction of form criticism: "[Both presentist and cultural-system models] of social memory as articulated by professional academics in the area of memory studies [have] a striking similarity to the perspectives of the early form critics. That is, any underlying historical connections have either been subsumed or heavily transformed to serve contemporary community needs" (197). Since at least the late 1980s this view of memory has been critiqued as "one-sided" and a "half-truth"; see, e.g., Michael Schudson, "The Present in the Past versus the Past in the Present," *Communication* 11 (1989): 105–13; Barry Schwartz, "Social Change and Collective Memory: The Democratization of George Washington," *American Sociological Review* 56 (1991): 221–36; Schwartz, *Abraham Lincoln and the Forge of National Memory* (Chicago: University of Chicago Press, 2000); Nachman Ben-Yehuda, *Masada Myth: Collective Memory and Mythmaking in Israel* (Madison: University of Wisconsin Press, 1995).

though no contemporaneous evidence suggests Jesus ever served in the temple.[4] We can, however, see the author working within the constraints of Jesus's established reputation as a descendant of Judah and not of Levi (see Heb 7:11–28). The point is not just what *kind* of priest the Judahite Jesus might have been; the point is also *how* Jesus's followers might incorporate priestly elements into their commemorative traditions of Jesus. More subtle innovations in the tradition, like shaping Jesus's appearance in Nazareth into a programmatic scene or attributing to him scribal literacy and authority (see Luke 4:16–30), must similarly vie for reception among communities with established perceptions of Jesus.[5]

Second, the dynamics of production and reception affected oral expressions of the Jesus tradition just as they did written expressions. Scholarly discussion often focuses on continuities or differences between oral and written traditional media. The form critics accepted meaningful distinctions between oral and literary tradition, but their identification of the gospels as *Kleinliteratur* and, therefore, unliterary led them to treat the written Jesus tradition as similar to, or a species of, the oral Jesus tradition. In 1983, Werner Kelber questioned this aspect of form-critical historiography.[6] In Kelber's view, the move from oral to written media introduced a transformation—a *disjunction*—into the tradition.[7] Whatever the precise relations and interactions between written and oral traditions, our point is that images of Jesus in both oral and written expressions have to be *available* to performers and authors to conceive in the first place and *plausible* (or capable of being rendered plausible) for audiences or readers to receive them.

Third, when we are talking about the production and reception of commemorative images, we are talking about how flesh-and-blood, embodied human beings

4. For discussion, see Rafael Rodríguez, *Jesus Darkly: Remembering Jesus with the New Testament* (Nashville: Abingdon, 2018), 129–40.

5. For discussions that explain Lukan redaction in Luke 4:16–30 as part of the reception of Jesus, see Rafael Rodríguez, *Structuring Early Christian Memory: Jesus in Tradition, Performance, and Text*, LNTS 407 (London: T&T Clark, 2010), 138–73; Chris Keith, *Jesus against the Scribal Elite: The Origins of the Conflict* (Grand Rapids: Baker Academic, 2014), 59–64.

6. Werner H. Kelber, *The Oral and the Written Gospel: The Hermeneutics of Speaking and Writing in the Synoptic Tradition, Mark, Paul, and Q* (Philadelphia: Fortress, 1983); see also Kelber, "Apostolic Tradition and the Form of the Gospel," in *Discipleship in the New Testament*, ed. Fernando F. Segovia (Philadelphia: Fortress, 1985), 24–46, republished in Kelber, *Imprints, Voiceprints, and Footprints of Memory: Collected Essays of Werner H. Kelber*, RBS 74 (Atlanta: SBL Press, 2013), 11–32 (references are to the 2013 republished edition).

7. The view that "oral and written media are fundamentally different and distinct" is known as the Great Divide theory; see Rafael Rodríguez, "Great Divide," in *The Dictionary of the Bible and Ancient Media*, ed. Tom Thatcher et al. (London: Bloomsbury, 2017), 163–64 (quote from 164).

lived within and experienced the tradition.[8] For anthropologists researching actual oral traditions, this point is obvious because every expression of the tradition requires at least one person to recite the tradition. New Testament scholarship often neglects how a performer's or author's previous experiences with the Jesus tradition might constrain the present performance (including the writing of a written gospel's text).[9] A traditional text—that is, a written text whose contents express or are related to material with which its audiences are already familiar, perhaps even deeply—continues to rely upon reception strategies that are also traditional among audiences. In such cases, the text signals to both the reader or performer and the audience that it is but another species of an already-familiar genus, especially inasmuch as the experience of the text—whether via public reading, recitation, or performance—is facilitated by a social event.[10]

Luke's Gospel, for example, identifies itself as and locates itself in relation to other *diēgēseis* "accounts," of the events of Jesus's life and teaching (see Luke 1:1–4). Whatever the merits of those other accounts, Luke is not writing a new kind of text so much as he is offering another expression of a known tradition (*tōn peplērophorēmenōn en hēmin pragmatōn*).[11] Even in the case of Mark, our earliest gospel, an audience with as much as four decades' experience with the tradition would have brought that experience to bear upon their reception and interpretation of Mark's apparently epoch-making accomplishment (i.e., the creation of a unified *written* account of Jesus's story). Even this genuine *novum* is subject to a "continuity of reception."[12] Not that "the tradition" prevented innovative claims

8. See Taylor Petrey's chapter, "Bodies and Embodiment," in the present volume.

9. Rodríguez, *Structuring*, 129–31. Also helpful in this regard is Alan Kirk's discussion of the gospel writers as "tradents" in *Q in Matthew: Ancient Media, Memory, and Early Scribal Transmission of the Jesus Tradition*, LNTS 564 (London: T&T Clark, 2016), 40–42.

10. As Kelber writes: "ancient chirographs came to life, both from the angle of composition and from the angle of reception, *in an environment saturated with verbal communication and orally performed activities.*" See "Jesus and Tradition: Words in Time, Words in Space," *Semeia* 65 (1995): 139–67, republished in Kelber, *Imprints*, 103–32 (107 cited above; my emphasis; references are to the republished edition).

11. See Loveday Alexander, *The Preface to Luke's Gospel: Literary Convention and Social Context in Luke 1.1–4 and Acts 1.1*, SNTSMS 78 (Cambridge: Cambridge University Press, 1993), 106–16.

12. According to Kelber ("Jesus and Tradition," 106), the uniformity and textual stability afforded by the innovation of movable type "depersonalized words and gave language the appearance of incontestable detachment." We are trying to resist that depersonalization in the present chapter. New Testament media critics too often reify written texts as social objects, as if they had certain essential consequences apart from the flesh-and-blood human beings gazing upon, listening to, or behaving in reference to the written object in their midst. See, e.g., Samuel Byrskog, *Jesus the Only Teacher: Didactic Authority and Transmission in Ancient Israel, Ancient Judaism and the Matthean Community*, ConBNT 24 (Stockholm: Almqvist & Wiksell,

from being created and accepted by those who recounted Jesus's words and deeds in the years between Jesus's life and the gospels' accounts thereof. The history of commemorating Jesus, however, did constrain both what could be said about him and how claims about him were received by auditors or readers. Not even Mark's Gospel—and certainly not those of Matthew, Luke, John, or Thomas—was produced or received apart from the history of the tradition and its portrayals and deployments of Jesus.

When we focus on the production *and reception* of images of Jesus among actual human beings whose experiences with the Jesus tradition antedate the written gospels, the form-critical distinction between the Jesus of history and the early Christian kerygma begins to blur. The kerygmatic message of Jesus's followers requires explanation as a historical phenomenon, and one of the factors contributing to the shape and content of that message was the communities' history of commemorating Jesus.[13] While historians cannot simply extract the historical Jesus from the kerygma as expressed in the written gospels, neither can they simply subtract that kerygma to reveal the historical Jesus. If historians hope to know anything about Jesus as a historical figure, we will do so *by means of* the earliest Christians' interpretive work with the Jesus tradition, not despite it.

A Multiform Jesus and a Multiform Tradition

The form-critical historiography of previous "quests" for the historical Jesus relied on the problematic method of isolating individual gospel pericopes from their narrative contexts. Historians of Jesus would then filter those pericopes through a battery of "criteria of authenticity" in hopes of separating authentic material from later, secondary material that reflected the creativity of the early Christians. The procedure did not work with the forms of the tradition found in our written gospels. Instead, historians would reconstruct the earliest recoverable form of a pericope, and that reconstructed form would be run through the criteria of au-

---

1994), 338–39. For the term "continuity of reception" (and the related "tradition of reception"), which places the written object within the context of a social group that could draw upon its experience with the nonwritten tradition in its reception of the written actualization of the tradition, see John Miles Foley, *The Singer of Tales in Performance*, Voices in Performance and Text (Bloomington: Indiana University Press, 1995).

13. Samuel Byrskog, *Story as History—History as Story: The Gospel Tradition in the Context of Ancient Oral History*, WUNT 123 (Tübingen: Mohr Siebeck, 2000), 3–6, in a critique of both narrative and form criticism, uses the double reference "kerygma as history—history as kerygma": "*the kerygma, the story of the present Lord, remains, after all, intrinsically linked with the Jesus of the past*" (6).

thenticity. The problems with this method have been explored elsewhere.[14] This section lays out critiques of the notion of "original form" and the tradition-critical procedures used to reconstruct that form on the basis of the later forms recorded in our written texts.

As E. P. Sanders demonstrated more than half a century ago, the Jesus tradition did not develop unilinearly, with certain features (e.g., Semitisms, names, length) indicative of earlier tradition.[15] More recently, media criticism in biblical studies and other fields (anthropology, folkloristics, etc.) has problematized the notion of an "original form," either in oral tradition or in written texts with roots in oral tradition. John Miles Foley refers to the "iterative quality of traditional oral narrative," that quality of repetition by which multiple expressions of a singular tradition are perceived as variants (or multiforms) of a singular tradition.[16] These multiple expressions are not laid down one after another, seriatim, with each expression editing or altering the features of immediately prior expressions. Tradition is a species of language, in which multiple expressions sit alongside one another as autonomous and simultaneously authentic actualizations of their encompassing tradition.[17]

Perhaps the most striking example of this multiformity of authentic tradition is the encounter between the risen Jesus and Saul as the latter approached Damascus (Acts 9:1–19; 22:1–21; 26:4–23).[18] Here we have three accounts that are immediately recognizable as versions of the same story. They are all written by the same author, so we are not dealing with redactional changes that reflect the

---

14. In addition to the materials cited in nn. 1 and 2, above, see Rafael Rodríguez, "Authenticating Criteria: The Use and Misuse of a Critical Method," *JSHJ* 7 (2009): 152–67.

15. See E. P. Sanders, *The Tendencies of the Synoptic Tradition*, SNTSMS 9 (Cambridge: Cambridge University Press, 1969). Sanders's dissertation has been eclipsed by his other contributions to Pauline and historical Jesus scholarship and is, therefore, often overlooked or inadequately heeded. For examples, see Stanley E. Porter and Andrew W. Pitts, "The Pre-Citation Fallacy in New Testament Scholarship and Sanders's Tendencies of the Synoptic Tradition," in *Christian Origins and the Establishment of the Early Jesus Movement*, ed. Stanley E. Porter and Andrew W. Pitts, TENTS 12 (Leiden. Brill, 2018), 89 107.

16. Foley, *Singer*, 2.

17. Foley, *Singer*, 83.

18. My reference to "authentic tradition" does not suggest the events of Saul's encounter with Jesus happened exactly as narrated; it would be difficult to envision a historical event in which "the men who were traveling with [Saul] . . . heard the voice but saw no one" (Acts 9:7) and, at the same time, "saw the light but did not hear the voice of the one who was speaking to [Saul]" (22:9). Rather, the term "authentic tradition" refers to the tradition's *social value*, in which the author and, presumably, the readers and hearers of both Acts 9 and 22 perceived the account being performed or read as legitimate, acceptable expressions of the story.

idiosyncratic styles or theologies of different authors. The differences between the three accounts are not insubstantial, but those differences are all the more interesting because the singular author seems not to conceive of the substance of the tradition in terms of the details that vary across the three accounts. No version is "earlier" or "more original" than the others, except in the pedantic sense that Acts 9 was written before Acts 22 and 26. James Dunn discusses "the conversion of Saul" and its patterns of stability and variability as an example of "the oral traditioning process itself," though the multiformity in which we are interested appears to be a feature of the *tradition* more than of its *orality*.[19] Recent discussions of both New Testament textual criticism and the textual development of Hebrew biblical texts, especially among the texts and fragments discovered in the Judean desert, have demonstrated the variability of scribal, chirographic tradition.[20] Our focus here is not on the verbal or structural dynamics of the texts themselves, though on the level of words and order we have ample evidence that biblical texts during the first centuries BCE and CE remained relatively fluid.[21] Our point is not textual but *sociological*: the scribes and their community at Qumran experienced different "versions" of scriptural texts as authentic expressions of scriptural tradition.[22] The

19. See James D. G. Dunn, *Jesus Remembered*, vol. 1 of *Christianity in the Making* (Grand Rapids: Eerdmans, 2003), 210–12. For more detailed discussion, see Rafael Rodríguez, *Oral Tradition and the New Testament: A Guide for the Perplexed* (London: T&T Clark, 2014), esp. 64–66.

20. The discussion in both fields is vast; for New Testament textual criticism, see D. C. Parker, *The Living Text of the Gospels* (Cambridge: Cambridge University Press, 1997). For the textual development of Hebrew biblical texts, see Michael Segal, "Between Bible and Rewritten Bible," in *Biblical Interpretation at Qumran*, ed. Matthias Henze (Grand Rapids: Eerdmans, 2005), 10–28; Sidnie White Crawford, *Rewriting Scripture in Second Temple Times* (Grand Rapids: Eerdmans, 2008); Crawford, *Scribes and Scrolls at Qumran* (Grand Rapids: Eerdmans, 2019); Eugene Ulrich, "The Jewish Scriptures: Texts, Versions, Canons," in *Early Judaism: A Comprehensive Overview*, ed. John J. Collins and Daniel C. Harlow (Grand Rapids: Eerdmans, 2012), 121–50; see also the essays republished in George J. Brooke, *Reading the Dead Sea Scrolls: Essays in Method*, EJL 39 (Atlanta: Society of Biblical Literature, 2013).

21. Eugene Ulrich ("Jewish Scriptures," 141) refers to "a measured pluriformity in the scriptural texts."

22. See n. 19 above. As Novakovic writes: "Textual pluriformity at Qumran was not an exception but a common feature of the Second Temple milieu. What is surprising, however, is the preservation of the variant readings of the scriptural books within the same community. *No evidence suggests that the Qumranites saw the presence of textual variants as a problem or that the group had a preference for a particular textual tradition.* . . . Such a pluriformity of textual versions indicates that it was a particular book, not its textual form, that was considered authoritative." See "The Scriptures and Scriptural Interpretation," in *The World of the New Testament: Cultural, Social, and Historical Contexts*, ed. Joel B. Green and Lee Martin McDonald (Grand Rapids: Baker Academic, 2013), 85–104 (quote from 88; my emphasis).

three accounts of Saul's encounter with Jesus, with all their differences and their agreements, exhibit the same multiformity by which textually distinctive versions are experienced by their authors or performers and their readers or audiences as authentic expressions of that tradition. There are no "layers" to peel back or to dig through, nor are there "earlier" or "later" forms of the tradition.

The tradition's multiformity is neither controversial nor difficult to see. What to do with that multiformity, however, has created considerable havoc, particularly inasmuch as multiformity has been contorted into evolutionary development. We will return to the question of the tradition's multiformity shortly. Werner Kelber, however, first notes the historically improper assumption that multiformity is a distortion of the original singularity of the historical Jesus. "To be sure, reiteration and variation of words and stories must be assumed for Jesus' own proclamation as well."[23] If we imagine in the beginning was the *ipsissima verba*, a singular and definitive collocation of words spoken by Jesus himself, and, further, that variations of those *ipsissima verba* are distortions of the tradition, we deceive ourselves and the truth is not in us.[24]

> When [Jesus] pronounced a saying at one place, and subsequently chose to deliver it elsewhere, neither he nor his hearers could have perceived this other rendition as a secondhand version of the first one. Each saying was an autonomous speech act. . . . No one saying was elevated to the privileged position of *ipsissimum verbum* at the expense of any other saying.[25] In the absence of a chart arranging materials in parallel columns and a trajectory inviting comparative analysis, each saying constituted an original and authentic intention that was actualized in social contextuality.[26]

Kelber insists on this irreducible multiformity of the Jesus tradition even from its origins: *"Jesus' proclamation was irreducible to ipsissimum verbum [sic]; it occurred in multiformity that was tantamount to multioriginality."*[27] If historians are

23. Kelber, "Jesus and Tradition," 113.

24. Kelber would insist on the singular, *ipsissimum verbum*, because he is speaking of *verbum* as a saying of Jesus rather than the *verba* that comprise that saying. My use of the plural is not a correction of Kelber but rather a nod to the standard use among historians of Jesus.

25. In context, Kelber is not talking about different sayings, one of which might be—but was not—privileged above the others, but rather of various expressions of a single saying, with one expression being the authoritative, canonical expression and the others epiphenomenal variants of the first.

26. Kelber, "Jesus and Tradition," 114–15. Kelber goes on to say: "multiple original sayings are a fact of oral life, but the search for the single, original, correct saying is pointless."

27. Kelber, "Jesus and Tradition," 118–19. In the original 1995 version of this essay in *Semeia* 65, only the words "*ipsissimum verbum*" were italicized (see 151).

questing for the actual teachings—if not quite the very words—of Jesus, it makes no sense to mark one of Jesus's expressions of, say, the parable of the sower as authentic and to relegate Jesus's other expressions of the same parable to secondary status.[28] In this sense, every expression of the parable of the sower that Jesus spoke is "authentic"; those expressions in all their variability are *equiprimordial* and, as Kelber says, "*the* original version."[29] What we find in the gospels, then, are not edited versions of sayings Jesus said on singular and specific occasions, but rather representations of the kinds of things Jesus said in the various kinds of interactions in which he found himself. As Ulric Neisser argued after comparing the Nixon tapes with John Dean's testimony of conversations that were recorded on those tapes, what appears to be the memory of a specific event is often the interpreted, schematized, and conflated memories "of repeated experiences, a sequence of events that the single recollection merely typifies or represents."[30]

The multiformity characterizing the very origins of the Jesus tradition undermines any attempt to subject later expressions to tradition-critical analyses. Certainly the later tradition was capable of taking Jesus's teachings in new directions or applying them to new situations, so we should be careful of attributing "multi*originality*" to the expressions of Jesus's followers. But if the sayings before the tradition were not uniform, then the tradition after the sayings cannot be reduced to uniformity.[31] The better procedure, instead of a misguided attempt at reconstructing chimeric tradition histories, is to offer multipronged analyses that

---

28. Jacques Schlosser, "Scholarly Rigor and Intuition in Historical Research into Jesus," in Holmén and Porter, *Handbook*, 1:493.

29. Kelber, "Jesus and Tradition," 119. In the original 1995 version of this essay, the entire phrase "*the original version*" was italicized (151). In 2014, I mildly chastised Kelber for "going too far" and "speaking too strongly" of *equi*primordiality (see Rodríguez, *Oral Tradition*, 38–39). Inasmuch as Kelber is speaking specifically of Jesus and not of the Jesus tradition after Jesus, Kelber's original point is appropriate and my correction of him misplaced.

30. Ulric Neisser, "John Dean's Memory: A Case Study," in *Introductory Readings for Cognitive Psychology*, ed. Richard P. Honeck (Guilford, CT: Duskin, 1994), 114. Neisser refers to this as "repisodic memory," that is, memory not of "the 'gist' of a single episode by itself, but [of] the common characteristics of a whole series of events."

31. James Dunn (*Jesus Remembered*, 211) refers to "the harmoniser's hypothesis of different episodes to explain differences between parallel accounts." The hypothesis of multiformity that I am proposing here differs from this "harmoniser's hypothesis" in that I am not claiming that Jesus said each of the forms of parallel sayings attributed to him in the gospels. The point here, instead, is that many (most?) of Jesus's significant sayings and many of his actions were already multiform before being handed down in the traditioning processes of his later followers. The multiforms we see in the tradition reflect the multiformity of Jesus's teachings and actions *as well as* the discrete, specific occasions in the life of Jesus and the influence of later, secondary contexts. *Multiformity is not harmonization.*

account for multiple expressions of a tradition in their specific contexts, exploring how each might function as an expression of the historical Jesus and also how each functions as an expression of the later Jesus tradition.[32]

Finally, historians of Jesus need to abandon the reflexive assumption that written tradition is stable in ways that oral tradition is not, or even that variability (or a peculiar combination of variability and stability) is a function of oral performance and tradition.[33] We have already discussed the variability even of written tradition, especially in the thrice-narrated account of Saul's encounter with the risen Jesus.[34] In 1972, French medievalist Paul Zumthor referred to manuscript variability as *mouvance* and differentiated a "work" from the "texts" that actualize that work.[35] Even before Zumthor, the famed Harvard classicist and folklorist Albert Lord made a similar distinction between "songs and the song."[36] *Mouvance* does not refer to the "scribal interventions," whether intentional or accidental, endemic to the handwritten reproduction of written texts. It is, rather, a different order of variability, in which a tradition (or work or song) exists as an untextualizable, intangible set of potentialities that are actualized in specific, particular, localized expressions (oral, written, or otherwise).[37] In the case of ancient traditions,

32. See my proposal in Rafael Rodríguez, "Your Will Be Done: Remembering Jesus' Submission to the Father," in *"To Recover What Has Been Lost": Essays on Eschatology, Intertextuality, and Reception History in Honor of Dale C. Allison Jr.*, ed. Tucker S. Ferda, Daniel Frayer-Griggs, and Nathan C. Johnson, NovTSup 183 (Leiden: Brill, 2021), 314.

33. See especially Dunn, *Jesus Remembered*; Terence C. Mournet, *Oral Tradition and Literary Dependency: Variability and Stability in the Synoptic Tradition and Q*, WUNT 195 (Tübingen: Mohr Siebeck, 2005). For an interesting corrective based on empirical analyses, see Travis M. Derico, *Oral Tradition and Synoptic Verbal Agreement: Evaluating the Empirical Evidence for Literary Dependence* (Eugene, OR: Pickwick, 2016).

34. See also n. 19 above.

35. Paul Zumthor, *Essai de poétique médiévale* (Paris: Seuil, 1972), 68–74.

36. Albert B. Lord, *The Singer of Tales* (Cambridge: Harvard University Press, 1960), 99–123; see also Foley, *Singer*, 48 n. 44: "any performance/version is fundamentally a 'tale within a tale,' with the avenues of implication necessarily running both ways. The present tale both enriches and is enriched by the larger, implied tale—itself unperformed (and unperformable) but metonymically present to the performer and audience."

37. This is what it means to say, with John Miles Foley (cited above), that tradition is a "species of language" (see n. 17 above). See also Rodríguez, *Structuring Early Christian Memory*, 83–86: "If we may import an analogy from structural linguistics, the tradition exists as *langue*; performance forges *parole*. That is, 'the tradition,' as *langue*, refers to the semiotic system within which and according to which individual expressions generate meaning; the 'text-in-performance,' as *parole*, refers to individual utterances that instantiate the larger system. . . . A linguistic system does not exist apart from its actualizations in concrete, individual utterances, but that system transcends and contextualizes individual utterances" (86).

the actualizations in written texts—including monumental and other inscriptions—are all that remain; oral, ritual, and other media of traditional expression evanesced with the passage of time.[38] These unwritten, now-vanished expressions of the tradition, however, were part of the encompassing "circumambient tradition" that contextualized our texts' originating authorship as well as their earliest receptions.[39] And though these unwritten expressions are unrecoverable today, our analyses of the written gospels sever the links connecting the texts and their life-sustaining tradition if we imagine they are—or were—discrete, serialized expressions of a linearly evolving phenomenon.[40]

Speaking in the Temple

Some critics have complained that studies appealing to memory studies and media criticism have a penchant for abstract, theoretical discussion.[41] When (or if) these studies examine specific texts and traditions, their high-level reflections on historiography have little bearing on detailed analyses of those texts and traditions.[42] That complaint is, at best, only selectively accurate.[43] The remainder of

38. John Miles Foley offers a fourfold taxonomy of "oral-derived texts," works of verbal art that have some manner of connection with a tradition of oral performance; see "The Riddle of Q: Oral Ancestor, Textual Precedent, or Ideological Creation?," in *Oral Performance, Popular Tradition, and Hidden Transcript in Q*, ed. Richard A. Horsley, SemeiaSt 60 (Atlanta: SBL Press, 2006), 123–40 esp. 137–39; see also Foley, *How to Read an Oral Poem* (Urbana: University of Illinois Press, 2002), 38–53; Rodríguez, *Oral Tradition*, 83–85.

39. Kelber ("Jesus and Tradition," 127) describes tradition as "a circumambient contextuality or *biosphere*" (italics not in 1995 edition); see also Rodríguez, *Oral Tradition*, 17, 39, 106–7.

40. See also Kirk, *Q in Matthew*, 123–31, though Kirk continues to identify variability as "the index feature of oral tradition" and also refers to (but does not specify) *"properties of the written medium"* (123). For a similar recognition of the simultaneous unrecoverability and vital importance of extratextual forms of the tradition, see Byrskog, *Jesus*, 331–49.

41. One often encounters the term "orality" (and "orality studies"), though there is little agreement on what this term means and, worse, not much evidence that it refers to anything at all. It is an apophatic term, meaning little more than the negation of literacy, written texts, and their alleged psychological and sociocultural accoutrements. See Rodríguez, *Oral Tradition*, 6–8.

42. Critiques of this nature include Alexander J. M. Wedderburn, *Jesus and the Historians*, WUNT 269 (Tübingen: Mohr Siebeck, 2010), esp. 93–143; Foster, "Memory," 198.

43. To pick just four counterexamples, Anthony Le Donne examines Son of David traditions in *The Historiographical Jesus: Memory, Typology, and the Son of David* (Waco, TX: Baylor University Press, 2009). In Rodríguez, *Structuring*, I examine the historical value of the healings and exorcisms in the Synoptic sayings tradition. Dale C. Allison Jr., in *Constructing Jesus: Memory, Imagination, and History* (Grand Rapids: Baker Academic, 2010), offers a historiographical principle (i.e., "recurrent attestation") and examines a number of principal themes in the Jesus tradition. Chris Keith provides detailed analyses of Jesus's perceived authority, literacy, and

this essay will offer a detailed discussion of the words attributed to Jesus during the temple confrontation (Mark 11:17; Matt 21:13, 16; Luke 19:46; John 2:16, 19).[44] As we will see, the tradents' interpretive lenses certainly affect the shape and content of the tradition, but those lenses are themselves shaped by the Jesus of history and the communities' traditions of commemorating Jesus and his confrontation with the temple authorities.

E. P. Sanders opened his analysis of "Jesus and the temple" both emphatically and cautiously: "It is overwhelmingly probable that Jesus did something in the temple and said something about its destruction."[45] Famously, Sanders is not ambivalent about the temple incident; it is the basis with which he begins his historical reconstruction of the historical Jesus.[46] We will consider three sayings:[47]

1. "Is it not written, 'My house shall be called a house of prayer for all the nations' [Isa 56:7]? But you have made it a 'den of bandits' [Jer 7:11]" (Mark 11:17; see parallels, with variations, in Matt 21:13; Luke 19:46).[48]

2. "Take these things away from here! Do not make the house of my Father a house of commerce!" (John 2:16).

3. "Destroy this sanctuary, and in three days I will raise it" (John 2:19).

The first saying appears in all three Synoptic Gospels in the context of Jesus's disruptive action in the temple courts. The second is often treated as a variant of the first, though they have in common only the double reference to an *oikos* and the genitive pronoun *mou*. Even here the differences outweigh the similarities. In John, *oikos* is used negatively the second time ("a house *of commerce*"), whereas in the Synoptics it remains positive ("a house *of prayer*"). Also, in John *mou* relates Jesus to God ("the house of *my* Father"), whereas in the Synoptics *mou* relates the

---

confrontations with his opponents; see, among other works, *Jesus' Literacy: Scribal Culture and the Teacher from Galilee*, LNTS 413 (London: T&T Clark, 2011); Keith, *Scribal Elite*.

44. For an analysis of the temple incident in John 2 (especially the narrator's citation of Ps 69:9 in 2:17), see Rafael Rodríguez, "Zeal That Consumed: Memory of Jerusalem's Temple and Jesus's Body in the Gospel of John," in *The Gospel of John*, ed. Thomas R. Hatina, vol. 4 of *Biblical Interpretation in Early Christian Gospels*, LNTS 613 (London: T&T Clark, 2020), 201–18.

45. E. P. Sanders, *Jesus and Judaism* (Philadelphia: Fortress, 1985), 61.

46. The chapter "Jesus and the Temple" begins with the following words: "*Having named Jesus' activity in the temple as the surest starting point for our investigation*, I must hasten to say that the question of Jesus and the temple brings with it the amount of uncertainty which is usual in the study of the Gospels." See Sanders, *Jesus and Judaism*, 61 (my emphasis).

47. For reasons of space, we will not discuss Matt 21:16 ("Yes. Have you never read, 'Out of the mouth of babies and nursing infants you prepared praise' [Ps 8:2]?").

48. All translations are my own, unless noted otherwise.

temple to God ("*my* house"). For these reasons, I do not treat the second saying as a multiform of the first. The similarities between the first and second sayings may have resulted in the latter being *received* as an instance of the former, but it is unlikely the second was *created* as an expression of the first. The second saying, therefore, lacks any parallels in the extant Jesus tradition.[49]

The third saying has the most diverse set of parallels. Variants of this saying appear in Mark's and Matthew's accounts of Jesus's trial before Jewish authorities (Mark 14:58 // Matt 26:61), and a Lukan variant can be found in Acts 6:14, where Stephen is accused of attributing to Jesus the same threat reported in Mark's and Matthew's trial scenes. The tradition appears again when witnesses to Jesus's crucifixion mock him (Mark 15:29 // Matt 27:40). A fragmentary parallel appears in Gos. Thom. 71, where Jesus says, "I will destroy this house, and no-one will be able to rebuild it. . . ."[50] These are the sayings that appear in extant commemorations of Jesus's action in the temple (and, related to that action, in Jesus's trial and related traditions).[51]

The various expressions are so thoroughly woven into the tradition of Jesus's confrontation with the temple authorities, his (and Stephen's) trial before those authorities, and the mocking of his adversaries at the crucifixion that we should probably say, with Allison, that rejecting them "should leave one thoroughly skeptical about the mnemonic competence of the tradition."[52] If Jesus did not say

49. John's description of the corrupted temple as a house *emporiou* is likewise unique in the New Testament. Matthew uses the related noun *emporia* in his account of the parable of the wedding feast (22:5). Although Matthew recounts this parable within the temple, the parable never uses the *oik-* stem. The verb *emporeuomai*, like the adjective and the noun, is used negatively in Jas 4:13 and 2 Pet 2:3, neither of which has any other resonances with John 2:16.

50. Simon Gathercole, *The Gospel of Thomas: Introduction and Commentary*, TENTS 11 (Leiden: Brill, 2014), 477–80. Translation from Gathercole.

51. As Gathercole notes in reference to Gos. Thom. 71, "Jesus is probably envisaged by the author [of Gos. Thom.] in, or in the vicinity of, the temple" (*Gospel of Thomas*, 479). Earlier in his *The Composition of the Gospel of Thomas: Original Language and Influences*, SNTSMS 151 (Cambridge: Cambridge University Press, 2012) Gathercole incorrectly claimed "only the fragmentary beginning ('I will dest[roy thi]s house') is paralleled in the Synoptics" (221). Every reference in the gospels to "destroying" (*katalyō* or *lyō*) the temple mentions "the sanctuary" (*ton naon*; Mark 15:29 // Matt 27:40), "this sanctuary" (*ton naon touton*; Mark 14:58), or "the sanctuary of God" (*ton naon tou theou*; Matt 26:61). In Acts, Stephen's adversaries accuse him of "speaking words against [this] holy place" (*kata tou topou tou hagiou* [*toutou*]) and repeating a prophecy that Jesus would "destroy this place" (*katalysei ton topon touton*; Acts 6:13–14). John 2:19, of course, has the imperative, "Destroy this sanctuary" (*lysate ton naon touton*). None of Jesus's references to the temple as an *oikos* or *oikia* also speak of "destroying" (*lyō* or *katalyō*) the "house." In the New Testament, the only co-occurrence of *katalyō* and *oikos/oikia* is in 2 Cor 5:1.

52. Allison, *Constructing Jesus*, 47. Allison continues: "If secondary accretions that seriously

something like the sayings recorded in the gospels, then the creation of these sayings entered the tradition too early and too widely for us to be able to detect the innovation.[53]

In the historiographical program sketched above, it would make no sense to ask, for example, if Mark's inclusion of "for all the nations" from Isa 56:7 is more or less original than Matthew's and Luke's (Q?) omission of the phrase.[54] Neither the Matthean nor Lukan expressions deny the Isaianic expression to Jesus's saying, as if the latter Synoptists imagined Jesus invoking Isaiah to claim the temple as a house of prayer, *but not for all the nations!*[55] If the Matthean and Lukan multiforms of the first saying were meant as corrections either to Mark or Isaiah, their redaction is too subtle to make the point for anyone not looking at a gospels synopsis.[56] Nothing in the Matthean or Lukan multiforms discourages readers or hearers familiar with Mark (as were the authors of Matthew and Luke) or even only with LXX Isaiah from supplying, metonymically, "for all the nations" in their reception of the current multiform.[57] If we must evaluate these variants chronologically,

---

misrepresent Jesus attached themselves to the tradition in such abundance from the beginning, then maybe he is gone for good. Sometimes parasites kill the host." See also John P. Meier, *A Marginal Jew: Rethinking the Historical Jesus*, AYBRL (New Haven: Yale University Press, 1991–2016), 2:630, cited by Allison.

53. Even the Jesus Seminar, in its discussion of Gos. Thom. 71, concedes: "Jesus could have predicted the destruction of the temple and its replacement by another 'not made with hands.' And [the Seminar Fellows] agreed that some such saying must have circulated as an independent remark during the oral period, since it appears in three independent sources." See Robert W. Funk and Roy W. Hoover, *The Five Gospels: What Did Jesus Really Say? The Search for the Authentic Words of Jesus* (San Francisco: HarperCollins, 1993), 513. Why, then, did they rate every expression of these traditions gray (Mark 11:17 parr.; John 2:16b; see also Mark 14:58 [!]) or black (Matt 21:16; John 2:16c, 19; Gos. Thom. 71; see also Matt 26:61)? They continue, "Yet [the Fellows] were hesitant to identify its original form." Despite taking "the safe course," even the hyperskeptical Seminar concludes, "its content probably goes back to Jesus." Similarly, see Crossan, *Historical Jesus*, 355–60, 437.

54. It would be similarly nonsensical to ask if Luke edits Mark's (and LXX Isaiah's) *klēthēsetai*, or if his *estai* comes from a non-Markan source.

55. In the MT tradition, Isa 56:7 envisions the house of God being called a house of prayer *ləkol hā'amîm* rather than *ləkol hagôyim*, which might affect how an author familiar with Hebrew *Vorlagen* (as was Matthew) understood the LXX's *pasin tois ethnesin*. The overlap and differentiation between *'am* and *gôy* are beyond the scope of this paper.

56. Identifying and interpreting redactions is a difficult enterprise, and we scholars working with multiple texts open before us are especially prone to overinterpret minute differences. For an example, see Zola's critique of Francis Watson in Nicholas Zola, "Evangelizing Tatian: The Diatessaron's Place in the Emergence of the Fourfold Gospel Canon," *PRSt* 43 (2016): 410–11.

57. For "metonymic (or *pars pro toto*) signification," see John Miles Foley, "Traditional Signs and Homeric Art," in *Written Voices, Spoken Signs: Tradition, Performance, and the Epic Text*, ed.

Matt 21:13 // Luke 19:46 (without *pasin tois ethnesin*) is later than Isa 56:7 LXX, so Mark 11:17 (which agrees verbatim with Isa 56:7 LXX, excepting the conjunction *gar*) is earlier than the Matthean and Lukan multiforms. But this judgment means nothing in a traditional setting, with a performer or reader actualizing the tradition in the presence of an audience, whether through dramatic performance or through actual reading (i.e., decoding signs inscribed on parchment or papyrus). All three Synoptic multiforms *are* the temple saying, leveled by Jesus as a critique against the temple leadership.

We should briefly comment on the fact that all three Synoptic Gospels include the tradition found in Mark 11:17 // Matt 21:13 // Luke 19:46. In form-critical Jesus historiography, these three variants are a "single attestation" of the tradition because, as far as we can verify, the later authors (Matthew and Luke) found Jesus's citations from Isa 56:7 and Jer 7:11 in Mark rather than in pre- or non-Markan tradition. Matthew 21:13 and Luke 19:46, in other words, are disqualified as evidence that Jesus actually quoted Isa 56:7 and Jer 7:11 in the temple; all that we can conclude is that the Matthean and Lukan evangelists preserved the references to Isa 56:7 and Jer 7:11 that they found in their source. This is correct as far as it goes, but it does not go far enough. When we expand our vision of the tradition from ink-and-parchment textuality to consider the flesh-and-blood, embodied experience of tradition, Matthew's and Luke's decisions tell us more about the Jesus tradition in the late first century than simply what they found in Mark. That each author retains the quotations from Isaiah and Jeremiah shows that, for both Matthew and Luke (whom we described, above, as tradents with prior experience with the Jesus tradition), the tradition they knew prior to their encounter with Mark's Gospel either contained a critique of the temple in similar terms or could feasibly be molded to include such a critique. In other words, Mark's account of the temple saying *made sense* to the two earliest tradents of Mark's Gospel for whom we have evidence. Matthew and Luke are not merely *repetitions* of Mark; they are evidence for the *reception* of Mark.

When we turn to the third saying (John 2:19), we arrive at conclusions that are perhaps most at odds with form-critical Jesus historiography. John 2:19 is the most complicated temple saying because (1) it occurs in the Gospel of John, the latest of the canonical gospels and the one often considered the most heavily reworked by later theological perspectives; (2) it occurs in a Synoptic-like story that has been transposed from the end to the beginning of Jesus's public activity; (3) none

---

Egbert J. Bakker and Ahuvia Kahane (Cambridge: Harvard University Press, 1997), 56–82; Foley, *Oral Tradition and the Internet: Pathways of the Mind* (Urbana: University of Illinois Press, 2012), 57: "always immanent."

of its parallels occur in the context of the temple incident; and (4) the saying is thoroughly worked into post-Easter, Johannine interpretation (see John 2:22). John 2:19 is so thoroughly reworked by Johannine theology that its historical value is highly suspect.

And yet, even here, it is not difficult to see how Johannine interpretive processes are vehicles for our historical knowledge rather than obstacles to it.[58] In all the Synoptic multiforms of the third saying (including Acts 6:14), the words are attributed to Jesus by adversaries. The accusation that Jesus said something like, "I will destroy this sanctuary made with hands and, in three days, build another, not made with hands" (Mark 14:58), or "I am able to destroy the sanctuary of God and, in three days, to [re]build [another]" (Matt 26:61), is portrayed clearly, even emphatically, by all three Synoptists as "false."[59] It is not exactly clear what about this charge is characterized as "false" by the Synoptists, and the Fourth Gospel's attribution of words so similar to this "false testimony" to Jesus is certainly intriguing.[60] Perhaps the Synoptists are rejecting something Jesus actually or purportedly said.[61] Perhaps they are rejecting the idea that Jesus ever threatened the temple, though the fact that all three attribute to Jesus a threat against the temple—even using the verb *katalyō*!—makes this unlikely (see Mark 13:2 // Matt 24:2 // Luke 21:6). Perhaps the falsity of the witnesses' testimony, according to the Synoptists, is the claim that *Jesus* would be the agent of the temple's destruction. The Synoptic Jesus expresses the threat to the temple in passive verbs, leaving open the possibility that God would wreak the temple's destruction (in quotidian terms, of course, the Romans were responsible for destroying the temple). John's second-person imperative, "*Destroy* this sanctuary" (*lysate ton naon touton*), does not attribute the temple's destruction to Jesus's interlocutors, as if Jesus were saying, "You are destroying (or, you will destroy) this sanctuary," so

---

58. See Rodríguez, "Zeal That Consumed"; see also Rodríguez, "What Is History? Reading John 1 as Historical Representation," *JSHJ* 16 (2018): 31–51.

59. Mark uses the verb *pseudomartyreō* twice (14:56–57), while Matthew uses the nouns *pseudomartyria* (26:59) and *pseudomartys* (26:60). The author of Luke-Acts uses the attributive phrase *martyres pseudeis* (Acts 6:13) as well as the negative verbs *hypoballō* (6:11) and *synkineō* (6:12).

60. As mentioned above (see n. 53), the Jesus Seminar printed Mark 14:58 in gray rather than black and said the content of the saying "probably goes back to Jesus."

61. "One should not, Mark insists, believe either false witnesses or mocking enemies. But all of that intensive damage control in Mark 13–15 simply underlines the fact that certain Christian circles, first, believed Jesus had said or done something concerning his [*sic*] destruction of the Temple and, second, interpreted that as the conjunction of siege and parousia in 70 C. E." See Crossan, *Historical Jesus*, 357. According to Crossan, this idea came from the event-and-saying in Mark 11:15–19.

much as it invites or dares those interlocutors to act.[62] Not until Gos. Thom. 71 does the extant tradition portray Jesus threatening to destroy the temple himself. In the Synoptic tradition at least, and perhaps also in the Johannine tradition, Jesus announces but does not execute the threat to the temple.

We might, finally, take notice of the earliest expression of this tradition, if in fact we were to decide it is a multiform of the temple saying. In 2 Cor 5:1, Paul entertains the possibility of the destruction (*katalyō*) of "our earthly house [*oikia*], this tent [*skēnos*]." Both *oikia* and *skēnos* can be used to refer to the dwelling place of God, whether the temple or, earlier, the tabernacle. Paul bridges the theological use of dwelling-as-temple and the metaphorical use of dwelling-as-body in 1 Cor 3:16–17 (see also 6:19), which uses *naos* and *oikeō* to link the holiness of God's dwelling within the Corinthians' bodies. Paul is certainly not performing or actualizing the tradition of Jesus's temple saying. But we should probably see the traditional links between *naos* and *oikos/oikia*, the danger of *katalyō* for the sanctuary (or house), and the metaphorical transferability of temple imagery to the human body as the tools with which Paul thinks as he addresses a very different situation.[63]

In the Johannine temple incident, destroying (*lyō*) the temple becomes a metaphor for killing Jesus: "he was speaking about the sanctuary of his body" (*tou naou tou sōmatos autou*; John 2:21). Despite the clear and dramatic reinterpretation of the temple incident (including the temple saying) in John, then, we nevertheless can see the past of Jesus's life and the commemorative tradition of recalling and recounting that past providing both the components and the constraints that enable Johannine interpretation. We can also understand how John's innovative work with the tradition might find willing reception among an audience already familiar with the Jesus tradition. Though John 2:16, 19 differ substantially from their Synoptic parallels, the Johannine sayings nevertheless make sense as a "repisode" of the kind of thing Jesus would say about Jerusalem's temple.[64] The various multiforms and versions of "the temple saying" we find in our sources convey the "common characteristics of a whole series of events," namely, Jesus's critique of the temple.[65]

62. According to BDF §387.2: "The imperative can simply be the equivalent of a concessive clause." The authors cite John 2:19 as their example, paraphrasing *lysate* as *ean kai lysēte*.

63. For a similar examination of applying Jesus tradition to very different contexts, see Rodríguez, "Your Will," 306–9; see also James F. McGrath, "Obedient unto Death: Philippians 2:8, Gethsemane, and the Historical Jesus," *JSHJ* 14 (2016): 223–40.

64. See Neisser, "John Dean's Memory," cited in n. 30 above.

65. Neisser, "John Dean's Memory," 114.

Decoding the Richly Encoded Jesus Tradition

The Next Quest for the historical Jesus must account for the irreducibility of the early Jesus tradition to only one medium: the handwritten text. The tradition did not grow up, layer upon layer, like an ancient tel encrusting the original, singular Jesus beneath accumulating detritus and debris. Tradition is never so unilinear. Instead, the Jesus tradition infused multiple media, including informal conversations, debates and disputations, public proclamation, worship, scriptural interpretation, ethics, ritual, song, prayer, art (both public and private), and much else besides. The texts with which we have to work are nearly all that remains of the vibrant, multimedia experience of the Jesus tradition.

While we cannot really recover what has been lost, neither can we ignore the thick connections that once gave our textual remains their social significance. In the first-century media cultures of earliest Christianity, the images of Jesus inscribed in the gospels both enriched and were enriched by "the larger, implied tale [here, the larger, totalizing image of Jesus]—itself unperformed (and unperformable) but metonymically present to the performer and audience."[66] As historians, we are not merely examining how words were added to other words, how words advanced or retreated, how new words were written and heaped upon old words, sometimes transforming them and sometimes burying them. The Jesus tradition is less an old fossil and more an old, unknown language. Like westerners before the secrets of the Rosetta Stone were unlocked, we can see the signs of the Jesus tradition but are often unable to hear them in anything like their original, living settings.[67] But as with ancient Egyptian hieroglyphs, we hope that somewhere amid our evidence is the key for unlocking those signs' signification.

The conceptual apparatus by which the form critics attempted to recover the pregospel Jesus tradition were insufficient for the complexity of the task. It led them into the cul-de-sac of differentiating earlier from later traditions and chasing a chimeric "original form" of the sayings in our texts. It also prevented them from noticing that the interpretive features they sought to excise from the material were the means by which historical knowledge about Jesus was formulated, transmitted, and preserved.[68] As we saw with the temple saying in Mark 11:17 parr. and John 2:16, 19, this does not mean that Jesus said each (or even any!) of the exact

66. Foley, *Singer of Tales*, 48 n. 44 (cited in n. 37 above).
67. "Without audiences and readers willing and able to listen, the most splendid old oak will make no sound when it falls, and the most densely coded traditional utterance may appear only pedestrian or awkward—Homer or the Old English poet 'nodding.'" See Foley, *Singer*, 183.
68. Zimmermann, *Puzzling*, 76–80.

phrases attributed to him in our various sources. Instead, it means those sources become the means by which we hear Jesus speaking, enacting, and explaining the threat against the temple. We also offered a suggestion about how Jesus was *mis*heard by his contemporaries, at least some of whom may have been motivated to mishear him because of their opposition to him, his message, his movement, or to all three at once. Finally, we suggested at least one instance in which the traditions of Jesus in the temple may have offered Paul tools for thinking about his own experience.

In none of these instances was the past swallowed up by the conditions of the present, even if, at the same time, the present was never swallowed up by the past to which it turned to make sense of itself. Instead, the various media mediating Jesus to his followers brought them in touch with a man they both already knew and sought to know anew. All this is too much to restrict merely to *written* tradition; it is the domain of tradition in all its sensorial variety. In the Next Quest, therefore, historians of Jesus will have to account for the tradition's irreducibility to handwritten texts.

6

BEYOND WHAT IS BEHIND

Chris Keith

The Next Quest for the historical Jesus must account for the inaccessibility of the past. This subject is somehow widely acknowledged and still underappreciated in our little corner of academia.[1] I would even hazard a guess that the widespread acknowledgment of the inaccessibility of the past contributes on some level to underappreciation of its significance, since the regularity of scholarly admissions that the past is past can obscure the degree to which the conviction that we can somehow *reach* an earlier stage of history animated both the discourse and practice of historical Jesus scholarship through most of its history.

With this observation in the background, my argument in this chapter can be stated in both general and specific ways. Generally, scholars should abandon the notion that they can "get behind" the Gospels and embrace a more robust role for the scholarly informed historical imagination of the past. Specifically, and among other procedural implications, scholars should abandon focusing on individual units of the Jesus tradition and instead focus on asking and answering—to the extent that they can—general questions about the historical Jesus and his socio-

---

1. Jens Schröter, "The Criteria of Authenticity in Jesus Research and Historiographical Method," in *Jesus, Criteria, and the Demise of Authenticity*, ed. Chris Keith and Anthony Le Donne (London: T&T Clark, 2012), 61–62: "It is a trivial insight . . . but nevertheless important to keep in mind, that the past itself is over and can only be represented by way of interpretation of what remains from bygone times in the present."

historical contexts. Some readers may already be objecting that they and other scholars have affirmed these points for some while. They would be right. As only one prominent example, Allison's 2010 argument for focusing our initial inquiries upon the "general impression," "big picture," and "gist" has been largely successful and pressed both these points.[2] What I distinctly emphasize in this essay, however, is the connection between these two matters, that is, how previous stages of the quest have been cloistered imaginatively precisely *because* they quested for the historical Jesus predominantly by attempting to verify particular passages of the gospels. In so doing, I indicate the potential for Next Quest research by embracing the role of the historical imagination and all means of informing that imagination.

In order to illustrate these points, I begin with three twentieth-century German Jesus scholars: Rudolf Bultmann and his two students, Ernst Käsemann and Günther Bornkamm. Although it is unquestionably one of the goals of the Next Quest to move on from needless recycling of "the same scholarly authorities of yesteryear," in this case it is necessary to start with them, and especially with a particular curiosity in the work of Bultmann and Bornkamm.[3] Doing so will allow us to appreciate how some contemporary scholars remain under their influence even when they think they do not. It will also allow us to appreciate that what we now foreground in the Next Quest was not altogether absent in earlier historical Jesus scholarship but was inadequately pursued.

BEHIND THE GOSPELS

The aforementioned curiosity in the work of Bultmann and Bornkamm is that they affirmed the historical likelihood of particular scenarios described by certain gospel texts while simultaneously rejecting the historical value of the texts that describe those scenarios. And though I can summarize this state of affairs in a way that makes their assessments seem somewhat nonsensical, it has to be appreci-

---

2. Dale C. Allison Jr., *Constructing Jesus: Memory, Imagination, and History* (Grand Rapids: Baker Academic, 2010): "We can learn some important things about the historical Jesus without resorting to the standard criteria and without, for the most part, trying to decide whether he authored this or that saying or whether this or that particular event actually happened" (10). Allison later writes: "The modern study of memory moves me to differentiate myself from those who, proceeding by subtraction, presuppose that we can learn about Jesus chiefly on the basis of a handful of parables and a small collection of aphorisms deemed, after a critical sorting, to be authentic" (14). For his own account of his abandonment of the atomistic criteria approach, see Dale C. Allison Jr., "It Don't Come Easy: A History of Disillusionment," in Keith and Le Donne, *Demise of Authenticity*, 186–99.

3. Quote from James G. Crossley, "The Next Quest for the Historical Jesus," *JSHJ* 19 (2021): 261.

ated that in the scholarly framework in which they were made, the assessments made complete sense. This curiosity reveals a difference between *kinds* of historical assessment—assessing the likelihood (or not) of a generalized claim versus assessing the historical status of a unit of tradition—that has become important in contemporary Jesus studies.

Bultmann and the Controversy Narratives

Bultmann walked this distinct exegetical and historical tightrope with regard to the controversy narratives, which portray Jesus and other Jewish teachers in conflict. According to Bultmann, "Controversy dialogues are all of them imaginary scenes."[4] The "historical life" in which they "have their proper place" is not that of the historical Jesus, but "in the apologetic polemic of the Palestinian Church."[5] He explains further, "In the form in which we have them the controversy dialogues are imaginary scenes illustrating in some concrete occasion a principle which the Church ascribed to Jesus."[6]

Bultmann's emphasis on these conflict stories as a literary genre and as they appear in the Gospels—"in the form in which we have them"—is important to notice because, on the more general question of whether the historical Jesus is likely to have engaged in such activities, he is more bullish: "Of course it is quite possible that he did; indeed, very probable."[7] He expresses this similar mixture of positions on the "scholastic dialogues" category of literary forms, which also feature Jesus as teacher: "It is in itself highly probable that Jesus was asked questions about the way to life, or about the greatest commandment, but it is quite another thing to ask whether the scenes which relate those questions are historical reports or not. They are such only in the sense that the Church formulated such scenes entirely in the spirit of Jesus."[8] Bultmann only teases the fascinating possibility that the early church fabricated tradition under the impact of the historical Jesus ("entirely in the spirit of Jesus"), that is, that Jesus himself might have contributed in some way to the production of tradition that Bultmann could not attribute to him methodologically.[9] The various strands of this complex knot have only become

---

4. Rudolf Bultmann, *History of the Synoptic Tradition*, trans. John Marsh (Oxford: Blackwell, 1963), 40.

5. Bultmann, *History*, 40–41.

6. Bultmann, *History*, 41.

7. Bultmann, *History*, 40. He also writes on the same page: "but the first question to be asked, methodically speaking, must be about the literary form of the controversy dialogue, and its origin as a literary device."

8. Bultmann, *History*, 54.

9. For a similar formulation, see Günther Bornkamm, "The Significance of the Historical

more important in the almost thirty years since Schröter called for a reception-history approach to the Jesus tradition in 1997.[10] I will return to this point below, but for now it will suffice to observe Bultmann's opinion that, generally speaking, scholars can be confident that such a historical scenario occurred, though they cannot—or at least should not—be confident in the historical value of the gospel texts that narrate those scenarios.

Bornkamm and the Passion-Resurrection Predictions

Thirty-five years after Bultmann's statements, Bornkamm followed his teacher's approach when it came to the passion-resurrection predictions in the Gospel of Mark (8:31; 9:31; 10:32–34).[11] He states, "That the road to Jerusalem had to lead to new and serious conflicts with the spiritual and temporal rulers, and that Jesus had to reckon with the possibility of his own violent end, we have no reason to doubt, however justified our grounds for disputing the historical validity of the individual prophecies concerning his suffering and resurrection."[12] If anything, then, Bornkamm is even more succinct than Bultmann. For Bornkamm, scholars can have confidence that Jesus contemplated his impending death in Jerusalem, but cannot have confidence in the passages that claim he did so.[13]

Jesus for Faith," in *What Can We Know about Jesus?* by Ferdinand Hahn, Wenzel Lohff, and Günther Bornkamm, trans. Grover Foley (Edinburgh: Saint Andrew Press, 1969), 76: "I could also say that Jesus himself, his history and personality, imposed and forced this method of presentation upon the bearers of the first tradition and the gospel writers, who later (in the last third of the first century A.D.) collected and molded this tradition!" The exclamation point is not present in the original German; see Günther Bornkamm, "Die Bedeutung des historischen Jesus für den Glauben," in *Die Frage nach dem historischen Jesus* by Ferdinand Hahn, Wenzel Lohff, and Günther Bornkamm, 2nd ed. (Göttingen: Vandenhoeck & Ruprecht, 1966), 63.

10. Jens Schröter, *Erinnerung an Jesu Worte: Studien zur Rezeption der Logienüberlieferung in Markus, Q und Thomas*, WMANT 76 (Neukirchen-Vluyn: Neukirchener, 1997), 485. Schröter here distinguishes between such an approach and methodological attempts to authenticate a "secured 'minimal stock'" (*gesicherten "Minimalbestand"*), thereby anticipating more recent shifts within historical Jesus studies.

11. Holly J. Carey, *Jesus' Cry from the Cross: Towards a First-Century Understanding of the Intertextual Relationship between Psalm 22 and the Narrative of Mark's Gospel*, LNTS 398 (London: T&T Clark, 2009), 46–49, rightly argues that scholarly nomenclature has tended to underemphasize the presence of the resurrection in these predictions, which she terms "passion-resurrection predictions" (48).

12. Günther Bornkamm, *Jesus of Nazareth*, trans. Irene and Fraser McLuskey with James M. Robinson (New York: Harper & Row, 1960), 154–55; see also 55.

13. Bornkamm, *Jesus*, 49, similarly expresses great confidence in the "fact" that Jesus was baptized by John the Baptist and that Jesus's meeting the Baptist was one of the most consequential events of "far-reaching importance" of his life. Nevertheless, for Bornkamm, "Tradition has

The Fascinating Unsaid

Most fascinating in these Bultmann and Bornkamm quotations for our present purposes is what remains unsaid. They do not attempt to explain the relationship between the status of the individual traditions and the general image they offer. That is, the general impression is composed of the individual units, and the individual units collectively yield the general impression, but how do they relate to one another? Unclear also is *how* or *why* their contrasting scholarly judgments relate to one another as constituent parts of an argument.[14] By what means do they conclude that the transmission, engine, brakes, and tires do not function . . . but the car runs just fine?

For the sake of clarity, I am not necessarily criticizing Bultmann and Bornkamm. It is the case that I do not share their confidence that we can know much about individual units of tradition, but here I am simply observing the odd scholarly scenario that results from this kind of historical assessment. I suggest that this resultant scenario is necessarily a byproduct of their predetermined commitment to focus predominantly and atomistically on individual units of tradition in their method, and I will return to this matter, too, shortly. Worth noting, however, is that in their unexplained and unargued affirmations of the general scenarios portrayed in multiple texts, they function more intuitively as historians, temporarily dropping the act of scientists who apply a litmus test to each individual element of the tradition.

At a more general level, these examples from Bultmann and Bornkamm, both of whose studies exerted an enormous influence on New Testament scholarship, illustrate perfectly the difference between questing for the historical Jesus by assessing general claims of the text (e.g., "Jesus was in conflict with other Jewish teachers" or "Jesus foresaw his death in Jerusalem") and focusing narrowly on the

---

altogether transformed the story into a testimony to the Christ, so that we cannot gather from it what baptism meant for Jesus himself, for his decisions and for his inner development" (54).

14. Bornkamm and Hahn, however, both opine on the fact that historical investigation of the Gospels is not restricted to what critical study labels "authentic" or "inauthentic" tradition (Bornkamm, *Jesus*, 11, 20–21), with Hahn even distinguishing between two quests: the quest for the historical Jesus and the quest for the earthly Jesus. See Ferdinand Hahn, "The Quest of the Historical Jesus and the Special Character of the Sources Available to Us," in *What Can We Know about Jesus?*, 30–33, 44–45. For further discussion, see Chris Keith, "Die Evangelien als 'kerygmatische Erzählungen' über Jesus und die 'Kriterien' in der Jesusforschung," in *Jesus Handbuch*, ed. Jens Schröter and Christine Jacobi, trans. Matthias Müller (Tübingen: Mohr Siebeck, 2017), 86–98; also Keith, "The Narratives of the Gospels and the Historical Jesus: Current Debates, Prior Debates, and the Goal of Historical Jesus Research," *JSNT* 38.4 (2016): 445–48.

status of particular traditions (for example, Matt 12:1–8 or Mark 9:31).[15] Although both kinds of historical investigation were theoretically available to scholars, proceeding from the house of Bultmann and 1950s German scholarship, mainstream Gospels scholarship in the German- and English-speaking worlds for the next several decades overwhelmingly donned its lab coat and threw its efforts into the verification of individual units of tradition by developing criteria of authenticity. I and others have traced this development in depth elsewhere and I need not repeat it here.[16] We do, however, have to recognize the astounding influence of this methodological approach. Questing for the historical Jesus by placing individual units of tradition over the criteriological Bunsen burner extends well into the present. Meier was not (formally) a form critic, but his fifth volume of *A Marginal Jew* (2016), which focuses on the parables, continues to defend the criteria of authenticity and specifically addresses the parables as "unit[s] of tradition."[17] Unsurprisingly, then, Meier's book exhibits the Bultmann-Bornkamm historiographical curiosity, affirming that the historical Jesus told parables but announcing already in the introduction that scholars cannot attribute the overwhelming majority of parable traditions to the historical Jesus: "In most cases, no criterion of historicity can argue convincingly for the origin of a parable in the mouth of the historical Jesus."[18] For Meier, like Bultmann and Bornkamm, Jesus likely did the kind of thing attributed to him in the gospel traditions, but historians cannot trust the gospel traditions that attribute that kind of thing to him.

15. Bultmann's *Geschichte des synoptischen Tradition* is arguably the most important book of New Testament scholarship of the twentieth century, and an even stronger case could be made that it is the most important book of Gospels scholarship of the twentieth century. Bornkamm's *Jesus von Nazaret* had at least fifteen German editions.

16. Chris Keith, *Jesus' Literacy: Scribal Culture and the Teacher from Galilee*, LNTS 413 (London: T&T Clark, 2011), 27–70; Keith, "The Indebtedness of the Criteria Approach to Form Criticism and Recent Attempts to Rehabilitate the Search for an Authentic Jesus," in Keith and Le Donne, *Demise of Authenticity*, 25–48; Anthony Le Donne, "The Rise of the Quest for an Authentic Jesus: An Introduction to the Crumbling Foundations of Jesus Research," in Keith and Le Donne, *Demise of Authenticity*, 3–17.

17. Regarding the criteria of authenticity, see John P. Meier, *A Marginal Jew: Rethinking the Historical Jesus*, AYBRL (New Haven: Yale University Press, 1991–2016), 5:6, 12–21. Quotation from 5:5.

18. Meier, *Marginal Jew*, 5:5. He attributes only four parables to the historical Jesus (5:8). For a more methodologically appropriate treatment of Jesus and the parables, see Ruben Zimmermann, *Puzzling the Parables of Jesus: Methods and Interpretation* (Minneapolis: Fortress, 2015), esp. 57–103.

History and the Individual Units

On display in this curiosity shared between Bultmann, Bornkamm, and Meier is the protracted *historiographical* influence of a specific *tradition* model. This focus on individual units of tradition was an inheritance from form criticism, a methodological behemoth in which the individual unit of tradition played the starring role in what was a fully developed theory of gospel transmission (the generating, passing on, collecting, developing, shaping, and eventual textualizing of the oral Jesus tradition into the written, Koine Gospels). Bultmann opened his famous study by emphasizing the significance of "the individual units of tradition" and insisting (contra Dibelius) that form criticism as a transmission theory had historical implications: "Form-criticism . . . must also lead to judgements about facts (like the genuineness of a saying, the historicity of a report and the like)."[19] Bornkamm similarly opened his book by affirming form criticism's "laws of tradition" and their relevance for his historical conclusions: "Observing these laws is an excellent aid in distinguishing the essential from the non-essential in any passage. . . . The critical exegete and the historian is therefore obliged, in questions concerning the history of tradition, to speak often of 'authentic' or 'inauthentic' words of Jesus and thus to distinguish words of the historical Jesus from 'creations of the Church.'"[20] He emphasized the individual units of tradition again after explicitly invoking form criticism's "laws":

> One observation is of special significance. It is that at the beginning of the tradition we find, not a historical sequence of events, but the individual pericope—the individual parable, the individual saying or story, which only in the gospels, often in very different ways, is given its setting and, with a very modest editing, arranged coherently. These little individual parts of the tradition have to be considered by themselves.[21]

These statements by Bornkamm warrant full quotation because they nicely encapsulate this approach to critical studies of the Gospels that has absolutely dominated Jesus studies for a century. Once more, on display is the *historical relevance* of the tradition model. The historical roots of each individual tradition must be traced or otherwise tested because the earliest past that a scholar can reach comes

19. Bultmann, *History*, 3–5 (quotation from 5).
20. Bornkamm, *Jesus*, 20.
21. Bornkamm, *Jesus*, 218.

in the shape of those individual units of tradition. They were, in the words of Bornkamm, "at the beginning."

I remain convinced, therefore, that one of the single most decisive developments in Jesus and Gospels studies in the previous century was the adoption of form criticism's theory for the transmission of the Jesus tradition by those questing for the person of Jesus of Nazareth in the mid-twentieth century.[22] Even when contemporary scholars believe they have left the theory formally behind, its residual effects remain, as can be seen in Meier's work on the parables. The Quest for the historical Jesus (so defined and carried out) was both enabled by and constrained by the affirmation that scholars can get "behind the Gospels" by means of individual units of tradition.

This state of affairs is observable elsewhere in this general period of scholarship in Käsemann's articulation of what became the criterion of dissimilarity in his famous essay "The Problem of the Historical Jesus," which was a lecture originally delivered in 1953. Käsemann states that his renewed call to historical Jesus research starts with form criticism and focuses upon "the individual unit of material."[23] He claims that "the historical credibility of the Synoptic tradition has become doubtful all along the line" and that there is "almost complete lack of satisfactory and water-tight criteria for this material" with a singular exception: "In only one case do we have more or less safe ground under our feet: when there are no grounds either for deriving a tradition from Judaism or for ascribing it to primitive Christianity, and especially when Jewish Christianity has mitigated or modified the received tradition, as having found it too bold for its taste."[24]

Much has been rightly written on the inherently anti-Semitic results of this

---

22. Keith, *Jesus' Literacy*, 27–41, esp. 38–40; Keith, "Narratives of the Gospels," 431–33, 437–40. For a sample of scholars explicitly stating their dependence upon form criticism for the quest for the historical Jesus, see, in chronological order, Ernst Käsemann, "The Problem of the Historical Jesus," in *Essays on New Testament Themes*, trans. W. J. Montague, SBT 41 (London: SCM, 1964), 34; Bornkamm, *Jesus*, 20, 218; Norman Perrin, *What Is Redaction Criticism?* (London: SPCK, 1970), 70–71; Reginald H. Fuller, "The Criterion of Dissimilarity: The Wrong Tool?," in *Christological Perspectives: Essays in Honor of Harvey K. McArthur*, ed. Robert F. Berkey and Sarah A. Edwards (New York: Pilgrim, 1982), 42; Ferdinand Hahn, "Methodological Reflections on the Historical Investigation of Jesus," in *Historical Investigation and New Testament Faith*, ed. Edgard Krentz, trans. Robert Maddox (Philadephia: Fortress, 1983), 47.

23. Käsemann, "Problem," 34: "With the work of the Form-Critics as a basis, our questioning has sharpened and widened until the obligation now laid upon us is to investigate and make credible not the possible unauthenicity of the individual unit of material but, on the contrary, its genuineness."

24. Käsemann, "Problem," 36–37.

formulation since it severs the historical Jesus from Judaism.[25] It also, however, attests an important substitution—the substitution of the historical Jesus for an earlier state of the tradition as the object of historical recovery. Bultmann had previously articulated a version of this criterion as a means of asserting "a genuine similitude of Jesus," that is, a literary form of a saying of Jesus: "We can count on possessing a genuine similitude of Jesus where, on the one hand, expression is given to the contrast between Jewish morality and piety and the distinctive eschatological temper which characterized the preaching of Jesus; and where on the other hand we find no specifically Christian features."[26] Käsemann and others expanded the formulation beyond a focus on a literary form to the Synoptic tradition in general and appropriated it as a means of questing for the person of Jesus, not just the earliest literary expression of a saying attributed to him.[27]

Once more, my point at present is not to pretend that I have caught these scholars in a sleight of hand that they made no attempt to hide in the first place. To the contrary, my point is to observe the ease with which the move was made and accepted, the unquestioned nature of the assumption that they could get to the historical Jesus and conclusions about him by way of their tradition criticism. These assumptions about the Gospels and the historical Jesus gave way to a full-blown cottage industry of the criteria of authenticity in the so-called Third Quest for the historical Jesus from the 1980s to the early 2010s.

What we should not miss, though, is that many of these mid-twentieth- and late twentieth-century scholars and their students genuinely believed that the Quest so defined could yield *access* to the past of Jesus in some form. Rigorous interrogation of individual units of the tradition could, they thought, take them "behind the Gospels." Bornkamm opened his *Jesus von Nazaret* by stating that his goal was to move beyond "mere tradition" and to "break through it and seek behind it to see the thing itself."[28] Likewise, and perhaps more emphatic, is Hahn, who was a student of Käsemann and Bornkamm and also defined "strictly isolated pieces" of the tradition as his starting point.[29] Hahn writes: "When I speak of the historical Jesus *I go behind all the statements of the community*, limit myself to

25. Dagmar Winter, "Saving the Quest for Authenticity from the Criterion of Dissimilarity: History and Plausibility," in *Demise*, 115–31; as well as her earlier landmark study Gerd Theissen and Dagmar Winter, *The Quest for the Plausible Jesus: The Question of Criteria*, trans. M. Eugene Boring (Louisville: WJK, 2002).

26. Bultmann, *History*, 205.

27. Noted earlier by Stanley E. Porter, *The Criteria for Authenticity in Historical-Jesus Research*, LNTS 191 (London: T&T Clark, 2000), 71–72.

28. Bornkamm, *Jesus of Nazareth*, 9.

29. Hahn, "Quest," 42.

the facts of his earthly life, his ministry and proclamation, and attempt to gain a picture which is free from all post-resurrection conceptions in order to grasp the history of Jesus in its own terms."[30] Hahn elsewhere describes clearly the identification of "authentic traditions about Jesus" as the path to the historical Jesus: "For it is only when *stages of the transmission* after Jesus can be definitely established that we can *gain access to Jesus himself.*"[31] The italicized portions of this quotation from Hahn exhibit precisely my earlier claim that, for these scholars, how they approach the historical Jesus is necessarily a byproduct of their transmission theory for the gospel tradition. From this perspective, one can easily understand why a focus on testing individual units of tradition has been so popular for so long. For many scholars, nothing less than direct access to the historical Jesus was at stake.

IMAGINING THE PAST IN FRONT OF THE SOURCES

What does the Quest for the historical Jesus look like now that scholars not only recognize but embrace that we cannot actually get "behind the Gospels," much less by usage of pseudoscientific criteria of authenticity? Before considering answers to that question, I first note that Next Quest Jesus scholars are hardly the first to ask it, which only reinforces the point that the question must be brought to the fore and overlooked no longer.

Predecessors

Already in the 1970s, Morna Hooker was famously questioning the usefulness of form criticism for historical inquiries.[32] In a 2000 publication that is often overlooked, Schüssler Fiorenza argued against an authentic/inauthentic dichotomy and the illusion of "scientific certainty" that it provides. Anticipating the memory approach and the surge of reception studies, she argued for a "critical retrieval and articulation of memory" whereby historical re-presentations feature the reception of Jesus by his rememberers.[33] As a reminder, at least in practice,

---

30. Hahn, "Quest," 45 (emphasis added).

31. Hahn, "Methodological," 41–42 (emphases added).

32. Morna D. Hooker, "Christology and Method," *NTS* 17.4 (1971): 480–87; Hooker, "On Using the Wrong Tool," *Theology* 75 (1972): 574–81.

33. Elisabeth Schüssler Fiorenza, *Jesus and the Politics of Interpretation* (New York: Continuum, 2000), 75, 78, 136. I drew attention to this work from Schüssler Fiorenza in Keith, *Jesus' Literacy*, 48. See now also Amy M. Walters, "Elisabeth Schüssler Fiorenza and the Quest for the Historical Jesus," *Open Theology* 6 (2020): 468–74.

Bultmann and Bornkamm were already making generalized pronouncements independently of their interrogation of individual units of tradition in the early and mid-twentieth century.

Die Schröterbahn

In my estimation, however, there is no scholar whose work is more consequential for a quest that abandons the attempt to "get behind" the Gospels than Jens Schröter. In addition to his 1997 *Erinnerung an Jesu Worte* and other publications, in a collection of essays from the early 2000s (translated into English in 2013) Schröter lays the methodological and hermeneutical foundations that precipitated the demise of the criteria of authenticity and make possible the Next Quest methodologically. He explicitly positions his perspective against the atomistic approach of form criticism and consistently draws attention to the fact that historical scholarship amounts to re-presenting the past as a hypothesis about what it might have been, not an attainment of, or access to, the actual past:[34]

> Viewed epistemologically, every conception of history is therefore a hypothesis about the meaning of what happened in the past that is oriented to the surviving traces of the past, which it orders and interprets.[35]

> Apart from this interpretation [of a historian] there is no history, but only dead material. Therefore, a text first becomes a historical "source" when it is read, interpreted, and placed in relation to other materials. The goal of history writing is thus not *reconstruction of the past* but *construction of history*: it constructs a picture of the past that has relative validity, dependent on the plausibility of the interpretation of reality that is currently valid, determined by the state of knowledge of the researchers, and determined by the view that the interpreter sets forth with the aid of the known material.[36]

---

34. Jens Schröter, *From Jesus to the New Testament: Early Christian Theology and the Origin of the New Testament Canon*, trans. Wayne Coppins, BMSEC (Waco, TX: Baylor University Press, 2013), 28–32. On p. 30 he writes: "We are thus advised to understand these as Jesus narratives with historical reference and consequently not to answer the historical question without regard for the 'framework' and not to restrict it to the individual units."

35. Schröter, *From Jesus to the New Testament*, 23.

36. Schröter, *From Jesus to the New Testament*, 35. Emphases original to German; see Jens Schröter, *Von Jesus zum Neuen Testament*, WUNT 204 (Tübingen: Mohr Siebeck, 2007), 39.

A conception of history based on critical examination is also, of course, a hypothesis about how it could have been that serves the interpretation of present reality.[37]

Every interpretation of the material is a hypothetical, falsifiable conception for understanding reality; historical truth is therefore a regulative idea, which these conceptions seek to approach.[38]

In these quotations and throughout his body of historical Jesus research, Schröter rightly emphasizes that the historian is only ever in front of the texts he or she is accounting for, offering hypotheses about a possible past based on his or her accumulated, tendentious knowledge, and from his or her present perspective. The remains of the past, as well as the historian's knowledge, viewpoint, and imagination, may restrain the historian's hypotheses, but they equally make those hypotheses possible in the first place. Furthermore, describing our theories of the past as "hypotheses" is not lamentable, but a rightful recognition that hypothetical is all that any portrayal of the past ever is. If we have no access to the past, if we cannot get "behind the Gospels," then we have not lost the objectivity with which past historians operated. Rather, we have acknowledged that our predecessors who intimated objectivity were not objective at all. Take, for instance, Meier's proposed "unpapal conclave" behind his *A Marginal Jew*:

Suppose that a Catholic, a Protestant, a Jew, and an agnostic—all honest historians cognizant of 1st-century religious movements—were locked up in the bowels of the Harvard Divinity School library, put on a spartan diet, and not allowed to emerge until they had hammered out a consensus document on who Jesus of Nazareth was and what he intended in his own time and place.[39]

This conclave was, it turns out, exactly what he called it—a "fantasy."[40] It was a ventriloquist act by one scholar. Meier's contributions are substantial, perhaps even era-defining, but they are not and never were the ideological average of Jews, Christians, and agnostics, and Harvard Divinity is hardly the only or ideal place one can study the historical Jesus. It should probably tell us something that, when

---

37. Schröter, *From Jesus to the New Testament*, 39.
38. Schröter, *From Jesus to the New Testament*, 47.
39. Meier, *Marginal Jew*, 1:1.
40. Meier, *Marginal Jew*, 1:1; 5:11.

scholarly and religious neutrality is imagined, it is imaginatively located in the elite universities of the northeast United States. Yet scholarship is not actually a consensus document, thankfully.

An Inexhaustive List of Characteristics in the Next Quest

The contribution of the Next Quest for the historical Jesus to this general trend away from atomistic assessments of the Jesus tradition is that the affirmation that the historian's task is to hypothesize the past from his or her position in front of the sources is *programmatic*. That affirmation will inevitably manifest in a variety of ways. What follows is an inexhaustive list of only a few characteristics, which other chapters in this volume and future contributions to the Next Quest will flesh out further.

First, reception histories will play a prominent role in the Next Quest for the historical Jesus.[41] At least two kinds of reception-historical approaches—both instrumental in questing for the historical Jesus—should be mentioned here. In one kind of reception-historical approach, scholars acknowledge that the portrayals of Jesus that come to us in our earliest sources are already part of the complex reception history of the historical Jesus.[42] They cannot be removed from that reception history without severing their umbilical cord, and this affirmation stands in direct contrast to the assumption that individual units of tradition must be assessed as decontextualized entities, sanitized of interpretive influence. For the sake of clarity, and because this point can be easily misunderstood or mischaracterized by others as an attempt to sneak claims for historicity in through the reception-historical backdoor, I underscore that approaching the earliest sources as part of the reception history of the historical Jesus is not the same as claiming that the historical Jesus is portrayed accurately in it. This approach asserts only that the historical Jesus set in motion all kinds of perceptions—and misperceptions—of him that eventually come to expression partly in the earliest sources as particular instantiations of that broader reception history. Unquestionably, that reception history includes misunderstandings of Jesus, misidentifications, embellishments, images that contradict other images, and inaccuracies along with any portrayals that we might judge as holding historical value. The operative point is—again—not that the historical Jesus did everything the Gospels say he did, but that *the reception history and the interpretations of Jesus that comprise it are historical artifacts in their own rights*, products of historical forces and processes

---

41. See further the chapter by Halvor Moxnes in this volume and the introduction.
42. Cf. Schröter, *Erinnerung*, 485.

that can be investigated *historically* as such. Historical truths and historical un-truths are equally products of particular sociohistorical circumstances, produced by the same kinds of processes, cultural conditions, and agents. Their distinction resides in our scholarly judgments about them, not the media mechanics of their transmission, as if one is clouded by ancient interpretive frameworks and the other clean and clear. The appropriate initial scholarly question is not, then, "What is the status of this tradition, authentic or inauthentic?" but "How have the ancients portrayed the past?" and then, "Why might they have portrayed it in the ways they did?" Likewise, we proceed, therefore, not with a limited "minimal stock" of sanitized traditions, but by acknowledging that we stand before this complex reception history. We then proceed to imagine a variety of ways that this reception history might have come before us. We gain ground in our knowledge by adjudicating between the possibilities, arguing for some and against others, but not with a litmus test applied to isolated sayings or actions.

Certainly, in providing answers to the question of how and why the ancients portrayed the past as they did, we may be able to affirm a historical likelihood or unlikelihood, but we must also acknowledge that there is a vast amount of historical knowledge to be gained apart from pronouncing on historical (un)likelihoods. Mere affirmation or rejection of historical portrayals does not exhaust our ability to learn historical information. As an example, even if we come to affirm that something in the Gospels happened, questions remain concerning why it—and not thousands of other words and events and ideas that also happened—gained traction among Jesus's followers. Alternatively, even if we come to reject that something in the Gospels happened, questions remain about why Jesus's earliest followers thought it did. If we think Jesus's followers misunderstood something, what led to the misunderstanding and why was it convincing? If we think they lied, why this lie and not another? There are any number of historical factors and forces that contributed to the transmission of the particular reception histories that have come down from antiquity, and anemic investigations about whether something did or did not happen come nowhere near capturing the full breadth of those factors and forces.

If I could indict atomistic approaches to the historical Jesus for one thing, it would be that their attempts to recover tradition *out of* the narrative frameworks of the Gospels treat those frameworks as ahistorical products, theological castles in the sky that appeared as miraculously as the Jesus they portray. Let us take the attribution of the title "Son of God" to Jesus as an example. Later followers of Jesus may have fabricated traditions about Jesus that describe him as the Son of God because they were already convinced that he was the Son of God, in which case their portrayal of the past amounts to a retrojective narrativization of their present theological convictions. But merely observing this dynamic of narrativization does not alleviate the historian from his or her task. This kind of thing happens all the time with narratives of the past, and it should not surprise anyone that it happens in these narratives as well. Yet the historian's task is not to dismiss interpretations *as* interpretations, but to explain why they exist in the first place. Why were there followers of Jesus (at all) who were convinced he was the Son of God? Why did they come to think of him as such? Maybe they were liars. Maybe he was a liar. Maybe they were telling the truth and he was too. Maybe they thought he was the Son of God because he told them he was. Maybe he did not really think that but wanted them to think it. Maybe he really thought it. Maybe he did not initially think it but came to think it later. Maybe he was just pulling a prank and it got out of hand. Maybe he told them one thing and they heard another, only to repeat it ad nauseam en route to the canon and creeds. Maybe he thought no such thing about himself but they lied and said he did. Maybe he did not know he was the Son of God and did not claim it for himself but they came to think it sincerely. Maybe they thought it insincerely. Maybe he told him he was the Son of God and they heard him say he was the Son of God but they thought he meant something different than he really did. Maybe he meant Psalm 2 and they meant Hercules or just a human or Adam. Maybe Jesus and his earliest followers agreed that the title Son of God meant one thing but later followers twisted it into something else.

Scholars have offered variants of all these proposals, and all assume some historical sequence or sequences. *But whatever we decide, the theological claim that Jesus was the Son of God that appears in the earliest sources about him arose in (a) particular historical context(s), as a result of historical processes, and thus requires a historical explanation* or at least an attempt at one. Labeling interpretive categories as "theological" does not change the fact of the categories' historical emergence, production, and acceptance. And somewhere at the beginning of that reception history is the person of Jesus, inaccessible but responsible at least in part for a reception history that is accessible. Trying to account for how we got from point A to point B is the fascinating task that we get to pursue; that is, unless you are a mythicist who thinks there was no Jesus at all, but even here I think there is a need to explain why the name "Jesus" was chosen to foist these ideas upon instead of "Beauregard."

The second kind of reception-historical approach that holds a prominent role in the Next Quest for the historical Jesus acknowledges that the historian him- or herself stands in a reception history, a particular social, cultural, global, and economic context. The focus in this approach is on the sociohistorical situatedness of the scholar in front of the text, complementing the aforementioned focus on the text in front of the scholar. Like the early perceivers of Jesus and the early tradents of the Jesus tradition, historical Jesus scholars—while holding different epistemological convictions—are similarly influenced in a variety of ways by the present from which they imagine the past, which includes the influence of the received past and, in this case, includes previous scholarship. Just as we may ask why particular images of Jesus did (or did not) take hold among his earliest followers, we can ask why particular issues do (or do not) take hold in particular periods of scholarly activity. Recent scholarship has made great advances along these lines, such as Heschel's study of the Aryan Jesus produced during the Third Reich, Crossley's studies on twentieth-century Jesus scholarship (*Jesus in an Age of Terror* and *Jesus in an Age of Neoliberalism*), or Moxnes's study of nationalism and the nineteenth-century Quest.[43] Scholars have sometimes too easily relegated such studies outside the boundaries of "historical Jesus studies" proper by describing them as "history of scholarship" or "history of interpretation." Although not technically an inaccurate description, this relegation reflects a traditional understanding of "historical Jesus studies" as quintessentially, or even solely, concerned with giving individual traditions in the Gospels a historical thumbs-up or thumbs-down. Yet, if Schröter is correct that the scholar's own tendentious knowledge and perspective are necessary elements in the production of a critical hypothesis about the past of Jesus—and Schröter is—then we can no longer relegate these "histories of interpretation" to the margins of the discourse. They must be fully accepted as part of the work taking place under the banner of historical Jesus studies. And when it comes to the potential to make new contributions to the discussion and learn new things about the historical Jesus from such approaches, the harvest is plentiful but the workers are few. We eagerly anticipate new insights that such scholarship will yield.

Moving beyond the important role of reception-historical approaches in the Next Quest, a second characteristic of the Next Quest, as I have mentioned already, is that we foreground the fact that thinking about the past is fundamentally, and inescapably, an imaginative act. That is not to say it is not scholarly, learned, critical, or rigorous. But it is to acknowledge that we need to bring to bear all the resources on our trained historical imaginations that we can. In this sense, boring old sociohistorical, contextual studies on Second Temple Judaism and the ancient Mediterranean remain as fundamentally important as they ever were. Like recep-

43. Susannah Heschel, *The Aryan Jesus: Christian Theologians and the Bible in Nazi Germany* (Princeton: Princeton University Press, 2008); James G. Crossley, *Jesus in an Age of Terror: Scholarly Projects for a New American Century* (London: Routledge, 2008); James G. Crossley, *Jesus in an Age of Neoliberalism: Quests, Scholarship and Ideology*, BibleWorld (Durham: Acumen, 2012); Halvor Moxnes, *Jesus and the Rise of Nationalism: A New Quest for the Nineteenth-Century Historical Jesus* (London: I. B. Tauris, 2012), respectively.

tion histories, these sociohistorical studies of ancient cultures are tools for our imaginations. Cross-cultural comparative studies must be recognized under the banner of historical Jesus studies for exactly the same reason, as we saw in the introduction. Modern scholarship on gender, sexuality, race, trauma, and ancient religion that have not previously had a home in Jesus studies should also be welcomed as part of the broader *historical* tool box, since they all force contributors to the discussion to consider factors that we might otherwise overlook in the texts that come before us and the "us" we bring before the texts.

Third, if we are only ever in front of the text, hypothesizing what might have been, we must be more honest about all we do not know (see Goodacre's chapter in this volume). We can make historical pronouncements on some issues, but we cannot possibly hope to answer other questions. Asking whether it is likely that Jesus was crucified by Romans is not the same as asking whether the transfiguration happened in space and time. Furthermore, it is not a zero-sum game of affirmation or rejection. We may have more confidence in some parts of our historical knowledge than others, as should be the case given the vagaries of antiquity. There are limits to our historical knowledge and historical imaginations, and there is simply so much about the ancient world that we do not know.

Yet there is also so much to know, and none of what I have mentioned is a reason to abandon the quest. The Next Quest for the historical Jesus will take on many more characteristics than the three that I have mentioned here. Generally speaking, however, accepting that we are only ever hypothesizing antiquity from a position in front of the sources should shape what we think we are doing when we "quest" for the historical Jesus. The Next Quest will therefore be purposefully inclusive of more voices and perspectives, humbler in its conclusions, more curious in its questions.

7

MISSING PIECES

Mark Goodacre

The Next Quest for the historical Jesus must consider the missing pieces, which vastly outnumber the slivers of information historians possess about Jesus. Scholars should stop behaving as if all the really important information about the historical Jesus can be found somewhere, somehow, among the materials that have survived antiquity. Ancient history is vastly different from modern history. Where the modern historian frequently faces the problem of navigating through oceans of primary sources, the ancient historian is more often stuck gazing into the gaps and longing for more material. Yet in spite of the fact that historical Jesus scholars know this, or claim to know this, they frequently behave as if it is irrelevant, continually finding new ways to rake over the same old materials as if they will reveal some kind of complete picture of the life of the historical Jesus. In this essay, I would like to reflect on the importance of taking the missing pieces seriously, looking at their potential to keep us honest, to stimulate our imagination, and to behave ethically.

Rudolf Bultmann's notorious claim that "I do indeed think we can now know almost nothing concerning the life and personality of Jesus" is, on one level, overstated and easy to dismiss.[1] There are lots of things that we can know about the life

---

1. Rudolf Bultmann, *Jesus and the Word,* trans. Louise Pettibone Smith and Erminie Huntress (New York: Scribner & Sons, 1934), 8. Bultmann makes the remark in appreciation of Schweitzer: "I do indeed think that we can now know almost nothing concerning the life and personality

of Jesus with a degree of confidence, including his connection to John the Baptist, his proclamation of the kingdom, the call of disciples who continued the movement after his arrest and crucifixion, and so on. There is no difficulty in producing a good sketch of things that can be known about Jesus, and E. P. Sanders has illustrated how much the historian can do with even a handful of key data when they are integrated into an informed understanding of Jesus's historical context.[2]

But knowing things about the historical Jesus is not the same as being able to write his biography. Bultmann's point is that we do not have the data available to trace his psychological development in the manner of contemporary biography. Yet by placing Bultmann's thinking into the disparaging (and in fact nonexistent) category of "No Quest" and getting overexcited about a supposed "Third Quest," scholars have expressed an increasing confidence in our ability to paint something approaching a complete picture of Jesus's life and personality, as if all the relevant and necessary materials for that complete picture must be available somewhere.[3] It just takes a bit of effort to get at them, whether that means being overoptimistic about the potential for second- and third-century gospels to yield historical Jesus data, or whether it means finely tuning special criteria in order to hone and sift through earlier materials because we feel that the literary deposit is somewhere bound to contain all the material of real importance. There is a sense that only matters peripheral to the task of reconstructing the key elements in Jesus's life could have disappeared.

This thinking may have developed out of an unrealistic perspective on the task. We proceed as if we are doing the work of restoration, clearing the dirt, removing the rust, repairing the damage, in order to reveal the real Jesus.[4] But historical Jesus research cannot be about restoration. As a discipline rooted in the study of ancient history, Jesus research should constantly involve the reminder that massive amounts of key data must be missing.

of Jesus, since the early Christian sources show no interest in either, are moreover fragmentary and often legendary; and other sources about Jesus do not exist. Except for the purely critical research, what has been written in the last hundred and fifty years on the life of Jesus, his personality and the development of his inner life, is fantastic and romantic. Whoever reads Albert Schweitzer's brilliantly written *Quest of the Historical Jesus* . . . must vividly realize this."

2. E. P. Sanders, *Jesus and Judaism* (Philadelphia: Fortress, 1985).

3. On the problems with the idea of "No Quest," see Dale C. Allison Jr., *Resurrecting Jesus: The Earliest Christian Tradition and Its Interpreters* (London: T&T Clark, 2005), 1–26, esp. 2–10 and 23–25.

4. Joachim Jeremias's approach typifies this; see, e.g., *The Parables of Jesus*, trans. S. H. Hooke, 2nd ed. (New York: Scribner's Sons, 1972), 13: "At a very early stage the process of treating the parables as allegories had begun, a process which for centuries concealed the meaning of the parables under a thick layer of dust."

CONSCIOUSNESS OF SELECTIVITY IN THE EARLY MATERIALS

The reminder about absent data is constantly present in the earliest materials themselves. One of our best and earliest data sets for the historical Jesus, the surviving epistles of Paul, are explicitly selective in the information they provide about Jesus. While Paul is able to provide a relevant saying of Jesus about divorce and remarriage (1 Cor 7:10–11), he has nothing relevant from Jesus on divorce of unbelieving spouses, and he has to offer his own advice (7:12–16). Mark's Gospel is similarly clear about its own selective nature. At his arrest, Jesus says, "Day after day I was with you in the temple teaching, and you did not arrest me" (Mark 14:49), but only a selection of those multiple days of teaching is provided by Mark.[5] And this coheres with a related element in Mark, where the narrator presents Jesus's teaching as something extracted from a larger mass of material:

> Mark 4:2: He began to teach them *many things* in parables, and *in his teaching he said* to them . . .

> Mark 4:33: With *many such parables* he spoke the word to them as they were able to hear it.[6]

The same point could be made from non-Markan material in Matthew and Luke, which presupposes extensive activities that are not narrated in either gospel, perhaps most obviously Jesus's woes on the unrepentant cities:

> Matt 11:21 // Luke 10:13: "Woe to you, Chorazin! Woe to you, Bethsaida! For if the deeds of power done in you had been done in Tyre and Sidon, they would have repented long ago in sackcloth and ashes."

What happened in Chorazin? We have no idea. There is little enough written about Bethsaida—only the healing of a blind man, which is omitted by Matthew and Luke (Mark 8:22–26), and Luke's problematic resetting of the feeding of the five thousand (Luke 9:10–17). The Synoptics repeatedly mention multiple healings, but they give only a handful of examples.[7] In other words, all three Synoptic evangelists give the impression of being self-consciously selective.

---

5. Translations are NRSVue except where otherwise stated.

6. See also similarly Mark 12:35 and 12:38.

7. Reported healings include Mark 1:32–34; 3:10; 6:13, 53–56; Matt 4:23–25; 8:16–17; 11:4–6; 12:15; 14:14, 34–36; 15:29–31; 21:14; Luke 4:40–41; 5:15; 6:17–19; 7:21–23; 8:2; 9:6; 10:17; 19:37.

The narrator in Luke seems particularly keen to depict incidents as examples and illustrations from among many that he could have chosen. Although Luke gives some chronological indicators (e.g., 9:28: *hōsei hēmerai oktō*, "about eight days"), more often he avoids threading stories together as if they happened one after another in sequence, as Bultmann pointed out.[8] Nor is the situation any different if we turn to the Gospels of John or Thomas. The latter famously provides no kind of connective or chronological markers, and its literary conceit is that of a collection of sayings that is highly and purposely selective. Similarly, John clearly indicates that the Gospel gives just a few representative incidents, "signs" that are chosen for their theological potential. And if the reader were in any doubt, the last verse of the gospel shines a light on the data that are not included:

> John 21.25: But there are also many other things that Jesus did; if every one of them were written down, I suppose that the world itself could not contain the books that would be written.

Awareness of the Problem

Many scholars are aware of the selective nature of the source material as well as the narratives that have not survived and those that were never written. Some historical Jesus scholars remind their readers of the partial nature of the source material. Robert Miller often underlines the problem of missing data. He lists among the fundamental difficulties of engaging in the quest that "Our evidence is spotty, sparse, and amenable to multiple interpretations," and that "Our understanding of the historical context is sufficiently incomplete that we have to rely on educated guesswork to fill in the many gaps."[9] Moreover, it is an issue flagged repeatedly in literature that dates to the earlier twentieth century, but which is now sidelined because it dates to the alleged "No Quest" period.[10] Henry Cadbury warned in 1937:

---

8. Rudolf Bultmann, *History of the Synoptic Tradition*, trans. John Marsh (Oxford: Blackwell, 1963), 360: "Luke knows that the few stories that have been passed on do not completely fit the course of events, but are only examples and illustrations; and so he frequently draws attention in some introductory phrase to the fact that the following section is really within a larger context. For this purpose he chooses a familiar formula from the LXX, *kai egeneto*, which is particularly used in Luke for introducing many stories from Mark." Bultmann's examples are Luke 1:5, 8; 3:21; 5:1, 12, 17; 8:22; 9:18, 51; 11:1; 14:1; 17:11; 18:35; 20:1.

9. Robert J. Miller, "When It's Futile to Argue about the Historical Jesus," *JSHJ* 9 (2011): 88. Cf. Robert J. Miller, "The Domain and Function of Epistemological Humility in Historical Jesus Studies," *JSHJ* 12 (2014): 131: "the data are frustratingly sparse."

10. See n. 3 above.

Probably the real difficulty on each side is the unwillingness to leave Jesus unknown and unexplained. The gaps in our knowledge of him are many. Both Jesus and his reporters are often silent just when we should like to know. Some of the most significant questions about him, not only external details like the year of his birth and of his death, but inward questions like his real attitude to Messiahship, are left to us unsolved problems. Let us recall the words of the inscrutable Jesus himself, 'No one knows the Son, save the Father.' He promises no further exception.[11]

But many scholars are not satisfied with admitting their ignorance, or being clear about the limits of the discipline. Morton Scott Enslin, in the same era, underscored the problems with the quest, while noting that many see these problems as an invitation to attempt the impossible:

> It is fast becoming a truism among New Testament critics that it is a hopeless task to attempt to write a life or history of Jesus in any approved sense of these terms. The materials for such a study are totally inadequate. Yet it is equally true that there seems little reason to believe that men will ever forego the attempt. Perhaps the very fact of the insuperable difficulties lends enthusiasm to the task. And so biographies and near-biographies are appearing with bewildering regularity. It cannot be done, so we try to do it.[12]

Enslin was surely right about the challenge presented by historical Jesus research. It is in large part because of the paucity of the literary deposit that certain scholars feel so keenly the need to attempt to tease every possible detail out of what little we have. In fact, the consciousness of the partial nature of the historical record informs one of the most popular metaphors in recent historical Jesus research: the image of the incomplete jigsaw puzzle.

The Incomplete Jigsaw Puzzle

Geza Vermes explains that "The historian's task is to assemble a monumental jigsaw puzzle of which many parts are still missing."[13] As well as striking a sur-

---

11. Henry J. Cadbury, *The Peril of Modernising Jesus* (New York: Macmillan, 1937), 48.

12. Morton Scott Enslin, "An Additional Step toward the Understanding of Jesus," *JR* 9 (1929): 419. Enslin's comments about the "bewildering regularity" of lives of Jesus in this era are also a witness to the problematic notion that this was a period of "No Quest."

13. Geza Vermes, *Searching for the Real Jesus: Jesus, the Dead Sea Scrolls and Other Religious Themes* (London: SCM, 2009), 51.

prisingly optimistic note in the use of the term "still," Vermes's use of the word "many" is something of an understatement. Stephen Patterson points out that the majority of the pieces are missing: "Above all, one can see that any attempt to find in the gospels anything like a complete portrait of Jesus will be somewhat of a disappointment. The portrait will not be a portrait at all, but a fragmentary picture—like a jigsaw puzzle with most of the pieces missing."[14]

But how many is "most"? Robert Webb is more precise. He suggests that engaging in historical Jesus research is like possessing a three-thousand-piece jigsaw puzzle, of which only three hundred pieces survive. He adds that there are also fifty pieces from another puzzle, and he is the one scholar who remembers to make clear that the picture has come off the box![15] But how realistic are these estimates? Do we have three hundred perfect pieces of a three-thousand-piece puzzle? Are we lucky enough to have 10 percent of all the relevant data? And do we only have fifty aberrant pieces, less than 2 percent contamination? What is surprising here is the sense of confidence even in the face of an image that is attempting to underline the difficulty of the task. In William Loader's similar use of the metaphor, he explains: "We are far from just having emptied the box onto the table and exposed 1000 or 2000 fragments. From the musings of many generations of scholars we can identify clusters, larger pieces of the puzzle. For many of us the constellation of unfinished work as its stands is already enough to suggest meaningful contours."[16]

The jigsaw metaphor can be pedagogically helpful, especially when it comes to finding a straightforward way of reminding introductory students of the difficulties of doing ancient history, all the more among students who have not begun to think about studying the historical Jesus and Christian origins as aspects of ancient history, and who may have thought that we know everything we might need to know about Jesus. In an introductory class, what better image could there be to explain that there are far too many missing pieces to be able to construct anything like a complete picture? The danger of the metaphor, however, is that it suggests that there is somehow a complete picture available out there, if only we have enough ingenuity to find it and to fill in the missing pieces of the puzzle. It encourages us to imagine the possibility that enough key pieces are present, so we can make informed judgments about how the whole puzzle might be resolved. A particularly skilled historian might be able to crack this puzzle—or at least to

14. Stephen J. Patterson, "The Historical Jesus and the Search for God," *HTS* 54 (1998): 488.
15. Robert L. Webb, "The Rules of the Game: History and Historical Method in the Context of Faith: The Via Media of Methodological Naturalism," *JSHJ* 9 (2011): 63–64.
16. William R. G. Loader, "The Historical Jesus Puzzle," *Colloquium* 29.2 (1997): 145.

get so close to cracking it that a major leap forward would be made. Yet the image might more reasonably be used to challenge this kind of thinking. Luke Johnson uses the metaphor negatively in this way: "Historians of early Christianity begin to appear like jigsaw puzzle solvers who are presented with twenty-seven pieces of a thousand-piece puzzle and find that only six or seven of the pieces even fit together. The reasonable thing to do would be to put those pieces together, make some guess about what that part of the puzzle might be about, and then modestly decline overspeculation about the pieces that don't fit."[17] Even though he said this a generation ago in the attempt to quell the excited, overconfident claims made in the first phase of the Jesus Seminar's research, Johnson's warning remains pertinent.

The difficulty is that it is far easier to see and to think about the pieces that we do have. It can seem more interesting and more stimulating to the scholarly mind, as opposed to the artistic mind, to find fresh analyses about existing materials than it is to speculate about what is absent. Yet any informed discussion of the historical Jesus must surely take seriously those absences.

JESUS'S INFLUENCES

Perhaps the most effective way to make the point is to reflect on an element that is present in every good biography: an exploration of the subject's major influences. According to almost everyone, one of the most certain things that we can know about the historical Jesus is that he was a disciple of John the Baptist. For many scholars, this is bedrock. But even if this is right—and there are good reasons to think that it is—it does not help us with assessing how influential John might have been in comparison to other people in Jesus's life.[18] We only know about the possible link between the two men because John the Baptist was himself famous and the gospel tradition remembers the association between the two men. Although we will probably never know what Josephus said about Jesus, it is likely that he devoted more time to John than he did to Jesus (*A.J.* 18.5.2).

But even among the elites, a person's influences are seldom restricted to only other famous people. Perhaps the major influence on Jesus was his grandfather Heli, whose fascination with Daniel 7 and Enochic literature informed Jesus's

17. Luke Timothy Johnson, *The Real Jesus: The Misguided Quest for the Historical Jesus and the Truth of the Traditional Gospels* (San Francisco: HarperSanFrancisco, 1996), 95.

18. For question marks on this consensus, see Morton Scott Enslin, "John and Jesus," *ZNW* 66 (1975): 1–18; William Arnal, "Major Episodes in the Biography of Jesus: An Assessment of the Historicity of the Narrative Tradition," *TJT* 13.2 (1997): 202–6. If Enslin and Arnal are right, we know even less about Jesus's influences.

apocalyptic mindset. Or could it have been Rabbi Matia in the Capernaum synagogue, who used to enjoy telling stories drawn from local agriculture? Was it Jesus's Aunt Salome, the person who gave Jesus his love of gendered couplets in poetry and parable? Or perhaps it was that crazy wandering Galilean exorcist Lebbaeus, who used to talk about casting out demons by the Spirit of God. The fact is that we just don't know. We can't know. Knowledge about Jesus is always and inevitably partial.

PLACING THE EXTANT PIECES

Yet even this underestimates the extent of the problem. It is not just that so many pieces are missing. It is that we do not know where to place the pieces that we do have. We are probably taking pieces and placing them wrongly, and our partial record does not allow us to see when, how, and where we are doing this. The point is best made with a different analogy. Gideon Mantell (1790–1852) was a British paleontologist whose name is attached to the discovery of the fossilized bones of a huge dinosaur he named "Iguanodon." His wife, Mary Ann Mantell (née Woodhouse, 1795–1869), actually discovered the bone, and in his reconstruction Gideon imagined it to be the dinosaur's horn and placed it on the animal's nose.[19] However, further discoveries later in the century made it clear that Mantell's guess was wrong. The bone was not a horn but was instead the dinosaur's pointed thumb!

Nor do the difficulties end here. Even where paleontologists have excellent fossil records, and where they know how to arrange the bones, there are cases where they may have placed the animals in the wrong poses. For many years, the Diplodocus stood proudly in the Natural History Museum in London with its neck stooping horizontally until, in 2009, Mike Taylor suggested that the dinosaur would in fact have held its head high.[20]

What if earlier questers were taking pieces of data and misapplying them? How would we be able to know? In the case of the Iguanodon, further discoveries corrected earlier reconstructions, and in the case of the Diplodocus, further

19. William Ashworth, "The Iguanodon 'Horn,' 1840," *Paper Dinosaurs 1824–1969*, Linda Hall Library, January 2009, https://dino.lindahall.org/man1840a.shtml. For a recent summary of the story, see Darren Naish, *Dinopedia: A Brief Compendium of Dinosaur Lore* (Princeton: Princeton University Press, 2021), 78–81.

20. For the news item, see Victoria Gill, "Giant Dinosaurs 'Held Heads High'," *BBC News*, May 29, 2009, http://news.bbc.co.uk/2/hi/science/nature/8068789.stm. For the research, see especially Michael P. Taylor, Mathew J. Wedel, and Darren Naish, "Head and Neck Posture in Sauropod Dinosaurs Inferred from Extant Animals," *Acta Palaeontologica Polonica* 54.2 (2009): 213–20.

research clarified earlier theories. Absent of more discoveries of relevant data relating to the historical Jesus, how can we know where we are putting good data into the wrong places? To take another metaphor favored by historical Jesus scholars—"joining the dots" or, in American English, "connecting the dots"—what kind of reconstruction of Jesus's life is possible when only a few of the dots have been given to us? What kind of distorted picture might we be painting?

In historical Jesus research, this point can be made by returning again to John the Baptist and, specifically, his baptism of Jesus. This is generally regarded as one of the most secure pieces of data we have about the historical Jesus, and many use it as a key piece in their reconstructions. For the sake of argument, let us assume that it is indeed a good piece of data, the equivalent of finding a dinosaur fossil, and ask how we integrate it into the picture as a whole. Most reconstructions place this event at the beginning of what they call Jesus's "public ministry," which is itself arguably a problematic construct of historical Jesus scholarship. Paul Achtemeier, for example, states that "Jesus went out into the wilderness to be baptized by John. The fact that we know almost nothing of Jesus' life prior to his baptism by John suggests that John's baptismal ministry inaugurated Jesus' own public work."[21] The placing of the baptism at the beginning of Jesus's public work is, however, just a guess based on its positioning in the Synoptic Gospels. To assume that the baptism took place at the beginning of Jesus's public life is simply to accept the chronology of Mark's Gospel at face value. Form criticism may now be out of fashion, but its skepticism about the accurate, chronological, biographical framework of the gospels has not been successfully challenged.

There are, after all, obvious literary and theological factors influencing Mark's placement of the baptism at the beginning of the gospel. In his narrative, John the Baptist is the Elijah figure who prepares the way for the messiah to whom he is subordinated. In this construction, Mark is hardly going to position the baptism story halfway through his narrative, even if it actually occurred much later in Jesus's life. And, of course, the evangelist may have had no idea when it happened. The narrative structure is designed to subordinate John to Jesus, to make him the forerunner, who is arrested before Jesus begins preaching and healing in Galilee (Mark 1:14), separating the two men both geographically and temporally.

In other words, the quotation of Achtemeier above, which is fairly typical of historical Jesus research, simply assumes that the baptism is the first major event in Jesus's life that we know about. The argument tends to be focused on estab-

---

21. Paul J. Achtemeier, Joel B. Green, and Marianne Meye Thompson, eds., *Introducing the New Testament: Its Literature and Theology*, 2nd ed. (Grand Rapids: Eerdmans, 2001), 211.

lishing its historicity. Once that has been established, scholars simply assume the Markan chronology and do not take time to argue for it as having taken place before the beginning of what is conceptualized as Jesus's public ministry. The fact that we, as readers, have not heard anything about Jesus's life before the baptism does not make the baptism the first thing of note that happened in the historical Jesus's life, any more than it makes the transfiguration (Mark 9:2–13) chronologically the midpoint of Jesus's historical career. Moreover, there are hints that this is indeed a Markan construct and that the two men were active at the same time. John 3:22–26 depicts Jesus baptizing alongside John with the acknowledgment that the two men had parallel careers, at least for some time. Other traditions like Mark 2:18, which mentions the disciples of John fasting as a present reality, also appear to witness their overlapping careers. The premise of Jesus's response (Mark 2:19–20) is that fasting should only take place after the departure of the disciples' master.

It is easy to imagine a historical scenario that does not place the baptism at the beginning of Jesus's itinerant work. Jesus was engaged in some kind of public activity in and around Galilee for a year or so before he met John the Baptist. After he hears about John, like several others he makes pilgrimage to the Jordan River to see him. Jesus has an epiphany there, a confirmation that he has been doing the right thing by leaving family and home and preaching and healing. Jesus then returns to Galilee strengthened in his resolve, renewed in his thinking, and more passionate than ever. Perhaps things happened like this; perhaps they did not. The point is not to argue for a different reconstruction but rather to draw attention to our ignorance about where to place the data and how to do our reconstruction.

The difficulty in large part is that when we fail to think about the missing pieces, it becomes easier to default into accepting the narrative framework of the canonical gospels as the historical framework of Jesus's life. Thus Darrell Bock, when reflecting on "the date of Jesus' ministry," says that it "depends in part on the date of the start of John the Baptist's ministry, since John baptized Jesus before the start of Jesus' ministry."[22] Or Maurice Casey, though retaining some caution about precise details, reads Mark's ordering as outlining the aspects of Jesus's career, even retaining a sense of the urgency with which Jesus acts in Mark: "Immediately after he exorcized the demoniac in the synagogue at Capernaum, Jesus went to the house of Simeon the Rock and his brother Andrew, with Jacob and John, the sons of Zebedee."[23] So too Colin Brown is confident, in criticizing Crossan,

---

22. Darrell Bock, *Studying the Historical Jesus: A Guide to Sources and Methods* (Grand Rapids: Baker, 2002), 71.

23. Maurice Casey, *Jesus of Nazareth: An Independent Historian's Account of His Life and*

about the ordering of events in the historical Jesus's life: "By characterizing Jesus' activity as essentially itinerant, Crossan overlooked the fact that it was initially based in Capernaum. Only after the Beelzebul charge did it enter the itinerant phase. By then it was a matter of necessity in order to avoid arrest and capital punishment."[24] Brown's reconstruction relies so heavily on Mark's chronology that it even fills in elements in the Markan structure that Mark does not specify, like the location of the Beelzebul controversy.[25]

Totality and Uniqueness

Confidence about individual details like these, though, is perhaps less remarkable than the confidence that many scholars have about the totality of what Jesus thought, said, and did. James Charlesworth is representative: "Jesus was driven by one desire: to obey God at all times and in all ways. For him, not one word of Torah may be ignored or compromised. To what extent does this man, Jesus of Nazareth, stand out as one of the most Jewish Jews of the first century? Readers will be able to answer that question as they ponder the issues raised in the following chapters."[26] Similarly, John Meier, in spite of some caution about gaps in our knowledge, speaks about the total pattern of Jesus's activity:[27]

> I would suggest that, if we are to continue to use the problematic category of "unique" in describing the historical Jesus, perhaps it is best to use it not so much of individual sayings or deeds of Jesus as of the total *Gestalt*, the total configuration or pattern of this Jew who proclaimed the present yet future

---

Teaching (London: T&T Clark, 2010), 256. Elsewhere Casey writes: "Jesus continued in the wilderness after his baptism. After John was arrested by Herod Antipas, Jesus went straight back into Galilee, Herod's territory" (197) and "At some stage Jesus moved to the Jewish town of Capernaum, beside the lake of Galilee, which became the centre of his prophetic ministry. Some time after his baptism, Jesus called the Twelve" (501).

24. Colin Brown, *A History of the Quests for the Historical Jesus*, ed. Craig Evans (Grand Rapids: Zondervan Academic, 2022), 2:389.

25. Neither Matthew (12:22–32) nor Luke (11:14–23) specifies where it takes place, and in Luke, it is in the post-Galilean central section.

26. James H. Charlesworth, *The Historical Jesus: An Essential Guide* (Nashville: Abingdon, 2008), xiii.

27. See, for example, John Meier, *The Roots of the Problem and the Person*, vol. 1 of *A Marginal Jew*, AYBRL (New York: Doubleday, 1991), 22: "And yet the vast majority of these deeds and words, the 'reasonably complete' record of the 'real' Jesus, is irrevocably lost to us today. This is no new insight of modern agnostic scholars. Traditionally Christianity has spoken of 'the hidden years' of Jesus' life—which amounted to all but three or four of them!"

kingdom, who was also an itinerant prophet and miracle worker in the guise of Elijah, who was also a teacher and interpreter of the Mosaic Law, who was also a charismatic leader who called disciples to follow him at great price, who was also a religious personage whose perceived messianic claims wound up getting him crucified by the Roman prefect, in the end, a crucified religious figure who was soon proclaimed by his followers as risen from the dead and Lord of all. It is this total and astounding configuration of traits and claims that makes for the uniqueness of Jesus as a historical figure within 1st-century Judaism.[28]

In context, Meier is making a broader point about Jesus's uniqueness and how that uniqueness can be understood, but in the course of making the point, he works with a presumption that it is possible to generate a "total" configuration or pattern for Jesus. Such claims assume that all the really important elements about Jesus were retained somewhere in the tradition and that these enable us to make claims with a degree of confidence about some kind of complete picture.

The desire to draw a complete picture is in fact necessary to the claims about Jesus's uniqueness. If key pieces of data are missing, we are not able to speak confidently about his "uniqueness," as Morna Hooker effectively pointed out over fifty years ago in a stinging critique of the criteria of authenticity, and especially "dissimilarity," which has only been fully appreciated in more recent scholarship.[29] The resistance to Hooker's critique for such a long time may have something to do with the theological utility of the claims of uniqueness, as Dennis Nineham warned over forty years ago in his "Epilogue" at the end of *The Myth of God Incarnate*, a piece that effectively undermined many of the claims made in the earlier part of that famous collection of essays.[30] Where the essayists often spoke about Jesus's unique relationship with God, Nineham questioned whether such claims could be made with any kind of confidence in responsible historical research.

MORE "JESUS" THAN "HISTORY"

There are no doubt other ideological interests at play in our failure to pursue this question properly, even after all these years. Those ideological interests are many,

28. John Meier, "The Present State of the 'Third Quest' for the Historical Jesus," *Biblica* 80 (1999): 476–77.

29. Morna Hooker, "On Using the Wrong Tool," *Theology* 75 (1972): 570–81. Regarding the criteria of authenticity, see especially Chris Keith and Anthony Le Donne, eds., *Jesus, Criteria, and the Demise of Authenticity* (London: T&T Clark, 2012), including Hooker's "Foreword: Forty Years On" (xiii–xvii).

30. Dennis Nineham, "Epilogue," in *The Myth of God Incarnate*, ed. John Hick (London: SCM, 1977), 186–204. See especially 188–89 and 195. Nineham, however, does not cite Hooker.

varied, and sometimes only questions of guesswork, but the same kind of optimistic assumptions about the data set are shared by those whose faith commitments compel them to regard the scriptural deposit as definitive, as well as those for whom the quest is a means of recovering a Jesus who is uncongenial to later Christian orthodoxy, for whom the relevant literary deposit extends more widely.

Moreover, most historical Jesus research is more about "Jesus" than it is about "history." It is surprisingly rare to find reflection on the nature of "history" in scholarship on the historical Jesus. As Luke Johnson suggests: "Perhaps the most problematic aspect of the spate of Historical Jesus books is their authors' assumption that 'history' is unproblematic. They apparently think that there is no need to define what is meant when the term history is used, since none of them bothers to do so."[31] Johnson adds that "records of human events" are "inevitably selective," such that: "Not everything that happens is recorded, nor is everything that is recorded preserved. Not everything preserved is edited, translated, read, or understood. The documentary basis of our historical knowledge of some 'great events' is astonishingly slender. Some events from antiquity are known only by a single sentence in a single work, preserved in a single manuscript."[32]

The historian who does not reflect on what is missing risks seeing history as heading on a predetermined, inevitable course, as if the way that things are remembered and represented is the only way that events could have transpired. It fails to see history as fully contingent and to think about how events might have turned out differently, which is even more of a problem in a subdiscipline like historical Jesus studies, where so many of the practitioners are people with a strong religious commitment of one kind or another, for whom doing history can be entwined with their own sense of a divine guiding hand.

Why They Matter

Missing pieces matter. Perhaps most importantly, missing pieces are missing people. One of the reasons that historical Jesus research remains a male-dominated area is that the literary deposit is dominated by tales of a male hero, his male students, and his male opponents, and many of the male scholars who inhabit this world simply perpetuate the androcentric perspective. While feminist scholars have done stellar work in hearing the voices of the women who appear in the texts as well as in building contexts for those who do not, reflection on missing people is essential for a feminist perspective on the historical Jesus. The same

31. Johnson, *Real Jesus*, 81.
32. Johnson, *Real Jesus*, 83.

point can be extended to the presence of other missing people—enslaved people, children, and so on.

Another important ethical issue relates to data that distorts historical inquiry, in particular the problem of forgeries and misleading popular culture. Whether we are talking about the James Ossuary, the Gospel of Jesus's Wife, or the sensationalist claims surrounding the Talpiot Tomb, the failure to reflect seriously on the missing pieces can lead to an overly optimistic assessment of data that offers false promises of filling the gaps. There will, no doubt, be further discoveries that are relevant to the historical Jesus, but the difficulty is that the forgers and the sensationalists pour their work into the gaps left by the surviving record. For them, the missing pieces are their opportunity to dupe the academy. If we spent longer thinking about those missing pieces, perhaps we would be less credulous whenever new claims emerge. To take the claims about the Talpiot Tomb as an example, if we had regularly reminded ourselves about how little we know about Jesus's family relationships, perhaps we would have been less excited about a particular conglomeration of details that only partly correspond to the evidence we do have.

Further, serious reflection on absent data might have helped us to be more informed about the challenge from so-called mythicists, whose stock-in-trade is the relatively limited data set. If we were more used to thinking seriously about the limits of our knowledge about the historical Jesus, perhaps we would be able to engage the ever more popular mythicist scholarship in a less condescending fashion. It is easy to respond to the mythicists by arguing that the data set is massive, convincing, and historically robust, but this kind of response can easily ignore mythicists, who are pointing to serious issues in the literary deposit, even if they make conclusions from this that are problematic.

WHAT WE CAN DO

The obvious difficulty with an essay of this nature is that it orientates itself not only to problems in the primary literature by drawing attention to the missing pieces in the literary deposit but also to problems in the secondary literature by drawing attention to the overly optimistic attempts to overcome the natural deficiencies in the primary texts. If the Next Quest for the historical Jesus is not going to be an entirely negative enterprise, burning down existing structures while offering nothing by way of new hope, some reflection on how to engage with missing data is worthwhile.

There are ways in which contemplation of the missing pieces could energize Jesus scholarship and contribute to the Next Quest, and a key point is the use of historical imagination. Scholars of Christian origins have on the whole been reluctant to embrace the study of counterfactual history, for example, but this has the potential to help us to think about ways in which the movement that became Christianity could have evolved differently. What if Mark had not survived?[33] What if the Egerton Gospel had survived? What if Q is rediscovered? What if Matthew and Luke had never come across Mark? What if Apollos had written letters, and Paul had not? The questions are underexplored in spite of their potential to stimulate our imaginations and to write different histories.

The difficulty with asking questions like these is that our imaginations are limited by our familiarity with the literary deposit, and our sense that everything was somehow destined to come out in the way that it did. Perhaps Saidiya Hartman's evocative "critical fabulation" could help us to think about the lost voices of those who surrounded the historical Jesus, those who influenced him, those whom he influenced, and the world in which he lived.[34] And where our imaginations are limited, we may need to overcome our distaste for historical fiction and engage critically with artistic imaginations in Jesus films, dramas, and novels. Perhaps too, as part of the Next Quest, we will write some of these ourselves.

33. For an attempt at imagining this, see Mark Goodacre, "A World without Mark: An Experiment in Erasure History," *BibInt* 31 (2023): 120–34.

34. Saidiya Hartman, *Lose Your Mother: A Journey along the Atlantic Slave Route* (New York: Farrar, Straus and Giroux, 2008); Hartman, "Venus in Two Acts," *Small Axe* 26 (2008): 1–14. For an application of Hartman's work to an ancient text, see Candida Moss, "Between the Lines: Looking for the Contributions of Enslaved Literate Laborers in a Second-Century Text (P. Berol. 11632)," *Studies in Late Antiquity* 5.3 (2021): 432–52.

8

Material and Visual Culture

Joan Taylor

The Next Quest for the historical Jesus should account for material and visual culture. In many ways, one may think, this goes without saying, because surely scholars have accounted for ancient material culture for a very long time. This material culture is often labeled "archaeology," rather than that which is revealed by archaeology, so that one "takes account of the archaeology" in terms of historical proposals. We have long been used to discussions about archaeology, often revolving around questions of "truth" in the Bible in relation to "truth" in archaeology, though generally the locus of the discussion has rested on questions about the foundations of Israel, centering mainly on the exodus, the biblical conquest model, or the Davidic monarchy.[1]

There have been numerous books specifically about Jesus and archaeology, or ones that focus particularly on Galilee's or Jerusalem's archaeology in regard to the events of Jesus's time there.[2] The *Biblical Archaeology Review* has been the foremost

---

1. See for example Israel Finkelstein and Neil Silberman, *The Bible Unearthed: Archaeology's New Vision of Ancient Israel and the Origin of Its Sacred Texts* (New York: Free Press, 2000).

2. James H. Charlesworth, ed., *Jesus and Archaeology* (Grand Rapids: Eerdmans, 2006); Craig A. Evans, *Jesus and the Remains of His Day: Studies in Jesus and the Evidence of Material Culture* (Peabody, MA: Hendrickson, 2015); Evans, *Jesus and His World: The Archaeological Evidence* (Louisville: Westminster John Knox, 2012); Jack Finegan, *The Archaeology of the New Testament: The Life of Jesus and the Beginning of the Early Church*, rev. ed. (Princeton: Princeton University Press, 1993); Shimon Gibson, *The Final Days of Jesus: The Archaeological Evidence* (New York:

publisher of studies for the general public on this subject.[3] My own PhD thesis was specifically about archaeology attributed to early Jewish-Christians who allegedly preserved memories about where Jesus went. I have also worked on the archaeology of Golgotha through time and various other gospel sites, with the sense that understanding a site can enable us to understand history better.[4] In comparison with what is written about archaeology and the Hebrew Bible, however, there have been fewer major points of contention or issues that have arisen in Jesus studies as a result of archaeological research, and those that have—like the Jesus Family Tomb or the so-called ossuary of James "the brother of Jesus"—tend to dissolve once the sensationalist aspects or even false claims are weeded out.[5]

Initially the use of archaeology was largely illustrative. It formed part of what used to be called "New Testament background." Archaeology allowed everyone to better walk in the footsteps of Jesus in Galilee and Jerusalem, and that model of

---

HarperOne, 2009); Jonathan L. Reed, *Archaeology and the Galilean Jesus: A Re-Examination of the Evidence* (Harrisburg, PA: Trinity Press International, 2000); Reed, *The HarperCollins Visual Guide to the New Testament: What Archaeology Reveals about the First Christians* (New York: HarperCollins, 2007); John Dominic Crossan and Jonathan L. Reed, *Excavating Jesus: Beneath the Stones, Behind the Texts*, rev. ed. (San Francisco: HarperSanFrancisco, 2002); John J. Rousseau, and Rami Arav, *Jesus and His World: An Archaeological and Cultural Dictionary* (Minneapolis: Fortress, 1995); John Donald Wilkinson, *Jerusalem as Jesus Knew It: Archaeology as Evidence* (London: Thames and Hudson, 1978).

3. E.g., Hershel Shanks and Dan B. Cole, eds., *Archaeology in the World of Herod, Jesus and Paul*, vol. 2 of *Archaeology and the Bible* (Washington, DC: Biblical Archaeology Society, 1990).

4. Joan E. Taylor, *Christians and the Holy Places: The Myth of Jewish-Christian Origins*, rev. ed. (Oxford: Clarendon, 2003); Taylor, "Golgotha: A Reconsideration of the Evidence for the Sites of Jesus' Crucifixion and Burial," *NTS* 44 (1998): 180–203; Taylor, "Missing Magdala and the Name of Mary 'Magdalene'," *PEQ* 146.3 (2014): 205–23; and also, more popularly, Taylor, "The Garden of Gethsemane—Not the Place of Jesus' Arrest," *BAR* 21.4 (1995): 26–35. This article is also on CD-ROM as one of fifty articles from the archives of *Biblical Archaeological Review*, and has been reprinted as "Where Was Gethsemane?," in *Jesus: The Last Day*, ed. Molly Dewsnap Meinhardt (Washington, DC: Biblical Archaeology Society, 2003), 23–38 as well as in *Where Christianity Was Born*, ed. Hershel Shanks (Washington, DC: Biblical Archaeological Society, 2006), 116–27. See also Taylor, "Magdala's Mistaken Identity," *BAR* 48.3 (2022): 55–58; Taylor with Shimon Gibson, *Beneath the Church of the Holy Sepulchre: The Archaeology and Early History of Traditional Golgotha* (London: Palestine Exploration Fund, 1994).

5. Simcha Jacobovici and Charles Pellegrino, *The Jesus Family Tomb: The Discovery, the Investigation, and the Evidence That Could Change History* (San Francisco: HarperCollins 2007); Hershel Shanks and Ben Witherington, *The Brother of Jesus: The Dramatic Story and Meaning of the First Archaeological Link to Jesus and His Family* (San Francisco: HarperCollins, 2003); and see for critique Ryan Byrne and Bernadette McNary-Zak, eds., *Resurrecting the Brother of Jesus* (Chapel Hill: University of North Carolina Press, 2009). The James Ossuary was proven to be a complex mix of a real archaeological object with a fake inscription.

archaeology remains alive and well today.[6] However, the writers of more recent reliable books on Jesus and archaeology have been foremost scholars who are leading lights in the so-called Third Quest (e.g., Charlesworth, Crossan), scholars who are particularly interested in understanding Jesus's world and his context and situating him within this world. If we move forward into a Next Quest, then, what needs to be done?

Fundamentally, in the Next Quest we need to be aware of how the study of the historical Jesus has used material culture not only of the past but also of the present. This is because we internalize various models formed from material culture when we visualize Jesus and his world, and our visualizations can create frameworks for what we think is possible or impossible, or what is right or wrong.

Seeking for the Material Past

To begin with, let us remember that the idea that the realia of the ancient world can enable us to better understand the gospels is very old. It arises in the wake of the Protestant revolution and is found particularly from the sixteenth century onward. At this time we get Bible tools such as cartography and explanations of terms, places, meanings. These appear in the Geneva Bible (1560) and the King James Bible (1611), the latter having "Genealogies" including "A Description of Canaan, and the bordering Countries," with a map by one John Speed.[7] A map creates a conceptual frame for a story, but Speed's map also includes drawings of the realia of the temple. Although there are also various sea monsters and a mermaid—in line with conventions of real maps of the time—surrounded by appropriate European ships, the message was that this was a real map. Speed used knowledge gleaned from travelers to Palestine about where certain places were found not only from the Old Testament but also from the New. Thus his map of "Canaan" has a quote from John 1 appearing right underneath the title, and Galilee is identified as the Galilee of Jesus, with sites plotted loosely around Lake Gennesareth (see fig. 8.1). With this map in hand, one can follow the story and imagine there is (or was) such a land "out there," where the story can be situated and reached by a modern ship. Such tools are assembled alongside a growing interest in the ruins

6. There will invariably be continuing books aimed at the pilgrim market; see for example Michael Hesemann, *Jesus of Nazareth: Archaeologists Retracing the Footsteps of Christ* (San Francisco: Ignatius, 2021).

7. Joan E. Taylor, "John Speed's 'Canaan' and British Travel to Palestine: A Journey with Maps," in *The King James Version at 400: Assessing Its Genius as Bible Translation and Its Literary Influence*, ed. David G. Burke, John F. Kutsko, and Philip H. Towner (Atlanta: SBL Press, 2013), 103–23.

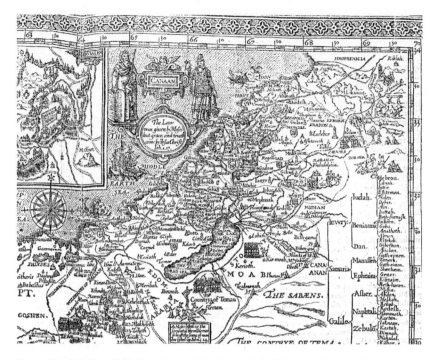

Figure 8.1. *John Speed's "A Description of Canaan, and the Bordering Countries" (detail). ARC A13.1G/1607. Image courtesy of Lambeth Palace Library, London.*

and relics of the ancient world at this time, collected into cabinets of curiosities or visited by intrepid scholars and adventurers.[8]

Given such a map, by implication "Canaan" lies behind "Palestine" as a kind of foundation for the present day. There were ancient names that remained, after all, even if Arabized. So surely, it was thought, it would be possible to somehow find in this land useful information that would illuminate Scripture. Protestants had not totally eschewed travel to Palestine, whether as part of business dealings connected with the Levant Company in Aleppo or out of general interest. There was a sense that being in this place was going to make a difference in understanding. This was not the same program as the dominant Catholic or Orthodox one that had established holy places where pilgrims could come to pray, step in the footsteps of the saints, and recall scriptural stories. The Protestant mentality was

8. See Joan E. Taylor, *The Englishman, the Moor and the Holy City: The True Adventures of an Elizabethan Traveller* (Stroud: Tempus, 2006).

more forensic in seeking these places as tools for the interpretation of Scripture rather than moments of prayerful piety and memory. And indeed these two different attitudes to such sites remain today, though they are no longer so much divided on denominational grounds.

The contemporary quest for a reliable material culture to inform biblical interpretation is founded on the work of such notables as Edward Robinson, a minister of the Congregationalist Church and classical and biblical scholar of Cambridge, Massachusetts, who, with Eli Smith, spent three months in Palestine in 1838.[9] In his monumental geographical studies, published in three volumes as *Biblical Researches in Palestine and Adjacent Countries*, Robinson identified many biblical places and noted many ruins—including what is now referred to as "Robinson's Arch," one of the arches supporting the monumental stairway leading up to Herod's Temple platform from the Tyropoeon Valley—bringing far more information into the "tool box" of realia than had previously been done.[10] The underlying quest here for Robinson was so that his labors would affirm Christian truth, meaning the truth of the Bible and ultimately of the revelation of Jesus. If sites could be identified, somehow this truth could be supported. The world of the Bible would be real, not some fantasy land.

Robinson was a frontrunner, but many other scholars soon found their ways to Ottoman Palestine to study relics of the past. In 1864, Melchior de Vogüé published a detailed study of what was, on the basis of his book title, the "Temple of Jerusalem," but was in fact an extensive record of the architecture and decoration of the eleventh-century Mosque of Omar on the Haram esh-Sharif.[11] This paved the way for existing Palestinian architecture to be considered representative of the architecture of the past, even if it was in vogue over a millennium after the time of Jesus. Less than ten years later, Charles Clermont-Ganneau, however, had a more antiquarian eye in looking for true ancient relics. Greatly encouraged by his discovery of a stele from Herod's Temple courtyard forbidding non-Jews from passing beyond the *soreg*, he embarked on extensive travels.[12] His two-volume *Archaeological Researches in Palestine during the Years 1873–1874*, published in English

9. Yehoshua Ben-Arieh, *The Rediscovery of the Holy Land in the Nineteenth Century* (Jerusalem: Magnes, 1979); Renaud Soler, *Edward Robinson (1794–1863) et l'émergence de l'archéologie biblique* (Paris: Geuthner, 2014).

10. Edward Robinson, *Biblical Researches in Palestine and Adjacent Countries*, 3 vols. (London: John Murray, 1841).

11. Melchior de Vogüé, *Le Temple de Jerusalem: Monographie du Haram-ech-Chérif. Suivie d'un essai sur la topographie de la Ville-Sainte* (Paris: Noblet & Baudry, 1864).

12. Charles Clermont-Ganneau, "Discovery of a Tablet from Herod's Temple," *Palestinian Exploration Fund Quarterly Statement* 3.3 (1871): 132–34.

in 1896, was a compendium of Clermont-Ganneau's notes as he observed ancient (or possibly ancient) architecture and material remains—some of which were randomly dug up with the help of local workmen—and recorded local traditions (i.e., folklore).[13]

One could go on concerning the recording of such explorations, but what is more interesting for our subject is that such a quest for truth via material culture also went in another direction. Europeans and North Americans began observing the behaviors and material culture of contemporary Palestinians as the nearest available parallel to the life experienced by biblical figures, and thus Palestine itself became a vast "tool" for the study of the Bible. Soon a whole host of additional tools were available for scholars, including photographic albums of Palestinian scenes.

This quest for material authenticity wove together both the relics of the ancient world and the contemporary culture of Palestine and directly fed into the Jesus Quest of the nineteenth century in looking to find a more authentic Jesus than the Christ of tradition. This then stepped into the influential work of Joseph Ernest Renan, who sought to imagine Jesus as a simple Galilean preacher. Renan's *Vie de Jésus*, which was published in 1863 and had thirteen editions in the year of publication, was fundamentally about situating Jesus in a supposed ancient cultural milieu (prefiguring the Third Quest), but it was much influenced also by the contemporary Palestinian milieu that Renan encountered.

Renan himself was a highly trained linguist, but he was also an archaeologist and French colonialist. In 1860, three years before he published his book on Jesus, he led Napoleon III's archaeological mission to find remains of ancient Phoenicia to ship back to the Louvre in Paris, publishing the results in the highly esteemed volume *Mission de Phénicie*.[14] It was from his base in Syria that he took the journey to Palestine, during which he was already writing his *Vie de Jésus*.[15] Material culture both past and present therefore played a major part in his construction of Jesus as a Galilean.

In this pathway, material culture represents a different kind of tool used not to support an interpretation of the Bible but as a foundation of an alternative historical presentation. The material and social-economic culture being resourced

13. Charles Clermont-Ganneau, *Archaeological Researches in Palestine during the Years 1873–1874* (London: Palestine Exploration Fund, 1896).

14. Ernest Renan, *Mission de Phénicie* (Paris: Imprimerie impériale, 1864).

15. Robert D. Priest, *The Gospel according to Renan: Reading, Writing, and Religion in Nineteenth-Century France*, Oxford Historical Monographs (Oxford: Oxford University Press, 2015) and see Halvor Moxnes, *Jesus and the Rise of Nationalism: A New Quest for the Nineteenth-Century Historical Jesus* (London: I. B. Tauris, 2012), 121–47; Geoffrey Nash, "Death and Resurrection: The Renans in Syria (1860–61)," in *Knowledge Is Light: Travellers in the Near East*, ed. Katherine Salahi (Oxford: Oxbow, 2011), 69–77.

for authentic context was not only (or not primarily) archaeological but also contemporaneous Palestinian culture.

Individual scholarship on the material culture appropriate to Jesus's world was supported by the establishment of European and American institutions in Jerusalem that promoted studies of material relating to the Bible. For example, after British surveyors had gone to work in Ottoman Jerusalem to work on a water supply project, a project largely intended to create safety and comfort for the burgeoning numbers of tourists and pilgrims, they were also making ad hoc discoveries from the distant past. As a result of this, in 1865 the Palestine Exploration Fund was created to supersede the scholarly Palestine Association as a surprising alliance of scientifically minded surveyors and Anglican clerics. The Palestine Exploration Fund was at the outset curiously committed not only to the toolkit designed to aid interpretation and biblical illustration but also to the scientific method, implying indeed (two years after Renan's book) that there may well be a historical truth that does not perfectly align with the words of the Bible or tradition. Ancient remains, topography, zoology, botany, and contemporary Palestinian culture were all key subjects for its scholars, as any of these might furnish (scientific) data for biblical interpretation and history.[16]

The Palestinian context was perhaps the most important aspect. The prime scholarship was the compendium of Gustaf Dalman's *Arbeit und Sitte in Palästina*, which, as a brilliant study of ethnography, furnished an extremely valuable mass of information about technology, farming, and objects, as if such data might provide a window into the ways of life and material reality of figures of the biblical past.[17] A Lutheran scholar, Dalman was a stellar expert on Semitic languages and literature and also the director of the *Deutsches Evangelisches Institut für Altertumswissenschaft des heiligen Landes zu Jerusalem*, established in 1900. It was axiomatic that contemporary Palestine would inform his understanding of Jesus, and in many ways he preempted the Third Quest by over half a century in looking to context as the bedrock of any interpretation. The translator of a collection of his 1922 studies on Jesus, Paul Levertoff, lamented that many, "even scholarly, works on the Gospels often show that their authors lack a first-hand knowledge of contemporary Palestinian life and thought," but not so Dalman's work.[18]

---

16. Ruth Kark and Haim Goren, "Pioneering British Exploration and Scriptural Geography: The Syrian Society/The Palestine Association," *The Geographical Journal* 177 (2011): 264–74; John J. Moscrop, *Measuring Jerusalem: The Palestine Exploration Fund and British Interests in the Holy Land* (Leicester: Leicester University Press, 1999); Shimon Gibson, "British Archaeological Institutions in Mandatory Palestine, 1917–1948," *PEQ* 131 (1999): 115–43.

17. Gustaf Dalman, *Arbeit und Sitte in Palästina*, 7 vols. (Gütersloh: C. Bertelsmann, 1928–1942).

18. See Levertoff's "Note by the Translator" in Gustaf Dalman, *Jesus-Jeshua: Studies in the Gospels*, trans. Paul Levertoff (London: SPCK, 1929), ix.

Looking to contemporary Palestine filled in part something of a hole in terms of the archaeological material of this era. In his book *Sacred Sites and Ways* (1924; Eng. 1935), which concentrated on gospel places, Dalman himself noted that "Prehistoric, Canaanitish, Israelitish periods have been explored; but the time of the Herodians, that most important epoch for Christians, has been neglected. We are still, for instance, only partly informed concerning the architectural styles and technique of that period. When this is remedied, we shall be in a better position to know the Land of Jesus."[19] In the meantime, Dalman had contemporary Palestine. He used it to speculate about Jesus's birth, for example, effectively fitting the Lukan birth story into Palestinian buildings:

In the East to-day the dwelling-place of man and beast is often in one and the same room. It is quite the usual thing among the peasants for the family to live, eat, and sleep on a kind of raised terrace (Arab. *mastaba*) in the one room of the house, while the cattle, particularly donkeys and oxen, have their place below on the actual floor (*Ka' el-Bet*) near the door; this part sometimes is continued along under the terrace as a kind of low vault. On this floor the mangers are fixed, either to the floor, or to the wall, or at the edge of the terrace. But this is not how the Evangelist conceived it to have been; he imagines that the manger was outside the inn, that is to say, in some particular stable, such as are used to-day for camels, sometimes, but more rarely for sheep. He takes it for granted that the stable was empty, as would be natural during the time when sheep spent the night in the open. In it must be imagined a manger up on the wall, which was to do duty as a crib for the Babe. It must be remembered that the Palestinian country folk know nothing of bedsteads, but their nightly couch is spread every evening anew upon the terrace of the house. It would hardly do to lay sucklings in this same fashion on the floor, where they would be in danger of being trodden on by men and beasts, and where it would be difficult to keep them clean. [20]

Accuracy and truth were understood to be the guiding principles here, and there was no doubt that contemporary Palestinian ways continued very ancient practices of the land. In making this observation, I do not mean to criticize this method unduly, because in many ways the Palestinians were indeed much closer to the lifestyle of people in the time of Jesus than the lifestyle of nineteenth- and

19. Gustaf Dalman, *Sacred Sites and Ways: Studies in the Topography of the Gospels*, trans. Paul Levertoff (London: SPCK, 1935), 14. That comment may actually ask us to reflect on what we have learned from Herodian architecture.

20. Dalman, *Sacred Sites and Ways*, 41.

twentieth-century Europeans and white Americans. However, the limits of what could or could not be used as evidence were not interrogated, since there was no archaeological base with which to compare the domestic houses of nineteenth-century Palestinians and first-century Judeans or historical ethnographical examinations.

MATERIAL CULTURE IN VISUAL CULTURE

From Robinson onward, the quest for authentic realia became an artist's toolkit to create different images of Jesus and his world akin to those of the Renaissance tradition. In the wake of travelers such as Robinson and authors such as Renan, realist artists painted work that showed the actual stones of Jerusalem behind their visualizations of Jesus. From the neoclassical turn of the seventeenth century onward, artists such as Nicholas Poussin had looked to classical visual culture, especially ruins, to reimagine stories from Greek and Roman legend. But neoclassical artists did not usually source ancient visual culture of the Roman East for their biblical depictions; this was the "Orient." The classical world was, to them, Western, and Jesus was simply "brand Jesus" (i.e., European, long hair, bearded, long robes) and recognizable in the crowd even when they were loosely styled in characteristically Ottoman-period Palestinian clothing. Members of Jesus's opposition among the Judaean hierarchy were styled invariably as elite "Orientals," often with large turbans and ornate garments.[21]

With a boom of American, Russian, and European travelers to Palestine, Jesus began to be depicted by realist painters in a nontraditional way, by reference to the people of contemporary Palestine, with the materiality of their dress and houses redeployed for an ancient story. Vasiliy Polenov (1844–1927), a Russian artist, traveled to Palestine and used scholarship, ruins, and the elements of the appearance of contemporary Palestinians in order to create a radically different picture of Jesus in his time, one that was supposed to be more accurate. Like Renan, Polenov strongly distinguished between the Jesus of history and the traditional Christ of the Russian Orthodox Church.[22] In his large painting of Jesus and the adulteress, *Christ and the Woman Taken in Adultery*, first shown in 1887, we have a remarkably indistinguishable Jesus that makes us aware of the legacy

21. Katie Turner, *Costuming Christ: Re-Dressing First-Century 'Christians' and 'Jews' in Passion Drama*, LNTS (London: T&T Clark, forthcoming).

22. See Jefferson J. A. Gattrall, *The Real and the Sacred: Picturing Jesus in Nineteenth-Century Fiction* (Ann Arbor: University of Michigan Press, 2014), 80.

of the traditional image today.[23] We are so wedded in fact to that "brand Jesus" image we cannot even immediately spot which figure is Jesus; he is identified not by looks but by the fact that those who would accuse the woman direct their attention to him, and—to help us a little—he is in a small pool of sunlight and has nothing on his head. In the background there is a grand structure supposed to represent the Jerusalem Temple. Polenov here overtly claimed to show "Christ as he was in reality," and compiled sixty pages of notes to support his depiction, including references to the work of Melchior de Vogüé's work on the Mosque of Omar and Clermont-Ganneau's discovery of the inscription forbidding non-Jews from going into the temple proper.[24]

Polenov was still rare in actually presenting Jesus as an ethnically Jewish Palestinian with quite short hair and light brown skin.[25] More commonly, despite using the realia of ancient ruins and contemporary Palestinian material culture, in most art of the nineteenth and twentieth century Jesus and his disciples were depicted as northern Europeans, even though Jesus may be dressed in quasi-Palestinian attire with various accoutrements of local styling.

Such visualizations also find their way into Bibles, particularly thanks to the influential work of Evelyn Stuart Hardy (1865–1935), since her illustrations formed part of the widely known Collins King James Bible, first published in 1934 (see fig. 8.2 on p. 138, below).[26] This gave readers a visual template for their historical imagination, and this template would ultimately find its way into TV documentaries and films, even in the present day. Thus we see a Jesus that, for Hardy, was European, implying an "ownership" (or at least understandability) in regard to Jesus and his disciples. Hardy's Jesus has pale skin and light brown hair. Jesus is one of "us" to Hardy, and therefore knowable. Yet Jesus is also Palestinian in "culture" and therefore different in attire, with some Oriental window dressing. But we may remember that after the First World War under the British Mandate, Palestine itself came under the colonial embrace of the British Empire. Hardy's Jesus is thus a colonial Jesus but also "brand Jesus."

We are today alert to issues surrounding race, but the wrongness of Hardy's showing of the story of the raising of Jairus's daughter is not just about the girl's blonde hair color or the figures' skin color. We need to remember that even the

23. Polenov's *Christ and the Woman Taken in Adultery*, now in the State Russian Museum, St. Petersburg, can be viewed online at https://www.artbible.info/art/large/118.html.

24. Gattrall, *Real and the Sacred*, 80–81 and see 262 nn. 64 and 66.

25. Jesus was apparently to have had a white *kippa* but Polenov removed it days before the exhibition; see Gattrall, *Real and the Sacred*, 82.

26. David Wootten, *The Illustrators: The British Art of Illustration, 1780–1993* (London: Beetles, 1993), 81.

Figure 8.2. *Evelyn Hardy (1865–1935), Raising of Jairus' Daughter, from the* Holy Bible, King James Version *(London: Collins, 1958), picture insert. Photograph of printed image.*

"Oriental" Jesus of the nineteenth and twentieth centuries is nothing like what men actually looked like in the first century. It has been my contention that by using the actual material and visual culture that provides us with information about the likely ancient dress Jesus wore, and by really visualizing Jesus's Judean ethnicity, we move a step toward a more authentic Jesus.[27]

Since the establishment of the State of Israel in 1948 and the further changes occurring after the Six-Day War of 1967, Palestine has experienced rapid cultural transformation and substantial alteration in terms of population settlements. When I first went to the region as a young kibbutz volunteer forty years ago, I was able to visit a Druze household where women baked flatbread using a dung oven on an earth floor and see for myself the kind of lifestyle that was so evocative to people like Dalman. However, we now have fewer places to see such traditional practices, as modern technology has replaced the old ways. For all its anachronisms, Dalman's work might yet be essential reading for the Next Quest in simply reminding everyone that the past is a foreign country, and the past of a foreign country is another planet.

27. See Joan E. Taylor, *What Did Jesus Look Like?* (London: Bloomsbury, 2018).

Packaging Material Culture

The toolkit of archaeology has been used to buttress claims for trusting the Bible as a source of accurate information about the past. This way of doing archaeology influences how we may see the value placed on ancient material culture when it comes to historical Jesus studies. The news media itself plays into the narrative of "true" or "false" with various discoveries. The Pilate inscription found in Caesarea in 1964 proves the biblical account true, whereas the "Jesus Family Tomb" was packaged as questioning biblical truth, as indicated by the subtitle of the popular book on the tomb by Simcha Jacobovici and Charles Pellegrino: "Evidence That Could Change History."[28] Actually, such evidence has not changed history at all, because history is always contingent. Historians question the accuracy of literary accounts and reframe history all the time. The point of Jacobovici and Pellegrino's book was actually to question the Bible as being an accurate representation of what took place.

Methodologically, such questions of true or false arising from finds are extremely simple. On the truth-claiming side, evidence of someone mentioned in the gospels as being a real person is supposed to mean that the account can be trusted. For example, we can point to Pontius Pilate as a real person, because we have coins and an inscription. But should we not then apply the same criterion of truth to the work of early Christian literature like the Gospel of Nicodemus where Pilate appears? In reality, mention of real people actually proves nothing in terms of the reliability of any account. Far more important is what the archaeology tells us about such people, and it can shed direct light on the rhetoric and choices made in our texts.[29]

Methodologically, it is the naysayers who have the logical clout. Anthony Frendo, the Maltese archaeologist who has more than anyone teased out how archaeology and texts relate in terms of history, has coherently explained that archaeological evidence cannot ever prove an account true; it can only correlate with an account.[30] Even when it correlates, it may be possible to create multiple historical scenarios to account for correlations, so that the biblical account is just one potential scenario. However, positive archaeological evidence that does *not*

28. Jacobovici and Pellegrino, *Jesus Family Tomb*.

29. For an examination of this in regard to Pilate, see Joan E. Taylor, "Pontius Pilate and the Imperial Cult in Roman Judaea," *NTS* 52 (2006): 555–82.

30. Anthony Frendo, *Pre-Exilic Israel, the Hebrew Bible, and Archaeology: Integrating Text and Artefact* (London: T&T Clark, 2011), 5.

correlate with a biblical account is much more damaging. This is the principle of falsification rather than verification, because two contradictory statements cannot both be true at the same time. As an example, an inscription on a first-century Jewish ossuary excavated under strict archaeological conditions in, say, Bethlehem, that referenced "Jesus son of Joseph, son of David, called the 'Christ,'" with the ossuary containing a skeleton showing evidence of crucifixion, would indeed be a challenge to accepting the accuracy of our gospel stories. A simple "Jesus son of Joseph," on an ossuary, when both these names are extremely common, does not give us such noncorrelating evidence for a falsification. The main point is that if something did take place historically, then existing archaeological evidence should correlate with this, even if other interpretations are also possible.[31]

When we think of material culture bearing upon the Quest for the historical Jesus there are additional elements that influence how it is presented. The first matter is sheer sensationalism: the media love good stories that will provide clickbait on numerous platforms. The marketing of both the Jesus Family Tomb and James Ossuary stories provides high-profile examples of what can happen. As Jonathan Reed has explored, publishers are all too willing to promote books that present items as new relics, largely for the evangelical Christian market. An archaeological object gains holy relic status by being a tangible link to Jesus.[32]

There is also tourism focused in Galilee and the sites in Jerusalem concerned with Jesus's death, burial, and resurrection. Because tourism is a huge industry, it has a direct impact on what is excavated and how excavations are presented. If archaeologists excavate a site linked with Jesus or his disciples, like Bethsaida or Magdala, they know well that they will get funding for future digs and analyses, because the sites could be developed for Christian tourism and people could charge fees. In coming to such sites, Christians are asked to accept the "truth" of the reliability of the site identification, and it is all about then embedding a certain narrative into a location so that newcomers can visualize the familiar story and feel more closely connected to that story.

Thus we visit "Capernaum the town of Jesus" (fig. 8.3). The presentation of the site is focused on what draws tourists, with a large church over a house venerated in the fourth century as the house of Peter.[33] The fact that there is a beautiful limestone synagogue of the fourth or fifth century CE becomes subsumed into this narrative of the "town of Jesus," because Christians know that there was a synagogue

31. Frendo, *Pre-Exilic Israel*, 105.
32. Jonathan Reed, "Overcoming the James Ossuary and the Legacy of Biblical Archaeology," in Byrne and McNary-Zak, *Resurrecting*, 187–206.
33. Taylor, *Christians and the Holy Places*, 268–94.

Figure 8.3. *The entrance to the archaeological site of Capernaum today. Photo by author.*

in Capernaum Jesus visited (Matt 4:13; Mark 1:21–28; Luke 4:16–37; John 6:22–59), and therefore prayer groups can gather here and "remember" Jesus's miracles enacted in this place. The material culture of the Capernaum synagogue is therefore an anachronistic backdrop, but it functions as a stage for Christian devotion.

New discoveries are announced in media, websites, and social media, sites are turned into tourist attractions and holy places, and narratives that create significance for such places can even trump actual historical work. This is now very much the case in regard to Magdala, which—as the ancient city of Tarichaea—is a very important site, but its identification as the "birthplace of Mary Magdalene" has become far more important.[34] This is no wonder when we consider that tour buses have made it an essential stop on the route around the lake, bringing economic benefits to the area. Again, the discourse gets directed toward a simple "truth."

34. Richard Bauckham, ed., *Magdala of Galilee: A Jewish City in the Hellenistic and Roman Period* (Waco, TX: Baylor University Press, 2018); Richard Bauckham and Stefano de Luca, "Magdala as We Now Know It," *Early Christianity* 6 (2015): 91–118; and see Taylor, "Missing Magdala"; Taylor, "Magdala."

In such visits we are led back into the pattern of walking in the footsteps of Jesus and remembering Bible stories. The experience is one of a truth, but it is one that takes place within the vision and imagination of the viewer. As historians of Jesus and his world, any visits to Galilee or Jerusalem mean we participate in the Christian tourism industry. Gone are the nineteenth-century Palestinian scenes of people threshing wheat or mending nets. Instead, they are replaced with boards and signage directing us to focus our imaginations in a particular way. We don't see people living a life we can imagine as "biblical." We see ourselves, with cameras and sun hats, and bare walls that act like a stage.

Using Material Culture to Think With

So, given all this, to what extent does such material culture matter, in any Quest for the historical Jesus? What exactly does it challenge? What does it illuminate?

Clearly, there are inherent problems with the notion of "biblical archaeology" itself, if it is conceptualized in line with "proof" thinking.[35] Some conservative scholars may yet still look to archaeology to explain better what is in the gospels almost as a visual aid.[36] But Jonathan Reed pushes a way forward "beyond the shadow of biblical archaeology" to a different approach: "this approach looks at wider patterns in the material culture, assesses aspects of the general cultural, social, or political trends at the time, and only then turns to how that evidence helps us understand the New Testament."[37] Thus, Byron McCabe's study of the socioeconomics of burial practices at the time of Jesus is given by Reed as an example of how taking the archaeology seriously leads us to ask different questions, so that the archaeology leads us to texts rather than the other way around.[38] Reed himself has shown how Galilean archaeology as a whole has greatly illuminated the socioeconomic context of Jesus.[39] In any form of the Next Quest, it is important to resist any simple "proof" language, true-false paradigms, or simple illustrations to explain the gospels, but rather promote a method of using material

35. Reed, "Overcoming."

36. Reed uses the example of Craig Evans, *Jesus and the Ossuaries: What Jewish Burial Practices Reveal about the Beginning of Christianity* (Waco, TX: Baylor University Press, 2003), 193–94.

37. Reed, "Overcoming," 195.

38. Reed, "Overcoming," 196, and see Reed's chapter "How to Bury a King" in Crossan and Reed, *Excavating Jesus*, 230–70.

39. Reed, *Archaeology and the Galilean Jesus*; and also Reed, "The Archaeological Contributions to the Study of Jesus and the Gospels," in *The Historical Jesus in Context*, ed. Amy-Jill Levine, Dale C. Allison Jr., and John Dominic Crossan (Princeton: Princeton University Press, 2007), 40–54.

culture to think about the gospels. This requires a more courageous and creative approach. It also requires us to be aware of the history of the study of material culture, and how it has created its own visual culture. We also need to be aware of our own suppositions or internalization of artistic images as we imagine the world of the past. So, for example, when visiting Capernaum as historians, we should not simply consider it as a resource to supply an illustrative context in which to place our "Jesus," but ask what Capernaum tells us about Jesus and the people who hosted and followed him in this town. We might ask: why did Jesus, a man from Nazareth, choose Capernaum? Is there anything else distinctive here that could possibly explain it? While a prophet may well not have honor in his own country (Luke 4:24; John 4:44), why did Capernaum, or other places, recognize Jesus? Can the stones speak to us?

One obvious point is that Capernaum was on the water. Federico Adinolfi and I have argued that proximity to water is a key narrative motif in the Gospel of Mark, implying but not highlighting Jesus's own baptismal mission.[40] But more than that, why choose Capernaum, then, of all the towns and villages on the lake? Why did Jesus not base himself in Jewish cities on the lake like Tarichaea or Tiberias? Indeed, these were the cities in which Josephus and his associates would concentrate their attentions during the First Judean Revolt. These are the places that mattered militarily and economically. So it is quite incredible that in the story of Jesus by the Sea of Galilee there is no mention of them. Comparatively speaking it is as if the gospels are describing someone with a mission in southern California whose base is not in Los Angeles or San Diego but in Oxnard in Ventura County. Or, to use a British example, it is as if someone engaging in a vital and urgent mission to reach all of England used Bedford as their main base.

We might then look to any distinctiveness in the archaeology of this town that made it essential for Jesus to be here, and indeed Capernaum is quite fundamentally different from neighboring cities like Tarichaea and Tiberias. In both Tiberias and Tarichaea (the latter known as Magdala in the Byzantine period) archaeology has revealed impressive material culture: well-laid-out streets; good limestone and basalt that has been well cut, dressed, and laid; nice public buildings like the theater in Tiberias or the synagogue in Tarichaea; water works; luxury villas like the House of Dice in Tarichaea with even inbuilt "mod cons" like personal *miqvaot* (fig. 8.4). Such elements imply an elite culture that sought to invest their funds in both private and public improvements.

40. Joan E. Taylor and Federico Adinolfi, "John the Baptist and Jesus the Baptist: A Narrative Critical Approach," *JSHJ* 10 (2012): 247–84.

Figure 8.4. *Roman-period private immersion pools in Tarichaea (contemporary Migdal). Photo by author.*

One of the most obvious things about Capernaum in the early Roman period is that the masonry of its dwellings does not include the finely cut stonework reserved for the much later white synagogue that we presently see. The early Roman walls are built of the local, black basalt field stones. The housing compounds are densely packed with no discernible luxury villas, and certainly no inbuilt *miqvaot*. Instead, they include more basalt grinding stones and basins that indicate that people did much of their own food processing at home. The courtyard paving is rough (fig. 8.5). The overall impression we get of early Roman Capernaum is that it was a much poorer town than the cities of Tiberias and Tarichaea.[41]

41. See Joan E. Taylor, "The Historical Brian: Reception Exegesis in Practice," in *Jesus and Brian: Exploring the Historical Jesus and His Times via Monty Python's Life of Brian*, ed. Joan E. Taylor (London: Bloomsbury, 2015), 93–106; and "Jesus as News: Crises of Health and Overpopulation in Galilee," *JSNT* 44.1 (2021): 8–30.

Figure 8.5. *Roman-period fieldstone structures in Capernaum. Photo by author.*

We may ask the question then: where are the poor in Jesus's world? Where do we look for economic privation? From the evidence of material culture, these cities housed a wealthy elite channeling funds into architecture, infrastructure, industry, and charity, whereas the densely populated rural villages and small towns of Galilee housed agricultural day laborers. Might this explain why Jesus does not really go to cities at all? When Jesus said "Blessed are the poor" (Luke 6:20), what would that have said about the relationship between a town like Capernaum and a town like Tiberias? That Jesus settled in a fisherman's house in Capernaum, of all places, would itself advertise something about his mission.

Conclusion

So, in conclusion, here I have reflected briefly on how material culture has been used to form ideas about Jesus at the time of the European and American questers of the nineteenth and early twentieth centuries, who traveled to Palestine with a wish to see a more authentic Jesus, informed in part by ancient remains but also by the material culture and practices of contemporary Palestine. Visual representations followed suit in imagining a "Palestinian" Jesus, but European visual culture would pull back from too Jewish-Palestinian a Jesus ethnically, even with quasi-Palestinian clothing. In the latter part of the twentieth century with its widescale modernization and cultural transformations, the archaeological study of Jesus has been embedded not only in the academy but also in a social context of contemporary pilgrimage and tourism in Israel, Palestine, and Jordan.

In the introduction to this volume, James Crossley has identified that the Next Quest must "move beyond searching for an uninterpreted reality 'behind' the texts and hypothesize the historical Jesus by means of the cultural and historical processes by which particular images of Jesus were produced and transmitted." Overall, in our study of ancient material culture we need to be alert to how it is being used to create a social reality or a visual culture today, even before we take a first step. Imaginative visual templates may well influence how we allow ourselves to see the past. At every stage, we need to ask how ancient material culture can "talk" to questions we have about the historical Jesus, or even lead us toward asking certain questions in the first place. As we imagine Jesus in the first-century context of Galilee, we need at the very outset to be aware of what we see and where our own image comes from, because that primary imaging itself can limit what we consider possible.

9

RELIGION, VISIONS, AND ALTERNATIVE HISTORICITY

Deane Galbraith

The Next Quest for the historical Jesus must account for the broader study of religion, culture, society, cognition, and historical consciousness.

In this chapter, I identify and discuss a few important current approaches in religious studies that I believe to be underutilized in the critical study of the historical Jesus, and which accordingly offer potential avenues for future questing. To make the discussion more concrete, I will sketch how these approaches might be applied to one key source for the historical Jesus: the story of Jesus's empty tomb (in Mark 16:1–8 and parallels)—perhaps at first blush an unusual choice for anything related to the Jesus of history, yet one that follows Fredric Jameson's injunction to "always historicise!"[1] In so doing, I find that visionary elements are far more extensive in Mark 16:1–8 than usually perceived, and indeed that visionary sources pervade Mark's Gospel, furnishing it with many of its most significant episodes. The presence of extensive visionary experiences in the early Jesus movement introduces a radical indeterminacy to any Quest for the historical Jesus and invites consideration of the pluriform character of historical consciousness.

---

1. Fredric Jameson, *The Political Unconscious: Narrative as a Socially Symbolic Act* (Ithaca: Cornell University Press, 1981), ix.

FUNNELING JESUS

It is very difficult to find any approach, method, criticism, or substantive finding within religious studies that has not already been seized upon and employed by biblical scholars eager to say something new about Jesus. As in scenes from the television shows *Shark Tank* or *Dragon's Den*, biblical scholars can sometimes appear like budding entrepreneurs racing to be the first to present their subtle innovations to the guild's gatekeepers in the desperate hope of gaining some eagerly sought-after academic capital. Stephen Moore and Yvonne Sherwood criticize the "obsession with method" within contemporary biblical studies, observing how it results in the production of endless "dreary" books and articles, each sounding something like this: "first in numbing dry detail is my method; now watch and be amazed while I apply it woodenly to this unsuspecting biblical text."[2] While Moore and Sherwood's pointed criticism does not of course apply to everything in the field, it too often hits its mark.

In respect of historical Jesus studies, I dub this approach "the Jesus funnel": it sucks in all the methods and findings from the humanities, social sciences, and other disciplines, with no other goal than to create the next innovative portrait of Jesus. And once a new conclusion about Jesus is generated, then rinse and repeat: one uses the methodology to analyse some other, equally unsuspecting biblical text.

Instead—and here I borrow a concept employed by our colleagues in marketing—the Next Quest should employ the Double-Funnel Jesus, a funnel wide at the top to engage with ideas current in the broader humanities, then narrowing to consider the historical Jesus and his sociohistorical context, before widening again to contribute those findings back to the humanities. The ultimate aim of the Double-Funnel Jesus is not the production of an infinite array of Jesuses differentiated according to every possible hermeneutical lens—homologous with consumer capitalism's provision of an ever-expanding range of choices for the expression of ever-multiplying niche identity politics. To paraphrase William Arnal's argument, Jesus scholars must instead offer academic conclusions of such sufficiently far-reaching application and generalizability that scholars working on the same methodology in another field will feel compelled to take that Jesus scholarship into account.[3] That may be the principal benefit religious studies offers

2. Stephen D. Moore and Yvonne Sherwood, *The Invention of the Biblical Scholar: A Critical Manifesto* (Minneapolis: Fortress, 2011), 40–41.
3. William Arnal, "What Branches Grow Out of This Stony Rubbish? Christian Origins and the Study of Religion," *SR* 39.4 (2010): 549–72.

biblical studies as opposed to any substantive or methodological contributions. It does not mean that historical Jesus scholarship should neglect its trademark close attention to primary sources. Yet also, and most crucially, we need to treat Jesus as a tool.

FOUR RELIGIOUS STUDIES APPROACHES FOR THE NEXT QUEST

To this end, I first outline four religious studies approaches whose potential has been underrealized within gospel scholarship: the cognitive science of religion; lived religion; the ontological turn; and indigenous research methodologies. I will then apply the approaches to Mark's empty tomb narrative and, finally, engage a wider academic conversation currently taking place about the variegated forms of historicity among diverse cultures.

Cognitive Science of Religion

The cognitive science of religion (CSR) has its origins in the 1980s and '90s, a period in which social constructionist explanations of religion were increasingly questioned and, conversely, a time in which advances in the study of human cognition and evolutionary history made it clear that religious behavior and belief are in part determined by universal psychological tendencies. Religious universals exist, as Claire White argues, because human minds are not sponges that indiscriminately absorb cultural information, but filters actively selecting and distorting information.[4] In order to explain how culture and religion function, therefore, we must not only understand social and environmental factors, but also how the human mind is structured to acquire, process, and transmit ideas.[5]

The same point may be made in a negative way: if we wrongly attribute natural tendencies to social or discursive origins, we will yield incorrect explanations and interpretations. For example, Cindel White et al. find that belief in karma—that the universe is inherently just—cannot be fully explained by local cultural or religious beliefs, but rests on four universal cognitive mechanisms: "intuitive thinking, mentalizing, dualism, and teleological thinking."[6] While belief in karma was higher in countries where karma was a normative concept, innate cognitive

---

4. Claire White, *An Introduction to the Cognitive Science of Religion: Connecting Evolution, Brain, Cognition, and Culture* (Abingdon: Routledge, 2021), 6.

5. White, *Cognitive Science of Religion*, 6.

6. Cindel J. M. White et al., "Cognitive Pathways to Belief in Karma and Belief in God," *Cognitive Science* 45.1 (2021): 1–42.

mechanisms account for belief in karma "above and beyond the variability explained by cultural learning about karma across cultures."[7] To draw a straight line from cultural particularities to belief in karma, therefore, would produce incorrect interpretations. As a further example, it has long been observed that, cross-culturally, women are prevalent among visionaries. Given that empathic and mentalizing abilities correlate positively with visionary behaviour, and given women score higher on average at empathy and mentalizing, this aggregate sex difference is what we might expect as a cross-cultural phenomenon. Emma Cohen thus criticizes earlier approaches to visionary practices that limited explanation and interpretation of female visionaries to social and cultural determinants alone.[8] CSR allows us to identify aspects of religious behavior that result from natural dispositions, and conversely isolate and better understand culturally contingent aspects that do not.

Furthermore, over the last three decades, CSR has created a storehouse of data on almost every facet of religion that has been largely untapped by biblical studies.[9] Armin Geertz recently compiled a long list of topics explored by CSR, which covers almost every topic in religious studies including morality, identity, gender, power relations, the nature of supernatural beings, death, rituals, prayer, dreaming, memory, violence, and much more.[10] CSR has also developed clear albeit technical methodologies for testing hypotheses. Studies employ a variety of methods, including experiments in controlled environments, longitudinal studies, and cross-cultural ethnography in both large-scale and small-scale societies.[11] To this end, CSR has also developed large datasets for the study of religion, such as *Pulotu* (on Pacific religious practices and beliefs) and *Seshat* (on ancient practices and beliefs).[12]

---

7. White et al., "Cognitive Pathways," 34.

8. Emma Cohen, *The Mind Possessed: The Cognition of Spirit Possession in an Afro-Brazilian Religious Tradition* (Oxford: Oxford University Press, 2007), 200–204.

9. There are exceptions, in particular the work of István Czachesz, e.g., in *Mind, Morality and Magic: Cognitive Science Approaches in Biblical Studies*, ed. István Czachesz and Risto Uro (London: Routledge, 2014).

10. Armin W. Geertz, "How Did Ignorance Become Fact in American Religious Studies? A Reluctant Reply to Ivan Strenski," *Studi e Materiali di Storia delle Religioni* 86, no. 1 (2020): 365–403.

11. For experiments in controlled environments, see, e.g., Marc Andersen et al., "Mystical Experience in the Lab," *MTSR* 26.3 (2014): 217–45. For an example of a longitudinal study, see John H. Shaver et al., "News Exposure Predicts Anti-Muslim Prejudice," *PLoS One* 12.3 (2017): 1–19. For an example of cross-cultural ethnography, see, e.g., Cindel J. M. White, Michael Muthukrishna, and Ara Norenzayan, "Cultural Similarity among Coreligionists within and between Countries," *Proceedings of the National Academy of the Sciences* 118.37 (2021): 1–9.

12. See Joseph Watts et al., "Pulotu: Database of Austronesian Supernatural Beliefs and Prac-

Most practitioners of CSR take a "building block" approach to the definition of religion, viewing it polythetically as a complex of components found in similar combinations across cultures. Richard Sosis, for example, identifies the building blocks of religious systems as comprising ritual, taboo, authority, myth, the sacred, a supernatural agent or agents, moral obligations, and purpose or meaning.[13] In turn, underlying these building blocks are a complex of cognitive mechanisms, which justify treating the term "religion" as a cross-cultural phenomenon manifested in different ways according to contextual and environmental factors.[14] CSR is in agreement with social constructionist approaches that the category religion is historically contingent, derived from folk terminology, and not native to the premodern world, and that before modernity religion was differently distinguished from the rest of human culture, if at all.[15] Yet CSR makes the additional claim that each building block of religion is derived from universal psychological mechanisms that combine in comparable ways cross-culturally.[16] If discursive analysis limits its subject matter to the *symbolic* dimension of language, CSR recuperates language's *iconic* dimension: language's ability to capture degrees of resemblance,

---

tices," *PLoS One* 10.9 (2015): 1–17; Peter Turchin et al., "Seshat: The Global History Databank," *Cliodynamics* 6.1 (2015): 77–107.

13. Richard Sosis, "The Building Blocks of Religious Systems: Approaching Religion as a Complex Adaptive System," in *Evolution, Development and Complexity: Multiscale Evolutionary Models of Complex Adaptive Systems*, ed. Georgi Yordanov Georgiev et al. (New York: Springer, 2018), 423–27. Yet see the critique in Deane Galbraith, "Religion without Scare Quotes: Cognitive Science of Religion and the Humanities," *Religion, Brain and Behavior* (2023): 1–8, https://doi.org/10.1080/2153599X.2023.2234441.

14. Benjamin G. Purzycki and Richard Sosis, *Religion Evolving: Cultural, Cognitive, and Ecological Dynamics* (Sheffield: Equinox, 2022), 171–89.

15. Recent studies have demonstrated that analogues to religion already existed in many cultures before the term was developed in the modern West. Rushain Abbasi argues that the Muslim concept of *dīn* was akin to the modern sense of "religion" long before the rise of the West; see "Islam and the Invention of Religion: A Study of Medieval Muslim Discourses on *Dīn*," *Studia Islamica* 116 (2021): 1–106. Will Sweetman argues that, prior to European contact, Indians already employed conceptions of pan-Indian Hinduism and distinguished Hinduism from Buddhism and Jainism. We should turn the "invention thesis" around, and say that the European term "Hinduism" was developed from precontact Indian precedents. See Will Sweetman, *Mapping Hinduism: "Hinduism" and the Study of Indian Religions, 1600–1776*, Neue Hallesche Berichte 4 (Halle: Franckeschen Stiftungen zu Halle, 2003). Robert Ford Company also identifies a category analogous to "religion" in premodern China; see "'Religious' as a Category: A Comparative Case Study," *Numen* 65 (2018): 338, 339; cf. Kevin Schilbrack, "A Realist Social Ontology of Religion," *Religion* 47.2 (2017): 161–78.

16. Joseph Bulbulia, "Áre There Any Religions? An Evolutionary Exploration," *MTSR* 17.2 (2005): 71–100.

comparison, similarity, or correspondence with reality.[17] If discourse theorists ask how concepts and categories are employed to create and authenticate human practices, CSR complements that analysis by asking why humans are motivated to adopt some practices and not others in the first place, and how cognitive mechanisms structure and shape contemporary religious practices and beliefs.[18] Human behavior is determined not only by a history of the social, but by a deeper history: our biological and phylogenetic history.[19] CSR's principal task is to examine that latter aspect.

Lived Religion

A second trend in religious studies still underemployed in the study of the historical Jesus is the lived religion paradigm.[20] Lived religion, as Meredith McGuire defines it, refers to "the actual experiences, practices, and beliefs of religious persons" as expressed in people's "everyday lives." It contrasts with "theologically correct" beliefs and practices prescribed by official religion.[21] Rather than making generalizing abstractions from the variegated beliefs, practices, and institutions of a particular religion, lived religion pays attention to the particular ways people "concretize" the imagined world of the supernatural, "materializing the [constructed] sacred" realm.[22] Lived religion is diverse and frequently shot through with inconsistencies; it responds urgently and unsystematically to the demands and circumstances of day-to-day life. It privileges practice over belief and the

17. On the symbolic versus iconic distinction (along with the indexical), see Charles S. Peirce, *Collected Papers of Charles Sanders Peirce*, ed. C. Hartshome, P. Weiss, and A. Burks (Cambridge: Harvard University Press, 1931–1958), 2:276; Galbraith, "Religion without Scare Quotes," 2–3.

18. Teemu Taira, *Taking "Religion" Seriously: Essays on the Discursive Study of Religion* (Leiden: Brill, 2022).

19. See Purzycki and Sosis, *Religion Evolving*, 12.

20. Lived religion has, however, been applied to the study of Manichaeans, late antiquity, and the Shepherd of Hermas, among other topics. See Mattias Brand, *Religion and the Everyday Life of Manichaeans in Kellis: Beyond Light and Darkness*, NHMS 102 (Leiden: Brill, 2022); Kristina Sessa, *Daily Life in Late Antiquity* (Cambridge: Cambridge University Press, 2018); Valentino Gasparini, Maik Patzelt, and Rubina Raja, eds., *Lived Religion in the Ancient Mediterranean World: Approaching Religious Transformations from Archaeology, History and Classics* (Berlin: de Gruyter, 2020); Angela Kim Harkins, "Looking at the *Shepherd of Hermas* through the Experience of Lived Religion," in Gasparini, Patzelt, and Raja, *Lived Religion*, 49.

21. Meredith B. McGuire, *Lived Religion: Faith and Practice in Everyday Life* (Oxford: Oxford University Press, 2008), 12.

22. Robert A. Orsi, *Between Heaven and Earth: The Religious Worlds People Make and the Scholars Who Study Them* (Princeton: Princeton University Press, 2005), 74.

body and emotions over abstract thought.[23] Lived religion is actualized across religious boundaries, such as those erected between Jews, Christians, or "pagans," in the messiness and exigencies of everyday life, and it recognizes that a person can assume several different and inconsistent identities according to the demands of different situations.[24]

Lived religion therefore challenges those approaches in scholarly monographs that tackle the meaning of, say, a single verse within the New Testament only after an exhaustive survey and distillation of (chapter 1) the Hebrew Bible, (chapter 2) Jewish pseudepigrapha, (chapter 3) Dead Sea scrolls, (chapter 4) Pauline Epistles, (chapter 5) the Four Gospels, (chapter 6) other early Christian literature, and (chapter 7) some Greek comparisons. Rather than dealing with synthesized abstractions of religion, the lived religion paradigm seeks out those religious traditions that contend and struggle with the challenges of everyday life, that struggle to fit in the received tradition, that force a reevaluation or adaptation of the tradition for the demands of current and contingent circumstances.[25] Such analysis must focus on "a particular culture, within a particular social environment (status, milieu, etc.), and within the specific moment and social gathering in which they are evoked, negotiated, and communicated."[26] It thus first requires reconstruction—despite the inherent limitations—of the historical record, of cultural, social, economic, and situational contexts.[27]

In addition, lived religion requires study of the ways that memories were fashioned, and of historical aesthetics and modes of religious experiences. For example, in her examination of the Shepherd of Hermas, Angela Kim Harkins asks readers to imagine from the textual clues "how texts were experienced and performed by people—what kind of affective response was had."[28] Drawing on cognitive science, Harkins analyses how the vision reports in the Shepherd of Hermas could have generated "enactive reading" experiences: scripting responses in listeners that re-create the experience described in the text, enabling them to feel the sensations described in or implied by the text.[29]

---

23. McGuire, *Lived Religion*, 39–41.

24. See the introduction of Gasparini, Patzelt, and Raja, *Lived Religion*, 2; cf. Brand, *Everyday Life of Manichaeans*, 23–24; Paula Fredriksen, "What Does It Mean to See Paul 'within Judaism'?," *JBL* 141.2 (2022): 359–80.

25. Brand, *Everyday Life of Manichaeans*, 29.

26. Maik Patzelt, "Introduction to Section 1," in Gasparini, Patzelt, and Raja, *Lived Religion*, 12.

27. Patzelt, "Introduction to Section 1," 12.

28. Harkins, "Looking," 49.

29. Harkins, "Looking," 53.

Ontological Turn

A third approach in recent studies of religion involves the so-called ontological turn in anthropology. Ontologists differ from traditional anthropologists in refusing to explain differences between peoples as a matter of *worldview* or *belief*, and instead treat the differences as real, as involving different *ontologies*.[30] For example, when Māori of Aotearoa New Zealand speak about mountains as ancestors, ontologists would not say that Māori *believe* mountains are ancestors and then attempt to explain how they can hold to these (implicitly deemed irrational) beliefs (e.g., for political reasons, due to cosmological beliefs, or for society to function harmoniously). Although not necessarily incorrect in themselves, all of these explanations tend to exoticize Māori ontologies. Instead ontologists "take seriously" indigenous ontologies, and as a result ask what analytical categories and methods must change *for the anthropologist* when they identify and contemplate differing ontologies.[31] Anthropologists may then "arrive at concepts that will allow them to describe and analyse their ethnographic data more cogently and precisely."[32] In so doing, the ontological approach, as Martin Holbraad and Morten Axel Pedersen frame it, aims to see what "one would not otherwise have been able to see."[33]

For example, when Cuban diviners who employ a certain powder in their séances state that "powder is power," Holbraad contends that we should not assume powder is the real thing and our task is to interpret how Cuban diviners connect it with their concept of power. We should instead consider the theoretical implications of how materiality and power (i.e., "powerful powder") may be a single thing. Conversely, we should avoid the temptation to explain it away by saying "they can't really believe that" or "they do believe that, but because of social pathology or schizophrenia," which would shut down unforeseen theoretical possibilities.[34] The ontological shift potentially, therefore, opens up dimensions of religious behavior that previously were underthematized or even entirely missed.

---

30. Martin Palacek, "The Ontological Turn Revisited: Theoretical Decline; Why Cannot Ontologists Fulfil Their Promise?," *Anthropological Theory* 22.2 (2022): 155.

31. Martin Holbraad and Morten Axel Pedersen, *The Ontological Turn: An Anthropological Exposition*, New Departures in Anthropology (Cambridge: Cambridge University Press, 2017), 2–3, citing Mauss on Māori gift exchange.

32. Holbraad and Pedersen, *Ontological Turn*, 13–14.

33. Holbraad and Pedersen, *Ontological Turn*, 4.

34. Amiria Henare, Martin Holbraad, and Sari Wastell, "Introduction: Thinking through Things," in *Thinking Through Things: Theorising Artefacts Ethnographically*, ed. Amiria Henare, Martin Holbraad, and Sari Wastell (London: Routledge, 2007), 5, 13–16; Martin Holbraad, "The Power of Powder: Multiplicity and Motion in the Divinatory Cosmology of Cuban Ifá (or *Mana*, Again)," in *Thinking through Things*, 189–225.

Indigenous Research Methodologies

A nascent area in religious studies, and one that complements the ontological turn, is the introduction of indigenous research methodologies into the academy.[35] It arises from the now widespread recognition that academia is not a neutral institution, but one that serves certain hegemonic interests, including whiteness, ableism, capitalism, neoliberalism, Eurocentrism, and patriarchy, among others. Indigenous research methodologies allow indigenous people in the academy to conduct research on *indigenous* terms, rather than terms set by the hegemonic ideology (that typically denies it *is* an ideology). For Nêhiyaw-Saulteaux scholar Margaret Kovach, indigenous methodologies begin with "Indigenous conceptual framing to focus, make visible, and uphold Indigenous knowledge systems."[36] The aim is to let indigenous researchers *be* indigenous, empowering indigenous peoples, as Ngāti Rangiwewehi scholar Rangimarie Māhuika phrases it, to "assert our cultural beliefs and practices, our way of knowing and being and our right to both live and maintain them."[37] Thus Opaskwayak Cree scholar Shawn Wilson defines "indigenous research" as "research that is conducted by or for Indigenous peoples."[38] In broader perspective, the aim of indigenous research methodologies is to decolonize and indigenize academia.[39]

Immersion in indigenous epistemologies offers *a third place* from which to evaluate the often invisible Eurocentrism prevailing in historical Jesus studies.[40] The necessity of an outsider's vantage point beyond scholarship's hegemonic center and removed from the object of study is illustrated, for example, by Meredith McGuire's critique of the way Rodney Stark and Roger Finke uncritically impose religious norms from modern western Europe to evaluate "religiosity" in

35. Linda Tuhiwai Smith, *Decolonizing Methodologies: Research and Indigenous Peoples*, 2nd ed. (London: Zed, 2012).

36. Margaret Kovach, *Indigenous Methodologies: Characteristics, Conversations, and Contexts*, 2nd ed. (Toronto: University of Toronto Press, 2021).

37. Rangimarie Māhuika, "Kaupapa Māori Theory Is Critical and Anti-Colonial," *MAI Review* 3.4 (2008): 1.

38. Shawn Wilson, *Research Is Ceremony: Indigenous Research Methods* (Black Point: Fernwood, 2008), 15. Cf. Smith, *Decolonizing Methodologies*; Kovach, *Indigenous Methodologies*; Bagele Chilesa, *Indigenous Research Methodologies*, 2nd ed. (Los Angeles: SAGE, 2020).

39. Kovach, *Indigenous Methodologies*.

40. Ekaputra Tupamahu, "The Stubborn Invisibility of Whiteness in Biblical Scholarship," *Political Theology Network*, November 12, 2020, https://politicaltheology.com/the-stubborn-invisibility-of-whiteness-in-biblical-scholarship/; Wongi Park, "Multiracial Biblical Studies," *JBL* 140.3 (2021): 425–59.

the medieval period.[41] Judged by Stark and Finke's own modern norms, the medieval church misleadingly appears irreligious. By contrast, a perspective from a third place—whether medieval thought or indigenous worldviews—intervenes to denaturalize unnoticed Eurocentricities within the study of the early Jesus movement; it challenges the imposition of one's unexamined assumptions. More radically, it challenges the modern Western conception of historicity itself, revealing the operation of alternative forms of historical consciousness, of the perhaps incommensurable ways in which the early Jesus movement might have conceived its relationship with the past.

THE VISION OF AN EMPTY TOMB

How might we draw on cognitive science, lived religion, the ontological turn, and indigenous research methodologies to examine the historical Jesus and do so in a way that contributes to the wider humanities? To this end—and following the remit to concentrate on "what's next?" in historical Jesus studies—I enter the empty tomb of Mark 16 in a manner intended to be exploratory, open-ended, and suggestive, rather than in any way definitive.[42]

The Ontology of Visions

The appearance of a young man dressed in white to a group of women at Jesus's empty tomb has been frequently interpreted as an indicator of a visionary experience, perhaps an angelophany. That is already Luke's interpretation when the two disciples on the road to Emmaus summarize that the women at the tomb had "seen a vision of angels" (24:23: *optasian angelōn heōrakenai*). Many commentators, including Martin Albertz, Rudolf Bultmann, David Catchpole, Holly Hearon, and Dale Allison, have identified a number of visionary "elements" within Mark 16, in particular in the women's vision of the young man or angel in the tomb. But they hold back, maintaining that these are *limited* elements, such as the *angelus interpres* that Bultmann identifies in verse 6.[43] The commentators are

---

41. McGuire, *Lived Religion*, 23–24.

42. Mark Goodacre rightly observes that Jesus's tomb, if representative of similar contemporary tombs, probably held multiple other people, so was not technically "empty"; see "How Empty Was the Tomb," *JSNT* 44.1 (2021): 134–48. Yet a tomb in a vision is different. Visionscapes are usually partial; in this vision report the women see only an empty tomb, vacated by Jesus, because that is all that concerns the female visionary.

43. Rudolf Bultmann, *History of the Synoptic Tradition*, trans. John Marsh (Oxford: Blackwell, 1963), 290; Martin Albertz, "Zur Formgeschichte der Auferstehungsberichte," *ZAW* 21 (1922):

keen to return to the reassuring reality they perceive in the frame of the story: the women's early morning visit to the tomb, the physicality of the tomb itself, and their fleeing from the tomb. The apparent assumption behind most discussions of the visionary experience is that vision accounts are less truthful than stories from waking life, that visions concern the internal realm of imagination versus the external realm of reality.

Some conservative Christian commentators go further, refusing any hint of a visionary experience in relation to resurrection appearances. N. T. Wright even asserts that people in "the ancient world," presumably much like his refined modern acquaintances, simply "knew the difference between visions and things that happen in the 'real' world."[44] Stephen T. Davis piles up reasons: "there is no denying" that there are no visionary experiences behind the appearance stories; such a conclusion is clear from "a quick and pre-critical reading"; the facts lead "naturally" to this conclusion; the "natural impression" and "plain sense" of the stories make this interpretation certain.[45] We may rightly criticize Wright and Davis as overtly anachronistic in their (modernist) failure to see that other peoples treat visions as affording insight into reality. Yet in carefully restricting the number of visionary elements in the empty tomb story, even less dogmatic commentators impose modern ontologies onto the text. The usual governing assumption is that visionary aspects are restricted to what the women saw *within* the tomb. But if we embrace the ancient ontology of visions, a compelling possibility is that the tradition in Mark 16:1–8 derives *in its entirety* from a vision.[46] Whether or not Jesus was really buried in a tomb, the tomb described in Mark 16:1–8 existed only in a visionary experience.

Indigenous knowledge provides a critical corrective, breaking the imposition of the modern ontological binary in which waking life is coextensive with reality, and visions coextensive with imagination. In *mātauranga Māori*, for example,

---

265; cf. David Catchpole, "The Fearful Silence of the Women at the Tomb: A Study in Markan Theology," *Journal of Theology for Southern Africa* 18 (1977): 9; Holly E. Hearon, *The Mary Magdalene Tradition: Witness and Counter-Witness in Early Christian Communities* (Collegeville, MN: Liturgical, 2004), 69; Dale C. Allison Jr., *The Resurrection of Jesus: Apologetics, Polemics, History* (London: T&T Clark, 2021), 166.

44. N. T. Wright, *The Resurrection of the Son of God* (London: SPCK, 2003), 690.

45. Stephen T. Davis, "'Seeing' the Risen Jesus," in *The Resurrection: An Interdisciplinary Symposium on the Resurrection of Jesus*, ed. Stephen T. Davis, Daniel Kendall, and Gerald O'Collins (Oxford: Oxford University Press, 1997), 129.

46. Mark has added features to 16:1–8 to incorporate the vision report into his wider narrative, in particular parts of 16:1 (with 15:40–41, 47) and much of 16:7 (to connect it to the saying of Jesus in 14:28). Yet as the components of the underlying visionary source are substantially preserved, I refer here simply to Mark 16:1–8 as the vision report.

a *moemoeā* ("vision" or "dream") is something really experienced by one's *wairua* (spirit) during sleep—not a thing your *wairua* imagines but something in which it *really* participates.[47] As with ancient Near Eastern terminology for dreams and visions, a *moemoeā* is not something that is *had* (i.e., "I had a dream"), but an event seen and felt.[48] Although trivial dreams are regularly attributed to imagination, significant dreams and visions are considered to reveal the deeper dimensions of reality, believed to be sent by *atua* (metapersons/ancestors/gods), especially to warn about the future.[49] Māori vision-worlds can radically merge and interweave with waking life, so that you don't know where one begins and the other ends. One is reminded of Peter's confusion, in the narrative of Acts 12, as to whether he is in a dream or waking life. Māori *matakite* (seer) Egan Bidois relates how he dreamed that he gave comfort to a troubled, suicidal friend. On subsequently meeting him in real life, his friend claimed he had heard the same words of comfort in his waking life, and also in the same place as in Bidois's dream.[50] All this was considered normal and expected. Bidois explains that dreams "can be the doorways in and out of various realms of existence where we are removed from the physical self." In dreams, he claims, "we are more what I believe is our true selves, our true forms, which are first and foremost spirit."[51] Within dreams, ancestors frequently provide insight, help, and guidance for the future. Anituatua Black recalls a time that her deceased husband's *wairua* descended on her, just before daylight while she was in a half-asleep, half-awake state, to assist with a restless spirit at a neighbor's house.[52] As in many other indigenous cultures, "dreaming and waking reality are not fully segmented or compartmentalized worlds but are rather overlapping experiences."[53] So too, dreams in the ancient world, as Robert Gnuse summarizes, "were no less real for many people than the impressions received during the wak-

47. As observed by Hono Rangi Huirama in *Wairua*, series 1 episode 4, produced by Ngatapa Black, aired on Māori Television on August 9, 2010, https://www.maoritelevision.com/shows/wairua/S01E004/wairua-series-1-episode-4.

48. Frances Flannery-Dailey, *Dreamers, Scribes, and Priests: Jewish Dreams in the Hellenistic and Roman Eras*, JSJSup 90 (Leiden: Brill, 2004), 1, 46.

49. Richard Taylor, *Te Ika a Maui* (London: Wertheim and Macintosh, 1855), 160.

50. Egan Bidois quoted in Michael Robbins, *The Primordial Mind in Health and Illness: A Cross-Cultural Perspective* (London: Routledge, 2011), 107.

51. Bidois quoted in Robbins, *Primordial Mind*, 104.

52. Quoted from *Wairua*, series 1 episode 4.

53. Barbara Tedlock, "Dreaming and Dream Research," in *Dreaming: Anthropological and Psychological Interpretations*, ed. Barbara Tedlock (Santa Fe, NM: School of American Research Press, 1992), 5; cf. T. Christopher Hoklotubbe, "(En)Visioning Creator's Revelation on Turtle Island: On Dreams, Visions and Decolonizing Biblicism," in *Multiracial Biblical Studies*, ed. Wongi Park, SemeiaSt (Atlanta: SBL Press, forthcoming).

ing hours. Dreams were viewed not as psychological experiences of the mind but as phenomena with a special reality of their own."[54]

Indigenous knowledge disrupts modern, Western assumptions concerning dreams and visions. The point is not to collapse indigenous knowledge onto the perspectives in the ancient world, but to be alert to possible alternative ontologies that may be operative within the text.

The Vision-Report Form and Its Extent

Taking indigenous vision ontologies seriously leads us to reevaluate the formal characteristics of Mark 16:1–8 in their entirety. Form-critical analyses of Mark 16:1–8 seldom account for more than a few of its features. Holly Hearon for example offers a minimal structure, describing its form as a typical narrative with a beginning, middle and end.[55] For David Catchpole, the *angelus interpres* and the women's reaction of "fear and silence" (16:5, 8) show that it "belongs to the structure of epiphany."[56] Martin Albertz and Dale Allison each identify an original Christophany behind the angel's message in Mark 16:5–6.[57] Gerd Lüdemann points out that there is more than one element of vision reports present in Mark 16:1–8, for "the angel does not just interpret but at the same time proclaims, and the women are terrified at his appearance."[58] Jane Schaberg offers the most comprehensive argument for viewing Mark 16:1–8 as a visionary experience. She argues that Mark 16:1–8 takes the form of an *apocalyptic* vision, identifying a long list of similarities between Mark 16:1–8 and Dan 7: the initial grief situation; the strange vision; the resulting amazement; the explanation by an angelic interpreter; a commission to tell others; and the final terror and silence.[59] While this lengthy list suggests extensive overlap between the empty tomb narrative and apocalyptic vision narratives, it struggles to explain why Mark 16 lacks distinctively *apocalyptic* features.

I argue that the entire form of Mark 16:1–8 comes closest to the form of *an ancient vision report*, a form found with remarkable consistency in the ancient

---

54. Robert Karl Gnuse, *Dreams and Dream Reports in the Writings of Josephus: A Traditio-Historical Analysis*, AGJU 36 (Leiden: Brill, 1996), 34.

55. Hearon, *Mary Magdalene Tradition*, 69.

56. Catchpole, "Fearful Silence," 9; cf. Mark 9:6, 15.

57. Albertz, "Zur Formgeschichte der Auferstehungsberichte," 265; Allison, *Resurrection of Jesus*, 166.

58. Gerd Lüdemann, *The Resurrection of Jesus: History, Experience, Theology* (London: SCM Press, 1994).

59. Jane Schaberg, *The Resurrection of Mary Magdalene: Legends, Apocrypha, and the Christian Testament* (New York: Continuum, 2003), 257, 286–88.

Near East, Judea, early Christianity, at Qumran, and in Philo and Josephus.[60] Mark 16:1–8 follows, in all essential details, the typical message vision report's threefold form—introduction (16:1–3), central body (16:4–6[7]), and ending (16:8)—and contains most of the distinctive vision motifs found in each part.[61]

I briefly outline the vision motifs found in every one of the three main sections of Mark 16:1–8. The reference to the women in Mark 16:1 identifies the visionaries, reflecting the fact that cross-culturally women are overrepresented among visionaries.[62] The liminal timing is stereotypical of night visions, the most prevalent time for hypnopompic visionary experiences common in REM sleep.[63] The reference to this time in Mark 16:2 is overdetermined and lacks logical consistency, a frequent feature of visionary logic. It is described both as *lian prōi* (a time before dawn) and as *anateilantos tou hēliou* (after the sun had already risen). Supernatural visions are often triggered by trauma, and although not mentioned by Mark it is clearly implicit in the violent death of Jesus and subsequent mourning rites.[64] Yet it could equally fit with participation in an early Christian ritual centered on reenacting Jesus's death, such as the Last Supper rite, which offered mystical unification with Jesus in his death. If the latter is the case, the women's vision of an empty tomb might plausibly date many years after Jesus's burial.

The number of verbs of sight throughout the vision body in verses 4–7 is striking and also indicative of its visionary source: *anablepsasai, theōrousin, eidon, ide,*

60. John S. Hanson, "Dreams and Visions in the Graeco-Roman World and Early Christianity," *ANRW* 23.2:1395–427; A. Leo Oppenheim, *The Interpretation of Dreams in the Ancient Near East: With a Translation of an Assyrian Dream-Book*, TAPS 46.3 (Philadelphia: American Philosophical Society, 1956); Flannery-Dailey, *Dreamers*; Susan Niditch, *The Symbolic Vision in Biblical Tradition*, HSM 30 (Chico, CA: Scholars Press, 1980); Klaus Seybold, "Der Traum in der Bibel," in *Traum und Träumen: Traumanalysen in Wissenschaft, Religion und Kunst*, ed. Therese Wagner-Simon and Gaetano Benedetti (Göttingen: Vandenhoeck & Ruprecht, 1984), 32–54; Andrew B. Perrin, *The Dynamics of Dream-Vision Revelation in the Aramaic Dead Sea Scrolls*, JAJSup 19 (Göttingen: Vandenhoeck & Ruprecht, 2017); David M. Hay, "Politics and Exegesis in Philo's Treatise on Dreams," in *Society of Biblical Literature 1987 Seminar Papers*, ed. Kent H. Richards, SBLSP 26 (Atlanta: Scholars Press, 1987), 429–38.

61. E.g., Robert H. Stein identifies a similar three-part structure in 16:1–4, 5–7, 8; see *Mark*, BECNT (Grand Rapids: Baker Academic, 2008), 728.

62. E.g., Janice P. Boddy, *Wombs and Alien Spirits: Women, Men, and the Zār Cult in Northern Sudan*, New Directions in Anthropological Writing (Madison: University of Wisconsin Press, 1989); Michael Lambek, *Knowledge and Practice in Mayotte: Local Discourses of Islam, Sorcery and Spirit Possession*, Anthropological Horizons (Toronto: University of Toronto Press, 1993).

63. Cf. Dan 7:2; 9:20–27; 1QapGen XIX, 14; XXI, 8; 4 Ezra 13:1; 2 Bar. 36:1; LAB 9:10; 28:4; Acts 16:9.

64. Carolyn Osiek, "The Women at the Tomb: What Are They Doing There?," *Ex Auditu* 9 (1993): 98; Kathleen E. Corley, *Women and the Historical Jesus: Feminist Myths of Christian Origins* (Santa Rosa, CA: Polebridge, 2002), 123–28. Cf. Ep. Apos. 9–10; Gos. Pet. 12–13.

and *opsesthe*. The young man in white clothing who delivers knowledge of Jesus's resurrection to the women (16:5) is plausibly an angelic messenger, as expected from Hellenistic Jewish message dreams and visions.[65]

Finally, the peculiar ending in Mark 16:8 makes good sense as the stereotypical response of dreamers and visionaries: they are filled with terror and are dumb-founded, almost ubiquitous reactions that in the vision-report genre serve to con-firm the veridical nature of a divine vision.[66] The whole of Mark 16:1–8, therefore, in structure, content, and language, conforms most closely to the typical form of an ancient vision report.

The Mutual Attraction of Mary and Jesus

While biblical scholarship has largely "cleansed" Mary Magdalene of her tradi-tional association with sinfulness and sex work, commentators still uncritically accept the gospels' claim that Mary had been "*exorcised* from demon possession" by Jesus or "*cured* from sickness" by him (Luke 8:1–3; cf 24:10). Catherine Keller asserts, for example, that Mary Magdalene's "encounter with Jesus was power-ful therapy for a many-layered and troubled psyche."[67] Possession behaviour is pathologized as something that Jesus wanted to get rid of and, as for Keller, is often assumed really to be an unwanted mental illness.

Giovanni Bazzana's recent analysis of possession behavior in the Jesus move-ment provides grounds to resist such an ableist conclusion, which sits uneasily with ontologies of possession in both the ancient world and contemporary eth-nologies. The possessed, cross-culturally, do not often stop channeling messages, healing, or engaging in mantic behaviour when they are exorcised or change religious affiliation; they typically just carry on exhibiting similar behaviour for their new group. Mary arguably was no exception. "Despite a later theologizing attempt to present [exorcisms] as signs of Jesus's apocalyptic defeat of evil," Baz-zana writes, "the typical result of Jesus's exorcisms is not the destruction of the demons but more simply their removal and displacement with the implicit as-sumption that they might return."[68] Bazzana cites the example in Zakaria Rhani's ethnography of exorcisms carried out near the tomb of Moroccan *marabout* Ben

65. Flannery-Dailey, *Dreamers*, 202–4, 242.

66. E.g., Gen 28:17 (Jacob); Dan 4:5 (Nebuchadnezzar); 1QapGen XIX, 19 (Abram).

67. Catherine Keller, "'She Talks Too Much': Magdalene Meditations," in *Toward a Theology of Eros: Transfiguring Passion at the Limits of Discipline*, ed. Virginia Burrus and Catherine Keller (New York: Fordham University Press, 2006), 241.

68. Giovanni B. Bazzana, *Having the Spirit of Christ: Spirit Possession and Exorcism in the Early Christ Groups* (New Haven: Yale University Press, 2020), 36.

Yeffou. Typical of such exorcisms, one woman referred to as "B" was exorcised of malevolent spirits that had caused her condition for fifteen years, only for them to be replaced by benign spirits that provided her with exorcistic powers.[69] The more likely conclusion is that, after encountering Jesus, Mary was now deemed possessed by the "right" spirit(s) for the benefit of the "right" side.

In addition, as Virginia Burrus has argued, Luke portrays the relationship between Jesus and the women, including Mary Magdalene, as one of a client serving wealthy patrons.[70] It follows that Mary and other "cured" women had the freedom and independence to choose their way of life; they did not need rescuing by Jesus, but presumably found what he offered to be beneficial.[71] The attraction may have been mutual: both Jesus and Mary carried out practices that others identified as possession behavior. Jesus was likewise accused of having an unclean spirit, even Beelzebul himself, and of being out of his mind (Mark 3:20–30).[72] The power balance between Jesus and Mary is thus ambiguous and probably multifaceted—who was following whom?

Christopher Rowland, in his book *The Open Heaven*, lists further events in the gospels that plausibly have origins *not* in the waking world but in the visionary experiences of Jesus and his movement. These include his baptism experience, his desert temptations, his sighting of Satan falling from heaven (Luke 10:18), and the transfiguration (Mark 9:2–8).[73] At his baptism, the heavens open and Jesus hears the voice of God. The personal and private nature of this divine vision is evident in God's address of Jesus as "you." By contrast, the literary development evident in Matthew turns that trace of a first-person vision report into a public event reported in the third person.[74] The boundaries between waking life and vision are fluid, and therefore challenge modern oppositions between reality and nonreality. The subsequent account of Jesus interacting with Satan and being

69. Zakaria Rhani, "Le chérif et la possédée: Sainteté, rituel et pouvoir au Maroc," *L'homme* 190 (2009): 27–50, cited in Bazzana, *Having the Spirit of Christ*, 50.

70. Virginia Burrus, "The Gospel of Luke and the Acts of the Apostles," in *A Postcolonial Commentary on the New Testament Writings*, ed. Fernando F. Segovia and R. S. Sugirtharajah (London: T&T Clark, 2009), 142–44.

71. As an example of the "client-with-benefits" relationship that elite women had with Jesus, Luke's Jesus heals and exorcises every one of his wealthy patrons (8:1–3). Luke also names some or perhaps all of these other women as present at the empty tomb: Joanna, Chuza's wife, and Susanna among "many others" (24:10).

72. See Bazzana, *Having the Spirit of Christ*, 24–59.

73. Christopher Rowland, *The Open Heaven: A Study of Apocalyptic in Judaism and Early Christianity* (London: SPCK, 1982), 358–66.

74. Martin Dibelius, *From Tradition to Gospel*, trans. Bertram Lee Woolf (New York: Scribner's Sons, 1935), 272; Rowland, *Open Heaven*, 360.

cared for by angels is brief and not explicitly described as a visionary experience. Yet Jesus's forty days of self-deprivation and his spirit possession during his baptism are each strongly reminiscent of ancient techniques to induce visions.[75] In addition, Jesus's ability to see all the kingdoms of the earth all at once from a very high mountain (described in Matt 4:8) reflects something not literally able to be experienced in waking life. It likewise indicates that "Jesus might have told of his battle with temptation as he experienced it."[76]

Just as Luke's Emmaus Road story explicitly interprets the women's sight of an angel inside the empty tomb as occurring in a "vision" (24:23: *optasian*), Matthew explicitly interprets Jesus's transfiguration as a "vision" (17:9: *horama*), presumably witnessed by the recipients of the vision (Peter, James, and John).[77] Luke indicates from the outset that the transfiguration is a visionary experience by referring to the visionaries as "overcome with sleep" (9:32), a common introductory visionary motif.[78] In Mark, the combination of multiple elements from ancient vision reports makes this visionary background implicit. The disciples know immediately yet without explanation that they see Moses and Elijah, just as in dreams and visions we feel we immediately know the identity of people.[79] Following the disciples' otherworldly experiences, there is a sudden shift in perception, as is common to visionary reports: the disciples look up and see nobody but Jesus.[80] The vision's content is revelatory: Jesus is the beloved Son of God, seemingly superior to Moses and Elijah.[81] The reaction of the disciples is typical of the outcome of a vision, as shared by the women in Mark 16:8: fear (9:6) and silence or difficulty in speaking (9:6, 9).[82] This central, hinge episode in Mark's Gospel requires purported access to the deeper reality that is provided by visionary experience, as will be the case for the report of Jesus's empty tomb.

Both the transfiguration and empty tomb narratives suspiciously declare that they were told to others only at some later time.[83] We may combine this observa-

---

75. Cf. Torsten Löfstedt, "Myths, Visions, and Related Literary Forms in the Gospels," *SEÅ* 80 (2015): 115.

76. Löfstedt, "Myths," 115.

77. Edith M. Humphrey, *And I Turned to See the Voice: The Rhetoric of Vision in the New Testament* (Grand Rapids: Baker Academic, 2007), 137; Derek S. Dodson, *Reading Dreams: An Audience-Critical Approach to the Dreams in the Gospel of Matthew*, LNTS 397 (London: T&T Clark, 2009), 177.

78. Humphrey, *And I Turned*, 143.

79. Löfstedt, "Myths," 116.

80. Löfstedt, "Myths," 116.

81. Humphrey, *And I Turned*, 143.

82. Catchpole, "Fearful Silence," 9.

83. James G. Crossley, "Against the Historical Plausibility of the Empty Tomb Story and the Bodily Resurrection of Jesus: A Response to N. T. Wright," *JSHJ* 3.2 (2005): 177, 186.

tion with other factors often noted: (1) the absence of any mention of the tomb or women in Paul; (2) the awkward and secondary fit of Mark 16:1–8 after the passion narrative; (3) the obviously secondary nature of the women characters in 15:40–41, 47, and (4) the visionary origins of both transfiguration and empty tomb reports. The evidence is admittedly cumulative rather than conclusive. Yet a pattern appears to exist in Mark in which insights into events that had occurred earlier in time (including during the lifetime of Jesus) in fact originate in visions experienced subsequent to his death, and in which the lateness of these traditions is defended as veridical by highlighting the motifs of dumbfoundedness and silence from the underlying vision reports.

Are there other gospel episodes that derive from visions? The sighting of Jesus walking on the water is a likely candidate. Indicia of oneiric or visionary origins include the early morning setting, the misrecognition of Jesus as a ghost, the disciples' terror, and Jesus' admonition (like other dream or vision figures) not to fear.[84] Martin Dibelius noted the epiphanic motif of Jesus first appearing to "pass them by" (Mark 6:48) was reminiscent of Moses's vision of Yahweh's passing rear view (Exod 33:18–23).

Rowland makes the further point that, although relatively few in number, each of the visionary events he enumerates are of central "importance" to Mark's account of Jesus's public life.[85] If so, I would add that this importance is precisely what we would expect from gospel writers who selected visions as their sources. Visions were usually only recorded if they revealed something of great significance. Confounding the modern binary in which waking life equates to reality and visions to the imaginary realm, ancient supernatural visions were seen to offer access to more profound knowledge, a deeper level of reality accessible only via divine revelation.[86] Modern aversion to visions has led most commentators to either wholesale reject or minimize the extent of visions in the gospels. The ontological approach, by contrast, asks not how to explain away these visions, but how to reassess literature that incorporates both dimensions as aspects of reality.[87] Mark would have understood that these supernatural vision reports provided access to

---

84. Löfstedt, "Myths," 116.

85. Rowland, *Open Heaven*, 366.

86. Oppenheim, "Interpretation of Dreams," 238; Flannery-Dailey, *Dreamers*, 35, 77.

87. I have argued elsewhere that, even among scholars who embrace the apocalyptically minded Jesus, there is an aversion to ascribing to him the more irrational, allegedly "crazy" aspects of apocalyptic thought, including its possession cult; calculations of end-times time-tables; visionary practices; revelations; heavenly ascents; achievement of mystical union with God. See Deane Galbraith, "Jeremiah Never Saw That Coming: How Jesus Miscalculated the End Times," in *Jeremiah in History and Tradition*, ed. Jim West and Niels Peter Lemche (Abingdon: Routledge, 2020), 150–75.

a superior reality not available in waking life. It is for this reason, I contend, that he chose a vision report as most befitting the climax to his work, as most able to guarantee the veracity of Jesus's resurrection and heavenly status.

If Jesus and his companions shared these practices and vision experiences, how many other episodes in the gospels originated with visions from Jesus's visionary cult? The possible influence of visions on other gospel traditions is rarely explored in Jesus scholarship, at least in comparison with the more rationalistic (and very Protestant) interest in detecting every faint trace of Scripture that has influenced gospel compositions. Yet one very likely example of a visionary origin for a Jesus tradition was identified by Hans Lietzmann—the Last Supper ritual. Paul claims that it was handed down by "the Lord" to him (1 Cor 11:23), indicating some private revelatory visionary or auditory experience that he later communicated to his churches. These are not traditions being handed down by living humans but directly by the Lord.[88] Combining this observation with the mystical identification with Jesus that appears to have taken place, the Last Supper ritual as we know it from the gospels must first have been celebrated sometime *after* Jesus's death, following the divine revelation to Paul of what had purportedly occurred in the life of Jesus.[89]

Dreams and visions as well as historicized Scriptures offered sources that could posthumously enhance Jesus's character and actions. It is notable in this regard that the two sections of Matthew's Gospel containing the most novel additions to Mark— the nativity and postresurrection appearance stories—are also based extensively on dreams and visions (the former also employing historicized Scriptures, in particular in the formula quotations).[90] Visionary experiences were arguably central to the formulation of many more historical Jesus traditions than is usually recognized.

Resurrection of the Subelite

In a series of studies, Justin Barrett has demonstrated that, while reflective and highly considered thoughts about God and other supernatural agents tend to

88. Hans Lietzmann, *Messe und Herrenmahl: Eine Studie zur Geschichte der Liturgie* (Bonn: Marcus and Weber, 1926), 255. Lietzmann wryly observes that we never find a comparable account within the many rabbinic transmissions of tradition that proceeds in this fashion: "Rabbi Akiba received [the tradition] *from Yahweh* and handed it on to Rabbi Meir" (255 n. 1). Cf. James Edward Harding, "Understanding in All Things: The Revelation and Transmission of Divine Insight in the Qumran Scrolls and the New Testament" (PhD diss., University of Sheffield, 2001), 268–96.

89. So too, Paul's vision or audition of the Lord's instruction about divorce (1 Cor 7:10) may have been the basis for constructing Jesus's instructions in Mark 10:2–12. The resulting separation of 1 Cor 7:10 from its original context (in Paul) in Mark 10:9 produces what is seemingly Jesus's more absolutist stance on divorce.

90. On dreams in Matthew, see Dodson, *Reading Dreams*.

be "theologically correct," when faced with time constraints or trauma, people resort to intuitive thought and "theologically incorrect" ideas.[91] Faced with remembrance of the traumatic death of their eschatological agent Jesus, we would expect his followers' conceptions of Jesus's afterlife would have been unsystematized, intuitive, responsive to the demands of everyday life, and prone to ad hoc rationalization and cognitive dissonance reduction.

We should therefore privilege, especially, the remarkable record of the crowds' attempts to establish the identity of Jesus soon after the death of John the Baptist, in which they posit that Jesus is John the Baptist or some other prophet resurrected to life (Mark 6:14–16). These reflect, if not actual debates, at least the type of debate that Mark thought was representative of everyday contemporaries. It is here, in lived religion, that we should *begin* to analyze developing resurrection beliefs of the Jesus movement, rather than following the typical approach of monographs that extrapolate the views of Jesus's followers from compendia of ancient sources on resurrection.[92] It is notable, in this regard, that resurrection was attributed to all three first-century eschatological agents who we know are connected with the Baptist movement—John the Baptist, Jesus, and Dositheos the Samaritan—each of whom inspired separate messianic movements that endured for centuries (i.e., the followers of John referred to in the Pseudo-Clementines, Mandaeans, Christians, and Dositheans).[93]

From the privileged starting point in Mark 6, it is clear that ordinary people, or at least a nonreligious specialist in the case of Herod, expected that individual righteous martyrs such as John the Baptist would individually experience bodily resurrection. Mark never mentions any universal (general) resurrection.[94] The

91. Justin L. Barrett, "Cognitive Constraints on Hindu Concepts of the Divine," *JSSR* 37 (1998): 608–19; Barrett, "Theological Correctness: Cognitive Constraint and the Study of Religion," *MTSR* 11 (1999): 325–39; Barrett and Frank C. Keil, "Conceptualizing a Nonnatural Entity: Anthropomorphism in God Concepts," *Cognitive Psychology* 31.3 (1996): 219–47.

92. Yet the excellent recent surveys of resurrection belief by Dag Øistein Endsjø and Outi Lehtipuu demonstrate the great variety of ancient Jewish and Greek views on resurrection, correcting oversimplifications of ancient resurrection beliefs that usually have the apologetic aim of contrasting Jesus's resurrection as something novel and exceptional. See Dag Øistein Endsjø, *Greek Resurrection Beliefs and the Success of Christianity* (New York: Palgrave MacMillan, 2009); Outi Lehtipuu, *Debates over the Resurrection of the Dead: Constructing Early Christian Identity* (Oxford: Oxford University Press, 2015).

93. While much New Testament scholarship considers the Mandaean John to be late and a secondary addition within Mandaeism, that view is opposed by Mandaean scholars. See Charles G. Häberl and James F. McGrath, eds., *The Mandaean Book of John: Critical Edition, Translation, and Commentary* (Berlin: de Gruyter, 2020), 9, 356–59.

94. The Samaritan question to Jesus concerning resurrection (Mark 12:18–27) is sometimes cited as evidence for belief in a general resurrection. But, even if historical, it cannot be used to

restriction of resurrection to the righteous is also the dominant view in Jewish sources before ca. 100 CE.[95] Mark's focus was on the resurrection of the righteous few, as the Jesus sectarians defined them. When a new eschatological prophet like Jesus came on the scene, the only question for debate was which resurrected prophet was he: John the Baptist, Elijah, or some other prophet? Similarly, Jesus anticipated that he and the living righteous of his own elect group would join the ranks of righteous elites from the past, the resurrected Abraham, Isaac, and Jacob (Matt 8:11–12). The historical Jesus anticipated the rule of a rival elite of righteous men: his twelve disciples seated on heavenly thrones, scrapping over who would be viceroy (Matt 19:28; Mark 10:35–45). This ideal reflects the movement's counter-elitist or "dissident" class aspirations as well as its actual patronage from an existing "subelite" or "local elite" that included Mary of Magdala and other women.[96] The historical Jesus's teaching about the resurrection of his followers as the righteous elite made it almost inevitable that, following his death, his followers would attribute an individual and especial form of resurrection to Jesus himself.

The lived-religion approach reveals a basic continuity in this regard between what Jesus taught about the role of elite righteous persons in the anticipated kingdom of God on earth and his followers' understanding of Jesus as an elite righteous person deserving of individual resurrection. The empty tomb narrative therefore contains valuable historical data insofar as its visionary production by a local elite patron (Mary of Magdala) corroborates Jesus's own counterelite ideology of a rival hierarchical kingdom to be established on earth whose membership would be strongly sectarian.[97] Jesus's view that resurrection would be restricted to an al-

---

mirror-read Jesus's understanding, as it is a hypothetical and ridiculing ad absurdum question. More relevant for understanding Jesus's understanding of resurrection is his abrupt shift to limiting discussion of resurrection to just three elite righteous men: Abraham, Isaac, and Jacob. Pace John P. Meier, "The Debate on the Resurrection of the Dead: An Incident from the Ministry of the Historical Jesus?," *JSNT* 77 (2000): 15.

95. For resurrection by righteous individuals, see 1 En. 22:1–4; 51:1–2; 61:4; 62:14–16; 91:10; 92:3; 108:9–12; Dan 12:1–3; 2 Macc 6–7, 15; Pss. Sol. 2:31; 3:10–12, 13–14; 4Q385; 4Q521; 2 Bar. 30:1; 50:2–3, 10–12. For general resurrection from the late first century onward, see 4 Ezra 7:32, 37; T. Benj. 10:6–8; LAE 13:3b–6 (Israel only); LAB 3:10; Sib. Or. 4:183–192.

96. Terminology from Milton Moreland, "The Jesus Movement in the Villages of Roman Galilee: Archaeology, Q, and Modern Anthropological Theory," in *Oral Performance, Popular Tradition, and Hidden Transcript in Q*, ed. Richard A. Horsley (Atlanta: SBL Press, 2006), 163; Giovanni B. Bazzana, *Kingdom of Bureaucracy: The Political Theology of Village Scribes in the Sayings Gospel Q*, BETL 274 (Leuven: Peeters, 2015), 4; Sarah E. Rollens, *Framing Social Criticism in the Jesus Movement*, WUNT 2.374 (Tübingen: Mohr Siebeck, 2014), 197; cf. William E. Arnal, *Jesus and the Village Scribes: Galilean Conflicts and the Setting of Q* (Minneapolis: Fortress, 2001), 159.

97. Cf., e.g., James G. Crossley, *Jesus and the Chaos of History: Redirecting the Life of the Historical Jesus* (Oxford: Oxford University Press, 2015), 64–95, 193–201.

leged righteous remnant dominated by his own followers became the grounds for his followers to proclaim that Jesus himself had been raised to the highest ranks of the righteous dead. Furthermore, the especial resurrection of a righteous rival elite (the Jesus movement) stands in continuity with earlier and contemporary Jewish expectations that righteous persons would be especial recipients of resurrection, a claim typically made in the absence of any conception of a universal end-times resurrection.[98] The local-elitist assumptions that underlie Mary Magdalene's vision of the empty tomb, therefore, provide corroboration that the early Jesus movement constituted a group of elite pretenders, a wannabe counterelite.

Alternative Historicity

These conclusions should now be developed and generalized with the aim of contributing back to the humanities. The possibilities here are numerous, dependent as they are on the particular interest of each researcher, which might include such foci as decolonizing the text, analyzing the gendered aspects of visionary experiences, class analysis, ableist assumptions about Mary Magdalene's "healing," or cross-cultural comparison of vision ontologies, among dozens of other potential options. Mary Magdalene's upper-class identity and Jesus's pretensions to that class lend support, for example, to Emma Cohen's findings that the higher involvement of women in religious possession behavior is not wholly reducible to women's repression in society. As a member of the Ngāpuhi and Te Rarawa peoples, I have a special interest in the way that Māori conceptions of *moemoeā* (visions/dreams) might draw out unstated presuppositions that operate in more Eurocentric visionary and oneiric ontologies.

I wish here, however, to conclude by reflecting on some implications of the visionary basis of Mark 16 for our analysis of the gospel's historicity. If we accept that early Christians lent a very high estimation to visionary sources when formulating and transmitting traditions about Jesus, this introduces a *fundamental uncertainty* to any modern reconstruction of the Jesus of history. Past quests have

98. E.g., Jeremiah and Onias (2 Macc 15:12–16); an army of righteous dead alongside the angelic army (1QM XII, 1–2, 7–8; XV, 15; see Deane Galbraith, "The Origin of Archangels: Ideological Mystification of Nobility," in *Class Struggle in the New Testament*, ed. Robert J. Myles [Lanham, MD: Lexington/Fortress Academic, 2019], 209–40); Adam, Abel, Abraham (T. Ab. 11; 13); various early human ancestors (1 En. 70:4; cf. Apoc. Pet. 4–6); Enoch, Seth, Abraham, Isaac and Jacob, then the twelve sons of Jacob, then other righteous Jews (T. Benj. 10:6–10). See generally Klaus Berger, *Die Auferstehung des Propheten und die Erhöhung des Menschensohnes: Traditionsgeschichtliche Untersuchungen zur Deutung des Geschickes Jesu in frühchristlichen Texten*, SUNT 13 (Göttingen: Vandenhoeck & Ruprecht, 1976); Rudolf Pesch, "Zur Entstehung des Glaubens an die Auferstehung Jesu: Ein Vorschlag zur Diskussion," *Theologische Quartalschrift* 153.3 (1973): 201–28.

greatly underestimated, and sometimes even disregarded, the radical epistemic limitations entailed by the existence of the many and important visionary sources that underlie the gospels. Moreover, when we are dealing with a visionary community, there are probably many "known unknowns": traditions that originated from visionary sources but which in their current form no longer contain clear indicia of visionary experiences. The early Jesus movement valorized their visionary sources as a royal road to the knowledge of some of the most important episodes in their biographies of Jesus. What was really worth saying about Jesus would be known from visions. For these reasons, visionary sources disrupt modern attempts to distinguish what is veridical and nonveridical within early Jesus traditions.

Yet we can view this conclusion positively *if* Jesus scholarship is prepared to expand its historical inquiry to consider alternative cultural conceptions of historicity. What first presents as fundamental uncertainty may resurrect this dead-end of scholarship by offering a contribution to a wider discussion taking place about non-Western and nonhegemonic forms of historical consciousness.

Anthropologist Charles Stewart relates how villagers of Naxos recount, on the basis of dream visions, how Egyptian Christians arrived there in late antiquity. These visions continued to be received intermittently for two centuries, inspiring searches for lost and buried icons allegedly belonging to the Egyptians.[99] In this process, the villagers do not *remember* the past; they *create* the past via visions and then *re-create* the past in rituals such as digging for icons. Compare the early Jesus movement's rituals such as the Lord's Supper and baptism, which not only dissolve members into Jesus but in this process blur past and present. As at Naxos, "affective resonance rather than chronology holds various events together."[100] In contrast to modern historical archives, which "objectivize and fix the past," the Jesus movement and Naxos villagers mobilize the "mythic power" of the past, which is thereby "reexperienced in the present."[101] The origins of Christianity are always already multitemporal and heterochronous, frustrating modernist attempts to distinguish the historical Jesus from his (later) cultic manifestations, yet they also provide rich resources for considering alternative constructions of historicity.[102]

Furthermore, the empty tomb vision-narrative presents a different *mode* of historytelling, due to its claim to be revealed by a visionary figure. When two Afro-Cubans informed anthropologist Stephan Palmié that they saw the ghost of an elderly slave Tomás had attached himself to him, he did not "transcribe" these

99. Charles Stewart, *Dreaming and Historical Consciousness in Island Greece* (Chicago: University of Chicago Press, 2017).

100. Stewart, *Dreaming*, 2.

101. Stewart, *Dreaming*, 2.

102. Cf. Maurice Halbwachs, *On Collective Memory*, ed. and trans. Lewis A. Coser (Chicago: University of Chicago Press, 1992), 118.

reports into more rational explanations, as the apologist and counterapologist might try to rationalize Jesus's resurrection accounts. Palmié instead analyzed their vision as historical discourse that was "encoded in an idiom different from the one with which we feel at home."[103] Such an idiom does not present a past "ontologically sealed off from the present," which would then necessitate our representation of that past.[104] It is rather an idiom in which the dead are still active in presenting their story to us, a melding of present and past generations (*Generationenverschmelzung*).[105] History's alternative idioms also include possession behavior, as for the Sakalava commemorations studied by Michael Lambek. Possessions of youthful mediums by brigand ancestral spirits constitute one mode of Sakalava historytelling. It is a mode "constituted by means of a different historicity," in which the ancestral world becomes ontologically present through the possessed youths, merging past and present. Sakalava possession thereby offers "a different way of collectively being in time."[106] Likewise, through visionary sources, the early Jesus movement participated in and produced its past within its own present.

Early Christian visions of the past created a historicity that afforded direct access to the life of Jesus in a manner that was simultaneously constitutive of their present-day community. A well-known Māori proverb encapsulates this blending of past and present, its commitment to the past which at once builds a communal hope for the future: *Kia whakatōmuri te haere whakamua* "I walk backwards into the future with my eyes fixed on my past." As I have begun to do here, the Next Quest for the historical Jesus should continue to investigate the alternative historical consciousness that produced the early Jesus movement's visionary sources, including the distinct ontology and temporality it entails, as one way of contributing to a broader conversation about historical consciousness taking place within the humanities.

103. Stephan Palmié, *Wizards and Scientists: Explorations in Afro-Cuban Modernity and Tradition* (Durham: Duke University Press, 2002), 3.

104. Palmié, *Wizards and Scientists*, 3.

105. Norbert Lohfink employs this (Gadamer-inspired?) term to describe the multitemporality he assumes underlies Deut 5; see *Die Väter Israels im Deuteronomium: Mit einer Stellungnahme von Thomas Römer*, OBO 111 (Göttingen: Vandenhoeck & Ruprecht, 1991), 20.

106. Michael Lambek, "On Being Present to History: Historicity and Brigand Spirits in Madagascar," *Hau: Journal of Ethnographic Theory* 6.1 (2016): 317–41.

10

Myth and Mythmaking

Stephen Young

At the risk of adapting what must be an exhausted Morpheus from *The Matrix* for yet another new setting, "What if I told you" that there was a figure from Mediterranean antiquity who had a boundless capacity to generate textual afterlives with overwhelming cultural significance in the history of Europe and its violent colonial legacies? While Jesus of Nazareth fits the bill, ancient historians could be forgiven for thinking first of Homer. As one such historian put it, "the greatest of the early poets gave rise to an unappeasable biographical itch. As with nature, so too with Homer: literary history abhors a vacuum."[1] Within this vacuum, mythmaking about Homer flourished and "Homer had to be equipped with a genealogy, a pedigree, a place of origin, a *curriculum vitae*, a list of titles, a knowable death, and a place of burial. Out of necessity sprang an entire genre of writings about the life of Homer . . . that flourished throughout antiquity and spread into early modernity."[2] Such literary activity about Homer was sometimes competitive: stories about the poet serve to claim his legacy—and its considerable legitimacy—for cities, institutions, writers, and leaders.[3] Ancient writers did not simply reuse

---

1. James Porter, *Homer: The Very Idea* (Chicago: University of Chicago Press, 2021), 63.
2. Porter, *Homer*, 63.
3. To stick with Porter, see his discussion of Athenian claims to Homer: "Everything points to an attempt by Athens to claim and control the legacy of Homer and to reap cultural, ideological, and political benefits from this move, which is exactly what happened" (*Homer*, 20).

the myths attributed to Homer. They repeated, adapted, and wove myths about the poet that often captured just as much attention as the poet's own work while reshaping how his epic poetry was read.

Why bring up Homer in a chapter for a historical Jesus volume? When one writes about Homer, the category of myth, however one defines it, is by necessity included. Homer was known both to write and be the subject of extensive myth-making.[4] This recognition goes back to Greek writings of the classical through Roman periods. While the meanings of *mythos* shifted throughout this timeframe, Homer's association with myth remained constant.[5] Whether a Roman-period Greek philosopher like (pseudo-)Heraclitus having to distance Homer from any "stain of abominable myth" (i.e., unethical depictions of the gods) in his *Homeric Problems* (2.1), or modern scholars like Sarah Iles Johnston explaining Greek mythic networks, Homer is the critical node in Greek mythology.[6] One cannot discuss Greco-Roman myth without Homer.

Comparing Jesus to Homer raises the specter of myth. When it comes to early Christian writings, relevant similarities between Jesus and Homer press themselves upon us: one cannot discuss these texts' own myths about Christian origins without Jesus. He was both the source and subject of seemingly endless mythmaking. Though it was not common for the earliest Christian authors to attribute writings to Jesus, as a character in their narrative and dialogue texts he was a preeminent source of mythological content—similar to other nonwriters like Socrates, the Alexander of Plutarch's *On the Fortune or Virtue of Alexander*, and the Pauls of the Acts of the Apostles and the Acts of Paul and Thecla.[7] Early narrative texts about Jesus also engage in mythmaking about him similarly to the profusion of sources about Homer: they furnish him with genealogies, pedigrees, places of origin, a *curriculum vitae*, titles (in the loose sense) and roles, a know-

---

4. In writing that Homer was known as a preeminent source of mythology, I do not presume his personal historical existence. Debates about and (re)creations of Homer commenced already by the sixth century BCE. On "the Homeric question," see Barbara Graziosi, *Inventing Homer: The Early Reception of Epic* (Cambridge: Cambridge University Press, 2002). M. L. West's classic article illustrates the early profusion of mythmaking about Homer; see "The Invention of Homer," *CQ* 49 (1999): 364–82.

5. See Bruce Lincoln's discussion of the shifting understandings of *mythos*'s relationship to truth or history in *Theorizing Myth: Narrative, Ideology, and Scholarship* (Chicago: University of Chicago Press, 1999), 3–45.

6. Sarah Iles Johnston, *The Story of Myth* (Cambridge: Harvard University Press, 2018).

7. For detailed discussion of depictions of a scribal-literate Jesus, which become more common in late antique Christian sources, see Chris Keith, *Jesus' Literacy: Scribal Culture and the Teacher from Galilee*, LNTS 413 (London: T&T Clark, 2011), 156–63.

able death, and even places of burial.[8] As with the phenomenon Eva Mroczek elucidates in early Jewish literature, we find a Jesus in search of stories, texts, and character development within ancient Christian literate exchange.[9] In other words, and given how scholars of religious studies think about myth, we find a Jesus in search of myths.

MYTH AND DECISIVE STEPS WE MUST TAKE FOR STUDYING JESUS

Myth unfortunately remains underappreciated and misdirected in the study of Jesus. Discussion of the so-called mythicists who deny his historical existence overshadows the terminology. With the exception of David Litwa's *How the Gospels Became History: Jesus and Mediterranean Myths*, engagements with mythicists are often more the stuff of polemics than arenas that experiment with new avenues for thinking about Jesus.[10] While these are sometimes entertaining polemics, discussions of mythicism are a space where trained academics often have the instinct to ask everyone to calm down and think about basic nonpositivist methods for doing history. Accordingly, scholars who research the early narrative literature about Jesus can emerge with a suspicion of the category of myth. Why not leave well enough alone since myth has receded as a scholarly category in the study of Jesus anyway?

The Next Quest for the Historical Jesus should align historical Jesus studies with an array of conversations, categories, and questions that find traction in scholarly arenas beyond the usual field of historical Jesus. As is well known, it has long been a field whose conventions sync more with idiosyncrasies of New Testament studies than with conversations that animate the broader study of history, ancient Mediterranean religion, and literary theories. To adapt Musa Dube's arguments about biblical studies for the Next Quest's intervention in scholarship, this is why interest in criteria of authenticity, redaction criticism, and Great Men has come more instinctively to historical Jesus studies' (often) white male participants than attention to narrative strategies, imperial ideology, ethnicity, gender, hierarchy,

8. Helen Bond emphasizes alignments between the earliest extant narrative writing we have about Jesus, the Gospel of Mark, and biographical conventions for famous (even legendary) philosophers, poets, and leaders in Greco-Roman literary culture; see *The First Biography of Jesus: Genre and Meaning in Mark's Gospel* (Grand Rapids: Eerdmans, 2020), 38–71.

9. Eva Mroczek, *The Literary Imagination in Jewish Antiquity* (Oxford: Oxford University Press, 2016), 16, 53–58, 87–88.

10. Litwa engages with and critiques the mythicists in chapter 1 of his book, using the discussion to highlight mythicist neglect of actually interpreting early narratives about Jesus in the context of ancient mythological materials. See *How the Gospels Became History: Jesus and Mediterranean Myths* (New Haven: Yale University Press, 2019), 22–45.

class, and questions about whose voices are—and are not—represented in the production of New Testament gospel texts.[11]

Adjusting what counts as default or "normal" scholarship may *feel* radical to our traditional demographics of scholars who research Jesus, as though so-called niche "area studies" like gender, hierarchy, and ethnicity are displacing the questions of scholarship. But as Blossom Stefaniw explains in her article about feminist scholarship and the study of early Christianity: "It is not radical, it is simply *accurate*, to take very decisive steps toward fully feminist historiography given that patriarchal historiography ignores not just half the population, but is necessarily also colonial and racist and homophobic and ableist and classist historiography, treating the vast majority of the earth's population, past and present, as the scenery through which great men stride."[12] The Next Quest is about normalizing such decisive steps so that scholarship on Jesus can become more truthful, inclusive, and focused on history instead of reproducing the erasures, exploitations, and contortions necessary to make the study of Jesus an arena that ignores the masculine, imperial, and even enslaving ideologies that permeate the sources about him and structure their meanings.[13]

The categories of myth and mythmaking are resources that can facilitate our decisive steps. First, disciplined attention to myth orients our gaze around comparison (see also Meggitt's chapter). The category highlights the relevance of overlooked examples of religious, philosophical, and teacher figures who wielded myths—thus also displacing Great Man approaches to Jesus since he becomes one among others. Second, mythmaking forefronts questions about gender, ideology, and the strategies available for naturalizing different institutions, hierarchies

11. Musa Dube, *Postcolonial Feminist Interpretation of the Bible* (St. Louis: Chalice, 2000), esp. 15–21, and then, for focus on Jesus and scholarship about him, 127–95. On the typical Great Man orientation and neglect of class, see James Crossley and Robert J. Myles, *Jesus: A Life in Class Conflict* (Winchester: Zero, 2023), ix, 2–4, 14–20; Robert J. Myles, ed., *Class Struggle in the New Testament* (Lanham, MD: Lexington/Fortress Academic, 2019). For critical interrogation of criteria of authenticity, see Chris Keith and Anthony Le Donne, eds., *Jesus, Criteria, and the Demise of Authenticity* (London: T&T Clark, 2012).

12. Blossom Stefaniw, "Feminist Historiography and Uses of the Past," *Studies in Late Antiquity* 4 (2020): 282. See also the important article by Sara Parks, "'The Brooten Phenomenon': Moving Women from the Margins in Second-Temple and New Testament Scholarship," *BCT* 15 (2019): 46–64.

13. Since the examples discussed in this chapter do not focus on gender and enslaving, see Ronald Charles, *The Silencing of Slaves in Early Jewish and Christian Texts* (New York: Routledge, 2020), 103–31; Colleen Conway, *Behold the Man: Jesus and Greco-Roman Masculinity* (Oxford: Oxford University Press, 2008), 89–157; James Crossley, *Jesus and the Chaos of History: Redirecting the Life of the Historical Jesus* (Oxford: Oxford University Press, 2015), 134–62; J. Albert Harrill, *Slaves in the New Testament: Literary, Social, and Moral Dimensions* (Minneapolis: Fortress, 2006), 66–85.

of authority, and values. From this perspective, the Jesus of our sources himself emerges as a male Jewish mythmaker among others. Like Theudas, John the Baptizer, and Paul, Jesus adapts mythological materials, such as narratives about God and beginnings, to promote his legitimacy and expertise, to elaborate upon and naturalize his claims about the Jewish deity's eschatological plans, and to make his novel program of action and social hierarchies—with him at the top—feel traditional. Third, our texts about Jesus themselves emerge as examples of myth-making. Together these suggestions facilitate reimagining how Jesus's contemporaries plausibly conceptualized him. The competitive claims of distinction or even uniqueness made for Jesus within our sources thus emerge as decidedly ordinary or expected strategies, not as evidence to take at face value while reproducing Great Man approaches to history.[14] Myth helps make Jesus and the writings about him fit in their world while also urging the decisive reorienting steps we need in our scholarship.

MYTH, MYTHMAKING, AND ASKING QUESTIONS ABOUT JESUS

To define myth is implicitly to offer a theory of it.[15] A definition already presumes which questions, interests, and even voices get to have a say in framing what is being defined.[16] Reflecting the interests of scholars in religious studies, it is common to distinguish between the content and the function of myth when engineering a definition. In other words, some researchers define myth by asking what kinds of things have to be talked about for something to be a myth. Common candidates have included gods, stories about the creation of the cosmos, narratives about the origins of a nation, and tales about the ancient ancestors of a people or founders of a city. Meanwhile, others urge that it is best to define myth by asking what social or political function myths serve. Do they promote social cohesion, create group identity, elevate one class of people above others, authorize certain institutions

14. For a brief accessible discussion of how "Great Man" approaches to history result in uncritical and untruthful erases of history, see Sarah Maza, *Thinking about History* (Chicago: University of Chicago Press, 2017), 10–44.

15. For an extended version of the following discussion of myth and mythmaking, see the introduction in Stephen Young, *Paul among the Mythmakers: Sins, Gods, and Scriptures* (Edinburgh: Edinburgh University Press, forthcoming).

16. For an important discussion that emphasizes how to offer a definition is also to theorize, see Russell McCutcheon, "Myth," in *Guide to the Study of Religion*, ed. W. Braun and R. T. McCutcheon (New York: Cassell, 2000), 190–208. For collections of essays that interrogate and advocate a variety of approaches to myth, see Laurie Patton and Wendy Doniger, eds., *Myth and Method* (Charlottesville: University of Virginia Press, 1996); Kevin Schilbrack, ed., *Thinking through Myths: Philosophical Perspectives* (New York: Routledge, 2002).

and practices, entertain, or explain parts of lived reality?[17] Rather than accepting this dichotomy, it is better to explore myth's content and function together in order to see how they can facilitate reimagining Jesus and the early narratives about him.

Content must be examined first. For this chapter, myth means a story involving gods or other superhuman agents. Right away this is a fraught definition. To offer a parallel example, there are well-known critiques of assuming that religion must involve gods.[18] What about "religions" that do not feature beliefs about gods, so the critique goes? Similarly, to circumscribe myth with gods is contested. Following an important path in religious studies, this chapter deploys myth as an etic and redescriptive or "second-order" category.[19] In other words, its use of myth need not reflect how ancient people wrote about *mythos* or *fabula*, which would be an emic, as opposed to etic, approach.[20] Scholars need not pretend that our definitions of myth arise inductively from studying everything anyone has categorized as a myth. This chapter's approach is thus not invalidated by examples of things that have been called myth but lack gods. It is more useful to specify a range of materials and explain how putting them together is productive.[21] Focusing on stories involving gods or other superhuman agents, how they communicate, whom they appoint, their temples, their ethnic affiliations, and their plans highlights the vast array of comparative opportunities between narrative literature about Jesus and other Jewish, Greek, and Roman ancient Mediterranean sources.

17. For discussions of interests in content versus function in the history of scholarship, see Robert Segal, *Myth: A Very Short Introduction* (Oxford: Oxford University Press, 2004), 1–10. For an example in biblical studies, see Debra Scoggins Ballentine, *The Conflict Myth and the Biblical Tradition* (Oxford: Oxford University Press, 2015), 2–3.

18. An important internal critique of religious studies focuses on its history of reinscribing Western (esp. Protestant Christian) norms for what "religion" is via its construction of categories like religion or world religions that incessantly focus on "beliefs" about gods. See Timothy Fitzgerald, *The Ideology of Religious Studies* (Oxford: Oxford University Press, 2000); Tomoko Masuzawa, *The Invention of World Religions* (Chicago: University of Chicago Press, 2005).

19. For a recent discussion of comparison and the usefulness of etic, second-order categories in the study of early Christianity, see John Kloppenborg, *Christ's Associations: Connecting and Belonging in the Ancient City* (New Haven: Yale University Press, 2019), 4–8, 18–19.

20. See Litwa's discussion of how ancient writers theorized *mythos* and *fabula* in relation to *historia* in *Jesus and Mediterranean Myths*, 1–19.

21. This approach follows Jonathan Z. Smith's argument that we should approach the concepts we use for analysis (e.g., "religion") as second-order categories that we create for the purposes of comparison; see *Imagining Religion: From Babylon to Jonestown* (Chicago: University of Chicago Press, 1982), xi. For a helpful discussion of what Smith advocates, and how it is not a denial of the reality of religious practices outside of scholarly naming of them, see Kevin Schilbrack, "A Realist Social Ontology of Religion," *Religion* 47 (2017): 161–78.

Having focused on content, we turn now to function. Research in religious studies has increasingly attended to the politics of myth. For example, Bruce Lincoln's influential work analyzes myth as "ideology in narrative form."[22] This marks a turn to questions about social significance. Myth becomes what people do when authorizing something, creating or reproducing social hierarchies, or engaging in other activities that can be labeled as social formation.[23] Thus, Russell McCutcheon advocates for an approach to myth as "a *technique* or *strategy*" and "as a class of *social argumentation* found in all human cultures," such that we should "entertain the possibility that myths are not things akin to nouns, but *active processes* akin to verbs."[24]

If myth is a "class of social argumentation," we can explore the various forms it takes. It turns out there is a limited selection of discursive strategies for transforming "a contingent set of human preferences advanced by interested actors" into "the product of nature and necessity"—a process called naturalization.[25] Let's say you prefer, benefit from, or just feel comfortable with a particular institution (e.g., your mosque, church, or synagogue), set of values (e.g., no sex outside of marriage), social hierarchy (e.g., men in authority over women), or even collection of categories for thinking about your world (e.g., everyone is either a man or a woman). You may then gravitate toward narratives in which these things are not

---

22. Lincoln, *Theorizing Myth*.

23. For what McCutcheon means by social formation: "'Social formation' is of use not only in the study of how new social organizations develop but also when studying how they are institutionalized, maintained over time and place, how they are contested, and, eventually, come to an end . . . 'social formation' nicely represents not only the ongoing work of bringing an imagined social group into existence but also the sleight of hand in making it appear always to have existed." See *Critics Not Caretakers: Redescribing the Public Study of Religion* (Albany: SUNY Press, 2001), 25. Jason Redden critically overviews how McCutcheon and Burton Mack deploy the category of social formation, noting in particular that their analyses operate at the level of groups and not individual actors in "Social Formation in the Study of Religion," *Religion Compass* 9 (2015): 501–11. For a well-theorized discussion of social formation that interrogates the relevant individual actors and strategies involved in creating groupness, see Rogers Brubaker, *Ethnicity without Groups* (Cambridge: Harvard University Press, 2004), 7–63.

24. McCutcheon, "Myth," 199–200.

25. Lincoln, *Theorizing Myth*, 149 (for the quotations). On naturalization, see Craig Martin, *A Critical Introduction to the Study of Religion*, 2nd ed. (New York: Routledge, 2017), 74–83; Erin Roberts, "Myth, Our Bloodless Battleground," in *Christian Tourist Attractions, Mythmaking, and Identity Formation*, ed. Erin Roberts and Jennifer Eyl (London: Bloomsbury, 2019), 9–17. See also McCutcheon's point that naturalization treats "specific social values *as if* they were inevitable and universal. . . . Myths present *one particular* and therefore contestable viewpoint as if it were an 'agreement that has been reached' by 'we the people' . . . By means of a disguised or undetected ideological slippage, 'is' becomes 'ought'" ("Myth," 204).

your preferences because you inherited or benefit from them. No, instead they are universal and foundational, part of the fabric of reality from the beginning. For an example of such a narrative, "Men are more naturally leaders because God made men bolder and women more emotional from the beginning." In this way a social hierarchy with men at the top transforms into an expression of "just the way things are," and it gets attached to a variety of other norms. This contested hierarchy thus becomes seemingly natural through the strategy of depicting its social arrangements as divinely established in our origins.

Such ways of imagining the world are strategies for naturalization, and enacting them is what scholars refer to as mythmaking. As Erin Roberts emphasizes, mythmaking often involves stories about cosmic, ethnic, or institutional origins.[26] Stories about origins are one strategy for naturalization. A related and often overlapping strategy is to depict something as divinely established and planned, or to present it as prefigured or commanded in sacred, foundational, or ancient texts. The earliest writings about Jesus exemplify both mythic strategies for naturalization.

JESUS THE MYTHMAKER AMONG OTHER INDEPENDENT JEWISH MYTHMAKERS

The New Testament gospels depict Jesus as an independent, noninstitutionally authorized Jewish mythmaker. This is how contemporaries—whether Jesus's own or, more to the point, audiences of the gospels—would have recognized him. There is a broad ancient Mediterranean phenomenon here.[27] A variety of religious and philosophical experts innovatively wove together mythic materials that were known among their consumers. Often these materials were prestigious myths: characters, stories, locations, gods, and texts that were already charged with ethnic, civic, or notable heritage importance.

Sarah Iles Johnston and Fritz Graf influentially sketched a related model for the experts in the afterlife behind the Bacchic gold tablets.[28] These tablets were inscribed sheets whose texts position an initiate within a web of repurposed mythological allusions to Orpheus, Eleusis, Dionysus, Persephone, underworld geography, and ideas about the situations a deceased soul may face there. The experts wove these mythic resources together to present a scenario in which potential initiates have a condition to which they can offer a solution and thus a superior

---

26. Roberts, "Myth."

27. See chapter 1 of Young, *Paul among the Mythmakers*.

28. Fritz Graf and Sarah Iles Johnston, *Ritual Texts for the Afterlife: Orpheus and the Bacchic Gold Tablets*, 2nd ed. (New York: Routledge, 2013), 66–135.

experience in the afterlife. As such, the self-styled Orphic experts tied their after-life ritual into known, established, and prestigious loci of mythic authority.[29] The effect was the promotion, legitimatization, and naturalization of their service.

Johnston further argues that differences between the eschatological details across the tablets do not simply indicate variation due to geographical or temporal distance between them. The variations are marks of competition: these afterlife experts had to compete for recognition. Some divergences between parallel details in tablets may indicate competitive modification. In other words, if you want to promote yourself as the true expert in knowledge of the underworld against an-other self-styled Orphic expert on the other side of the marketplace, you might alter the location of a key tree in the underworld and demonstrate your superior expertise accordingly.[30] As I have argued elsewhere, Alexander of Abonoteichus, the apostle Paul, and Christian teachers like Valentinus and Marcus are likewise notable examples of independent, freelance, or self-authorized religious experts who competitively adapted myths to promote their expertise.[31]

Jewish sources beyond Paul's Letters likewise feature self-authorized myth-makers. To offer a few examples: in his *Jewish Antiquities*, Josephus writes of "a certain imposter" (*goēs tis*) who "persuaded the majority of the masses to take up their possessions and to follow him to the Jordan River. He stated that he was a prophet and that at his command the river would be parted and would provide them an easy passage" (*A.J.* 20.97 [Feldman, LCL]). We lack further evidence for Theudas beyond this passage in a hostile source. It is plausible to speculate that his claims about parting the Jordan drew on Jewish mythological lore relating

---

29. On understanding claims about Orpheus and Orphism as authority-conferring strategies for competitive positions and rituals about the afterlife, divine world, and related matters, see Radcliffe G. Edmonds, "Extra-Ordinary People: Mystai and Magoi, Magicians and Orphics in the Derveni Papyrus," *CP* 103 (2008): 27, 30–36. Notably, Edmonds has repeatedly critiqued the understandings of Dionysus mythology operative for scholars like Graf and Johnston; see his "Tearing Apart the Zagreus Myth: A Few Disparaging Remarks on Orphism and Original Sin," *ClAnt* 18 (1999): 35–73; responded to by Alberto Bernabé, "La toile de Pénélope: A-t-il existé un mythe orphique sur Dionysos et les Titans?," *RHR* 219 (2002): 401–33. Even so, Edmonds and Graf and Johnston converge when it comes to explaining the Bacchic gold tablets' mythmaking and "Orphic" expertise as strategies for legitimacy.

30. For their model of competitive innovation, see Graf and Johnson, *Ritual Texts for the Afterlife*, 71–73, 80, 94, 111, 119, 194.

31. Young, *Paul among the Mythmakers*; see also Young, "The Marcosian Redemption: Myth-making, the Afterlife, and Early Christian Religiosity," *JECH* 6 (2016): 77–110. See also Heidi Wendt's excellent study of self-authorized religious expertise in the Roman period Mediterra-nean, on which my work and others' build: *At the Temple Gates: The Religion of Freelance Experts in the Roman Empire* (Oxford: Oxford University Press, 2016).

both to the exodus and the entry into the promised land through the Jordan River (Josh 3–4), which itself is a reuse of exodus myths. In this way Theudas adapts the exodus and promised-land-entry myths in ways that further resonate with mythology about a divine warrior with control over the sea and waters who may share that authority with his human agent.[32]

Similarly with the so-called Egyptian, according to Josephus's discussion in his *Jewish Antiquities*, he called himself a prophet and led his followers to the Mount of Olives outside Jerusalem, where he claimed that at his command the city's walls would fall (*A.J.* 20.168–172; the account of the Egyptian in *B.J.* 2.259–263 lacks the material about Jerusalem's walls). The impression is an eschatological reuse of Israelite conquest mythology.[33] We can also redescribe John the Baptizer as an independent teacher who adapted prominent ancestral myths about the wilderness, the Jordan River, exile, and restoration in his eschatological religious practices.[34]

When discussing Jesus himself and myth, it is important to disrupt the durable Judaism versus Hellenism dichotomy, which, "despite decades of critiques," as Annette Yoshiko Reed explains, "remains re-inscribed by habituated patterns of selectivity in scholarly training and practice."[35] Myth should not be understood as something essentially Hellenistic in opposition to story or history, which are then taken as Jewish. Models such as the "borrowing" of ideas or "influence" often accompany the Judaism-versus-Hellenism dichotomy, as though we require a special explanation for how Jewish writers like Paul or the author of the Gospel of Mark could have wielded Greek and Roman mythological materials.[36] Our models should not presume that Greek and Roman mythological presences in writings about Jesus indicate "borrowing" or being "influenced" by something from the

32. For discussion of relevant passages, especially Ps 88:26 LXX and the Josephus passage about Theudas, see J. R. Daniel Kirk and Stephen L. Young, "'I Will Set His Hand to the Sea': Psalm 88:26 LXX and Christology in Mark," *JBL* 133 (2014): 333–40; on mythology about divine warriors and the sea, see Ballentine, *Conflict Myth*.

33. E. P. Sanders makes this eschatological point about both the Egyptian for conquest mythology and Theudas for exodus mythology in *Jesus and Judaism* (Philadelphia: Fortress, 1985), 171–72.

34. Joan Taylor exemplifies this common point about John and the Jewish mythological framework for his program in *The Immerser: John the Baptist within Second Temple Judaism* (Grand Rapids: Eerdmans, 1997), 101–49; see also Tucker Ferda, "John the Baptist, Isaiah 40, and the Ingathering of the Exiles," *JSHJ* 10 (2012): 154–88; Sanders, *Jesus and Judaism*, 92–93.

35. Annette Yoshiko Reed, "Writing Jewish Astronomy in the Early Hellenistic Age: The Enochic *Astronomical Book* as Aramaic Wisdom and Archival Impulse," *DSD* 24 (2017): 4–5.

36. For a fuller critique of Judaism versus Hellenism and associated models like borrowing or influence, see Stephen Young, "'Let's Take the Text Seriously': The Protectionist Doxa of Mainstream New Testament Studies," *MTSR* 32 (2020): 345–54.

outside. As Robyn Walsh emphasizes, the writers of New Testament Gospels were literate men who wrote within Greco-Roman literary cultures wherein knowledge of Homer and other foundational texts in educational practices (e.g., Hesiod, Euripides) were basic in the literate repertoire.[37] It is thus unsurprising that interpreters elucidate all manner of reuses, resonances, competitive allusions, and engagements with Homeric and other Greco-Roman myths in the gospels.[38]

Given that it is easy for readers to think of resonances with Homeric epic in the gospels as myth, in what follows I focus instead on Jewish myths given the long-standing aversion in biblical studies to thinking about Jewish materials as myth. The point is to think of Jesus's own reuses of Jewish stories about his ancestral deity, that deity's eschatological plans, ethnic and cultic lore, and prophetic paradigms as, in fact, Jesus's mythmaking—and not just as his theology, "use of Scripture," or other categories internal to New Testament studies.

In the Gospel of Mark, Jesus adapts Israelite myths to explain his actions, naturalize hierarchies with himself at the top, delegitimize his opponents, and authorize some of his positions about the Jewish high God and his temple. In Mark 1:14–15 he announces the dictatorship or empire of God—a concept that itself rings bells from Jewish ancestral texts—in his proclamation of the eschatological good news of God (see also the chapters by Galbraith and Crossley on apocalypticism and millenarianism respectively). As numerous interpreters have shown, the significance of the good news here resonates with a series of Jewish myths about God's long-term imperial plans and with royal ideologies of kings who administer theocratic empires on behalf of gods who appointed them. This is not a Jesus who "subverts" imperial ideologies, but one who mobilizes them on behalf of his God's own imperial and theocratic empire.[39]

---

37. Robyn Walsh, *The Origins of Early Christian Literature: Contextualizing the New Testament within Greco-Roman Literary Culture* (Cambridge: Cambridge University Press, 2021), 108–9, 117–18, 127–28, 135–36, 141–43. For Walsh's broader point about the writers of the New Testament Gospels as participants in wider literary culture, see 105–200. See also Dennis MacDonald, *The Homeric Epics and the Gospel of Mark* (New Haven: Yale University Press, 2000), 4–14. Walsh and MacDonald are developing what is a basic point about the place of Homer's poetry in Greco-Roman literate educational practices; e.g., Raffaella Cribiore, *Gymnastics of the Mind: Greek Education in Hellenistic and Roman Egypt* (Princeton: Princeton University Press, 2001), 197–98; Richard Hunter, *The Measure of Homer: The Ancient Reception of the Iliad and the Odyssey* (Cambridge: Cambridge University Press, 2018), 4–8, 15–24.

38. In particular, see Marianne Bonz, *The Past as Legacy: Luke-Acts and Ancient Epic* (Minneapolis: Fortress, 2000); Litwa, *Jesus and Mediterranean Myths*; Litwa, *Iesus Deus: The Early Christian Depiction of Jesus as a Mediterranean God* (Minneapolis: Fortress, 2014); MacDonald, *Homeric Epics.*

39. James Crossley argues for wielding more overtly imperial, dictatorial, and theocratic

In Mark 4:10–12, Jesus presents his enigmatic teaching as an enactment of Isa 6:8–10, as though his God is fulfilling a prophesied threat through Jesus. Jesus casts himself as a significant actor in a Jewish eschatological scheme that draws on ethnic mythological lore about Elijah and the Son of Man in Mark 9:12–13. His temple tantrum in Mark 11:15–18 mobilizes Jeremiah 7 to present his actions in terms of God's judgment on temple leadership. And Mark 12:10–11 has Jesus re-using material from Ps 118 about God's temple to frame the significance of what's happening when competing Jewish leaders reject him. Jesus combines novel adaptation of mythic materials (presenting his presence as the fulfillment of a return from exile and *Christos* myth from Isa 61) with demonstrations of literary expertise involving a sacred book in Luke 4:16–30.[40]

A thread running through many of these passages in which Jesus wields Jewish mythological resources is competitive polemic against his fellow Jewish opponents: Jesus naturalizes his expertise, movement, and teachings about Israel's God by positioning himself as a prophesied actor in Jewish eschatological myths. This necessarily delegitimizes his opponents (more on them below) since, according to Jesus's competitive rhetoric, they do not understand their ancestral deity's plans and laws, ultimately oppose him, and thus do not credibly represent God.[41]

It has become so second nature for most readers of the New Testament Gospels to identify with Jesus that his claims about divine authorization have become unremarkable. So too has the fact that he interprets sacred ancestral texts and proffers versions of ethnic history. But it is important to let the familiar become unfamiliar; for the unremarkable to be remarked upon. Jesus's claims to divine authorization are performing the invisible work of making his legitimacy feel obvious. This is why critical scholars should ask questions about naturalization: what strategies make certain hierarchies, attributions of authoritative status, and even understandings of God feel natural? From this perspective, it should be notable that the early narratives about Jesus constantly depict him claiming

---

terms to replace "kingdom of God" given the latter's domestication in contemporary discourse that empties it of its authoritarian and empire resonances; see *Jesus and the Chaos of History*, 63–95; see also Crossley and Myles, *Jesus*, 21, 106–9. Dube similarly emphasizes the importance of not effacing the imperial and violently hierarchical nature of Jesus's proclamation (*Postcolonial Feminist*, 127–95). For critiques of the dominance of a Jesus who subverts imperial and other hegemonic ideologies in New Testament studies, see Robert J. Myles, "The Fetish for a Subversive Jesus," *JSHJ* 14 (2016): 52–70.

40. For discussion of how this passage's representation of Jesus's literate skills would have resonated, see Keith, *Jesus' Literacy*, 142–45.

41. See also Mark 2:8–12, 23–28. Chris Keith likewise highlights the competitive contours of Jesus's rhetoric, also focusing on Matt 23 (*Jesus against the Scribal Elite: The Origins of the Conflict* [Grand Rapids: Baker Academic, 2014], 4, 58, 116–17).

divine authorization and crafting versions of Israelite history that culminate in the dictatorship of the God he proclaims, his role in its realization, and his "values" while invalidating his opponents or even the possibility of legitimate dissent.

This chapter's stress on Jesus as a specifically independent mythmaker develops the social theorist Pierre Bourdieu's insistence that a hierarchy of positions characterizes each field of cultural production and competition.[42] The hierarchy spans those on the dominant versus the dominated side. One's position in the field shapes not only their dispositions and tastes, but also the strategies available for establishing distinction and accumulating the available forms of capital.[43]

To use Bourdieu's best-known example, in an artistic field the dominant actors are the art dealers, museum administrators, and the artists patronized by them. They control institutional access and economic resources. Their ways of communicating, including the very categories they use, reflect their dominant positions and tend to naturalize the status quo's distribution of power (which favors them) through making it always feel natural and obvious as opposed to (socially) arbitrary.[44] Artists not associated with such institutions, however, occupy dominated positions in the field. Their strategies for distinction reflect the options available to them. Bourdieu highlights in particular the common rhetoric of disinterest among the dominated. They make a virtue of necessity (i.e., their dissociation from dominant institutions) and represent themselves as not doing art for business, money, or other interested reasons (like the sellout, impure artists patronized by museums), but instead art for art's sake. They do not produce art for the curators of the dominant institutions, but only for other legitimate (read: disinterested) people.

As Stanley Stowers has argued, we find a similar distribution of strategies for establishing distinction and accumulating different forms of capital among ancient Mediterranean religious experts.[45] Independent, freelance, or self-authorized (i.e., the nondominant) religious experts had a limited set of strategies available.[46]

42. See especially Pierre Bourdieu, *The Field of Cultural Production: Essays on Art and Literature*, ed. Randal Johnson (New York: Columbia University Press, 1993), 38–73, 82–86, 131–41.

43. Bourdieu, *Field of Cultural Production*, 38, 83–84.

44. On what Bourdieu means by (socially) arbitrary, see *Masculine Domination*, trans. R. Nice (Stanford: Stanford University Press, 1998), 3, 9.

45. Arguing for the utility of approaching ancient Mediterranean religion—including early Christianity—in terms of such fields and their dominant versus dominated experts has been a major focus of Stowers's recent work; see, e.g., "The Religion of Plant and Animal Offerings versus the Religion of Meanings, Essences, and Textual Mysteries," in *Ancient Mediterranean Sacrifice*, ed. J. W. Knust and Z. Várhelyi (Oxford: Oxford University Press, 2011), 35–56.

46. Wendt, *At the Temple Gates*, develops Stowers for a more full-orbed mapping of dominated (i.e., freelance) religious expertise in the ancient Mediterranean, while Walsh similarly

These actors gravitate to displays of textual mastery, works of power, and specialized knowledge, leveraging any prestigious ethnic or cultic statuses they could and also (I would add) reusing myths.[47]

It is instructive to think about portraits of Jesus in the gospels from this vantage point, and here Chris Keith's *Jesus against the Scribal Elite* proceeds in a similar direction. In the New Testament Gospels, Jesus is not a member of an established class that administers the temple. He is instead a newly arrived teacher in a Jewish field of competition.[48] Jesus clashes with other independent experts, the Pharisees, who, though also not inhabiting dominant positions, are more established in the field than Jesus. One of the ways Jesus contests their more established authority is to attack their disinterest, which is an expected strategy for distinction among intellectual experts. Think of Mark 7:6–13, Matt 23, and many of the other passages about Jesus's mythmaking briefly mentioned above. Jesus polemically delegitimates the Pharisees as hypocrites who reject God in favor of their own interests and greed. Unlike Jesus, they do not really understand their ancestral God, his laws, or eschatological plans. These gospels also depict a clash between Jesus and dominant Jewish figures with institutional position: the Sadducees and priests. In this case too, Jesus contests their authority and institutional legitimacy through attacks on their disinterest (e.g., Mark 11:27–33). Throughout these narratives Jesus naturalizes his expertise, often against his competitors, via the strategies available to independent experts: displays of interpretive and ethnic-historical expertise, works of power, claims of divine authorization and revelation, esoteric enigmatic teachings, and reuse of established myths.[49] Some, many, all, or none of these passages may reflect events that took place during the life of Jesus. The key point for the Next Quest, however, is that our earliest narratives about Jesus, despite their often competitive differences, conspicuously present him as a kind of myth-wielding expert that would have been recognizable or understandable to their readers. This image of Jesus is not incidental in these gospels.

---

develops such research to discuss the relative positions of different kinds of literate experts (*Early Christian Literature*, 121–27).

47. See Young, *Paul among the Mythmakers*. Keith correctly emphasizes that making a performance of using a text did not necessarily imply the literacy skills necessary to read it (*Jesus against the Scribal Elite*, 25–29).

48. See Sanders's similar point: *Jesus and Judaism*, 287–88.

49. On works of power and divinatory actions as another characteristic practice of independent religious experts in the ancient Mediterranean, see Jennifer Eyl, *Signs, Wonders, and Gifts: Divination in the Letters of Paul* (Oxford: Oxford University Press, 2019).

New Testament Gospels as Mythmaking about Jesus

While the New Testament Gospels present Jesus as a mythmaker, it is also important to imagine these texts as themselves mythmaking about Jesus. In terms of
content, these gospels are narratives about Jesus that relate him, his actions, and
his death to gods. They draw upon a limited set of characters and connect Jesus to
a network of wider mythological materials (i.e., Jewish Scriptures, eschatological
schemes, and scripts about their God) while setting Jesus in the originary period
of their movements. Their stories are furthermore tied to geographically specific
places. One can thus classify the gospels as mythological texts about Jesus that
align with key ways scholars of Greco-Roman antiquity define myth.[50] In other
words, if the New Testament Gospels were any other writings from the ancient
Mediterranean, readers would not hesitate to think of them as mythological texts
and to read them in comparison with others.

The New Testament Gospels are also ideology in narrative form. Each gospel
strategically crafts a founding figure (Jesus) whose actions and connections to
God legitimate the versions of cultural prestige, hierarchies, heritage in Israel's
sacred lore, and competitive interests favored by their writer(s) and the Christ
teachers with whom they associate.[51] This is not to say that every ideological effect
of these writings was reflectively intended by the writers, or that their operations
of power are always overt or repressive. Such flawed approaches to power prioritize individuals and their intentions while shifting our gaze away from questions
about structures, rhetorical effects, and the varied but intersecting gender, class,
ethnic, or free-enslaved positions people occupied that differently shaped the
significance a New Testament Gospel and its mythmaking about Jesus could have
for them.[52] Nor is focusing on ideological effects to sanction an allegorical interpretive method that privileges any possible social significance within historical
analysis, as though Matt 16:18–19 necessarily indicates it was a writing of "early
Catholicism" that fabricated a Petrine lineage for future popes. Interrogating the
narrative strategies of or potential competitive relationships between the gos-

50. For example, Johnston, *Story of Myth*, 8–11.

51. For a similar model for thinking about the Synoptic Gospels, see Stanley Stowers, "The
Concept of 'Community' and the History of Early Christianity," *MTSR* 25 (2011): 249–53; Walsh,
Origins of Early Christian Literature, 5–7, 14, 131–33, 134–94.

52. As Candida Moss has shown, these differing positions of privilege include the asymmetrical relationships between collaborative parties in the writing process of early Christian texts,
e.g., "authors" and their enslaved "secretary" laborers who contributed to the meanings of the
texts. See "The Secretary: Enslaved Workers, Stenography, and the Production of Early Christian
Literature," *JTS* 74.1 (2023): 22–23, 54–56.

pels is gloriously complicated, speculative, and experimental just like all ancient historical study.

To offer one example, I align with a group of scholars who think the Gospel of Mark does not require adherence to Jewish laws among (gentile?) followers of Jesus, whereas a key goal of the writer of Matthew was to usurp, redirect, or otherwise competitively rewrite Mark's position on this and other matters. If one follows this line of thought, it matters that Mark 7:19's *katharizōn panta ta brōmata* seems to interpret Mark 7's story about Jesus's legal competition with Pharisees and scribes about ceremonial washing to mean Jesus set aside some of his ancestral dietary laws.[53] The writer of Matthew, conversely, not only deletes the *katharizōn panta ta brōmata* interpretation of Jesus's action in his rewriting of the story (Matt 15:1–20), but also—and uniquely in the New Testament Gospels—has Jesus proclaim the permanence of the law while polemicizing against anyone who teaches others they can relax even the smallest of its commands (Matt 5:18–19). Matthew 28:20 even concludes the Gospel with Jesus's imperial instructions that involve teaching future disciples "to keep all which I commanded you," which, as the writer has already made a point of emphasizing, includes all parts of Jewish law. Some interpreters venture further and explain that the Gospel of Mark was "a biographical expression not just of concepts central to Paul, but of Paul's own persona . . . Mark primes audience expectations to Paul's advantage . . . [and] was quite deliberate and consistent in forging such connections" whereas the Gospel of Matthew was a polemical rewriting of Mark because its writer opposed Pauline influence.[54] In any version of these scenarios, the writers of Mark and Matthew (re)wrote narratives about Jesus that made their competing positions simply expressions of or obedience to their divinely appointed founding figure:

53. This is an incredibly complicated and debated issue. Numerous questions must be distinguished. Did Jesus himself obviate divinely revealed ethnic dietary laws? Did Jesus and others even think he was doing so or just taking a position in a Jewish legal debate? Does Mark 7:19 attribute significance to Jesus's actions that Jesus himself would have rejected? For a discussion that takes seriously how Jesus himself, as best we can tell, did not "reject" Jewish laws, see Matthew Thiessen, *Jesus and the Forces of Death: The Gospels' Portrayal of Ritual Impurity within First-Century Judaism* (Grand Rapids: Baker Academic, 2020), 1–42, 187–96.

54. For the quote, see Heidi Wendt, "Secrecy as Pauline Influence on the Gospel of Mark," *JBL* 140 (2021): 580. There is a long history of interpreting Mark as written in support of, allegorically rewriting, or in general "influenced by" Paul. For recent discussion, Eve-Marie Becker, Troels Engberg-Pedersen, and Mogens Müller, eds., *Mark and Paul: Comparative Essays Part II, For and Against Pauline Influence on Mark*, BZNW 199 (Berlin: de Gruyter, 2014). On Matthew as a rejection of Mark as too Pauline, see David Sim, "Matthew's Use of Mark: Did Matthew Intend to Supplement or to Replace His Primary Source?," *NTS* 57 (2011): 178; Sim, "Matthew 7.21–23: Further Evidence of Its Anti-Pauline Perspective," *NTS* 53 (2007): 325–43.

Jesus. Mark and Matthew are thus themselves forms of mythmaking about Jesus that naturalize the social hierarchies, values, and understandings of God their writers preferred.

These approaches to Mark, Matthew, Jewish law, and competition over Paul's legacy are by no means accepted by all critical scholars. But regardless of one's position on the topic, as Chris Keith has shown, the writers of the New Testament Gospels were engaged in a project of "competitive textualization" that sometimes involved "usurping" or "cannibalizing" earlier established texts (e.g., Matthew's use of Mark and Jewish sacred texts) to "siphon" or otherwise redirect their authority.[55] Sometimes the competitive textualization was polemical, other times not, but it did involve writers positioning their texts as authoritative access points to earlier prestigious texts.[56] A key strategy for allowing Christ teachers to siphon, or even monopolize, the authority of Jewish Scriptures plus Israel's prestigious heritage was by depicting Jesus, his actions, and teachings as their own prophesied culmination. Paula Fredriksen memorably explains this phenomenon: early writers about Jesus gave him "an aura of inevitability, by appeal to ancient writings . . . by retrofitting [his] biographical incidents to themes, images, and prophecies in traditional Scriptures, his earliest followers grounded Jesus' mission and message in sacred history."[57] The writer of Luke even has Jesus explicitly theorize these "competitive textualization" moves when Jesus presents himself and his disciples' commanded proclamation of him to all nations as the true subject of Jewish Scriptures (Luke 24:25–27, 32, 44–47).

The phenomenon of early Christ teachers treating Jewish Scriptures as their own has become so familiar that the work necessary to make this practice feel legitimate easily becomes invisible. Thinking of the New Testament Gospels as mythmaking refocuses our gaze on that work: repeated stories about Jesus that allude to, continue, or eschatologically fulfill Jewish writings in combination with stories of Jesus also teaching others that these sacred writings are supposed to be interpreted thus. This is ideology in narrative form. Such narratives naturalize the writers of specific gospel texts and their associates as legitimate (or, *the* legitimate) inheritors of the ancient and authoritative capital of Jewish Scriptures. In this way the writers of the gospels participated in the ideals of dominant Greek and Roman literary cultures, wherein legitimacy was sought by staking out privileged connec-

55. Chris Keith, *The Gospel as Manuscript: An Early History of the Jesus Tradition as Material Artifact* (Oxford: Oxford University Press, 2020), 100–130; see esp. 121–23 on "Matthew's Posture toward Mark."

56. Keith, *Gospel as Manuscript*, 104, 112–14, 122.

57. Paula Fredriksen, *When Christians Were Jews: The First Generation* (New Haven: Yale University Press, 2018), 102–3.

tions to a prestigious past and demonstrating that the proper interpretation of ancient, sacred, or exotic texts revealed a truth aligning with you.[58] Mythmaking about Jesus made this ideological work possible and simultaneously invisible so it could feel natural.

To reimagine the New Testament Gospels as mythmaking about Jesus is to promote a set of questions for thinking about them that align more with the paths scholars in other subfields navigate when they study history and texts. A focus on mythmaking helps deexceptionalize the study of these gospels and the Jesus presented in each one.[59] The gospels and their portraits of Jesus can still be distinctive in various ways, but they no longer have the privilege of special methods that set their study uniquely apart from other writings about gods, people appointed by them, founding figures, and hegemonic gender and imperial ideologies in the ancient Mediterranean. These are the kinds of decisive steps urged for the field of biblical and early Christian studies by scholars like Dube and Stefaniw.[60] In other words, to think of Jesus and the New Testament Gospels in dialogue with myth does not end the conversation, but suggests new directions for it, which is a key goal for the Next Quest.

58. See Walsh, *Origins of Early Christian Literature*. On such roles for sacred or ancient texts, see chapter 5 of Young, *Paul among the Mythmakers*.

59. On the importance of deexceptionalizing the study of the gospels, Jesus, and early Christianity, see Crossley, *Jesus and the Chaos of History*; Shaily Shashikant Patel, *Smoke and Mirrors: Discourses of Magic in Early Petrine Traditions* (New York: Oxford University Press, forthcoming); Jared Secord, *Christian Intellectuals and the Roman Empire: From Justin Martyr to Origen* (University Park: Pennsylvania State University Press, 2020), 3–6; Stowers, "Concept of Community"; Walsh, *Origins of Early Christian Literature*, 4–15, 97–99, 136, 142.

60. Dube, *Postcolonial Feminist Interpretation*; Stefaniw, "Feminist Historiography." See the discussion in the opening section of this chapter.

2

BEGINNINGS OF A NEXT QUEST

11

THE LATE LATIN QUEST

Paula Fredriksen

The Next Quest for the historical Jesus should acknowledge that the Quest did not begin in Enlightenment Germany but was already underway in late Roman North Africa. The historical Jesus was a construct contested by two rhetorically trained, hermeneutically sophisticated fourth-century readers of Latin New Testament texts: the Manichaean *electus* and bishop, Faustus, and his younger contemporary and quondam co-religionist, Augustine of Hippo. They fought on terrain not unfamiliar to our twenty-first-century selves: the criteria of responsible historical narration; the reading of the gospels comparatively and critically; the past as a species of nonbeing and, thus, history itself as a type of discursive construction; and the inevitable indeterminacy of working with texts, whose transmission and whose meanings are themselves intrinsically unstable.

ANTECEDENTS

Augustine had addressed some of these issues in an early work on biblical interpretation, *De doctrina Christiana* (begun ca. 397, though not completed until decades later). And he had explored the ontological status of the past as a species of nonbeing especially in book 11 of his *Confessions* (begun also in 397). In that latter masterwork, time emerged as the great divide between humans—intrinsically time-bound and, thus, caught up in confounding problems of interpretation, be it of experience, of language, or of biblical texts—and the timeless god for whom the restless soul longed (*Conf.* 1.1.1).[1] But thanks to Faustus's own attacks on catholic biblical interpretation, the *Capitula,* with its sophisticated challenge to the catholic double canon and the doctrine of incarnation, these issues came urgently to the fore. And much of their argument focused on their respective constructions of Jesus of Nazareth, that figure who, for both men, represented the crucial historical and anthropological juncture between heaven and earth.

The doctrines of their contesting churches set the plumb lines for each man's arguments, thus of their depictions of the figure of Christ. For the purposes of their respective quests for the historical Jesus, however, their textual commitments differed significantly. Manichaeism had its own canon, those revelations written and preserved by its inspired founder, Mani.[2] The New Testament, for Manichees, was a type of apocrypha, a nonauthoritative assemblage sprinkled here and there with christological truths where these could be discerned to confirm and to conform to Manichaean teachings.[3] Yet it was the sacred texts of the catholic church that dominate Faustus's *Capitula.* In that work, Faustus never expounds specifically Manichaean teachings. Instead, he focuses resolutely on critical readings of catholic Scriptures. Disallowing to Jewish writings (i.e., the catholic Old Testament) any positive religious relevance, Faustus maintained that Judaizers had corrupted the content of the New Testament. One could accordingly glean Christian truth—that is, Manichaean truth—from these writings only through careful sifting and critical reading.

Faustus's arguments put Augustine on the defensive. The younger man responded to this challenge with overwhelming force: a massive refutation in thirty-three books entitled *Contra Faustum Manichaeum* (ca. 399?).[4] Emerging from the fog of battle were two quite distinct images of a historical Jesus. Faustus established his in part by reading the Four Gospels and Paul's Letters comparatively and critically. Augustine established his by insisting on assessing Scripture

1. For a discussion of Augustine's views on texts, time, and biblical interpretation, see Paula Fredriksen, *Augustine and the Jews* (New Haven: Yale University Press, 2010), 190–210.

2. For an excellent introduction to Mani and Manichaeism, see Iain Gardner and Samuel Lieu, *Manichaean Texts from the Roman Empire* (Cambridge: Cambridge University Press, 2004).

3. On the status of New Testament texts for Manichaean Christianity, see Michel Tardieu, "Exégèse Manichéenne du Nouveau Testament," in *Les règles de l'interprétation,* ed. M. Tardieu (Paris: Cerf, 1987), 123–46.

4. I draw on the translation of *Against Faustus* by R. Stothert in *Nicene and Post-Nicene Fathers,* (Grand Rapids: Eerdmans, 1974), 1:135–345. Augustine himself characterized this as a *grande opus* "a huge work" (*Retract.* 2.7.1). Augustine was aided by the fact that he controlled the "debate." By the time that the *Capitula* came into his hands, Faustus himself was dead, and Augustine presented Faustus's case "as if Faustus had stated his opinions himself, and I had replied to him" (*Faust.* 1.1). The text, in brief, is an ersatz disputation.

"according to its historical sense" (*secundum historicam proprietatis* or *ad litteram* or *proprie*) as a report of things that were actually done (*facta; Faust.* 12.7). Faustus's literary-critical approach bears a striking resemblance to the ways that New Testament scholars still work; so too do Augustine's ideas about time, texts, and historical writing. Let us follow each man's quest for their respective historical Jesuses, attending to their methods and to their a priori principles as well as to their concluding results.

FAUSTUS AS CRITICAL READER

Faustus starts from the principled position that the Old Testament has nothing to do with the New Testament. The morally defective god of Jewish Scripture was not the deity revealed by Christ (e.g., *Faust.* 22.4). That god's law had been renounced by Christ and by his apostle, Paul.[5] Accordingly, Faustus dismissed the Old Testament for the purposes of constructive theology: only the New Testament merited Manichaean exegesis.[6] What sense, then, could be made of those places in Paul's Epistles or in the Four Gospels that seemed to resonate positively with Jewish traditions?

Faustus begins by asserting that primary evidence—Paul's Letters—is to be prioritized over secondary evidence, namely, the Four Gospels. We have no primary evidence from Jesus: he left no writings. Paul at least wrote his letters. Though they had manifestly been partly corrupted by later Judaizing interpolations, Faustus observes, they still represented a cache of his own words. The task of the critical reader was to sort out the wheat of Paul's actual teachings from the chaff of Paul's earlier erroneous opinions and of these later Judaizing

---

5. We see here Mani's debts to the work of the second-century theologian Marcion. Mani's revelations occurred in Mesopotamia, where communities of Marcionite Christians had long been established. Both communities considered the "New Testament" to consist primarily of Paul's Letters, though the sequence and selection of epistles differed. See Tardieu, "Exégèse manichéenne," 143 for a comparative chart. On the Manichaean reuse of Marcionite traditions, see Jason BeDuhn, "Biblical Antitheses, Adda, and the *Acts of Archelaus*," in *Frontiers of Faith: The Christian Encounter with Manichaeism in the Acta of Archelaus*, ed. J. BeDuhn and P. Mirecki (Leiden: Brill, 2007), 131–47.

6. To do this, however, Faustus had to labor long and hard to delegitimize Old Testament texts and traditions: fully fourteen books out of Augustine's thirty-three are given over to Faustus's thoroughgoing and detailed critique of the themes, commandments, personages, and practices in Jewish texts. As Faustus himself states, "We [Manichees] are enemies not of the Law, but of Judaism" (*Faust.* 22.2). For a counterargument interpreting Faustus as more sympathetic to Jews and Judaism than was Augustine, see Jason BeDuhn, "Augustine, Faustus, and the Jews," *Manichaeism and Early Christianity*, ed. J. Van Oort, NHMS 99 (Leiden: Brill, 2021), 295–316.

interpolations (*Faust.* 11.1). The Gospels, more complicated, were in a different category. Later than Paul, their stories about Jesus were the work of anonymous authors (33.3: unknown *semi-Judaeis* "half-Jews"). Paul's statements—with their famed polarizing of gospel and law—therefore had the interpretive priority when working to reconstruct the revelation of Christ.

Faustus had composed the *Capitula* as if he were responding to a series of challenges put to him by a catholic interlocutor. For example, book 11 opens with the question, "Do you accept the authority of the Apostle Paul? . . . *Et maxime!*" Why, then, did Faustus not hold to what Paul said, namely, that Christ was the Son of David according to the flesh (Rom 1:3; *Faust.* 11.1)? Such a statement is objectionable, in the Manichaean view, on two grounds. First, it holds that Christ was actually incarnate (Manichaean Christology was docetic). Second, it links Christ to the unsavory Old Testament figure of David (cf. *Faust.* 22.5). Pointing to 2 Corinthians—in the Manichaean order, an epistle composed after Romans— Faustus praises Paul for coming to a more enlightened understanding: "Even though we once knew Christ *secundum carnem*, we know him that way no longer" (2 Cor 5:16). Paul had corrected himself, realizing that Christ was not fleshly. Manichaean hermeneutics left room for such Pauline improvements. If catholics disputed this, Faustus continued, well and good: in that case, then Paul did not write Rom 1:3, but a later Judaizing interpolator did (*Faust.* 11.1).

The Four Gospels were another matter. They were not written by Jesus, but only about him. Sayings attributed by the evangelists to Jesus, Faustus notes, appear in quite different contexts. Compare, for example, Matt 8:5–13 and Luke 7:2–10. Only Matthew relates the saying about the eschatological table of Abraham, Isaac and Jacob in this scene. The two gospel writers shape differently how the centurion requests a cure, and Luke places the tradition about the eschatological table in a different context entirely (Luke 13:29). "Given how uncertain we must be about the [narrative] context of this saying," concludes Faustus, "there is no reason *not* to question whether Jesus ever said it at all" (*Faust.* 33.2–3). Faustus, in short, reads the Four Gospels "horizontally," comparing similar passages across these traditions, thereby analyzing the sayings and scenarios of each text the way that we do when reading in parallel columns. And he concludes, as modern critics have done, that the evangelists, well after the historical Jesus's lifetime, had inherited traditions variously and embedded them differently in their different accounts. The result, urges Faustus, is that each saying attributed to Jesus has to be weighed and judged for authenticity—the criteria of authenticity contingent, ultimately, upon conforming to Manichaean revelation (18.3; 33.3).[7]

7. Tardieu, "Exégèse Manichéenne," 131–32.

One criterion of authenticity for a teaching or saying of Jesus is whether it speaks against Jewish tradition.[8] Faustus refuses in principle to believe—or to believe that Jesus had believed—that the old (namely, Judaism) should be mixed with the new (that is, Christianity; *Faust.* 8.1, cf. 16.6). The more hostile to Jews and to Judaism an evangelical scene or saying is—Jesus's repeated violations of the Sabbath; his action against merchants in the temple courtyard; his contestations with Jewish authorities, who in any case planned, plotted and effected his execution—the more *likely* its authenticity. This hermeneutical rule of thumb is the Manichaean version of the criteria of dissimilarity and of coherence. And such an anti-Jewish Jesus, gleaned from these secondary texts, coheres with the primary evidence of the anti-Jewish Paul, who himself had abandoned the law to found the church of the gentiles. In this sense, Mani had continued and accomplished what was preached by Christ and begun by Paul: the establishment of a (completely) law-free community, liberated from the old (Judaism) and oriented around the newness of the proclamation of God's kingdom.[9]

What then of the Four Gospels? Do they provide any useful and usable information about Christ? The conflicting genealogies of Matthew and of Luke got things off to a bad start, noted Faustus, reinforcing Manichaean arguments that the catholic doctrine of incarnation was both late and wrong (*Faust.* 3.1). What about where Jesus seems to speak positively of law, say, at Matt 5:17? There, context matters for interpretation. At that point, Faustus explains, Christ spoke of the laws prior to Sinai, laws held in regard by all peoples, including heroic ancients like Seth and Enoch. Those are the laws that Jesus came to fulfill (19.3). These four techniques of literary criticism—first, that Paul himself later corrected his own earlier erroneous teachings; second, that different narrative contexts indicated the redactional activity of the evangelists, ipso facto calling into question the reliability of the imputed tradition; third, that context could determine a positively meaningful teaching attributed by the evangelists to Jesus; and, fourth, that intractably Jewish passages were the work of later Judaizing interpolators—enabled Faustus to retrieve a New Testament Jesus consistent with the revelations of Mani. The law had nothing to do with the gospel. Christ had nothing to do with Judaism, which he in all cases condemned. Christ himself was uninvolved with human flesh, which was itself outside the scope of redemption.

8. "We think," says Faustus, that "*Christum in destructionem legis ac prophetarum venisse*" (*Faust.* 18.1).

9. Faustus's interpretation was very close to—indeed, borrowed from—the supersessionist theologies embodied in North African (retrospectively) catholic tradition by Tertullian and Cyprian; see Fredriksen, *Augustine*, 223–27, 231–32.

AUGUSTINE AS HISTORICAL THINKER

Earlier work on thinking historically and on reading the Bible historically had serendipitously prepared Augustine for the serious challenge that he now faced from Faustus. In *De doctrina Christiana*, contemplating the semiotics of biblical language, Augustine had considered the correspondence between scriptural texts, historical events, and biblical interpretation. But he also began working at a more fundamental level on the correspondence between language and meaning.

How can one determine the proper referent of Scripture's language? Words are *signa*, signs that point toward something. Those informed by intentionality (*signa data*) can point in two different directions: to specific things or ideas within their own immediate interpretive context (*signa propria*, "proper" or "literal" or "self-referring" signs), or to things or ideas outside of their immediate context, that is, toward something else (*signa translata*, "referred-away" or "metaphorical" signs; *Doctr. chr.* 2.10.15). But the Bible is a special instance of *signa data* because of its unique double authorship: the timeless, eternal God who is its source, and the historically contingent human beings who were its medium (*Doctr. chr.* 2.2.3). Its *signa*, accordingly, are both *propria* and *translata*, both historical and metaphorical or typological. But the Bible's spiritual meanings, Augustine insists, can never undermine its "plain" or "historical" meanings. In other words, no matter how elevating the spiritual meaning, Scripture must also always be understood *proprie* and *ad litteram* and *quam verba sonant* within its own context, historically, according to its plain sense, "just as the words say."

But what do the words say? Augustine was well aware of the diversity and very variable quality of Latin translations and manuscripts (*Doctr. chr.* 2.11.16). But he offsets this unnerving realization by holding that the Bible *in any language* represented a "translation" from the timeless God to the historical and linguistic contingencies of its human authors. The texts themselves—the question of particular translations aside—were thus intrinsically and infinitely interpretable. The only way for fallen, time-bound humanity to know the eternal word of God (or, indeed, anything) was to wrestle with interpretation, always imperfectly mediated through language.[10]

The authority of catholic doctrine determined the limits of acceptable interpretation for Augustine, but it also underscored the importance of considering

---

10. "Reading and writing were among the labours imposed on the first couple as a result of their disobedience in the garden of Eden. They were the consequences of human curiosity and pride. Before the fall, there was no need for such cumbersome instruments of communication. God spoke to Adam and Eve directly, as he did to the Hebrew prophets, or he made his will known without the use of language." Brian Stock, *Augustine the Reader: Meditation, Self-Knowledge and the Ethics of Interpretation* (Cambridge: Harvard University Press, 1996), 15.

the historical context when discerning the meaning of any biblical passage. If the catholic double canon—the law of Moses and the grace and truth of Jesus Christ (John 1:17; *Faust.* 22.6)—represented one continuous divine initiative of redemption, then its particular teachings had to make sense within their original historical context, both pre- and postincarnation. Augustine thus argues, for example, that sacrificing animals had never been an improper way to worship God.[11] Indeed, God had commanded it, and the Jews had been right to obey that command and to enact those *sacramenta* (*Doctr. chr.* 3.6.10). As *signa translata*, such sacrifices may have been codes for Christ; but as *signa propria*, they were also straightforward commandments about required pious behaviors appropriate to their own historical period. For Augustine, in other words, historical context matters for correct textual interpretation (*Doctr. chr.* 3.10.15–12.20).

Working on his commentary on Galatians (ca. 394–395) several years before his encounter with Faustus's *Capitula*, Augustine had also had the benefit of a run-in with Jerome. The latter, in his own commentary on Galatians, had floated an interpretation of Paul and Peter's famous falling out in Antioch (Gal 2:11–14), wherein the two apostles had only pretended to argue for the edification of their audience. Of course Peter had known that the law had been abrogated by Christ: he merely pretended to say otherwise, Jerome explained, in order to provide Paul with the opportunity to pronounce that teaching forthrightly.[12]

The falsehood, in Augustine's view, was double: the apostolic fight was itself faked, and then Paul had written up a false account of the fight in his letter. He objected strenuously (*Ep.* 28.3.4–5). If the truthfulness of the biblical text was itself called into question, so then was the authority of the Bible as a whole—exactly as the Manichees had done. Several years later, still awaiting a reply from Jerome (unknown to both men, Augustine's first letter had gone missing), Augustine wrote that there had been nothing wrong *in principle* with these Jewish apostles still living according to Jewish law in any case (*Ep.* 40.4.4). At issue in Antioch was the question whether *gentiles* needed, also, to live according to the law as if it were

---

11. This position put Augustine at loggerheads with a long proto-orthodox criticism of Jewish blood sacrifices. Drawing on an originally pagan critique of animal sacrifices—that is, that high gods have no need of such, though lower gods welcomed them—these earlier fathers had argued that God gave the laws of sacrifice to Jews in order to distract them from their perennial propensity to worship idols (e.g., Justin, *Dial.* 19.5; cf. Tertullian, *Marc.* 2.18.3). For the *contra Iudaeos* trope of blood sacrifices being intrinsically linked to idol-worship, see Fredriksen, *Augustine*, 227–34.

12. For a lively review of this controversy between Augustine and Jerome, see Eric Plumer, *Augustine's Commentary on Galatians* (Oxford: Oxford University Press, 2003), 41–43.

necessary for salvation. Peter had thought yes. Paul argued no. Peter, corrected, conceded the point.

Augustine's interpretation sat within a larger argument: no matter how many symbolic meanings Holy Scripture might contain, it also served as a genuine record of *gesta*, things that happened (contra Jerome) in the way that the text relates. Thus, if the Old Testament depicted God as giving the law and as praising Israel for keeping the law, then keeping the law was good from the time of its reception through the first generation of the church when Christ and, postresurrection, his apostles (Paul included) had continued to abide by its instructions. The law was a benefit and a privilege (*Faust.* 12.3), its importance enduring because it led to Christ (12.4 and 7)—"not the Christ produced by the Manichees, but the Christ of the Hebrew prophets." Accordingly, Paul himself had lauded God's giving of Israel's law (Rom 9:4). "If the law had been bad, the Apostle would not have praised Israel for having it" (*Faust.* 12.3). God, in other words, had charged Israel with more than preserving the text of his book. He had charged them as well to enact its commandments, *secundum carnem*, within historical time (4.2).

Augustine's polemic against Faustus, as with his argument with Jerome, occasioned his most positive pronouncements on the law. But in the case of Faustus, it also caused him to reset his own prior depictions of the historical Jesus. As recently as in his commentary on Galatians and in *De doctrina Christiana*, Augustine had maintained that Jesus had alienated Jewish contemporaries by his violations of and flagrant disregard for Jewish law (e.g., *Exp. Gal.* 22.1; *Doctr. chr.* 3.6.10). Now, against Faustus, Augustine sees the "historical Jesus" in quite a different way. "Christ never tried to turn Israel away from the Law; but he charged *them* with being turned from the law" (*Faust.* 16.24). Christ had criticized the Pharisees not because they were *too* scrupulous, but because they were not scrupulous enough. Jesus, he asserts, never broke a single one of God's commandments according to Jewish custom, "but he found fault with those around him who did" (*Faust.* 16.24). Jesus was circumcised and brought as an infant to the temple (32.18 and 22); he offered sacrifices in the temple; he was vigilant in his Sabbath observance, even to the point of not rising from the dead until after the Sabbath was finished (16.29). Augustine's "historical Jesus" is more than an incarnate Jesus. He is a law-observant Jewish Jesus because—again, contra Faustus—there had never been anything wrong in the first place with Jewish law or with the Jewish observance of Jewish law. Understood in light of (true) Christian revelation, the Jewish Scriptures were the books of the (true) church.

"The past is gone," Augustine observes, "and the truth of what is past lies in our own judgment, not in the past event itself" (*Faust.* 26.5). If we must assess whether a report of a past event is true, Augustine insists, our *sententiae* must rest upon the authority of our sources. For Augustine, the truth of the past as reported in Scripture is guaranteed by the authority of the catholic church, ensured by the succession from apostles to bishops to councils (11.2; 13.5). Therefore, he concludes, "we believe both that Christ really was born and that he truly died because the Gospel is truth. . . . And we can confirm with confidence that what happened in the past (*factum*) was nothing other than what the Gospel truth teaches" (26.7).

The Late Latin "Historical Jesus"

What can we say, in summary, about the work of these two great combat theologians? Both constructed a historical Jesus who embodied the theological principles of their respective churches. Faustus's Jesus was never incarnate; he had renounced Jewish law with its demonic god and its unsavory spokesmen in favor of a new revelation of redemption, a revelation that had been finally, reliably stabilized in the writings of Mani. Augustine's Jesus was truly incarnate, because flesh was the creation of the good God. His Jesus lived a Jewish life because the source of the law and the source of redemption was the same God, Creator, and Father. And the saving message of the gospel with its promise of the resurrection of the fleshly body rested on the foundation of the law and was truly and reliably related in the authoritative canon of the catholic church.

Both Christs generated by this argument, in other words, *served a fundamentally apologetic purpose.* No surprise there. What is interesting, however, is the way that both antagonists mobilized arguments about the past and about how to read texts historically in order to present their respective Christs. For Faustus, immediate literary context was key; for Augustine, past historical context was key. "History" for neither man is a secular concept. It serves, rather, to illumine and to fortify their respective a priori theological positions. In this sense, they use "the past" to validate the present.

For both men, the figure of the historical Jesus is crucial to their case. This fact gives their arguments, despite their foreign antiquity, a curious familiarity. Faustus's techniques of literary criticism, his doctrinal motivations aside, are immediately familiar to current questers, who use many similar critical and comparative readings to assess historical materials about the figure of Jesus in New Testament sources. Augustine's acute awareness of the infinite interpretability of texts (though not his solution to the problem) approaches a postmodern sensibility. And his Jesus fits into his Jewish historical context—albeit for fourth-century doctrinal reasons—in ways that recall the conclusions of many recent questers.

Each man conjures a "historical" Jesus, in other words, because of its tactical importance. Each historical Jesus served as a concentrated *pars pro toto* of two huge and incommensurate theological systems. Each Jesus authorizes their pre-senter's theological position. And interestingly, in configuring his Jesus, each man also takes a stand on the relevance of Judaism to "true" Christianity. Faustus the Manichee, appealing to Paul, had the less complicated position: the one (Judaism) had nothing to do with the other (true Christianity). Augustine the ex-Manichee, more interestingly, by appealing to the catholic double canon, thought himself into a theological novum. He reimagined the relationship of God to Israel, of Jesus to Judaism, and thus reimagined, as well, the relationship of his own church, past and present, to the Jews.[13]

13. Fredriksen, *Augustine and the Jews*, 213–375.

12

Chartism and Forgotten Quests

James Crossley

The Next Quest for the historical Jesus will need to look at forgotten quests in archives, newspapers, pamphlets, and other such sources if we want more new data to help explain the history of the Quest as a cultural phenomenon. Because of the sheer breadth of possibilities, in this essay I will provide some examples from a specific, though formative, era of the quest through contextualizing working-class and dissenting radicalism of mid-nineteenth-century England. Foregrounding previously overlooked history from below is laudable enough, but this sort of material can also show how the micro helps explain the macro, in this instance how a quest for the historical Jesus from below can help us understand social and economic changes taking place in the nineteenth century. Halvor Moxnes and Dieter Georgi have previously shown how the famous lives of Jesus in the late eighteenth and nineteenth centuries (e.g., those of Reimarus, Schleiermacher, and Strauss) were part of emerging bourgeois nationalism in challenging the dominance of the aristocratic Christ of the old feudal order, to put it crudely. The nineteenth-century bourgeois version of "Great Men" biographies was integral to the emerging lives of Jesus, and the politically and theologically controversial contrast between the human Jesus and the divine Christ reflected the tensions between bourgeois citizenship and traditional monarchical power. Christ the King now faced the challenge of Jesus the statesman, enlightened citizen, or autonomous leader and teacher in his geographical, political, social, cultural, and national context and in relation to a people and to colonialism. This larger-than-life charismatic Jesus provided a model for inspirational individuals who would help shape this new world in the nineteenth century.[1]

In this essay, I want to look at the other side of these developments. Emerging bourgeois thought was not the only use to which the historical Jesus could be put as European capitalism consolidated its power; where emerging bourgeois thinkers were in tension with outgoing order, the emerging proletariat could both join in *and* turn the tradition of this "human" Jesus against bourgeois dominance as part of an influential reading of the historical Jesus as an oppositional figure. To do this, I will focus particularly on the mid-nineteenth-century movement known as Chartism and its precursors in English radicalism from below. I will end with comments on research into archival and related material and its relationship to a bigger history of Jesus and the Quest.

David Friedrich Strauss, George Eliot, and Charles Hennell

While we can always forgive the overlooking of niche archival material about the history of the Quest, perhaps less mercy can be shown in the case of English working-class radicalism of the mid-nineteenth century for the simple reason that we were told about their interest in the historical Jesus. In *The Condition of the Working Class in England*, first published in German in 1845, Engels commented on the role of socialists in the education of workers, including the supply of cheap translations of French and German literature. One such translation, Engels noted, was David Friedrich Strauss's *Life of Jesus*, first published a decade earlier (1835–1836).[2] A key figure involved in this English translation was the journalist and radical dissenting Christian, rationalist, and freethinker, Henry Hetherington, with

---

1. Dieter Georgi, "The Interest in Life of Jesus Theology as a Paradigm for the Social History of Biblical Criticism," *HTR* 85.1 (1992): 51–83; Halvor Moxnes, *Jesus and the Rise of Nationalism: A New Quest for the Nineteenth Century Historical Jesus* (London: I. B. Tauris, 2011). The story is, of course, more nuanced than my generalization and something resembling the Quest predates the French Revolution. For wider recent discussion, see Jonathan C. P. Birch, "The Road to Reimarus: Origins of the Quest for the Historical Jesus," in *Holy Land as Homeland? Models for Constructing the Historic Landscapes of Jesus*, ed. Keith Whitelam (Sheffield: Phoenix, 2011), 19–47; Birch, *Jesus in an Age of Enlightenment: Radical Gospels from Thomas Hobbes to Thomas Jefferson* (New York: Palgrave Macmillan, 2019); Birch, "Revolutionary Contexts for the Quest: Jesus in the Rhetoric and Methods of Early Modern Intellectual History," *JSHJ* 17.1–2 (2019): 35–80; Cristiana Facchini, "Jesus the Pharisee: Leon Modena, the Historical Jesus, and Renaissance Venice," *JSHJ* 17.1–2 (2019): 81–101; Miriam Benfatto, "The Work of Isaac Ben Abraham Troki (16th Century): On the Place of the Sefer Hizzuq Emunah in the Quest for the Historical Jesus," *JSHJ* 17.1–2 (2019): 102–20.

2. Friedrich Engels, *The Condition of the Working Class in England*, trans. Florence Kelley

editions coming out in the first half of the 1840s.[3] The fourth edition of Strauss's *Life of Jesus* was given a considerably more famous English translation by the novelist George Eliot (Mary Ann Evans) in 1846.[4] However, during the process of establishing the translator and carrying out the translation, there was a lack of awareness of the Hetherington version. This was partly due to the respective translations representing or being marketed to different audiences. As Valerie Dodd showed, Hetherington's four-volume version was printed on cheap paper while Eliot's was on paper of good quality; Eliot "envisaged a middle-class market, whereas Hetherington was aiming his project at the impoverished workers." The two different translations point further to two strands of theological and political radicalism: "One was composed of enlightened, middle-class dissenters, the other of the urban working class."[5]

These two strands, though distinct, overlapped and their Jesuses give us insight into the interests and influence of, and anxieties about, the emerging working-class movement. The story of the historical Jesus of the English middle-class dissenting tradition is known, even if not always foregrounded, in historical Jesus scholarship and was represented not just by Eliot's translation but previously by (for instance) Charles Hennell. Hennell, who came from a mercantile and Unitarian background, was part of Eliot's network pushing for the translation of Strauss's *Das Leben Jesu*.[6] But Hennell had also published *Inquiry concerning the Origin of Christianity* in 1838 and it was written independently of Strauss's book, though the authors soon interacted and

---

Wischnewetzky (London: Sonnenschein & Co., 1892), 239–40. See also Thomas Carlyle, *The Life of John Sterling* (London: Chapman and Hall, 1851), 271.

3. See David Friedrich Strauss, *The Life of Jesus, or, A Critical Examination of His History*, 4 vols. (London: Hetherington, 1842–1844). Cf. J. R. Beard, preface to *Voices of the Church in Reply to Dr D. F. Strauss, Author of "Das Leben Jesu"*, ed. J. R. Beard (London: Simpkin, Marshall, and Co., 1845), v–xiv: "There has been one translation of the Leben Jesu into our tongue, published in penny numbers, and designed for circulation among the working classes, under the auspices of HETHERINGTON. The work . . . has not the slightest literary value whatever; being obviously brought out to supply food to the unhappily depraved appetite for sceptical productions, so prevalent in these times among our manufacturing populations" (xiii). For discussion of the complexities of the versions available see Margaret Anne Crowther, *Church Embattled* (Newton Abbot: David & Charles, 1970), 47–48; Valerie A. Dodd, "Strauss's English Propagandists and the Politics of Unitarianism, 1841–1845," *Church History* 50.4 (1981): 415–35, esp. 425–28.

4. David Friedrich Strauss, *The Life of Jesus, Critically Examined by Dr David Friedrich Strauss. Translated from the Fourth German Edition*, trans. George Eliot, vol. 1 (London: Chapman Brothers, 1846).

5. Dodd, "Strauss's English Propagandists," 426.

6. For an overview of Hennell's life, see Ian Sellers, "Hennell, Charles Christian (1809–1850)," in *Oxford Dictionary of National Biography*, September 23, 2004, https://www.oxforddnb.com /display/10.1093/ref:odnb/9780198614128.001.0001/odnb-9780198614128-e-12939.

were aware of their similarities.[7] Much of Hennell's reconstruction of Jesus, shorn of the miraculous, was conventional enough in radical, dissenting, and Unitarian traditions, and was of course in line with some of the general tendencies in Germanic reconstructions of the historical Jesus. This earthly Jesus was a moral and intellectual leader, an independent thinker, a good man, benevolent, refined, dignified, liberal, enlightened, bold, imaginative, and a representative of human virtue.

While these traits attributed to Jesus may have been typical of the time, it is worth noting that Hennell also contributed to the positive rhetoric about Jews and Judaism that has become the hallmark of contemporary historical Jesus scholarship and distinct from the dark path that influential Jesus scholarship would take in the nineteenth and early twentieth centuries. Hennell saw similarities between Jesus and the Essenes in terms of moral purity and simplicity, adding that "Jesus was a Jew" who "spent his life amongst his own nation."[8] By the time of *Inquiry*, he had long-held interest in reading Josephus and Jewish history and reading them critically alongside the New Testament.[9] Certainly, for Hennell, Jesus left his own stamp on intellectual authorities and on the local Jewish ideas, and there are some indications of Hennell constructing a distinctiveness in relation to known Jewish ideas. Even so, Hennell grounded the influence of Jesus in a context where such ideas were acceptable (21–23). Jesus's independence and re-formist inclination might have meant he clashed with the Pharisees and scribes over the interpretation of law and tradition, but this was typically constructed by Hennell in terms of a clash with the "established authorities" and put him in a different strand of Jewish thought, notably stemming from the prophets (310–11). This Jesus still observed the law of Moses (including the "ritual" law) and was more conservative than others, such as Judas the Galilean (311). Similar ideas to those of Jesus were not just to be found in the Old Testament but also in texts like Sirach and rabbinic tradition and the familiar ideas they were said to represent. Indeed, Hennell further dedicated a whole section and chapter to comparative Jewish texts (219, 317–25, 334–56). Hennell even mentioned Mendelsohn's claim that "intelligent Jews consider Jesus as a generous enthusiast" (417).

7. Charles C. Hennell, *Inquiry concerning the Origin of Christianity* (London: Smallfield and Son, 1838). On the interaction between Hennell and Strauss, see David Friedrich Strauss, "Vorwort von Dr Strauss," in Charles C. Hennell, *Untersuchung über den Ursprung des Christenhums: Aus dem Englischen* (Stuttgart: Hallberger, 1840), iii–viii; Charles C. Hennell, "Preface to the Second Edition," in *Inquiry concerning the Origin of Christianity* (London: Allman, 1841), xi–xii; Strauss, *Life of Jesus, Critically Examined*, vii–viii.

8. Hennell, *Inquiry*, 8–19, 313–14. Subsequent citations of Hennell, *Inquiry* appear in-text.

9. Sara S. Hennell, *A Memoir of Charles Christian Hennell* (privately published, 1899), 13, 60–61. Cf. Strauss, "Vorwort," v.

Though ideas about an improvement of Judaism remained (as they implicitly have in much scholarship to this day), Hennell's Jesus was firmly, positively, and emphatically presented in the context of Jewish ideas. This was in line with positive English Unitarian interactions with Jews, including in Unitarian circles such as in Manchester where Hennell was born and in Hackney where Hennell was educated as a boy.[10] While Hennell provided one of the most rhetorically positive constructions of Jews and Judaism in the English dissenting tradition, he was not alone. As we will see, the emphatically class-based and antiestablishment constructions of Jesus in English radicalism from below could sometimes mean that the emerging ethnically and biologically racialized understandings were avoided, and questions of religious superiority were downgraded (though not eliminated). While Hennell may have been guided by his own personal background in Jewish studies, interactions with Jews, and universalist interests, his reconstruction of Jesus and Christian origins was also a part of nineteenth-century discussions about class and revolution.

In terms of class and revolution, there is a constant tension in Hennell's presentation of Jesus, which works on two levels and tells us something about the context in which *Inquiry* was written. The tension is between, on the one hand, Jesus the prophet expecting imminent divine intervention and, on the other, Jesus the great moral teacher. On one level, the issue is the overly supernatural beliefs associated with this understanding of Jesus, which was in tension with Hennell's rationalistic Unitarian background. To deal with this tension, Hennell prioritized one part of his reconstruction of Jesus over another. He suggested that the expectation of an extraordinary event that would bring about "national regeneration" was, in fact, "quite unnecessary" for the introduction of a "purer creed of religion and morals" (301–2). The authorities in Jerusalem were more urgently concerned not with what was "superior and more innocuous" in Jesus's teaching but with what Jesus might have meant about this imminent coming kingdom and how the crowds might react. Yet such things were for Hennell and his implied readers "of least importance to us" (303–4). Jesus was also excused by Hennell because the premodern context meant that his enthusiasm for thinking himself the predestined king "was by no means irrational" on its own terms. The "strictest reasoner" must accept that Jesus's views were "well grounded," and it was "merely a sign of mental vigour, that he acted according to them" (298; cf. 329). In other words, such rationalism could be extracted from an irrational context.

10. John Seed, "Unitarianism, Political Economy and the Antinomies of Liberal Culture in Manchester, 1830–50," *Social History* 7.1 (1982): 3; Dodd, "Strauss's English Propagandists," 425; Sellers, "Hennell."

On another level, this tension effectively functions as another type of sympathetic but anxious middle-class commentary on the disturbances surrounding working-class agitation and demands toward the mid-nineteenth century with a clear steer toward nonviolent action in the present. The idea that God's people were "slaves" to "powerful masters" was understood, Hennell argued, as a source of "grief and indignation" (5–8). Jesus shared the enthusiasm of many "patriotic Jews" about the miraculous emancipation and exaltation of Israel and for the coming kingdom where a Jewish holy nation would become the "empire of the world." Jesus expected to assume the character of the messiah and become the Mosaic prophet and prince who would soon sit on the throne of David (21–23). Jesus was thus described by Hennell not only as a "reformer" but also a "revolutionist" (300, 305–8, 310–11). Nevertheless, Hennell's Jesus was emphatically not a violent revolutionist in the sense that he would lead an "armed rebellion against the Romans" to achieve his goals (308–9). In this respect, Hennell contrasted Jesus with Judas the Galilean and his notion of violent resistance. Judas was likewise a "political and religious reformer," but Jesus "abstained from the evidently useless attempt of armed opposition" and provided an alternative (5–8, 22–23, 26). Jesus instead preferred the idea of divine intervention as had happened in the past: as God had freed the Israelites from Egyptian slavery, so God would free Israel from the "taskmasters" of Rome (308–9).

This distinction between armed insurrection and divine intervention allowed Hennell to maintain his positive portrait of Jesus and cope with his reservations about ancient irrationalism. As great figures in his position were wont to do, this Jesus held himself with great magnanimity in the face of death. He began to contemplate the possibility of martyrdom and developed ideas that the messiah must suffer before he reigns (28–29, 31). Jesus saw that without supernatural intervention there was no chance against the might of the Romans and, with Essene-like submission to providence, carried on into Jerusalem (30, 298–99). Nevertheless (or furthermore), this involved Hennell restressing his view about the dignity of Jesus and allowing his historical reconstruction to blur into commentary on Jesus's contemporary relevance. While Jesus may have taken the messianic route, the character of prophet and teacher "seems to have agreed better with his temper and habits of thought" and was more suited to contemplation and imagination than the "coarser turmoils of the world." More a Nathan or an Isaiah than a Joshua or a Gideon, Jesus worked better "dilating" on the prospects of the kingdom rather than "in entering into those political intrigues and daring enterprises which form the gratification of ordinary revolutionists." Moreover, Jesus's parables and discourses were to be preferred over driving out the buyers and the sellers in the temple when he accepted the "dangerous homage of the multitude." Messiahship may have brought with it political views, but "the character of a moral and intellectual leader was more natural to him" (30, 309–10). If we translate this into the debates within Chartism (see below), the *mass* working-class movement of the mid-nineteenth century, this Jesus was ultimately more "moral force" than "physical force," as we might expect of someone from Hennell's context.

There are further class dimensions to Hennell's Jesus that were partly driven by related well-meaning concerns about the working class toward the middle of the nineteenth century. His description of Jesus's social status would not be out of place in a middle-class construction of a palatable and idealized working-class leader in the making in the early to mid-nineteenth century and in the face of anxieties about working-class violent agitation.[11] This kind of leader must take on the sorts of traits more readily available to middle-class thinkers and leaders. Accordingly, this Jesus studied intensely "the literature within the reach of Jewish peasants" but it was "impossible" for him to remain a carpenter at Nazareth his whole life. As the usual routes to greatness were "closed to the lower ranks" except for "heading a revolt," this provided insight into the emergence of Jesus according to Hennell (22–23). As his reputation grew, Jesus was followed by the multitudes, including those further up the social scale. "Some of the better sort of Jews" who looked to a national revival and even "a few of the nobles, who partook of the popular feeling" saw this new prophet as "more than a common pretender"— indeed, some of the disciples themselves may have come from a more prosperous background (cf. Matt 19:29), Hennell suggested (26, 31).[12]

Hennell and Eliot are part of the story of the emergence of the Quest as a product of middle-class dissent, reacting against or transforming the monarchical, ele-

---

11. For a near contemporary comparison of middle-class construction of a palatable working-class religious leader, see Mrs O'Neill, *The Bondman: A Story of the Days of Wat Tyler* (London: Smith, Elder, and Co., 1833); James Crossley, *Spectres of John Ball: The Peasants' Revolt in English Political History, 1381–2020* (Sheffield: Equinox, 2022), 190–98. In this respect, we might note extended editorial from the *Poor Man's Guardian* (then edited by Hetherington himself) from October 5, 1833, which claimed that Jesus's opponents were cunning enough to give him an ignoble death to deter other reformers. They did not impeach Jesus for, or highlight, his political views or his preaching on usury, extortion, and hypocrisy because if they did the people would have defended Jesus and "inflicted summary justice on the wretches."

12. Cf. S. Hennell, *Memoir*, 46. This contextualizing of Hennell in debates surrounding working-class and middle-class radicalism and reformism may partly explain a key difference between Hennell and Strauss noted in the preface to the second edition of *Inquiry*: "He hesitates to ascribe to Jesus the political aim included in the Jewish notion of the Messiahship, but seems inclined to consider his views directed exclusively to spiritual dominion" (xii). See also S. Hennell, *Memoir*, 77, in Hennell's letter to his daughter, Sara: "I have read half the second vol. of Strauss, and am surprised to find that he thinks Jesus took a spiritual view of his kingdom. I really think he is not so just or profound *on this point* as I am."

vated Christ of the old feudal and aristocratic order, as Moxnes and Georgi show (see above). But Hennell's anxieties in his presentation of Jesus's revolutionary and class-based interests hint strongly toward the popularity of the other side of this story, the story of the Jesus of working-class radicalism that is barely known in historical Jesus studies. That this story is forgotten in academic theological circles is understandable given that the kind of evidence that survives (especially books) is much more likely to come from middle-class circles. It is telling in this respect that when the rationalist critique from below of traditional ideas about religion does get noticed, it is in the pamphleteering tradition.[13] But there is also evidence of previously overlooked working-class radical Jesuses from the cheap, widely circulated newspapers now readily available in digitized archives. Beyond Engels's passing comment, newspaper archives reveal what sorts of things were being done with Jesus in English working-class radicalism of the time.

JESUS CHARTIST

As noted, the major working-class movement in England of the mid-nineteenth century—as observed by Engels—was Chartism. Chartism was concerned with universal male suffrage, electoral reform, middle-class betrayal of the working class, workplace reform, and wage rises accompanied by widespread strike action, arrests of leaders, mass public meetings, conflict with the authorities, riots, conspiracies, insurrectionary activity, and deportations. In terms of religious identities, there were Chartist congregations as Christianity (of different denominations) and Chartism overlapped. There were popular Chartist hymns, biblical allusions were frequent, and the idea of a form of the "social gospel" was common and infused with anticlericalism. In the popular imagination at least, the famed firebrand preacher of workplace and social reform, Joseph Rayner Stephens, was associated with the movement.[14] Nevertheless, Malcolm Chase

13. We might note the comments of an unimpressed Owen Chadwick, *The Victorian Church: Part I, 1829–1859* (Oxford: Oxford University Press, 1966): 530: "Older deism in England assumed that Christianity was an imposture. This short way of dismissing the New Testament descended to many working-class atheist pamphleteers of the thirties and forties."

14. Michael S. Edwards, *Purge This Realm: A Life of Joseph Rayner Stephens* (London: Epworth, 1994). On popular connections between Stephens and Chartism or Chartist ideas, see, e.g., *Northern Star*, September 29, 1838; *Northern Liberator*, April 25, 1840; Pierce Egan the Younger, *Wat Tyler; Or, the Rebellion of 1381* (London: Peirce, 1847), 835–38. See also the discussion in Dorothy Thompson, *The Chartists: Popular Politics in the Industrial Revolution* (New York: Pantheon, 1984), 116–17; 195, 239, 322–23; Dodd, "Strauss's English Propagandists," 430–31; Malcolm Chase, *Chartism: A New History* (Manchester: Manchester University Press, 2007), 50–53, 79, 97–98, 118, 120–21, 141, 260, 263, 268–69, 338, 362 n. 12.

suggests a difference between English and Scottish Chartism. For Chase, many of the approximately twenty English Chartist churches were "ephemeral," and the "English congregations also tended towards religious humanism whereas the Scottish churches were more theologically orthodox," not least on questions of Christ's divinity and resurrection and the Bible as the "complete revelation of God's will."[15] This generalization helps explain the popularity of the more radical works on religion and Jesus in the Chartist press (see below). However, we still need to be careful about reading too much into passing statements about Jesus because of the relative diversity and often conventionality of devotional commitments in English Chartism.

Jesus was an obvious authority to be invoked in articles, lectures, sermons, and outbursts among Chartists and their precursors in the 1830s, and some references give us some insight into the sort of contexts which would have been receptive of historical Jesus work. Here I now summarize the results of many relevant newspaper articles. There is recurring emphasis on the "earthly" or "human" Jesus, with minimal concern for the miraculous, hard divinity, or resurrection, and with a consistent stress on the relevance of Jesus for the politics of the present. The presentation is also largely consistent, whatever the religious affiliation of Chartists—the differences typically involve whether to emphasize violence or not. The picture is one of Jesus, the anticlerical class warrior, who was sometimes a laborer and who was from and cared for the poor, vagrants, and oppressed. He spoke out against usury, avarice, hypocrisy, tyranny, plunder, exploitation, and the rich. Jesus's opponents were the perceived exploitative and hypocritical middle and upper *classes* of his day, especially the priests and sometimes the Pharisees. They were not generalized as Jewish or religious opposition as such but rather instances of Jewish opposition within first-century Jewish society stratified like any other society. Put another way, like-minded groups across time and place effectively slot into their class-based position in the exploitative system. Opposition in Jesus's time was thus seen to be paralleled in the present among hostility from Whigs, Tories, aristocrats, and church authorities of various stripes (Church of England, Catholic, Nonconformist). In the face of such aggressive opposition, the stress lay on the impressiveness of Jesus's teachings, egalitarianism, virtue, morality, humility, discipline, neighborliness, and dignity.[16]

15. Chase, *Chartism*, 52; cf. 141, 250.
16. See, e.g., *Poor Man's Guardian*, November 19, 1831; March 3, 1832; May 26, 1832; November 24, 1832; March 16, 1833; April 6, 1833; April 27, 1833; August 31, 1833; September 7, 1833; November 23, 1833; March 22, 1834; June 7, 1834; October 25, 1834; December 20, 1834; January 3, 1835; February 21, 1835; April 25, 1835; May 2, 1835; June 27, 1835; November 7, 1835; *Northern Star*, April 21, 1838; *Northern Liberator*, September 1, 1838; December 8, 1838; July 6, 1839; September 21,

Jesus's death was regularly understood as an example of the unjust end that always awaits the benevolent reformer, though this Jesus did not always passively accept his fate. The question of Jesus and violence depended on the stance of the Chartist interpreter and reflected the tension in Chartism between "moral force" and "physical force." That is, sometimes the Chartist emphasis was on peace; on other occasions there was a hint of Chartist menace. To take a colorful example of the latter, when a clergyman was giving a sermon on the "virtues and excellence" of Jesus to the prisoners of Durham County Prison, an inmate called Laing (a.k.a. "Radical Jack" of Stockton) stood up and proclaimed, "Sir, Jesus Christ was the first Chartist. He was the best man that ever came into the world. He taught the doctrines of humility and equality, and even instructed men to sell their garments and buy a sword." For this outburst, poor Radical Jack received three days' solitary confinement.[17]

While such understandings of Jesus were not always the lives of Jesus in scholarly imaginations, there are indications that emerging ideas about the historical Jesus influenced the thinking of the Chartists and their precursors in the 1830s. In newspapers, and in addition to pamphleteering, there is evidence of awareness of Germanic "skepticism" and academic theology (as Engels implied) and reports and advertised books for sale relating to lives of Jesus and controversial approaches to the Bible, including Strauss's reconstruction and reports of the mistreatment of Strauss, Thomas Paine's work, and the English translation of Baron d'Holbach's scathingly critical account of Jesus.[18]

We also have a specific example of the influence of critical scholarship on Chartist understandings of Jesus and the gospels. In 1842, the Chartist lecturer and poet John Watkins published a series of lectures, including an extended lecture on Jesus, Christianity, and Chartism.[19] Watkins gave an outline of Jesus's life that harmonized the gospels and argued the first followers of Jesus were able to preserve this outline because it was "found in tradition and contemporary testi-

---

1839; March 21, 1840; May 2, 1840; *Northern Star*, August 14, 1841; December 11, 1841; November 5, 1842; January 7, 1843; June 10, 1843; December 6, 1843; December 6, 1845; January 2, 1847; August 11, 1849; May 15, 1852; May 22, 1852. Cf. *The Charter*, September 22, 1839.

17. *Northern Liberator*, September 7, 1839; *The Charter*, September 15, 1839. For inevitably brief speculation about Radical Jack's background, see Thompson, *Chartists*, 158.

18. E.g., *Poor Man's Guardian*, February 16, 1833; March 23, 1833; August 17, 1833; November 30, 1833; February 22, 1834; *Northern Star*, February 18, 1843; December 6, 1845; October 24, 1846; November 21, 1846; December 5, 1846; April 17, 1847; December 18, 1847; February 12, 1848; September 9, 1848; September 23, 1848; December 29, 1849; May 18, 1850.

19. *Northern Star*, April 9, 1842. All references to Watkins's lecture are taken from *Northern Star*, June 11, 1842, and June 18, 1842. On Watkins's life, see Thompson, *Chartists*, 43, 56, 118, 125, 157–58; Chase, *Chartism*, 117–25.

mony" and was later narrated by the evangelists and preached about by Paul and others. We also find overlapping rhetoric with bourgeois lives of Jesus. Jesus was the "most memorable man that ever lived ... a good man, if ever there was a great man, a man of genius and of virtue ... a gentleman in the true sense of the word." Nevertheless, this great man Jesus was seen as relevant to lower order radicalism. We learn that Jesus was born of "poor parents," who were forced to flee Herod, and that after "wandering from country to country, probably in search of work," they eventually settled in Nazareth. As a "poor man ... a working man," the "son followed his father's trade of a carpenter," before his public preaching. Note here the emphasis on the *this-worldly* father-son relationship, which is followed by a stress on how resurrection was *not* about the miraculous return to physical life from physical death. Rather, the attempt to extinguish the life of Jesus was countered by "his fame [that] rose from his own ashes." The christologically elevated Jesus this is not.

Whereas Hennell saw Jesus break through the apparent constraints of his class, Watkins's Chartist Jesus remained a class warrior of the lower orders. Even though Watkins himself may not have had a working-class upbringing, at this stage of his Chartist career his ideas were embedded in such working-class interests. For him, Jesus's first companions were "poor fishermen" and he spoke in language that the common people understood: parables. Jesus's unpaid reformist preaching involved fearless denunciation of the "inhuman rich." Explicit hostility toward the wealthy and the exploiters picked up on a common enough Chartist theme. Jesus himself was dedicated, loyal, and disciplined in his duty to "justice and humanity" in stark contrast to his opponents made up of "usurpers," "monopolizers," and "oppressors," enemies he wanted to help but who, in return, resented and killed him. In line with Chartist martyrology, and indeed with understandings of masculinity in some strands of nineteenth-century lives of Jesus, Watkins cast (in some detail) Jesus as a "man of sorrow, of suffering, and of sacrifice" who endured as long as he did because of his "very goodness, his very greatness, his very genius and virtue."[20] Even at the end, cruelly humiliated and shamed by his (unnamed) executioners, Jesus still took his ordeal with dignity.

After Jesus's death, his followers then spread Jesus's "principles" while "doing justice to his motives, to his conduct, to his character." They likewise faced persecution to the point of Watkins labeling them "Blessed martyrs!" These brave martyrs enabled the spread of Christianity until it was corrupted by pomp, power, and the "unholy alliance" of church and state, which produced the "bastard progeny"

---

20. Regarding notions of masculinity in nineteenth-century lives of Jesus, see Moxnes, *Jesus and the Rise of Nationalism*, 34–37.

of bishops and assorted clergy, whether Catholic or Protestant. The very system Jesus had tried to overthrow had returned but was now even worse. Put differently, this was an unashamedly self-conscious construction of Jesus in light of the nineteenth-century present and historic ongoing class and political relations. And so, as politics had led Christianity astray, so politics could return Christianity to its first principles through a complementary movement: Chartism. Both were deemed "essentially democratic" and "opposed to class-legislation, class-distinctions, usurpations and oppressions." Thus, for Watkins, Jesus was a preacher of a timeless truth promoting human welfare and happiness for which "many heroes and martyrs" have fought and died. This tradition, he argued, continued in England in the dissident tradition of the eighteenth and nineteenth centuries, culminating with the Chartists who acted Jesus-like in the face of persecution and ridicule from latter day "platter-scaping scribes and Pharisees," who among the priests were the *class* representatives of opposition to Jesus in Chartist imaginations. Little surprise that Watkins claimed (as he did elsewhere) that "no man can be a Christian unless he be a Chartist, and *vice versa.*"[21]

Such clear blurring of past and present does not mean that we should avoid seeing this reconstruction in the tradition of familiar historical Jesus studies. For a start, we should recall that there are indications that the Chartist Jesus was (or at least could sometimes be) a Jesus who is accessible because ideas about him were transmitted by a preexisting gospel tradition. We have also noted how bourgeois lives of Jesus were engaged with the political questions of their day. The portrayal of Jesus as a virtuous Great Man in opposition to the ruling classes of his day may have been given a spin in light of working-class interests among Chartists, but the general portrayal is hardly out of place in the familiar nineteenth-century reconstructions of Jesus. Furthermore, we have some clear antecedents in English radicalism that are crucial for illuminating what we find in the snippets of Chartist understandings of Jesus. The translation of Strauss and the awareness of Germanic theology already provide important indications of the background to the interest in this human or historical Jesus among English radicals and dissidents. But Chartists were tapping into preexisting influences from the historical Jesus work carried out in English radical traditions, particularly those following the French revolution onward, which constructed the Jesus movement and its opposition in terms of class conflict and political relations. Of especial importance here is the best-known example: the republican revolutionary from an artisan background, Thomas Paine, who was a major influence on English radicalism and dissent (in-

---

21. As we might expect, Watkins's thinking elsewhere was steeped in Chartist martyrology. See Chase, *Chartism*, 117, 121.

cluding Chartism) and whose work on Jesus was acknowledged by Hennell in his *Inquiry* (21–22, 303–4, 309–11, 316–17, 333, 357).[22]

Thomas Paine

In *The Age of Reason* (part 1 published in 1794; part 2 in 1795), Paine argued that the gospels were written many years after the purported events. [23] They were *not* written by Matthew, Mark, Luke, and John and they provide contradictory, disordered, and distorted accounts, some with conspicuous silences and omissions when read side by side, thereby suggesting that they were written by "unconnected individuals" who were not eyewitnesses (2:70, 81, 85–86, 88). Worth recalling concerning the embellishment of ideas about Jesus is Paine's famous criticism of the historical accuracy of miracle stories and prophecies. For Paine, these stories were dubious in and of themselves, but his skepticism was also based on a critical reading of the gospel texts and pushing their logic to absurdist positions. For instance, Paine could sarcastically dismiss the story of the devil showing and promising Jesus all the kingdoms of the world (Luke 4:1–13) by pointing out that if this had really happened, then there is a surprising lack of interest in the discovery of America (1:55; cf. 2:69).

If we can get to the "real character" of Jesus, then this must be something different than the gospel presentations. While Chartism lacked Paine's polemics toward the biblical texts, there were comments made about Jesus that were inherited by the Chartists. For Paine, all we can know about Jesus was that he was a "virtuous and amiable man," a "reformer and revolutionist" who preached a benevolent morality (1:7–8).[24] Jesus preached the "equality of man" and was against the "corruption and avarice of the Jewish priests," which in turn brought the vengeance of the priesthood against him. The priests accused him of sedition and conspiracy against the Romans. But, as with Chartism, there is no indiscriminate Jewish

22. Cf. S. Hennell, *Memoirs*, 31, 74–75.

23. Thomas Paine, *The Age of Reason: Being an Investigation of True and of Fabulous Theology* (Boston: Hall, 1794), 8–9, 23; Paine, *The Age of Reason: Being an Investigation of True and of Fabulous Theology. Part the Second* (London: Symonds, 1795), 71–81. Subsequent citations of *Age of Reason* appear in-text. Paine later wrote what would become known as the third part of *Age of Reason, Examination of the Passages in the New Testament*, where the focus was primarily on dealing with the issue of prophecy. See *Examination of the Passages in the New Testament, Quoted from the Old and Called Prophecies concerning Jesus Christ* (New York: Paine, 1807). *Age of Reason* and related miscellaneous pieces were later brought together in Thomas Paine, *The Theological Works* (London: Carlile, 1819) and led to a legal and political storm.

24. Later, Paine is more tentative still about what we can know about the existence of Jesus (e.g., *Age of Reason*, 2:65; *Examination*, 48).

blame here. The Romans had subjugated the Jews and demanded taxation. Thus, Jesus likely contemplated "the delivery of the Jewish nation from the bondage of the Romans" and the Romans were therefore likely to have had issues with the Jewish Jesus too (2:71–73). Indeed, upon this earthly Jesus, Paine argued that "Christian mythologists" constructed Jesus Christ as both God and man, as ancient gentile mythology regularly claimed that extraordinary people were deified sons of their gods and the result of intercourse between gods and women. Post-Jesus Christianity was, then, a product of such gentile and "heathen" thinking (1:7). The gospels were part of this process and so are now limited in what they can tell us about what we would call the historical Jesus.

In terms of lasting influence, we should recall how popular Paine's work was. Despite, or because of, attempts to suppress it in Britain, *Age of Reason* became a sensational international hit going through multiple editions. As well as arousing unsympathetic responses, *Age of Reason* was cheap and known among miners, laborers, and artisans as well as political radicals.[25] Moreover, the varied discontents ranging from reformist to revolutionary in reaction to the economic hardships following the Napoleonic Wars gave the Paine-style Jesus a renewed impetus. A provocative and likewise controversial presentation of such a Jesus that engaged Paine's work came from Thomas Evans: a printcolorer, bracemaker, and product of 1790s London radicalism, the revolutionary ideas of Thomas Spence, and popular millenarianism.[26]

Thomas Evans

Evans's controversial work *Christian Policy, the Salvation of the Empire* was published in 1816. Here he attacked impoverishment and made the case for dramatic

---

25. John Keane, *Tom Paine: A Political Life* (London: Bloomsbury, 1995), 396–400; Patrick W. Hughes, "Irreligion Made Easy: The Reaction to Thomas Paine's *The Age of Reason*," in *New Directions in Thomas Paine Studies*, ed. Scott Cleary and Ivy Linton Stabell (New York: Palgrave Macmillan, 2016), 109–31; see also E. P. Thompson, *The Making of the English Working Class* (London: Penguin, 1963), 105–7, 544, 846.

26. For further details on Evans and his context, see Thompson, *Making of the English Working Class*, 171, 177–78, 182, 187–88, 191, 672–73, 736, 852, 886; Gregory Claeys, "Thomas Evans and the Development of Spenceanism, 1815–16," *Bulletin of the Society for the Study of Labour History* 48 (1984): 24–30; Iain McCalman, *Radical Underworld: Prophets, Revolutionaries, and Pornographers in London, 1795–1840* (Cambridge: Cambridge University Press, 1988); Malcolm Chase, *"The People's Farm": English Radical Agrarianism, 1775–1840* (Oxford: Clarendon, 1988); Malcolm Chase, "Evans, Thomas (b. 1763, d. in or before 1831)," in *Oxford Dictionary of National Biography*, January 3, 2008, https://www.oxforddnb.com/display/10.1093/ref:odnb/9780198614128.001.0001 /odnb-9780198614128-e-47140; Edward Royle, *Revolutionary Britannia? Reflections on the Threat of Revolution in Britain, 1789–1848* (Manchester: Manchester University Press, 2000), 44–45.

agrarian transformation with a specifically politicized understanding of "paganism" providing the negative foil. Evans harked back to the popular myth, also inherited by the Chartists (though rejected by Paine) of a golden era of Saxon constitutional liberties spoiled by the feudalism of the "pagan" Norman Conquest of 1066. The "pagan" Norman Conquest could not fully obliterate these constitutional rights, and the English, "like the Jews," continued to struggle for a better world.[27] This was part of wider ideas about the struggle against the tyrannical landowning descendants of the Normans in the following centuries, an impulse toward freedom that was understood, then, as part of a tradition of English constitutionalism from below.[28] The accompanying myth of the Norman yoke in the English radicalism of the late eighteenth and nineteenth centuries was often framed in terms of political, economic, behavioral, and cultural values, and it would later provide an alternative version of English identity to ideas of a biologically or racialized Victorian English or British identity.[29]

While not undermining their difference from the common enough anti-Jewish remarks of the time (by radicals or not), we should not romanticize the rhetoric of these English radicals on issues of race (clunky language, dubious comments, and stereotypes remain as we might expect). And, although Jews and Judaism were presented positively by Evans and others, there remained limitations when they compared Judaism with Christianity and (the Jewish) Jesus, even if the continuities were also acknowledged.[30] Nevertheless, this was still a myth that later

27. Thomas Evans, *Christian Policy, the Salvation of the Empire* (London: Seale and Bates, 1816), 9–14.

28. For discussion, see Christopher Hill, "The Norman Yoke," in *Democracy and the Labour Movement: Essays in Honour of Dona Torr*, ed. John Saville (London: Lawrence and Wishart, 1954), 11–66; John Belchem, "Republicanism, Popular Constitutionalism and the Radical Platform in Early Nineteenth-Century England," *Social History* 6 (1981): 1–32; Billie Melman, "Claiming the Nation's Past: The Invention of an Anglo-Saxon Tradition," *Journal of Contemporary History* 26 (1991): 575–95; James Epstein, *Radical Expression: Political Language, Ritual, and Symbol in England, 1790–1850* (Oxford: Oxford University Press, 1994), 1–32; James Epstein, "'Our Real Constitution': Trial Defence and Radical Memory in the Age of Revolution," in *Re-Reading the Constitution: New Narratives in the Political History of England's Long Nineteenth Century*, ed. James Vernon (Cambridge: Cambridge University Press, 1996), 22–51; Benjamin Weinstein, "Popular Constitutionalism and the London Corresponding Society," *Albion* 34 (2002): 37–57; Josh Gibson, "The Chartists and the Constitution: Revisiting British Popular Constitutionalism," *Journal of British Studies* 56 (2017): 70–90; Gibson, "Natural Right and the Intellectual Context of Early Chartist Thought," *History Workshop Journal* 84 (2017): 194–213.

29. For discussion, see Chris R. Vanden Bossche, *Reform Acts: Chartism, Social Agency and the Victorian Novel, 1832–1867* (Baltimore: Johns Hopkins University Press, 2014), 38–49; Crossley, *Spectres of John Ball*, 207–17, 224–25.

30. Concern for a "more just and equitable mode of dividing the rent or produce of the

helped incorporate Irish-background Chartists in the movement. It also meant a figure like the tailor William Cuffay, who came from a slave family background, could be seen as a Chartist hero and the greatest Englishman because of his behavior, cultured use of language, musical ability, and political leanings, while the establishment and satirical press were simultaneously publishing racist abuse about him.[31] And this background myth contributed to the positive use of generalizing language about Jews and Judaism in relation to the human figure of Jesus in English radicalism.

Evans's Jesus needs to be understood through his reading of this sort of history. For Evans (and others) there were three great eras of liberty in human history standing against, and corrupted by, the oppression of "paganism": (1) Moses and his agrarian republic; (2) the Christian republican epoch grounded in the principles of the first Christians (who were also enslaved Jews, Evans added) when everything was held in common and inspired by Jesus; and (3) Anglo-Saxon England when led by another "great, good, and virtuous man . . . Alfred the Great, Alfred the Good . . . the third saviour of the world." Evans argued that the "territory of a nation is the people's farm" but, in the present, the people starve in the midst of plenty "produced by their own labour" and are in the "condition of slaves." Similar to what would soon be seen with Chartism, the remedy required a return to the basic principles of Christianity, in Evans's case so that "all feudality be abolished, and the territory of these realms be declared to be the people's farm."[32]

In this context we can understand Evans's development of the Paine-style Jesus as, once again, a "good and virtuous man." Jesus was so because he observed the laws of Moses to reproduce "that harmony and brotherhood so necessary for the well being of society." As with Paine, it was the "pagan Greeks" who made Jesus a "divinity," not the first followers or "the Jews," because "the Jews were commanded to deify no man." Evans then adds what was at that time an incendiary comment, one that went further than the familiar Paine-style understanding of Jesus:

---

land" makes Christianity "so much more superior to Judaism." While the "great philosopher and lawgiver" Moses put people in possession of the land, Jesus (i.e., "Joshua, the son of Joseph and Mary") established the division of the rents of the land. See Evans, *Christian Policy*, 21; cf. 20, 39: "the God of the Jews, of the Christians, a good God. . . . For if Judaism and Christianity be a revelation from the Deity, it is, in both instances, a revelation of a particular system of policy to be observed for the administration of the things of this world amongst Jews and Christians; and whoever will not conform to this policy, rebel against God."

31. For discussion with bibliography, see Crossley, *Spectres of John Ball*, 213–17.

32. Evans, *Christian Policy*, 9, 14, 25. On comparable views in Chartism, see Chase, *Chartism*, 337–38.

This man, a Roman slave, crucified as a slave, (the mode of execution peculiar to Roman slaves) for preaching the seditious doctrine that God was the proprietor of the earth, and not the Romans; that all men were equal in his sight, and consequently ought not to be slaves to one another, nor to the Romans; for which he was crucified by the Romans. His Hebrew name was Joshua, being a Jew. His name as given us in Greek, being Jesus, for Joshua, and Christ for the Anointed. Our account of him is also Greek; the first council, called by the emperor Constantine, having destroyed all the Hebrew writings, to put down the laws of Moses, and introduce a new theology acceptable to the court, by whom they were overawed, and under whose influence they were induced to adopt the Greek or pagan gospels, or writings, and reject the Hebrew.[33]

The argument that an enslaved Jesus had contemporary ramifications was the sort of claim echoed in Chartism (and elsewhere) and in their clunky, if well-meaning, comparisons and associations between chattel slavery and wage slavery.[34]

Evans may not have had the same lasting level of fame as Paine, but his work on Jesus attained a significant degree of publicity and notoriety that meant it could not be ignored. The subversive potential of Evans's work was immediately noted by prominent establishment figures, including the Poet Laureate Robert Southey in his infamous, provocative, and seemingly anonymous piece in *Quarterly Review* (dated October 1816 but published February 11, 1817), which critiqued ideas about parliamentary reform, popular democracy, oppositional journalism, and radical Christianity.[35] Another report felt that Evans's proposals were really advocating a system of "universal robbery, blasphemy, and infidelity." Like the "seditions and blasphemies" of people such as Paine, there was potential for Ev-

33. Evans, *Christian Policy*, 10.

34. Thompson, *Chartists*, 189–91; Richard Bradbury, "Frederick Douglass and the Chartists," in *Liberating Sojourn: Frederick Douglass and Transnational Reform*, ed. Alan Rice and Martin Crawford (Athens: University of Georgia Press, 1999), 169–86; Kelly J. Mays, "Slaves in Heaven, Laborers in Hell: Chartist Poets' Ambivalent Identification with the (Black) Slave," *Victorian Poetry* 39 (2001): 137–63; Mike Sanders, *The Poetry of Chartism: Aesthetics, Politics, History* (Cambridge: Cambridge University Press, 2009), 93–94; Richard Huzzey, *Freedom Burning: Anti-Slavery and Empire in Victorian Britain* (Ithaca: Cornell University Press, 2012), 89–90; Martin Hoyles, *William Cuffay: The Life and Times of a Chartist Leader* (Hertford: Hansib, 2013), 97–98; Chase, *Chartism*, 307–8.

35. *Quarterly Review* 16 (October 1816): 225–78; "Robert Southey to Thomas Southey (21 December 1816)," *The Collected Letters of Robert Southey: Part Five, 1816–1818*, ed. Ian Packer, Tim Fulford, and Lynda Pratt (Romantic Circles, 2016), https://romantic-circles.org/editions/southey_letters/Part_Five/HTML/letterEEd.26.2882.html.

ans's "dangerous delusions" to "seduce the still more ignorant," and thus this sorry episode might require the intervention of the attorney general.[36]

John Ball/Jesus

Paine and Evans, with their ideas about religion and the Bible, were two of the more influential figures on lower order and working-class radicalism of the nineteenth century. And, of course, the politically radical Jesuses did not end there or with their ongoing receptions, and examples from many more interpreters could be given. But to get a general sense of the wider diffusion, influence, and popularity of politically radical and potentially violent "human" Jesus tropes influenced by Paine, Evans, and others, we can turn to another figure of the Chartist past whose exemplary life was merged with Jesus's: the priest of the 1381 English uprising, John Ball.[37] The uprising had at this point been largely vilified for four hundred years, but by the end of the eighteenth century it was starting to be sympathetically understood not just as an expression of justified concerns but as an English expression of revolution and social change along the lines of Jacobin idealism and radicalism in 1790s London.

Southey himself had contributed significantly to this reassessment in an unexpected but influential way. As a young Jacobin and Paine sympathizer, Southey wrote the dramatic poem or play *Wat Tyler* in 1794. Despite the title, much of the focus of *Wat Tyler* is on the priest John Ball, who was typically assumed by friendly and hostile interpreters alike as the ideologue of the uprising. In *Wat Tyler*, Ball is a critic of wealth inequality and oppression, a promoter of human equality and justice, a philosopher of revolutionary violence, and a selfless martyr for the cause. As this already implies, Ball is also presented like or as emulating the earthly, historical Jesuses emerging at the time, shorn as ever of the miraculous. Ball is of the people and came to serve, not command, and reminds people that the Son of God came as the humble and lowly man from Nazareth. Ball preaches the "law of Christ," discourages violent revenge, delivers "woes" to the rich, gives commands to sell possessions and give to the poor, notes that the sun shines on all people and God provides for them, attacks the "blood-purpled robes" of a royalty who turn the laboring classes to poverty, stands in contrast to the church authorities, observes an avaricious "high priest," receives an unfair trial, and advocates mercy, justice, and love.[38]

---

36. *Saint James's Chronicle*, December 14, 1816; *Hereford Journal*, December 25, 1816. Cf. *Champion*, December 29, 1816; *Carlisle Patriot*, January 11, 1817; *Manchester Mercury*, January 14, 1817.

37. Crossley, *Spectres of John Ball*, 155–297.

38. Robert Southey, *Wat Tyler* (London: Hone, 1817), 23–33, 40, 47–69.

But *Wat Tyler* was not published in the 1790s and Southey went on to become Poet Laurate, an establishment figure and high-profile critic of people like his younger self. However, just as Southey's provocative critique of radicals like Evans was published in *Quarterly Review*, *Wat Tyler* was somehow obtained, pirated, and repeatedly published by Southey's opponents from February 13, 1817, onward.[39] *Wat Tyler* provoked a scandal in the press and in Parliament, and was the source of much embarrassment for Southey. Unfortunately for Southey, it became a popular success, and seven editions were produced in 1817 alone and 60,000 copies sold, as it was republished cheaply and widely.[40] Against the backdrop of agitation, insurgency, dissent, and conspiracy in the early nineteenth century (including in Evans's networks), *Wat Tyler* was performed on stage and Southey (with the pertinent extracts from *Wat Tyler*) was satirized in popular publications, the press, and Parliament.[41]

By the time of Chartism, Southey's reading of the Jesus-like John Ball effectively became *the* John Ball in radical and dissenting working-class and middle-class circles of the first half of the nineteenth century, as both figures served similar authorizing functions. This Ball was invoked in protests, newspaper columns, poetry, and on the stage.[42] There was even a performance of Southey's *Wat Tyler* at Darlington Theatre with proceeds to be donated in "support of Durham political prisoners" who, we might reasonably speculate, could have included Radical

39. It is not entirely clear how the manuscript got into the hands of Southey's enemies. For discussion, including of the legal details, see, Frank Taliaferro Hoadley, "The Controversy over Southey's *Wat Tyler*," *Studies in Philology* 38 (1941): 85; "Robert Southey to Edith Fricker (c. 12 January 1795)," in *New Letters of Robert Southey: Volume I*, ed. Kenneth Curry (New York: Columbia University Press, 1965), 90–92; Ralph Anthony Manogue, "Southey and William Wordsworth: New Light on an Old Quarrel," *Charles Lamb Bulletin* 38 (1982): 105–14; W. A. Speck, *Robert Southey: Entire Man of Letters* (New Haven: Yale University Press, 2006), 170–71; Megan Richardson, *The Right to Privacy: Origins and Influence of a Nineteenth-Century Idea* (Cambridge: Cambridge University Press, 2017), 15–20.

40. For discussion of the reception of *Wat Tyler*, with bibliography, see Crossley, *Spectres of John Ball*, 173–205.

41. Zachary Zealoushead, *Plots and Placemen, or Green Bag Glory, an Historical Melo Drama, in Two Acts: As Performed at the Boroughmonger's Private Theatre* (London: Seale, 1817), 21–24; *Morning Chronicle*, March 15, 1817; *The Black Dwarf*, March 26, 1817; *The Republican*, March 29, 1817; *Chester Chronicle*, July 25, 1817; *Oxford University and City Herald*, July 26, 1817; *Liverpool Mercury*, August 8, 1817.

42. See *Cleave's Penny Gazette of Variety and Amusement*, March 10, 1838; *Northern Star*, May 29, 1841; October 16, 1841; April 9, 1842; November 19, 1842; December 2, 1843; February 28, 1846; Benjamin Brierley, *Home Memories and Recollections of a Life* (Manchester: Heywood & Son, 1886), 41.

Jack, the aforementioned promoter of a menacing Chartist Jesus.[43] That Jesus and Ball served a similar purpose in Chartism gains further support from the Chartist thinker of Christian origins John Watkins, discussed above, as he also wrote a play about Ball, though it is no longer extant.[44] Put another way, the tropes associated with the historical Jesus we have seen here were spread beyond the straightforward presentations of Jesus and were among the basic assumptions of Chartism.

Moving Beyond

This is, of course, a snippet both of the story of the English Quest for the historical Jesus from below and popular radical uses of historical Jesus scholarship at a time when the subject flourished. Furthermore, what I have discussed here is likely only scratching the surface of a huge amount of data concerning working-class, dissenting, and radical history over the nineteenth century, into the twentieth, and beyond, and in different geographical locations. As ever, some of this research has been carried out.[45] But we are in a position where more can be done (see Massey's chapter). Change in scholarly readings of the Quest is now easier partly because newspaper archives are often (though certainly not always) digitized unlike much archival material. One of my ongoing regrets as I currently work on English radical history away from Chartism in nondigitized archives (e.g., Labour History Archive, Working Class Movement Library, Marx Memorial Library) is not being able to collect and analyze the recurring references to and discussions of the historical Jesus. But the material is there for those willing, and no doubt the same could be said for countless archives across the world.

Nevertheless, we can still see a coherent outline of a popular English historical Jesus emerging in the first half of the nineteenth century. For all the idiosyncrasies of given writers, we see repeated traits associated with the historical Jesus: a virtuous, egalitarian, anticlerical, revolutionary, Jewish, antislavery, class warrior and martyr with an ambiguous attitude toward violence and who was unjustly killed because of competing class interests. By the time of Chartism, this was a firmly established class-based English radical tradition from below that was conducive to reinterpreting Strauss's controversial work and was part of the tradition

43. *Northern Star*, October 31, 1840.

44. Reports remain, however. See, e.g., *Yorkshire Gazette*, March 16, 1839; *Northern Star*, December 10, 1842; Ebenezer Elliott, *The Poetical Works of Ebenezer Elliott, the Corn-Law Rhymer* (Edinburgh: Tait, 1840), 163.

45. For American radicalism after the period discussed here, see David Burns, *The Life and Death of the Radical Historical Jesus* (Oxford: Oxford University Press, 2013).

of a radical reading of the moderately liberal Strauss.[46] The scholarly histories of English historical Jesus scholarship will typically focus on the influence of deists on Reimarus and how establishment Anglican intellectuals dismissed, ignored, and eventually compromised with Germanic developments in historical Jesus studies, with occasional mention of middle-class dissenters like Hennell. But in between were the working-class political dissenters and their advocates from the nineteenth century who now deserve their place in the history of the Quest for the historical Jesus.

Reclaiming history from below is a worthy exercise, but this enterprise was not always just about representation of the marginalized. It was much more. What has been lost in interdisciplinary histories from below is that it was developed by some of its famed practitioners to explain agency, structure, and change in history and the historical-materialist processes in the transformation from, for example, feudalism to capitalism.[47] Here we have noted, via Moxnes and Georgi, how the human, historical Jesus became a bourgeois project, challenging the dominance of the aristocratic Christ of the old order. What delving into the world of English working-class radicalism shows us is the emerging contradictions in capitalism between owners and workers, and how the radical human figure of Jesus emerging in the Enlightenment was carried on and developed by and for the English working class. Where this line of thinking might be developed further in historical-materialist terms is in the imperialist phase of capitalism and the colonial enterprise, and *not* only how the emerging bourgeois Jesuses were part of that. As suggested in the introduction to this volume, the Next Quest should also support the detailed historical and archival work on presentations of the historical or "human" Jesus in colonial entanglements across a range of cultural contexts.

46. Dodd, "Strauss's English Propagandists," 423. For an overview of Strauss's politics in relation to his version of the historical Jesus, including different political receptions of Strauss, see Moxnes, *Jesus and the Rise of Nationalism*, 95–120.

47. Jonathan White, *Making Our Own History: A User's Guide to Marx's Historical Materialism* (Glasgow: Praxis, 2021), 103–11.

13

FAME AND AURA

Matthew G. Whitlock

The Next Quest for the historical Jesus must account for the fame and aura that *precede* the historical Jesus of Nazareth. Intuitively, we assume that fame *follows* the early life and origins of an ancient, historical figure, especially the "humble origins" of Jesus of Nazareth. Yet when we approach these origins, we only do so because we *first* knew of Jesus's fame, not the concrete reality of the historical Jesus of Nazareth. In other words, we view—no matter how hard we try not to— the historical Jesus through and because of the lens of fame, a lens that *precedes* the Jesus of history.[1]

A brief excursus into Don DeLillo's 1986 novel *White Noise* helps illustrate this point.[2] In the third chapter of the novel, college professors Jack Gladney and Murray Siskind visit a famous tourist attraction, a barn in the countryside outside the fictional town of Farmington. On their way, they pass a procession of road signs at every turn: "THE MOST PHOTOGRAPHED BARN IN AMERICA." Once there, they

---

1. Here I draw from Claire Colebrook and her analysis of simulacra and simulation in the work of Jean Baudrillard and Gilles Deleuze, as reflected in Don DeLillo's novel. See Claire Colebrook, *Gilles Deleuze*, Routledge Critical Thinkers (Abingdon: Routledge, 2002), 97. The concept of simulacra preceding the real comes from Baudrillard's chapter "The Precession of Simulacra" in *Simulacra and Simulation*, trans. Sheila Faria Glaser (Ann Arbor: University of Michigan Press, 1994), 1: "The territory no longer precedes the map, nor does it survive it. It is nevertheless the map that precedes the territory—precession of simulacra—that engenders the territory."

2. Don DeLillo, *White Noise* (New York: Penguin, 1986), 12–13.

park alongside numerous cars and a tour bus and walk up a path to an elevated site for photographing the barn, where postcards are also sold. They view people taking photographs of the barn: they are "taking pictures of taking pictures." At this site Murray observes, "no one sees the barn" and then makes several observations. First, "Once you've seen the signs about the barn, it becomes impossible to see the barn." Second, "We're not here to capture an image. We're here to maintain one. Every photograph reinforces the aura . . . an accumulation of nameless energies." Third, "We only see what others see. The thousands who were here in the past, those who will come in the future. We've agreed to become part of a collective perception. This literally colors our vision. A religious experience in a way, like all tourism." Fourth, "What was the barn like before it was photographed? . . . What did it look like? . . . We can't answer these questions because we've read these signs, seen the people snapping the pictures. We can't get outside the aura. We're part of the aura." [3]

DeLillo's insights about the barn can just as easily apply to the fame and aura of Jesus of Nazareth. While not the most photographed figure, he is one of the most painted, written about, and sung about ones in the Western world. And even outside of the realm of religion, he remains the standard of fame, as we witnessed in John Lennon's proclamation about the Beatles: "We're more popular than Jesus now," or Amy Finnerty's comment about Kurt Cobain after Nirvana's famous MTV Unplugged show where Cobain sang "Jesus Doesn't Want Me for a Sunbeam." After the show, Cobain complained, "No one liked it." Finnerty retorted, "Kurt, they think you are Jesus Christ."[4]

We encounter a procession of signs on the way to the historical Jesus of Nazareth, *a collective perception* from actors, singers, television shows, gospels writers, and scholars: John Legend, Jim Caviezel, Lady Gaga's "Black Jesus," Southpark's "Jesus and Pals," John's Jesus, Paul's Jesus, Mark's Jesus, Matthew's Jesus, a Facebook response to a *Review of Biblical Literature* article about the most recent book on Luke's Jesus. We are *taking pictures of taking pictures*. Then there is art, from da Vinci's Last Supper to Warner Sallman's *The Head of Christ*, the 1940 picture by "an illustrator for advertising agencies and religious publishers," duplicated millions of times in "church bulletins, calendars, posters, bookmarks, prayer cards,

---

3. See Colebrook, *Gilles Deleuze*, 97: "what the tourists are going to see is not what the barn *is* in concrete reality, but what the barn has become through repeated simulation." On the surface, the pilgrimage to the barn seems to be an experience of the unique, singular, concrete reality of the barn, but the experience of the barn itself is and will always be of "the barn in that famous photograph."

4. Charles R. Cross, *Heavier Than Heaven: A Biography of Kurt Cobain* (New York: Hachette, 2019), 306. Cobain's "Jesus Doesn't Want Me for a Sunbeam" is his own rendition of the Vaselines' "Jesus Wants Me for a Sunbeam."

tracts, buttons, stickers and stationary," and the subject of a 1994 *New York Times* article "The Man Who Rendered Jesus for the Age of Duplication."[5] *We only see what others see. The thousands who were here in the past . . .* What's more, this procession of signs certainly has not been a drive to the countryside for multitudes over time. Colonialism, anti-Semitism, racism, white supremacy, homophobia, transphobia, ableism, the negation of reproductive rights—all have received a stamp of approval from Jesus's aura and fame. Colonialism is not only the result of Jesus's fame, but also an unjust cause. And from a posthuman standpoint, the environment itself has felt drastic effects of a particular procession of signs from Jesus's aura.

We stand in front of a massive accumulation of signs about Jesus. From this, an aura expands and maintains itself. *We can't get outside the aura. We're part of the aura.* Yet, unlike Professor Siskind, who stands directly in front of the barn, we can never stand in front of the concrete reality of the historical Jesus of Nazareth. And if Professor Siskind claims not to see the barn but only its aura when he stands directly in front of the barn, what then can we say, unable to stand in front of the concrete reality of the historical Jesus of Nazareth? And how do this distance and absence of the historical Jesus enhance Jesus's aura?

It is the concept of aura and its relation to distance that I want to explore in this chapter, theorizing how early Christian writers created and maintained Jesus's aura and fame through a rhetoric of distance, and how scholarship has maintained it. Such an exploration certainly applies more broadly to reception history of Jesus or, more properly, perception history. But here I concentrate chiefly on early Christian texts and modern scholarship. In doing so, I mediate between our time and the first century with Walter Benjamin's theory on aura and distance found in his essay "The Work of Art in the Age of Its Technological Reproducibility."[6] First, I outline Benjamin's theory of aura and distance and its relation to the historical Jesus and fame; second, I suggest how early Christian texts created and maintained Jesus's aura and fame through a rhetoric of distance; third, I suggest how modern scholarship has maintained this aura. In this third section, I argue for why it is vital for the Quest for the historical Jesus to continue in this rapidly changing technological and political landscape, asserting that rigorous scholarship, informed by Benjamin's theory, can move us away from aura maintenance.

5. William Grimes, "The Man Who Rendered Jesus for the Age of Duplication," *New York Times*, October 12, 1994. See also David Morgan, *Icons of American Protestantism: The Art of Warner Sallman* (New Haven: Yale University Press, 1996).

6. All citations of Walter Benjamin's works, unless otherwise noted, are from *Selected Writings*, ed. Michael W. Jennings et al., trans. Rodney Livingstone et al., 4 vols. (Cambridge: Belknap, 1991–1999).

DISTANCE: THE CREATION AND MAINTENANCE OF AURA AND FAME

How are aura and fame constructed and maintained? Here I turn to Walter Benjamin's theory on aura and distance, delineating the context and relevancy of his theory, defining his theory, applying his theory to the study of the historical Jesus, and further unpacking his theory with cognitive science research.

Walter Benjamin and Aura: Context and Relevancy

Before explaining Benjamin's theory on aura, I note two important contextual factors: the context of Benjamin's theory and the theory's relevance to our own context and subject matter, Jesus of Nazareth. First, although Benjamin's essay focuses on art and technology, his chief concern is much broader than aesthetics.[7] He begins and ends with a Marxist critique of the superstructure, populist politics, and fascism, outlining the ways in which all three use aesthetics, including the traditional concepts of creativity, genius, eternal value, and mystery, for their own interests.[8] Then in the body of the essay he suggests how the aura, authenticity, and authority of art serve these fascist interests, and how, on the other hand, modern technological reproduction can decay the aura, authenticity, and authority of the art and serve the interests of the proletariat. Benjamin, therefore, does not bemoan the decay of aura in its complex relationship with fame, a point I will return to at the end of this chapter. Second, Benjamin's focus on art and its technological reproducibility is particularly relevant to our subject. For we derive our perceptions of Jesus chiefly through literature and art, and through their manifold reproductions and effects up to the present moment, a moment of rapid reproduction and simulacrum of images. Although the "original" Jesus in the Quest for the historical Jesus is the historical person of Jesus of Nazareth—and not a work of art—Benjamin's insights help us come to grips with how this "original," whom we will never see, is reproduced in literature and art, and how Jesus's aura is created and maintained (and perhaps decayed in the future) as our modes of technological reproduction change over time.

---

7. See Miriam Bratu Hansen, "Benjamin's Aura," *Critical Inquiry* 34.2 (2008): 336–75; Susan Buck-Morss, "Aesthetics and Anaesthetics: Walter Benjamin's Artwork Essay Reconsidered," *October* 62 (1992): 3–41.

8. See Hansen, "Benjamin's Aura," 356: "The diverse practices of aura simulation converged and culminated . . . in supplying the means for resurrecting the aura's undead remains in the arena of national-populist and fascist politics."

Walter Benjamin and Aura: A Theory of Distance

What is aura and how is it created and maintained? Aura is grounded in the object's or person's unique, historical existence—their authenticity and authority.[9] Aura is then created and maintained by establishing a distance from this unique existence.[10] So Benjamin defines aura as "the unique apparition of a *distance*, however near [the object] may be."[11] Aura is not dependent on spatial distance of the object, according to Benjamin, hence, "however near it may be." Rather, aura depends also on spatiotemporal distance in connection with human perception as it is affected in turn by technology, the main thrust of Benjamin's argument. Hence, Murray Siskind can stand directly in front of the barn and only see its aura as first established by the famous photograph. To sum up in Benjamin's words: aura is "a strange weave of space and time: the unique appearance of a distance, no matter how near it may be."[12] Historical existence, authenticity, authority, and distance (spatiotemporally perceived) all interact together in the formation and maintenance of aura, according to Benjamin. If one is taken away, aura *may* decay. This leads to the heart of Benjamin's argument: the potential decay of aura through technological reproduction and changes in human perception, a decay he celebrates.

Benjamin asserts that aura decays in at least four ways, largely due to how technological reproducibility has affected human perception of the object over time. First, the object loses its cult value. It moves from being "an instrument of magic" to "a work of art," from the sacred to the secular. However—and this is key for what I assert later about the Quest for the historical Jesus—this transition from sacred to secular *alone* does not contribute to loss of aura.[13] Second, the object's aura decays as it becomes reproduced and popular. Objects become reproduced for the public

9. Although Benjamin's chief focus is on the aura of artwork in his "Work of Art" essay, it is noteworthy that the first example he uses grounds aura in nature: "To follow with the eye—while resting on a summer afternoon—a mountain range on the horizon or a branch that casts its shadow on the beholder is to breathe the aura of those mountains, of that branch." See Walter Benjamin, "The Work of Art in the Age of Technological Reproducibility (Third Version)," in *Selected Writings*, 4:255. Throughout his writings, aura is not limited to artwork and covers human subjects, such as the human aura in photographs. See Hansen, "Benjamin's Aura."

10. I recognize the nuances of the term "object" here. Overall, I aim to avoid the false dichotomy between subject and object. In her work on Benjamin, Susan Buck-Morss ("Aesthetics and Anaesthetics," 12) offers a more holistic view connecting the perceiver and perceived, avoiding the dichotomy between subject and object, which she calls a "constant plague of classical philosophy."

11. Benjamin, "Work of Art," 4:255.

12. Walter Benjamin, "Little History of Photography," in *Selected Writings*, 2:518.

13. On the false assumptions about secularization taking away the aura of religious figures,

and are no longer confined to sacred spaces, private ownership of the elite, or photographs only seen by families, all of which contribute to exclusivity, scarcity, and
distance—and hence aura.[14] It is "the desire of the present-day masses to 'get closer'
to things spatially and humanly, and their equally passionate concern for overcoming each thing's uniqueness by assimilating it as a reproduction."[15] Reproduction
extracts sameness from uniqueness. The masses are drawn to the "uniqueness"
as a result of first encountering the reproduction, the sameness; and sameness is
further extracted as the masses investigate the uniqueness. "The stripping of the
veil from the object, the destruction of the aura, is the signature of a perception
whose 'sense for the sameness in the world' has so increased that, by means of
reproduction, it extracts sameness from even what is unique."[16] Third, technology
produces new ways of viewing the original. The artists and perceivers move from
being magicians to surgeons. For example, photography allows for close-ups and
film allows for slow motion, both new ways of viewing reality. Fourth, a modern
artwork produced solely for mass reproduction is not fetishized. There is no original
copy of value. Hence, modern, reproducible artifacts are not connected with the
aura and authenticity of an original, nor is there an overly strong desire among the
masses to find the original negative or film roll, for example.[17]

Jesus of Nazareth and Aura: A Theory of Distance

Contrary to Benjamin's theory, Jesus's aura remains despite massive technological
reproduction and technological changes in perception. Why is this the case? On
the surface, Jesus's religious cult value seems to provide one answer. Unlike other
historical figures (e.g., Roman emperors), Jesus's religious value remains today. Jesus
remains a part of religious practice, not just an image in art, literature, and history.
However, Jesus's aura may not decay even if secularized, even if viewed apart from
religious tradition. Hence, the distinction in prior quests between the "earthly"
and "heavenly" Jesus is not entirely helpful when discussing Jesus's aura and fame
and their influence on scholarship, nor is the distinction between "the historical
Jesus" and "the Jesus of faith." Both the earthly and historical Jesus, according to

---

see Cavan W. Concannon, *Profaning Paul*, Class 200: New Studies in Religion (Chicago: University of Chicago Press, 2021), 95–96.

14. "In the cult of remembrance of dead or absent loved ones, the cult value of the image
finds its last refuge." See Benjamin, "Work of Art," 4:258.

15. Benjamin, "Work of Art," 4:255.

16. Benjamin, "Work of Art," 4:255–56.

17. Note that there are three versions of Benjamin's artwork essay, and Benjamin scholars
do not argue about which one is more "authentic."

Benjamin's argument, can retain aura and fame just as much as the heavenly one and the one of faith—for earthly figures and objects maintain auras despite having little religious value. Even famous barns maintain aura. Famous figures in history maintain auras, even rock stars, especially if they die young.[18] In *The Frenzy of the Renown: Fame and Its History*, Leo Braudy notes that today, "through the technology of image reproduction and information reproduction, our relation to the increasing number of faces we see every day becomes more and more transitory."[19] In our modern context of mass production, uniqueness, therefore, is all the more important. It is the unique and repeated faces or names, Braudy continues, that stand out, often the most historical and distant ones: "Alexander, Caesar, Cleopatra, Jesus, Mohammed, Joan of Arc, Shakespeare." Braudy asserts how fame "celebrates uniqueness, and in part it requires that uniqueness be exemplary and reproducible."[20] Fame survives, in other words, as long as it maintains uniqueness in light of mass reproduction. It is on this point that Benjamin is most helpful: the paradoxical relationships between uniqueness and sameness, singularity and reproducibility. As long as spatiotemporal distance preserves aura, preserves Jesus's uniqueness, Jesus's aura remains no matter how much Jesus is reproduced, no matter how "near" the masses or scholarship comes. No matter how much he is reproduced, Jesus provides, in Benjamin's words, a "gaze that will never get its fill."[21]

Cognitive Science: Aura and Halo, Distance and Uniqueness

Cognitive science research on the "halo effect" is particularly helpful in unpacking Benjamin's theory on aura for the twenty-first century. Benjamin himself, in his early writings, links halo and aura together. Miriam Bratu Hansen notes how Benjamin sees "aura as an elusive phenomenal substance, ether, or *halo* that surrounds a person or object of perception, encapsulating their individuality and authenticity."[22] Cognitive science, like Benjamin's work on aura, studies how halos can be illusionary and affect the way one views another object or person, whether a present or a historical one. According to Joseph Forgas:

18. Early death certainly has played a role in creating aura through distance. See my eighth lens for further analysis—*The Rhetoric of Early Death*—later in this chapter.

19. Leo Braudy, *The Frenzy of the Renown: Fame and Its History* (New York: Vintage, 1980), 5. Braudy notes several key factors in modern fame construction: mass production, visual media (i.e., television and film), the expansion of audiences beyond the elite, the demise of the monarchy, and the Industrial Revolution (584–87).

20. Braudy, *Frenzy of the Renown*, 5. See also 585 on "the desire to be different but familiar."

21. Walter Benjamin, "On Some Motifs in Baudelaire," in *Selected Writings*, 4:338.

22. Hansen, "Benjamin's Aura," 340.

Halo effects refer to the widespread human tendency to make unwarranted inferences about a person's unknown characteristics on the basis of known but often irrelevant information. It seems as if known traits radiate a "halo" influencing how unrelated qualities are perceived. Halo effects differ from stereotype effects in that, in the case of halo effects, it is a person's *unique traits* or characteristics that give rise to unwarranted inferences.[23]

A distant Jesus, whose real and historical characteristics are widely unknown, has been quite vulnerable to the "halo effect." The few known, unique traits about Jesus (e.g., his early death on a cross) become the basis for unwarranted inferences about who he was wholly and historically, a tendency that has proliferated in both early Christian texts and scholarship, which I argue below. Taking what little we know about Jesus, looking at him from a spatiotemporal distance, and weaving together these few known and unique elements, creates a halo and aura. Below I argue that the earliest texts about Jesus created his aura in this fashion, and that the twenty-first century continues to maintain it.

The Rhetoric of Distance: Jesus's Aura and Fame in Early Christian Texts

How were Jesus's aura and fame constructed and maintained in early Christian texts? Media studies offer pathways for considering how early technology expanded early Christianity while preserving Jesus's uniqueness.[24] And Greco-Roman studies are ripe with examples of how ancient peoples sought to gain and maintain fame at the time when early Christian texts began to proliferate.[25] These two lenses call for extended studies. But here I focus on Benjamin's theory in relation to early Christian texts. Below I suggest ten lenses for further analysis of the rhetoric of distance and aura in early Christian texts:

---

23. J. P. Forgas, "She Just Doesn't Look Like a Philosopher . . . ? Affective Influences on the Halo Effect in Impression Formation," *European Journal of Social Psychology* 41 (2011): 812. Emphasis is my own.

24. Peter Horsfield, *From Jesus to the Internet: A History of Christianity and Media* (West Sussex: Wiley-Blackwell, 2015).

25. See Robert Garland, *Celebrity in Antiquity: From Media Tarts to Tabloid Queens*, Classical Inter/Faces (London: Bristol Classical Press, 2012); Braudy, *Frenzy of the Renown*, 55–189. Jewish writings are also ripe with examples of aura and fame: Philo, Josephus, the Dead Sea Scrolls, Jubilees, 1 Enoch.

1. *The Rhetoric of Spatiotemporal Distance.* Both Paul and the author of Luke, for example, freely acknowledge distance from the historical Jesus of Nazareth as they articulate their gospels (Gal 1:18; Luke 1:1–4).

2. *The Rhetoric of Intimacy at a Distance.* This phrase comes from a famous study from 1956 by Horton and Wohl, which became the foundation for parasocial interaction studies, an entire subfield in Communication Science.[26] It involves "'the simulacrum of conversational give and take' that takes place between users and mass media performers."[27] The rhetoric of intimacy at a distance can be analyzed in gospel reception history, especially Jesus's intimate words received at a distance. Moreover, it can be analyzed in the Pauline Letters once they began to be copied, read, and heard conversationally by later, unintended audiences. Deutero-Pauline works apply here as well. Marketing research on influencers is quite interested in the concept of creating "intimacy as a distance." "Jesus as an influencer" may not be grossly anachronistic here.

3. *The Rhetoric of Fame and Distance in the City.* In Vergil (book 4 of the *Aeneid*), the goddess Fama visits cities, not rarely traveled areas. The city is the chief, technological force for expanding one's celebrity and fame in the Greco-Roman world, but also a large place for being unknown enough to establish distance.[28] Paul's city strategy plays well into his goal to make Jesus's name above every name (Phil 2:9), although Jesus himself is distant. And Acts of the Apostles later employs this rhetoric of fame and city from Jerusalem to Rome.

4. *The Rhetoric of a Humble Distance from Fame.* Kurt Cobain is famous for being reluctantly famous in public, even though fame seems to be part of his private goal.[29] We see similar strategies in Greco-Roman literature.[30] In early Christian literature we find the rhetoric of Jesus's own self-emptying origins (Phil 2:7), despite the ultimate aim of attaining "a name above every name" (2:9).

5. *The Rhetoric of Secrecy.* The secrecy and hiddenness motifs (e.g., the secrecy motif in the Gospel of Mark; Matt 11:25–30; Gospel of Thomas) establish distance, mystery, and scarcity, thereby creating aura.

6. *The Rhetoric of Veiling.* The concept of veiled glory (2 Cor 3:12–18)—whether fading or too intense—plays well into aura-creating-distance, even if there is a promise of a full unveiling, constancy, and nearness.

26. D. Horton and R. Wohl, "Mass Communication and Para-Social Interaction: Observations on Intimacy at a Distance," *Psychiatry* 19 (1956): 215–29.

27. Tilo Hartmann and Charlotte Goldhoorn, "Horton and Wohl Revisited: Exploring Viewers' Experience of Parasocial Interaction," *Journal of Communication* 61 (2011): 1104.

28. Garland, *Celebrity in Antiquity*, 8.

29. Cross, *Heavier Than Heaven*, 363.

30. See Garland, *Celebrity in Antiquity*, 9, for "strategic self-presentation."

7. *The Rhetoric of Eternal Value of the Object.* The eternal value of the unveiled object creates infinite possibility, hence temporal distance yet sameness (Heb 13:8). The unsearchable, eternal value of Jesus (Eph 3:8–9) offers a distance and, in Benjamin's words, a "gaze that will never get its fill."[31]

8. *The Rhetoric of Early Death.* Greco-Roman literature was quite aware of how early death established distance for creating and maintaining fame.[32] Jesus's early exit from among his followers created an appropriate distance for their gospels, revitalizing the movement.

9. *The Rhetoric of Famous Yet Distant Heroes.* Plutarch's *Lives* is the Greco-Roman exemplar here. Early Christian texts also used the distance of past heroes, including Jesus, to create and maintain aura, substantiating a single trait or a grouping of traits (Heb 11:1–12:4).

10. *The Rhetoric of Famous Yet Distant Authors.* The anonymity, pseudonymity, and distance of early Christian authors created aura in their writings and ultimately their subject matter: Jesus.

Aside from identifying distancing rhetoric in early Christian texts, the Next Quest can also apply Benjamin's distancing effect to theories about the earliest, pretextual receptions of the Jesus movement.[33] If aura is constructed by *the unique appearance of a distance, no matter how near it may be*, then this distancing effect certainly includes the earliest receptions of Jesus, no matter how near they may have been, rightly underscoring aura's effects on the earliest receptions. "No one sees the barn," even those who stand directly in front of it. Furthermore, work needs to be done on distance and aura in the gospel narratives, especially as they relate to other first-century literature and practices (i.e., a leader's spatiotemporal relationship between followers and crowds). Whether follower or part of the crowd, one's reception and encounter in many cases are based *first* on word of mouth (e.g., Mark 6:14). And when people encounter Jesus, Jesus sometimes distances himself by being alone (Mark 6:46–47; Matt 14:23; Luke 6:12–13) or with his immediate followers (Mark 6:30–34; Luke 9:18), or by standing at a distance in front of the crowds (Mark 3:9–10; 4:1–2; Matt 13:1–2; Luke 5:1–3).

---

31. Walter Benjamin, "On Some Motifs in Baudelaire," 4:338.

32. For example, see Garland, *Celebrity in Antiquity*, 36, on Alexander.

33. Willi Braun delineates well the levels of filtering that take place during the earliest points of pre-textual reception. See "The Past as Simulacrum in the Canonical Narratives of Christian Origins," *R&T* 8 (2001): 213–28. The earliest, pre-textual receptions in relation to projection theory also are ripe for examination.

MODERN SCHOLARSHIP'S ROLE IN THE MAINTENANCE
AND DECAY OF JESUS'S AURA

I now turn to the final question: How are Jesus's aura and fame reinforced and maintained in modern scholarship, especially the prior Quests? From this I ask, so what? Why is it important to be aware of, and even disrupt, Jesus's aura? In answering this question, I conclude with suggestions about why and how—in light of Jesus's aura and fame—we ought to continue the Quest.

The Maintenance of Aura in Modern Scholarship

While the Next Quest is moving beyond the use of criteria, I believe it is important to think about the criteria in light of Jesus's fame and aura. It is not simply that the criteria have failed to lead us to the concrete reality of Jesus of Nazareth. Rather, the criteria have propagated and maintained Jesus's aura and authority. The spatiotemporal distance in any phase of the Quests is a given. But this distance creates and maintains aura—"a unique apparition at a distance"—when combined with claims of authenticity, which are based on criteria that focus on uniqueness: embarrassment, discontinuity, and rejection and execution. These "known" and unique characteristics are then propagated by criteria of multiple attestation and coherence, which really are early (multiple attestation) and modern (coherence) ways of reproducing a seemingly cohesive image of Jesus for a mass audience.[34] An "authentic" aura of Jesus is created from a distance, repeated in modern publications and from early Christian texts. As Forgas's research warned above, we make unwarranted inferences about a person's unknown characteristics on the basis of the known and unique.

Narrative approaches also repeat the aura-making of early Christian texts, maintaining aura within an uninterrupted and protected loop. While they are helpful for understanding how early Christian narratives function in creating worlds within the illusory walls of the text and its diverse readers, these approaches are not substitutes for the concrete reality of Jesus of Nazareth and of the worlds outside the texts, the ancient world and our own. A retreat into narrative approaches without consideration of the historical Jesus simply repeats and maintains Jesus's aura and fame for the twenty-first century. Benjamin was quite suspicious of such syntheses in history, literature, and art—especially cohesive narratives. I will address this suspicion in more detail below.

---

34. Though this process is common throughout the so-called Third Quest, I derive this set of criteria from John P. Meier's *The Roots of the Problem and the Person*, vol. 1 of *A Marginal Jew: Rethinking the Historical Jesus*, AYBRL (New York: Doubleday, 1991), 167–95.

Why Aura Maintenance in Modern Scholarship Is an Issue

The promulgation and maintenance of Jesus's aura and fame is a vital issue for modern scholarship to address. The context of Benjamin's "Work of Art" essay, as I noted above, provides the reason. In the face of fascism, racism, and anti-Semitism in Europe, Benjamin saw firsthand the effects of aura on political life, in his words, "the aestheticizing of political life."[35] As Miriam Bratu Hansen notes: "Benjamin's call to the demolition [of aura] was aimed at the technologically enhanced fabrication, from the mid-nineteenth century on, of auratic effects on a mass scale."[36] I have listed here and elsewhere how Jesus's aura has justified and is justifying grave injustices on a mass scale.[37] Scholarship has an ethical and civic responsibility for interrupting auras and their authority in relation to the historical Jesus and early Christian texts. This does not involve an ideological battle, which too often involves using Jesus's aura for good causes in order to counter destructive ones; instead, this involves scholarship's duty of "closing the distance" to the object or person of study (akin to Benjamin's point on photography's disruption of aura), continuing on to the Next Quest, as I outline in the final section below.

Why the Quest Must Continue in the Shadow of Jesus's Aura and Fame

Given what we know about aura and fame, should we continue the Quest? I unequivocally assert yes, even if the concrete reality of Jesus of Nazareth is irrecoverable and in pieces. We must continue to gather, but not fallaciously connect, these pieces. When we cynically give up on the task of "closing the distance," aura is maintained. This is precisely where I see danger in giving up on the Next Quest. Giving up on this quest is a move to maintain Jesus's aura. Brian Massumi, in his essay on "Realer Than Real," describes the modern dilemma of having copies without the actual, concrete realities.[38] First, we can fall into *cynicism* that everything we see in the technologically mediated world is no longer real. Second, we can fall into *nostalgia*, in our case, for "the lost" Jesus, what Massumi would call "a nostalgia for the old reality so intense that it has difformed [our] vision of everything outside of it."[39] Both cynicism and nostalgia maintain Jesus's aura.

35. Benjamin, "Work of Art," 269.

36. Hansen, "Benjamin's Aura," 335–36.

37. See my "Introduction: Making Early Christian Texts Strange (Again)," in *Critical Theory and Early Christianity*, ed. Matthew G. Whitlock (Sheffield: Equinox, 2022), esp. 5 n. 16.

38. Brian Massumi, "Realer Than Real: The Simulacrum according to Deleuze and Guattari," *Copyright* 1 (1987): 90–97.

39. Massumi, "Realer Than Real," 95.

Instead, I suggest moving forward with the Next Quest to "close the distance," with Benjamin's help. I end by naming four Jesuses to consider for the twenty-first century, a montage of Benjamin's ideas: the distracted Jesus, the common Jesus, the fragmented Jesus, and the profane Jesus.

The Distracted Jesus

Auras are broken through distraction, not contemplation, a key point in Benjamin's "Work of Art" essay: "The painting invites the viewer to contemplation; before it he can give himself to his train of associations."[40] The aura of the artwork invites associations, much like the unique known of the halo invites unwarranted connections. Distraction aims to break these associations, associations which are merely assimilated into existing paradigms, reinforcing aura. Dadaist art, for example, aims to distract the viewer by distracting assimilative thinking and demanding accommodation to new, disruptive details. For example, the indigenous artwork on the posters for the Next Quest project in the summer of 2022 does this: distracting us from the associations the West wants to make with Jesus's aura. Cognitive science has buttressed Benjamin's thoughts on distraction. In many instances, negative, distracted thinking is more beneficial than positive thinking; cognitive diffusion is more beneficial than a fusion of ideas. Joseph Forgas has found that simple awareness of the processes of "halo effect" does not affect the way one views a person. Awareness of the aura alone does not stop the effects aura. Participants in studies of the halo effect were given the details about how the halo effect influences judgments; this knowledge did not help them avoid the effects on their judgments. Instead, research found that bad moods, not awareness, break halo effects.[41] I am not suggesting simply studying the historical Jesus in a bad mood; what I am suggesting is committing to the disruption of Jesus's aura through the study of what is disruptive: the common, fragmented, and profane, all of which are expected from historical scholarship.

The Common Jesus

Benjamin points to common, material objects as a means of distraction, preferring "haptic nearness" of common objects to "contemplative distance" of sacred or scarce objects.[42] The common is preferred over the unique and famous. This

---

40. Benjamin, "Work of Art," 4:266–67. See also Howard Eiland, "Reception in Distraction," *Boundary* 2 (2003): 51–66.

41. Joseph P. Forgas and Simon M. Lahan, "Halo Effects," in *Cognitive Illusions: Intriguing Phenomena in Thinking, Judgment and Memory*, ed. Rüdiger F. Pohl (London: Routledge, 2017), 276–90.

42. See Hansen, "Benjamin's Aura," 352.

is where work on material culture adds value to the Next Quest, moving us away from Jesus's aura, rightly distracting us with what is common and usual in the concrete world of Jesus of Nazareth, including how he—along with many others—would have dressed, as Joan Taylor has done in her research.[43] It is not Jesus's actual garments (i.e., the traditional interest of auratic and religious quests) that interest scholarship, but first-century, common garments.

The Fragmented Jesus

For Benjamin and the Frankfurt School, montage and fragments are valued over unity and synthesis. Adorno's comparison of impressionism with montage is helpful here: "Impressionism dissolved objects . . . into their smallest elements in order to synthesize them gaplessly into the dynamic continuum. It wanted aesthetically to redeem the alienated and heterogenous in the replica. . . . It was against this that montage protested, which developed out of the pasted-in newspaper clippings and the like during the heroic years of cubism."[44] Likewise, in scholarship it is tempting to take the smallest elements of what we probably do know about Jesus of Nazareth and connect them to what we deem as unique, gaplessly intergrating them into a larger, dynamic continuum, claiming an accurate and authoritative "replica" of Jesus (see Forgas's research above). In contrast, pasted clippings of incomplete lists (e.g., Sanders's "almost indisputable facts") and scattered sources serve to disrupt Jesus's aura.[45] Incompletion and a diffusion of contradictory yet diverse sources do not serve Jesus's aura and fame, but they are hallmarks of rigorous scholarship. Historical Jesus scholarship must value multiple pieces without synthesis. We are not obligated to provide a complete, unified picture of Jesus. Mitzi Smith and Yung Suk Kim in *Toward Decentering the New Testament*, for example, thoughtfully discuss "The Danger of a Single Story" when they present the diverse gospel stories and their diverse sources.[46] Scholarship

43. Joan Taylor, *What Did Jesus Look Like?* (London: Bloomsbury, 2018). Benjamin and Hansen both discuss how objects can have a metonymic relationship with the aura of a person, and therefore have aura, such as the philosopher Schelling's coat. See Hansen, "Benjamin's Aura," 340.

44. Theodor Adorno, *Aesthetic Theory*, ed. Gretel Adorno and Rolf Tiedemann, trans. Robert Hullot-Kentor, Theory and History of Literature 88 (Minneapolis: University of Minnesota Press, 1997), 154–55. Note that Adorno was not happy with Benjamin's celebration of aura decay. See Hansen, "Benjamin's Aura," 357.

45. E. P. Sanders, *Jesus and Judaism* (Philadelphia: Fortress, 1985), 11.

46. Mitzi J. Smith and Yung Suk Kim, *Toward Decentering the New Testament* (Eugene, OR: Cascade, 2018). Smith and Kim derive "The Danger of a Single Story" from the 2009 TED Talk of award-winning Nigerian novelist Chimamanda Ngozi Adichie.

must avoid a single story about Jesus of Nazareth and instead present a diverse and fragmented Jesus.

The Profane Jesus

From his earliest writings, Benjamin highlighted the profane along with the common "in the advertising kiosk and in the criminal," as he says in his early work "The Religious Position of the New Youth," where he praises the religious skepticism of youth.[47] Centering the common and profane breaks auras. What makes an analysis of the profane in Jesus's life difficult, however, is the distance. What can we name as profane if all we have is aura? Even more, what do we do with a Jesus whose few "profane" qualities—captured as "unique" by historical Jesus scholarship—have created and maintained his aura? By contrast, Paul at least provides us with a firsthand testimony (even if the historical Paul hides behind his own rhetoric), the groundwork for a reception history in which we can trace and locate the profane, as Cavin Concannon does in *Profaning Paul*. Given these circumstances, however, I still suggest continuing a quest to find what is profane-but-not-unique about the historical Jesus of Nazareth, that is, what is common and profane about first-century daily life in Nazareth, daily life that is not in discontinuity with Jesus of Nazareth: sexual habits, gender identities, daily routines, defecation, flatulence, humor, vulgarities, norms, and prejudices. It is through distracting Jesus's aura with the profane and common that his aura is no longer actively maintained by scholarship. So, I end with a quote from *Profaning Paul*, where Concannon cites a key interpreter of Benjamin, Giorgio Agamben: "Profanation, however, neutralizes what it profanes. Once profaned, that which was unavailable and separate loses its aura and is returned to use. . . . [It] deactivates the apparatuses of power and returns to common use the spaces the power had seized."[48]

47. Walter Benjamin, "The Religious Position of the New Youth," in *Walter Benjamin: Early Writings, 1910–1917*, ed. Howard Eiland, trans. Howard Eiland et al. (Cambridge: Belknap, 2011), 169.

48. Giorgio Agamben, *Profanations*, trans. Jeff Fort (New York: Zone, 2015), 77. Quoted in Concannon, *Profaning Paul*, 96.

14

NETWORKS

John S. Kloppenborg

During much of the Quest for the historical Jesus the focus has been on isolating the intellectual and moral virtuosity of a single figure and mapping the distinctive moments that gave literary expression to the beliefs and practices of the Jesus movement—the Sayings Gospel Q, Paul, Mark, Matthew, Luke, John, and the many later literary articulations. The methods employed in the various quests—the criteria of dissimilarity, embarrassment, multiple attestation, and coherence—were aimed at isolating a single voice, while the method of redaction criticism was designed to isolate the thought and literary intentions of individual author-editors who employed sources, manipulating and shaping them to create coherent versions of "the gospel."

The heuristic model of several discrete and determinate nodes that can be isolated with some measure of plausibility has produced rich and, in many respects, compelling results. I have no intention of dismissing them. Nevertheless, it is also true that these methods have also produced competing voices of Jesus—Jesus the apocalypticist, the wisdom teacher, the restorationist, the Cynic-like prophet—and significant variety in the identification of the theological, cultural, and even literary profiles of each of the evangelists. These various portraits and editorial reconstructions might indicate that the tools and methods we use are not equal to the task of isolating single moments in a matrix. Equipment such as spectrometers are efficient in measuring the wavelength of electromagnetic radiation but not well suited to cope with its particle-like features. It might be that the urge to arrive at logically coherent and discrete sets of beliefs and attitudes about Jesus (or the competing theologies of Q, Mark, etc.) is an unrealistic imposition, and we should expect fuzzier and less consistent pictures. Or variations might point to the existence at many stages of multiple voices or collective inputs that create "noise" in the system.

In the last twenty-five years of research into Christian origins, there have been a few gestures that imagine the Jesus movement not as a set of discrete and determinate nodes but in more collective terms with multiple agents at work. In 2005 Melanie Johnson-Debaufre published *Jesus among her Children: Q, Eschatology, and the Construction of Christian Origins*, in which she challenged the then-current view that the singular and unique role of Jesus was a (perhaps *the*) major preoccupation of the Jesus people.[1] A singular coherent portrait of Jesus was no doubt the goal for Paul, Mark, and John as well as the apologists in the second century, even if it is difficult for us to specify what that portrait was. But was it, she asks, for Q? And did the articulation of the identity of Jesus constitute the fault line that divided the Jesus people from others? Johnson-DeBaufre's contention is that it did not.

Johnson-Debaufre begins with the premise that decisions about how to construe Q's principal interests—Christology, the elaboration of the nature of the kingdom, futuristic or presentist eschatology—do not flow automatically from the contents of Q but inhere in contemporary theological habits. Recent debates about Q's eschatology or its cultural inclinations are less about the data and more a meta-debate about theological authority. As a kind of thought experiment, she argues against placing Jesus's identity at the heart of Q's interest and instead treats Q as a text that seeks to shape "the community's self-understanding as unified around a common vision" (44).

Johnson-Debaufre strives to displace Christology from the center of Q and see as its center a communal and cooperative vision of the *basileia*. This entails regarding the language of judgment, so common in Q, not as a rhetorical strategy aimed at "creating group boundary lines between insiders and outsiders . . . but intent on persuading those groups to recognize their common cause" (80). For Johnson-Debaufre, Q 3:16–17 is not about the judgment of opponents; instead, it uses judgment language to underscore "the urgency and significance of enacting the vision of the *basileia* of God in the life of the community" (112). The well-known tension that seems to exist between Q 11:19, which seems to recognize

1. Melanie Johnson-DeBaufre, *Jesus among Her Children: Q, Eschatology, and the Construction of Christian Origins*, HTS 55 (Cambridge: Harvard University Press, 2005). Subsequent citations of Johnson-DeBaufre appear in-text.

activity in Judean exorcists as expressions of God's spirit, and Q 11:20, which appears to claim the exclusive mediation of the kingdom for Jesus, is in Johnson-DeBaufre's view not a tension at all, but (following Tertullian) makes a case "for the communal vision of the *basileia* of god over against the *basileia* of Satan" (167). Likewise, Johnson-DeBaufre stresses in Q 11:31–32 that what is greater than Jonah or Solomon is not a some*one* but a some*thing—the presence of the basileia.*

The twentieth-century exclusive focus on Christology as *the* preoccupation of Q is probably the legacy of a combination of the theological commitment to the uniqueness of Jesus coupled with the "Great Man" model of the nineteenth century—the historiographic conviction that history is moved by individuals endowed with special attributes, superior intellect, courage, charismatic leadership abilities, or divine features. For Johnson-Debaufre, however, the center of Q was disbursed—not only that it was not preoccupied with the identity of a single agent, but also that the *basileia* was a collective, communal project of transformation.

Scholarship on Q had also moved away from the models inherited from the twentieth century of a single agent (Jesus) and the "Q community," the latter understood as a discrete entity whose existence could be traced back to Jesus and set contrastively against other social formations (the apostolic church, the Hellenistic synagogue, the Pharisaic synagogue, etc.). Clare Rothschild argues that a significant portion of Q was in fact Baptist in origin.[2] If this thesis can be sustained, it implies that Markan and post-Markan developments have "purified" the tradition of its Baptist elements and that the "Quest of the historical Jesus" should perhaps be reconceived as the quest of John the Baptist and Jesus. As for the supposed "Q community," Paul Hoffmann eschews the language of "community" entirely. As early as 1972 Hoffmann refused the term *Gemeinde*, since it implied far too much about those persons associated with the Sayings Gospel Q, mainly, that they constituted a "community" with a set of distinct ritual practices, a "theology," and a historical and spatial setting. He preferred the less determinate *Q Gruppe*.[3] For much of Q scholarship thereafter, "community" and "*Gemeinde*" were eschewed, as were scholars such as Kloppenborg who began to speak of "a group or network

2. Clare K. Rothschild, *Baptist Traditions and Q*, WUNT 190 (Tübingen: Mohr Siebeck, 2005).

3. Paul Hoffmann, *Studien zur Theologie der Logienquelle*, NTAbh 8 (Münster: Aschendorff, 1972), 10: "Mit Absicht spreche ich nicht von der hinter Q stehenden 'Gemeinde', sondern wähle in der Regel den theologisch unbelasteten Begriff 'Gruppe'; dies geschieht nicht, weil ich die theologische Bedeutung der christlichen Gemeinde in Frage stellen, sondern nur, weil ich nicht ungeprüft diese oder jene Gemeindekonzeption in die Logienquelle eintragen möchte. Außerdem soll die Wahl dieses Begriffes daran erinnern, daß es sich hier um *eine* christliche Gruppe der frühen Christenheit handelt, nicht aber um die christliche Gemeinde schlechthin."

of groups."[4] At about the same time, the terms *Jesusbewegung* and "Jesus move-ment" entered the language of Christian origins, evidently as a way to capture the disbursed and diverse natures of the social groupings that variously associated themselves with Jesus and to avoid the implication that "Christianity" existed as a discrete intellectual and social formation distinguishable from "Judaism."[5]

Although I had earlier spoken of a "network" to describe the social formation in which Q circulated, the term was used naively and without any theorization. In this paper, as a contribution to the Next Quest for the historical Jesus, I would like to take this occasion to think more carefully about how network theory might provide a more disciplined way to look at the Jesus movement and the Quest of the historical Jesus.

Networks are ways to visualize the relationships among persons, institutions, locations, and other things (nodes) and the variety of links (edges) between those nodes. Network maps help to understand how information, influence, power, and various resources cluster and flow, the effects of clustering, the most (and least) probable directions of flow, and in some cases the particular conditions that account for propagation (of ideas, infections, resilience, power) throughout a network.

Social network analysis does not merely map the relationship among nodes. Network analysis begins with the premise that "social life is created primarily

4. John S. Kloppenborg, "Literary Convention, Self-Evidence, and the Social History of the Q People," *Semeia* 55 (1991): 78, 86, 90. See also Kloppenborg, *Excavating Q: The History and Setting of the Sayings Gospel* (Minneapolis: Fortress, 2000), 170–71: "The term 'community' (*Gemeinde*) is problematic insofar as it is used to refer to a discrete and bounded 'church' with a clear membership, identity rituals, and the means by which to distinguish its members from other persons residing in the same locale. The existence of such 'churches' is scarcely conceivable in a village (which typically consists of 80–100 nuclear families representing two to four clans) and barely possible in a large town." Later he writes: "Instead of imagining with Theissen that the early Jesus movement represented by Q comprised itinerants with their sometime supporters, it seems more likely that there was a network of local groups and local leaders, perhaps household heads, and that the mobile workers were dependent upon the households both materially and for the legitimation of their roles" (211).

5. The term, perhaps borrowed from the revival of Christianity in the late 1960s and early 1970s in North America and Germany, was first used of the ancient Mediterranean phenom-enon by Gerd Theissen, *Soziologie der Jesusbewegung: Ein Beitrag zur Entstehungsgeschichte des Urchristentums*, Theologische Existenz Heute 194 (Munich: Kaiser, 1977), and subsequently by Richard A. Horsley, *Sociology and the Jesus Movement* (New York: Crossroad, 1989) and Paul Hoffmann, *Studien zur Frühgeschichte der Jesus-Bewegung*, SBAB 17 (Stuttgart: Katholisches Bi-belwerk, 1994). The English translation of Ekkehard W. Stegemann and Wolfgang Stegemann, *Urchristliche Sozialgeschichte: Die Anfänge im Judentum und die Christusgemeinden in der med-iterranen Welt* (Stuttgart: Kohlhammer, 1995) appeared as *The Jesus Movement: A Social History of Its First Century*, trans. O. C. Dean (Minneapolis: Fortress, 1999).

and most importantly by relations and the patterns formed by these relations."[6] Instead of focusing on individual agents, their qualities, and their contributions to a social phenomenon, network analysis begins with the constellation of relationships among members of a network as a way to understand a particular phenomenon. Social innovations are not merely the result of independent persons acting independently or even many imitating the behavior of one agent, but rather represent the behaviors that emerge from the complex relationships that exist among those individuals. We might conceive of the *basileia theou* as an emergent quality that arises from the network of Jesus, John, and their followers, rather than the achievement of a single individual.

There are at least two types of subnetworks that might be relevant to understanding the "Jesus movement" and the positions occupied by Jesus (and John): material and economic networks, and information networks.

Material and Economic Networks

In an earlier essay, I discussed the several material and economic subnetworks that were implicated in the fishing industry on Kinneret.[7] Several important results came from examining fishing as a networked activity that involved material exchange.

Although there is almost no direct data from Roman Palestine about the structure of the fishing industry, comparative data exist from Ptolemaic and early Roman Egypt that likely applied also to Palestine.[8]

First is the issue of who controlled fishing in the region. The gospels tell us nothing about who owned or controlled the shores of the Kinneret. Other sources indicate, however, that while the open sea was treated as *res nullius*—and for this purpose the Kinneret was not a sea—shorelines and riverbanks were typically owned and therefore leased to fishermen, either for a fixed fee or for a share of the

6. Alexandra Marin and Barry Wellman, "Social Network Analysis: An Introduction," in *The SAGE Handbook of Social Network Analysis*, ed. John Scott and Peter J. Carrington (London: SAGE, 2014), 11.

7. John S. Kloppenborg, "Jesus, Fishermen and Tax Collectors: Papyrology and the Construction of the Ancient Economy of Roman Palestine," *ETL* 94.4 (2018): 571–99.

8. See Facundo Daniel Troche, "Fishing in the Lake of Galilee and the Socio-Economic Context of Jesus' Movement," in *Texts, Practices, and Groups: Multidisciplinary Approaches to the History of Jesus' Followers in the First Two Centurie; First Annual Meeting of Bertinoro (2–5 October 2014)*, ed. Adriana Destro and Mauro Pesce, Judaïsme ancien et origines du christianisme 10 (Turnhout: Brepols, 2017), 81–107.

catch.[9] This means that fishermen were necessarily entangled in a fiscal network of leases and rent collection.

Second, fishing depended on multiple material networks, since most of the material needs of fishing were supplied by others. The analysis of the fishing boat discovered near Kibbutz Ginnosar in 1986 showed that the planking was Lebanese cedar, not local timber. This implies either that the planks had been imported through a trade network or that the boat itself was manufactured elsewhere and shipped to the Kinneret.[10] The manufacturing techniques are those of an expert shipwright, presumably not those of local fishermen.[11] The many repairs on the boat, however, lack the same level of competence, and the use of various types of local wood and several techniques of joins suggest that the repairs were both local and nonprofessional.[12]

The boat may have been owned by the fishermen or leased by an owner. Both models are attested in Egypt, where the documentation on fishing is much more plentiful than for Jewish Palestine. It is critical to recognize, however, that a boat was a significant capital investment. It would be used for fishing, especially in the winter when the outflow of the Upper Jordan was strong and the springs at Heptapegon oxygenated the water, which resulted in a significant increase in the mass of phytoplankton.[13] During the summer and fall, however, boats could not be left idle, since one of the methods of tax extraction was to tax fishermen by the number of boats they owned or operated. This means that it was in the interests of boat owners to keep the boats active, even when there was little fishing, for example, by transporting people or supplies across the Kinneret. The multiple crossings of the Kinneret that are part of the fabric of Mark's Gospel, therefore, are not desultory voyages, but reflect the financial need to have fishing boats double

---

9. On this point, see the discussion in Kloppenborg, "Jesus, Fishermen and Tax Collectors," 582–84.

10. Ella Werker, "Identification of the Wood," in *The Excavations of an Ancient Boat in the Sea of Galilee (Lake Kinneret)*, ed. Shelley Wachsmann, Atiqot 19 (Jerusalem: Israel Antiquities Authority, 1990), 65–75.

11. J. Richard Steffy, "The Boat: A Preliminary Study of Its Construction," in Wachsmann, *Excavations of an Ancient Boat*, 29–47.

12. I rely on the judgment of Jerome Hall (Anthropology, UCSD) who has for several years been studying and restoring the boat. On the wood used for patches, see Werker, "Identification of the Wood," and, in general, William H. Charlton, "Building a Model of the Kinneret Boat," *INA Quarterly* 19.3 (1992): 3–7.

13. On tropic levels in the Kinneret, see Moshe Gophen, "Fisheries Management in Lake Kinneret (Israel)," *Lake and Reservoir Management* 2.1 (1986): 327–32; on fishing season, see Facundo Daniel Troche, "Il sistema della pesca nel lago di Galilea al tempo di Gesù. Indagine sulla base dei papiri documentari e dei dati archeologici e letterari" (PhD diss., Università di Bologna, 2015), 87–89.

as water taxis. This in turn would bring fishermen into contact with other local networks on both sides of the Kinneret.

Third, fishing required a variety of other materials: nets and sails, typically manufactured from linen. Bethsaida at the north end of the Kinneret is known to be a site of flax production and, presumably, linen.[14] The work of mending nets no doubt fell to the fishermen, as Mark 1:19 suggests. But the bronze net tools would have been manufactured elsewhere.[15]

Fishermen also typically needed hooks, normally fabricated from bronze, net weights of either lead or drilled stone, as well as anchors (large drilled stones). Since lead is not found in Palestine, it had to be imported from such sites as Laurion (Attica), Macedonia, Cilicia, Cyprus, North Africa, Sardinia, and even Spain.[16] Molds and casts for net weights have been found in among fishing paraphernalia in Jewish Palestine. We might conclude accordingly that lead was imported as ingots and cast into weights in the Galilee. In addition, fishing required ropes— probably manufactured from hemp—and baskets for holding and transporting the catch. Whether rope was of local manufacture is uncertain, although it is known that rope was a major export of Egypt.[17]

These are all upstream requirements of the fishing industry and presuppose a thick network of lessors and local suppliers of wood, nets, sails, bronze hooks, lead net weights, anchors, and ropes, some of whom were connected more distantly to timber producers, lead mines, bronze smelting, flax processing, and rope manufacture. The frequency of interaction with such suppliers no doubt varied considerably. Since a well-constructed boat likely lasted a decade or more, the interaction with shipwrights was probably infrequent. Nets could be mended, but since linen is not especially durable, periodic interaction with linen weavers would be necessary to replace nets that were beyond repair.[18] Bronze net tools may have lasted a con-

14. Rami Arav (personal communication; September 20, 2017) notes that flax production dropped at the beginning of the Hasmonean period when the economic orientation of Bethsaida shifted from the coastal cities to the Galilee. Nevertheless flax has been found in storerooms, and even if linen production declined somewhat, Bethsaida as a fishing village would have required linen nets.

15. Ehud Galili, Avshalom Zemer, and Baruch Rosen, "Ancient Fishing Gear and Associated Artifacts from Underwater Explorations in Israel—A Comparative Study," *Archaeofauna* 22 (2013): 145–66.

16. Jean David C. Boulakia, "Lead in the Roman World," *American Journal of Archaeology* 76.2 (1972): 139–44. Ezekiel 27:12 reports that lead was imported by Tyre from Tarshish (Spain).

17. Daniel Sperber, "Objects of Trade Between Palestine and Egypt in Roman Times," *JESHO* 19.2 (1976): 132–33.

18. Annalisa Marzano, *Harvesting the Sea: The Exploitation of Marine Resources in the Roman Mediterranean*, Oxford Studies on the Roman Economy (Oxford: Oxford University Press, 2013), 29.

siderable time, but hooks and net weights, which are frequently lost, would have required more frequent interaction with the artisans who produced them. Ropes and baskets likely required frequent interaction with artisans. And of course, interaction with those who leased out the shoreline would have been at least yearly, if the lease was for a fixed sum (presumably payable either at the signing of the lease or at some point in the fishing season). If the lease called for a percentage of the catch, interaction with a lessor or their agents would be more frequent.

The downstream requirements of the fishing industry of course included the need to access to markets, and this required transportation from the lake to sites of consumption, or to the facilities for the salting and pickling of fish or the production of garum (perhaps Tarichaeae/Migdal). The most distinctive downstream requirement of fishing, however, flowed from the perishable nature of fish. Unlike agricultural crops which matured (and therefore were taxed) only in specific times during the year, the fishing season was long and fish began to rot as soon as they were taken from the water. Hence, the catch had to be marketed or sent for salting, pickling, or garum production almost immediately. This also meant that leaseholders and tax officials were engaged as soon as fishermen landed their catches.

The intensity of interaction with tax officials is illustrated by a papyrus from Oxyrhynchus. Dating from the second century, P.Oxy. 49.3495 is either a fisherman's account or, more likely, the report of an *epitērētēs* (tax supervisor) for the daily catches of a fisherman for twenty-one days during the period from Paophi 11 to Hathyr 1 (October 8–28). The account records the income, taxes due, and lease payments (all in drachmae), and is divided into "casts" (*boloi*). The account indicates that there were between three and eleven "casts" per day. During the fishing season in the fall and winter (in Egypt) the value of each cast was assessed before it was removed to market, and the taxes and lease payments calculated and deducted. In Egypt, and probably in Palestine, this allowed the market value of the produce immediately to be deposited in a bank and the relevant taxes and lease charges to be deducted. While tax officials might be present yearly at a grain field or vineyard at the time of the harvest or vintage, the *epitērētai* continuously surveilled fishing activities. This of course meant that fishermen and *epitērētai* were in constant interaction or, in the language of network analysis, fishermen and tax agents had strong and short ties.

Figure 1 offers a visualization of the upstream and downstream networks of fishermen and illustrates the dense connections (line width) that fishermen had with various suppliers of materials, consumers, and especially tax agents.

The network map of fishermen suggests that the appearance in the Jesus tradition of fishermen along with tax collectors—the only two occupations to be mentioned in Mark—is not adventitious. The nature of fishing meant that of the

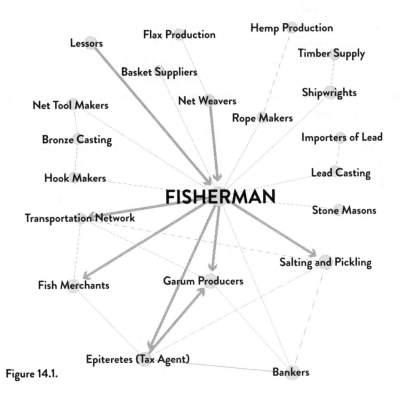

Figure 14.1.

various producers found in agrarian societies, fishermen had among the highest levels of interaction with tax agents. Aliyah El Mansy has recently suggested that Levi son of Alphaeus, often thought to be a customs agent, was plausibly responsible for collecting the fish tax.[19] It is also to be noted that such tax agents were typically *local* persons, hence Galileans. The use of Levi's patronym in Mark 2:14 perhaps indicates that this was a local tradition (from Capernaum), which identified a specific individual.[20] Whoever Levi was, he was no doubt well known to the fishermen of Capernaum.[21]

19. Aliyah El Mansy, "Τελῶναι im Neuen Testament—Zwischen sozialer Realität und literarischem Stereotyp" (Habilitationsschrift, Philipps-Universität Marburg, 2021), 268. She cites for comparison I.Eph. 20 = GRA II 127 (Ephesus, 54–59 CE), the construction of a tax office (*to telōnion tēs ichthuikēs*) in the harbor of Ephesus.

20. Compare Nemesion son of Zoilos, the praktor of Philadelphia in the early first century CE. See Willy Clarysse, "Nemesion Son of Zolios," *Leuven Homepage of Papyrus Collections*, ArchID 149, 2012, https://www.trismegistos.org/arch/archives/pdf/149.pdf.

21. It is now widely recognized that the *telōnai* of the gospels were not *publicani*. Direct

The earliest phases of the Jesus movement were located within networks of suppliers to fishermen and their downstream markets and networks of tax agents with whom they were intimately connected. It is likely that the movement spread initially at least within these networks.[22] Unfortunately, the Jesus tradition is silent on the occupations of others (apart from the general term *ergatai*, day laborers) and hence it is difficult to work out other networks that may have operated within the early Jesus movement.

Neither fishermen nor tax agents were in the marginally economic sectors of Jewish Palestine. Fish was an important protein source but supplementary to the Mediterranean staples of grain, oil, and wine. Archaeological evidence suggests that fish from the Kinneret were consumed not only in such nearby centers as Sepphoris and Tiberias, but were distributed to the south and even to the Madaba plain.[23] Evidence from Egypt indicates that the income generated from fishing, even when one takes into account taxation and leasing expenditures, would have put fishermen significantly above subsistence-level agriculture.[24] The same can be said for tax agents. The role of *telōnēs*, at least in Egypt and probably in Palestine, had become a liturgy at least by the time of Claudius, which implies that *telōnai* had sufficient wealth to be susceptible for compulsory service.[25]

Thus, a network analysis of the early traditions about Jesus and his earliest followers suggests that the Jesus movement originated in a highly networked sector of the Galilean economy and that it flourished not among the economically marginal, but among persons who had some access to modest levels of wealth.

taxes were collected by the prefect or in the territories controlled by the Herodians, including Antipas and Philip. Indirect taxes were contracted to local agents. It is possible that this form of collection might have become a liturgy as early as the first century. See John R. Donahue, "Tax Collectors and Sinners: An Attempt at an Identification," *CBQ* 33 (1971): 39–61; and especially El Mansy, "Τελῶναι."

22. As, for example, Q 7:29, 34; Mark 2:16; Luke 15:1; 18:10–13; and 19:2–10 suggest.

23. Angela von den Driesch and Joachim Boessneck, "Final Report on the Zooarchaeological Investigation of Animal Bone Finds from Tell Hesban," in *Faunal Remains: Taphonomical and Zooarchaeological Studies of the Animal Remains from Tell Hesban and Vicinity*, ed. Øystein S. LaBianca and Angela von den Driesch, Hesban 13 (Berrien Springs, MI: Andrews University Press, 1995), 65–108; Arlene Fradkin, "Long-Distance Trade in the Lower Galilee: New Evidence from Sepphoris," in *Archaeology and the Galilee: Texts and Contexts in the Graeco-Roman and Byzantine Periods*, ed. Douglas R. Edwards and C. Thomas McCollough (Atlanta: Scholars Press, 1997), 107–16.

24. Kloppenborg, "Jesus, Fishermen and Tax Collectors," 596–97.

25. El Mansy, "Τελῶναι," 125, 153, in reference to the Nemesion archive (30–61 CE).

KNOWLEDGE NETWORKS

To the extent that the earliest Jesus movement in Palestine propagated through oral (nonliterary) channels, it remains invisible to us. It is clear, however, that it quickly became connected with scribal networks, which has left a significant imprint on the literature it produced.

It was argued at least two decades ago that the framers of Q were low-level scribes. Kloppenborg had originally observed that Q (or at least its formative stratum) adopted the distinctively scribal genre of the "instruction," and that the rather basic level of organization of Q suggested composition by scribes of relatively modest accomplishment. Moreover, Q was concerned not only with the *content* of instruction but with the *origin, nature, transmission,* and *means* by which wisdom was obtained—all typically scribal preoccupations.[26] More recently, it has been pointed out that Q shows awareness of typically scribal forms and their logics—for example, the distinctive form of the agricultural loan, which was used as the basis for the measure-for-measure aphorism, and the structure of the Lord's Prayer, which adheres to the form of an official petition.[27] Even more recently, Giovanni Bazzana has shown that "the linguistic makeup of the Sayings Gospel Q contains several elements, which can be confidently traced back to the activities and the terminological habits of κωμογραμματεῖς or of other sub-elite functionaries operating at the same or at a comparable administrative level."[28]

Scribes, whether the village clerks (*kōmogrammateis*) or other literate persons connected to village administration, rarely operated in isolation. They were typically connected laterally to the *kōmarchēs* (mayor) and various tax agents, registrars, and other functionaries, and vertically to nome officials and ultimately to the *dioikētēs, stratēgos,* and the *basilikos grammateus.* Many of the lower-level functions were liturgies, which meant that such officials met the census requirements for office. They were also locals, and hence naturally had many connections with family and neighbors. It was only in the latter part of the second century CE that a *kōmogrammateus* could not serve in his own village.

26. Kloppenborg, "Literary Convention." See further William E. Arnal, *Jesus and the Village Scribes: Galilean Conflicts and the Setting of Q* (Minneapolis: Fortress, 2001).

27. John S. Kloppenborg, "Agrarian Discourse in the Sayings of Jesus," in *Engaging Economics: New Testament Scenarios and Early Christian Interpretation,* ed. Bruce Longenecker and Kelly Liebengood (Grand Rapids: Eerdmans, 2009), 104–28; Alan Kirk, "Administrative Writing, Oral Tradition, and Q" (paper presented at the Annual Meeting of the Society of Biblical Literature, Q Section, San Antonio, TX, 2004).

28. Giovanni Battista Bazzana, *Kingdom of Bureaucracy: The Political Theology of Galilean Village Scribes,* BETL 274 (Leuven: Peeters, 2015), 85.

Papyrus archives from Egypt indicate how these low-level functionaries were connected in networks that included other functionaries in the same village, parallel functionaries in adjacent villages, nome officials, and senior administrators in Alexandria. An example of the interconnectedness of a scribal network is provided by the archive of Sokrates son of Sarapion from mid-second-century Karanis.[29]

Approximately two hundred papyri fragments were recovered in the University of Michigan excavations at Karanis in 1926, including those belonging to a scribal archive in houses B16–18 and B2. Sokrates was a *praktōr argyrikōn* (collector of money taxes) and at one time, a *laographos* (census official) in Karanis, and the son of an *eklēmptōr* (tax farmer). He was married to the sister of M. Sempronius Gemellus, a Roman citizen and gymnasiarch (of Alexandria?). The couple had twin sons, Sarapion (aka M. Sempronius Sarapion) and Sokrates (aka M. Sempronius Sokrates).[30] One served as a *sitologos* (in charge of the granaries) and the other as a *praktōr argyrikōn* like his father. Sokrates and Gemella also had a daughter, Tasoucharion.

It is likely that Sokrates had a half brother on his mother's side, Kastor, who served as the *kōmogrammateus* of the nearby village, Ptolemais Nea. Kastor had two sons, Achillas, a *kōmogrammateus*, and Ptolemaios. Ptolemaios had five children, one of whom is named as a *horiodeiktēs* (boundary official). Figure 2 illustrates visually Sokrates's family connections.

In addition to familial connections Sokrates's network included Roman citizens—not only Sempronia Gemella but also Gaius Valerius Gemellus, who had enlisted in the Roman fleet, and his ex-wife, Demetria (P.Mich. 7.442 = *ChLA* 5.295) along with various officials from Karanis (the *kōmogrammateus*, *SB* 18.13306) and adjacent villages (the *sitologos* of Ptolemais Nea, *SB* 6.9433), and a group of *kōmo-*

---

29. Kalilien Geens, "ArchID 109. Sokrates, Tax Collector, and Family," in Katelijn Vandorpe, Willy Clarysse, and H. Verreth, *Graeco-Roman Archives from the Fayum*, Collectanea Hellenistica – KVAB 6 (Leuven: Peeters, 2015) and Mohamed Gaber El-Maghrabi and Cornelia Römer, eds., *Texts from the "Archive" of Socrates, the Tax Collector, and Other Contexts at Karanis (P. Cair. Mich. II)*, Archiv für Papyrusforschung und verwandte Gebiete – Beihefte 35 (Berlin: de Gruyter, 2015); Mohamed Gaber El-Maghrabi and Cornelia Römer, eds., *More Texts from the Archive of Socrates. Papyri from House 17, Level B, in Karanis (P. Cair. Mich. III)*, Archiv für Papyrusforschung und verwandte Gebiete – Beihefte 45 (Berlin: de Gruyter, 2021).

30. A birth certificate for the twins (P.Mich. 3.169, 154 CE) by the mother (Sempronia Gemella) lists them as *ex inç[ert]o paṭṛẹ*, either because the father could not contract a legal marriage (a soldier, for example), or because he was of lower status than Gemella. Henry A. Sanders, "Two Fragmentary Birth-Certificates from the Michigan Collection," *Memoirs of the American Academy in Rome* 9 (1931): 61–80, takes the view that Gemella was a freedwoman and the mistress of her guardian (Gaius Iulius Saturninus), while Geens argues that the impediment to a legitimate birth was that Sokrates was not a Roman citizen.

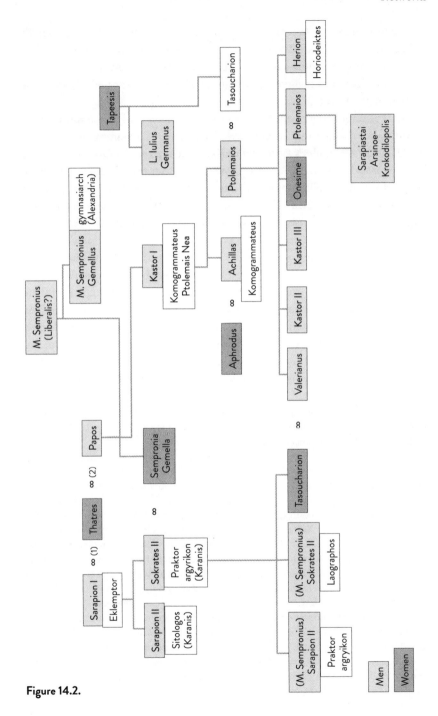

Figure 14.2.

grammateis and *presbyteroi* who wrote jointly to the governor of the division of Herakleides (*SB* 12.11104). The archive contains administrative documents and personal letters, including a letter from Kastor's son, Ptolemaios, telling his father that he had been invited to join a group of Sarapiastai as their *agoranomos* (P.Mich. 8.511 = *GRA* 3.240).

What is interesting about Sokrates's archive is not only his multiple connections, but the fact that he possessed literary texts: a grammatical papyrus (LDAB 4764); Menander's *Epitrepontes* (LDAB 2643); the *Acta Alexandrinorum* (LDAB 15); and Kallimachos's *Aitia* (LDAB 477). Other texts found in proximity to Sokrates and Gemella's houses include copies of the *Iliad* (A, B, Δ, Γ, H, Ξ, Φ); a commentary on *Iliad* A; a list of titles of comedies; Demosthenes's *De corona*; a surgical treatise; Epictetus's *Discourses*; and an oracle question addressed to the "greatest god Soxis Pnepheros."[31]

The presence of such a rich collection of literary texts in the archive of a village administrator suggests that Sokrates (and his family) were what Gugliermo Cavallo has called "free readers," literate persons who read not as a part of their occupation but for pleasure, not for *utilitas* but *voluptas*, as Cicero puts it.[32] It should not be surprizing that these free readers exchanged literature with each other.[33] Nor should it be surprising that these readers also made copies of the literature they possessed or that they composed their own literature.[34] These free readers supply the bridge between the activities of administrative and tax officials

31. See Peter van Minnen, "House-to-House Enquiries: An Interdisciplinary Approach to Roman Karanis," *ZPE* 100 (1994): 227–51; El-Maghrabi and Römer, *Texts from the "Archive" of Socrates*; El-Maghrabi and Römer, *More Texts from the Archive of Socrates*.

32. Gugliermo Cavallo, "Discorsi sul libro," in *La produzione e la circolazione del testo. 3. I Greci e Roma*, ed. Giuseppe Cambiano, Luciano Canfora, and Diego Lanza, vol. 1 of *Lo Spazio letterario della Grecia antica* (Roma: Salerno editrice, 1994), 613–47, citing Cicero, *De finibus bonorum et malorum* 5.52.

33. See P.Oxy. 18.2192; a Christian example is P.Oxy. 58.4365, in which the writer asks the recipient to lend a copy of "Esdras" (4 Ezra) recalling that the sender had lent the recipient "the little Genesis" (Jubilees). See Thomas J. Kraus, "The Lending of Books in the Fourth Century C. E. P. Oxy. LXIII 4365—A Letter on Papyrus and the Reciprocal Lending of Literature Having Become Apocryphal," in *Ad Fontes: Original Manuscripts and Their Significance for Studying Early Christianity, Selected Essays*, TENTS 3 (Leiden: Brill, 2007), 185–206. See also Giovanni Battista Bazzana, "'You Will Write Two Booklets and Send One to Clement and One to Grapte': Formal Features, Circulation, and Social Function of Ancient Apocalyptic Literature," in *Scribal Practices and Social Structures among Jesus Adherents: Essays in Honour of John S. Kloppenborg*, ed. William E. Arnal et al., BETL 285 (Leuven: Peeters, 2016), 43–70.

34. E.g., P.Oxy. 2.209. See AnneMarie Luijendijk, "A New Testament Papyrus and Its Documentary Context: An Early Christian Writing Exercise from the Archive of Leonides (P.Oxy. II 209/p[10])," *JBL* 129.3 (2011): 575–96.

found in every village and the reflective and theological discourse found in some of the Jesus tradition.

As I have argued elsewhere, the measure-for-measure aphorism begins from the fact that seed grain was measured out (*metreō*) with a grain scoop (*metron*) and, in order to ensure parity in lending and borrowing, measured back by the same *metron* of the granary from which it was originally measured.[35] Dozens of lease agreements prepared by scribes take the form, "I, NN, have measured out to you, NN, by the grain scoop [*metron*] of the third granary of Karnis, *x artabae* of grain and you will measure it back to me, on (date) by the same *metron* of the third granary of Karanis" (or a similar form, mutatis mutandis, framed from the perspective of the borrower). The measure-for-measure aphorism in Q mobilizes this scribal knowledge, but applies it to an injunction to show mercy:

> Be merciful as your father is merciful. Do not judge and you will not be judged
> [[for with the judgment that you judge, you will be judged]] and with the mea-
> sure that you measure our, it will be measured back to you. (Q 6:36–38)[36]

What is noteworthy in this aphorism is that it takes the perspective of the *lender*, who in financial transactions knows that the system of lending and repayment guarantees equivalence through the use of the same *metron*. This system of borrowing served the interests of the lender, ensuring that repayment would always use the same terms as the initial loan. But the aphorism applies the same guarantee to those who are in a position to show mercy (i.e., by forgiving loans? by showing leniency?) and employs the same logic: those who show mercy will benefit by the very system of exchange that has guaranteed them profits and return on their investments. This is surely an appeal to self-interest, but one that brings economic principles into the domain of moral interaction.

There are other examples of this crossover between scribal knowledge, scribal formulae, and the moral knowledge found in the Jesus tradition.[37] My point here is that the early Jesus tradition was located in the nexus of "religious" or moral knowledge and administrative scribal knowledge, precisely because the agents of these forms of knowledge were, inter alia, scribes. These scribes were not merely pencil pushers, but persons who *also* valued and read the literature, literature that

35. Kloppenborg, "Agrarian Discourse."

36. This reconstruction is that of the International Q project; see James M. Robinson, Paul Hoffmann, and John S. Kloppenborg, *The Critical Edition of Q*, Hermeneia (Minneapolis: Fortress, 2000). The double brackets mark words that are ascribed to Q only with hesitation.

37. See especially Bazzana, *Kingdom of Bureaucracy*.

was in fact that basis of moral reasoning in the ancient world—Homer, Menander, Epictetus, and others. One might assume that the scribes of Roman Palestine also had in their houses copies of the Tanakh, Sirach, or other Judaean writings. This literature supplied the scribe with moral foundation that could be mobilized in expressions of the Jesus tradition.

Conclusion

The burden of this paper has been to show that social and literary innovations often exist in social networks that undergird and reinforce that innovation. The tendency of scholarship on Christian origins to date has been to promote the notion that the Jesus tradition can be traced to an individual genius. There is no doubt that Jesus was an innovator. But without supporting and creative social networks, that innovation would never have survived. Attention to social and economic networks in early Roman Palestine might assist us in thinking about the constitution of the earliest Jesus devotees, including their socioeconomic status. And the scribal networks that all acknowledge as instrumental in the codification and transmission of the Jesus tradition were likely more than simple tradents, but persons who contributed materially to the Jesus tradition by mobilizing their professional knowledge and their knowledge as "free readers" to contribute to that tradition.

15

Scribal Galilee

Sarah E. Rollens

Although it is against my nature to fall into line when given instructions, I must begin this chapter by insisting that the Next Quest for the historical Jesus must account for scribal activity in Roman Galilee. The most important textual source that we can use to illustrate this claim is the Sayings Gospel Q (or simply, Q). Indeed, when we survey the terrain of early written Jesus traditions, the only one that stands a chance of stemming from Roman Galilee before the First Jewish War is Q.[1] While I am personally less than sanguine about our ability to mine the *ipsissima vox* of Jesus from Q, many scholars of the historical Jesus have viewed Q (often along with Mark's Gospel) as some of our best evidence for Jesus's core teachings.[2] Regardless of where one falls on the question of the historical Jesus proper, the topic of "scribal Galilee" and the early Jesus movement is, to my mind,

---

1. I try deliberately to avoid terminology such as "Christian" or "Christian community." As will be clear, the arguments that I make about the author(s) of Q does not require them to be in any sort of organized "religious" group or even to possess any kind of firm identity associated with Jesus—rather, they were interested authors who advanced a particular social vision within the Q source and used Jesus as a spokesperson.

2. As in James M. Robinson, *The Gospel of Jesus: In Search of the Original Good News* (San Francisco: HarperOne, 2005); John Dominic Crossan, *The Historical Jesus: The Life of a Mediterranean Jewish Peasant* (San Francisco: HarperCollins, 1991). But for some of the problems with this enterprise, see John S. Kloppenborg, "The Sayings Gospel Q and the Quest of the Historical Jesus," *HTR* 89.4 (1996): 307–44.

only relevant to Q, because when we turn to the later gospels, we are dealing with cultural expressions of a translocal movement that have lost much of their regional specificity and that have begun to show marks of more elite forms of literature. What this means, then, is that Q provides us with some of the most relevant data for understanding scribal Galilee close to the time and place of the historical Jesus and the bureaucratic perpetuation of ideas in his name.

Before turning to Q and scribalism, it is useful to set the stage with some remarks on the challenges of talking about scribes in New Testament studies. Ancient scribes, to borrow the apt words of Kim Haines-Eitzen, "were a necessary, indeed indispensable, part of Roman-era society in which few people learned to read and write."[3] Of course, stories and sayings of wise teachers were being shared orally in this period and people communicated all manner of topics by word of mouth, yet we should not go so far as to claim the Roman Empire was an "oral society," strictly speaking. It depended strongly on the written word, and scribal figures, operating in a range of social locations, facilitated this dependence.[4] Yet New Testament scholars have often been reticent to envision scribes playing a role in the early Jesus movement. In part, this is because many have uncritically taken over the gospels' negative portrayals of scribes and assumed that they were singularly opposed to Jesus.[5] This is a consequence, in turn, of scholars not fully appreciating the varying levels and activities of scribalism in the Roman Empire. For instance, elite Judean scribes may have lacked sympathies with Jesus, but such figures do not exhaust all the possible types of scribes in this context.

To be sure, this is not all on us. The term scribe, as Alan Kirk has noted, is a "notoriously imprecise" term in antiquity.[6] Not only were there important regional differences among ancient scribes, but also there were scribes to be found at every rung of the social ladder carrying out a range of practices. For instance, profes-

---

3. Kim Haines-Eitzen, *Guardians of Letters: Literacy, Power, and the Transmitters of Early Christian Literature* (Oxford: Oxford University Press, 2000), 15.

4. Carol Bakhos, "Orality and Writing," in *The Oxford Handbook of Jewish Daily Life in Roman Palestine*, ed. Catherine Hezser (Oxford: Oxford University Press, 2010), 485. See also William E. Arnal, "The Trouble with Q," *Foundations & Facets Forum* 2.1 (2013): 31–32.

5. Chris Keith has shown that the negative depictions of elite scribes in the canonical gospels are in service of demonstrating that Jesus was understood to be in competition with the Judean scribes' authority; see *Jesus against the Scribal Elite: The Origins of the Conflict*, 2nd ed. (London: T&T Clark, 2020). Unfortunately, many other scholars have taken the gospels' depictions as evidence for scribes (of all varieties) being completely separate from the Jesus movement.

6. Alan Kirk, "The Scribe as Tradent," in *Scribal Practices and Social Structures among Jesus' Adherents: Essays in Honour of John S. Kloppenborg*, ed. William E. Arnal et al., BETL 285 (Leuven: Peeters, 2016), 97.

sional accountants who worked in elite Roman households operated much differently than the administrative functionaries found in villages in Roman Egypt and Palestine, who in turn operated much differently from aristocratic Judean scribes trained extensively in matters of Jewish law. The literate capacities of scribes, moreover, could range from possessing barely the skills to spell their own name to showcasing the ability to compose brand new literature, replete with allusions to existing Greco-Roman classics.[7] Against the idea (based largely in the gospels themselves) that scribes were singularly opposed to the Jesus movement, I will pull together important scholarship on the Q source to show that its authors were familiar with a rather distinct form of scribal activity and that we should thus not drive a firm wedge between "scribes" and "followers of Jesus."

Before proceeding, let us also recognize that Q is a very *localized* ideological project, evincing particular interest in Galilee. Evidence for the localized nature of Q in Galilee is admittedly somewhat limited, but it is not nonexistent. Jonathan L. Reed, for instance, has charted the "social map" of Q, finding that it centers on Galilee and radiates outward, becoming increasingly abstract and mythic as it moves away from the actual villages with which the authors appear to have been familiar.[8] Other Q commentators have pointed out that Q seems intimately aware of Galilean village networks, fixating with heightened emotion on a cluster of cities on the northern rim of the lake of Galilee.[9] The vitriol against Chorazin, especially, is telling, for the village is practically unknown in other literature before this point. Indeed, the assumption of negative interaction and hostile reception there (e.g., Q 10:13)—especially for an obscure settlement with perhaps seven hundred people in the early first century—suggests a native familiarity. In the words of one Q commentator, then, "the provenance of Q is without much doubt

---

7. Two famous examples will suffice to illustrate this range. The well-known papyrus P.Petaus 121 records the formulaic practice lines of a village scribe named Petaus, who may have been only partially literate, as he makes spelling mistakes when practicing his stock phrases. In this case, his scribal competency might have been a function of his ability to memorize and construct documentary formulae. At the other end of the spectrum is the example of Chariton of Aphrodisas, who refers to himself as a *hypographeus* (a secretary, which was, in many cases, functionally equivalent to a scribe) and appears to have written an extensive novel called *Chaereas and Callirhoe*.

8. Jonathan L. Reed, "The Social Map of Q," in *Conflict and Invention: Literary, Rhetorical, and Social Studies on the Sayings Gospel Q*, ed. John S. Kloppenborg (Valley Forge, PA: Trinity Press International, 1995), 17–36.

9. John S. Kloppenborg, "Q, Bethsaida, Khorazin, and Capernaum," in *Q in Context II: Social Setting and Archaeological Background of the Sayings Source*, ed. Markus Tiwald, BBB 173 (Bonn: Bonn University Press, 2015), 60–90.

the Galilee of Jesus."[10] The present discussion will therefore consider Q a text stemming from in or around Galilee prior to the First Jewish War (66–73 CE).[11]

To return to scribalism, a number of studies have sought to create helpful typologies of scribal figures, but unfortunately, these typologies go only so far in clarifying social characteristics and experiences of scribes on the ground.[12] Scribes appear to have occupied very fluid positions in the Roman Empire, and many of the binaries used to organize scribal differences (e.g., urban versus rural; public versus private; documentary versus literary) are "fraught with problems."[13] These issues of categorization, however, will not concern us here. Suffice to say that scribes were diverse and "operated at a number of different socioeconomic levels and within a variety of social and cultural contexts . . . [they are found at] nearly all levels of society."[14] Our focus will be on a very particular sort of mid-level scribalism, the type that shows familiarity with administrative practices and other local civic matters, sometimes shorthanded in Q scholarship as "village scribes" (*kōmogrammateis*), though such terminology can be somewhat misleading. In documentary archives, these sorts of middling administrative figures encompass all manner of roles, including tax collectors, clerks, agricultural supervisors, and petty functionaries who produce petitions and contracts.[15] The remainder of this

10. Douglas E. Oakman, *The Radical Jesus, the Bible, and the Great Transformation* (Eugene, OR: Cascade, 2021), 97. On the Galilean provenance of Q, see also John S. Kloppenborg, *Excavating Q: The History and Setting of the Sayings Gospel* (Minneapolis: Fortress, 2000), 214–61; William E. Arnal, *Jesus and the Village Scribes: Galilean Conflicts and the Setting of Q* (Minneapolis: Fortress, 2001); Reed, "Social Map of Q"; Richard A. Horsley, "The Historical Context of Q," in *Whoever Hears You Hears Me? Prophets, Performance, and Tradition in Q*, ed. Richard A. Horsley (Harrisburg, PA: Trinity Press International, 1999), 46–60.

11. On the date of Q, see Matti Myllykoski, "The Social History of Q and the Jewish War," in *Symbols and Strata: Essays on the Sayings Gospel Q*, ed. Risto Uro (Helsinki: Finnish Exegetical Society, 1996), 143–99; Arnal, *Jesus and the Village Scribes*, 165–68; Sarah E. Rollens, *Framing Social Criticism in the Jesus Movement: The Ideological Project in the Sayings Gospel Q*, WUNT 2.374 (Tübingen: Mohr Siebeck, 2014), 94–100. Despite my agreement with this specific setting of Q, my argument will not change much if Q is situated after the First Jewish War, as in Robyn Faith Walsh, "Q and the 'Big Bang' Theory of Christian Origins," in *Redescribing the Gospel of Mark*, ed. Barry S. Crawford and Merrill P. Miller, ECL 22 (Atlanta: SBL Press, 2017), 483–534.

12. For discussions of the relevant literature on organizing scribes into various categories, see Rollens, *Framing Social Criticism*, 131–38; Sarah E. Rollens, "Why We Have Failed to Theorize Scribes in Antiquity," in Arnal, *Scribal Practices and Social Structures*, 117–33.

13. Haines-Eitzen, *Guardians of Letters*, 22.

14. Haines-Eitzen, *Guardians of Letters*, 7–8. At least in the Egyptian context, which can probably be fruitfully compared to Roman Palestine, scribes worked "at every level of the administration" (27).

15. So also, Giovanni B. Bazzana, "Galilean Village Scribes as the Author of the Sayings Gos-

chapter will focus on showing that the Q source—the text that stands in close proximity to the historical Jesus—bears evident marks of scribalism. If we want to grapple with the written sources for the earliest Palestinian Jesus movement, we have to think about how scribalism leaves its imprint on our evidence.

CONSIDERATIONS OF CONTENT

The evidence for the mid-level scribal provenance of Q comes in two main varieties: the *content* of the text and the *form* of the text. We will begin with what is, in my view, the weaker of the two varieties of evidence: the content of Q.

Some of the classical studies of the Q source have found that in terms of genre, the text shares affinities with Near Eastern instructional literature.[16] Ancient instructions tend to contain practical wisdom and moral guidance, as opposed to mythic narratives, dialogues, biographies, or other sorts of content. In the Near Eastern context, most instructional texts were certainly produced by relatively elite scribal figures, who were regularly allied with the political elite and who were interested in authorizing their own pursuit of knowledge acquisition, their practices of self-reflection and judgment, and the connection of such qualities with divine personae. Texts such as Sirach and Proverbs are two prototypical instances of these elite, idealized forms of instructional literature. While Q is somewhat limited in scope in comparison, it nevertheless appears to be at least *aspirational* in such a direction. Not only does Jesus spout numerous ethical teachings in Q, but in general his wise sayings valorize "clarity of perception," "guidance," "good speech," and "moral examples," which reflect, as one Q expert notes, "the self-consciously 'public' nature of the scribal pursuit [in these sorts of texts]."[17] In other words, the

---

pel Q," in Tiward, *Q in Context II*, 133: "'village scribes' must be understood in a loose sense ... [including] many other individuals trained in writing, such as managers of private estates, priests of local shrines, and even people who would offer limited expertise for hire to the illiterate majority." In trying to insulate the Jesus movement from these sorts of petty intellectuals, a number of scholars (though increasingly fewer of late) have sought to argue that Jewish society educated children in literacy skills at a higher rate than wider Roman society and thus that it is plausible that some of Jesus's first followers could have composed stories about Jesus. This seems to be a misreading of the evidence, an imposition of later rabbinic evidence, and probably a bit of wishful thinking (see the overview of the issues in Keith, *Jesus against the Scribal Elite*, 20–27).

16. John S. Kloppenborg, *The Formation of Q: Trajectories in Ancient Wisdom Collections* (Minneapolis: Fortress, 1987); Robinson, "LOGOI SOPHON: On the Gattung of Q," in *Trajectories through Early Christianity*, ed. James M. Robinson and Helmut Koester (Philadelphia: Fortress, 1971), 71–113.

17. John S. Kloppenborg, "Literary Convention, Self-Evidence and the Social History of the

content of Q reflects precisely the scribal, intellectual values that other sapiential, instructional literature does.

There are other details in Q's content that suggest a distinct kind of administrative scribal competency. In particular, many of the examples that Q uses throughout Jesus's sayings are *topoi* drawn from the world of urban administration.[18] For instance, Q appeals to the legalities of marriage (Q 16:18); loan agreements and debts (6:30, 38, 11:4); courts and lawsuits (6:29; 12:58–59); the organization of (not just the activities involved in) agricultural harvests (10:2; 3:17); the mechanics of dividing inheritance (12:13–14, 24, 33–34); estate management (12:42–46); and recordkeeping, taxation, and accounting (6:32; 11:50–51; 12:6–7; 19:12–26).[19] These curious references, mobilized not just to describe but to *persuade*, betray a world of experience that is best associated with mid-level bureaucratic figures. It is not *impossible* that people from a different social location would be familiar with such phenomena, but to use them so consistently and with so little reflection on their appropriateness seems to suggest we are dealing with authors who saw these sorts of situations on a day-to-day basis and who considered these scenarios the most appropriate ones with which to argue.

We can be even more specific. Even Q's idea of debt remission, while certainly having roots in Jewish tradition (e.g., Deut. 15), also embodies a distinct kind of ideology that the scribes who were responsible for village administration were routinely used to associating with royal figures. Giovanni B. Bazzana's outstanding work on Q has shown fascinating similarities between the ideological contours of debt remission and amnesty offers imparted under some Ptolemaic rulers (see, for instance, P.Tebt. 1.5 [Kerkeosiris, 118 CE]) and Q's vision of divine forgiveness in the kingdom of God (as in Q 11:1–4 [the Lord's Prayer]). Put differently, the release of debts and the communal harmony imagined in the kingdom of God look quite a lot like the idyllic state of affairs that Ptolemaic amnesty decrees purported to enact. The point, to reiterate, is that a number of *topoi* Q draws upon presuppose a rather distinct familiarity with language and ideals of urban administration.

A final area of content I want to highlight is somewhat more speculative, but also, I think, rather curious. Bazzana has also shown that Q's authors have a

---

Q People," *Semeia* 55 (1991): 83. Kloppenborg discusses numerous textual examples to illustrate these themes in Q. Cf. Oakman, *Radical Jesus*, 93.

18. The Greek term means generally "topic," but in formal Greco-Roman rhetoric it refers to specific topics that an author self-consciously uses to organize the form of their written work.

19. A curious observation about the motif of tax collectors in early Jesus traditions is made by Kloppenborg: "any essential mention or interest in *telonai* [tax-collectors, those contracted to collect taxes in a specific region] related to Jesus disappears from early Christian literature after the Synoptic Gospels. References to *telonai* supply a very important index in evaluating the social contexts of the earliest Jesus-scribes" (*Excavating Q*, 212–13).

penchant for using storage metaphors in Jesus's parables and sayings (Q 12:12–21, 33–34). What kind of people, Bazzana wonders, would use examples of proper storage, of all possible *topoi*, to animate what is essentially an ethical and political textual project? Rural peasants, who likely produced just enough beyond the subsistence level in order to afford taxes and tributes, were likely not able to accumulate enough foodstuffs or commodities to have to worry about storing them anywhere for any amount of time.[20] Elite figures, on the other hand, who *did* accumulate goods and needed to both inventory and store them, did not actually do the inventory and storage operations themselves. It turns out that the maintenance and ongoing awareness of things in storage is *once again* the domain of administrative scribal figures. Thus, we have yet another *topos* that seems somewhat unextraordinary at first glance but probably betrays the social positionality of a very particular group of literate people.

To be sure, comparing the content of Q with the administrative materials produced by village scribes or similar mid-level functionaries operates in the realm of speculation (albeit a disciplined speculation). After all, a skilled writer could *masquerade* as representing the perspective of any social location, simply by manipulating language. For that reason, this discussion has focused on examples that reveal the *unstated assumptions* of the authors or the experiences that they (apparently) assume to be self-evidently persuasive. Many of these happen to be scenarios with which village scribes would have been intimately familiar.

CONSIDERATIONS OF FORM

The more persuasive body of evidence for connecting Q with scribal figures, to my mind, concerns the actual *form* that the document takes. The form that a particular document takes, especially its compositional and organizational techniques, often illuminates its author's (or authors') implicit assumptions about the appropriate presentation of its ideas; these, in turn, are closely related to their education, training, and, accordingly, their social location. For this reason, I suggest that the scribal competency of the authors has left an indelible mark on the form of Q.

New Testament scholars have reconstructed the text of Q by extracting the material common to Matthew and Luke that does not derive from Mark.[21] The re-

---

20. As argued extensively by scholars such as Douglas E. Oakman, *Jesus and the Peasants* (Eugene, OR: Wipf & Stock, 2008); Richard A. Horsley, *Jesus and the Spiral of Violence: Popular Jewish Resistance in Roman Palestine* (Minneapolis: Fortress, 1993). Both of these distinguished scholars have produced some of the foundational scholarship for understanding peasantry in Roman Palestine during the first century.

21. The process is somewhat more complex than the above phrasing suggests. On the

sulting text is a Greek text with some sophistication, though it is not a complex or intricately structured narrative like, for instance, the Acts of the Apostles. It nevertheless shows marks of deliberate organization, framing, and redaction.[22] Q is thus no random or haphazard list of sayings stemming from Jesus; it is a deliberate composition that requires a particular set of skills and technologies to craft.

Yet the literary forms present in Q are even more specific than most readers realize. Several examples demonstrate that Q shows knowledge of compositional techniques that were common in documentary papyri produced by mid-level scribes. The first concerns the Lord's Prayer (Q 11:1–4). We have already seen that the ideas of debt remission in this prayer resonate with royal ideologies promoted in some legal documents. In addition, Bazzana has argued persuasively that the *form* of the prayer in Q seems to reflect the structure of legal petitions.[23] Alan Kirk has independently but similarly argued that a kind of "scribal screen" is imposed on the Lord's Prayer, which causes it to evince structural affinities with petitions in documentary papyri.[24] Neither Kirk nor Bazzana goes so far as to suggest that the Lord's Prayer was *invented* wholesale by the authors, but rather that when Q's authors decided to write this down, they drew on their repertoire of knowledge for what official documents and records looked like.

Still drawing on Bazzana's important work, he has shown that specific lexical items in Q reflect the "highly formulaic documents" that administrative officials regularly penned.[25] One example is the terminology of *ekballō* in Q 10:2, which is the request in the so-called mission discourse to send out workers for the great harvest. Not only is *ekballō* a strange term to use here, especially when *apostellō* is what one might expect, but *ekballō* is precisely the term that managers and foremen use in documentary papyri to request or commission laborers (134). It is "the term employed to indicate compulsory work" (136). This lexical item, Bazzana

---

methodological approach and scholarly assumptions involved in the reconstruction of Q, see James M. Robinson, Paul Hoffmann, and John S. Kloppenborg, *The Critical Edition of Q*, Hermeneia (Minneapolis: Fortress, 2000).

22. Kloppenborg, *Formation of Q*; Alan Kirk, *The Composition of the Sayings Source: Genre, Synchrony, and Wisdom Redaction in Q*, NovTSup 91 (Leiden: Brill, 2014); Arland Jacobson, "The Literary Unity of Q," *JBL* 101.3 (1982): 365–89.

23. Giovanni B. Bazzana, *Kingdom of Bureaucracy: The Political Theology of Village Scribes in the Sayings Gospel Q*, BETL 274 (Leuven: Peeters, 2015), 165–211; Giovanni B. Bazzana, "*Basileia* and Debt Relief: The Forgiveness of Debts in the Lord's Prayer in the Light of Documentary Papyri," *CBQ* 73 (2011): 511–25.

24. Alan Kirk, "Administrative Writing, Oral Tradition, and Q" (paper presented at the Annual Meeting of the Society of Biblical Literature, Q Session, San Antonio, TX, 2004).

25. Bazzana, "Galilean Village Scribes," 141. Subsequent citations of Bazzana, "Galilean Village Scribes," appear in-text.

argues, "makes the most sense if we think that the authors of Q were people acquainted with specific terminology of liturgies" (139). Such is also the case with the term *phthanō* used in Q 11:20 to describe the kingdom of God "reaching" people. This word, too, is part of stock phrasing that scribal figures used; in this case, it was deployed to praise superior figures, usually with phrasing similar to "your love or beneficence reaches us all" (139–40). This particular terminology thus is another indicator that the authors were "well acquainted with the typical expressions of royal ideology embedded in highly formulaic documents" (141).

Coming at this issue from another angle, William E. Arnal has convincingly demonstrated that Q uses the compositional technique of gender pairing to structure many of its passages. Gender pairing is a scribal technique found in administrative and legal documents wherein the scribe employs a "male" example and a "female" example of a given situation to exhaust all possible cases.[26] Q has several instances of this pairing (e.g., the two men in the field and the two women in the mill in 17:34–35; the queen of the South and the men of Nineveh in 11:31–32; the man planting the mustard seed and the woman adding yeast to flour in 13:18–21). Some scholars have taken these examples as instances of Q's gender inclusivity or evidence for women in the so-called Q community.[27] But as Arnal maintains (and I agree), Q shows no real interest in the experiences or perspectives of actual women. Instead, the technique of gender pairing should be taken as evidence that the authors were familiar with a useful technique that scribes employed to signal how all-encompassing a legal situation was. The presence of petition-like passages, particular administrative terminology, and gender pairing together illustrate that some of the language of Q derives from rather "formulaic diction" so common among the extensive extant documentary papyri produced by middling administrative figures in regions like Palestine and Egypt.[28]

26. William E. Arnal, "Gendered Couplets in Q and Legal Formulations: From the Rhetoric to Social History," *JBL* 116.1 (1997): 75–94.

27. Tal Ilan, "The Women of the Q Community within Early Judaism," in Tiward, *Q in Context II*, 195–212; Amy-Jill Levine, "Who's Catering the Q Affair? Feminist Observations on Q Paraenesis," *Semeia* 50 (1990): 145–61; Levine, "Women in the Q Communit(ies) and Traditions," in *Women and Christian Origins*, ed. Ross S. Kraemer and Mary Rose D'Angelo (Oxford: Oxford University Press, 1999); Sara Parks, *Women in Q: Gender in the Rhetoric of Jesus* (Minneapolis: Fortress, 2019). Granted the presence of such language could function inclusively at a later point in the Jesus movement, but my point is that it was not originally included and intended to speak to the experiences of women.

28. For "formulaic diction," see Kirk, "Scribe as Tradent," 98. In terms of politics and society, Palestine and Egypt were structurally similar: they had a native population that was ruled by the (often distant) Roman regime. Retainer figures, often drawn from the native population, facilitated this colonial situation, which understandably generated resentment from the people

In addition to drawing on formal, compositional techniques regularly found in documentary papyri, we should also entertain another interesting hypothesis about Q's form. In an essay that has implications for the Q source, Gregg Schwendner begins with the question: "why were so many early Christian texts written in plain, non-cursive documentary script rather than book script?"[29] Looking at texts from the Egyptian context, he observes that the earliest Christian manuscripts "are not written in formal book hands popular in the first-second centuries, but in informal hands, rather styleless and plain."[30] This "styleless and plain" writing is that which we happen to find in documentary papyri, he notes, often to facilitate accessibility to readers with a range of literate competencies. Based on this evidence, his provocative suggestion is that by the second century "readers expected Christian books to be written in quasi-documentary style."[31] How does this connect to Q, for which we admittedly have no manuscript evidence? Schwendner makes the interesting, and I think plausible, suggestion that "if the original version of Q were written in bureaucratic style"—and we have certainly seen this based on the discussions of form and content above—"[then] subsequent copies might adhere to the format and writing style of the original," such that the form becomes expected later.[32]

Kim Haines-Eitzen makes similar observations to Schwendner, though in a slightly different way. Focusing on Christian papyri in the second and third centuries, she finds an "overlap" in documentary and literary styles.[33] Put differently, these documents "manifest a distinct dual influence between literary and documentary styles of writing."[34] For her, this confirms the role that professional scribes played in copying early Christian manuscripts. Both Haines-Eitzen and Schwendner invite us, then, in different ways to consider how these bureaucratic, documentary writing habits entered the Jesus traditions. The evidence I have discussed above suggests that these habits were present as early as Q.

Thus, like the content of Q, the form of the document shows signs of being produced by people with some sort of subelite scribal competency. Again, in my view, the formal similarities amount to a stronger argument than an argument based

---

being oppressed. In addition, Rome similarly extracted agricultural produce, taxes, and tributes from both of these regions, which necessitated a robust bureaucratic structure to be effective. Because of these points of similarity, the analogous nature of these two regions is assumed by most papyrologists; see Bazzana, "Galilean Village Scribes," 134.

29. Gregg Schwendner, "Greek Writ Plain: Village Scribes, Q, and the Palaeography of the Earliest Christian Papyri," in *Scribes and Their Remains*, ed. Craig A. Evans and Jeremiah J. Johnston (London: Bloomsbury, 2020), 88.

30. Schwendner, "Greek Writ Plain," 98.

31. Schwendner, "Greek Writ Plain," 102.

32. Schwendner, "Greek Writ Plain," 102.

33. Haines-Eitzen, *Guardians of Letters*, 63.

34. Haines-Eitzen, *Guardians of Letters*, 63.

on content alone (after all, mimicking content and taking over literary themes and imagery are somewhat simple), but to literally *shape* texts in such a peculiar way—indeed, in a way that only a tiny segment of the population would have the skills and training to do—tells us much about authorship. It would help, then, to place this hypothesis about the people behind Q in historical and cultural context before thinking about its implications for the historical Jesus.

GALILEAN SCRIBALISM AND THE EARLY JESUS MOVEMENT

This scenario of mid-level administrative scribal figures showing interest in recording and circulating an early collection of Jesus traditions (especially those that ideologically undergird their [aspirational] role as public intellectuals and learned sages) makes particularly good sense in pre-70 Roman Palestine, especially when we think about who actually had the skills and interest to write down such a collection of traditions. While literacy rates in the Roman Empire could be as high as 10 percent of the population, estimates for Roman Palestine are much lower, perhaps as low as 3 percent—some have even hypothesized that the rate was under 1 percent in rural areas.[35]

The question we have yet to answer is, *Why* would these middling scribal figures be interested in recording traditions associated with Jesus? My basic answer—which I explored at length in my monograph on Q[36]—is that it is precisely these middling administrative figures, drawn from the native population and acting in service of, but nevertheless alienated from, local elites, who would be in the best position to sympathize with Jesus's teachings. We may speculate, moreover, that they recognized the value of their skills of literacy and networks and took it upon themselves to record these traditions and circulate them through their networks. What's more, my cross-cultural research on social movements in structurally similar social contexts suggests that there are good reasons to think that middling administrative figures would have *wanted* to support a movement like Jesus's movement. Due to their precarious position on the cusp of two social classes, especially in an increasingly fragile socioeconomic situation, the Q scribes may have even imagined themselves as spokespeople for those villagers struggling to live in and accommodate the might of Rome and the demands of the native elite.[37] In other words, what we have is the "perfect storm" of educated, literate

---

35. Catherine Hezser, *Jewish Literacy in Roman Palestine*, TSAJ 81 (Tübingen: Mohr Siebeck, 2001), 496.

36. Rollens, *Framing Social Criticism*.

37. Arnal provides an excellent overview of the important economic changes in Galilee in the early first century (*Jesus and the Village Scribes*, 97–155), before showing how Q's rhetoric reflects an experience of disruption and "uprootedness" (157–203).

people acting as custodians for a body of tradition, rife with social critique, that they either invented wholesale or, at the very least, stamped with their particular ideological imprint.

To return to New Testament scholars' unfortunate habit of homogenizing scribes in the world of Jesus, there is little reason to assume that the Q scribes were elite Judean scribes associated with the temple or the Judean aristocracy. For one, the vitriolic rhetoric against Jerusalem and what it stands for suggests otherwise (Q 13:34–35).[38] For another, while Q is a literate product, it is not an elite piece of literature that texts like Sirach or Proverbs are, and it certainly does not ideologically align with the temple apparatus or with traditional religious authorities (e.g., Pharisees or Sadducees). The compositional techniques of the document, as we have noted, betray habits associated with mundane administrative writing: drafting petitions, creating contracts, recording inventories of storage caches, and the like.[39]

Moreover, ancient evidence is clear that administrative figures also read, copied, and even sometimes wrote literature.[40] C. H. Roberts, for instance, has noted that "the same scribe might copy manuscripts for a living and himself be a frequent writer of letters . . . or a slave might be trained to make copies of literary works for his own and at the same time keep his owner's memoranda and accounts."[41] Likewise, Alan Kirk has found cases of "grammarian-level teachers (so possessing some *paideia*) earning extra money by supplying scribal and clerical services."[42] Bazzana has drawn our attention to a fascinating document from Egypt that has a land survey on the *verso*—the product of administrative officials—but a primitive sayings collection on the *recto* with sayings drawn from numerous well-known sources. Of this he writes that this example "will suffice to establish that a group

---

38. Chris Keith has also found that the Palestinian Jesus movement, at least as depicted in the textual evidence that purports to represent it, was largely hostile to elite scribal figures; see *Jesus against the Scribal Elite*. So also, Oakman acknowledges that the scribes of the Jesus movement "manifested both points of ideological conflict with other known scribal groups in first-century Palestine as well as significant differences" (*Radical Jesus*, 111). It is unfortunate for us that the gospels use generic language of "scribes" to define such a large swathe of Jesus's opponents, because many scholars have simply taken that language to imply that scribes—of all varieties—were singularly opposed to the Jesus movement. See my discussion in Rollens, "Scribes in Antiquity."

39. The majority of Q scholars avoid treating Q as very elite literature. A notable exception is Alan Kirk, whose work has focused on situating Q alongside other elite wisdom literature. See Kirk, *Composition of the Sayings Source*.

40. Haines-Eitzen, *Guardians of Letters*, 8, 32–34.

41. C. H. Roberts, as cited in Haines-Eitzen, *Guardians of Letters*, 12–13.

42. Kirk, "Scribe as Tradent," 99.

of arguably professional scribes of documentary texts decided to reemploy an unwritten papyrus piece cut out from an old survey of flooded land that was lying about in their office."[43] In addition, Haines-Eitzen has argued that there is evidence that "these same scribes—who were trained to prepare documents, contracts, letters, and so on—could be called upon to copy literary texts."[44] She includes the fascinating case of one Chariton, identified as a clerk or secretary (*hypographeus*) in the employ of a lawyer (*rhētōr*), who penned an ancient novel called *Chaereas and Callirhoe*. Chariton, she surmises, "is precisely the character who appears in so many papyrological documents as one whose basic function was to verify the contents of a document and write a subscription on behalf of someone who was illiterate."[45] These characters, in turn, are exactly the sorts of figures, I argue, who were responsible for Q. Thus, we have compelling evidence that figures like the thousands of nameless writers responsible for documentary papyri did indeed aspire to write literary texts.[46]

What's more, translocal scribal networks would have provided an excellent source of ready-made pathways to share ideas about Jesus in and around Galilee and Judea.[47] Haines-Eitzen argues that early Christian literature moved through scribal networks in the second and third centuries: "[S]ocial networks among early Christians provided the framework by which Christian literature was transcribed, transmitted, and disseminated. More precisely, . . . scribes who copied early Christian literature did so from *within private scribal networks*."[48] The role of scribes, she contends, goes beyond just writing and copying: "their *relationships* (or links or connections) were integral to the reproduction and circulation of early Christian

43. Bazzana, "Galilean Village Scribes," 148.

44. Haines-Eitzen, *Guardians of Letters*, 6. So also, on the diverse tasks of professional scribes, Bakhos, "Orality and Writing," 4–5.

45. Haines-Eitzen, *Guardians of Letters*, 33.

46. Cf. the discussion focused on scribalism in antiquity in Leila Avrin's *Scribes, Script, and Books: The Book Arts from Antiquity to the Renaissance* (Chicago: American Library Association, 1991).

47. Elite literary networks, of the kind populated by Pliny the Younger, Tacitus, or Martial, likely did not exist in any meaningful way for most Galileans. It is possible that they appeared in some form among the Judean aristocracy, but such networks were probably largely oriented toward the temple and its intellectuals, toward which Jesus traditions show a great deal of hostility. On elite literary networks, see Raymond J. Starr, "The Circulation of Literary Texts in the Roman World," *ClQ* 37.1 (1987): 213–23; Kendra Eshleman, *The Social World of Intellectuals in the Roman Empire: Sophists, Philosophers, and Christians*, Greek Culture in the Roman World (Cambridge: Cambridge University Press, 2012).

48. Haines-Eitzen, *Guardians of Letters*, 78.

literature."[49] Now, I ask: why shouldn't this diffusion through scribal networks be the case much earlier, in the first decades after the life of Jesus, especially when the text itself already shows evidence of administrative influence?

Christina Gousopoulos has looked closely at the intravillage scribal networks attested in documentary papyri and argued that "village administrators were one of the significant vectors for the creation, copying, and dissemination of literary texts, including the vital texts that established the cult of Christ as a textual community."[50] She examines the remarkable example of the archive of one Akousilaos, a *sitologos demosios* (granary supervisor). Not only does his archive contain the requisite administrative documents that one would imagine for his administrative role, but it also contains a curious booklist that includes several well-known classical authors. It is hard to surmise the purpose of this book list but possibilities include: a list for inheritance, a list for convenience, and finally—most importantly—"a list to present to his companions and fellow *literati* a convenient reference to the books he currently possessed and the ones he was still intent on acquiring."[51] Gousopoulos finds the latter option compelling, which thus provides us with an instance of administrative figures, connected translocally to their counterparts in other towns and villages, sharing aspirations to own and (presumably) to read elite literature. Against the idealized picture of how the Jesus movement spread in the Four Gospels, Acts, and Eusebius's idealized narrative, the collaboration, communication, and spread of ideas through preexisting scribal networks simply make more sense than any other romanticized idea of apostles transporting texts around as part of their "mission" in first-century Roman Palestine.

IMPLICATIONS FOR THE HISTORICAL JESUS

Why does any of this matter for the historical Jesus? Put simply, the earliest source for the Jesus movement (Q) shows signs, in both form and content, of being penned by subelite scribal figures. In other words, we do not have an unmediated Jesus tradition. One concern that might be emerging from this discussion is: if the form and content bear so many marks of scribalism, does this imply Jesus did not say what Q says it did? Perhaps.[52] But it also could mean that the Q scribes encountered and "wrote up" these ideas in the way that made the best sense to

49. Haines-Eitzen, *Guardians of Letters*, 81, my emphasis.

50. Christina Gousopoulos, "Sub-Elite Readers and the Transmission of Christian Literary Texts," *ETL* 97.1 (2021): 39.

51. Gousopoulos, "Sub-Elite Readers," 46. Akousilaos's frequent contact with elite figures, she suspects, "may have ... provided him an exemplar of a library to emulate in his own home" (51).

52. And in some cases, I would certainly answer in the affirmative. My interests in the

them.[53] At this point in the history of critical scholarship on early Christianity, it should not be controversial to conclude that ancient texts bear the ideological marks of their authors. However, when we are dealing with religious texts, it often remains difficult to *truly* appreciate this. Especially with the long-standing Protestant emphasis on the unmediated word of God and its presence in inspired texts, it is tricky to say that this bit or that bit was put into a religious text simply because of the author's education or training. Yet, to be sure, that is what I am suggesting. Rather than see this as a *problem* for studying the historical Jesus, though, we might do well to use it as evidence for the *kinds of people* who wanted to preserve the traditions associated with him, which gives us a window into a certain kind of reception history.

This kind of argument also questions the widespread assumption that the Jesus tradition is a *popular* tradition, appealing to the masses and drawing directly from or reflecting their immediate experiences. In its most extreme form, this myth of origins simply takes over the gospel accounts and Acts' later narrative about agrarian workers learning straight from the mouth of Jesus and then teaching others and so on and so forth. But even its more modest form imagines that these stories and sayings about Jesus were preserved by unlettered, humble peasants, who loyally preserved them in oral form until a literate member of their religious community wrote them down for largely pious reasons. This portrait of Christian origins often relies on romanticized notions of peasants and makes very little sense in the social landscape of first-century Palestine, especially considering literacy rates, education levels, and the like. What we need is a realistic hypothesis for the *kinds of people* involved in preserving and transmitting the sayings of Jesus. As I have shown, Q uses a cache of imagery and literary techniques that makes sense originating among middling administrative figures.[54] We should thus abandon the idea that illiterate peasants kept the Jesus traditions alive simply by telling stories for decades until the gospels were written. Rather, we can agree with Douglas Oakman that "Jesus of Nazareth entered the pages of history due to the work of sympathetic scribes."[55]

Furthermore, translocal scribal networks, which we know existed from Egyptian evidence, may have facilitated the first networks of the Jesus movement.

---

present paper, however, are somewhat broader than likelihoods of invention or fabrication of Jesus traditions.

53. Rollens, *Framing Social Criticism*, 200.

54. As I have argued in my monograph on Q, the authors also draw imagery from the worldview of the peasantry, but it is *framed* with their distinct perspective and compositional techniques. See *Framing Social Criticism*, 142–58.

55. Oakman, *Radical Jesus*, 89.

We mentioned earlier the example of Akousilaos, the granary manager, and his archive. Gousopoulos finds fascinating evidence that *sitologoi* were often well connected to agricultural workers, figures in the transportation business, and figures in higher-level administrative offices.[56] In short, *village administrators truly might have been some of the most well-connected people in the social landscape of the Roman Empire*—akin to the axial figures and mediating intellectuals that we often find facilitating the spread of social and political movements throughout history.[57] The movement of ideas and people through these sorts of networks makes much more sense than simply taking over the gospel myths themselves and concluding that we are dealing with radical itinerant preachers or a cadre of charismatic wonder-workers. Yes, that is what the texts are *about*, but we are not obliged to accept this as a viable historical explanation for the development of the tradition.[58]

In closing, if we are going to take the Q source seriously as early evidence for the Palestinian Jesus movement, we will need to account for its strong affinities with administrative and bureaucratic writing.[59] That may be underwhelming or uninteresting for some, threatening for others, and possibly annoying for still others. Such reactions, however, do not change the fact that these influences are present in the text and that scholars of the historical Jesus must wrestle with the implications of their presence. These influences, as we have seen in this chapter, frame and color the earliest memories of the historical Jesus in Galilee.

56. Gousopoulos, "Sub-Elite Readers," 47–49. On scribal networks, see also Rollens, *Framing Social Criticism*, 136–37.

57. See my extensive cross-cultural comparison of other social movements with Q in Rollens, *Framing Social Criticism*, 44–79.

58. Bruce Lincoln, "Theses on Method," *MTSR* 8 (1996): 225–27. Thesis 13 reads: "When one permits those whom one studies to define the terms in which they will be understood, suspends one's interest in the temporal and contingent, or fails to distinguish between 'truths,' 'truth-claims,' and 'regimes of truth,' one has ceased to function as historian or scholar. In that moment, a variety of roles are available: some perfectly respectable (amanuensis, collector, friend and advocate), and some less appealing (cheerleader, voyeur, retailer of import goods). None, however, should be confused with scholarship."

59. Cf. Douglas Oakman: "Scholarship must reckon with an initial match of interests that could explain why any scribe or scribes would be concerned with the words and activities of an illiterate peasant" (*Radical Jesus*, 92).

16

Synagogues

Anders Runesson

The Next Quest for the historical Jesus must account for the physical, social, and discursive nature of the ancient institutions we refer to as "synagogues." This is simply because almost all other approaches and themes listed in this book are dependent to some degree on knowledge that can be distilled from these communal settings, within which Jesus chose to enact and communicate his message and, indeed, to embody his purpose. It is the structures of these institutions themselves, rather than the many and varied applications of the ancestral traditions that emerged from them, that allow us, in the midst of profound diversity, to speak of "Second Temple Judaism" as a category and the matrix within which we define Jesus socially, culturally, politically, economically, and "religiously."

You Need a Body to Locate a Soul

Since we as modern scholars researching the historical Jesus are part of the reception history of both Jesus and the institutions he proclaimed his message within, we need to begin our discussion by considering a question I believe is essential to all Quests: who wants the field of historical Jesus studies to move

A version of this chapter was presented at the 2023 meeting of the SNTS in Vienna, Austria. I'm grateful to the participants of the Social History and the New Testament seminar, and especially Sarah E. Rollens, who responded to the paper, for their comments and questions.

forward in the first place, and why? Many would probably think that this type of research would be very Christian and theological in nature, but then again, historical reconstructions, for most Christians, can hardly attain normative status.[1] As John P. Meier notes, "The more we appreciate what Jesus meant in his own time and place, the more 'alien' he will seem to us."[2] Already Albert Schweitzer wrote in a similar vein, "There is a deep significance in the fact that whenever we hear the sayings of Jesus we have to enter a realm of thought which is not ours."[3] E. P. Sanders also famously stated, "I am a liberal, modern, secularized Protestant, brought up in a church dominated by low christology and the social gospel. I am proud of the things that that religious tradition stands for. I am not bold enough, however, to suppose that Jesus came to establish it, or that he died for the sake of its principles."[4]

History may be best described, then, as a countercultural exercise, through which we aim to perceive things in ways unfamiliar to us; it is the conscious effort to disentangle what we think we know from our own discursive habits and seek enlightenment through glimpsing into worlds otherwise unknown. It is our longing to hear voices not our own and to learn from them that brings the historical into being. Seeing our world from the "outside"—to the degree that this is at all possible—through these voices highlights both the normal and the normative as part of trajectories of variously shaped receptions otherwise forgotten; it destabilizes our sense of how things are or must necessarily be and thus contributes to the larger discussion of what could or even should be. Herein lies for many, I believe, the basic impulse to join historical conversations orbiting the Jesus figure. Precisely how these conversations are modeled, however, is the subject of a continuing debate, which now enters its next phase.

1. See, e.g., John P. Meier, *The Roots of the Problem and the Person*, vol. 1 of *A Marginal Jew: Re-Thinking the Historical Jesus*, AYBRL (New York: Doubleday), 197: "The Jesus of history is not and cannot be the object of Christian faith." Cf. Raymond E. Brown, *The Critical Meaning of the Bible: How a Modern Reading of the Bible Challenges Christians, the Church, and the Churches* (New York: Paulist, 1981), x: "While the biblical 'word of God' is inspired (and thus of God and not merely about Him), every word of it comes from human beings and is conditioned by their limitations. Because of the human element, one needs scientific, literary, and historical methods to determine what the ancient authors meant when they wrote—that knowledge does not come from revelation." If, from a Christian perspective, such an argument applies already to the study of the biblical texts, how much more relevance would it not have for scholarly reconstructions of a historical figure mentioned in those texts!

2. Meier, *Marginal Jew*, 1:200.

3. Albert Schweitzer, *Out of My Life and Thought: An Autobiography*, trans. C. T. Campion (New York: Mentor, 1953), 47–48.

4. E. P. Sanders, *Jesus and Judaism* (London: SCM, 1985), 334.

For me, understanding Jesus historically—that is, as the Other whom we would not have recognized had we met him on the street[5]—necessarily entails resurrecting the Jewish world of the eastern Mediterranean, within which he once made sense. In other words, it is an exercise in contextual plausibility. You need a socioreligious, cultural, political, and economic body to locate a soul. But how are we to proceed with this task if, as has been convincingly shown in recent research, Second Temple Judaism "was marked by a staggering diversity that challenges attempts to define what Judaism or being Judaic in antiquity was"?[6] It is the argument of this chapter that one of the few ways to identify that which was shared among ancient Jews is to focus on settings where, as the Gospel of John claims, "all the Jews come together" (18:20): the Jerusalem temple but, even more importantly, the "synagogues," since the latter represent the local contexts within which people—men and women—met and interacted on a regular basis. These Jewish institutions, which were ubiquitous in the ancient Mediterranean world and, importantly, can be reconstructed based on sources both beyond and within the New Testament texts, thus provide us with a critical entry point into the world of Jesus, as he shared it with his contemporaries. Indeed, it is within these types of settings that we should locate his earliest followers too, as well as the transmission and textualization of traditions preserving his memory; "synagogues" offer us nothing less than access to important clues not only about the person but also about how his memory and message were preserved and shaped. Elsewhere, I have called this approach, through which we may also learn about ancient theology and ideology based on the institutional contexts within which they were formed, "institution criticism."[7] Such a procedure opens up, too, for understanding historical change beyond viewing the individual as its prime mover, the importance of which is emphasized by James Crossley in his introduction to this volume.

It is, of course, impossible to address in any detail such monumental issues in a brief chapter. The first question, however, as we begin the process of defamiliariza-

---

5. Any historical reconstruction that results in familiar scenes or scenarios is, many would say, inherently unlikely, or, at the very least, should be the object of careful examination.

6. Loren Stuckenbruck, "What Is Second Temple Judaism?," in *T&T Clark Encyclopedia of Second Temple Judaism*, ed. Daniel M. Gurtner and Loren Stuckenbruck (London: T&T Clark, 2020), 1:19.

7. See Anders Runesson, "The Historical Jesus, the Gospels, and First-Century Jewish Society: The Importance of the Synagogue for Understanding the New Testament," in *A City Set on a Hill: Essays in Honor of James F. Strange*, ed. Daniel Warner and Donald D. Binder (Mountain Home, AR: BorderStone, 2014), 293; and, in a bit more detail, Anders Runesson, "Placing Paul: Institutional Structures and Theological Strategy in the World of the Early Christ-Believers," *SEÅ* 80 (2015), 44 n. 2; revised and updated as chapter 7 in Anders Runesson and Rebecca Runesson, *Judaism for Gentiles: Reading Paul beyond the Parting of the Ways Paradigm*, WUNT 494 (Tübingen: Mohr Siebeck, 2022), 175–93.

tion that may lead us to appreciate Jesus as the historical Other arguably needs to be: what was a "synagogue" in the first century? As it turns out, answers to this question will destabilize any understanding of antiquity based on later definitions of "synagogue," and erase simplistic dichotomies between "politics and religion," "church and synagogue," "Christians and Jews," "slave and free," and "men and women," just to mention a few of the many aspects differentiating "us" from "them." In the following, I shall present a reconstruction of these "synagogue" institutions and then proceed to outline some implications of this reconstruction for how we understand Jesus and his program. Doing so, I shall also comment on how changes in institutional setting may shed light on how the late antique and medieval "church" and "synagogue" came into being, and how this may have led to more general shifts in how the message was understood. The bottom line is that it is hardly possible to ask the questions "who was Jesus and what did he want to achieve?" without also having to respond to the query "what was a first-century synagogue?"

Reconstructing an (Institutional) World without Rabbis and Christians

Mainstream Judaism today, in all its varieties, developed from rabbinic Judaism and its institutions, which did not exist in the time of Jesus. Christianity did not exist either, of course, and this forces us to locate sources to be used as evidence in our effort to reconstruct the nature of Second Temple–period "synagogues" primarily beyond those authored within any of these traditions. Such restrictions do not affect texts later included in the New Testament, though, since they were authored apart from the process of canonization and belong to the early period. Some Christian texts authored in the second century onward should be used with caution, however. The main reason for this is not that "synagogues" developed significantly after 70 CE (they did not).[8] Rather, by then we see the beginnings of Christian sociorhetorical efforts to place the Jesus movement and its *ekklēsia* in direct opposition to the *synagōgai* of the Jews, the latter being imagined as the reverse image of "the church."[9] In addition to first-century literary texts, our

---

8. See Anders Runesson and Wally V. Cirafesi, "Reassessing the Impact of 70 CE on the Origins and Development of Palestinian Synagogues," in *The Synagogue in Ancient Palestine: Current Issues and Emerging Trends*, ed. Rick Bonnie, Raimo Hakola, and Ulla Tervahauta, FRLANT 279 (Göttingen: Vandenhoeck & Ruprecht, 2020), 37–57.

9. See discussion by Judith Lieu, "The Synagogue and the Separation of the Christians," in *The Ancient Synagogue from Its Origins until 200 CE: Papers Presented at an International Conference at Lund University, October 14–17, 2001*, ed. Birger Olsson and Magnus Zetterholm, ConBNT 39 (Stockholm: Almqvist & Wiksell, 2003), 190–95, who notes that it was still rare before 200 CE

evidence consists of inscriptions, papyri, and archaeological remains, all of which should be part of the analytical work.[10]

While the Greek term used to designate Jewish institutions eventually boiled down to *synagōgē* (which then enters the English language as "synagogue") and *ekklēsia* emerged as the preferred term used by Christians to designate their institutions (translated in most contexts into English as "church"), in the first century no such terminological distinctions along denominational boundaries is discernable.[11] Indeed, as many scholars have noted, the institutions we uniformily today call "synagogues" were designated by multiple terms in antiquity—with some overlap, at least seventeen in Greek, five in Hebrew, and three in Latin.[12] The most common of these were *synagōgē, proseuchē*, and, notably, *ekklēsia*.[13] Without taking this terminological diversity into account, it is impossible to identify the relevant source material. Furthermore, as this material is collected and analyzed, it seems clear that, as I and others have previously argued, behind these terms we find two basic types of institution, inhabiting distinct social spheres of ancient societies: a civic type and an associative type.[14] Since we lack English terminology to differentiate between these types, and the English word "synagogue"

to use the dichotomy "*synagōgē* versus *ekklēsia*" to indicate Christianity and Judaism as two separate entities.

10. Sources have been collected, translated, and interpreted in Anders Runesson, Donald D. Binder, and Birger Olsson, *The Ancient Synagogue: From Its Origins to 200 CE: A Source Book*, AJEC 72 (Leiden: Brill, 2008) (hereafter *ASSB*). Since its publication, new archaeological evidence has emerged, and new interpretations of synagogue terminology have been added to the discussion; we are currently working on updating the book to reflect this.

11. Despite the fact that the term "church" comes from a different Greek word (*kyriakos*) meaning "that which belongs to the lord," or simply "of the lord." The translation of *ekklēsia* that comes closest to its first-century usage is "assembly," signaling also its contemporary Greek—and Jewish—political nuances.

12. For sources, see the terminological index in *ASSB*, 328.

13. For *ekklēsia* as a synagogue term, see the comprehensive analysis by Ralph J. Korner, *The Origin and Meaning of Ekklēsia in the Early Jesus Movement*, AJEC 98 (Leiden: Brill, 2017), esp. 81–149, and also Andrew R. Krause's analysis of Josephus's use of the term, *Synagogues in the Works of Flavius Josephus: Rhetoric, Spatiality, and First-Century Institutions*, AJEC 97 (Leiden: Brill, 2017), esp. 98–114, 193–95. *ASSB* does not deal with all occurrences of *ekklēsia* as a synagogue term. Also lacking in this regard are Lee I. Levine, *The Ancient Synagogue: The First Thousand Years*, 2nd ed. (New Haven: Yale University Press, 2005); Anders Runesson, *The Origins of the Synagogue: A Socio-Historical Study* (Stockholm: Almqvist & Wiksell, 2001); Donald D. Binder, *Into the Temple Courts: The Place of the Synagogues in the Second Temple Period*, SBLDS 169 (Atlanta: Society of Biblical Literature, 1999).

14. Runesson, *Origins*; Jordan J. Ryan, *The Role of the Synagogue in the Aims of Jesus* (Minneapolis: Fortress, 2017). For other examples, see Ryan, "The Socio-Political Context of Public Synagogue Debates in the Second Temple Period," in Bonnie et al., *Synagogue in Ancient Pales-*

conceals this difference, we may, for convenience, call them "public synagogues" and "association synagogues."

"Synagogue" terms were applied to these two types of institution indiscriminately, and this is true also of the titles of officials associated with respective institutions. In this way, the Jewish socio-terminological situation mirrors rather closely the Greco-Roman one, as non-Jewish societies also displayed institutions on civic and associative levels, and the latter had a tendency of imitating the terms used in the former.[15] To take one example, in the Greco-Roman world *ekklēsia* was used as a term identifying both civic and associative institutions, even though the former vastly outnumbers the latter in our sources. In the Jewish world, which was socioculturally intertwined with the larger Mediterranean world, we see a similar situation. Here, the usage of *ekklēsia* could be referring either to Jewish civic institutions (i.e., "public synagogues") or, less often, to Jewish associations. For the latter, Philo provides some material (*Spec.* 1.324–325; *Deo* 111; *Virt.* 108).[16] As for the "public synagogues," the material includes Josephus, who often uses this term, and Sirach, who applies the term frequently to the public assemblies of the land.[17] The same word is used in 1 Macc 14:18 and Jdt 6:16, 14:6, and in LAB 11:8 we find the Latin equivalent (*ecclesia*).[18] In the gospels, however, we find almost exclusively the use of *synagōgē* for civic institutions. Here *ekklēsia* is applied three times in only two contexts in Matthew's Gospel, designating an associative setting run by Jesus-oriented Jews (Matt 16:18; 18:17). *Synagōgē* could, however, also designate an association, as seen in the Theodotos inscription and in Philo's description of the *synagōgē* of the Essenes.[19] Examples could be multiplied. My point is simple: the terminological diversity and interchangeability that applies to institutions designated by synagogue terms means that context becomes key for the interpretive endeavor.

The archaeological material is perhaps easier as far as the identification of either type of institution is concerned. Due to limitations of space, I will comment here only on some of the key distinguishing architectural elements of

tine, 134–35 n. 9. On the definition of the synagogue as a semipublic association, see esp. Peter Richardson, *Building Jewish in the Roman East* (Waco, TX: Baylor University Press, 2004), 207–21.

15. On Greco-Roman associations and the place of Christ groups in relation to them, see most recently John S. Kloppenborg, *Christ's Associations: Connecting and Belonging in the Ancient City* (New Haven: Yale University Press, 2019) and Richard Last and Philip A. Harland, *Group Survival in the Ancient Mediterranean: Rethinking Material Conditions in the Landscape of Jews and Christians* (London: T&T Clark, 2020).

16. For text and commentary, see *ASSB*, nos. 201–203.

17. For Josephus, see, e.g., *A.J.* 16.62; 19.332; *B.J.* 1.550, 654; 4.159, 162, 255; 7.412; *Vita* 267–268; for Sirach, see, e.g., 15:5; 21:17; 23:24; 31:11; 33:19; 38:32–33; 39:9–10; 44:15.

18. For text and commentary, see *ASSB*, no. 64.

19. See *ASSB*, nos. 26 (*CIJ* 2.1404), and 40 (Philo, *Prob.* 80–83), respectively.

Figure 16.1. *The Gamla synagogue, looking southwest. Photo by author (2010).*

the buildings used in the two social contexts. As for the civic institutions, the placement of stepped benches lining three or four walls of the main hall of these buildings is crucial for identification. The Gamla synagogue in the Golan Heights (see fig. 16.1) is a good example of this architectural solution, echoing the Greek council halls (*bouleutēria*).[20] The focal point of this type of spatial arrangement is the empty space at the center of the room, from where Torah was likely read (see further below), but the construction as such is designed for interaction between those present.[21]

20. For this and other examples of public buildings identified as synagogues, see *ASSB*. While new finds have been made and are currently discussed, the following are important: Magdala, Capernaum I, Gamla, Cana (*ASSB*, no. 2; see also Tom McCollough, "The Synagogue at Khirbet Qana in Its Village Context," in Bonnie et al., *Synagogue in Ancient Palestine*, 81–95), Qiryat Sefer, Modiʿin, Herodion, Masada. For the Gamla synagogue, see also the reconstruction in figure 4.143 in Anders Runesson, "Synagogue," in Gurtner and Stuckenbruck, *T&T Clark Companion to Second Temple Judaism*, 2:748.

21. The closest modern architectural parallel would be the design of the space in which the British Parliament convenes, with its very effective focus on precisely interaction.

Adding to the archive of evidence, such archaeological remains are associated with the institutions that Josephus (for instance) often designates *ekklēsiai*, echoing the political, democratic Greek institutions that were, according to him, later copies of the Jewish original.[22] We have good grounds, in my view, for understanding this space, in which we find both men and women, as a locally run religiopolitical institution.[23]

The situation looks different as we turn to associative spatial contexts. While we find benches in main halls here too, architectural solutions for housing these groups were more diverse.[24] When groups had the (economic) opportunity to gather in purpose-built structures, we find multipurpose buildings that often include several additional rooms such as those mentioned in the Theodotos inscription.[25] Since common meals were part of association activities, both Greco-Roman and Jewish and among those engaged in Christ devotion (whether Jewish or not), the presence of cooking and dining facilities—such as in the Ostia and Jericho "synagogues" as well as the assembly spaces of the covenanters at Qumran[26]— distinguish between architectural remains related to associations and those used by civic assemblies. Still, these small face-to-face groups facilitated communication and discussion, just as the architecture of the civic institutions did, albeit in different ways. In both types of settings, we must reckon with broadly defined participation by both women and men in the processes in which ancestral traditions were interpreted, shaped, and actualized.[27] And this, in turn, may shed light on why one of the terms chosen by first-century authors to identify these types of institutions, too, was the Greek political term *ekklēsia*, signaling shared concerns for communal affairs and responsibility in decision-making. Importantly, this term also indicates a sense of shared religiopolitical group identity or peoplehood.

In terms of distribution, if we combine all source types, we find that first-century "synagogues" cluster in the Galilee and the coastal region (e.g., Caesarea)

22. See discussion by Krause, *Synagogues*, 112–14, 193–95.

23. On mixed assemblies of men and women, see Josephus, *A.J.* 4.209–210, 256–261; Luke 13:10–21; Acts 16:13–16; 17:1–9, 10–14; 18:24–26. Note also the book of Judith and how Judith is said to interact in public assemblies (*ekklēsiai*, Jud 6:21); see discussion in Korner, *Origin and Meaning of Ekklēsia*, 97–98, 104. Regarding the synagogue as a religiopolitical institution, see Ryan, "Socio-Political Context."

24. See Edward Adams, *The Earliest Christian Meeting Places: Almost Exclusively Houses?*, rev. ed., LNTS 450 (London: Bloomsbury, 2016), which includes discussion of spaces used by Jews.

25. See n. 19. Rooms included hostel functions.

26. *ASSB*, nos. 179, 15, 41. On gathering for meals in Jewish associative settings, see also the permission of Caesar for the Jews to do so in Josephus, *A.J.* 14.216.

27. For mixed assemblies in the diaspora, see, e.g. Josephus, *A.J.* 14.256–261; Philo, *Contempl.* 30–33.

as well as in Judea, excluding Samaria.[28] We also have sources that mention the general presence of these institutions in the land, but which do not associate them with specific towns or cities. This type of evidence is important as it shows the general prevalence of "synagogues" in the land. While we know of the existence of Samaritan synagogues in the diaspora dating to as early as the third or second century BCE, the earliest remains in the land date to the fourth century CE.[29] It is possible, even likely, that Samaritans maintained their own civic and associative institutions in Samaria in the first century CE, but due to present lack of evidence this assumption cannot be proven.

What activities were taking place in these different types of institutions? While the civic institutions dealt with city and town administration, including juridicial functions, Jewish associations catered to their specific membership and recruited through specific networks.[30] Around the first century CE, however, we find several activities that were shared between them. The most important for our purposes here is the communal reading and teaching of Torah followed by debate or discussion.[31] While it is difficult to say exactly when such readings, which were unique to the Jews in antiquity, began to take place on a weekly basis,[32] public readings of

28. For an overview, see the foldout map in *ASSB*.

29. The third- or second-century BCE evidence is found in *ASSB* no. 100. For the fourth-century CE evidence, see Reinhard Pummer, "Samaritan Synagogues and Jewish Synagogues: Similarities and Differences," in *Jews, Christians, and Polytheists in the Ancient Synagogue: Cultural Interaction during the Greco-Roman Period*, ed. Steve Fine (New York: Routledge, 1999), 105–42.

30. Associations in the ancient Mediterranean can be categorized according to the networks through which they recruited members, and whose everyday lives they facilitated (e.g., occupational, neighborhood, domestic, cultic, or immigrant networks). For discussion, see Kloppenborg, *Christ's Associations*, 23–40; Last and Harland, *Group Survival*, 9–13.

31. See, e.g., Philo, *Prob.* 81; *Hypoth.* 7.11–14; *Spec.* 2.62; *Decal.* 40; *Somn.* 2.127; *Mos.* 2.216; *Legat.* 156; Josephus, *B.J.* 2.289; *A.J.* 16.42–43, 164; Acts 9:20; 13:14; 15:21; 17:1; 18:4. See also the Theodotos inscription (*ASSB*, no. 26). On debate after readings, see Carl Mosser, "Torah Instruction, Discussion, and Prophecy in First-Century Synagogues," in *Christian Origins and Hellenistic Judaism: Social and Literary Contexts for the New Testament*, ed. Stanley E. Porter and Andrew Pitts, TENTS 10 (Leiden: Brill, 2013), 550.

32. On the weekly Sabbath rhythm of these assemblies, see esp. Josephus, *C. Ap.* 2.175; *B.J.* 2.289; Philo, *Opif.* 128; *Hypoth.* 7.11–14; *Spec.* 2.62; Mark 1:21; Luke 4:16; Acts 13:14. It is difficult to say when exactly communal reading of the Torah began to take place on a weekly basis, as the earliest unambiguous evidence of this seven-day cycle is limited to the first century CE. I have argued elsewhere, however, that it is a reasonable assumption that this custom was introduced by the Hasmoneans as a strategic tool in their nation building; see chapter 4 of Runesson, *Origins*. To be sure, while the evidence for communal readings is overwhelming, we know very little about *how* they were performed; we have no evidence suggesting that later practices, such as *lectio continua* or other strategies, were implemented already in the first century.

Torah as a phenomenon originated in civic settings in the Persian period, the time when we, indeed, may place the forerunners of the "public synagogues" we find in the first century.[33] Prayer is much more difficult to identify as related to civic assemblies on Sabbaths. However, prayer rituals could be part of liturgies on other days for special reasons, such as public fasts (Josephus, *Vita* 295), and people could use "synagogue" buildings for their individual prayers at any time, which indicates the public status of these buildings (cf. Matt 6:5). The situation is different for the associative settings where communal prayer is evidenced for some association synagogues in the land (e.g., 4Q503) as well as for diaspora "synagogues."[34]

Another difference between civic and associative institutions concerns their nature, as perceived, as far as we can tell, by the ancients. While, as shown by the Theodotos inscription and Philo's and Josephus's descriptions of the Essenes, reading, expounding, and teaching Torah stood at the center of activities linked to "association synagogues," such associations could be regarded by their members as holy places, as in the cases of the covenanters at Qumran and the Essenes more broadly.[35] This idea of "synagogue" buildings as holy space was not, in my opinion, applied to public "synagogues" in the land, but there are plenty of diasporic sources from this time claiming that Jewish association buildings were understood as sacred.[36] This is important to note when we consider the institutional contexts in which Jesus operated and whom he met, or could meet, there.

---

33. So Runesson, *Origins*, 237–400, but see also Levine, *Ancient Synagogue*, 21–44, and Binder, *Into the Temple Courts*, 204–26. Interestingly, already the Targum understood the institution assembling in the city gate to be the same type of institution as the public institution called "synagogue" (*bêt knîštêhôn*) in the author's own time; see Tg. Neb. Amos 5:12, and note the court setting. On the Targum in the context of synagogues, cf. Per Å Bengtsson, *Passover in the Targum Pseudo-Jonathan Genesis: The Connection of Early Biblical Events with Passover in Targum Pseudo-Jonathan in a Synagogue Setting* (Lund: Royal Society of Letters, 2001), esp. 21–25, 74–76.

34. Josephus, *A.J.* 14.260; Philo, *Deus* 8–9; *Spec.* 3.169–171; Justin Martyr, *Dial.* 137. See discussion of these passages in *ASSB*, nos. 113, 161, 169, 217.

35. Philo, *Prob.* 81; cf. Josephus *B.J.* 2.128–132; CD XI, 22–XII, 1; cf. Steven Fine, *This Holy Place: On the Sanctity of the Synagogue During the Greco-Roman Period* (Notre Dame: University of Notre Dame Press, 1997).

36. So also Levine, *Ancient Synagogue*. There is an interesting example, however, with regard to synagogues as holy space in the land: the "synagogue" building in Caesarea Maritima mentioned by Josephus (*B.J.* 2.289). This synagogue is said to have been "desecrated" (*miainō*) when a non-Jew performed a sacrifice of birds just in front of its entrance. This seems to imply that the building was seen, by Josephus, as sacred. Caesarea Maritima was, however, a non-Jewish city, in which the Jewish population was allowed to construct a "synagogue" for specific purposes and gatherings, notably not including local city administration, which was otherwise part of the activities of public "synagogues" in the land. This means that the Caesarea Maritima "synagogue" should be understood as more related to diaspora "synagogues," and thus to how

Equally important, but from a different perspective, is identifying the institutional structures embodied by officials and leaders. In the past, many scholars assumed that the Pharisees were in charge of "synagogues" (without further defining which type of institution was meant) and, after locating Jesus in this milieu, proceeded to theorize about possible reasons behind conflicts noted in the gospels. The Pharisees, of course, led their own assemblies or associations.[37] However, as Lee Levine and many others have noted, "the truth of the matter is, the Pharisees had little or nothing to do with the early synagogue, and there is not one shred of evidence pointing to a connection between the two. No references associate the early Pharisees (the 'Pairs' and others) with the synagogue, nor is there anything in early synagogue liturgy that is particularly Pharisaic."[38] The rabbis did not exist as a group in the time of Jesus, but even as they were later consolidating their own group(s), early rabbinic literature shows little interest in "public synagogues." It is not until around the third or fourth century that such interest emerges, and it took even longer before the rabbis were able to implement their definition of Judaism in institutions shared with other Jews.[39]

Looking at titles associated with "synagogue" officials in the land of Israel, we find the following in the sources:

> *archisynagōgos* (ruler of the synagogue; Mark 5:22)
> *archōn* (ruler; Matt 9:18; Josephus, *Vita* 278, 294; *A.J.* 4.214)
> *hypēretēs* (Hebrew: *ḥazzān* = attendant; Luke 4:20)

---

such "synagogues" were understood to inhabit the associative sphere of society. The issue of the sanctity of "synagogues" in the land and in the diaspora is discussed by Susan Haber in dialogue with the work of Ed Sanders in *They Shall Purify Themselves: Essays on Purity in Early Judaism* (Atlanta: Society of Biblical Literature, 2008), 161–79, esp. 175–78.

37. As for the Pharisees, from the gospels and Acts we learn that their associations included members who were scribes (Mark 2:16; Luke 5:30; 23:9). One of them, a teacher of the law (*nomodidaskalos*), is mentioned by name in Acts 5:34 (Gamaliel). Matthew 22:35 also mentions a *nomikos* (a scribe who was an expert in Jewish law) as a member of a Pharisaic association (cf. Mark 12:38, who writes *grammateus* and does not indicate the person's affiliation with any association). For a possible reference to a Pharisaic "association synagogue" in Matt 12:9, see Runesson, *Origins*, 355–57.

38. Levine, *Ancient Synagogue*, 41. Note here that Levine defines "synagogue" as a public institution. Cf. Shaye J. D. Cohen, "Were Pharisees and Rabbis the Leaders of Communal Prayer and Torah Study in Antiquity? The Evidence of the New Testament, Josephus, and the Early Church Fathers," in *Evolution of the Synagogue: Problems and Progress*, ed. Howard Clark Kee and Lynn H. Cohick (Harrisburg, PA: Trinity Press International, 1999), 89–105.

39. Cf. Chad S. Spigel, *Ancient Synagogue Seating Capacities: Methodology, Analysis and Limits*, TSAJ 149 (Tübingen: Mohr Siebeck, 2012), 3 n. 13 and literature referred to there.

grammateus (scribe; Mark 1:21–22)

presbyteros (elder; *ASSB*, no. 26; cf. Luke 7:3–5)

dynatos (possibly, see Josephus, *B.J.* 2.287, 292)

Hiereus (priest) was a hereditary title related to the temple cult and did not in itself indicate a particular position in synagogues. However, priests were often leaders in and benefactors of synagogues.[40] In fact, if any group could be said to have been closely aligned to "synagogues," it would be the priests. As Matthew Grey has shown,

> priests were often integrated into Judea's national institutions and into the local leadership structures of the cities, towns, and villages where they resided when they were not on duty at the Jerusalem temple. This integration was promoted by Pentateuchal legislation, which appointed priests to be custodians of divine law whose legal expertise and gifts of divination also qualified them to serve as judges over a variety of civic, ritual, and religious matters within the Judean community.[41]

It is debated what exactly the titles of synagogue officials implied in terms of responsibilities, and we should note that any such office could be, and likely was, often held by a priest. It seems certain, however, that the *archisynagōgos* and the *archōn* enjoyed the highest status, while the *grammateus* (scribe) was associated with teaching at Sabbath gatherings (cf. Mark 1:21–22). Possibly, scribes were also teaching children at other occasions.[42] Their duties varied in different time periods. As for first-century Jewish society, scribes were low or middle level officials and judges in cities, towns, and villages working as bureaucrats and experts in Jewish law. Consequently, they were involved in village administration and thus must have worked within the setting of "public synagogues." They were not an autonomous group with a specific political agenda but could vary in background and allegiances on the local level.[43] Thus, as with priests, we could find among the scribes some with Pharisaic leanings and others who had joined the Jesus movement (cf. Matt 13:52). Reading and teaching in "public synagogues" were

---

40. *ASSB*, no. 26; cf. Philo, *Hypoth.* 7.13. For discussion of priestly involvement in "synagogues," see Levine, *Ancient Synagogue*, 519–29.

41. Matthew Grey, "Priests, Judean Community Assemblies, and Synagogue Development in the Second Temple Period," in Bonnie et al., *Synagogue in Ancient Palestine*, 125.

42. If such activities did take place in "synagogues"; cf. Josephus, *C. Ap.* 2.204.

43. See Anthony J. Saldarini, *Pharisees, Scribes, and Sadducees in Palestinian Society: A Sociological Approach* (Grand Rapids: Eerdmans, 2001).

not, however, linked exclusively to a specific office; anyone who was able seems to have been allowed to perform such tasks.[44] In an association setting, Philo notes that among the Essenes, one person read from Scripture and another person, "of especial proficiency," expounded what had been read.[45]

Taken together, these various aspects of "synagogue" activities open up space for reconstructing a context within which we may understand competition between Jewish groups for dominance in Jewish society, whether they were Pharisees, Herodians, Jesus followers, or followers of Judas the Galilean. Civic institutions provided a platform of sorts for debates and interaction, and the promotion of certain goals through specific interpretations of Torah. In fact, once we have digested the otherness of the prerabbinic, civic institutional setting in which Jesus made sense and noted the influence of priests, who traveled on a regular basis between their hometown and Jerusalem, Jesus's own focus, according to the gospels, first on the "synagogues" of Galilee and then, after gathering a following, on Jerusalem (cf. Matt 19:1–2) emerges as historically quite interesting.[46]

RESURRECTING A FIRST-CENTURY KINGDOM

Against this background, it seems to me methodologically unwise to ignore the institutional setting—the civic institutions through which towns and villages organized their communal lives—where the oldest and only direct evidence to which we have access (i.e., the canonical gospels) claim Jesus operated as he proclaimed and enacted his message about a coming kingdom. Taking a wider horizon as point of departure, Philip Harland has argued that

> certain social dimensions of group life among Judean (Jewish) gatherings and Christian congregations, including issues of identity, are better understood when we place these groups within the framework of unofficial associations in the Greco-Roman world. Despite their position as cultural minority groups, synagogues and congregations should not be studied in isolation from analogous social structures of that world.[47]

44. See Mosser, "Torah Instruction," 550. This would be the type of setting in which we should imagine Luke's description of Jesus reading and interpreting of Torah in the *synagōgē* of Nazareth, and the debate that follows in Luke 4:16–30.

45. Philo, *Prob.* 82; cf. *Spec.* 2.62.

46. E.g., Mark 1:39; Matt 4:23; 9:35; cf. Luke 6:6; 13:10. Luke 4:44 suggests that Jesus also taught in the civic institutions of Judea.

47. Philip A. Harland, *Dynamics of Identity in the World of the Early Christians* (New York: T&T Clark, 2009), 25.

The Greco-Roman association context to which Harland refers is closely related to both Christian and Jewish origins but not, to put it succinctly, to Jesus. For the researcher, associations with their varied member-based networks will shed light on how the movement spread after Jesus's death and provide us with a social and discursive space within which we may consider the process of transmission and (con)textualization of tradition. Indeed, the very seed that became the church was sown here, just as the medieval and modern synagogue finds its (rabbinic) origins in this type of unofficial institutional context. But, based on what we know about the institutional realities in Galilee and Judea, specifically the civic institutions designated by "synagogue" terms and the archaeological remains that can be associated with those terms, this was not the type of setting within which the historical Jesus operated.

While the nature of the source material itself needs to be studied and understood against the background of what we know about unofficial group formation and network analysis in the ancient Mediterranean, the content of these same sources guides us away from precisely those semiprivate settings when we seek the historical Jesus: away from the social sphere between the public and the private and into the political world of first-century Judaism. This is crucial precisely because the political is what will, in these settings, carry the explanatory force as we seek to understand this historical figure in his place, be it his life, his purpose, or his death.[48]

So far, few scholars have engaged the Quest for the historical Jesus through the lens of recent synagogue studies.[49] But when such interdisciplinary work *is* undertaken, critical insights emerge that would otherwise have remained obscure. With Jordan Ryan's vitally important 2017 study *The Role of the Synagogue in the Aims of Jesus*—the most comprehensive investigation merging synagogue studies with historical Jesus research published to date—scholarship on Jesus has moved forward in a range of significant ways. Indeed, it is through synagogue studies in particular that we may perceive that which was shared among Jews,

48. To be sure, there was no such thing in antiquity as politics without "religion"; any reference to the political therefore needs to include consideration of the ancestral traditions interwoven with it and vice versa.

49. But see Chris Keith's excellent study, *Jesus against the Scribal Elite: The Origins of the Conflict*, 2nd ed. (London: T&T Clark, 2020), in which he contrasts the social status of Jesus with that of the officials working in these institutional settings. Considering issues of social class and literacy, Keith concludes that the status discrepancy in and of itself would have been enough to provoke conflict, regardless of the details of the message proclaimed. See also Jonathan Bernier, *Aposynagōgos and the Historical Jesus in John: Rethinking the Historicity of the Johannine Expulsion Passages*, BIS 122 (Leiden: Brill, 2013).

and this makes Jesus's program emerge in greater clarity. In the midst of the radical diversity of Second Temple Judaism, studying these physical, social, and discursive spaces, the institutional—that is, the "agreement" around which and through which people operationalized their communal lives—will increase our knowledge of issues orbiting gender, class, literacy, politics, ethnicity and ethnic diversity, matters of social inclusion and exclusion, slavery, purity and impurity, and health (demon possession, exorcism, skin disease, etc.). Even larger matters, such as what defines "religion" and "theology" and how these phenomena relate to the social and the political, may surface in new light when seen from within these institutional parameters.[50] Returning Jesus and his message to these settings will restore a vision of a kingdom lost in the mist of time. What we will do with that kingdom beyond placing it on a bookshelf is a hermeneutical question, however, that cannot, and should not, be answered by historians alone. But the Next Quest can hardly ignore it.

50. I have discussed this in some detail in Anders Runesson, "Synagogues at the Intersection of Text and Archaeology: The Genesis and Framework of Second Temple Judaism," in *Second Temple Judaism in Scholarly Perspective: Integration of Recent Developments*, ed. Dan M. Gurtner and Loren T. Stuckenbruck (London: T&T Clark, 2024).

Armies and Soldiers

Christopher B. Zeichmann

The Next Quest for the historical Jesus must account for armies and soldiers.[1] The military occupies a strange place in the study of the New Testament. It is both everywhere and nowhere; it is a matter of consensus and abstract debate. No one doubts that it was a profoundly negative force in the lives of ancient Palestinians, but what does one make of the seemingly positive interactions between soldiers and early Christians? What did the centurion at the cross mean when he said Jesus was "(a) God's son"? Did soldiers abandon their poor treatment of Jewish civilians (as John the Baptist demands in Luke 3:14) or continue in their ways as usual? What does one make of the demon named "Legion" in Mark 5:1–20—is it a veiled criticism of Roman military rule? What might Jesus's own posture toward the military have been?

Thanks to Fernando Bermejo-Rubio for his collaboration on some of the content in "The When and Where of Military Personnel" section of this chapter and granting permission to use it here.

1. A quick note of clarification. "Palestine" in this chapter heuristically designates the region that includes Herodian principalities of Judea, Galilee, Perea, and Batanea as well as the Decapolis and independent cities of the south coast (e.g., Ascalon). Though the military was experienced in different ways across these locations, they are usefully grouped together due to their shared and overlapping military-political history. Notably, this encompasses nearly the entire region where the canonical gospels depict Jesus—with the exceptions of the regions of Tyre and Sidon (e.g., Mark 7:24–31).

On the one hand, a scholar with no less pedigree than E. P. Sanders confidently dismisses its relevance on the grounds that Rome did not rule Palestine "by occupation."[2] Insofar as no legions garrisoned the region before the First Jewish War (66–73 CE), Rome's methods of rule are to be found elsewhere: foremost, the proxy rule of client kings and the assurance of inevitable victory of Roman might. On the other hand, early twenty-first-century New Testament interpretation has had a strong anti-imperial and postcolonial inflection, leading scholars to maintain that the military was a major aspect of daily life in prewar Palestine. Representative of this more recent trend is Richard Horsley: "The "forceful suasion" of Roman military power functioned through the perceptions of subject peoples. The Romans simply terrorized peoples into submission and, they hoped, submissiveness through the ruthless devastation of the land and towns, slaughter and enslavement of the people, and crucifixion of people along the roadways or in public places."[3] With esteemed scholars diametrically opposed concerning the military's role in early Roman Palestine, it is little surprise that commentators often avoid the topic completely. For all the talk of "empire," there is little discussion of the military itself in historical Jesus scholarship.

In this chapter, I would like to suggest briefly two ways the study of the historical Jesus might benefit from recent advances in the study of the militaries of the eastern Mediterranean. First is the counterintuitive insight that there was no monolithic "Roman army." Rather, there were a variety of military forces in early Roman Palestine—forces that had little in common by way of purpose and demographics. Civilians, including the New Testament evangelists and likely the historical Jesus, were cognizant of these distinctions and held differing opinions about such forces, unlike the modern tendency to homogenize them under the aegis of a singular "Roman army." Second, there has been extensive archaeological work on fortlets, forts, road stations, and other sites where Palestinian soldiers were located. Discussion of these sites is often monadic, such that their broader significance in relation to each other is unclear. How might we understand the military networks of Palestine in a comparative perspective? What might this indicate about their role in Jesus's life and death?

---

2. E. P. Sanders, "Jesus' Galilee," in *Fair Play: Diversity and Conflicts in Early Christianity; Essays in Honour of Heikki Räisänen*, ed. Ismo Dunderberg, Christopher M. Tuckett, and Kari Syreeni, NovTSup 103 (Leiden: Brill, 2002), 10.

3. Richard A. Horsley, *Galilee: History, Politics, People* (Valley Forge, PA: Trinity Press International, 1995), 116. The first sentence is an unattributed quotation from Edward N. Luttwak, *The Grand Strategy of the Roman Empire from the First Century A.D. to the Third* (Baltimore: Johns Hopkins University Press, 1976), 33.

There Was No "Roman Army"

One should differentiate between three types of soldiers in Palestine during the period 37 BCE–130 CE (i.e., from Herod the Great until the formation of Syria Palaestina). Best known are legionaries, who differed from other soldiers in several respects. First, legionaries were employed by Rome itself. Their allegiances were to the emperor and whichever general they served, not to any particular king, religious group, or province. Unlike almost all other soldiers, legionaries were Roman citizens before they were recruited. Though a legionary could hypothetically hail from anywhere within the empire, the requirement of Roman citizenship limited their demographics. Legionaries were more likely to speak Latin than other soldiers. They were usually recruited from the most heavily Romanized cities and provinces, and their citizenship afforded them privilege over both civilians and other types of soldiers. Legions primarily garrisoned in major imperial provinces such as Syria, Belgica, Pannonia, and postwar Judea. Legionaries were prevalent throughout the province of Judea beginning with the First Jewish War and only served as the occupying force following the war's conclusion. There is no reason to think the historical Jesus ever encountered a legionary, despite the ubiquity of such soldiers in the popular imagination of Roman antiquity.

Roughly equal in number to the legionary soldiers across the empire were auxiliaries. Auxiliaries, like legionaries, served the government of Rome but were divided into two distinct military types: *cohors* (*speira*) and *ala* (*eilē*)—infantry and cavalry, respectively—with a few mixed units termed *cohors equitata* as well. Auxiliary soldiers were almost exclusively noncitizens who became soldiers under the promise of receiving Roman citizenship in exchange for their military service; this citizenship grant was indicated by the gift of a "diploma"—a formulaic bronze tablet listing the conditions of retirement and information about the soldier receiving that particular diploma (e.g., DMIPERP 202–296).[4] Auxiliary soldiers were significantly less Romanized than legionaries: auxiliary soldiers from eastern provinces spoke the lingua franca of Greek along with local languages (e.g., Aramaic), bearing little if any competence in Latin. Though auxiliaries often served in major imperial provinces alongside legionaries, they also served in minor provinces or specific regions within major provinces as well. Thus, provinces or subprovinces with a governor of equestrian status (e.g., Raetia, Noricum, prewar Judea) had

---

4. Database of Military Inscriptions and Papyri of Early Roman Palestine (DMIPERP) can be found at https://armyofromanpalestine.com/. For a print edition, see Christopher B. Zeichmann, ed., *Database of Military Inscriptions and Papyri of Early Roman Palestine with Map and Gazetteer of Military Sites*, revised and updated ed., Aquila Legionis 24–25 (Madrid: Signifer, 2022).

no legions but only auxiliaries. Auxiliary soldiers were present in the province of Judea (6–40, 44–66 CE) as the only soldiers in the region. Importantly, these soldiers were recruited from within Judea, especially the cities of Caesarea Maritima and Sebaste, which is to say that they were locals.[5] After Judea was promoted to a consular province in 70 CE, the auxiliaries that had been recruited in Judea were sent elsewhere in the empire and were replaced by a variety of foreign auxiliaries who had no connection with the local populace and served alongside legionaries.[6] The Decapolis also garrisoned auxiliaries recruited from abroad, though they were also being supplemented by legionaries once they were annexed to the province Arabia in 106 CE. Any soldiers Jesus encountered in either the province of Judea or the Decapolis were auxiliaries, as were the soldiers that crucified him.

There were also royal forces that did not directly serve Rome but were under the authority of a client king. The periphery of the Roman Empire was peppered with kingdoms allied with Rome that were permitted to maintain their own militaries (e.g., Nabatea, Antipas's Galilee, Agrippa I's Judea). These armies differed in their hierarchies, pay scale, functions, and recruitment strategies, among other features, from kingdom to kingdom.[7] Emperors occasionally asked kings to contribute their soldiers to Roman campaigns as signs of loyalty, a request that was rarely refused. These soldiers were almost always recruited from within that particular kingdom and had no prospect of eventual citizenship either. With little invested in Romanness, royal soldiers spoke the local lingua franca and rarely had knowledge of Latin or other aspects of Roman culture. Josephus mentions Hesbonitis and Gaba as military colonies that Antipas inherited from Herod the Great (*A.J.* 15.294; *B.J.* 3.36); soldiers were likely recruited from Sepphoris and Tiberias too, not to mention whoever could be mustered from rural areas. These soldiers were locals in every sense of the word, almost certainly spending their entire military career in their home kingdom.[8] All Herodian dynasts had their own royal army, including Antipas, Agrippa I, and Herod the Great himself. In the gospels, the centurion at Capernaum (Luke 7:1–10), as well as Herod's purported slaughter

---

5. See Josephus, *A.J.* 15.296; 20.122, 176; *B.J.* 1.403; 2.52, 58, 74, 236; 3.66.

6. For more details, see Christopher B. Zeichmann, "Military Forces in Judaea 6–130 CE: The *Status Quaestionis* and Relevance for New Testament Studies," *CBR* 17 (2018): 86–120.

7. Samuel Rocca, *Herod's Judaea: A Mediterranean State in the Classical World*, TSAJ 122 (Tübingen: Mohr Siebeck, 2008), 133–96; Israel Shatzman, *The Armies of the Hasmonaeans and Herod: From Hellenistic to Roman Frameworks*, TSAJ 25 (Tübingen: Mohr Siebeck, 1991), 129–316.

8. See the discussion in Christopher B. Zeichmann, *The Roman Army and the New Testament* (Lanham, MD: Lexington/Fortress Academic, 2018), 3–7; Jonathan P. Roth, "Jewish Military Forces in the Roman Service," in *Essential Essays for the Study of the Military in New Testament Palestine*, ed. Christopher B. Zeichmann (Eugene, OR: Wipf & Stock, 2019), 83–88.

of innocents (Matt 2:16–18) all involved royal soldiers, albeit of different armies. Any unmentioned soldiers Jesus may have encountered in Batanea, Perea, and Galilee were royal soldiers.

It may not be entirely obvious why these distinctions warrant such fuss—yes, the soldiers may have differed in meaningful ways, but didn't they ultimately serve "Rome" in some sense? On this point, Simon James demonstrates in a series of brilliant articles that the notion of a singular "Roman army" is entirely anachronistic to the Roman Principate.[9] James contends that the concept of *"the* Roman army" is problematic because it retrojects modern notions of the "war machine" into antiquity and purports a unified military structure that did not exist at the time. James notes that there was not even a word that communicated the notion of a single, monolithic military in the early Common Era:

> "Army" (*exercitus*), singular, was used for a particular grouping of forces, such as the standing army of a province or a corps specially assembled for a particular campaign. When generalising about the military, they employed plurals, writing of "the armies" (*exercitus*), "the legions" (*legiones*), "the regiments" (*numeri*), etc., and not least of "the soldiers" (*milites*), denoting a socio-political category.[10]

The same can be said of Greek. *Stratia* and *stratopedon* were used in a manner similar to *exercitus*, and generalizations about military units are consistently pluralized—such as *speirai, teloi, lochoi,* and *stratiōtai*—rather than operating with any singular and unified referent. This not only operated on a linguistic level but as a matter of individual perceptions, sympathies, and antipathies: soldiers understood themselves to be clients of their specific general, and individual generals likewise understood themselves to be patrons of their soldiers. The effects of these social relations were abundantly evident under the triumvirates and during the Year of the Four Emperors (68–69 CE), but at a more mundane level. When auxiliaries became Roman citizens and could choose their new Roman name with the *tria nomina*, they commonly did so to align themselves with their generals. One man from Philadelphia in the Decapolis gave up his Semitic birthname and

9. Simon James, "The Community of the Soldiers: A Major Identity and Centre of Power in the Roman Empire," in *Proceedings of the Eighth Theoretical Roman Archaeology Conference*, ed. Patricia Baker et al. (Oxford: Oxbow, 1999), 14–25; James, "Soldiers and Civilians: Identity and Interaction in Roman Britain," in *Britons and Romans: Advancing an Archaeological Agenda*, ed. Simon James and Martin Millett, Council for British Archaeology Research Report 125 (York: Council for British Archaeology, 2001), 77–89.

10. James, "Community of the Soldiers," 14.

not only took the name of his general, Gnaeus Domitius Corbulo, but claimed to be his son as well, becoming "Domitius son of Domitius."[11] It was simply not feasible for emperors to act as patron over the entire army, thereby precluding any panimperial military unity.

Thus, while contemporary scholars may understand these units to be part of a single Roman military apparatus, this conceptualization is entirely anachronistic to antiquity. Civilians were aware of the differences between the prewar and post-war garrison, the different Herodian royal armies, and so on. If one is to engage in a thorough, or even tenable description of the military in the gospels, it is necessary to attend to the differences between the units and the garrisons of which they were a part. The Gospel of Luke is egregious in this regard. Rather than offering a single depiction of "the military," it depicts Antipas's soldiers as being as capricious and cruel as their monarch (Luke 23:11; cf. Acts 12:1–19 with Agrippa I), whereas auxiliaries (especially their officers) are depicted more moderately (Luke 23:47; cf. Acts 10:1–48; 23:1–35; 27:1–28:31). Indeed, the soldiers are often mere append-ages of their commander (e.g., Pilate in Mark 15:2, 15). This is not to mention the sharp distinctions that were made within the ranks: how status prejudices led footsoldiers (*pedites*) to be construed as an unruly mob, whereas centurions and tribunes are generally depicted as sympathetic figures in gospel literature.[12] There is nothing to suggest that the evangelists or any of the figures in their narratives conceived of a single "Roman army"; moreover, I would suggest that attending to the politics of military representation would be a fruitful exercise for both those who study the gospels and those studying the historical Jesus, such that one avoids simply reinscribing the prejudices of our written sources.

The differences between the types of soldiers might flag several things to one interested in the study of the historical Jesus. Take, for instance, some readings of the centurion at Capernaum (Matt 8:5–13; Luke 7:1–10), which imagine a straight-forward identification between the centurion and the Roman Empire. Fritz Kun-kel claims that in this pericope, "two empires meet; and curiously enough, they are pleased with one another. Jesus, marvelling at the captain's faith, predicts in his excitement a vast spread of the teaching to 'many from east and west.'"[13] This sort of reading—wherein the event is an encounter between Jesus and Rome—is not viable, not least because the centurion did not represent any actual "empire,"

---

11. DMIPERP 295 with Benjamin Isaac, "The Decapolis in Syria: A Neglected Inscription," *ZPE* 44 (1981): 72–73.

12. Zeichmann, *Roman Army*, 49–106.

13. Fritz Kunkel, *Creation Continues: A Psychological Interpretation of Matthew* (Mahwah, NJ: Paulist, 1989), 120–21.

Herod the Great (Greatest Extent)

Judaea

Galilee-Peraea

Batanaea

Nabataea

Mazra'at Jebel Siri
Paneas
Qeren Naphtali
Giscala
Kul'at Shuneh
Gamla
Ya'ad   Yuvalim
Capernaum   Bethsaida
Iotapata   Mount Nitai
Tarichaea
Sepphoris   Tiberias   Hippos
Gaba   Gadara
Ramat Hanadiv
Caesarea Maritima   Qasr e-Lejah
Scythopolis
Tel Zeror   Pella
Narbata
Gerasa
Sebaste
Kafr Sur
Khirbet el-Kiliya
Khirbet Najar
Tel Michal   Khirbet 'Urmeh
Antipatris   Khirbet Fitdusi   Alexandrium
Jaffa   Ofarim
Gadora
Khirbet el-Maqatir   Philade
Khirbet ad-Daliya   Bethel
Jamnia   Rujum Abu Hashabe   Horval Kefira   Jericho   Bakarat   al-Habbasa
Emmaus   Aqed   Kypros   Julias
Azotus   Horvat Mazad   Khirbet al-Atrash
Jerusalem
Bethar
Herodium
Ascalon   Ein el-Taraba
Capharabis   Rujum el-Kase
Khirbet al-Qatt   Machaerus
Khirbet Canan
Anthedon   Khirbet el-Muraq   Kiryat Arba   Khirbet el-Kaser
Gaza   Rujum el-Dir   Oresa   Ein Gedi
Khirbet Hamas   Rujum el-Hamiri
Bank of Eshtemoa
Gittha
Giv'at Nahal Yattir   Tel 'Arad   Masada
Tel Sharuhen   Beersheba   Harei 'Anim
Moleatha
Horvat Uza
Aroer

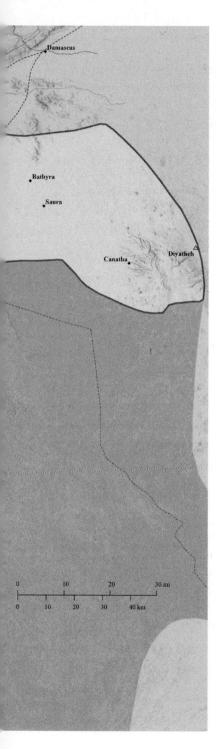

Figure 17.1. Map of known Palestinian military sites during the pre-War period (6–66 CE). A cross (+) indicates 8 or fewer soldiers (one contubernium), an open triangle (△) indicates 9–80 soldiers (less than one centuria), and a black diamond (◆) indicates 80+ soldiers (more than one centuria). These are, it should be emphasized, estimates. See DMIPERP for details about individual sites.

but the principality of a Herodian tetrarch. It is, of course, possible that Matthew and Luke anachronistically understood the centurion to be an auxiliary or legionary (seeing as how they were writing several decades after most of Galilee was annexed to the province of Judea and thus garrisoned auxiliaries and legionaries). This, however, has nothing to do with the situation of the historical Jesus.

One might also consider Mark 5:1–20, the incident where Jesus exorcises a demon named "Legion." It has been common to read this as a sly criticism of Roman occupation of Judea, citing a constellation of imagery that evokes *legio X Fretensis*—the unit that garrisoned Jerusalem after the Jewish War. In addition to the word "legion" itself, commentators have observed that the standard of *legio X Fretensis* depicted a boar and that the unit commonly used aquatic imagery as well (e.g., Poseidon, war galley).[14] Familiarity with the armies of Roman Palestine would cue to readers that this sort of critique cannot be attributed to the historical Jesus for a number of reasons: Gerasa was not in Judea or Galilee, there were no legions in Gerasa or anywhere else in the Decapolis during the life of Jesus, and *legio X Fretensis* was not in Jerusalem (itself 110 km away from Gerasa) until the Jewish War. All of this would suggest that such subtexts, if they are indeed present in Mark's Gospel, do not represent Jesus's own politics but must result from a postwar tradition.

THE WHEN AND WHERE OF MILITARY PERSONNEL

There is a common misconception, thanks to Josephus, early Christian literature, and popular culture, that the military in prewar Palestine was largely confined to its largest cities, especially Caesarea Maritima and Jerusalem. Josephus overwhelmingly associates the Palestinian garrison with Caesarea and Sebaste, but narrates a number of military incidents in Jerusalem, most of which are related to the temple. The New Testament Gospels and Acts likewise associate almost every military character with either Caesarea or Jerusalem: the crucifixion and burial of Jesus (Mark 15 and parallels), the conversion of the centurion Cornelius (Acts 10), the arrest of Peter (Acts 12), Paul's trial (Acts 21–23), and the escort of Paul to Rome (Acts 27–28). Josephus's works exhibit similar tendencies. Josephus's most memorable military anecdotes include when Pilate's men brought a "standard"

14. See, e.g., Warren Carter, "Cross-Gendered Romans and Mark's Jesus: Legion Enters the Pigs (Mark 5:1–20)," *JBL* 133 (2015): 139–55; Richard A. Horsley, "'By the Finger of God': Jesus and Imperial Violence," in *Violence in the New Testament*, ed. Shelly Matthews and E. Leigh Gibson (London: T&T Clark, 2005), 51–80; Matthias Klinghardt, "Legionsschweine in Gerasa: Lokalkolorit und historischer Hintergrund von Mk 5,1–20," *ZNW* 98 (2007): 28–48.

from Caesarea to Jerusalem (*A.J.* 18.55–59; cf. Philo, *Legat.* 299–305), when a soldier "flashed" temple attendees shortly before the Jewish War (*A.J.* 20.108; *B.J.* 2.224), and when soldiers intervened in interethnic conflict at Caesarea (*A.J.* 20.173–178). To be sure, these cities quartered a considerable number of soldiers. The Antonia fortress, adjacent to the Jerusalem temple, probably served as barracks for an entire six-hundred-man cohort during Jesus's life.

The supposition that the military was a largely *urban* phenomenon before the Jewish War, however, is flatly contradicted by the archaeological evidence. Rather, the vast majority of soldiers were located in small rural garrisons and seemed to have served as more of a patrolling force than the sort of occupying power they are commonly imagined to be. The size and distribution of Palestinian fortlets, watchtowers, and road stations often held little correlation with the density of nearby civilian settlements, meaning the military did not simply serve to suppress restless populations (see figure 17.1). These fortlets and watchtowers seem to have served a similar purpose to those in Egypt. Egyptian ostraca document two guards of low rank at each watchtower: one spending the day up in the tower and the other monitoring the traffic along the road.[15] The size and design of Palestinian watchtowers suggest they were manned similarly. To be sure, governors often placed military structures within ten kilometers of fortified cities at satellite villages (e.g., three or possibly four were west of Jerusalem, another one or possibly two were near Emmaus). These fortifications both served as support to larger garrisons (with evidence, for instance, of facilities to aid in construction found near Emmaus) but also to ensure lines of communication remained open and secure.

Why would Herodian tetrarchs—but especially the governors of Judea—adopt such an approach? From the time of the prefects until the outbreak of the Jewish War, there were no significant battles or wars in Judea, meaning few of its soldiers ever participated in combat operations. Soldiers in peaceful provinces were typically assigned to other duties, such as policing, patrolling, provincial construction projects (e.g., road paving), administrative labor, and intelligence gathering. There is ample evidence that soldiers in prewar Judea performed these duties. Consider, for instance, one anecdote related in a handful of rabbinic sources:

> Once the (Roman) government sent two soldiers and said to them, "Go and make yourselves Jews, and see what is the nature of their Torah." They went to

---

15. Richard Alston, *Soldier and Society in Roman Egypt: A Social History* (London: Routledge, 1995), 81–82, citing O.Amst. 8–14. Oddly, no archaeological remains of Egyptian watchtowers survive.

Rabbi Gamaliel in Usha, and they read Scripture, and they studied the Mishnah, midrash, laws, and narratives. When the time came for them to leave, they (the soldiers) said to them (the school of Rabbi Gamaliel), "All of the Torah is fine and praiseworthy, except for this one matter which you say, 'An object stolen from a gentile is permitted (to be used), but (an object stolen) from a Jew is prohibited,' but this matter we shall not report to the government" (Sifre Deut 344)[16]

A number of features might strike us about this narrative, such as the use of soldiers for Roman spying, not to mention the apparent ability of those soldiers to both successfully infiltrate Jewish social circles and understand their teachings, despite little prior experience with Judaism itself. Even if the narrative is fantastical, similar military duties are recounted elsewhere. Josephus, for instance, says that Pilate had his soldiers act as undercover agents during the aqueduct episode (*A.J.* 18.30–62; *B.J.* 2.175–177). Patrols after the First Jewish War also monitored road traffic during festivals, but given the influx of soldiers to deter unrest among the Judean pilgrims during festivals while the temple still stood, this was likely practiced before the war as well (see, e.g., Josephus, *B.J.* 2.224–227; *A.J.* 20.105–112).[17]

Such surveillance duties served several purposes, three of which are interrelated and worth highlighting for historical Jesus research: (1) to maintain peace in the province; (2) to mitigate potential rebellions; and (3) to implement policy changes that might have occurred after Varus's disaster in the battle of the Teutoburg Forest. The maintenance of peace in a given province was the primary duty of its garrison. This generally entailed a greater focus on preventing threats *within* the region than any foreign threats from *without*. In Judea and its environs, this tended to take the form of addressing banditry and quelling insurrectionist impulses, both of which are extensively discussed by Josephus and mentioned by other sources. Indeed, Strabo in his *Geographica* implies that Hasmonean tolerance of brigandage was the impetus for Rome's (temporary) annexation of Judea in the

16. Cf. y. B. Qam. 4.3, 4b; b. B. Qam. 38a. See the discussion of its complex tradition-history in Shaye J. D. Cohen, "'Those Who Say They Are Jews and Are Not': How Do You Know a Jew in Antiquity When You See One?," in *The Diasporas in Antiquity*, ed. Shaye J. D. Cohen and Ernest S. Frerich, BJS 288 (Atlanta: Scholars Press, 1993), 11, from which the translation above is taken. For more extensive discussion of the topic, see Zeichmann, *Roman Army*, 23–48.

17. Lam. Rab. 1.52; see Moshe Fischer, Benjamin Isaac, and Israel Roll, *Roman Roads in Judaea II: The Jaffa-Jerusalem Roads*, BAR International 628 (Oxford: Tempvs Reparatvm, 1996), 15–16: "Vespasian Caesar placed guards at eighteen miles from Pomais [=Emmaus?] and they would ask pilgrims and say, 'To whom do you belong?' and they would say, 'To Vespasian, to Trajan, to Hadrian.'"

first place: "the tyrannies [of the Hasmonaeans] were the cause of brigandage, for some rebelled and harassed the countryside, both their own and neighbouring lands, while others collaborated with the rulers and seized the possessions of others and subdued much of Syria and Phoenicia" (16.2.28).[18]

The question of how a governor might best address unrest can be understood by reference to the panimperial response to the battle of the Teutoburg Forest when Germanic tribes united under Arminius in rebellion against Rome in 9 CE. This led to the destruction of three legions and several auxiliary units not to mention the death of the Roman governor Varus. The defeat was largely attributed to failures of intelligence gathering and military-civilian interactions within Germania. The shock that reverberated from the Teutoburg disaster seems to have led to changes within the intelligence systems for *all* provincial governors. The outcome of Arminius's great victory had profound effects on Roman policies— losing three out of its total twenty-eight legions was a serious blow[19]—particularly the widespread assumption that legionary or auxiliary *presence* was sufficient in its own right to quell insurrectionist movements. If the *clades Variana* can best be understood as an intelligence failure—and there is every indication that it could, all the more so because Segestes had warned Varus of the impending attack[20]—it must have had some consequences in the gathering and processing of information in provinces identified as potentially troublesome. Roman historian and contemporary of Pontius Pilate, Velleius Paterculus, wrote that Arminius made use of Varus's negligence, "sagaciously seeing that no one could be more quickly overpowered than the man who feared nothing, and that the most common beginning of disaster is a sense of security."[21]

The incident prompted reflection among military men and administrators across the empire. There is a widespread tendency among Roman writers to reflect upon the battle and imply that Varus made crucial errors in his underestimation of Germania and that military commanders would do well to learn from his mis-

18. Translation from Benjamin Isaac, *The Limits of Empire: The Roman Army in the East*, rev. ed. (Oxford: Clarendon, 1992), 66.

19. That the memory of Teutoburg plagued the Roman consciousness for years is perceptible in many ways; for instance, the section devoted by Tacitus to that battle (*Ann.* 1.61–62) "is the most extended, self-contained flashback in the *Annales*, and it reaches across the greatest length of time, six years." Quote from Victoria E. Pagán, "Beyond Teutoburg: Transgression and Transformation in Tacitus *Annales* 1.61–62," *CP* 94 (1999): 303.

20. Rose Mary Sheldon, *Intelligence Activities in Ancient Rome: Trust in the Gods, but Verify* (London: Routledge, 2005), 175, 191–92.

21. Velleius Paterculus 2.118; translation from Shipley, LCL. Rose Mary Sheldon observes that "later Roman commanders in Germany are described as being aware of German 'secret arrangements.'" Sheldon, *Intelligence Activities*, 191, citing Tacitus, *Ann.* 2.20.

takes.[22] Strabo, for instance, generalizes about German deviousness and warns against trusting them in any capacity (*Geogr.* 7.1.4), Tacitus chastises Varus for ignoring the warnings about Arminius's treachery (*Ann.* 1.55), and Suetonius depicts wise commanders learning from Varus's mistakes (e.g., *Tib.* 18). Indeed, surveying the ample number of fortlets and watchtowers throughout prewar Palestine, Benjamin Isaac concludes that "the Romans in Judaea, it seems, intended to avoid the mistakes attributed to Varus in Germany."[23] That is, networks of military surveillance and communication are attested along the various roads of the prewar period—including the Jaffa-Jerusalem, Jaffa-Shechem, and Jerusalem-Philadelphia roads. This may not be a coincidence, given that Varus governed Syria (of which Judea was a part) before the revolt at Teutoburg—subsequent Syrian and Judean governors may have seen vulnerabilities in their own provincial charge, in light of Varus's rash policies. To be sure, this was hardly the only instance of intelligence failure by the Roman military (one thinks of the many native revolts, like that of Boudicca), though it was certainly remembered as one of the most disastrous and apparently prompted considerable reflection on military strategy.

This might prompt us to consider the sine qua non of the historical Jesus: his death by crucifixion at the hands of auxiliaries garrisoned in Judea. It is likely that Pilate had gathered some degree of intelligence regarding Jesus before their encounter in Jerusalem. This supposition is further reinforced by the fact that Roman administration partially relied on reports from allies for intelligence on enemies and troublemakers beyond their borders. Herodian rulers are a case in point, bearing close relationships with the emperors and their subordinates. In thinking of the historical Jesus, we might not only inquire what kind of person would be crucified, but what kind of person might warrant such intelligence gathering in the eyes of Pilate and the Herodians?

More broadly, one might note that in the prewar period, the military was not an occupying force but a policing force comprised of locals, as discussed above. Indeed, only a small portion of Palestinian soldiers would have participated in military combat (the devastation of Antipas's army in 37 CE being the most prominent instance; see Josephus, *A.J.* 18.119). This is not to suggest that the militaries

22. Note, however, that Jewish sources from Josephus through the rabbis show no knowledge of the battle of the Teutoburg Forest; see Hanan Eshel, "Publius Quinctilius Varus in Jewish Sources," *JJS* 59 (2008): 112–19.

23. Isaac, *Limits of Empire*, 107, especially contrasts postwar Palestine with the problems Cassius Dio attributed to Varus's planning: "He did not keep his legions together as was proper in a hostile country, but distributed many of the soldiers to helpless communities, which asked for them for the alleged purpose of guarding various points, arresting robbers or escorting provision trains" (*Hist. rom.* 56.19.1).

were benevolent or even benign presences, only that the relationship between civilians and soldiers was not one marked by the features of military occupation.[24] This situation was overhauled after the Jewish War when cities became the primary garrison sites for a number of reasons, replacing the economic motor of the temple after its destruction being just one factor.[25] That being said, the question still remains: to what extent do the evangelists anachronistically presume or represent this postwar situation in their tales of Jesus's life?

ACCOUNTING FOR ARMIES AND SOLDIERS

It is impossible to discuss the historical Jesus without understanding the role of the military within early Roman Palestine, not least because of his crucifixion and explicit interactions with soldiers in gospel literature. Beyond these concerns, the more mundane roles of soldiers warrant far greater consideration than it has been given, as there is a tendency to overlook the wide range of nonliterary sources for ascertaining the role of soldiers in the region, ranging from papyri and inscriptions to archaeological data.[26] While hardly free of bias, these nonliterary sources nevertheless can cast into relief the tendentious accounts of, say, Josephus and the evangelists, permitting consideration of alternate perspectives on soldier-civilian interactions and relating the sorts of interactions that the historical Jesus and his disciples may well have experienced apart from literary tropes that are sometimes credulously assumed to be representations of reality.

---

24. Papyri from Egypt indicate that such relationships were a mixed bag, typically favoring civilians of higher status. See most extensively Alston, *Soldier and Society*.

25. See Jonathan P. Roth, "The Army and the Economy in Judaea and Palaestina," in *The Roman Army and the Economy*, ed. Paul Erdkamp (Amsterdam: Gieben, 2002), 375–97.

26. My own effort to collect these into a single corpus and render them accessible is DMIPERP (armyofromanpalestine.com).

18

Class Conflict

Robert J. Myles

The Next Quest for the historical Jesus must adopt a hard approach to class and class conflict. This requires moving beyond soft approaches that tether possibilities for class conflict in first-century Galilee and Judea to sharp rises or falls in the general standard of living, and toward a more robust, dialectical, and theoretically rich approach that regards the activities and ideas of the early Jesus movement as *symptomatic* of their wider socioeconomic environment. After all, Jesus's historical life circumstances were interwoven with definite material premises and conditions; he was not only a product of his first-century Jewish milieu but also of the intersecting social and economic forces of a wider agrarian world. Irrespective of whether one argues for a Galilee that was hopelessly downtrodden or relatively peaceful and prosperous during the reign of Herod Antipas, it is incumbent upon the critical historian to explain (rather than explain away) how *this* material reality, and the antagonisms it produced, impacted the lives of Jesus and his compatriots, and how it *necessarily* serves as a plausible basis for the generation of the prominent ideas, perceptions, and activities of the early Jesus movement.

Given the complexity of this task, and the field's inclination toward theological reductionism (see below), it is little surprise that class and class conflict are frequently overlooked or misunderstood in historical Jesus research specifically and the study of Christian origins more generally.[1] It is still common to read of,

---

1. This is also possibly because of the associations of class conflict and historical materi-

or hear about, claims that class is a product of the Industrial Revolution, that it concerns modern capitalist issues of the proletariat and bourgeoisie, and so has no meaningful application to the agrarian and precapitalist social world of the early Jesus movement. In place of class, it has also become fashionable for scholars to speak of "social status," which (so it is asserted) is better at dealing with the multiplicity of conflicting and intersecting identity factors beyond one's own class position.[2] For example, while Jesus may have ranked lower on the social scale due to his being classed as a rural artisan, he also enjoyed certain privileges as a relatively erudite male.[3]

Concerns about anachronism and appropriateness are certainly warranted. What is sometimes missed in these critiques is how they might apply to any number of critical approaches. After all, all historical methods developed since the Enlightenment are inflected by the concerns and assumptions of modernity, but this does not mean they have no heuristic or analytical use value. This is particularly true if we understand the task of the historian as primarily an act of ideological translation, that is, to "present the past to the present in terms that will be meaningful *for* the present."[4] Likewise, discussions about the complexity of class obvi-

---

alism with Marxism. James Crossley has suggested that a fear or even hostility to Marxism is part of the problem for a Christian-dominated discipline in which many scholars may not be comfortable with Marxism's largely atheistic presuppositions and heritage. James G. Crossley, *Why Christianity Happened: A Sociohistorical Account of Christian Origins (26–50 CE)* (Louisville: Westminster John Knox, 2006), 9. Neil Elliott has similarly diagnosed the remarkable rarity of explicit reference to Marxist categories in Pauline scholarship as something of an "allergic reaction." Neil Elliott, "Diagnosing an Allergic Reaction: The Avoidance of Marx in Pauline Scholarship," *BCT* 8.2 (2012): 3–15.

2. As Roland Boer and Christina Petterson observe: "at a recent annual meeting of the Society of Biblical Literature, there were several panels devoted to the topic of class, with many scholars dismissing it as a useless and reductive term in the name of a liberalist focus on the individual." Roland Boer and Christina Petterson, "Hand of the Master: Of Slaveholders and the Slave-Relation," in *Class Struggle in the New Testament*, ed. Robert J. Myles (Lanham, MD: Lexington/Fortress Academic, 2019), 139.

3. Theoretically sophisticated versions of this approach have been developed within biblical studies such as that advocated by Elisabeth Schüssler Fiorenza, *Jesus and the Politics of Interpretation* (New York: Continuum, 2000). Through her body of work Schüssler Fiorenza deploys the term *kyriarchy* in place of *patriarchy* to describe the multifaceted domination of the emperor, lord, master, father, husband, and elite propertied male. *Kyriarchy* features as a heuristic or "analytic instrument that allows one to investigate the mulplicative interdependence of gender, race, and class stratifications as well as their discursive inscriptions and ideological reproductions." Elisabeth Schüssler Fiorenza, *Democratizing Biblical Studies: Toward an Emancipatory Educational Space* (Minneapolis: Fortress, 2009), 113.

4. William E. Arnal, *Jesus and the Village Scribes: Galilean Conflicts and the Setting of Q* (Minneapolis: Fortress, 2001), 65.

ously have their place and should continue as part of the work of the Next Quest. What a preference for "status" can sometimes end up doing though—especially when paired with North American–led interests in individualism and identity politics—is reduce class to an individual idiosyncrasy. Simply put, a focus on class as an identity with respect to the historical Jesus is to make class about Jesus rather than the structural forces and conflicts present in the society in which he lived.

It is for these reasons that I prefer to adopt *historical-materialist* notions of class and class conflict. From this vantage, "class" refers not so much to the social classes of modern bourgeois sociology or anthropology, but rather to how people relate to the productive forces of the mode of production of their day.[5] By "class conflict," then, I mean the competing material interests of these groups that generate ongoing antagonisms in society and are the ongoing basis of historical change. In this sense, class is not a static category to be measured solely through income levels or as a performed individual or collective identity (as interesting as such explorations might be). Rather, it is a way of thinking about and grouping together those who share common material and social interests broadly conceived. Such groups and conflicts may be obfuscated by ideology—whether ancient or modern—yet this does not mean that class conflict is absent, or that it does not function as a useful explanatory concept for understanding the emergence of the early Jesus movement, as we will see. Indeed, several contributors to this volume already adopt historical-materialist approaches—whether implicitly or explicitly—and it appears that historical materialism will emerge as a significant methodological feature of the Next Quest. Among other advantages, it offers us the possibility of uniting Jesus origins research with reception histories of Jesus from later periods and under different modes of production.

What I want to do for the rest of this chapter, then, is to highlight some of the prospects and challenges for historical Jesus scholars who want to incorporate historical-materialist approaches to class conflict as part of the Next Quest. This involves first situating Jesus within socioeconomic and material shifts as he was growing up in first-century Galilee under the reign of Herod Antipas. But it also requires progressing beyond idealist and theologically reductive accounts of class conflict, which have become the hallmark of recent scholarship on Galilee. Indeed, when the social context of the historical Jesus is discussed, it is normally

---

5. For recent treatments in respect of New Testament studies see, e.g., James Crossley, "Class Conflict and Galilee at the Time of Jesus," in *The Struggle over Class: Socioeconomic Analysis of Ancient Christian Texts*, ed. G. Anthony Keddie, Michael Flexsenhar III, and Steven J. Friesen (Atlanta: SBL Press, 2021), 163–85; Robert J. Myles, ed., *Class Struggle in the New Testament* (Lanham, MD: Lexington/Fortress Academic, 2019).

dominated by broad cultural discussion with minimal emphasis on class or economic factors, especially in terms of how such factors could have *produced* the early Jesus movement to begin with. Many scholars appear to be working from the idealist presumption that the world of ideas forms the background to, and is generative of, ideas. While this may in certain cases be true, it must also be acknowledged that people react, whether consciously or not, to material forces and use cultural (including religious) language and symbols in order to communicate those reactions.

Similarly, it is crucial to avoid the trap of economic determinism or what has often been labeled "vulgar Marxism." This is a reductive form of critique that understands the economic base as directly determining all aspects of social life in unmediated and deterministic fashion.[6] For all its apparent baggage, one of the many benefits of Marx's theory of history is that it compels us to explain the conditions under which a given social phenomenon emerges. Crucially, for Marx, one-to-one causal determinism—the idea that X causes Y in a linear way—cannot adequately explain social phenomena. Rather, we need to look to the totality of what is going on. Accordingly, my chapter will critically engage some influential work on Galilee and class which erroneously assumes a direct model of economic determinism to downplay the importance of class conflict for understanding the emergence of the early Jesus movement. As we will see, a historical-materialist approach—in which the ideas, perceptions, and activities of the early Jesus movement are held in dialectical tension with the economic situation of their time and place—is our best hope yet for a great leap forward in historical Jesus research of the Next Quest.

CLASS CONFLICTS IN GALILEE AS JESUS WAS GROWING UP

The materialist conception of history has typically sought to determine how class antagonisms and technological developments drove the transformation from feudalism to capitalism, but it has also sought to understand the transformation from ancient societies to feudal ones.[7] Obviously, this scope alone is too broad for under-

6. It was heavily attacked by "orthodox" Marxists such as Vladimir Lenin (as "economism"), Antonio Gramsci, and Georg Lukács. Vladimir Lenin, *What Is to Be Done?*, trans. Joe Fineberg and George Hanna (London: Penguin, 1988); Antonio Gramsci, "Some Theoretical and Practical Aspects of Economism," in *Selections from the Prison Notebooks*, trans. Quintin Hoare and Geoffrey Nowell-Smith, vol. 2 (New York: International Publishers, 1971); Georg Lukács, "What Is Orthodox Marxism?," in *History and Class Consciousness*, trans. Rodney Livingstone (Cambridge: MIT Press, 1971).

7. See, e.g., Chris Wickham, *Framing the Early Middle Ages: Europe and the Mediterranean 400–800* (Oxford: Oxford University Press, 2006).

standing the historical figure of Jesus but what this approach does mean is we can situate Jesus in relation to the class antagonisms of his time and place and with an eye to the social and cultural changes that were generated. The specific socioeconomic circumstances affecting the historical Jesus are thus not to be found solely in static descriptions of his rural Jewish setting—including romantic portrayals of village life or of his profession as a *tektōn*—but rather in the dynamic shifts and ruptures that characterized his wider agrarian world, including especially any significant disturbances to ordinary expectations of how daily life should be best lived around the time he was growing up and when he later became active as a religious organizer.[8]

The basic outline of this economic situation should be familiar to most biblical scholars: within an agrarian society, the smaller propertied class, by virtue of its control of the means of production, appropriated surplus off the larger class group made up of those who worked the land and water. Exploitation usually took its form in unfree labor (including slavery, medieval serfdom, and debt bondage), as well as in the form of taxes and tribute, and, more typical for first-century CE Palestine, the letting of land and house property to leasehold tenants in return for rent paid either in money, kind, or services.[9]

During the lifetime of Jesus, Herod Antipas was, of course, tetrarch of Galilee. The major economic drivers in Galilee during his reign—beyond the usual patterns of agrarian production of the land and water that sustained local populations—included a small number of sizable building projects. This was part of a broader and long-standing pattern in Palestine under a policy of Roman imperial development that attempted to bring Galilee and Judea into the empire's orbit to appropriate its surplus more efficiently through the mechanisms of tribute, taxes, rents, and loans. Antipas's father, Herod the Great, was well known for his own building projects in Judea, most notably the expansion of the Jerusalem temple and the founding of Caesarea Maritima. Antipas himself, following in his father's footsteps, sponsored at least two major urbanization projects in Galilee that we know about: the rebuilding of Sepphoris and the building of Tiberias.

Sepphoris had been destroyed by the Romans in 4 BCE during the turmoil surrounding Herod the Great's death. After he became tetrarch, Antipas had the

---

8. For more on the cross-cultural category of "religious organizers" see James Crossley and Robert J. Myles, *Jesus: A Life in Class Conflict* (Winchester: Zero, 2023), 47–49. Jesus's promise that the twelve would sit on thrones judging Israel and the request of James and John to sit on Jesus's right and left (Mark 10:35–40) constitute important and early evidence of organization by the Jesus movement.

9. See further G. E. M. de Ste. Croix, *The Class Struggle in the Ancient Greek World* (Ithaca: Cornell University Press, 1981); Roland Boer and Christina Petterson, *Time of Troubles: A New Economic Framework for Early Christianity* (Minneapolis: Fortress, 2017).

city rebuilt and refortified to the extent that Josephus could later refer to it as "the ornament of all Galilee" (*A.J.* 18.27). Sepphoris served as Antipas's capital until some years later when he founded the city of Tiberias on the western shore of the Sea of Galilee. Tiberias was completed around 20 CE and named in honor of the Roman Emperor Tiberius (*A.J.* 18.35–36). As Jonathan L. Reed notes, "No area of Galilee lies outside a 25-km radius of these new urban centers."[10] Accordingly, through the construction of these two cities, Antipas was able to extend his strategic and administrative influence over the entirety of Galilee, incorporating previously self-sustaining and mostly independent villages and towns into a more tightly integrated imperial economy.

The development of these cities obviously came at a cost. From a class perspective, that cost was disproportionately borne by the nonelite classes. Sepphoris, for instance, had complete dependence on the countryside for agricultural goods, which it was incapable of producing itself. This placed additional demands on local producers: surrounding villages (such as Nazareth) would have to contribute the labor and surplus to sustain it. Surplus could be expropriated "through outright seizure, forced services, taxes, rents, interest on loans, or fees for various services offered by the cities, including market and exchange services."[11] With the development of the water system, including during the time of Antipas, Sepphoris also dominated water resources in the area.[12] Similar inequitable dynamics between city and countryside structured the flow of resources and wealth in Tiberias.[13] For millennia, fishing on the Sea of Galilee had been a largely local, self-reliant, and seasonal affair in the lakeside villages. The founding of a major urban settlement on the lakeshore allowed better-connected elites to dominate the lake economy, placing additional demands on local fishermen in small villages like Capernaum and leading to an overall rise in productive and extractive activity as well as increased competition. Urban settlements like Sepphoris and Tiberias thus functioned as effective concentration points in which taxes, surplus, and other economic and power networks could operate more efficiently.

Antipas's urbanization projects would have had a significant impact on everyday life in Galilee as Jesus and his compatriots were growing up. The effect of these changes would have been felt acutely by those who lived in the surrounding villages whose socioeconomic activity was now oriented toward providing not

---

10. Jonathan L. Reed, *Archaeology and the Galilean Jesus: A Re-Examination of the Evidence* (Harrisburg, PA: Trinity Press International, 2000), 96.

11. Arnal, *Jesus and the Village Scribes*, 147.

12. Sean Freyne, *Jesus: A Jewish Galilean* (London: T&T Clark, 2004), 46–47.

13. See further Crossley and Myles, *Jesus*, 24–49.

only for their own subsistence but also toward servicing more extensive economic networks. Importantly, this would have produced a range of opportunities and misfortunes for the inhabitants of Galilee: displacement from traditional life patterns for some, an increased standard of living for others, and in many cases something in between. For small villages or towns like Nazareth or Capernaum, the character of social organization and hierarchy was itself forever changed in ways that would have generated a range of responses, even if the economic shifts ultimately led to an overall rise in prosperity, as we will see below.

DISTORTIONS OF CLASS CONFLICT IN HISTORICAL JESUS RESEARCH

Given the immense gulf between the elite and nonelite classes of antiquity, the social and economic changes that came about as a consequence of Antipas's urbanization projects suggest a context ripe for class conflict. Despite it being widely known that wealth in antiquity was concentrated among an aristocratic few, and that much of the peasantry and rural population lived on a knife's edge, class and class conflict are frequently distorted in recent scholarship on Galilee. There is a respectable and influential strand of scholarship that has argued that because the overall Galilean economy under Antipas was relatively prosperous, his building projects would have benefited the nonelite population, assuming a kind of "trickle-down" logic where even those at the bottom of the social and economic pyramid would have enjoyed a higher standard of living than the cliché oppressed peasant. Some prominent voices of the previous quest have even suggested that the nonelite population would have largely agreed with the elite about how well things were going for them.

While assessing the effectiveness of Antipas's rule, one of the most influential historical Jesus scholars from the past forty years, John P. Meier, suggested that "ordinary people judged the advantages of peace and a modest standard of living to outweigh the perilous promise of revolt."[14] He continued: "for all the inequities of life, the reign of Herod Antipas was relatively prosperous and peaceful, free of the severe social strife that proceeded and followed it . . . he was an able ruler who managed to live at peace with his people."[15] Another major figure of the previous quest, E. P. Sanders, concurred: "The lack of uprisings [during the 20s and 30s] also indicates that Antipas was not excessively oppressive and did not levy exorbitant taxes . . . he undertook large building projects that helped reduce

14. John P. Meier, *The Roots of the Problem and the Person*, vol. 1 of *A Marginal Jew: Rethinking the Historical Jesus*, AYBRL (New York: Doubleday, 1991), 283.
15. Meier, *Marginal Jew*, 1:282–83.

unemployment. Galileans in Jesus' lifetime did not feel that things most dear to them were seriously threatened: their religion, their national traditions and their livelihoods."[16] These romantic claims about how the nonelite perceived things under Antipas are clearly overstated and unsubstantiated. It is no great secret that our evidence for the ancient past tends to favor the imprint of elite society. The near absence of unmediated evidence for the attitudes and perceptions of ordinary people in Galilee restricts what we can and cannot say with confidence, and we ought to be more cautious when generalizing about what may have been a diverse set of responses. Indeed, speculations of the kind above risk rendering invisible the perceptions and experiences of the substantial numbers of people whose voices are simply not present in the archaeological or literary record, at least not in any direct, unmediated way.[17]

We should also problematize the related assumption that discontent among the nonelite population requires *explicit* evidence of uprisings. No doubt evidence of extensive material damage would help the case, but the disgruntled masses do not always destroy buildings (although sometimes they do). The weight of these kinds of arguments appears to rest on the tactful inclusion of the adverb "relatively." For instance, during Antipas's long reign things appeared *relatively* uneventful compared to before (during the reign of Herod the Great) or after (in the lead-up to the Jewish Revolt). While this may (or may not) be the case in terms of explicit instances of social upheaval, it appears the word "relatively" is doing far too much work here to be analytically useful. Likewise, so what if Antipas was not "excessively oppressive," as Sanders puts it? This does not undermine possibilities for class conflict, particularly when the drivers of such conflict remain deeply rooted in the class antagonisms and material imbalances of an agrarian society. Similar economic drivers from the time of Herod the Great, including a not dissimilar policy of building projects and Romanization of the Palestinian political economy, continued rather than receded during Antipas's reign.[18]

Even Josephus's account of the building of Tiberias does not shy away from class dimensions and, specifically, from the forced and violent displacements that took place as a consequence. Josephus explains that in the founding of Tiberias the new settlers, many of whom were Galilean and poor, were "by compulsion and with violent force" relocated to this new city to be its inhabitants. This compulsion was in part necessary because, according to Josephus, Tiberias had been built on the site of tombs (*A.J.* 18.36–38). It is curious that scholars advocating the pic-

16. E. P. Sanders, *The Historical Figure of Jesus* (London: Penguin, 1993), 21.
17. See further Robert C. Knapp, *Invisible Romans* (London: Profile, 2011).
18. See, e.g., Crossley and Myles, *Jesus*, 51–55.

ture of a relatively harmonious and agreeable Galilee under Antipas have largely overlooked this gruesome Josephan entry point into a world of class conflict as a consequence of urbanization, even when directly citing this passage.[19] Thinking back to Sanders's judgment above that Antipas was not "excessively oppressive," one wonders whether those who experienced this violent upheaval firsthand, and whose accounts we do not possess, would have agreed with him. Would those forcefully displaced from their hometowns due to socioeconomic changes agree with Sanders when he wrote that "Galileans in Jesus' time did not feel that things most dear to them were seriously threatened"?

Even claims that Antipas's urbanization projects reduced unemployment, or were not seriously threatening to rural peasants who benefited from more work opportunities, need to be tempered against what else we know of the broader dynamics of rural life within a stratified society. While building projects obviously required labor from surrounding villages, the assumption that villagers felt un-threatened or were not exploited is unfounded. We should also remember that for much of the population not directly impacted through displacement, the found-ing of these urban settlements likely resulted in an incremental deterioration of smallholders' circumstances. This would have taken place through a series of slow and gradual processes that were cumulative and methodical, such as through debt, monetization, trade, and the gradual loss of title to the land or ease of access to fishing rights. This is not to deny that some of the peasantry would have bene-fited materially from the changes, but others would not have fared quite so well. In a highly stratified society, any so-called benefits of urbanization would not be shared equally.[20] The case for a relatively prosperous Galilee in which ordinary people necessarily shared in all the spoils of a moderate increase in productivity under Antipas has been greatly exaggerated.

19. Note how Jensen (discussed in more detail below) possibly romanticizes Josephus's account of the upheaval: "The people dragged to live there are described as former slaves or tenants subjected to Antipas who actually received plots of land and fully furnished houses in Tiberias as compensation, granting Antipas the role of benefactor." Morten Hørning Jensen, *Herod Antipas in Galilee: The Literary and Archaeological Sources on the Reign of Herod Antipas and Its Socio-Economic Impact on Galilee*, WUNT 2.215 (Tübingen: Mohr Siebeck, 2006), 230.

20. Sharon L. Mattila has pointed out that there is not necessarily a correlation between population or commercial growth and greater prosperity on the part of the average individual. Sharon Lea Mattila, "Revisiting Jesus' Capernaum: A Village of Only Subsistence-Level Fishers and Farmers?," in *The Galilean Economy in the Time of Jesus*, ed. David A. Fiensy and Ralph K. Hawkins (Atlanta: SBL Press, 2013), 110.

VULGAR STRAWMEN AND THE CASE FOR CLASS CONFLICT

The tendency to posit an overall and "relatively" peaceful and prosperous realm under Antipas has continued in more recent scholarship on class and Galilee.[21] In some cases this has been mobilized by more contemporary scholars of the historical Jesus to downplay the importance of class conflict as a generative feature behind the emergence of the early Jesus movement.[22] Morten Hørning Jensen is worth singling out here in particular. Through an influential monograph and several articles, Jensen has made an important contribution to our understanding of the relationship between the reign of Antipas and the socioeconomic conditions of early first-century Galilee.[23] Attempting to be sensitive to conflict models while also not wanting them to dominate or obscure archaeological data, he synthesizes literary and archaeological data on Galilee to suggest an overall direction of health and "stability—if not moderate growth—rather than rapid change and/ or decline" and hence he finds himself "compelled to conclude that, since rapid change cannot be attested to any notable degree, the socio-economic conditions of rural life were most likely stable, as well, from a relative perspective."[24] Jensen seeks to break through the binary between casting Antipas as either a stabilizing influence on Galilee, protecting it from excessive Romanization, or a cause of class conflict resulting in banditry to survive. He instead articulates a softer position that "in all probability the impact of his reign on the socio-economic conditions of early first-century Galilee was moderate and adjusted too." Thus, he concludes his monograph by asserting that "Antipas was a minor ruler with a moderate impact."[25]

---

21. To date Morten Hørning Jensen (discussed below) and Anthony Keddie have offered the most robust articulations of this tendency. See Anthony Keddie, *Class and Power in Roman Palestine: The Socioeconomic Setting of Judaism and Christian Origins* (Cambridge: Cambridge University Press, 2019).

22. See, e.g., Helen K. Bond, *The Historical Jesus: A Guide for the Perplexed* (London: Bloomsbury, 2012), 77. Bond suggests that despite occasional city-rural disputes and nonviolent protests, "the picture that emerges of Antipas's Galilee is of a reasonably prosperous, stable realm, relatively at ease with its Jewish ruler."

23. Jensen, *Herod Antipas in Galilee*; Morten Hørning Jensen, "Herod Antipas in Galilee: Friend or Foe of the Historical Jesus?," *JSHJ* 5.1 (2007): 7–32; Jensen, "Rural Galilee and Rapid Changes: An Investigation of the Socio-Economic Dynamics and Developments in Roman Galilee," *Biblica* 93.1 (2012): 43–67; Jensen, "The Political History in Galilee from the First Century BCE to the End of the Second Century CE," in *Galilee in the Late Second Temple and Mishnaic Periods*, ed. David A. Fiensy and James Riley Strange (Minneapolis: Fortress, 2014), 1:51–77.

24. Jensen, "Rural Galilee and Rapid Changes," 66.

25. Jensen, *Herod Antipas in Galilee*, 254.

Similar methodological issues noted above concerning the imprint (or lack thereof) of the nonelite in the archaeological record also plague Jensen's analysis. For instance, what Jensen interprets as evidence for the flourishing of Galilean villages, such as the appearance of a few elite frescoed houses in rural areas "can also be described in terms of social elites arising under Antipas in the larger villages who expressed their wealth in a way that accentuated class divisions."[26] The assumption that excavated material remains and literary sources, which overwhelmingly originate from the elite strata, speak for the general population of a stratified cross section of society is, accordingly, both overstated and unwarranted. Jensen's dependency on this incomplete data to evaluate the overall picture of conflict in Galilee, without use of a theoretical framework—whether cross-cultural anthropological, social, or economic—"renders his analysis weak," according to Sarah E. Rollens.[27]

Despite the absence of a theoretical framework, Jensen nonetheless utilizes comparative evaluations internal to the history of ancient Galilee that facilitate his "relative" assessments about the level of social and economic antagonism at the time of Antipas. For example, the archaeological record suggests that Galilee flourished during Antipas's reign, with old towns growing in size and activity. Even so, under Antipas there was only modest urbanization compared with the lavish building programs that were the hallmark of Herod the Great. Compared to his father, then, "Antipas was much less of a builder, and the deteriorating effect he could have had on the Galilean economy was therefore also all the more limited."[28] Having extrapolated this overall picture of moderate growth and stability, Jensen then reasons that "the picture of the historical Jesus as provoked by and opposed to the reign of Antipas cannot be substantiated."[29] As a result of this speculation he even suggests we might look more to "religious motivation" instead of class conflict as a driving force behind the emergence of the early Jesus movement.[30]

All Jensen has done here, in dismissing the presentation of Jesus as reacting against certain socioeconomic phenomena, is attack a vulgar materialist strawman. Jensen ought to be strongly faulted for his idealist alternative, as presuming the primacy of (religious) ideas as generative of other ideas, irrespective of the material situation, is (in this case, theologically) reductive. As mentioned above,

---

26. Jonathan Reed, review of *Herod Antipas in Galilee* by Morten Hørning Jensen, *JSJ* 38.3 (2007): 405.

27. Sarah E. Rollens, *Framing Social Criticism in the Jesus Movement: The Ideological Project in the Sayings Gospel Q*, WUNT 2.374 (Tübingen: Mohr Siebeck, 2014), 27.

28. Jensen, "Political History in Galilee," 75.

29. Jensen, *Herod Antipas in Galilee*, 258.

30. Jensen, "Rural Galilee and Rapid Changes," 66.

for Marx the point of critique is to explain the conditions under which a given social phenomenon emerged, not to fetishize it in ways that mask the totality of what is going on. Through the materialist conception of history, our point of departure should be the material world and human activity itself in which such ideas are grounded and come into being.

In proper dialectical fashion, then, Jensen's suggestion should be turned on its head: if we were to start from an overall picture of moderate growth and stability in Galilee, how do we account for the prominent ideas, perceptions, and activities of the Jesus movement? Indeed, as Rosemary Luff has recently and correctly framed the contradiction: "Although the archaeological evidence indicates a prosperous and thriving Galilee in the early first century CE, the Gospel texts suggest a society under stress and one where the rich were flourishing at the expense of the poor."[31] This apparent contradiction needs to be critically interrogated rather than explained away. It may require reviewing previously held assumptions and giving more weight to previously neglected data such as Josephus's account of the upheaval surrounding the foundation of Tiberias.

But regardless of how one nuances the situation in Galilee we should also keep in mind the classic historical-materialist point typically ignored in such debates, that even cases of an overall material rise in living standards can still involve antagonisms between classes. Class conflict does not disappear just because some or even most people's material needs may be met. The situation of unequal distribution of resources remains; it will not satisfy all and rises for some can, in turn, lead to further demands. Reactions to changes in production, labor, household relocations, and land use because of urbanization could, then, take on many different, even contradictory, forms. In fact, as some social historians have argued, social unrest or rebellion and accompanying millenarianism is more likely to erupt in agrarian societies when urbanization, modest commercial activity, and accompanying demands intensified.[32]

A stress on *perception* is important here because much of the reductive discussion on Galilee and class conflict wrongly assumes a vulgar or direct correlation between a rise or fall in living standards and the temperament of the general population. Yet in the ornamentation of Sepphoris and the building of Tiberias, we should not underestimate how the socioeconomic world was significantly altered for rural Galileans and not everyone would have *perceived* such changes for the

31. Rosemary Margaret Luff, *The Impact of Jesus in First-Century Palestine* (Cambridge: Cambridge University Press, 2019), 1.

32. See further John Kautsky, *The Political Consequences of Modernization* (New York: Wiley, 1971); Crossley and Myles, *Jesus*, 31–47.

better. Whatever the consequences for the general standard of living, Antipas's urbanization projects marked a significant change, even if at the level of ideological construction of the world. Such changes unlocked inherited tensions and anxieties and arguably propelled various social and religious movements, such as the early Jesus movement, into existence. Discontent with the present world order, including condemnation of the rich and powerful deemed to be largely responsible for these material and ideological changes, appears to be a significant and well-attested theme through the gospels. This theme was also, presumably, popular across a wide cross section of Jewish society, enough so to attract people from varying class backgrounds in Galilee and Judea to the movement in the first place.[33]

Conclusion

Going forward in the Next Quest, the task of class analysis will require on the part of the critical historian a much more sophisticated exploration of how the prominent ideas, perceptions, and activities belonging to the early Jesus movement were *necessarily* grounded in, and responding to, concrete material circumstances, whether consciously or not. This means going beyond simplistic social profiling of Jesus as a *tektōn* (cf. Mark 6:3) and instead attempting to situate Jesus and the early Jesus movement dialectically within the broader social and material conflicts of their time and place. As we have seen, the changes and upheaval in Galilee as Jesus was growing up had clear connections to class and would have been experienced differently by different groups of people with differing solidarities. These socioeconomic changes could also result in displacements such as the one described by Josephus in his description of the founding of Tiberias, which would have dramatically exacerbated the fracturing of traditional social ties and norms. Irrespective of whether there was an overall rise in living standards, scholars of the Next Quest will still need to account for, rather than dismiss or explain away, the ways in which material factors and the generation of ideas, beliefs, and activities intersect. What conditions and contradictions triggered the early Jesus movement to say what it did, to do what it did, and to dream what it did?

33. See further Crossley and Myles, *Jesus,* 256–59.

19

Textiles, Sustenance, and Economy

Janelle Peters

The Quest for the historical Jesus must certainly continue to account for the economy. In the past, scholars such as Richard Horsley and John Dominic Crossan
examined possible rivalry between the cities and the more agrarian areas in which
Jesus traversed.[1] Sharon Lea Mattila has argued that the social complexity of such
civic environments in which ostensible carpenters operated may be carefully
mapped.[2] Marianne Sawicki has pointed out the ways in which modern Western
Protestant emphasis on nuclear households has obscured the mixed kinship work
and domestic arrangements of many in Judea and Galilee that was partially due
to economic necessity and partially out of sustained rethinking of family ties.[3]
The temple cleansing has been read in terms of the ongoing Jewish critiques of
the temple on religious terms but also on economic and anti-imperialist terms.

1. Richard Horsley, *Christian Origins* (Minneapolis: Fortress, 2010), 11; John Dominic Crossan,
The Historical Jesus: The Life of a Mediterranean Jewish Peasant (San Francisco: HarperCollins,
2010), 4.
2. Sharon Lea Mattila, "Revisiting Jesus' Capernaum: A Village of Only Subsistence-Level
Fishers and Farmers?," in *The Galilean Economy in the Time of Jesus*, ed. David A. Fiensy and
Ralph K. Hawkins (Atlanta: SBL Press, 2013), 75–138.
3. Marianne Sawicki, *Crossing Galilee: Architectures of Contact in the Occupied Land of Jesus*
(London: Bloomsbury, 2000), 20; Marianne Sawicki, "Who Wouldn't Marry Jesus?," in *A Wandering Galilean: Essays in Honour of Seán Freyne*, ed. Zuleika Rodgers, Margaret Daly-Denton,
and Anne Fitzpatrick-McKinley (Leiden: Brill, 2009), 301–20.

Jesus's famous saying to render to Caesar what is Caesar's and to God what is God's has pointed to the ongoing financial burden faced by Jesus's presumably lower-class audience, whether field-based farmer, independent weaver, city-centered carpenter, or seaward fisherman.

However, the Next Quest should also account for textile imagery and ideas of sustenance through which economic assumptions of the day were examined. I will argue that the earliest audiences of Jesus relied frequently on textile imagery to argue good standing in God's kingdom should not be based upon economic production and resources. This may be seen in episodes such as the saying shared by Matthew and Luke that exhorts listeners to consider the flowers that do not spin and the birds that do not reap. Jesus encourages people regardless of gender, class, and ethnicity to have access to God and divine providence without concern for economic status or work ethic. This attitude corresponds to actions attributed to the Markan Jesus such as the healing of the hemorrhaging woman who spent all of her money on physicians without finding a cure until, at last, she grabs onto Jesus's clothes and cures herself, forming a model upon whom some of those subsequently healed are based.[4] Repeatedly, the evangelists preserve earlier material that associates states of undress with possession and passion and dress as a sign of transfiguration and heavenly presence. God the Father, for Jesus and his various audiences, clothes the world in a way that prefigures the heavenly economy.

JESUS'S AUDIENCE

First, Jesus's audiences, as depicted by his near-contemporary evangelists, suggest that Jesus was considered authoritative by his listeners. Jesus is said to have taught with authority and not like the scribes (Mark 1:22). While the eschatological element of Jesus cannot be ignored, this authority is not simply divinely bestowed but comes into contrast with an influential socioeconomic class of men in Judean society. As Chris Keith notes, "the most plausible explanation for why the early Church remembered Jesus as both a scribal-literate teacher and a scribal-illiterate teacher is that Jesus did not hold scribal literacy, but managed to convince many in his audiences that he did."[5] Though the gospels partially present the rupture with Pharisees and scribes, the gospels depict Jesus as having access to the temple and

4. Amy-Jill Levine argues that Jesus turns the woman from a mother to a daughter, rendering her ritually pure by virtue of never menstruating. See Amy-Jill Levine, "The Gospel and Acts," in *The Oxford Handbook of New Testament, Gender, and Sexuality*, ed. Benjamin H. Dunning (Oxford: Oxford University Press, 2019), 295–314.

5. Chris Keith, *Jesus' Literacy: Scribal Culture and the Teacher from Galilee*, LNTS 413 (London: T&T Clark, 2011), 26.

synagogues where intellectual conversations are being had. One wonders if Jesus reflects what Shaye Cohen has deemed the democratization of Second Temple Judaism—empowered by daily prayers and accessible Torah instruction, Jesus worked out his own spiritual interpretation that he shared with fellow spiritual seekers outside of traditional cultic spaces such as the temple.[6] Just as Jesus did not have the benefit of a more formal education like Paul's Pharisaic education, or assume a more elevated status as Josephus did at Masada, Jesus encourages women such as Mary and Martha to deprioritize cooking and cleaning on behalf of guests for the sake of hospitality—Jesus wants both men and women to participate in informal intellectual settings according to our received literary tradition. The earliest community of Jesus is an informal school and salon, and Jesus himself is a teacher without an official title.

When situating the historical Jesus and his companions, this information about Jesus's educational attitudes is vital. Although many stories are set in the countryside—John the Baptist's ministry, the Sermons on the Mount and Plain, the multiple feeding stories—romanticizing the pastoral was also an elite pastime in the Hellenistic and Roman periods, as we can see in the ancient novel. The pastoral romance *Daphnis and Chloe*, for instance, features two foundlings raised by shepherds, following the example of goats. As they are left with tokens of recognition, their adopted parents give both the boy and the girl an equal education despite their current statuses as enslaved individuals whose parents are not known. These are details we don't see in the gospels, though admittedly Judea and Galilee are somewhat removed from the isle of Lesbos during the early Roman imperial period. Other evidence in the gospels—a reliance on somewhat folksy and gnomic sayings that may appeal to a wider range of audiences than a Lukan Homeric allusion, repeated scenes of living off the land in the countryside, and so on—suggests that Jesus's closest circles were indeed of a lower economic class than later generations of leadership in ancient churches.

Jesus and his companions are not the lowest economic classes—they are not sentenced to complete drudgery. In fact, they evidently have the free time and resources to choose to abandon work in order to take up ministry permanently. While they do not have the educational opportunities of wealthier contemporaries or later church fathers such as Augustine, they are able to engage in ministry at or above the subsistence level and, for the most part, without living off of locusts and honey like John the Baptist. Jesus's disciples have a degree of leisure to go and hear Jesus speak. They might know people who have sufficient economic means

---

6. Shaye Cohen, *From the Maccabees to the Mishnah*, 3rd ed. (Louisville: Westminster John Knox, 2014), 69.

to buy anointing oil worth a year of day laborer wages and people who can afford more upscale funerary arrangements. However, the apostles—even later ones like Paul—all have trades that require manual labor during the day at some point in their lives. Making money is a continual concern—there are not inheritances or funds that Jesus and the apostles can rely upon like favorite Roman authors and rhetoricians such as Cicero or Pliny. The lives of Jesus's companions in this economic periphery meant that the scrutiny of the Roman emperor did not directly impact their business and personal matters as much as other authors in our Roman literary record, including even Greek-speaking Josephus. Rather, they would have been nameless faces were a census to happen, and they would not have had to flee to Egypt with Jesus in the event of foreign prophets visiting their local king. No emperor was going to know they exist or would have personally ordered them to commit suicide in the manner of our beloved Stoic philosopher Seneca.

Debates continue about the independence of contemporary Jewish groups such as the community at Qumran, where one could argue that a much higher degree of literacy and signs of wealth are found. While several holiness groups such as the Therapeutae were known to exist, it is possible that some of the groups that have been assumed to be insular and completely separate from outsiders for purity reasons could have been joined for festivals by those who normally worked outside the community. Such is the proposal concerning Qumran, which could have been visited by other Essenes though possibly still not by camelhair-wearing and locust-and-honey-eating wild man John the Baptist. Given the Hasmonean project of bringing the Galilee and even Samaria into Jerusalem-based practices, it is quite possible that Jesus's relatively laissez-faire approach to purity matched those of many within Galilee and Samaria, particularly if Mordechai Aviam is correct about the converted gentile population.[7]

Economic anxiety among this audience appears to have been high. Many parables deal with the squabbles that ensue when all workers are paid the same day-wage or face the threat of debtors' prison, including the admonition that debtors who do not forgive other debtors will not receive heavenly favor (Matt 18:23–35). Stories about the ability of John the Baptist and Jesus to live off the land themselves point to alleviating these anxieties. Likewise, in the case of Jesus, providing lunch for thousands of others suggests that a subsistence lifestyle should be in reach for followers, even if it is only Jesus who is summoned to dine with Pharisees and then receives anointing with inordinately expensive oil by a woman Luke calls

---

7. Mordechai Aviam, "People, Land, Economy, and Belief in First-Century Galilee and Its Origins: A Comprehensive Archaeological Synthesis," in *The Galilean Economy in the Time of Jesus*, ed. David A. Fiensy and Ralph K. Hawkins (Atlanta: SBL Press, 2013), 5–48.

a "sinner" (Luke 7:36–50). Matthew's version of the Lord's Prayer uses the word "debts" (6:12) to follow the notion of "daily bread" (6:11), a mild extravagance but hardly luxury fare. The gospels take care to lead audiences into wide, open landscapes as much as possible. Repeatedly, this landscape is shown to be hospitable and sustaining—when Jesus's disciples worry that their teacher is not going to pay the temple tax, Jesus sends them to the sea to cast a single line that yields a stater that will pay for all of them (Matt 17:27). In this respect, Jesus is again similar to the ancient novel *Daphnis and Chloe*, where Daphnis is able to attempt to marry Chloe through the miraculous purse guarded by the stench of a dead dolphin (3.27–30). Daphnis's prize of three thousand drachmas is sufficiently large to purchase the freedom of himself and his bride in the late first or early second century CE.[8] By having a smaller amount, Jesus and the narrative might emphasize staying or surviving within existing socioeconomic confines, however arbitrary given the general "freedom" of Jesus and the disciples.

JESUS'S SAYING NOT TO WORRY

Speaking of bucolic landscapes, it is at this juncture that we should turn to Jesus's saying not to worry. Jesus says that people should look at how the birds do not reap and the flowers do not spin in order to know that God cares for them and their survival. This saying is widely attested among many of our earliest sources, and it seems to have been foundational for many groups of early Christ followers, who tended to fall among lower socioeconomic groups than later Christian leaders. The exhortation given by Jesus to look at nature for assurance of God's care for humans is found in Matthew, Luke, P.Oxy. 655, and the Coptic manuscript of the Gospel of Thomas from Nag Hammadi. In this saying, Jesus asks his audience to look at fields beyond their culinary value to even their ornamental value. Although the grain in the field could certainly feed disciples were Jesus not around to multiply loaves, there is sufficient abundance to not have all arable land devoted to agriculture for sustenance. Some land may harbor flowers, and those flowers may exist simply to be considered there in their lack of economic activity.

Flowers and Birds

Jesus seems to address cloth production in his saying not to worry. According to Matthew, Jesus directs the attention of his disciples to the "birds of the air" and

---

8. R. L. Hunter, *A Study of Daphnis and Chloe* (Cambridge: Cambridge University Press, 1983), 4.

the "wild flowers." Since the wild flowers do not spin and the birds of the air do not reap, it may be concluded that God will also take care of his followers regardless of their spinning and reaping success. According to Luke, Jesus points specifically to ravens and lilies, ravens being birds that must shift around and are thus found in stories like 1 Kings 17 where ravens bring Elijah food during a drought, and lilies being respectable and comforting flowers. According to P.Oxy. 655, only the flowers—not the birds—are in focus, and stature is also a provision of God. It is possible that this invokes notions of status that were intricately linked with garments in the Roman Empire in traditions around garments such as the toga. It is also possible that this refers to the fact that cloth was more precious in the preindustrial world, as we can see in New Testament stories involving the generous gifting of cloaks and the depraved gambling over Jesus's clothes. As Gos. Thom. 36.1–3 and NHC II 39.24–27 also lack the birds, James Robinson and Christoph Heil have suggested that the flowers-only form of the saying is the version closer to the language used by Jesus, though probably in Aramaic rather than Greek.[9] The Matthean and Lukan glosses on the glory of Solomon arrayed corroborate the flower primacy, in that the extended imagery for cloth seems to suggest that the cloth-producing flowers are the more important component of this pair.

Flowers were normally connected with the feminine in antiquity, but there is evidence that flowers could be associated with lower-class men being subordinated by elite males. The iconography of the Roman goddess Spes depicted her contemplating a flower. The Floralia was celebrated in honor of the Roman goddess Flora.[10] In trying to show the delicacy and feminine qualities of the enslaved protagonist Daphnis in *Daphnis and Chloe*, Longus compares his hair to the hyacinth. An even stronger connection to flowers occurs when Daphnis's romantic rival for the hand of his beloved Chloe destroys the flower garden Daphnis spent so long tending for the arrival of his master.[11] In the destruction of the flowers, Daphnis sees his own bodily demise, and it is the happy resolution of the novel that Daphnis ends by being redeemed by the father who exposed him when he seemed not to need the excess of an additional mouth to feed.[12] While

9. James M. Robinson and Christoph Heil, "The Lilies of the Field: Saying 36 of the Gospel of Thomas and Secondary Accretions in Q 12.22b–31," *NTS* 47 (2001): 1–25; Dirk Jongkind, "'The Lilies of the Field' Reconsidered: 'Codex Sinaiticus' and the Gospel of Thomas," *NovT* 48 (2006): 209–16.

10. Janelle Peters, "Gendered Activity and Jesus's Saying Not to Worry," *Neot* 50 (2016): 48.

11. Angeline Chiu, *Ovid's Women of the Year: Narratives of Roman Identity in the Fasti* (Ann Arbor: University of Michigan Press, 2016), 158.

12. Hunter notes that these poverty twists are a feature of New Comedy, perhaps aiming to induce audiences to rethink the social order. See Hunter, *Daphnis and Chloe*, 67.

it is certainly a possibility later and more elite audiences might have seen the imperative to allow the flowers to be unproductive as an exhortation to let Daphnis live, Jesus's own audiences could very well have seen a teaching that would let them live should their labor market effort be unremunerative for their masters and bosses.

Jesus's Location

In finding the historical Jesus, we must admit that we have a problem in this saying, insofar as that we do not know where Jesus is when he proclaims it. Matthew thinks Jesus gives this saying on a mountain in the context of ethical instruction that insists that no enslaved person can serve two masters, whether two competing businesspeople or God and wealth. Luke presents Jesus giving this saying outside of what we usually think of as his equivalent to Matthew's Sermon on the Mount (the Sermon on the Plain). Unlike Matthew's imagery of slavery, Luke connects this saying with problems over receiving inheritances—a much wealthier problem to have! With the appearance of this saying at Oxyrhynchus and Nag Hammadi, it appears that we do have a free-floating saying that formed the traditional *chreia* attributed to Jesus later reworked into more narrative literary productions like gospels. This saying is told by Jesus in various contexts in the gospels: city gatherings and countryside chats. However, its imagery points directly to natural processes that transcend human agricultural interventions: nature and God trump human labor and wealth.

There is really nothing political about this saying. It is more purely economic, if such a thing is possible. Jesus does not direct his audiences to go out and follow the example of John the Baptist, occasionally getting in trouble with the self-indulgent local ruler. Rather, in the midst of the struggle to provide for oneself, disciples are reminded that looking at nature will provide examples of more abundance than is perhaps strictly deserved. Like Jesus's closest disciples who literally pluck grain from fields they did not plant in the Synoptic tradition (Matt 12:1–8; Mark 2:23–28; Luke 6:1–5), all of the disciples may be assured that food and protection exist on this planet without their effort but for their benefit. Such a moral opposes the tendency of wisdom literature to insist that only solid effort results in good security and comfort.

Jesus's saying corresponds to a widely held expectation that those with means would share with those without in times of famine. Slightly later in the first century, Dio Chrysostom exonerated himself of grain hoarding when he was being threatened with death by neighbors in Prusa: "No man is more blameless than I am in connection with the present shortage. Have I produced the most grain of all and then put it under lock and key, raising the price?" (*Or.* 46.8). As Paul Erd-kamp notes, honorific inscriptions help us to interpret this discourse as a common occurrence, with Q. Popillius Python from Macedon being remarkable for selling grain at a market discount "in times of dearth."[13]

Both Matthew and Luke, who give Jesus sayings wider contexts as opposed to just the saying, place the saying about worry in instructions that advocate giving to the poor and not seeking excessive wealth. Before using nature as an example of divine providence and orientation, Matthew displays concern for the heart's orientation toward wealth—using the institution of slavery (6:24) and the bio-logical fact of moths, destroyers of food and cloth, as examples of the futility of accumulating worldly wealth (6:19–21). Matthew's Jesus calls worldly wealth by the Aramaic *mammon* (6:24), which is in the Q material and is placed in Luke 16 as the conclusion for the parable of the dishonest steward. Matthew notes that seek-ing after worldly comfort is a concern of "the nations" in the Hellenized world.[14] Luke's Jesus very clearly goes on to instruct disciples to give alms.

Although Jesus is surely anticipating an interest in education in asking his audiences to use their leisure time listening to his instruction, the saying itself does not direct male or female listeners to further education. It is nowhere near the length of Seneca's *On Divine Providence* (whatever its original form). Jesus does not spend a lot of time asking why theodicy is a part of the theological order. The value God has for humanity serves as an implicit contrast to that held for humanity by those who enacted social distinctions such as enslavement, which is made explicit in places like Matt 5:45 where Jesus notes rain falls on everyone regardless of good works and intentions or lack thereof.

Connection to Occupations of Jesus's Audiences

In giving his instruction not to worry, Jesus uses gendered metaphors from the area familiar to his audience: agricultural and cloth production. Jesus likely knew women who spun and wove within the space of the home and also outside of it, though outside of the home men are also known as commercial weavers.[15] Women weaving symbolized the social fabric in order since the archaic time of Penelope weaving a shroud for Laertes. Moreover, typical Roman scenes show men taking a very prom-

13. Paul Erdkamp, *The Grain Market in the Roman Empire: A Social, Political and Economic Study* (Cambridge: Cambridge University Press, 2005), 90.

14. Robert S. Kinney, *Hellenistic Dimensions of the Gospel of Matthew: Background and Rhet-oric* (Tübingen: Mohr Siebeck, 2016), 6–7.

15. William den Hollander, *Josephus, the Emperors, and the City of Rome: From Hostage to Historian* (Leiden: Brill, 2014), 299.

inent role in agricultural production and even commercial baking, but we do find women in the harvest in places ranging from the book of Ruth to *Daphnis and Chloe.* As Lauren Hackworth Petersen and Sandra Joshel have shown, men put up funerary monuments that recast their baking guild from one of possibly using the labor of enslaved people to one in which men are depicted—at least—as being truly equal. While this data from the tomb of Marcus Vergilius Eurysaces and the house of the baker read against the literary tradition and is thus Rome-centric, the idea of male baking as bringing together a number of social classes could have possibly extended over Jesus's eastern Mediterranean context.[16] Moreover, the bread itself, governed as it was by city male overseers, was a symbol of friendship and commensality in male-produced texts, leading to customs that keeping it whole preserved unity.[17]

Much has been made about the potential for these gendered pairs by scholars, including myself in a *Neotestamentica* article.[18] The spindle and the loom were technologies that demanded women's time, but they also allowed women the potential to support their families and to resist demands placed upon them. In the book of Tobit, Tobit's wife earns money for the family with her cloth production (2:11).[19] Joseph Fitzmyer notes that Tobit's wife would have been supporting the whole family.[20] Tobit has been found in various forms at Qumran, and scholars now agree that it was probably written initially in Aramaic around 200 BCE. Qumran lasted until the fall of the Second Temple, so this tradition of weaving women would have been current during the time of Jesus. Egyptian papyri show enslaved women apprenticed to women as old as fifty or sixty as well as enslaved men apprenticed to men in order to become weavers.[21] The association of women and weaving in the early Roman Empire led to late antique depictions of both Leto and the Virgin Mary as textile workers and mothers.[22] Spindles in funerary contexts appear with women, as they commemorate a pursuit of the deceased in life.[23]

16. Sandra Joshel and Lauren Hackworth Petersen, "Slaves in the Workshop," in *The Material Life of Roman Slaves* (Cambridge: Cambridge University Press, 2014), 118–61.

17. Justin Taylor, "Bread That Is Broken—And Unbroken," in Rodgers et al., *Wandering Galilean*, 525–37.

18. Peters, "Gendered Activity."

19. Samuel L. Adams, *Social and Economic Life in Second Temple Judea* (Louisville: Westminster John Knox, 2014), 49.

20. Joseph A. Fitzmyer, *Tobit* (Berlin: de Gruyter, 2003), 139.

21. Anna C. Kelley, "Searching for Professional Women in the Mid to Late Roman Textile Industry," *Past & Present* (2023): 23.

22. Catherine Gines Taylor, *Late Antique Images of the Virgin Annunciate Spinning: Allotting the Scarlet and the Purple* (Leiden: Brill, 2018), 38.

23. Lauren Hackworth Petersen, "The Baker, His Tomb, His Wife, and Her Breadbasket: The Monument of Eurysaces in Rome," *Art Bulletin* (2003): 230–57.

Spinning can even serve as a euphemism, sparing women the label of exploited sex worker or rape victim.[24] Later, as Anna Kelley notes, the church fathers such as John Chrysostom use textile work as an arena in which women are acknowledged to be talented, providing a contrast to activities such as spear throwing.[25]

When Jesus tells people they need not spin or weave to secure survival from God, he tells people to bloom. It is likely that most audiences would have thought first of the women who spun, carded, and wove. It is also possible that some male weavers might have thought of themselves. Jesus in this saying isn't staying within the bounds of his occupational guild—he is reaching across artisanal lines, just as he refuses to stay affiliated with only one synagogue. This picture of Jesus's economic vision shows a Jesus active in an agrarian society where grain is the primary foodstuff and cloth is precious enough to gamble for and steal.

Though the Jesus saying about flowers and birds is not found in Mark or John, neither gospel presents a Jesus that would contradict this ethic. Mark includes the disciples plucking heads of grain to make a path for Jesus, a pre-Markan tradition that also makes its way into Matthew and Luke.[26] When the Pharisees confront him, he points to the scriptural example of David and his companions eating the bread of offering that only priests could lawfully eat, recalling the importance of the law for self-definition as a people of Israel.[27] As highly trained but not always wealthy individuals, much like Paul the apostle and tentmaker, the Pharisees seem to have allowed this implicit critique of the economic favoritism toward already elite priests to stand. John's Samaritan woman meets Jesus at a well, where he promises her that she will receive living water that overrides the notion of practical drawn water. The woman is then empowered to go tell others, despite what seems to be an unluckily extraordinary number of marriages and live-in arrangements.

Overall Message

In telling audiences not to worry, Jesus appears in a familiar mode from contemporary philosophy in reminding people of divine providence. Jesus himself does

24. In Act I, scene 3 of Shakespeare's *Twelfth Night*, the housewife is envisioned as taking someone between her knees and "spinning" him.

25. John Chrysostom, *Quales ducendae sint uxores* (*CPG* 4379; PG 51:225–242); Kelley, "Searching for Professional Women," 1.

26. James Crossley, *The Date of Mark's Gospel: Insight from the Law in Earliest Christianity* (London: Bloomsbury, 2004), 161.

27. Mar Pérez i Diaz, *Mark, A Pauline Theologian: A Re-Reading of the Traditions of Jesus in the Light of Paul's Theology* (Tübingen: Mohr Siebeck, 2020), 92.

not have an occupation where he is permitted to become a philanthropist, and he does not come from a family with inherited wealth. He is not actually in a position personally to tap into his storehouses and feed the populace. Significant gains of funds in his socioeconomic context come from miracles, which are inaccessible to those in his audience who are neither Jesus nor apostles. Therefore, he admonishes his audiences to give to the poor and to consider the fields for their intrinsic worth as individual souls. This perhaps forms a contrast to those in Jesus's context like the Matthean centurion, who identifies with his enslaved helper only as he is about to lose him to illness. The field, baking, weaving, and cloth imagery inherent to the saying cuts across socioeconomic lines to speak to all people while simultaneously engendering individual self-worth, though individual consciousness in the sense of interiority must still await Augustine's time.

Economics and Clothing

Although not necessarily part of the historical Jesus's intention when giving the saying not to worry, clothes indicated social identity in antiquity, and the earliest stories of Christ followers make use of clothing to illustrate heavenly order. The woman with hemorrhages is able to touch Jesus's cloak tassels in order to pull power from his body.[28] Other healed individuals evidently also go after the cloak of Jesus, and they receive healing for their initiative through faith. The transfiguration changes the robes of Jesus into both elite and heavenly robes, giving Jesus a new identity like Christians "put on" a new identity at baptism.[29] Believers may give items such as extra cloaks as alms, indicating the value of clothing and the limited nature of material wealth among early Jesus followers. Just before Jesus's crucifixion, individuals run around naked (Mark 14:51–52), prefiguring perhaps Jesus's unwinding of the burial cloths that bound him in the tomb. Soldiers at Jesus's execution gamble over his clothes. Possible angels appear in his tomb fully clothed after his resurrection.

The simplicity of the clothing references—unremarkably colored clothing, sometimes with tassels, on earth and white clothing in heavenly space—gives us a sense of the socioeconomic conditions that the Jesus movement seems to have found normal: lower-class socioeconomic conditions where the latest hair-

28. Candida Moss, "The Man with the Flow of Power: Porous Bodies in Mark 5:25–34," *JBL* 129 (2010): 507–19.

29. Janelle Peters, "Robes of Transfiguration and Salvation in Early Christian Texts," in *Dress in Mediterranean Antiquity: Greeks, Romans, Jews, Christians*, ed. Alicia Batten and Kelly Olson (London: Bloomsbury, 2021), 279–88.

style trends of Roman empresses and the fake rings of would-be knights do not feature as they do in the mostly elite literature from Roman authors of the early imperial period. It is not until Acts 16:14 that Paul introduces Lydia, a dealer of purple cloth, into the set of believers. She represents someone who will be able to acquire resources to share directly or sell for fund redistribution in a way that is more repeatable than Jesus's miraculous feedings.[30] Lydia is important because she has an upper-class clientele that is legally allowed to wear purple according to Roman sumptuary laws. She herself, though, is just a socially climbing merchant who is either reaching down to the Jesus movement or bringing it up on the social ladder with her, albeit too late to support Jesus's ministry directly.

Reflecting on the data of the clothes in earliest Christian sources, we are able to view Jesus's statement about not worrying about what one is to wear or where one is to sleep in a new light. In addition to perhaps being more attractive to gospel audiences after the fall of the temple that led to some forced migration of Judeans, the Jesus saying about worry could be interpreted as inclusive of those with little or nothing to share. In a culture that valued hospitality and being able to bring a sacrifice, those living on the margins were unable to participate in basic cultural values. The touching story about the gods appearing to Baucis and Philemon in Ovid's *Metamorphoses* becomes decidedly inaccessible to many Roman audiences when one considers that not everyone would have held sufficient status to have a spouse and a household of one's own in which to entertain the gods with one's spouse. Those serving as domestic help and possibly having their every move planned and tracked, as Lauren Hackworth Petersen and Sandra Joshel have so masterfully demonstrated, certainly could not simply entertain gods or angels without the permission of their masters.[31] An exhortation to look at a natural field free of soldiers, wild beasts, famine-causing insects, and so forth in order to see the value placed upon each individual regardless of their economic status or output would have been inclusive in the only way available to a historical Jesus who was unable to bequeath worldly possessions and health to his followers.

Conclusion

In conclusion, the Next Quest for the historical Jesus should continue to consider the economy and do so with reference to textiles and ideas about sustenance. In the economic arrangements pictured in our texts, women and men are thrown into the mix, as they often are in households reliant upon enslaved labor. Jesus

30. Eben Scheffler, "Caring for the Needy in the Acts of the Apostles," *Neot* 50 (2016): 131–66.
31. Joshel and Petersen, "Slaves in the Workshop," 138.

reaches across occupations and social classes to provide a comprehensive vision of his agrarian economy. Invoking economic production at the core of civic values—bread and cloth production—Jesus encourages audiences instead to return to nature before such fabrication in order to see how birds and flowers do not have labor tasks and are nonetheless fed and clothed by God. This idea of the inherent worth and dignity of individuals coheres with Jesus's statements encouraging almsgiving in Q and the gospels. It refuses to shame those without resources to sacrifice at the temple or provide hospitality for guests according to traditional Mediterranean customs. It aligns with Jesus's own lack of economic resources, as he himself is only able to heal and feed thousands of people through divine power and miracles.

20

CITY AND COUNTRY

Robyn Faith Walsh

The Next Quest for the historical Jesus must account for city and country. In so doing, scholars of the New Testament and early Christianity are forced to confront that the gospels correspond coherently within an arch of imperial-era writing that centers "Rome" both culturally and conceptually, constructing that which is beyond its "city limits" as increasingly prone to the "exotic" and miraculous, characterized by *thauma* or *thaumata*—marvels or wonders.

Allied to genres like paradoxography, travelogue, bucolic literature (including the Greek and Roman novel), as well as the kind of ethnographic writing epitomized by later writers like Pausanias, the gospels present the reader with an account of a Judean or Galilean wonderworker and philosopher, innately knowledgeable and endowed with miraculous powers who, in his journeys from the pastoral countryside to the corrupting city, both encounters local wonders and, at times, enacts them. This is an exceedingly common Greek and Roman *literary* construction. The notion of the corrupting city, for instance, is nothing new to ancient Mediterranean storytelling;

This project would not have been possible without the insights and generosity of my former colleague at the University of Miami, Dr. James R. Townshend, whose work on Vergil's Camilla and the aesthetics of the grotesque (cited below) were formative in my analysis of Mark's Gospel. And a warm thank you to the members of the Antiquities Interdisciplinary Research Group (AIRG) at the University of Miami, the participants in the Next Quest conference in Bedford, UK, as well as Nancy Evans, Stephen Hebert, and Sarah Rollens for their help and advice on this piece. All translations are my own, unless otherwise noted.

as is often the case for philosophers or unconventional heroes like Aesop, urban spaces are, at best, "a distraction from the pursuit of philosophy," infested with "false prophets," and, at worst, deadly.[1] Plutarch likens cities—awash with diversions and conspicuous *graffito*—to the enticements of prostitutes in a brothel (*Mor.* 520c).[2] By contrast, utopian fictions like the novel often present innately virtuous characters, who have eschewed traditional *paideia*, opting to be educated by the gods in natural settings in blissful ignorance of the corruptions of urban life until they are thrust into the city—or the "city" comes to them via piracy or other villainy.[3]

Likewise, a common invective between authors in the ancient world was to label allies and competitors alike as writers of "miscellany [and] marvels."[4] Apion and Pliny the Elder, for instance, are routinely accused of being "sophistic producers of marvels" who attempt to "please the ear" of their audiences with "shabby . . . Greek wonder-tales."[5] More often than not, this impresses as the kind of complaint lodged against writers who had achieved a good deal of attention and circulation—what we might term "popularity." Not only were paradoxographical accounts and tales about miraculous happenings and healings by all accounts popular, Pausanias suggests that "everyone who has ever existed [*hoposoi . . . pephykasi*] enjoys hearing mythic tales and even heighten the marvel/wonder [*epiterateuesthai*], so that they sully truth [*alēthesin*] by mixing it with lies [*synkerannyntes auta epseusmenois*]" (*Descr.* 8.2.7).[6] From Aristotle to Herodotus and Pausanias, the amazement of *thaumata* is considered the result of either relative "rarity" or "lack of knowledge," sometimes both.[7] Moreover, writers of *thaumata*

---

1. The first quote is adapted from Stephanie Ann Frampton, "What to Do with Books in the 'De Finibus'," *TAPA* 146.1 (2016): 127. The second is adapted from Amiel Vardi, "Gellius against the Professors," *ZPE* 137 (2001): 43–44.

2. For more discussion on this passage, see Joseph Howley, *Aulus Gellius and Roman Reading Culture: Text, Presence, and Imperial Knowledge in the Noctes Atticae* (Cambridge: Cambridge University Press, 2018), 26.

3. Here I am, in part, revisiting an observation made in Robyn Faith Walsh, *The Origins of Early Christian Literature: Contextualizing the New Testament within Greco-Roman Literary Culture* (Cambridge: Cambridge University Press, 2021), 137–55.

4. Adapted from Wytse Keulen, *Gellius the Satirist: Roman Cultural Authority in Attic Nights* (Leiden: Brill, 2009), 238.

5. Adapted from Keulen, *Gellius the Satirist*, 238.

6. The context of this quote in Pausanias is the tale of Lycaon sacrificing a human baby on the altar of Lycaean Zeus, after which he is transformed into a wolf—a story that Pausanias claims he is apt to believe on the bases of antiquity (*ek palaiou*) and "probability" (*eikos*; *Descr.* 8.2.4). What prompts the critique cited are claims that griffins have leopard spots and that Tritons speak with human voices (8.2.7).

7. Lydia Langerwerf, "'Many Are the Wonders in Greece': Pausanias the Wandering Phi-

go to great (rhetorical) pains to substantiate their marvels with autopsy (that is, personal self-verification) or claims about eyewitnesses—eyewitnesses who are, at times, encoded in the narrative itself.

While tasked with reflecting on "city and country," you will not find me commenting on the historical Galilee and its famines, overpopulation, or droughts.[8] Nor will I comment on the so-called urbanization of Sepphoris or socioeconomic considerations of peasant classes.[9] Rather, allow me to begin in Victorian England by drawing briefly on some theoretical approaches to the work of E. M. Forster and, specifically, his book *Howards End*.[10] Published in 1910, the novel follows the lives of three families in London: the wealthy, capitalist Wilcoxes; the Schlegels, well-educated German-British siblings who are comfortably part of an upper middle class; and the Basts, a couple teetering on the edge of poverty. "Howards End" is the name of a relatively remote country home outside of London owned by the Wilcoxes that more or less becomes the subject of an ownership dispute between the protagonists. At the core of the tale is not simply the dichotomy between city and country living, but how writers create a sense of the past—often a past that never existed—one that "[elides] social realities" by simplifying or falsifying the past, "erasing its painful features."[11] The story reveals how writers commodify nostalgia through claims about the "commercial 'taint' of urban life" and how, by creating "fictitious histories," writers can take "nostalgic desire [as] a way to reach a wished-for past time, or a desired past space." These invented locations and moments "[seek] to sell" nostalgic desire back to the reader by compressing time and presenting people or places as symbolic representations of purity or by adopting "new ways of mapping time" or even, flatly, "things that never existed."[12] I suggest that the gospels and historical Jesus research offer a similar set of strategic goals. The more we uncritically accept the gospels' presentation of Jesus and Judea as a repository of possible, historical "fact"—that is, the more we take the

---

losopher," in *Recognizing Miracles in Antiquity and Beyond*, ed. Maria Gerolemou (Berlin: de Gruyter, 2018), 306.

8. Morten H. Jensen, "Climate, Droughts, Wars, and Famines in Galilee as a Background for Understanding the Historical Jesus," *JBL* 131.2 (2012): 307–24; Joan E. Taylor, "Jesus as News: Crises of Health and Overpopulation in Galilee," *JSNT* 44.1 (2021): 8–30.

9. Nathan Schumer, "The Population of Sepphoris: Rethinking Urbanization in Early and Middle Roman Galilee," *JAJ* 8.1 (2017): 90–111; Sharon Lea Mattila, "Jesus and the 'Middle Peasants'? Problematizing a Social-Scientific Concept," *CBQ* 72.2 (2010): 291–313.

10. Nota bene: I elected to draw this theoretical analogy because the Next Quest conference took place outside of London in the summer of 2022.

11. Elizabeth Outka, "Buying Time: *Howards End* and Commodified Nostaglia," *Modernisms* 36.3 (2003): 333.

12. Outka, "Buying Time," 331, 334–35.

gospels literally and not rhetorically—the more we miss the strategic goals of their authors. With *Howards End*, the conceit of the story is not "Who shall inherit this house?" as much as it is "Who shall inherit England?"—the native aristocracy or the aspirational classes? With the gospels, the question is not "Who is Jesus?" but "Who shall inherit the Kingdom?"—Judea or Rome?

In what follows, I offer a few words on my assumptions about approaching the gospels and the merits of the historical Jesus enterprise. I will then attempt to shed new light on Jesus's miracle working as a species of traditional imperial subject matter. As I have noted, I contend that the gospel writers are utilizing structural elements from genres like paradoxography in their presentation of these phenomena. Specifically, Jesus and his actions are presented as a series of strategic literary *thaumata*—wonders or marvels—designed to convince the reader, sometimes playfully, that the fantastic is plausible.

Focusing principally on the Gospel of Mark (with some supporting discussion of the Gospel of Luke) I will demonstrate that *thaumata*, paradox, and eyewitnesses or "autopsy" are presented in the text in a manner that corresponds to a larger and established imperial literary method designed to engage and entertain the reader simultaneously through an interplay of rhetorical gaslighting. The result is that the seemingly extraordinary is in fact quite ordinary in Mark. Mark employs a traditional means of "legitimizing" the claims he makes through well-executed technique and craft.

Rereading Mark in this way disrupts traditional methodologies that maintain claims—whether implicit or explicit—about the historical merits of Jesus's wonderworking. Namely, that authors like Mark consciously engage motifs or genres of writing that were known to be aesthetically successful, presumably for the purposes of interest and circulation. Such engagement was not necessarily dependent on subject matter; that is, Mark may be writing *thaumata* about Jesus, but he does not need Jesus to write about *thaumata*. Why he chooses to write about Jesus is a separate question, but one that does not address the more immediate observation that Mark is functioning within a circumscribed social network of what I have described elsewhere as "literate cultural producers."[13] While the skill level of a writer like Mark is not up to the distinction of a Vergil or Pausanias, Mark nonetheless demonstrates an awareness of that culturally elite level of discourse.[14] At the same

13. Walsh, *Origins of Early Christian Literature*. I am invoking the language of Pierre Bourdieu, to be discussed later.

14. Walsh, *Origins of Early Christian Literature*, 121–27. While I have selected Vergil as a comparative model for the brand of strategic wonder and bewilderment he ascribes to his eyewitnesses in the present piece, it is possible to trace this motif back to Homer as well, per the work of Dennis MacDonald and the failure to recognize Odysseus; see *The Homeric Epics and the*

time, his use of Koine Greek, coupled with certain elements of style, suggests a strategic writer intentionally appealing to an established literary marketplace.

Ultimately, acknowledging Mark's debt to craft serves three primary functions: (1) it locates Mark within a network of writers and allows for comparison with representatives of this formative social network; (2) it thus demonstrates that Mark's concern may not be relating an accurate or oral "religious" history, as much as detailing his subject matter according to literary expectation; and (3) it allows us to evaluate aesthetic value of Mark's choices as a writer relative to his literary field.[15]

Premises

An implicit assumption about the canonical gospels is that they self-consciously intend to communicate a developed or developing theology about the nature of Jesus. Subsequently, the majority of analyses begin from the premise that there is something at stake in the writing of gospels that pertain to either the viewpoint of a historical Christian community or the historical Jesus (or both). Elsewhere, I and others have troubled the notion of a religious "community" behind the production of the gospels.[16] Likewise, a great deal of critique of the historical Jesus paradigm exists, albeit largely in reference to theoretical issues concerning the

---

Gospel of Mark (New Haven: Yale University Press, 2000). Citing Homer as a primary model is tempting in that it resolves questions about the author of Mark being aware of a type of literary device found in a Latin author; moreover, the so-called recognition scenes in Homer may contain some worthy parallels between Odysseus's active deception and "testing" of his disbelieving addressees and the function of "faith" in Mark. That said, because Odysseus is prone in some of these scenes to give a false identity, actively deceive, or play off of a standing relationship with the characters with whom he interacts, I judged that the function of Homer's approach to misrecognition went beyond the discrete literary parameters of *thauma*-writing I am attempting to identify. On the recognition scenes in Homer, consider Peter Gainsford, "Formal Analysis of Recognition Scenes in the 'Odyssey,'" *JHS* 123 (2003): 41–59. On multilingualism in the imperial period, some useful sources include Elizabeth Rawson, *Intellectual Life in the Late Roman Republic* (London: Duckworth, 2002), 19 37; Eleanor Dickey, "Teaching Latin to Greek Speakers in Antiquity," in *Learning Latin and Greek From Antiquity to the Present*, ed. Elizabeth Archibald, William Brockliss, and Jonathan Gnoza (Cambridge: Cambridge University Press, 2015), 30–51. The scholarship on Mark's use of apparent "Latinisms" is vast and leaves open the question of whether the author was acquainted with the language; a useful source on this matter is Adela Yarbro Collins, *Mark: A Commentary*, Hermeneia (Minneapolis: Fortress, 2007), which chronicles several instances of Latin borrowings with bibliography (e.g., Mark 15:15).

15. Walsh, *Origins of Early Christian Literature*.

16. Walsh, *Origins of Early Christian Literature*; Stanley K. Stowers, "The Concept of 'Community' and the History of Early Christianity," *MTSR* 23 (2011): 238–56.

search for "Christian origins."[17] And while scholars often attend to the broader literary influences on the gospel writers in their analyses, functionally this is of secondary concern to questions of documenting belief in or knowledge of Jesus's life and teachings. The author-qua-author is marginalized in evaluations of the gospels precisely because questions of literary function, form, and social context do not serve the scholar particularly well when the objective is to marshal these writings into prooftext of and for Christianity.

Writers are confined to the technologies, trends, and tropes of their writing culture; they have their own forms of distinction and *habitus* that are dictated by conditions of education, social standing, geography, ethnicity, gender, ability or disability, and so forth. To illustrate this point, I have argued that one way we can reread the gospels in their imperial moment is as "captive literature"—that is, a class of literature aimed at critiquing Rome's colonialization of the ancient Mediterranean by focusing on the futile struggles of their so-called barbarian subjects.[18] This reframing disaggregates the gospels from protohagiography, demonstrating that more is at stake for these writers than the echo chamber of Christian narrative. The gospels are no more singularly concerned with chronicling the life of the historical Jesus than the *Aeneid* is a vessel for the historical Aeneas.[19] And, to the extent that they are engaged in a traditional form of *bios*-writing (see Bond's chapter), we would be well served to recognize that one-dimensional comparisons are insufficient to the task of explicating the who and why of the gospels. Jesus resembles Odysseus, Daniel, Moses, Socrates, Aesop, Alexander, Augustus, for example, not only because the author is trying to draw an analogy for the sake of proving Jesus's importance or authority and so forth, but also because the author is demonstrating their own ability and authority within the inherently competitive field of writing.[20] The gospel writers use numerous tricks of the trade that

17. Willi Braun, *Jesus and Addiction to Origins: Toward an Anthropocentric Study of Religion*, ed. Russell McCutcheon (Sheffield: Equinox, 2020); William Arnal, "The Collection and Synthesis of 'Tradition' and the Second-Century Invention of Christianity," *MTSR* 23 (2011): 193–215.

18. Robyn Faith Walsh, "IVDAEA DEVICTA: The Gospels as Imperial 'Captive Literature,'" in *Class Struggle in the New Testament*, ed. Robert J. Myles (Lanham, MD: Lexington/Fortress Academic, 2019), 89–114.

19. My gratitude to Sarah Rollens for articulating this observation in a private conversation.

20. Walsh, *Origins of Early Christian Literature*, 170–94; David Konstan and Robyn Faith Walsh, "Civic and Subversive Biography in Antiquity," in *Writing Biography in Greece and Rome: Narrative Technique and Fictionalization*, ed. Koen De Temmerman and Kristoffel Demoen (Cambridge: Cambridge University Press, 2016), 26–43; Adela Yarbro Collins, *Is Mark's Gospel a Life of Jesus? The Question of Genre* (Milwaukee: Marquette University Press, 1992); MacDonald, *Homeric Epics*; Johan Thom, "Cleanthes' Hymn to Zeus and Early Christian Literature," in *Antiquity and Humanity: Essays on Ancient Religion and Philosophy*, ed. Adela Yarbro Collins and

we are inclined to overlook when we prioritize seeking evidence for recension, interpolation, oral tradition, or the historical Jesus.

My reader will be familiar with the moments of "wonder" in Mark; therefore, I will begin with a description of the less-familiar motif of *thaumata* in imperial-aged literature. I will then demonstrate how Mark engages this trope in his writing, establishing the character of Jesus as a *thauma*. There are three elements or stages of the *thauma* that pertain both globally and to the specific account in Mark's Gospel: (1) the bewilderment or wonder of the crowd who observe the *thauma*; (2) eyewitness confirmation of the *thauma* fostering faith or belief; (3) the *thauma* paradoxically embodying an inversion or transgression of established expectation (e.g., a hero gruesomely crucified). By establishing a long arc of engagement for this particular literary trope, I demonstrate its usefulness and relative banality as a go-to means of communicating the power of impact of certain divine figures from the epics forward.

This rereading also offers a plausible, alternative understanding of the literary objectives of the author of the Gospel of Mark without appeals to anachronistic theological concepts (e.g., Mark's "Christology") or the Romantic idea of an assumed early Christian community informing the content of the Gospel (e.g., the Markan "church"). It also stands as a corrective to synthetic descriptions of Mark's Gospel along the lines of William Wrede's enduring concept of the "Messianic Secret" (*Das Messiasgeheimnis*) which, in part, attempts to harmonize Jesus's futile demands for silence among those who witness his miraculous deeds in order to delay the fulfillment of his messianic task.[21] Such approaches mystify the intentions of the gospel writer by centralizing the presumed theological aims of this motif at the expense of its literary function and influences. Put differently, by framing the action of the protagonist around presumptions about Jesus's so-

---

Margaret M. Mitchell (Tübingen: Mohr Siebeck, 2001), 477–99; Marianne Palmer Bonz, *The Past as Legacy: Luke-Acts and Ancient Epic* (Minneapolis: Fortress, 2000); Tuomas Rasimus, Troels Engberg-Pedersen, and Ismo Dunderberg, eds., *Stoicism in Early Christianity* (Grand Rapids: Baker Academic, 2010); Richard C. Miller, "Mark's Empty Tomb and Other Translation Fables in Classical Antiquity," *JBL* 129.4 (2010): 759–76; Ilaria Ramelli and David Konstan, "The Use of *XAPA* in the New Testament and Its Background in Hellenistic Moral Philosophy," *Exemplaria Classica* 14 (2010): 185–204; Runar Thorsteinsson, *Roman Christianity and Roman Stoicism: A Comparative Study of Ancient Morality* (Oxford: Oxford University Press, 2010); Karl Olav Sandes, *The Gospel "according to Homer and Virgil": Cento and Canon* (Leiden: Brill, 2011); M. David Litwa, *Iesus Deus: The Early Christian Depiction of Jesus as a Mediterranean God* (Minneapolis: Fortress, 2014); C. Kavin Rowe, *One True Life: The Stoics and Early Christians as Rival Traditions* (New Haven: Yale University Press, 2016). This list is by no means exhaustive.

21. William Wrede, *Das Messiasgeheimnis in den Evangelien: Zugleich ein Beitrag zum Verständnis des Markusevangeliums* (Göttingen: Vandenhoeck & Ruprecht, 1901).

called ministry, proponents of theories idiosyncratic to later Christian theology effectively foreground the quest for the historical Jesus when the only historical figure accessible in these writings is the author.

LITERARY *THAUMA*

Thauma can be a rather amorphous category. While the term can be deployed as a literary device or aesthetic strategy within a larger piece writing (e.g., Vergil's *Aeneid*, which I will discuss), it can also range into a more concrete and discrete classification as its own genre. Though the boundaries of literary *thaumata* are flexible, the practice nonetheless exhibits certain common features in isolation or combination: the presentation of a paradox, usually represented by an individual figure or character, who instills wonder, amazement, confusion, or fear, and the resolution of the initial paradox, sometimes in the form of a renewal or instilling of faith or belief (*pistis*) or, sometimes, the death of the *thauma*.

Among the writings one might classify in the genre of *thaumata*, Phlegon of Tralles's explicitly titled *On Marvels* (*Peri thaumasiōn*) stands out as a representative example.[22] Reputedly a freedman of Hadrian, Phlegon's compilation of wondrous phenomena, people, places, and events catalogs tales of the miraculously aged and the escapades of amorous ghosts (e.g., Philinnion of Amphipolis; *Mir.* 1.14–18), among other incredible tales.[23] Phlegon is also notable for his multiple accounts of resurrection or reanimation incidents, including Rufus of Philippi in Thessalonica among others (*Mir.* 1.1–2.1).[24] The length of Phlegon's vignettes

---

22. *Paradoxographorum Graecorum Reliquiae*, ed. Alexander Giannini (Milan: Istituto Editoriale Italiano, 1966); *Phlegon of Tralles' Book of Marvels*, ed. and trans. William Hansen (Exeter: University of Exeter Press, 1996), 66–68. Of note, the earliest extant use of the term "paradoxographer" dates to the twelfth-century scholar John Tzetzes; however, it is not in consistent use until the early nineteenth century with A. Westermann's edited *Scriptores Rerum Mirabilium Graeci* (1839). Jessica Priestley notes "The similarity of the ancient titles of the works included in the modern editions (almost all mention thaumasia or paradoxa ['marvels' or 'paradoxes']), as well as formal features which the works share, suggest that ancient writers and readers may have recognized certain conventions for these works. It is, however, important to be alert not only to the similarities between the texts which have led to their being grouped together by modern editors, but to variations between them also." See Jessica Priestley, *Herodotus and Hellenistic Culture: Literary Studies in the Reception of the Histories* (Oxford: Oxford University Press, 2014), 76.

23. Phlegon includes a stand-alone section titled *Peri makrobiōn* (*On Long-Lived Persons*) 5.2, 4 (*FGrHist* 257 F 37). See Hansen, *Phlegon of Tralles*, 50–57.

24. Incidentally for the study of the gospels, Rufus of Philippi, like the *Satyricon*'s widow of Ephesus, emerges from his grave after three days (although, admittedly, under very different circumstances). Likewise, the empty tomb of the maiden Philinnion is discovered on the third

varies; however, he is careful to classify his wonders and group them accordingly (e.g., birth narratives) as well as cite his sources (e.g., "Antigonos reports that in Alexandria"; *Mir.* 28.1).[25] Each of these groupings is characterized by immediacy and very little or no context, although each claim is strategically supported by either invoking testimony, witnesses, or citing the rulers in power at the time of the event.[26] Phlegon's work is particularly notable for this project in that his Greek is presented at a level of relative skill comparable to what we find in the gospels, and the spare and rapid-fire nature of his vignettes is not dissimilar from Mark's sense of immediacy (e.g., the repetition of *kai euthys*).

Thaumata are also akin to paradoxographical forms of writing as found in the catalogues of wondrous ephemera collected by Hellenistic authors like Archelaus or Apollonius.[27] Fantastic stories like Plutarch's fanciful descriptions of the moon (*Mor.* 920b) are arguably allied to this genre, albeit folded into works that usually classify as other forms of writing (e.g., *bioi*, declamation, essays).[28] As Tim Whitmarsh notes, while not a "coherent genre" in and of itself, the "focus on local history"—even if extraterrestrial—routinely allowed ancient authors "a locus for fictional thinking."[29] This "fictional thinking" might include ethnographic or historical details, meditations on virtue and vice, or ekphrasis. In each case, *thaumata* provided literary and strategic space to present the extraordinary or an extraordinary claim within the parameters of the possible.

Deliberating on the broader distinctions between history and fiction in Greek and Latin literature, Whitmarsh identifies *thaumata* specifically as "a peculiarly indeterminate epistemological position, between the plausible and the impossible" associated with the kind of storytelling and "exoticism" characteristic of writers like Herodotus.[30] Barbara Boyd similarly notes that "the more distant the land, the stranger the marvels tend to be" when it comes to *thaumata* in the eth-

---

day of her zombie-esque sojourn (*Mir.* 1.14–18). Thus, accounts of the astonishing reappearance or revivification of the dearly departed "after three days" may have been relatively commonplace for an imperial audience consuming this type of literature; see Miller, "Mark's Empty Tomb"; Robyn Faith Walsh, "The *Satyrica* and the Gospels in the Second Century," *ClQ* 70.1 (2020): 356–67.

25. "Headings" may not have been part of the earliest manuscript tradition; they do not appear in the *Paradoxographorum Graecorum Reliquiae*.

26. An approach which, incidentally, evokes associations with the Gospel of Luke, to be discussed.

27. Tim Whitmarsh, *Beyond the Second Sophistic: Adventures in Greek Postclassicism* (Berkeley: University of California Press, 2013), 21.

28. Cf. Robyn Faith Walsh, "*Argumentum ad lunam*: Pauline Discourse, 'Double Death,' and Competition on the Moon," *HTR*, forthcoming.

29. Whitmarsh, *Beyond the Second Sophistic*, 23. To clarify, Whitmarsh does not discuss extraterrestrial examples; that is my addition.

30. Whitmarsh, *Beyond the Second Sophistic*, 20.

nographic tradition.[31] Common to these variances in the presentation of *thaumata* are elements of spectacle; whether presented as a positive, unusual, or even troubling phenomenon, the *thauma* "strongly underlines the visual aspect of a thing."[32] Because the plausibility of a *thauma* is belied by relative circumstance and inaccessibility, the key to making it believable is either an incredibly detailed description of the subject or object or claims of eyewitness testimony.

Take, for example, Artemisia in Herodotus's *Histories*, who appears as a capstone to a comprehensive index of leaders and warriors as a "special wonder" (*malista thōma*; *Hist.* 7.99). Artemisia's position and the relative detail Herodotus provides about her "youthful willingness and manliness" (*neēnieō hypo lēmatos te kai andrēiēs*) to forge into battle is paradoxical precisely because she is a woman (*gynaikos*; 7.99). The marvel of this juxtaposition—a woman *and* a warrior—makes her story an ideal culmination for Herodotus's chronicles: "She is at the end of the list precisely because she is paradoxical; *seeing is believing*."[33]

Camilla cuts a similar figure in Vergil. A paradoxical or transgressive character as *bellatrix*, she emerges for the first time as the last in a catalogue of leaders allied in battle against Aeneas and the Trojans (*Aen.* 7.803–817).[34] Her subsequent appearances establish her as a woman who has eschewed femininity and feminine pursuits in favor of a decidedly masculine and martial existence. From her bold eagerness to march into battle (11.502–506), to her nearly blinding pursuit of spoils (11.778–784), she is likened to a hawk (*accipiter*) pursuing a dove "high in the clouds" (*sublimem in nube columbam*), holding it in its grasp and ruthlessly gutting it "with its hooked talons" (*eviscerat uncis*; 11.720–724). She is a creature of war, blooded and unaccustomed to the "baskets of Minerva" (*calathisve Minervae*; 7.805–807). James R. Townshend goes so far as to suggest that Vergil's Camilla as *thauma* embodies the poet's aesthetic interest in the grotesque.[35] In detailed vignettes on his *aspera virgo*, Vergil "treats [Camilla] as an aesthetic object by dramatizing audience reactions to her," thus, illustrating "the aesthetic response he expects his creation to generate"—namely, astonishment at her status as both man and woman, human and animal.[36]

31. Barbara Boyd, "Virgil's Camilla and the Traditions of Catalogue and Ecphrasis (Aeneid 7.803–17)," *AJP* 113.2 (1992): 222.

32. Boyd, "Virgil's Camilla," 222 n. 28.

33. Boyd, "Virgil's Camilla," 222, my emphasis.

34. Cf. on Camilla as interpolation, James R. Townshend, "Camilla and Virgil's Aesthetic of the Grotesque" (paper presented at the Antiquities Interdisciplinary Research Group at the University of Miami, 2020), 4–5.

35. Townshend, "Aesthetic of the Grotesque," 1–23.

36. Camilla is also described as being weaned by a wild mare in *Aen.* 11.570–572; Townshend, "Aesthetic of the Grotesque," 2.

Vergil is curiously explicit in his descriptions of Camilla's effect on those who view her—her eyewitnesses. Perhaps most pertinent to her role as *thauma* is *Aen.* 7.812–817:

> *illam omnis tectis agrisque effusa iuventus*
> *turbaque miratur matrum et prospectat euntem*
> *attonitis inhians animis, ut regius ostro*
> *velet honos levis umeros, ut fibula crinem*
> *auro internectat, Lyciam ut gerat ipsa pharetram*
> *et pastoralem praefixa cuspide myrtum.*

At her all the youth who have poured out of the houses and fields and the crowd of mothers marvel, and they watch her as she goes, mouths agape, minds astonished, how a royal ornament covers her smooth shoulders with purple, how a pin binds up her hair with gold, so that she herself carries a Lycian quiver and a shepherd's myrtle staff with a spear point fixed to the end.[37]

Camilla's appearance so transfixes those who see her that they are rendered "astonished," even dumbfounded. Elsewhere, she instills fear or terror (*territus*; 11.699–700) in those who witness her "frightful" appearance (*oculos horrenda in virgine fixus*; 11.507). Fear and bewilderment also characterize her death at the hands of Arruns; Arruns slays the warrior queen and finds himself fleeing "in confusion" (*turbidus*) like a predator that has overstepped its bounds (11.815). In each one of her appearances, Camilla's paradoxical nature and actions generate reactions from her onlookers in kind: amazement, wonder, fear, confusion.

These specific reactions are also echoed throughout Mark. Take the introductory account of Jesus's arrival in Capernaum (1:21–28): Jesus enters the synagogue and teaches with such power and influence (*exousian*) that the people in attendance are rendered astonished (*exeplēssonto*; 1:22). He proceeds to reprimand an unclean *pneuma* in their midst and, once again, the witnesses are described as "amazed" (*ethambēthēsan*) and are left questioning amongst themselves: "What is this (*Ti estin touto*)? . . . he commands the unclean spirits, and they obey him!" (*kai tois pneumasi tois akathartois epitassei, kai hypakouousin autō*; 1:27).[38] Thus, from the onset of the gospel, Jesus is established as an otherworldly figure—a "wonder"—and a puzzling rival to the local *grammatici* (*grammateis*; 1:22) and other

---

37. My translation is indebted to Townshend, with modifications.
38. Chris Keith also discusses the reception of Jesus in the Galilean synagogue in Mark and Jesus's "astounded" witnesses in Chris Keith, *Jesus' Literacy: Scribal Cultural and the Teacher from Galilee*, LNTS 413 (London: T&T Clark, 2011), esp. 124–34.

authorities. Mark is also able to achieve all of this through the "amazement" of his literary eyewitnesses who act as an avatar for the reader— indicating the proper response to these seemingly unusual events.

Returning to Camilla, incorporating an explicit audience or viewer into his text accomplishes twin goals for Vergil. First, it establishes Camilla as an object of epic fascination; as Boyd states, "Virgil is especially fond of incorporating a viewer or viewers into his visual narratives in order to emphasize that what he is describing is something meant to be understood in pictorial terms."[39] In other words, Vergil's graphic description of Camilla offers ample opportunity for what others have called "decorative writing" or the kind of embellished and descriptive writing characteristic of ekphrasis.[40] The detail provided of what it was like to see Camilla in the flesh is akin to what one would expect of a writer describing a fresco or a frieze. This is why Townshend can reliably link Camilla to the aesthetic tradition in Vergil: "for the external audience (i.e., the reader) . . . Camilla does not *appear* to be an artistic creation: that is precisely what she is."[41] Like Mark, Vergil is not content merely describing Camilla; he uses his embedded literary witnesses to illustrate the proper response to his *thauma* to the reader.

Second, her paradoxical nature as a woman warrior, easily capable of transfixing crowds or instilling wonder, fear, or confusion, renders her a "great marvel"—a *mega thauma*—and one for whom only a vivid description will suffice.[42] Without a detailed account, supported by the presence of reputed eyewitnesses, her very existence stretches credulity. If "seeing is believing," then the embedded or internal witness also offers a healthy measure of "you don't have to take *my* word for it."

The aforementioned Phlegon engages in a similar strategy by repeatedly invoking his sources, not out of a sense of fair attribution but out of necessity; what he presents to his reader is often so paradoxical, farfetched, or absurd that confirmation must be established from "outside" his narrative. Take, for example, his description of a hippocentaur found in Saune:[43]

τὸν δὲ ἱπποκένταυρον συλλαβὼν ὁ βασιλεὺς ζωὸν ἀποπέμπει σὺν ἑτέροις δώροις πρὸς Καίσαρα εἰς τὴν Αἴγυπτον . . . οὐ φέρων δὲ τὴν μεταβολὴν τοῦ ἀέρος τελευτᾷ, καὶ οὕτως ὁ ἔπαρχος τῆς Αἰγύπτου ταριχεύσας ἀπέστειλεν εἰς Ῥώμην . . .

39. Boyd, "Virgil's Camilla," 223.

40. Boyd, "Virgil's Camilla," 223, quoting R. D. Williams, "The Function and Structure of Virgil's Catalogue in *Aeneid* 7," *ClQ* 11 (1961): 149.

41. Townshend, "Aesthetic of the Grotesque," 17.

42. Boyd, "Virgil's Camilla," 223.

43. For the following block quotations from Phlegon and their interpretation, the Greek has been used rather than transliteration for purposes of comparison and ease.

Ἐν δὲ τῇ . . . πόλει Σαύῃ ἐλέγοντο καὶ ἕτεροι εἶναι ἱπποκένταυροι. τὸν δὲ πεμφθέντα εἰς Ῥώμην εἴ τις ἀπιστεῖ, δύναται ἱστορῆσαι· ἀπόκειται γὰρ ἐν τοῖς ὁρίοις τοῦ αὐτοκράτορος τεταριχευμένος, ὡς προεῖπον.

The king captured the hippocentaur [alive] and sent it, with other gifts, to Caesarea and Egypt . . . it did not tolerate the change of air, and died, so that the prefect of Egypt embalmed it and sent it to Rome . . .

There were also said to have been other hippocentaurs in the . . . city of Saune. So far as concerns the one sent to Rome, anyone who is skeptical can examine it for himself, since as I said above it has been embalmed and is kept in the [emperor's storehouse]. (*Mir.* 34.2–35.1)

Phlegon invokes the emperor's storehouse in a fine example of rhetorical gaslighting; what are the odds that the reader has the means or access to accept his challenge and confirm his claims? His challenge also serves as an authorizing strategy; if his designation as a freedman of Hadrian is correct, he communicates to the reader the unique nature of his access. Thus, both author and reader engage in a conceit that allows Phlegon to call the reader's bluff.

In addition to eyewitness framing, Phlegon turns to citing political figures as a rhetorical means of marking time and place:

Ἐγένετο σημεῖον παράδοξον ἐπὶ Ῥώμης, ἄρξοντος Ἀθήνησιν Δεινοφίλου, ὑπατευόντων ἐν Ῥώμῃ Κοΐντου Οὐηρανίου καὶ Γαΐου Πομπηΐου Γάλλου· Ῥαικίου γὰρ Ταύρου, ἀνδρὸς στρατηγικοῦ, τῆς γυναικὸς θεράπαινα τῶν τετιμημένων ἀπεκύησε πίθηκον.

Κορνηλίου Γαλλικανοῦ ἡ γυνὴ παιδίον ἔτεκεν κεφαλὴν ἔχον Ἀνούβιδος ἐπὶ Ῥώμης, ἄρξοντος Ἀθήνησιν Δημοστράτου, ὑπατευόντων ἐν Ῥώμῃ Αὔλου Λικιννίου Νερούα Σιλιανοῦ καὶ Μάρκου Οὐεστίνου Ἀττικοῦ.

An extraordinary omen occurred in Rome when the archon at Athens was Deinophilos and the consuls in Rome were Quintus Veranius and Gaius Pompeius Gallus. An honored enslaved woman belonging to the wife of Raecius Taurus, a man of praetorian rank, birthed a monkey.

The wife of Cornelius Gallicanus gave birth near Rome to a child having the head of Anubis, when the archon at Athens was Demostratos and the consuls in Rome were Aulus Licinius Nerva Silianus and Marcus Vestinus Atticus. (*Mir.* 22–23)

The gospels illustrate the persistence of this paradoxographical feature across imperial writing. The Gospel of Luke, for instance, uses a similar framing. Luke invokes the rule of both Augustus and the Syrian governor Quirinius in his infancy narrative in order to establish the believability of a heavily pregnant maiden traveling over one hundred and fifty kilometers on the back of a lumbering animal to give birth to the predicted messiah in an animal pen:

> It happened in those days [*egeneto de en tais hēmerais*] that a decree went out from Emperor Augustus that all the world should be registered [*apographesthai pasan tēn oikoumenēn*]. This was the first registration when Quirinius was governor [*hēgemoneuontos*] of Syria. (Luke 2:1–2)

Indeed, it is useful to pause here to consider also the kinship between timetelling in paradoxographical and gospel literature in order to reinforce the multiple points of contact within this class of literature beyond the use of a thaumatic structure. And as with the presentation of Jesus as a literary *thauma*, references to time in Luke have often been explained via anachronistic logic when, as best as we can tell, Luke's references to political leaders are hopelessly flawed. While some have attempted to resolve these errors by revisiting the imperial calendar in Luke's favor or by suggesting he intended to name a different Syrian leader, these efforts smack of special pleading.[44] More commonly, but not at all unrelatedly, scholars view Luke's claims in theological terms. In such formulations, naming Augustus and Quirinius is linked to the gospel writer's implicit Christology; Jesus represents a heavenly ruler come to supplant earthly rulers. In his Hermeneia commentary, for instance, François Bovon suggests that the passage reflects Luke's general "affinity for dates" and that the specific references to those in power "alludes to the historicity of salvation, but also has a polemical point: the 'political theology' of Augustus, supported particularly in the East by the religious worship of the ruler, is unmasked and invalidated by the Christological claim."[45] Others have suggested that Luke is earmarking "sacred events in secular time."[46] Yet these analyses fail to account adequately for the writer's intention, knowledge, or training. This is to say, these theories may reliably represent later theological understandings of Luke's use of political references, but, given Luke's knowledge of imperial writing habits and conventions, it is quite likely he is simply telling time in a fashion

44. Sabine R. Huebner, *Papyri and the Social World of the New Testament* (Cambridge: Cambridge University Press, 2019), 34–36, gives a history of interpretation of this motif since the sixteenth century.

45. François Bovon, *Luke 1: A Commentary on the Gospel of Luke 1:1–9:50*, Hermeneia (Minneapolis: Fortress, 2002), 83.

46. Paula Fredriksen, *From Jesus to Christ: The Origins of the New Testament Images of Jesus*, 2nd ed. (New Haven: Yale University Press, 2000), 31.

common to the era that also strategically engages in a tool of the confirming or "convincing" trade.[47]

In literary context, both Luke and Phlegon deploy their timekeeping in a manner that simultaneously anticipates and quells doubt; the claims they are making are so extraordinary, they strategically ground those claims in the (seemingly) concrete. They call upon the reader's faith that what they are about to reveal is at least plausible (*eikos*), even though it stretches credulity.[48] This approach is emblematic of the thaumatic paradigm. Given our contemporary familiarity with the Jesus story, it is useful to reiterate that the gospel writers are presenting their readers with a series of stories about a prophetically predicted, pneumatically endowed, wonderworking son of the high god of the ethnic Judeans who is routinely—and in Mark, mysteriously—performing remarkable acts. Even for the Son of Man, animating two thousand pigs with an unclean polymorphous legion and compelling them into a suicidal swan dive is extraordinary (Mark 5:1–20). Such strategies for presenting literary *thaumata* are, therefore, critical for these writers, regardless of whether their intentions are to convince or simply entertain.

Thus, in the Gospel of Mark we see an even more pronounced engagement with *thauma*-writing as Jesus elicits the same reactions from eyewitnesses in the text as Vergil's Camilla: wonder, fear, confusion. Again, this didactic writing style performs on two registers: the eyewitnesses validate the text's claims, and their actions and reactions illustrate for the reader both the significance of the wonders being described and the proper response to those wonders. Mark adds to his thaumatic construction the element of faith (*pistis*) as a precondition or consequence of Jesus's actions; however, faith is not unprecedented among paradoxographical authors.[49]

MARK'S WONDERWORKER

One need not be a particularly taxonomic observer to recognize that the Gospel of Mark presents numerous moments of "wonder." There are over twenty instances throughout the gospel in which Jesus elicits wonder, amazement, confusion, fear, or bewilderment among those he encounters with Mark using either *thauma* or its

47. For more on the use of references to political leaders as a strategy to mark time, see Walsh, *Popularizing Jesus*.

48. Note that *eikon* is the same term used by Pausanias in his description of Lycaean Zeus in the discussion of *Descr.* 8.2.7 above.

49. For more on the relationship between faith and *thauma* among other ancient Mediterranean authors: Walsh, *Popularizing Jesus*.

cognates.[50] Beyond Mark 1:22–27, I will bring forward three additional examples in order to demonstrate Mark's persistent use of this literary paradigm. Again, these exempla are by no means exhaustive but should suffice to locate Mark as a writer interested in portraying Jesus as a *thauma* embodying themes of paradox and ekphrasis akin to what is found in Vergil, Phlegon, and others. While Jesus's physical appearance remains largely unremarkable in the text—likely a literary strategy in itself[51]—paradox is communicated by other means and the same principles of literary witness obtain. Those who observe Jesus's comings and goings are mesmerized by his abilities and their reactions are didactic for the reader. Moreover, Jesus's actions—including his teachings—communicate that there is some "divine being at work" in Mark's Gospel as the bewildered supporting characters marvel at Jesus and dizzyingly muse over how he accomplishes his many feats.[52]

Following Jesus's first appearance in Mark's Gospel and the subsequent confusion and wonder this engenders (e.g., *ethambēthēsan*; 1:27), Jesus returns to his *pied-à-terre* in Capernaum and draws an inquisitive mob. They bring a paralyzed man to the scene and, when they are unable to enter at the door, they gain access through the roof (2:4). Jesus, "seeing their faith" (*idōn . . . tēn pistin autōn*; 2:5), while simultaneously perceiving "in his *pneuma*" (*tō pneumati autou*; 2:8) that some local *grammatici* (*tōn grammateōn*; 2:6) are questioning him, elects to reward the faithful and rebuke his doubters by healing the man (2:9–12). As he rises from his floor mat and heads for the door, everyone (*pantas*) is "astonished" (*existasthai*) and, praising God, exclaim "We've never seen anything like that before!" (*hoti houtōs oudepote eidomen*; 2:12). As with Camilla, the astonishment of the crowd is not resolved before the vignette closes; throughout the gospel one marvel is proceeded by another with the onlookers variously astounded or bewildered and left questioning—and sometimes fearing or resenting—what they have just seen and heard.

50. Cf. Mark 1:22, 27; 2:12; 3:21; 5:15, 20, 33, 42; 6:2, 51; 7:37; 9:6, 15, 32; 10:24, 26, 32; 11:18; 14:33; 16:8. Among the cognate terms are forms of *thambeō, histēmi, ekstasis, ekplēssō*.

51. Walsh, *Origins of Christian Literature*, 170–94; Joan E. Taylor, *What Did Jesus Look Like?* (London: Bloomsbury, 2018).

52. Notably, *thaumata* pertain to a wide range of phenomena: features of either the natural or built environment; art; technical achievements; and biological, physiological, zoological, or meteorological ephemera. They could also reference human disposition or action, for which the usual dichotomy of virtue and vice obtained: heroism or cowardice, wisdom or stupidity, and so forth. Included within this range were characters who "focalized" *thaumata* by "[provoking] wonder because of their behaviour or by uttering unexpected words . . . narrated in a way which suggests that they are an example of some divine being at work." See Priestley, *Herodotus and Hellenistic Culture*, 55–56.

Entering Gerasene territory, Jesus next encounters the "demoniac" (*daimoni-zomenon*)—a man possessed with "unclean *pneuma*" (*pneumati akahartō*; 5:2) calling themselves "Legion" (5:10). Legion asks Jesus to cast them out of the man and into "a great heard of feeding swine" (*agelē choirōn megalē boskomenē*; 5:11). Jesus obliges. The possessed swine hurdle down a precipice and into the sea and drown (5:13). The herdsmen (*boskontes*) "fled and told [what happened] in the city and the fields" (*ephygon kai apēngeilan eis tēn polin kai eis tous agrous*; 5:14), drawing a huge crowd back to Jesus. Seeing the demoniac "sitting, having been clothed and in his right mind" (*kathēmenon himatismenon kai sōphronounta*; 5:15) frightens the group (*ephobēthēsan*; 5:15) to the point that Jesus is asked to leave. The now-former demoniac attempts to join Jesus on his forward journey, but Jesus instructs him to return to Decapolis to tell his story. The episode tersely concludes with the phrase: "and all marveled" (*kai pantes ethaumazon*; 5:20)—using the direct terminology of *thauma*.

After the demoniac incident, Jesus crosses the sea and is asked to heal the daughter of one of the synagogue leaders, Jairus. He is pressed upon by a large crowd as he walks to Jairus's home and passively heals a woman suffering from hemorrhages (*gynē ousa en rhysei haimatos dōdeka etē*; 5:25) who grabs his cloak; Mark describes a "power" (*dynamin*; 5:30) emanating out of Jesus at the moment the woman touches his garment without any deliberate action on his part. When he arrives at the daughter's bedside she has already died; Jesus insists she is merely sleeping, a claim so seemingly preposterous that everyone begins to jeer (*kate-gelōn*; 5:40). Jesus takes the girl's hand and commands her to rise (*talitha koum*) and she begins to walk around (5:41). Everyone is immediately struck with "great amazement" (*exestēsan . . . megalē*) to such an extent that they nearly go out of their minds (*ekstasei*; 5:42).[53] In this case, the transparent apposition of life and death, and of Jesus being derided only to then be proven correct, represents pre-cisely the kind of paradox one might expect as a prelude to a "great marvel" in this kind of literature.

Jesus then heads back to Nazareth to teach (*didaskein*) in the synagogue, which astonishes those who hear him (*akouontes exeplēssonto*; 6:2). As was the case ear-

---

53. Mark uses a cognate accusative in this line to indicate the depth of the impact of this "marvel" on the attendees, which generates a certain repetitiveness. There is also a seemingly superfluous detail given about the girl's age that is a bit jarring to the modern reader. On the whole, the Greek is less transparent than traditional English translations would lead one to believe. A more literal translation would be something like: "And immediately the young girl stood up and walked around; for she was twelve years old. And they were amazed with great amazement" (5:42). I interpret *ekstasei* as a kind of bewilderment above in order to capture what I imagine may have been the function of the repetition of terms.

lier in the gospel, these observers begin questioning the paradoxographical nature of Jesus among themselves, ultimately taking offense at the juxtaposition of his power and wisdom given their familiarity with his background and family. After being rebuked, Jesus himself is "amazed" (*ethaumazen*)—again, *thauma*—by their disbelief or lack of faith (*apistian*; 6:6), a mutuality characteristic of dialogues for which wonder and paradox are key.

Astonishment strikes again later in the same chapter when Jesus, casually "walking on the sea" (*thalassēs peripatounta*; 6:49) during a windstorm, encounters the disciples on an imperiled boat. "Terrified" by this sight and thinking Jesus a ghost (*phantasma*), the disciples start screaming until Jesus instructs them to "pull yourselves together . . . do not be afraid" (*tharseite . . . mē phobeisthe*; 6:50). Once aboard, the winds calm, and the disciples are "very much exceedingly astounded" (*lian ek perissou . . . existanto*; 6:51). Jesus continues with them on their journey to Gennesaret ,where he is bombarded once more by throngs and continues to teach and perform healings, yet specifically withholds his *sēmeia* or "signs" from the Pharisees (8:11–13). Throughout the narrative the crowds are both awestruck (e.g., *exethambēthēsan*; 9:15) and questioning (e.g., "they were exceedingly astonished" [*perissōs exeplēssonto legontes pros heautous*]; 10:26).

Mark peppers these encounters with Herodotean-like "facts" about the Jewish sects (e.g., "For the Pharisees, and all the Jews, do not eat unless they thoroughly wash their hands," 7:3) and the territories Jesus visits in this eastern edge of the Roman Empire, with names and places frequently detailed (e.g., the Jordan River, Nazareth, the Sea of Galilee, Capernaum, Perea, Gennesaret, Gerasene, Decapolis, Bethsaida, Caesarea Philippi, Jerusalem, and so forth). Again, each of these episodes correspond structurally and thematically to the accounts of wonder found elsewhere in imperial literature, invoking the same motifs and framing found in writers like Herodotus, Phlegon, and Vergil.

CONCLUSION

This chapter has identified a set of literary tropes in the Gospel of Mark that were previously—and idiosyncratically—associated with both the historical Jesus and the gospel historicity paradigm. By dismantling these assumptions and demonstrating an alternative approach, I have illustrated how concepts like "city and country" functioned as a strategic choice for a writer like Mark, aimed at showcasing his relative skill and engagement with the literature of the age. Beyond this, allow me to add the following observations.

First, although obviously writing in the second century and, therefore, unmoored from the traditional dating of the gospels, Pausanias's negotiations throughout and descriptions of Greece stand out as a compelling corollary to accounts of Jesus. Both the Jesus of the gospels (as formulated by the gospel authors) and Pausanias as narrator present their homelands as "a place of sights [*idoi*] and wonders [*thaumatos*]." Both are "aimed at Greek readers."[54] Both present from the periphery of empire the local places, people, customs of a homeland that essentially resembles an ethnographic project.

Lydia Langerwerf describes Pausanias as a visitor to the "centre of his own world. Yet, through his evocation of the mythical and classical past, he is also traveling to a past no longer there."[55] I believe this observation has multiple applications to the gospels, not the least of which is imagining a Judea—and a Jerusalem temple—still standing in an era in which they had fallen.[56]

Second, I am influenced by Meghan Henning's contribution to this volume and the specific role of healing narratives in the gospels as part of the larger literary strategy I have attempted to identify. That is, in terms of imperial book culture, the notion of the book itself as *miracula*—as part of a larger wonder culture of the empire—impresses as another means of approaching writings like the gospels. Alexia Petsalis-Diomidis, for example, in her book *Truly beyond Wonders*, argues that "the treatment of books as valuable objects, even on occasion as *miracula*, to be collected, admired, and displayed parallels the viewing of bodies as *miracula*, and their collection in [spaces like] the Asklepieion."[57]

I suggest that paradoxography and the gospels share these features: presenting bodies, displaying them in the text, marveling at them, healing them, crucifying them, and resurrecting them. And the further away one gets from the "city"—from Rome—the more wondrous these miracles can be.

54. Langerwerf, "Wonders in Greece," 307.

55. Langerwerf, "Wonders in Greece," 311.

56. William Arnal, "The Gospel of Mark as Reflection on Exile and Identity," in *Introducing Religion: Essays in Honor of Jonathan Z. Smith*, ed. Willi Braun and Russell T. McCutcheon (London: Equinox, 2008), 57–67.

57. Alexia Petsalis-Diomidis, *Truly beyond Wonders: Aelius Aristides and the Cult of Asklepios* (Oxford: Oxford University Press, 2010), 219.

21

GALILEE AND JERUSALEM

Tucker S. Ferda

The Next Quest for the historical Jesus must account for the connection between the Galilean provenance of Jesus and the messianic movement that set up shop in Jerusalem only shortly after his death and believed that the restoration of Israel and Zion was underway. How did we get from here to there?

Discussion of "Galilee and Jerusalem" in Jesus research intersects with fundamental considerations of class, the economics of Palestine, and other sociopolitical realities. But given that other essays in this volume are devoted to these topics, my focus will be on two other matters that must remain important in the Next Quest for the historical Jesus. The first is the question of the relative chronology of Jesus's activity and its contours (namely, where he was, and for how long), and the second is the motive for Jesus's final journey to Jerusalem at the end of his life. Concerning the latter, it was Albert Schweitzer who noted that one can divide the old lives of Jesus in two based upon how they answer the question of why Jesus went up to Jerusalem for that final Passover: to work or to die.[1] The comment is as incisive now as it was then, even if we have for good reason abandoned any attempt to write a "biography" of Jesus. Moreover, in my estimation the much-needed advancement of systematic analysis and social history in Jesus research should not be pitted against an effort to reconstruct the general aims of Jesus, as

---

1. Albert Schweitzer, *The Quest of the Historical Jesus: A Critical Study of Its Progress from Reimarus to Wrede*, trans. William Montgomery (New York: Macmillan, 1950), 388–92.

though these angles of inquiry were somehow in tension with one another. Annette Merz memorably remarked in a 2015 SBL panel on "The Future for Historical Jesus Studies" that historical Jesus research must continue if for no other reason than Jesus remains a rare case from the ancient Mediterranean world in which historians might elevate the voice of one silenced by the military might of Rome and otherwise ignored by its elite storytellers.[2] There must be a place in the Next Quest for historians to attend to the agency of Jesus in the history he tried to make yet could not make as he pleased, operating as he was under circumstances that were not self-selected but existed already.[3]

I will focus first on the chronology and contours of Jesus's activity and then turn to look at the transition to the fateful last week with Schweitzer's maxim in mind.

CONTOURS AND CHRONOLOGY

It is probably only those who doubt that Jesus was a historical figure who would dispute that Jesus was from Nazareth of Galilee and that he died in Jerusalem on a Roman cross. But saying much about the events occurring between Nazareth and Jerusalem is challenging for the simple reason that the four sources that might be helpful for this task do not agree on the contours and chronology of the activity of Jesus.[4] I summarize the main claims of the Synoptics and John as follows in roughly chronological order, none of which should be particularly controversial:

- In Mark, Jesus comes "from Nazareth of Galilee" to the Judean wilderness and the Jordan for baptism (1:4–13), and then returns to the Galilee after John's arrest (1:14). The remainder of Mark's Gospel is a clear tale about two places: a Galilean ministry (beginning at 1:15) and its conclusion in Jerusalem during the Passover (beginning at 11:1). Moreover, this arrangement is significant for

2. Annette Merz, Respondent for "The Future for Historical Jesus Studies" (paper presented at the Annual Meeting of the Society of Biblical Literature, Atlanta, GA, November 23, 2015).

3. With allusions here of course to Karl Marx and Friedrich Engels, "The 18th Brumaire of Louis Bonaparte," in *The Marx-Engels Reader*, ed. Robert C. Tucker (New York: Norton, 1978), 595.

4. The Gospel of Thomas is likely dependent on the Synoptic Gospels and has denarrativized the tradition. Cf. Simon Gathercole, *The Gospel of Thomas: Introduction and Commentary*, TENTS 11 (Leiden: Brill, 2014). In the final form of Q there are some narrative elements and place names, but not enough to be of much help. The insightful study by Stephen Hultgren, *Narrative Elements in the Double Tradition: A Study of Their Place within the Framework of the Gospel Narrative*, BZNW 113 (Berlin: de Gruyter, 2002), ultimately goes beyond the evidence.

the plot development and narrative tension of Mark's story of Jesus as a whole: Mark "begins" (cf. *ērxato didaskein* at 8:31) to anticipate Jerusalem and Jesus's death very clearly after Peter's confession at 8:27–9:1, an episode which essentially divides the narrative in half.

- The Gospel of Matthew assumes and expands on the Markan skeleton. Matthew makes two significant changes to the Galilean material: adding a great deal of teaching material in blocks, and moving individual Markan episodes around. Both changes, however, do little to affect the main contours of the public activity of Jesus, which still has this exclusively Galilean ministry occurring before its climax in Jerusalem. Peter's confession maintains the pivotal location in this transition (16:13–27). Matthew follows Mark's order of events in Jerusalem fairly closely, mostly adding additional material at the appropriate Markan location.

- The Gospel of Luke assumes and expands on the Markan skeleton as well, but in a different way than Matthew does. Luke follows the sequence of episodes in Mark more closely than Matthew, while also adding to the Markan scheme material received from elsewhere. The most notable divergence is that in Luke the final journey to Jerusalem is vastly longer—almost ten modern chapters (9:51–19:28) as opposed to Mark's three—while the relative sequence in the larger movement is the same. In Luke, Peter's confession, while present, loses its transitional significance (9:18–27), and this prize goes to Jesus now sending his own followers before him on their mission (so the context of 9:51's "he set his face to go to Jerusalem"; note also the sending of the seventy in Luke 10). Luke also follows Mark's order of events in Jerusalem fairly closely, mostly adding additional material.

- The Gospel of John has Jesus (1) working contemporaneously to John the Baptist in Judea and Jerusalem before his arrest (see esp. 3:22–24), including his controversial temple action (2:13–25); and (2) spending most of his time in Judea and Jerusalem. This latter point needs to be stressed: Jesus spends almost as much time around the Jordan in the Fourth Gospel as in the Galilee, and if John 6 was not original to John (which I think is probable), the Galilean activity is reduced to almost nothing.[5] The narrative marks external time explicitly by

5. The only Galilean scenes include 2:1–13; 4:43–54; 6:1–7:9. After 7:9, Jesus is never said to be in Galilee again. Concerning the question of the originality of John 6, I make three points: (1) there is a nonsensical transition from 5:47 to 6:1 ("after this Jesus went to the other side of the sea of Galilee" [he was in Jerusalem in 5:47]), which is very different than the clear and logical narrative sequencing up to this point (cf. 1:29, 43; 2:1, 13; 3:22; 4:3, 43; 5:1). Cf. Raymond Brown, *The Gospel according to John*, AB 29–29A (Garden City, NY: Doubleday, 1966), 1:235–50. (2) John 6 contains the most abundant links to Synoptic Galilean tradition in the Fourth Gos-

making note of several pilgrimage festivals and having Jesus "go up" to Jerusalem multiple times (cf. 2:13; 5:1; 7:10; 10:22 [here not from Galilee]), but lacks any rising tension in Galilee or anticipation of a climactic arrival to Jerusalem.

Without mitigating the differences among the Synoptics themselves, it is clear that the most substantial variations emerge between John and the Synoptics. This famous dilemma has bearing on the length of Jesus's activity as well, as the Synoptic presentation could well occur within one year's time (though not necessarily so) while John's account requires at least two full years to run its course.[6] There was already discussion about this in the early church.[7] The highly debated question of John's knowledge of one or more of the Synoptics has some bearing on this question, but not a determinative one: even if John's Gospel was aware of or dependent on the Synoptics, the longer runtime and more frequent trips to Jerusalem could still stem from tradition.[8]

I am equally skeptical of two different paths forward: that we must choose between either John or the Synoptics, or that the Johannine and Synoptic presentations can be neatly harmonized in such a way that all the pieces fit together. The problem with both routes is twofold. First, they fail to acknowledge adequately the theological nature of all these accounts. That is, this is not a decision between

---

pel (in particular, feeding the multitude, walking on the water, teaching in "the synagogue in Capernaum," and the confession of messiahship by his closest followers). (3) The ending of the bread of life discourse, particularly in its emphasis on the "flesh" of Jesus and many disciples of Jesus "going away" (6:60–67), contains potentially striking parallels to developments in the Johannine community as evident in the Johannine Letters (cf. esp. 1 John 2:18–19; 4:1–6; 2 John 7–10). We can only speculate on how to put all this together, but here is my guess: Chapter 6 was added to the Fourth Gospel at a later point in light of and in response to later challenges and splintering in the Johannine community and in knowledge of the Synoptic tradition about Jesus in Galilee, supplementing a potential deficiency of the Fourth Gospel in this respect. This, of course, says nothing about the provenance of these materials. For additional discussion, see Jean Zumstein, *Das Johannesevangelium* (Göttingen: Vandenhoeck & Ruprecht, 2016), 240–82.

6. For good overviews, see John P. Meier, *The Roots of the Problem and the Person*, vol. 1 of *A Marginal Jew: Rethinking the Historical Jesus*, AYBRL (New York: Doubleday, 1991), 403–9; Gerd Theissen and Annette Merz, *The Historical Jesus: A Comprehensive Guide*, trans. John Bowden (Minneapolis: Fortress, 1998), 162–84; D. Moody Smith, "Jesus Tradition in the Gospel of John," in *Handbook for the Study of the Historical Jesus*, ed. Tom Holmén and Stanley E. Porter (Leiden: Brill, 2011), 3:1997–2040.

7. Cf. Ps.-Clem. *Hom.* 17.19; Irenaeus, *Haer.* 2.22.1–3; Clement of Alexandria, *Strom.* 1.21; Origen, *Hom. Luc.* 32.5; *Princ.* 4.5.

8. The twentieth-century consensus about Johannine independence is no more; for evidence of a significant shift of opinion, see Eve-Marie Becker, Helen K. Bond, and Catrin H. Williams, eds., *John's Transformation of Mark* (London: T&T Clark, 2021).

an untheological chronology and a theologized one, but between two highly stylized story patterns that have literary advantages peculiar to each. John wants Jesus in Jerusalem as much as possible because it advances his temple Christology and allows Jesus to declare his superiority to the particular pilgrimage festival in question. At the same time, the forward-looking and anticipatory Galilean period in the Synoptics invests the death and resurrection of Jesus, viewed retrospectively, with additional theological significance. Redaction-critical studies of the Synoptics have also shown that "Galilee" and "Jerusalem" have become thematically loaded in such a way that they almost become characters in the story.[9] The landscape—particularly borderlands and territorial divisions—can theologically signify post-Easter realities, especially the nature of the gentile mission.[10]

In addition to theology, there is, secondly, the challenge of form. Richard Bauckham wrote in *Jesus and the Eyewitnesses*: "That the individual units of the Synoptic Gospels are close to the oral forms in which they previously existed and that in oral transmission they were not necessarily linked together as they are in the Gospels remain, in my opinion, the most significant insights of form criticism and have not been refuted."[11] He is right. If Mark had found in his source(s) a relatively fixed chronology of Jesus's activity, then Matthew and Luke's use of Mark is difficult to explain, for they have no qualms about disturbing precedent with their adaptations of the Markan framework. And this is to say nothing of John. The flexible reordering we find in our narrative sources suggests that such reorganizations were common in the transmission of the tradition from likely the very beginning, and so we are certainly unable in our position to re-sort what has already been re-sorted. Now the reality of creative reorganization does not mean that the written gospels were the first to tell stories about Jesus; it means only that there was not "one way" to rehearse his activity. Some of the early form critics were wrong in attributing so quickly the specification of place and geographical location to a later stage in the transmission of the tradition. Bultmann, for instance, who thought that the earliest sayings tradition was essentially contextless, often regarded place and location detail as entering the tradition only later, either due to a sudden interest in history (which did not characterize the earlier tradition,

9. Willi Marxsen, *Der Evangelist Markus: Studien zur Redaktions-geschichte des Evangeliums*, 2nd ed. (Göttingen: Vandenhoeck & Ruprecht, 1959).

10. As in Mark 5:1–20 and 7:24–8:10, especially. Matthew 4:12–17 connects Jesus's move to Galilee with Isa 9's "Galilee of the gentiles," and makes other significant changes elsewhere (e.g., 8:33–9:1: no proclamation in the Decapolis; 15:21–22: Jesus does not enter the region of Tyre and Sidon).

11. Richard Bauckham, *Jesus and the Eyewitnesses: The Gospels as Eyewitness Testimony*, 2nd ed. (Grand Rapids: Eerdmans, 2017), 243.

he thought), or the requirements of "developed storytelling" as in the case of "folk tales" and "fairy tales."[12] Moreover, he thought that often setting was inferred from the saying in question, for example, "that Jesus was rejected in Nazareth is a conclusion from the saying on which the scene was built."[13] The data not only fail to support such inferences, but they suggest, to the contrary, that place and location, when specified for certain episodes, were important enough that they shaped the ways in which those stories were received and transmitted by later tradents. It is striking in the Synoptic tradition that concrete items (in terms of place) tend to stay concrete in reception.[14] Vague things (e.g., "a mountain," "a village," "by the sea," and so on) tend to stay vague.[15] Moreover, any noticeable change makes concrete things more vague, not vague things more concrete (as might be expected when increasing numbers of gospel readers had never been to Palestine).[16] We certainly have the rearrangement of order and variation in details (some small and some big), but place is not something that seems to have been treated with complete freedom by the evangelists.[17] This must vindicate the contention of C. H.

12. See Rudolf Bultmann, *History of the Synoptic Tradition*, trans. John Marsh (Oxford: Blackwell, 1963), 63–69. I write "often" because he does admit that, in certain cases, it is "not impossible for the early tradition itself to have passed on this or the other apothegm complete with localization" (65). But this is, for him, an aberration.

13. Bultmann, *History of the Synoptic Tradition*, 64.

14. Cf. Mark 1:29–31 and parr.; Mark 1:32–34 and parr.; Mark 5:1–20 and parr.; Mark 5:21–43 and parr. (though Matthew specifies the Markan "Gerasenes" as "Gadarenes"); Mark 6:1–5 and parr.; Mark 7:24–30 // Matt 15:21–28; Mark 10:46–52 and parr.

15. Cf. Mark 1:40 and parr.; Mark 2:13 and parr.; Mark 2:23–28 and parr.; Mark 3:1–6 and parr.; Mark 3:13–19 and parr.; Mark 4:1 and parr.; Mark 6:6–7 and parr.; Mark 9:2–8 and parr.; Luke 7:18–35 and Matt 11:2–9; Matt 10:5–42 and Luke 10:2–12.

16. Cf. Mark 2:1 // Matt 9:1 // Luke 5:17; Mark 3:19 //Matt 9:32 // Luke 11:14–23; Mark 7:31–37 and Matt 15:29–31; Mark 8:27–30 // Matt 16:13–20 // Luke 9:18–22; Mark 9:30–32 // Matt 17:22–23 // Luke 9:43–48. Three interesting exceptions: (1) the feeding of the five thousand (compare 6:45 and Luke 9:10; but this could be correcting the record about Bethsaida); (2) Mark 8:10's Dalmanutha becomes Magadan in Matt 15:39 (also likely correcting the record or using a different name for the same place); (3) the anointing story that appears in all four gospels (Mark 14:3–9; Matt 26:6–13; John 12:1–8; Luke 7:36–50)—here we probably have the unique situation of two originally independent stories that were nevertheless similar enough in details that their lines got crossed in transmission. For discussion see Richard Bauckham, "The Bethany Family in John 11–12: History or Fiction?," in *Aspects of Historicity in the Fourth Gospel*, vol. 2 of *John, Jesus, and History*, ed. Paul N. Anderson, Felix Just, and Tom Thatcher (Atlanta: SBL Press, 2009), 185–202.

17. It is instructive to note that Matthew, while rearranging much of the order of Mark before Peter's confession, nevertheless uses the situation of Markan material as a guiding tool of the reorganization, gathering together in chapter 9, for instance, varied "Capernaum" material, and here even attaching a loose Capernaum tradition (8:5–13) (from Q 7:1–10, I believe; it maintains its Capernaum roots in John 4:46–54). Luke does the same, even though he has a marked ten-

Dodd that the kerygma had a storied form, for place is meaningless in the absence of story (which is why the Gospel of Thomas lacks both), and some of these memories must go back to the very beginning, perhaps even reports circulating during the time of Jesus himself.[18]

In any case, notwithstanding the significance of place in the tradition, the freedom of reorganization cannot be denied, and so I do not think we are in position given the nature of our sources to say with much confidence how frequently Jesus was in Jerusalem before that fateful Passover and how long he was operative.[19] It seems that the Synoptics give hints that Jesus had more contacts in and around Jerusalem than their narratives adequately explain, which might suggest that John's Jerusalem-frequenting Jesus was not a creation ex nihilo.[20] We might best "account for" *both* John and the Synoptics if we assume they are different "memory refractions" of the activity of Jesus that centered in the Galilee (a fact John seems to assume) but also involved Jerusalem, especially during the pilgrimage festivals when other Galileans would have made the trek.[21] Following

---

dency to loosen the temporal connection between Markan pericopae (e.g., 5:12; 17; 8:22), and it is evident that most of his audience would have no idea where these places were (hence the need to explain that Capernaum was "a city in Galilee" in 4:13 and so on; cf. 8:26; 9:10). While place is less frequently specified in Q (while far more geographically rooted than the Gospel of Thomas), those locations critics have deemed authentic to Q are preserved in transmission even if the order is not (cf. 3:3; 4:16; 7:1). It may even be that Luke moved up Mark 6's rejection at Nazareth to an earlier point precisely because Q had originally made some note about "Nazareth" (note the spelling *Nazara*) at the beginning of Jesus's public appearance, which Matthew would too attest but does something different with it (Matt 4:13). See here Hultgren, *Narrative Elements in the Double Tradition*, 128–90.

18. C. H. Dodd, "The Framework of the Gospel Narrative," *ExpT* 43 (1931–32): 396–400; Dodd, *The Apostolic Preaching and Its Developments* (New York: Harper & Row, 1962).

19. See Theissen and Merz, *Historical Jesus*, 168.

20. Meier, *Marginal Jew*, 1:403: "scattered details in the Synoptic Gospels imply what John makes explicit." Note Mary and Martha appear in John 11 and also in Luke 10:38–42, and Jesus obviously knew someone—maybe the same group—in Bethany, where he consistently lodged leading up to the Passover (cf. Mark 11:11; 14:3). Personal contacts in Jerusalem may also explain the "upper room" for his last meal with his disciples. See also James D. G. Dunn, *Jesus Remembered*, vol. 1 of *Christianity in the Making* (Grand Rapids: Eerdmans, 2005), 323–24; Brian D. Johnson, "The Jewish Feasts and Questions of Historicity in John 5–12," in Anderson et al., *Aspects of Historicity in the Fourth Gospel*, 117–30; Michael Allen Daise, "Jesus and the Jewish Festivals: Methodological Reflections," in *Jesus Research: New Methodologies and Perceptions*, ed. James H. Charlesworth (Grand Rapids: Eerdmans, 2007), 283–304.

21. Anthony Le Donne, *The Historiographical Jesus: Memory, Typology, and the Son of David* (Waco, TX: Baylor University Press, 2009), 13. On Galilean pilgrimage to Jerusalem, note Josephus, *BJ* 2.43; *AJ* 17.254. On John's presumed knowledge of Jesus's Galilean activity, see 2:12; 3:24 (on the arrest of John); 4:3 (note *apēlthen palin*); 4:43 (and use of traditional rejection saying);

John in this way does not mean we must follow John in what he has Jesus doing in Jerusalem, however, which is basically talking about himself for all to hear. Indeed, based on John's portrait one would have to imagine that Jesus of Nazareth was for some time a household name in Jerusalem, and this cannot be historical.

But all of this adds up to a fairly meager harvest, and that is a problem for Jesus research that deserves further attention. The "so what" of the length-of-activity question might not be as weighty as sometimes assumed, to be sure, since one year versus two or three years is relatively a short timespan either way, and in general the same kind of activity and public response is possible given the size of Palestine. But our inability to discern how active Jesus was in Jerusalem before that final Passover has bearing on the nature of Jesus's following, his perception by the Jerusalem authorities, and possibly even how we understand his death. One recalls Paula Fredriksen's argument that the Romans knew quite well that Jesus was not a political threat partly because he was in Jerusalem more frequently than the Synoptics imply.[22] A different scenario emerges, naturally, if the first anyone of authority had heard of him was when he entered Jerusalem on an ass during the Passover, the time "when sedition is most likely to break out" (Josephus, *B.J.* 1.88). These are crucial issues that each generation of scholars must assess and reassess anew.

UP TO JERUSALEM

Ulrich Luz once penned a fascinating article with his key research question as the title: Why did Jesus go up to Jerusalem? His interest was not how many times Jesus was in Jerusalem, but the motive for what turned out to be his last visit.[23] Luz gave the following answer to his question: as the nineteenth-century lives of Jesus had contended, Jesus's activity was characterized by "two contrasting epochs"—a time of success and a time of failure—and he went up to Jerusalem expecting to suffer the onset of the eschatological tribulation and lose his life "for many." It is an interesting reboot of Albert Schweitzer's thesis that Jesus went up to Jerusalem not to work but to die.

---

71. It is also interesting that John assumes a more positive reception of Jesus in Galilee than in Judea and Jerusalem (4:45).

22. Paula Fredriksen, *Jesus of Nazareth: King of the Jews* (New York: Vintage, 1999), 28–34, 218–25, 238–41; Fredriksen, "The Historical Jesus, the Scene in the Temple, and the Gospel of John," in *Critical Appraisals of Critical Views*, vol. 1 of *John, Jesus, and History*, ed. Paul N. Anderson, Felix Just, and Tom Thatcher (Atlanta: SBL Press, 2007), 268, 272–76.

23. Ulrich Luz, "Warum zog Jesus nach Jerusalem?," and "Der unbequeme Jesus: Nochmals: Warum zog Jesus nach Jerusalem?," in *Exegetische Aufsätze*, WUNT 357 (Tübingen: Mohr Siebeck, 2016), 115–32, 133–50.

Luz's thesis is provocative because Jesus research since the advent of form criticism has generally been averse to big-picture questions such as this concerning the activity of Jesus. The success of the form-critical project is perhaps most clearly seen in the way in which subsequent Jesus research has focused on the authentication of specific sayings, deeds, or even themes in the tradition without feeling the need to explain how these parts fit together into some larger whole.[24] But Luz's essay shows, even if this was not his intention, that we cannot help but answer this question, even if we fail to acknowledge that this is what we are doing. There is no "non answer" to this—even to say that Jesus went up simply to observe the Passover like everyone else and got caught up in things he never expected *is* to answer the question. Further suggestions might be:

- he went up to proclaim the kingdom (e.g., basically continue what he did in Galilee, just in a different location);
- or he went up expecting the kingdom he had proclaimed to arrive in full on that particular Passover;
- or he went up to predict the temple's imminent demise and reconstitute a new community around himself;
- or he went up to be installed as the rightful king and messiah of Israel by force if necessary;
- or he went up expecting to die a martyr's death for the sake of his message, like one of the prophets of old;
- or he went up to die for the sins of his followers, of Israel, or of the world;
- or he went up to force Jerusalem and his followers to make a decision concerning him and his message and was uncertain what the result would be.

Historians are caught in the position of William James's hiker: we all have to jump. The question is not if we decide to answer Luz's question, but how we weigh the relative probability of various answers. What historical scenario makes the best sense of the most data, while also explaining, or "accounting for" the claims and behaviors of his followers after him?

I obviously cannot do justice to this complex topic in an essay of this length, but hopefully framing the issue in this manner demonstrates its importance for

---

24. See Tucker S. Ferda, *Jesus, the Gospels, and the Galilean Crisis*, LNTS 601 (London: Bloomsbury T&T Clark, 2019), 144. This is not the same as "coherence" as in the "criterion of coherence," which, in application, seems to be about conceptual or ideological harmony in the teaching of Jesus. For discussion see Anthony Le Donne, "The Criterion of Coherence: Its Development, Inevitability, and Historiographical Limitations," in *Jesus, Criteria, and the Demise of Authenticity*, ed. Chris Keith and Anthony Le Donne (London: T&T Clark, 2012), 95–114.

whatever comes "next" in Jesus research. In what remains I offer a few tentative suggestions that I must leave more on the level of reasonable assertion than
detailed argument.[25]

The weakest part of Luz's argument, it seems to me, is the way he seeks to connect the final journey to Jerusalem with the demise of Jesus's efforts in the Galilee.[26]
As I have written about elsewhere, I do not think there is sufficient reason to believe
that Jesus's Galilean activity was marked by a notable "crisis" of rejection that resembles "the Galilean Storms" of Renan, Keim, and others, or the failure of Jesus's
own expectations (as in Schweitzer's reconstruction based loosely on Matt 10:23).[27]
There are traditions that only make sense, it is true, if we assume they function as
responses to rejection, but it is an over reading to take the Galilean woes (Q 10:13–16),
as a particularly crucial example, and infer from this denouncement of three Galilean villages that Jesus's larger work in the Galilee had been largely unsuccessful and
come to an end in a way that explains his departure for Jerusalem.[28]

By contrast, the strongest part of Luz's argument is his attempt to make sense
of Jesus's final trip to Jerusalem eschatologically. The suggestion that Jesus expected to suffer in the eschatological tribulation specifically is reasonable because
there are other indications in the tradition that Jesus thought of the messianic
woes or tribulation as nigh or already at hand.[29] It further seems reasonable to
take Jesus's last journey to Jerusalem as an intentionally climactic one, meaning
that, unlike Jesus' various travels to and fro in the Galilee that did not fundamentally alter the nature of his mission, it is hard to see things "going back to normal"
should this Passover have ended without Jesus on a Roman cross. The tradition
is rife with claims about instigative behavior on Jesus's part. Does Jesus simply
return to Galilee after this festival to resume his activity there?

I wonder if we might approach the question of why Jesus went up to Jerusalem
not by moving forward from Galilee to Jerusalem but back from the beliefs and

---

25. See also Jens Schröter, *Jesus of Nazareth: Jew from Galilee, Savior of the World*, trans. Wayne
Coppins and S. Brian Pounds (Waco, TX: Baylor University Press, 2014), 179–99.

26. A similar argument appears in Eckhard Rau and Silke Petersen, *Perspektiven des Lebens
Jesu: Plädoyer für die Anknüpfung an eine schwierige Forschungstradition* (Stuttgart: Kohlhammer,
2013), 239–72.

27. Ferda, *Galilean Crisis*, 94–103, 134–44, 147–87.

28. Ferda, *Galilean Crisis*, 220–33.

29. Cf. Joachim Jeremias, *New Testament Theology: The Proclamation of Jesus*, trans. John
Bowden (New York: Scribner's Sons, 1971), 127–31, 241–44; Dale C. Allison Jr., "Q 12:51–53 and
Mark 9:11–13 and the Messianic Woes," in *Authenticating the Words of Jesus*, ed. Bruce Chilton
and Craig A. Evans (Leiden: Brill, 2002), 289–310; Brant Pitre, *Jesus, the Tribulation, and the End
of the Exile: Restoration Eschatology and the Origin of the Atonement*, WUNT 204 (Tübingen:
Mohr Siebeck, 2005), 163–76, 180–86, 212–16.

expectations of the post-Easter community. Per the approach of this volume, it seems to me that there are two facts that any reconstruction must "account for," and these stand in some tension with each other. On the one hand, Christians very early on were interested in the meaning of Jesus's death and they devised all kinds of different explanations not only to excuse the cross but to explain how it was actually fundamental to his mission.[30] While we should be leery of tracing all of these claims and their supporting scriptural exegeses back to Jesus, it remains highly unlikely that Jesus's death in Jerusalem caught him by complete surprise.[31] Assuming that Jesus believed in God and thought his mission was inspired by God, he must have had some way of making sense of that beforehand. On the other hand, and as noted at the outset of this essay, we must explain how shortly after the life of Jesus his followers (several of whom were native Galileans) had set up a new home base in Jerusalem, the very place where Jesus had been crucified. Since this early community made sense of their own present experiences by asserting the inaugurated fulfillment of long-awaited hopes for the restoration of Israel—e.g., the resurrection of the dead had begun, the eschatological spirit had been poured out, and the Isaianic "good news" of God's reign was being proclaimed—it makes good sense that we find traces in early Christian literature of the concomitant hope for the redemption and glorification of Jerusalem as expected in Scripture and its subsequent interpretation.[32] Between the "pillars" in Jerusalem (Gal 2:9) and the triumphant vision of the "new Jerusalem" at the end of Revelation (21–22), we even find Paul at the climax of Rom 9–11 asserting

---

30. See Barry D. Smith, *The Meaning of Jesus' Death: Reviewing the New Testament's Interpretations* (London: Bloomsbury, 2017).

31. Helpful here is Joachim Gnilka, "Wie urteilte Jesus über seinen Tod?," in *Der Tod Jesu*, ed. Karl Kertelge (Freiburg: Herder, 1976), 13–50, who distinguishes between readiness for death (*Todesbereitschaft*) and certainty of death (*Todesgewissheit*). For a more recent discussion see Alexander J. M. Wedderburn, *The Death of Jesus: Some Reflections on Jesus-Traditions and Paul*, WUNT 299 (Tübingen: Mohr Siebeck, 2013).

32. Most notably, where we hear from Isaiah about the exalted mountain of the Lord (2:1–22) and the pilgrimage of the nations (49:1–12, 22–23; 56:8–12; etc.); from Zechariah about the great battle over Zion (12–14); and from Ezekiel about the restored Jerusalem and its new, Eden-like temple (40–42). Cf. Tob 13:1–17; T. Dan 5:12; 2 Bar 32:1–7; 40:1–4; 4 Ezra 10:25–54; 13:36; 11Q18 [New Jerusalem] and 11Q19 [Temple Scroll]; Pss. Sol. 17:21–46 (the "Son of David" rules over a purged and purified Jerusalem). The occupiers of Jerusalem during the Jewish Roman War minted coins with inscriptions "for the redemption of Zion" and "Jerusalem the Holy"; cf. Donald T. Ariel, "Identifying the Mints, Minters and Meanings of the First Jewish Revolt Coins," in *The Jewish Revolt against Rome: Interdisciplinary Perspectives*, ed. Mladen Popović, JSJSup 154 (Leiden: Brill, 2011), 373–97. Note also the fourteenth petition in the Amidah: "have mercy, O Lord our God, on Jerusalem your city and on Zion the dwelling place of your glory and on the kingdom of the house of David your righteous messiah"; cf. y. Ber. 4.3.

and thus all Israel will be saved, just as it is written:
the redeemer will go out of Zion,
he will banish ungodliness from Jacob,
and this is my covenant with them,
when I take away their sins (11:26–27, my translation)

The apostle to the gentiles, who spent most of his career far away from the holy city, could not help but speak of Zion when imagining the future return of Jesus the messiah.[33]

Why did the followers of Jesus expect these things? Martin Hengel showed that Easter would not have turned Jesus into the messiah in the complete absence of a messianic claim on his part before Easter.[34] Easter functioned to confirm, rather than create, the messianism of the early Christian movement. The same is surely true for explaining the origin of this restoration eschatology linked to Zion in the early church, not least because of Jerusalem's negative associations with the crucifixion of Jesus and the diasporic pull of the gentile mission as it continued to ramp up.[35] The idea of the new Jerusalem descending from heaven at the end of Revelation did not itself descend from heaven. There is a great deal of material in the gospels that might be used to justify this interest, some of which I have mentioned already, but I list nine here:

1. the so-called triumphal entry of Jesus to Jerusalem on a donkey, which all the evangelists imply or explicitly state aimed to evoke Zech 9's prophecy about "the king" coming to Jerusalem;

2. the troublesome "temple saying" about its destruction and rebuilding in three days (Mark 14:57–58; Matt 26:61; John 2:18–22; Acts 6:14; Gos. Thom. 71), which the evangelists handle in very different ways, with some trying to distance Jesus from it;

---

33. See James D. G. Dunn, *Romans 9–16*, WBC 38B (Nashville: Nelson, 1988), 682. Cf. Peter Stuhlmacher, "Die Stellung Jesu und des Paulus zu Jerusalem: Versuch einer Erinnerung," *ZNW* 86 (1989): 140–56.

34. For the most extensive treatment see Martin Hengel and Anna Maria Schwemer, *Der messianische Anspruch Jesu und die Anfänge der Christologie*, WUNT 138 (Tübingen: Mohr Siebeck, 2001), esp. 1–80 ("Jesus der Messias Israels").

35. Jürgen Becker, *Jesus of Nazareth*, trans. James E. Crouch (Berlin: de Gruyter, 1998), 334: "If Jesus had predicted the destruction of the temple or had pronounced God's judgment on Jerusalem, the earliest post-Easter church would probably have established itself in Galilee rather than in Jerusalem." Cf. Allison, *Constructing Jesus*, 50–51. An important study is Kim Huat Tan, *The Zion Traditions and the Aims of Jesus*, SNTSMS 91 (Cambridge: Cambridge University Press, 1997), though he unfortunately builds his case rather precariously on the authenticity of specific sayings of Jesus.

3. the symbolic action in the temple that, despite its myriad interpretations, likely anticipates a new eschatological temple;

4. the Q saying (13:34–35) in which Jesus expresses his earnest desire to "gather" Jerusalem, and laments that it was thwarted;

5. the parable of the wicked tenants in which Jesus is sent to the vineyard and its keepers—read, the temple and its leadership—understood within the larger sweep of Israel's history (Mark 12:1–12 and parr.);

6. the identification of Jesus as the "one who comes in the name of the Lord" from Ps 118 (see Mark 11:9 and parr.; 12:10 and parr.; Q 13:35), who "comes" specifically to Jerusalem and the temple;

7. the uniquely Lukan saying that Jesus must "finish" his work in Jerusalem (13:32–34);

8. several Synoptic episodes that discuss the prospect of enthronement (Mark 10:35–45 and parr.; Matt 19:28; Luke 22:29–30); and

9. the crucifixion of Jesus as one having something deserving the mocking title "king of the Jews" (Mark 15:26 and parr.).

Critics will dispute the meaning and historicity of various items in this catalogue. But some common impressions emerge: Jesus's "coming" to Jerusalem is regarded as crucial for his overall mission, his arrival is framed as a climactic event, he speaks of the eschatological fate of the temple, and it is here, in Jerusalem, that we have the most clear messianic features of the tradition. We also should not miss that Isaiah's conjoining of the "good news" of God's salvation with the manifestation of God's "reign" or "rule" (which the Targum consistently takes as "the kingdom of the Lord being revealed") remains the closest parallel to the language of Jesus, and the focus of these oracles is Jerusalem.[36]

Conclusion

So, there is the tension in the question "why did Jesus go up to Jerusalem": two things that need "accounting for" but which cut in somewhat different directions. To return once more to Schweitzer's binary of to work or to die, both are onto something, and the trouble comes when one chooses one to the exclusion of

36. See Tg. Isa. 40:9; 52:7; and also 31:4. Note also Tg. Obad. 21 and Tg. Zech. 14:9. On Isaiah's influence see Craig A. Evans, "From Gospel to Gospel: The Function of Isaiah in the New Testament," in *Writing and Reading the Scroll of Isaiah: Studies of an Interpretive Tradition*, ed. Craig C. Broyles and Craig A. Evans (Leiden: Brill, 1997), 651–91. As Helen Bond writes, "Any Jewish preacher had to reckon with Jerusalem, particularly one who prophesied the restoration of Israel and looked for the establishment of God's kingdom on earth." See *The Historical Jesus: A Guide for the Perplexed* (London: Bloomsbury, 2012), 136.

the other (so Schweitzer himself, who made Jesus's final trip "a funeral march to victory").[37] But this only raises the question: how then does the prospect of death relate to Jesus's eschatological message about restoration? Perhaps this is something that the Next Quest for the historical Jesus can work out more clearly for us. Ironically, this might mean taking us forward by actually taking us back to some of the big-picture questions of the old lives of Jesus, albeit more humbly and with historical imaginations stretched by newly emerging fields of study.

37. See Albert Schweitzer, *The Mystery of the Kingdom of God,* trans. Walter Lowrie (Eugene, OR: Wipf & Stock, 1970), 267.

22

RACE, ETHNICITY, AND WHITENESS

Wongi Park

The Next Quest for the historical Jesus must account for how the politics of race, ethnicity, and whiteness invariably shape ancient constructions and modern representations of Jesus. I want to begin by thanking Chris Keith and James Crossley for the invitation to take part in this creative and collaborative exercise. In what follows, the hypothetical question I pose—and invite you, the reader, to consider—is both retrospective and prospective: how might historical Jesus studies be reoriented if the Next Quest more fully engaged with the discourse on race, ethnicity, and whiteness?

A few qualifications are in order before diving into this question. First, race, ethnicity, and whiteness are complex theories of identity and difference that span multiple disciplines in the humanities and social sciences. Each term covers a vast discursive terrain that could be treated individually on its own terms. To do justice to one, let alone all three, is an impossible task. Hence, the treatment that follows barely scratches the surface and does not claim to be comprehensive.

Second, I am coming into this conversation not as an expert in historical Jesus studies but as a curious observer. While I am appreciative of previous quests, I am also critical of the dominant methods of historical criticism on which much of historical Jesus scholarship relies. Indeed, as will be made clear in the following analysis, the very goal of determining that which is historically authentic, original, and irreducible creates far more problems than it solves. Recently, I have started to question how certain methods in the field are assumed and taken for granted.

Consequently, the following argument reflects how my thinking about historical criticism has evolved over time.

Third, I am neither a prophet nor the son of a prophet. But I know enough to know that you cannot put new wine into old wineskins (Matt 9:14–17). You need to first bind the strong man before plundering his house (Matt 12:29). A foolish man builds his house on sand, but a wise person builds his house on rock (Matt 7:24–27). In less Matthean lingo, it is not enough to simply brainstorm new ideas for the Next Quest. It is first necessary to cancel some things from previous quests. When posing this question at the virtual conference—what would you cancel from previous quests?—the chat box was flooded with suggestions: Great Man approaches to Jesus, the criteria of authenticity, anti-Semitism, anti-Judaism, N. T. Wright, objectivity, Q, Jesus as a unique figure in history, pitting Jesus against the Jews and Pharisees, Jesus as a white European, and much more.

Returning to the question with these qualifications in mind, the hypothetical answer I would like to explore is as follows. If the Next Quest took the discourse on race, ethnicity, and whiteness seriously, the dominant theories, ethnic terminology, and ethical aims of historical Jesus scholarship would need to be reassessed. Revising the traditions, categories, and conclusions of previous quests, I argue, is crucial for moving the conversation forward.

How and Where to Begin

When it comes to the issue of race and the historical Jesus, there are several avenues that could be explored. For instance, one possibility is to reconstruct how race and ethnicity operated in the first-century world to better appreciate the social, cultural, and ethnic challenges faced by the historical Jesus. Conversely, one could begin with an analysis of how racism and ethnocentrism operate in the modern world as a framework for understanding social hierarchies in the Greco-Roman world. Still another approach might be to leverage the insights of critical race theory and whiteness studies to probe certain texts, traditions, and interpretations concerning the historical Jesus.

All of these are promising possibilities that would yield a sharpened understanding of identity, power, and difference in the development of early Judaism and early Christianity. But the question I would like to use as a point of departure is related to the history of scholarship: how did modern racism impact and shape the development of scholarship on the historical Jesus? That is, how did certain racialized ideas influence the production of knowledge? Moreover, do these racialized notions have currency in the field today and, if so, how and where are they reproduced?

Deracializing Dominant Theories

Racism is a modern disease that has plagued the field of biblical studies since its inception. The roots of the problem have been diagnosed in various ways. Cain Hope Felder names the problem as Eurocentrism, which he defines as a form of "academic prejudice that the European way of doing things is 'objective' and somehow not culture bound."[1] Beneath the search for the original meaning lies a deeper issue: "Even the apparently nonprejudicial search for 'the original meaning' of a text is usually driven by a desire to demonstrate that the Eurocentric interpreter's own favored position is closest to that 'original meaning.' . . . What passes for normative hermeneutics is in fact white, male, Eurocentric hermeneutics."[2] According to this analysis, the historical-critical pursuit of the original meaning simultaneously conceals and universalizes "the European way of doing things."

For Shawn Kelley, the Enlightenment foundations of biblical studies from Hegel, Heidegger, and Bultmann are "trapped in a racialized discourse."[3] Deane Galbraith does not mince any words when he says, "Historical-critical scholarship is racialized scholarship."[4] Approaching the issue from a different angle, Susannah Heschel keenly shows how German anti-Semitism was used as a tool to manufacture whiteness as a byproduct of European orientalism, imperialism, and fascism.[5] These dynamics were mediated and passed down from generation to generation in the form of nineteenth- and twentieth-century German scholarship. This is what she refers to as the pathology of biblical studies.

With reference to the current makeup of the Society of Biblical Literature, Vincent Wimbush notes: "The paucity of black membership is due ultimately not to the bad faith and manners of members of the Society in the past but to something more profound—the (unrecognized, unacknowledged) racialized discursive practices and politics that have defined it."[6] Angela Parker connects these realities back to the origins of the field and the history of segregation. She writes,

1. Cain Hope Felder, introduction to *Stony the Road We Trod: African American Biblical Interpretation*, ed. Cain Hope Felder (Minneapolis: Fortress, 1991), 6.

2. Felder, introduction to *Stony the Road We Trod*, 6.

3. Shawn Kelley, *Racializing Jesus: Race, Ideology, and the Formation of Modern Biblical Scholarship* (London: Routledge, 2002), 211.

4. Deane Galbraith, "The Perpetuation of Racial Assumptions in Biblical Studies," in *History, Politics and the Bible from the Iron Age to the Media Age: Essays in Honour of Keith W. Whitelam*, ed. James G. Crossley and Jim West (London: Bloomsbury, 2016), 133–34.

5. Susannah Heschel, *Abraham Geiger and the Jewish Jesus* (Chicago: University of Chicago Press, 1998) and Heschel, *The Aryan Jesus: Christian Theologians and the Bible in Nazi Germany* (Princeton: Princeton University Press, 2008).

6. Vincent L. Wimbush, "Interpreters Enslaving/Enslaved/ Runagate," *JBL* 130 (2011): 8.

"Established in 1880 at a time where segregation was the norm and not everyone had access to membership or the education for critical biblical scholarship, White men established what the critical investigation of the Bible would entail. Scholars must never forget that founding identity and must push against the inherent biases of 'established' approaches."[7]

Ekaputra Tupamahu attributes the problem to doctorate-granting institutions that are predominantly white: "In the United States, a doctoral student has to pass a comprehensive or qualifying exam after their taking their coursework, and in many schools the materials for the comprehensive exams are a huge stack of books written by white scholars."[8] In order to earn a doctorate in biblical studies, one is required to master Western history, tools, and methods of interpretation. Similarly, Jacqueline Hidalgo reasons that the few number of Latina biblical scholars stems from a lack of doctorate programs that "provide a space in which US Latinas may study the questions, texts, practices, or issues that matter to many potential US Latina biblical scholars and their communities."[9] Suffice it to say, many other remarks from minoritized scholars of color could be included.

Building on this cloud of witnesses, I add my own observations phrased as blunt provocations:

> *Markan priority is anti-Semitic.*
> *Markan priority is anti-Catholic.*
> *Markan priority is racist.*

Phrased in a more diplomatic way, the theory of Markan priority and the Two Source Hypothesis stem from a racist context that openly denigrated Judaism and Catholicism in the interest of a pro-German Protestant white nationalism. William R. Farmer explains:

---

7. Angela N. Parker, "Invoking Paul's μὴ γένοιτο and Sofia's 'Hell No' against the Stubborn Whiteness of Biblical Scholarship," *Political Theology Network*, November 26, 2020, https://politcaltheology.com/invoking-pauls-μὴ-γένοιτο-and-sofias-hell-no-against-the-stubborn-whiteness-of-biblical-scholarship/.

8. Ekaputra Tupamahu, "The Stubborn Invisibility of Whiteness in Biblical Scholarship," *Political Theology Network*, November 12, 2020, https://politicaltheology.com/the-stubborn-invisibility-of-whiteness-in-biblical-scholarship/.

9. Jacqueline M. Hidalgo, "The Politics of Reading: US Latinas, Biblical Studies, and Retrofitted Memory in Demetria Martínez's Mother Tongue," *Journal of Feminist Studies of Religion* 29 (2013): 121.

The theory of Markan primacy has led to the academic practice of interpreting the text of the Gospel of Matthew, the foundational Gospel of the Church, in the light of Matthew's presumed changes to the text of Mark. The twist of Jesus' lips that followed from this paradigm shift diminished the Jewish content and character of his message. In this way Markan primacy ironically helped pave the way for anti-semitic German Christianity in the Third Reich.[10]

An important step of delegitimizing Judaism, as far as German biblical scholars and theologians were concerned, was developing a theory of Synoptic relations that justified and gave expression to their anti-Semitic and anti-Catholic sensibilities. Reordering the Synoptic Gospels to demote Matthew played a strategic role in that process. David Laird Dungan sheds light on what is at stake:

> It is not surprising, therefore, to see German Protestant biblical scholars, in the midst of the violent, national struggle with the forces of Roman Catholicism, create a *Gospel source hypothesis* that will sever "German Christianity" from its *Jewish roots*. With the Two Source Hypothesis in hand, that is, a historical scenario that locates the beginning of the Christian faith in the un-Jewish, pro-Pauline Gospel of Mark, accompanied by a theoretical Sayings Source having a conveniently non-Jewish message, German biblical scholars could *decanonize* the very Jewish Gospel of Matthew *and split* the New Testament from the Old in biblical theology. With Matthew effectively locked up in the basement, liberal German scholars—going all the way back to Schleiermacher and before—could feel natural in looking to the Hellenistic world for antecedents and parallels to the Gospels, as if early Christianity had had nothing to with Judaism or the Old Testament (emphasis original).[11]

How could nineteenth-century German Protestants dismiss Judaism and Catholicism in one fell swoop? A solution was provided by Heinrich Julius Holtzmann (1832–1910). By rendering Matthew as subordinate, secondary, and inferior, the Gospel of Mark was promoted to a superior status that mediated the life and ministry of Jesus from a more gentile and less Judean and Jewish perspective.

---

10. William R. Farmer, "State *Interesse* and Markan Primacy: 1870–1914," in *Biblical Studies and the Shifting of Paradigms, 1850–1914*, ed. Henning Graf Reventlow and William Farmer (Sheffield: Sheffield Academic, 1995), 15–16.

11. David Laird Dungan, *A History of the Synoptic Problem: The Canon, the Text, the Composition, and the Interpretation of the Gospels* (New York: Doubleday, 1999), 339.

To be clear, Holtzmann was certainly not the first to argue for Markan priority. However, his writings solidified Mark and Q's position in the Two Source Hypothesis.[12] In this way, German Protestantism was effectively deracialized of its Jewish and Judean roots. Decanonizing Matthew was all part of a broader pattern of eclipsing Catholicism and shoring up state interests as evident in the writings of Julius Wellhausen, Adolf von Harnack (1851–1930), and many others. The overall effect was a depiction of Christianity as universal, nonethnic, and unencumbered by the particularities of race and ethnicity. German Protestantism was thus depicted as antithetical to Judaism and superior to Catholicism.

Although Markan priority is the standard view in contemporary biblical studies, it is important to note that this was not always the case. In fact, the popularity of Matthew was well established in the earliest years of the Jesus movement. The frequent citations of Matthew in Clement of Alexandria, Ignatius, Jerome, Justin, Origen, and other writings such as the Didache, Gospel of Thomas, and Epistle of Barnabas attest to Matthew's early prominence. From a canonical perspective, Matthean priority is a far more natural fit. This is what made sense to the earliest followers of Jesus. Jesus's Judean and Jewish identity was not something to overcome, remove, or reconcile. That all started to change, however, in nineteenth-century Germany. While the racist origins do not necessarily invalidate the theory, it is important to bear in mind the larger cultural and ideological milieu in which Markan priority originated.

At this point, it is necessary to add some nuance to the argument. That the theory of Markan priority emerged out of a racist context does not automatically make it wrong. All the same, this does not make it right either. Nor am I suggesting that those who hold to Markan priority are somehow racist by default. Nevertheless, the line of questioning I am raising all points back to where the theory originated, whose interest it served, how it became the dominant view in contemporary biblical scholarship, and why. The most obvious problem with the Two Source Hypothesis is that the Q source (from the German *Quelle*) was never recovered. It is a hypothetical text that only exists in the minds of nineteenth-century German Protestants and those who continue to presuppose its validity today.

I am not yet ready to make a case for Matthean priority, but I am at a point where I am questioning why I subscribe to Markan priority and how I came to this understanding. Why do I assume that Mark precedes Matthew historically, even though Matthew is first canonically? Why do I assume that Matthew used Mark as

12. David Barrett Peabody, "H. J. Holtzmann and his European Colleagues: Aspects of the Nineteenth-Century Discussion of Gospel Origins," in Reventlow and Farmer, *Biblical Studies*, 50–131.

a source? Why is Mark central to my reading of Matthew as it is for many others? On a practical level, the answer to these questions is straightforward: I subscribe to Markan priority and the Two Source Hypothesis because that is what my professors in seminary and graduate school taught me—just as they have been taught by their professors before them. Indeed, virtually every standard biblical studies textbook published in the last century assumes Markan priority and posits Two Source Hypothesis as the consensus solution to the Synoptic problem.

But what exactly does the Q source give us? What kind of work does it do? Whom does it please? Whom does it harm? What would the Next Quest look like if the theory of Markan priority, Q, and the Two Source Hypothesis were altogether decentered and dismissed? For one, it would involve a less circular reading of Matthew without presupposing its dependence on Mark. If there is any merit to the connection between modern forms of racism and the emergence of Markan priority, there seem to be some remnants of white German Protestant bias that remain deeply embedded in the traditions and theories scholars assume. In other words, assuming Markan priority seems to be a modern problem imposed on the biblical text, rather than something that arises naturally out of the gospels themselves.

What does this all mean for the Next Quest? Minimally, it means that the Next Quest must somehow reckon with this history. It means that the Judean, Jewish, and Israelite traditions surrounding early Judaism and early Christianity must be reconsidered. It means that the influence of modern racism on the dominant traditions and theories of biblical scholarship must be reassessed. It means that the conclusions drawn from previous quests that prioritize Mark must be revisited. It means acknowledging how the Two Source Hypothesis has functioned to filter out Jewish and Catholic influences in the history of scholarship. If the racist legacy of Markan priority is passed down from one generation to the next, then a critical intervention is necessary in order to break the cycle.

RETHINKING ETHNIC TERMINOLOGY

Second, if the Next Quest took the discourse of ethnicity more fully into account, the terminology employed in historical Jesus studies might need to be reevaluated. To unpack this claim, I want to dig deeper into the Gospel of Matthew and examine the translation of the term *Ioudaios* as a case study. Strong's Dictionary (G2453) conflates various meanings by defining *Ioudaios* as "Jewish as respects birth, race, religion." Before the exile, such language was commonly used as a reference to citizens of the kingdom of Judah. By the time Matthew was written, the nationalistic undertones of the Greek term would have likely diminished. But the ethnic dimensions of the term in defining a group certainly did not. The term occurs five times in Matthew:

> Where is the child who has been born king of the *Jews*? For we observed his star in the east and have come to pay him homage. (2:2)

> Now Jesus stood before the governor, and the governor asked him, "Are you the king of the *Jews*?" Jesus said, "You say so." (27:11)

> And after twisting some thorns into a crown they put it on his head. They put a reed in his right hand and knelt before him and mocked him, saying, "Hail, King of the *Jews*!" (27:29)

> Over his head they put the charge against him, which read, "This is Jesus, the King of the *Jews*." (27:37)

> So they took the money and did as they were directed. And this story is still told among the *Judeans* to this day.[13] (28:15)

Most of the occurrences are in relation to Jesus and clustered in the passion narrative. But curiously, the term is used by those who are not regarded as *Ioudaios* as a descriptor for individuals in this group. That is, all of the occurrences of the term are by non-Judeans and non-Jews to describe Judeans and Jews. Related to this point, the NRSVue translates four of the occurrences as "Jews" but for some reason—perhaps to avoid the charge of anti-Semitism—translates the term in Matt 28:15 as "Judeans." Regardless of whether the term is translated as "Jew" or "Judean," gentile characters in Matthew view Jesus as being part of this group. Here in these examples the ethnic connotations of the term are clearly implied: Jesus is *Ioudaios* insofar as he was born in Bethlehem of Judea (Matt 2:1). To better appreciate the ethnic dimensions of *Ioudaios*, it is necessary to compare this term to other ethnic markers in the text of Matthew.

Another ethnic term that serves as a counterpoint to *Ioudaios* is *ethnos*. Again, Strong's Dictionary merges various meanings by defining *ethnos* as "race, tribe, Gentile, heathen, nation, people." There are numerous occurrences of *ethnos* in Matthew:

---

13. All translations come from the NRSVue unless otherwise noted.

Land of Zebulun, land of Naphtali, on the road by the sea, across the Jordan, Galilee of the *gentiles*. (4:15)

For it is the *gentiles* who seek all these things, and indeed your heavenly Father knows that you need all these things. (6:32)

These twelve Jesus sent out with the following instructions: "Do not take a road leading to *gentiles*, and do not enter a Samaritan town." (10:5)

And you will be dragged before governors and kings because of me, as a testimony to them and the *gentiles*. (10:18)

Here is my servant, whom I have chosen, my beloved, with whom my soul is well pleased. I will put my Spirit upon him, and he will proclaim justice to the *gentiles*. (Matt 12:18)

In his name the *gentiles* will hope. (12:21)

Then they will hand him over to the *gentiles* to be mocked and flogged and crucified, and on the third day he will be raised. (20:19)

But Jesus called them to him and said, "You know that the rulers of the *gentiles* lord it over them, and their great ones are tyrants over them." (20:25)

Therefore I tell you, the kingdom of God will be taken away from you and given to a *people* that produces its fruits. (21:43)

For *nation* will rise against *nation* and kingdom against kingdom, and there will be famines and earthquakes in various places. (24:7)

Then they will hand you over to be tortured and will put you to death, and you will be hated by all *nations* because of my name. (24:9)

And this good news of the kingdom will be proclaimed throughout the world, as a testimony to all the *nations*, and then the end will come. (24:14)

All the *nations* will be gathered before him, and he will separate people one from another as a shepherd separates the sheep from the goats. (25:32)

> Go therefore and make disciples of all *nations*, baptizing them in the name of the Father and of the Son and of the Holy Spirit. (28:19)

The most common translation of *ethnos* in Matthew is "gentile." Most of the occurrences focus on individuals or groups who are not characterized as *Ioudaios*. But two other translations are "people" (21:43) and "nation" (24:7, 9; 25:32; 28:19). Additionally, there are certain regions (4:15), roads (10:5), and places (20:19; 24:14) associated with gentiles.

A cognate term closely related to *ethnos* is *ethnikos*. According to Strong's Dictionary (G1482), the following definitions are offered: "adapted to the genius or customs of a people; suited to the manners or language of foreigners." The term occurs twice in Matthew and, like *ethnos*, is typically translated "Gentile":

> When you are praying, do not heap up empty phrases as the *gentiles* do, for they think that they will be heard because of their many words. (6:7)

> If that person refuses to listen to them, tell it to the church, and if the offender refuses to listen even to the church, let such a one be to you as a *gentile* and a tax collector. (18:17)

A final term for consideration in Matthew is *xenos*. The term is typically translated as "foreigner" or "stranger" and occurs five times in Matthew:

> I was hungry and you gave me food, I was thirsty and you gave me something to drink, I was a *stranger* and you welcomed me. (25:35)

> And when was it that we saw you a *stranger* and welcomed you or naked and gave you clothing? (25:38)

> I was a *stranger* and you did not welcome me, naked and you did not give me clothing, sick and in prison and you did not visit me. (25:43)

> Then they also will answer, "Lord, when was it that we saw you hungry or thirsty or a *stranger* or naked or sick or in prison and did not take care of you?" (25:44)

> After conferring together, they used them to buy the potter's field as a place to bury *foreigners*. (27:7)

The upshot in all of these examples is to appreciate the ethnocentric framework of Matthew's Gospel. There is a clear dividing line between those who are regarded as *Ioudaios* in contrast to those who are regarded as *ethnos* or *ethnikos*. Moreover, what distinguishes one group from another is not necessarily religious, at least not in the modern sense of the term. Indeed, if religious differences were primarily in view, Jesus and the Pharisees might be on opposing sides of the spectrum. The more pressing differentiation, rather, is ethnic in character. From the perspective of Jesus's teaching in the Sermon on the Mount (Matt 6:7), Jesus and his disciples are clearly part of a different ethnic group. This ethnocentric framework is made explicit at key points in the Matthean narrative, particularly when other ethnic identities come into play. The missionary discourse of Matt 10, the story of Jesus's encounter with the Canaanite woman in Matt 15:21–28, and the episode in which Peter is ethnically interpellated as being associated with the Galilean Jesus in Matt 26:69–74 are examples where ethnocentrism is explicit. Ethnic differentiation is clearly and consistently delineated in each of these scenes.

Based on the preceding analysis, ethnicity is a far more appropriate way of describing the insider versus outsider perspective that frames the Gospel of Matthew. Matthew begins with the inclusion of other ethnic identities in Jesus's genealogy: Tamar, who is Canaanite (Matt 1:3); Rahab, who is Canaanite (Matt 1:5); Ruth, who is Moabite (Matt 1:5); and Bathsheba, who is Hittite (Matt 1:6). Matthew concludes with a reversal of the ethnocentric mission in Matt 10. In the final concluding scene, the resurrected Jesus stands before his disciples and says:

> All authority in heaven and on earth has been given to me. Go therefore and make disciples of all nations [*panta ta ethnē*], baptizing them in the name of the Father and of the Son and of the Holy Spirit and teaching them to obey everything that I have commanded you. And remember, I am with you always, to the end of the age. (28:18–20)

The translation of *Ioudaios*, *ethnos*, *ethnikos*, and *xenos* is a prime example of how the modern concept of religion has overdetermined scholarly discussions on the historical Jesus. Translating these terms under the category of ethnicity, rather than religion, provides a deeper appreciation for the ethnic framework of the Matthean narrative. And if these points apply to Matthew, an early part of the presentation of the story about Jesus, then they likewise have ramifications for the study of the historical Jesus.

REDEFINING THE ETHICAL AIMS OF SCHOLARSHIP

Finally, if the Next Quest took the discourse on whiteness seriously, the ethical aims of historical Jesus scholarship would need to be reconsidered. The third and final topic is the most controversial of the three, the least connected to the historical Jesus on the surface, and yet the closest in proximity to the contemporary world of reading and reception. It is also a topic that hits close to home for me. Therefore, I begin with an incident that provides a contextual obligation and responsibility to address this issue directly and in a manner that does not give any more attention than it requires or deserves.

On April 27, 2019, a young white male Christian entered the Chabad of Poway synagogue with an AR-15 style rifle killing one individual and injuring three others in a racist, anti-Semitic attack. The shooter pleaded guilty and was sentenced to life in prison without the possibility of parole plus an additional 121 years and 16 years as part of a plea deal. Like other racially motivated hate crimes, the shooter left a manifesto explaining his motivations. The manifesto is filled with hateful slurs and racist rants that will not be reproduced here.

One of the more appalling details in the manifesto was the biblical justifications the shooter espoused for carrying out the attack. Astoundingly, the shooter articulated a crystal-clear understanding of the gospel message as traditionally understood in Protestant Christianity. Moreover, the shooter's theological belief that the church supersedes Israel, derived from covenant theology in the Reformed tradition, justified his actions. Five biblical passages are quoted verbatim in the manifesto from the KJV: Matt 27:24–25; John 8:37–45; 1 Thess 2:14–16; Rev 2:9; 3:9. The shooter's attack was a dramatic performance, a simulation and performative reenactment of the crucifixion, whereby all Jews everywhere are forever blamed for the death of Jesus:

> When Pilate saw that he could prevail nothing, but that rather a tumult was made, he took water, and washed his hands before the multitude, saying, I am innocent of the blood of this just person: see ye to it. Then answered all the people, and said, "His blood be on us, and on our children." (Matt 27:24–25 KJV)

As this disturbing example reveals, replacement theory goes hand in glove with replacement theology. Or in Rosemary Ruether's classic formulation, "Anti-Judaism in Christian theology stands as the left hand of Christology."[14] Another perplexing part of this story is that the shooter was a member in good standing at the local Orthodox Presbyterian Church. The church has strong ties to Westminster Seminary California, my alma mater, and gathers for Sunday worship in the chapel of the seminary on campus.

How could such a hateful act be perpetuated by someone who was a self-professing Christian? Many would be quick to dismiss this as an extremist act of

---

14. Rosemary R. Ruether, "Anti-Semitism in Christian Theology," *Theology Today* 30.4 (1974): 365–81. See also Ruether, *Faith and Fratricide* (New York: Seabury, 1974), 64.

the far right, and they would be correct in doing so. While it is certainly true that this was an extremist act, it is also necessary to probe the underlying biblical and theological justifications for Christian supersessionism. Crucially, the shooter's understanding of the gospel message did not hamper but actually provided a worldview that facilitated his actions. How was this possible? How did his biblical and theological understanding of Christianity serve as a vehicle for his racist ideology and extremism?

The answers to these questions lie at the intersection between Jesus, Protestant Christianity, the modern legacy of racism, and its counterpart, the construction of whiteness. The aims of historical Jesus scholarship must be broadened to address how representations of Jesus contribute to the modern disease of xenophobia and racism.

Conclusion

What, then, is the way forward? Canceling Markan priority is certainly one possibility for sure. Another solution is to change the terminology employed in historical Jesus studies to more fully capture how ethnic groups interacted with one another in the ancient world. A third possibility is to decenter whiteness in the field of biblical studies and to move from a monoracial to a multiracial approach to biblical interpretation.

The basic methodological orientation of historical Jesus studies is to go backward in time in order to recover the Jesus of history—Jesus as he actually was in his ancient first-century context. Central to this effort is the use of historical criticism: the rigorous use and application of scientific principles to render the most original, authentic, and superior historical reconstruction. There are of course different ways that this happens, and not all historical Jesus studies make the claim to authenticity to the same level or degree. Nevertheless, this is the basic orientation that dominates historical Jesus studies.

But I am not interested in retrieving the most historically accurate understanding of Jesus as he actually was in the ancient world of the first century. A far more productive move is to examine what kind of work these various reconstructions do in the present day. To say it another way, I am less concerned in where historical Jesus scholarship starts and ends and more interested in how it is used and where it goes. So, while debunking Markan priority and establishing Matthean priority would be fine and well, doing so under the claim of being most original, authentic, and unique is problematic. Such a claim repeats the ideology of whiteness and Eurocentrism.

The aim of this paper is not to offer any quick and easy solutions, but to present the problem anew as the burden, responsibility, and promise of the Next Quest.

The methodological principles that underlie the historical Jesus project need to fundamentally change. A different starting point is necessary. How might historical Jesus scholarship be disentangled from the biblical, theological, and ideological web of race, ethnicity, and whiteness? How might a different approach to biblical interpretation be developed to counteract the modern legacies of race, ethnicity, and whiteness? If the politics of race, ethnicity, and whiteness invariably shape ancient constructions and modern representations of Jesus, then the work is cut out for the Next Quest.

23

BORN OF A *DOULĒ*

Mitzi J. Smith

The Next Quest for the historical Jesus must take seriously the Lukan witness that a *doulē* (enslaved young female) named Mary gave birth to a baby boy named Jesus while she was still enslaved. It would not be lost on ancient readers—freeborn, enslaved, freed, male or female, or colonized under the Roman Empire—that a *doulē* can only birth an enslaved child, a *doulos* or *doulē*. In a slave society like Rome in the first and second centuries BCE and CE where the enslaved population was increased or repopulated primarily through war captives and breeding, colonized or enslaved Jewish peoples living under the Roman Empire would know that enslaved women, Jewish or not, give birth to enslaved children; Mary would be no exception. But dominant scholarship willfully rejects the material reality of Mary's enslavement signified by her self-identification as a *doulē* in favor of an exclusively metaphorical, if subversive, reading. The metaphorizing of *doulē* with the addition of the prepositional phrases "of God" or "of the Lord" need not preclude that Mary, in the Lukan birth narrative, testifies simultaneously to an existential dilemma or lived reality. It is inconceivable to modern dominant interpreters that Mary could be an enslaved female virgin who gives birth to an enslaved child named Jesus; it defies their cultural sensibilities. This inconceivableness is reified in the translation-interpretation of *doulē* in the Lukan birth narratives in the NRSV and quite disappointingly, but not unsurprisingly, in the NRSVue (revised and updated edition of the NRSV) that continues the conservative tradition of translating *doulē* as *servant*. This rejection of a material reality that ancient readers would not have dismissed so easily is sacralized in the biblical text. It matters who translates and who reads.

WINSOME MUNRO AND MARY'S ENSLAVEMENT

While feminist scholars like Jane Schaberg and Marianne Kartzow take seriously the coercion and violence Mary experiences and the historical context of enslavement signified by Mary's double self-identification as a *doulē*, they both conclude that it is absolutely metaphorical.[1] Both Kartzow and Jennifer Glancy in her book *Slavery in Early Christianity* mention the one scholar of whom I am aware, Winsome Munro, who treats Mary's identity as a *doulē* literally. Munro's book entitled *Jesus, Born a Slave: The Social and Economic Origins of Jesus' Message* was published posthumously in 1998 by Mellen Press.[2] Glancy finds Munro's hypothesis unconvincing and ambitious but provocative.[3] Kartzow states that while most scholars disagree with Munro she finds her ideas interesting and hopes "interpreters will follow up on her thoughts."[4]

A SERIOUS LOOK AT MUNRO AND LUKE'S MARY AND HER CHILD

I find Munro's proposal that Jesus was a *doulos* because his mother was a *doulē* more plausible than not. This is Luke's testimony in his most accurate and careful reconstruction of Jesus's life and ministry based on eyewitness testimonies (1:1–5)—Mary was a *doulē* who gave birth to a baby named Jesus. My doctoral dissertation advisor Professor François Bovon (1938–2013) once wisely told me that whether or not he agreed with an argument would not determine whether he would engage or publish it; he would ask whether it advanced the conversation. This stance was obviously not the scholarly response to Munro's *Jesus Born a Slave*.

Like Munro, I agree with womanist New Testament scholar Clarice Martin that the Greek words *doulos* and *doulē* should never be translated euphemistically.[5]

1. Jane Schaberg, *The Illegitimacy of Jesus: A Feminist Theological Interpretation of the Infancy Narratives* (Sheffield: Sheffield Academic, 1995); Marianne Bjelland Kartzow, *The Slave Metaphor and Gendered Enslavement in Early Christian Discourse: Double Trouble Embodied* (London: Routledge, 2018).

2. Winsome Munro, *Jesus, Born a Slave: The Social and Economic Origins of Jesus' Message* (Lewiston, NY: Mellen, 1998). Munro's colleague, William Poehlmann at St. Olaf College in Northville, Minnesota, prepared the completed manuscript for publication.

3. Jennifer Glancy, *Slavery in Early Christianity* (Oxford: Oxford University Press, 2002), 127.

4. Kartzow, *Slave Metaphor*, 17 n. 32. Kartzow is interested in how ancient audiences would have understood when hearing or reading the slave metaphors.

5. Clarice J. Martin, "Womanist Interpretations of the New Testament: The Quest for Holistic and Inclusive Translation and Interpretation," in *I Found God in Me: A Womanist Biblical*

Otherwise, too much violence and trauma are lost in translation. Munro's approach to reconstructing the historical Jesus uses the overall criterion of historical plausibility broken down into categories that include disparaging implications (against the grain), environmental plausibility (didn't occur in a vacuum—historical contexts ancient Jewish and Roman enslavement), multiple attestations, and so on. Unlike Munro I do not use the criteria of traditional historical Jesus Quests for a primeval Jesus behind the text. Honestly, I had no interest in the historical Jesus research until Amy-Jill Levine invited me and three other nonhistorical Jesus scholars to present papers on Jesus and enslavement for an SBL panel some years ago. More in line with Chris Keith's argument, I hypothesize a re-presentation or reconstruction of the historical Jesus in consideration of the gospels or more specifically in the narrative world of Luke's Gospel, written by an unknown elite man who, in my view, was likely also an enslaver or slave master.[6]

Munro considers the enslavement of Mary and her son Jesus to be "highly probable" even if we cannot supply absolute proof.[7] In my view, no constructions of the historical Jesus can be proven to be absolutely true. I argue that Munro did what she hoped to accomplish; I take her hypothesis "seriously as a viable possibility" that should not be "summarily dismissed as absurd."[8] Although Munro adeptly employed traditional historical Jesus tools to support her hypothesis, historical Jesus scholars, it appears, ignored her work and muted her voice on this subject. I could not locate a single review of Munro's book. Whose books are reviewed in a journal or in an SBL program unit is often a political affair and was even more so in the late twentieth century. Despite Munro being South African, her book was even ignored in Pieter J. J. Botha's 2009 essay "Historical Jesus Research and Relevance in South Africa."[9] Botha's review covers the period 1975–2009 and focuses on the works of Albert Nolan, Andrie B. du Toit, Willem S. Vorster, Andries G. van Aarde, and Pieter F. Craffert. Munro's work is not even worthy of a footnote in Botha's essay and thus absent from his bibliography. Apparently, not one peer

---

Hermeneutics Reader, ed. Mitzi J. Smith (Eugene, OR: Cascade, 2015), 19–41. Womanist scholar Raquel St. Claire Lettsome in "Mary's Slave Song: The Tensions and Turnarounds of Faithfully Reading Doulē in the Magnificat," *Int* 75.1 (2021): 6–18, translates *doulē* as slave and yet treats it metaphorically.

6. Chris Keith, "The Narratives of the Gospels and the Historical Jesus: Current Debates, Prior Debates and the Goal of Historical Jesus Research," *JSNT* 38.4 (2016): 448. See Mitzi J. Smith, "Howard Thurman and the Religion of Jesus: Survival of the Disinherited and Womanist Wisdom," *JSHJ* 17 (2019): 271–91.

7. Munro, *Jesus, Born of a Slave*, 10.

8. Munro, *Jesus, Born of a Slave*, 10.

9. Pieter J. J. Botha, "Historical Jesus Research and Relevance in South Africa," *HvTSt* 65.1 (2009): art. 154. Botha writes that historical Jesus research is atypical in New Testament scholarship in South Africa.

reviewer or the publishing journal required that Botha at least mention Munro's work. Women and scholars of color are often required to cite the works of white male scholars (and white women, depending on the journal), but the dominant can publish often without mentioning the pertinent scholarship or contributions of Black scholars, other scholars of color, and women. Botha was able to avoid noting or engaging Munro's work by limiting his survey to "influential" historical Jesus scholarship. But who determines what is "influential"?

All our constructions of Jesus (and of God) resemble the man, woman, or non-binary person reflected back to us in our proverbial mirrors. The dominant images of Jesus are whitewashed in that they are constructed primarily by dominant white male scholars and considered most legitimate, objective, nonideological, and culture-free, even by too many readers of color. Put differently, our constructions of Jesus are impacted by the tools we do or do not use, the conversation partners we engage or reject, and our cultural imaginary, sensibilities, and interests, which shape, focus, and hone our reading lenses. This is not to say that, for example, every Black and brown scholar would take Munro or my reconstruction of Jesus seriously because of how they identify themselves. And white scholars have identity; ignoring or refusing to acknowledge one's racial or cultural identity does not mean it does not exist and does not impact how we read and what we choose to read. It matters who interprets and translates!

It Matters Who Reads and Translates the Text

Before I provide a summary of my recent essay "Abolitionist Messiah: A Man Named Jesus Born of a Doule," I will discuss the impact of Munro's context on her historical Jesus research. Munro was conscious of and open about her own contextual and subjective reasons for writing, her willingness to consider seriously the possibility that Mary, the mother of Jesus, and Jesus himself were enslaved. She wrote the following about the impact of her personal and national context on her critical reading of Jesus:

> I do not deny that my personal background, experience, interests and commitments probably predispose me to consider my hypothesis plausible enough to investigate. As a woman, and longtime feminist of a third world racial elite, committed to the South African liberation movement, I am conscious of being by social location both an oppressor and oppressed. Though of a family deemed "white," I am descended both from a slave ancestress and from colonial slaveowners. Even before learning about my own slave connections a few years ago, I had long been aware of the profound influence of slavery on South

African society, and that on a submerged level of consciousness South African whites in general view and relate to "our black people" in much the same way that slave-owning populations have to their slaves through the centuries. The result is that I am predisposed to discern certain features of slave-type societies, and of slaveowner-slave interaction in the New Testament. My South African political background predisposes me to look for and to recognize the influence of materially-based class and ethnic interests and conflict, on the text, as well as the dynamics of structural power relations in and behind the text.[10]

In *Jesus, Born a Slave*, Munro shares more about her family background. She was a liberation activist exiled from her home country of South Africa. Johan Engelbrecht located Munro's sister in South Africa from whom he gathered lots of information. Few people knew Munro in her homeland; she was unwelcomed because of her political convictions. She attended a boarding school called Potchefstroom High School for Girls where she became a feminist and learned Latin. Munro studied Greek informally with a teacher at the school and a few other students. Thus, as a high school student, she was already reading the Greek text of the New Testament. Englebrecht states "she had already become aware that what she perceived as religious truth was shrouded by layers of interpretation, and that these interpretations were often coloured [sic] by racism and sexism."[11]

As a college student at the University of Witwatersrand (UW), Munro majored in English and Latin and minored in Greek, graduating in 1945. As chair of the Student Christian Association at UW, she integrated two African students among the representatives to a meeting at Stellenbosch, resulting in an uproar. After Munro completed her BA and started teaching, she continued fighting against racism, sexism, and poverty. She joined the Council of Africans and Europeans and would have joined the African National Council (ANC) if whites had been permitted to do so at the time.

From 1953 to 1959, Munro traveled and taught in Europe, returning to South Africa to lead the Christian Education Movement. She also joined the Congress of Democrats and visited activists who were imprisoned or detained under house arrest. In 1965 the police raided Munro's apartment. Shortly after the raid she moved to the United States where she exiled for twenty-six years and was refused a passport to return to her homeland where her family resided. Munro did not return to South Africa until 1991 to see her mother before she died, and she

10. Munro, *Jesus, Born of a Slave*, 14–15.
11. Johan Englebrecht, "In Memory of Her: The Life and Times of Winsome Munro," *R&T* 3.2 (1996): 86–92, esp. 88.

joined the ANC. In 1994 she returned to South Africa to participate in its first democratic election.[12]

Like Munro, I am committed to liberation and freedom, but I have never been personally exiled from my homeland. My African ancestors, however, were forcefully removed from the motherland and enslaved. I have never visited the homeland of my African ancestors. A rejection of Munro's hypothesis is not my first impulse. My cultural imaginary and sensibilities are not repulsed by or averse to taking seriously Mary's declaration that she is existentially a *doulē*. I, like Munro, am open to pursuing the possibility.

To reiterate, all scholars have identity and are impacted by their identities, regardless of whether they name their identities when constructing theology or doing biblical interpretation. I am an African American or Black woman who also identifies as a womanist. As a womanist biblical scholar, I am informed and shaped by my own cultural imaginary and sensibilities. When performing biblical interpretation, I center the voices, traditions, epistemologies, artifacts (including sacred texts such as the works of Toni Morrison and the Bible), and experiences of Black women and our communities. A womanist is also a globalist who is situated in and connected with the world and other human beings in it. Sometimes, as African Americans we "feel like a motherless child" a long way from home, which is how the Lukan Jesus is depicted. A child born to an enslaved mother is rendered motherless. Saidiya Hartman writes that "in every slave society, slave owners attempted to eradicate the slave's memory, that is, to erase all the evidence of an existence before slavery."[13] In the twenty-first century, some revisionists attempt to erase enslavement from the history books and classrooms in the United States. Hartman testifies that "everyone told me a different story about how the slaves began to forget their past [and while the particulars of the stories that circulated throughout West Africa varied] . . . all of them ended the same—the slave loses mother. Never did the captive choose to forget; she was always tricked or bewitched or coerced into forgetting."[14] It matters who controls the retelling or reinterpretation of the story and what version gets reified in a sacred text. Hartman states that "slavery made your mother into a myth, banished your father's name and exiled your siblings to the far corners of the earth."[15] Sometimes it is the theological myths (origin narratives), creeds, or traditions we create and deify

12. Englebrecht, "In Memory of Her," 88–91.

13. Saidiya Hartman, *Lost Your Mother: A Journey along the Atlantic Route* (New York: Farrar, Straus and Giroux, 2007), 155.

14. Hartman, *Lost Your Mother*, 155.

15. Hartman, *Lost Your Mother*, 103.

that fling (by pyre or other form of silencing) contrary possibilities beyond our hermeneutical imaginary so that they never rise again.

Munro's manuscript saw the light of day because Mellen Press agreed to publish it. Mellen informed Munro of their decision a week prior to her untimely death. In 1994, she died suddenly about four weeks after she had returned to her homeland of South Africa to participate in the free elections.[16] Consequently, William Poehlmann, Munro's colleague at St. Olaf College in Minnesota, graciously prepared the manuscript for final submission and publication posthumously. Munro wrote the following in *Jesus, Born a Slave*: "My goal in publishing my findings is not to produce unquestionable certainty [who can?]. If I can do no more than persuade my readers that my hypothesis is to be taken seriously as a viable possibility, and not summarily dismissed as absurd, I shall have achieved my end."[17]

READING LUKE'S MARY IN THE CONTEXT OF ANCIENT ENSLAVEMENT

In my recent essay "Abolitionist Messiah: A Man Named Jesus Born of a Doule" in *Bitter the Chastening Rod*, I build on Munro's research.[18] I confess I initially became open to the possibility that the Lukan Jesus was born enslaved while teaching a new course entitled "Ancient Slavery, the New Testament, and Modern Slave Narratives" at Columbia Theological Seminary in 2021. While taking seriously the characterization of Mary as *doulē* (enslaved girl), I emphasized the fact that any child born to an enslaved girl or woman in a slave society enters the world as a slave or enslaved. As we discussed Luke's birth narrative in the context of Jewish and Roman enslavement, DMin student Pastor J. Lee Hill blurted out, "Dr. Smith, we might be looking at a slave narrative." After a short pause, I responded enthusiastically, "Yes, indeed; we might be reading the biography of an enslaved man named Jesus." Subsequently, I decided to pursue the idea beginning with Jennifer Glancy's work on the enslaved in early Christianity. As noted above, although Glancy mentions Munro's work on the historical Jesus, she does not find it plausible.[19]

Like Munro, in "Abolitionist Messiah: A Man Named Jesus Born of a Doule," I read the Lukan slave biography of Jesus in the context of ancient Jewish and Roman enslavement. However, I begin the essay with the Black interpretative tra-

16. Englebrecht, "In Memory of Her," 91.

17. Munro, *Jesus, Born a Slave*, 10.

18. Mitzi J. Smith, "Abolitionist Messiah: A Man Named Jesus Born of a Doule," in *Bitter the Chastening Rod: Africana Biblical Interpretation after Stony the Road We Trod in the Age of BLM, SayHerName, and MeToo*, ed. Mitzi Smith, Angela Parker, and Ericka Dunbar (Lanham, MD: Lexington/Fortress Academic, 2022), 53–70.

19. Glancy, *Slavery in Early Christianity*.

dition that understands God and Jesus in ways consistent with the Black struggle for liberation, as articulated by James Cone in his book *Black Theology and Black Power*.[20] Like the enslaved African ancestors of African Americans and other Black peoples, God's son entered the world in stigmatized, or to use Zakiyyah Jackson's phrase "black(ened) flesh."[21] To summarize my argument, I propose that "Jesus lived in somatic and existential solidarity with other enslaved persons."[22] Like Munro, I examine the Christ hymn at Phil 2:6–11. I compare the hymn to Mary's hymn (Luke 1:46–55) noting the linguistic parallels and the reversal theme in both. I assert that "these two hymns derive from the same community, or Jesus's status as a child born of an enslaved woman was known or shared knowledge in several communities; others preferred to erase it from memory."[23] Mary names her material reality but scholars overwhelmingly argue that we should view it metaphorically. Next I turn to a contextual analysis of the Lukan birth narrative where Mary identifies herself as an enslaved young virgin and sings a song of reversal in which those of low status will be exalted and the rich are sent away empty. Can we view Mary's status as metaphorical and not that of the wealthy? We might think of status reversal for those living at the bottom of the socioeconomic ladder as manumission or emancipation but with the "forty acres and a mule." Jesus's mother Mary and his master and father Joseph perform the rituals prescribed in the law of Moses for an enslaved child born in a Jewish household, including circumcision and participation in the rites of purification. Jesus is manumitted, perhaps by last will and testament or some other legal means, at the age of thirty (an age of maturity and when under Roman law an enslaved man can be freed). Munro argues that Jesus was likely an enslaved man and later a fugitive slave, but I have proposed that Jesus could well have been freed at the age of thirty—the age of maturity and eligibility for manumission—at the death of Joseph, his father and master, and therefore free to engage in his itinerant healing and teaching ministry. Jesus is a healer or physician, which is one of the many diverse jobs that enslaved persons performed. In Luke's birth narrative, Jesus's birth is celebrated by lowly shepherds, who were often enslaved persons; Simeon, whose story reads like a manumission narrative and a prelude to Jesus's abolitionist anointing; and Anna, who might have been a temple slave and a widow. There are no wise men with gold and expensive gifts in Luke's Gospel. Finally, I argue that Jesus is at home

20. James Cone, *Black Theology and Black Power* (Maryknoll, NY: Orbis, 1997).

21. Zakiyyah Iman Jackson, *Becoming Human: Matter and Meaning in an Anti-Black World* (New York: New York University Press, 2020); see Smith, "Abolitionist Messiah," 54.

22. Smith, "Abolitionist Messiah," 56.

23. Smith, "Abolitionist Messiah," 62.

with sinners and tax collectors because as an enslaved person he is considered one of them, a "sinner."

WHAT DIFFERENCE DOES IT MAKE?

Sometime after my essay "Abolitionist Messiah" had been submitted for publication, I was invited to give a lecture in the department of religion at the University of Georgia.[24] I elected to share my reading of the Lukan Jesus as an enslaved man who begins his public ministry at the age of thirty years after he is freed. Often the first reaction of dominant students and scholars (and some persons of color) is to question the relevancy or necessity of the proposal or hypothesis that Jesus was born an enslaved man, which should imply that the biblical interpretations of dominant white students and scholars are also guided or influenced by what they determine is relevant to them. What readers deem relevant is always a factor in what and how we choose to interpret. However, most often Black liberationists, Black feminists, womanists, other scholars of color, and women bear the additional burden of articulating for the dominant how our scholarship is relevant to them. The presumption is that dominant scholarship should be treated as universally relevant, as if their identities do not impact what they deem relevant. Let me say that my reading of the Lukan Jesus (and Munro's) says to oppressed communities whose ancestors were enslaved and who live daily with their "backs against the wall"—including persons caught in the powerful contemporary epidemic of sex or human trafficking in the United States and globally—that God had flesh in the game! It says that God did not save or protect his "only begotten Son" from the evil of enslavement while failing to miraculously save many oppressed people. Jesus lived like the least of these. Toni Morrison reminds us of what Orlando Patterson documented in his book *Slavery as Social Death*, which is that most ethnic groups, if not all, have enslaved ancestors.[25] God did not spare God's own son from living like the most vulnerable in the world. Or as Allen Callahan argues, Jesus lived and died like a "thug" without shelter, inheritance, land, or net worth; he came into the world with nothing and left with nothing.[26]

24. Although the presentation was recorded, I never received a copy of the recording; it was somehow lost.

25. Toni Morrison, *The Source of Self-Regard* (New York: Vintage, 2019); Orlando Patterson, *Slavery and Social Death. A Comparative Study* (Cambridge: Harvard University Press, 2018).

26. Allen Callahan, "God's Only Begotten Thug," in Smith et al., *Bitter the Chastening Rod*, 39–52.

THE PROBLEM OF THE METAPHOR "ENSLAVED OF GOD/THE LORD"

I want to return to and expand the discussion of the ambivalent use of the Greek nouns *doulos* or *doulē* as both referencing the material reality of enslavement and the spiritual metaphorizing of that materiality. I argue that we can view the metaphorizing of *doulē*, which is accomplished by appending the prepositional phrase *tou theou* (of God) or *tou kuriou* (of the Lord) to *doulē*, as an attempt to subvert, mitigate, and survive violence, loss of autonomy, or vulnerability, especially in a moment or lifetime of violence and trauma, such as an announcement to a enslaved virgin girl that she will conceive and give birth to God's Son. In addition to the example of Hermes (in the Shepherd of Hermes), whose master sells him to a mistress named Rhoda, and our reading of the enslaved in the Joel quotation in the Acts of the Apostles (2:18), I discuss here the example of Thecla in the Acts of Paul and Thecla.[27] The freeborn woman Thecla is seized by Alexander, a leader and powerful man of the Antiochenes who wore a crown. The story says that for Alexander it was love at first sight, and it appears he attempts to purchase her from Paul with money and gifts. But Paul says he does not know her and she does not belong to him. Did Alexander presume her to be an enslaved woman? Did he put his hands on her, molest her in public to make her his own by force? Thecla's response to Alexander when he put his hands on her is to cry out in anguish for Paul (who seems to have abandoned her); she begs Alexander not to force himself on her. While in the throes of Alexander detaining her, Thecla cries out and identifies herself as an enslaved female (*doulē*) of God.[28] In that instance, she has been captured and like other enslaved women can be subjected to rape by a powerful master unless someone intervenes. Thecla spiritually mitigates and subverts the horrible reality of her predicament, envisioning and declaring herself to be enslaved to God as opposed to belonging to Alexander. Alexander has a strange type of love for Thecla, a self-centered privileged love. When Thecla grabs and rips his cloak and knocks the crown off his head in her attempt to break loose from his grip on her body, a dishonored Alexander drags an arrested Thecla before the governor to be tried and judged. She confesses and is condemned to tangle with the beasts and die in the arena. Thecla, the prisoner or enslaved of the state, again identifies

---

27. Regarding the quotation of Joel in Acts, see Smith, "Abolitionist Messiah," 61. R. McL. Wilson, trans., "Acts of Paul and Thecla," in *New Testament Apocrypha*, ed. Wilhelm Schneemelcher, rev. ed. (Louisville: Westminster John Knox, 1992), 2:239–46. Greek text of the Acts of Paul and Thecla from R. A. Lipdius, ed., *Acta Pauli et Theclae*, vol. 1 of *Acta Apostolorum Apocrypha* (Leipzig: Mendelssohn, 1891), §§26–38.

28. Translated "handmaid of God" in Wilson, "Acts of Paul and Thecla." See Lipdius, *Acta Pauli et Theclae*, §§26, 32.

herself as *hē doulē tou theou* in her prayer just before she is brought into the arena to be attacked by the beasts.[29] Thecla is stripped naked, given a girdle, and thrown into the theater where the lions, bears, and other animals attack each other but leave her untouched, to the shock of the spectators. The beasts respect Thecla in ways that Alexander did not. When Queen Tryphaena faints as the bulls are set loose on Thecla, her handmaids (*therapainidas*) believe her to be dead. Alexander panics and falls at the governor's feet and pleading for mercy tells the governor to free Thecla (*apolyson tēn thēriomachon*).[30] Thecla was not a free woman each time she declared herself to be the enslaved of God. Consequently, the governor summons Thecla from the stadium and asks her to identify herself in the context of what he witnessed. A not yet physically free Thecla responds, "I am the enslaved woman of the living God" (*egō men eimi theou tou zōntos doulē*); for the sake of God's Son in whom she believes, the beasts failed to touch her.[31] As the governor releases Thecla, he affirms her identity as *hē doulē tou theou*; her God proved more powerful than the beasts and the state. When the governor orders that clothes be brought to Thecla and tells her to clothe herself, she testifies that God clothed her when she was in the stadium and shall cover her with salvation on judgment day. Then Thecla dresses herself with the clothing. The metaphorical spiritual use of being clothed is not a substitute for being physically dressed. The metaphorical sense and the material reality coexist. The metaphorical is often evoked to subvert, mitigate, and survive a precarious material reality. Thecla's captivity started the minute the powerful Alexander grabbed her violently in an attempt to force her to be physically or sexually affectionate with him in public. The physical or material condition of enslavement or captivity often precedes a subversive, mitigative, and spiritual metaphorization of an oppressive existential reality. I argue that this is the case when Mary identifies herself as *hē doulē tou theou* in Luke's Gospel.

CONCLUSION

Luke's Jesus sees his ministry as proclaiming release to the captives. I see him as an abolitionist type. Abolitionists advocate for freedom in slave societies, even if they end up dead and never physically free anybody. He died a death typically reserved for the enslaved, which I have argued in my essay "'He Never Said a Mumbalin Word'" likely included castration.[32] He eats with "sinners and tax collectors"

---

29. Lipdius, *Acta Pauli et Theclae*, §31.
30. Lipdius, *Acta Pauli et Theclae*, §§26–38.
31. Lipdius, *Acts Pauli et Theclae*, §37.
32. Mitzi J. Smith, "'He Never Said a Mumbalin Word': A Womanist Perspective of Crucifixion,

because he is considered one of them. Josephus claims that God allowed the capture and enslavement of some Jewish persons on account of their sins. How shall we, therefore, read the parables of enslavement in Luke? This is complicated. Enslaved persons are hybrid persons who both resist and assimilate, to varying degrees, both unknowingly and intentionally. I have no need to justify Luke's slave parables. What might this reading of Jesus as an enslaved man later manumitted by his master say about the author? Is the author a reforming (as opposed to reformed) wealthy slave master trying to warn those of his class to change their ways? We cannot know for sure, but we can hypothesize. I encourage what I call *epistemological vulnerability* and *hermeneutical humility*. Hermeneutical humility is an interpretative disposition one has after developing or already holding an interpretation or hermeneutical hypothesis, which requires an openness to being wrong (in part or in whole) and to possibly changing one's hypothesis or interpretation. One can hold an interpretation or hypothesis with confidence but not treat it as if it is absolutely and objectively *the* gospel. Epistemological vulnerability is a disposition one assumes while doing a reinterpretation or interpretation of a passage. It is the attitude and openness with which one approaches the process of (re)interpretation or goes through the interpretative process. Since the Jesus of faith and the Jesus of history are intricately connected, we cannot tell with certainty where one begins and the other ends. And we are always dealing with ancient subjective testimonies from a past and culture we can only access imperfectly.

Sexual Violence, and Sacralized Silence," in *When Did We See You Naked? Jesus as a Victim of Sexual Violence*, ed. Jayme Reaves and David Tombs (London: SCM, 2021), 46–66.

24

Bodies and Embodiment

Taylor G. Petrey

The Next Quest for the historical Jesus has to account for the body and embodiment. Such a statement may seem surprising. Indeed, from one perspective it is possible to conclude that the tradition has been obsessed with Jesus's body. From questions about the sort of substance Jesus's body was made of, to how it was conceived, to its race, gender, and abilities, to the kinds of pains and pleasures it was capable of and participated in, to its other practices that have been scrutinized for theological and normative guidance, Jesus's body may be one of the most important and enduring theological topics up to the present day. The interest suggests that within this theological framework the truth of Jesus's body reveals something important about the truth of his identity. The Chalcedonian doctrine of the "two natures," the human and the divine, with all its limitations, proclaimed a serious commitment to the embodiment and flesh of Jesus. While this investment in Jesus's body is primarily a theological project, such ideas have even served as the basis for some confessional defense of the "historical" study of Jesus.[1]

Perhaps because of this long-standing theological investment, scholars of the historical Jesus have not clearly defined the body as a point of historical inquiry. Robert Orsi has argued that the theological question of Jesus's body was the defining question of modernity itself. Protestants embraced a paradigm of sym-

---

1. C. Stephen Evans, *The Historical Christ and the Jesus of Faith: The Incarnational Narrative as History* (Oxford: Oxford University Press, 1996).

bolic representation in their interpretation of Jesus's Eucharistic logion "this is my body." In this framework, Catholics held to an "anti-modernist" perspective that affirmed that the bread was the actual body of Christ transformed. Modernism emphasized absence and symbol while anti-modernism emphasized presence and reality. As Orsi summarizes the Catholic-Protestant wars in Europe and beyond, "rivers of blood have flowed over this theological difference."[2] Such ideas have been baked into the Protestant legacy of historical Jesus studies.

The Next Quest should reconsider its treatment of the body as a research area. Beginning in the 1980s, the somatic turn in sociological and historical fields denaturalized the body and increasingly saw it as a cultural product that could be studied in new ways. Questions of power, ontology, representation, bodily practices, health and healing, gender, sexuality, class, race, and more gave new data and interpretive insight to something that had previously been taken for granted. For several decades now, studies of the body have flourished in the closely related fields of classics, ancient Judaism, and early Christianity, as well as other areas of New Testament studies. The treatment of bodies and embodiment overlaps considerably with the important fields and topics covered in this volume. While each of these topics deserves special treatment, there is also some benefit from reflecting on the intersections and overlaps as they relate to the broader category of the body. A post-biographical Next Quest for the historical Jesus has much to gain from these questions.

HISTORY OF THE HISTORY OF THE BODY

It is useful to first define the terms "body" and "embodiment." This isn't straightforward. In fact, these are extremely contested theoretical questions. These terms seem like synonyms but have come to be a shorthand for a methodological division in this field. "The body" is the preferred term for social construction theories in sociological and humanistic analysis. By contrast, "embodiment" is the preferred term for phenomenological approaches to the subject. Some have argued that social constructionist approaches to the body that focus on the categories by which the body is defined and regulated are in tension with a phenomenological approach. The former is invested in politics and social conditions of "the body," while the latter might offer a richer understanding of how one navigates and experiences the world beyond the mind-body dichotomy.[3] The former sees the body as an epistemological,

---

2. Robert Orsi, "When 2+2=5," *The American Scholar*, March 1, 2007, https://theamerican scholar.org/when-2-2-5/.

3. Nick Crossley, "Phenomenology and the Body," and Darin Weinberg, "Social Construc-

discursive, or linguistic production while the latter sees the body as a lived, onto-logical reality. These debates are ongoing. For instance, trans theory has become one place where these competing approaches to the body are playing out.[4]

Phenomenologists reject the idea that one "has" a body, instead talking about the ways that one "is" a body. The body is central to how one experiences life and how one perceives the world. These approaches to the lived body have of-ten had a difficult time finding purchase in historical fields.[5] There is a lack of access to lived experiences because such experiences are not directly available to the historian and are often rarely found (depending on the era) in the sources themselves. Medical experiences have tended to be one important exception in historical phenomenology.[6] Emotion, pain, and the passions have been another. At the same time, experience is an unstable data point since that experience is interpreted and expressed through language and culture—the very things the cultural constructionists are seeking to analyze. As Joan W. Scott has argued in a classic article, historians should make "experience" an object of study rather than an unproblematic fact.[7]

The genealogy of constructionist ideas is extensive, but for religion scholars Mary Douglas's book *Purity and Danger*, as much as any other study in the last century, cemented a view of the body as a malleable social symbol. In Douglas's analysis, the body as a cultural object is a metaphor whose meaning exceeds it-self and becomes a microcosm for a whole range of social issues. Furthermore, the body's boundaries are seen as a symbol for the community's boundaries. The body is regulated and protected as a symbol of the regulation and protection of the community. Douglas had specifically analyzed Jewish notions of purity, mak-ing her work especially attractive to other historians and scholars interested in contextualizing ancient Jewish culture.[8]

French philosopher Michel Foucault's influence has certainly been felt in the study of religion as well. Among his most important insights was his articulation

---

tionism and the Body," in *Routledge Handbook of Body Studies*, ed. Bryan S. Turner (London: Routledge, 2012), 130–43 and 144–56 respectively.

4. See for instance, Gayle Salamon, *Assuming a Body: Transgender and the Rhetorics of Mate-riality* (New York: Columbia University Press, 2010); Jay Prosser, *Second Skins: The Body Narratives of Transsexuality* (New York: Columbia University Press, 1998).

5. Willemijn Ruberg, *History of the Body* (London: Red Globe, 2020), 79–85.

6. Barbara Duden, *The Woman beneath the Skin: A Doctor's Patients in Eighteenth-Century Germany* (Cambridge: Harvard University Press, 1991).

7. Joan W. Scott, "The Evidence of Experience," *Critical Inquiry* 17.4 (1991): 773–97.

8. Mary Douglas, *Purity and Danger: An Analysis of Concepts of Pollution and Taboo* (London: Routledge, 1966).

of the relationship between power and the body. Much of this analysis centered on the idea of how modern institutions, including hospitals, schools, factories, and prisons, developed new techniques to regulate bodies. But the insights also went further. Foucault suggested that power operates on and within the body to produce the body. The body is an effect. This approach suggests that we might critically investigate not "the body" as an empirical object that conveys its own truth, but rather how the body is managed, regulated, disciplined, and put into discourse. Such scholarship on the body then focuses on these techniques of power at the intersection of society and individual self-discipline. One might detect in any given historical moment a discourse of the body rather than a presumed natural, static conception of the body that persists throughout time.[9] Such approaches have been particularly influential on studies of gender, sexuality, race, ability, and more.

Yet another avenue into research on "the body" has been through practices, especially through the influence of Pierre Bourdieu. Bourdieu's major theoretical goals were to displace certain antinomies in social science, including subjective and objective modes of knowledge, the separation of the symbolic from the material, the disconnect between theory and research, and the dichotomy between structure and agency. He saw the antinomy between structure and agent, for example, as unproductive and believed that it failed to account for human behavior. He developed a theory of "practice" to articulate his ideas. This notion of practice focuses on transcending the artificial divide between symbol and meaning, individual and society, and mind and body. Most influential in this respect has been Bourdieu's development of the concept of *habitus*, or the adaptation and internalization of external social structures, such as the learned behaviors that communicate class, gender, and so on. Bourdieu's approach was designed to mediate between phenomenological "subjectivist" accounts of the self and disciplinary, externally imposed "objectivist" accounts of the self. It also provided space to consider adaptation and stylization of cultural norms. This allows one to study not what the body is or what it means in a given cultural context, but what the body does in a given cultural context.[10]

JESUS AND BODY AND EMBODIMENT STUDIES

The body and embodiment seem both ubiquitous and yet often invisible in the various Quests for the historical Jesus. This somatic turn in all of its varieties has

9. Michel Foucault, *Discipline and Punish: The Birth of the Prison*, trans. Alan Sheridan (New York: Vintage, 1977).

10. Pierre Bourdieu, *The Logic of Practice*, trans. Richard Nice (Stanford: Stanford University Press, 1990); Bourdieu, *Outline of a Theory of Practice*, trans. Richard Nice (Cambridge: Cambridge University Press, 1977).

not been entirely absent in studies of the historical Jesus, though its absence has been a point of commentary. In his essay on the topic of "body" in the influential volume *Critical Terms for Religious Studies* (1998), William R. LaFleur points to the early-twentieth-century approaches to the historical Jesus, especially Rudolf Bultmann's demythologization project, as removing "the pervasive, often embarrassing, *somaticity* of everything—including a bloody crucifixion—that had been important in the New Testament."[11] Bultmann, for instance, interpreted the public torture of Jesus's body as indicative of an "inner transformation" of the self. As Stephen Moore charges, "One would be hard pressed to find a Protestant New Testament scholar more squeamish about the blood of Jesus than Bultmann."[12]

If the somaticity of Jesus was downplayed in earlier quests—and it is probably worth revisiting more carefully whether and how this is the case—one can say that attention to bodies and embodiment has emerged as a feature of more contemporary studies. Body studies became mainstream in recent decades in closely related fields. In many respects, Peter Brown's *The Body and Society: Men, Women, and Sexual Renunciation in Early Christianity* (1988) brought significant interest to body studies not only in early Christianity but in religious studies more generally. However, it is significant that Brown begins his study with Paul, skipping over any analysis of Jesus and the canonical gospels. But the body was becoming firmly entrenched in the field. Such volumes as Sarah Coakley's *Religion and the Body* (1997) clarified the trend. Biblical studies was not spared. Books like Howard Eilberg-Schwartz's *People of the Body: Jews and Judaism from an Embodied Perspective* (1992) and Dale Martin's *The Corinthian Body* (1999) made important contributions to this topic.[13] Pauline studies have been especially productive territory for yielding scholarship on the body.[14] Jennifer A. Glancy's book *Corporal Knowledge: Early Christian Bodies* (2010) also demonstrates the maturation of the topic, bringing together the representational and phenomenological approaches to the body and embodiment.[15]

For whatever reason, it seems these studies have had little impact on historical Jesus scholarship—even when, for instance, Glancy discusses Jesus's miracles.

---

11. William R. LaFleur, "Body," in *Critical Terms in Religious Studies*, ed. Mark Taylor (Chicago: University of Chicago Press, 1998), 42.

12. Stephen Moore, *God's Gym: Divine Male Bodies of the Bible* (New York: Routledge, 1996), 23.

13. Dale Martin, *The Corinthian Body* (New Haven: Yale University Press, 1999); Howard Eilberg-Schwartz, *People of the Body: Jews and Judaism from an Embodied Perspective,* The Body in Culture, History, and Religion (New York: SUNY Press, 1992); Sarah Coakley, ed., *Religion and the Body* (Cambridge: Cambridge University Press, 1997).

14. See, for instance, Joseph Marchal, ed., *Bodies on the Verge: Queering Pauline Studies* (Atlanta: SBL Press, 2019).

15. Jennifer A. Glancy, *Corporal Knowledge: Early Christian Bodies* (Oxford: Oxford University Press, 2010).

The body seems yet to lurk around the edges of scholarship on Jesus. Consider the major trends that seek to locate Jesus within a Jewish social context. Scholars of the historical Jesus have given attention to reports about Jesus's life and death, including controversies over healing miracles and exorcisms, conflicts over table fellowship, ascetic practices, and disputes about purity laws.[16] These conflicts are often taken to be contesting ideas about the Torah or perhaps about who has the authority to teach at all.[17] But these studies often do not note that the terms on which these questions hinge—healing, purity, ritual, and so on—are bodily matters. The conflicts over these issues then cannot be fully understood if one does not consider how different theories of the body play a role in the disagreement. That is, many studies represent an intellectualizing trend in the analysis of Jesus and traditions about Jesus that see his location within Judaism as a matter of adherence to an intellectual framework, which continues to sideline the body as the matter at stake.

One contributing factor in the scholarship on early Christianity may be a tendency to perpetuate the idea that the body is not a particularly important site of reflection in the first century. Several scholars have suggested that there is a cultural shift with respect to the body in late antiquity. Susan Ashbrook Harvey and Patricia Cox Miller have argued that there is a "material turn" in the fourth century, when post-Constantinian Christianity engages the body and material objects in new ways. This shows up in new theological attention given to the body (such as the various christological disputes), but also new practices and sensory experiences.[18]

If this periodological assessment that identifies a new conceptualization of the body in the fourth century is correct (and I think that it is), it raises two important historiographical points relevant to the Quest for the historical Jesus. First, what conceptualizations of the body were operative in this earlier *epoche*? Second, what movements, precedents, and fissures that anticipate the material turn in the fourth century were already present that may help explain these new developments? If there was something distinctive about the body in late antique Christianity, framing it against an earlier period provides an important periodological intervention to sustain or nuance this model.

16. Craig S. Keener, *The Historical Jesus of the Gospels* (Grand Rapids: Eerdmans, 2009).

17. Chris Keith, *Jesus and the Scribal Elite: The Origins of the Conflict*, 2nd ed. (London: T&T Clark, 2020).

18. Susan Ashbrook Harvey, *Scenting Salvation: Ancient Christianity and the Olfactory Imagination* (Berkeley: University of California Press, 2006); Patricia Cox Miller, *The Corporeal Imagination: Signifying the Holy in Late Ancient Christianity* (Philadelphia: University of Pennsylvania Press, 2009).

Physiognomic Consciousness

Next, there is a narrower question about Jesus's body: when and why does interest in Jesus's appearance, his gestures, and a rich description of his body begin to matter? Obviously, the positivist approach to such a question, whether material or descriptive, runs into several limitations. But asking this question still might be useful. The gospel accounts of Jesus are replete with attention to bodies and embodiment. From Jesus's own miraculous conception and paternity, the "Word" becoming "flesh," healings and exorcisms, touch, travels, rituals, consumption of food and drink, transfiguration, corporeal punishment and execution, resurrection and transformation, the ability to pass through solid substance, appear, and disappear at will, the body is a persistent presence in the narrative.

At the same time, perhaps by some expectations any detailed descriptions of bodies seem glaringly absent in these texts. Physiognomy and ekphrasis were important rhetorical devices from Aristotle to the Second Sophistic.[19] A "physiognomic consciousness" in the ancient world connected character and appearance. Important treatises from Pseudo-Aristotle's *Physiognomica* in the third century BCE to Polemo's *De physionomica liber* in the second century CE explicitly theorized these observations. These were deeply influential on the rhetorical arts in the Roman era.[20] Inasmuch as these were tools used to deduce the character of a person because of the relationship between the body and soul, they were useful, if admittedly inexact, shortcuts of character assessment. These approaches focused not only on the body as an object—its dimensions and features—but also on the gestures and movement of the subject. Thus, the physiognomic observer should train their attention on the morphology of the body as well as its comportment. Class, gender, and fortitude, among other things were observable in the body and its performances.

Despite its strong influence in this era, physiognomy does not play much of a role in the early gospels. There is nothing comparable to the description of Paul's visage and stature in the Acts of Paul—bald, with a furrowed brow, bow-legged, short and round, with hollow eyes, appropriate physical qualities for his spiritual persona.[21] Callie Callon has demonstrated how other early Christians made ex-

19. Alessandro Stavru, "Pathos, Physiognomy, and Ekphrasis from Aristotle to the Second Sophistic," in *Visualizing the Invisible with the Human Body: Physiognomy and Ekphrasis in the Ancient World*, ed. J. Johnson and A. Stavru (Berlin: de Gruyter, 2019), 143–60.

20. Laetitia Marcucci, "Physiognomic Roots in the Rhetoric of Cicero and Quintilian," in Johnson and Stavru, *Visualizing the Invisible*, 183–201.

21. Bruce J. Malina and Jerome H. Neyrey, *Portraits of Paul: An Archaeology of Ancient Personality* (Louisville: Westminster John Knox Press, 1996); Callie Callon, "The Unibrow That Never

tensive use of bodily features in their rhetoric about the righteous, heretics, and martyrs.[22] Yet for Jesus, there is nothing that describes physiognomic qualities. Importantly, the only body part of Jesus that receives any description at all is his penis. Jesus was circumcised (Luke 2:21). It is also here, at the central site of Jesus's Jewishness, that we might consider the role of the body in memory about Jesus. As Andrew Jacobs has shown, this feature of Jesus's body was a source of profound discomfort for early Christians. Some sought to erase or negate it entirely, while others developed theories that Jesus's circumcision was evidence of his humility and sacrifice. Jesus's penis needed to be managed, explained, and contextualized.[23]

Otherwise, there is no ekphrasis or detailed description of either Jesus or any of the main characters of the gospels. Further, there are very few descriptions of gestures beyond touching, a turn, or an occasional mention of clothing. In the second to fourth centuries, there were Christian debates about whether or not Jesus was ugly, in part because there was no clear description of him.[24] Joan Taylor notes that it would have been possible to invent a tradition of Jesus's handsomeness. Further, if he were ugly, this too would have conformed to the suffering servant description that this individual would have "no form nor comeliness, and when we shall see him, there is not beauty that we should desire him" (Isa 53:2).[25] What might it mean to shift our question from the positivist approach to instead ask why this mattered and how different factions negotiated the question? What do we make of the bareness of detail about Jesus's body in the earliest literature and its renewed importance later?

The absence of close description of Jesus's body does appear to be puzzling. According to her classic study, Elizabeth Evans points out that the Hellenistic development of biography showed that "description of personal appearance" was "an essential feature" of at least some biographies.[26] Suetonius, for instance, made extensive use of such description in his *Lives of the Emperors* to convey whether

---

Was: Paul's Appearance in the Acts of Paul and Thecla," in *Dressing Jews and Christians in Antiquity*, ed. Alicia Batten, Carly Daniel-Hughes, and Kristi Upson-Saia (Surrey: Ashgate, 2014), 99–116.

22. Callie Callon, *Reading Bodies: Physiognomy as a Strategy of Persuasion in Early Christian Discourse* (London: T&T Clark, 2019).

23. Andrew S. Jacobs, *Christ Circumcised: A Study in Early Christian History and Difference* (Philadelphia: University of Pennsylvania Press, 2012).

24. Stephen Moore, *God's Beauty Parlor: And Other Queer Spaces in and around the Bible* (Stanford: Stanford University Press, 2001); Callon, *Reading Bodies*, 131–55.

25. Joan Taylor, *What Did Jesus Look Like?* (London: Bloomsbury, 2018), 12–13.

26. Elizabeth C. Evans, "Physiognomics in the Ancient World," TAPS 59.5 (1969): 50–51.

they were good or bad, placing such descriptions at the end of each biography.[27] Plutarch's biography of Alexander is another key example of the practice, where the physical description of Alexander is designed to underscore his claim to divinity. Ancient biographers and historians did make use of descriptions of the physical form of their subjects. Livy describes the appearance of Scipio Africanus as "tall and stately," "long hair added charm," "masculine and soldierly," "his age was exactly at the height of physical strength," and exhibiting a "youthful bloom" (*Ab urbe cond.* 28.35 [Moore, LCL]). Tacitus describes the elderly Tiberius in this way: "he possessed a tall, round shouldered, and abnormally slender figure, a head without a trace of hair, and an ulcerous face generally variegated with plasters" (*Ann.* 4.57 [Jackson, LCL]).

Other ancient writers, however, were uninterested in these descriptions. There was no universal expectation that biographies contain a linguistic portraiture, though the trope did gain gradual popularity.[28] What may be needed is a fresh study of the presence and absence of physiognomy in ancient *bios* literature. If we take Robyn Faith Walsh's hypothesis that the gospels were produced by "educated elites interested in Judean teachings, practices, and paradoxographical subjects" who may or may not have been devotees of Christ, what does the absence of physiognomy mean? How might we situate the relative inattention to Jesus's body in physiognomy and ekphrasis as a type of practice of ancient writers? Is this evidence that helps us to better locate the social situation of its authors? Further, how might we think about this lack of description as informing our ideas about memory? Is there an ideology of the body in its absence, in the lack of worry about it that we might detect?

Trauma is one way of thinking about the significance of the absence of Jesus's body. Michael J. Thate has recently explored this theme in Mark. He examines multiple instances in which the body of Jesus is "not here" (Mark 16:6). The experience of the empty tomb is at the heart of the story, which entangled the disciples in (another) trauma of the absence of Jesus. In the ending of Mark, the women who went to the tomb had *tromos kai ekstasis* overtake them. Jesus's somatic absence, depriving the disciples of a body to mourn, is the "originary trauma" that is expressed in this early gospel.[29] Though Thate's analysis depends heavily on the idea of the gospels as textualizations of communities, his focus on the body—

27. Gian Franco Chiai, "Good Emperors, Bad Emperors: The Fiction of Physiognomic Representation in Suetonius' *De vita Caesarum* and Common Sense Physiognomics," in Johnson and Stavru, *Visualizing the Invisible*, 203–26.

28. Evans, "Physiognomics," 46–58.

29. Michael J. Thate, *The Godman and the Sea: The Empty Tomb, the Trauma of the Jews, and the Gospel of Mark* (Philadelphia: University of Pennsylvania Press, 2019), 43–51.

especially its absences—models how attention to these topics provides a new locus of analysis.

There may be other ways that the gospels engage with the physiognomic consciousness. The presumed connection between body and soul suggested the body could be a guide to understanding the interiority of the person. The emotions, for instance, manifested on the body, especially the face, communicating the person's interior state without words. There are numerous telltale signs listed in physiognomic literature regarding the eyes, mouth, voice, skin, and more. But the most important sign of insanity is "extreme and convulsive mobility."[30] Frenetic gestures as opposed to slow, calm, and dignified movement read as madness to the keen interpreter. But this body is not wholly other. As Maria Gerolemou explains, as it appears in Greek tragedy and epic, "the mad body is depicted in ekphraseis neither as contemptible nor as alien; on the contrary, it becomes a source of knowledge concerning the darker sides of human existence."[31] Mikeal Parson's evaluation of Luke-Acts shows some possible examples here. Some of the healing stories, the Ethiopian eunuch, and others draw on this ancient physiognomic consciousness, he argues, in ways that subvert expectations by giving positive descriptions of these characters.[32] There is also in the teaching tradition of Jesus some distrust of the relationship between the inner and outer, the body and the soul. Jesus reportedly offers instructions on fasting that speak negatively of the "hypocrites" who "disfigure their faces so as to show others they are fasting." In contrast, Matthew's Jesus suggests that one should disguise their fasting by presenting oneself well to the outside world. God then will see and provide a reward, as opposed to receiving public attention for an act of piety (Matt 6:16–18).

Further assessment of the role of physiognomy in the traditions about Jesus holds a great deal of promise. Treatments of the history of this theme in classical literature and taxonomies of its usage and avoidance might offer more information about the sociohistorical context of the memory-making practices of the Jesus narratives. We might also consider whether and how the sparseness of description is itself its own literary trope. Finally, there might be greater attention to the political implications of the few descriptions of bodies that we do have, particularly considering questions of "subversion" and agency.

---

30. Maria Gerolemou, "Representing the Insane," in Johnson and Stavru, *Visualizing the Invisible*, 273.

31. Gerolemou, "Representing the Insane," 275.

32. Mikeal C. Parsons, *Body and Character in Luke and Acts: The Subversion of Physiognomy in Early Christianity* (Grand Rapids: Baker Academic, 2006).

Redesign of Self

The body as a site of formation of the self could be particularly relevant to how we might think about the presence of the body in the Jesus material. The idea of the body as a site of both productive and repressive power has been broadly influential in the humanities and social sciences in recent decades. In his essay from a quarter century ago advocating body studies in religion, LaFleur focuses in on what he calls "the practice of religious redesign of the body."[33] In this view, LaFleur points out how scholars might train their attention to the religious traditions that emphasize bodily modification. In this case, the body is conceived of as a laboratory for accessing experiential states. He contrasts this with another pole in religious practice that insists that the body not be modified or altered in any way.

Redesign of the self can also expand the way we think about the disputes in the Gospels about ritual, purity, health, asceticism, and resurrection. To illustrate what such attention might offer, I want to focus on a tension in the sayings tradition. On the one hand. Jesus enjoins the disciples: "Do not worry . . . about the body" (Matt 6:25; Luke 12:22). On the other hand, Jesus warns that a great amount of scrupulosity should be on the body, particularly its troublesome parts: "If your right hand offends you, cut it off." The advice continues regarding an offending foot and an offending eye (Mark 9:43–47; Matt 5:29–30; cf. Matt 18:8–9; Gos. Thom. 22; cf. Matt 6:22; Luke 11:34). But I want to tug at these sayings for how we might approach them from different angles in body studies to reveal something new.

The possibilities of and prohibitions against modification might be a window onto the ideologies of the relative fixity of social status. Cultural hierarchies are a key example of how bodies are encoded with differential value and naturalized. Certain bodies are deemed to be more suited for certain labor, power, or access to care. Age, ability, ethnicity, gender, health, class, and more mark difference and differential value based on the body. At the same time, the body is an unstable signifier, one which may be shaped and molded to traverse these very boundaries, including gender, class, ability, and more. If the body is culturally produced it can also be culturally reproduced.

One view that undergirds transforming the body is that the body, or the flesh, is the site of an irascible proclivity in the human being. The rational self must then exert control over this element that seeks to escape social constraints. Jesus's injunction to cut off and pluck out problematic body parts points to the ways that this regulation of the self, discipling and punishing it through scrupulous

33. LaFleur, "Body," 37.

attention, is one example. Such bodily modifications and practices might extend to circumcision, extreme fasting, virginity and celibacy, making oneself a eunuch, and so on. This vision of the body as a limitation is also a vision of the body as a source of potentiality, of becoming. The body is a tool of transformation.

These disciplinary techniques belong to a fascinating history. Michel Foucault argued that the transition from the medieval to the modern era deployed new, often more effective and insidious technologies to discipline and civilize bodies. These included surveillance and cultivation of the interior self. New social rules emerged for how bodies were to behave, including in relation to one another. Some bodily activities were increasingly hidden from public view, including violence, sex, and defecation. Disciplinary power fractured and proliferated in new and often overlooked or invisible ways to be concerned with an increasing number of practices and to manage modern society in productive ways from a variety of institutions.[34] The idea of the managed or disciplined self as a broadly effective program of incorporating social values has had a significant impact on the field. Stephen Moore has helped pioneer new analysis of the disciplinary regime imagined in the New Testament. Moore's account of Jesus's disciplined body in *God's Gym* takes a Foucauldian approach to (male) bodies and embodiment in the New Testament.[35]

One of the interesting debates that has emerged in recent decades focuses on how to evaluate these putatively disciplinary techniques when they also become the means by which individuals or groups may express agency. In these contexts, agency is often considered a practice of resistance to or within a cultural system. Yet, notions of agency as resistance have been overly reliant on the concept of the autonomous liberal subject. Is an individual reshaping themselves because of a dominating social structure that imposes itself on the body, or because they are engaged in an act of self-making? This relationship between agency and submission has occupied a central position in such thinkers as Saba Mahmood, Talal Asad, and R. Marie Griffith.[36] This sort of attention to the body has the potential to break out of some of the reigning binaries in historical Jesus studies, such as resistance and oppression, for thinking about a more expansive approach to considering and theorizing power.

34. Foucault, *Discipline and Punish*.
35. Moore, *God's Gym*.
36. Saba Mahmood, *Politics of Piety: The Islamic Revival and the Feminist Subject* (Princeton: Princeton University Press, 2005); Talal Asad, *Genealogies of Religion: Discipline and Reasons of Power in Christianity and Islam* (Baltimore: Johns Hopkins University Press, 1993); R. Marie Griffith, *God's Daughters: Evangelical Women and the Power of Submission* (Berkeley: University of California Press, 1997).

HEALTH AND HEALING

Another important area for the consideration of new possibilities in historical Jesus research concerns health and healing. LaFleur's recommendation includes looking at medicine as another major focus for the study of the body and embodiment in religion.[37] What would a body-centric account of disease and health look like?

One must surely register an extensive attention to sickness and healing in the stories of Jesus. Often studies of health in historical Jesus scholarship proceed from the attempt to identify whether such traditions may be associated with Jesus at all, or how they are interrelated with other traditions about his teaching. Jesus's power over the bodies of others is a frequent theme. Historical Jesus scholarship in the past few decades has examined a Jewish framework for such miracles. Eric Eve has offered a historical account of the miraculous deeds within first-century Judaism.[38] Ian Wallis's study has helped situate these disease ideologies as presented in the gospels in a theological and political social context.[39] Matthew Thiessen's work has further situated these healing miracles in the context of Jewish purity and a "law-observant Jesus." He argues, "Jesus does not abolish the ritual purity system; rather, he abolishes the force that creates the ritual impurity in the person he meets."[40] In contrast to a view of Jesus as "Jewish-lite," or as an internal critic of the law, this view sees the Jesus of the Synoptic Gospels as a "contagious force of holiness" for overcoming impurity.[41] These studies are primarily interested in Jesus's relationship to Judaism especially with respect to legal questions.

Some previous approaches to health and healing have looked to a wider context. Martin's *Corinthian Body*, focused on Paul, argues that there are two main disease etiologies in the ancient world: imbalance and invasion. The humoral theory of the body is the most prominent example of the imbalance system, where the body is an ecosystem that must be tempered. For invasion, the body is perceived as a penetrable and vulnerable entity that is fending off hostile forces. Martin argues, "The ideology of the body presupposed by most early Christian literature ... reflects the invasion etiology of disease."[42] Such a view of the body has driven a

37. LaFleur, "Body," 40–42.

38. Eric Eve, *The Jewish Context of Jesus's Miracles* (Sheffield: Sheffield Academic, 2002).

39. Ian Wallis, *The Galilean Wonderworker: Reassessing Jesus's Reputation for Healing and Exorcism* (Eugene, OR: Cascade, 2020).

40. Matthew Thiessen, *Jesus and the Forces of Death: The Gospels' Portrayal of Ritual Impurity within First-Century Judaism* (Grand Rapids: Baker Academic, 2020), 6.

41. Thiessen, *Jesus and the Forces of Death*, 179.

42. Martin, *Corinthian Body*, 163.

number of political readings of these texts from supporting hierarchies to resisting imperialism. These notions of invasive or contagious forces and contagious purity could be more fruitfully compared.

Exorcism fits in the broad category of health and healing, particularly for its conceptualization of the body and even its descriptions of embodiment. In these instances, the body is seen as a container that may be filled with different external forces, some good and some evil, that will affect how the body behaves. Giovanni Bazzana's book *Having the Spirit of Christ* brings these early Christian accounts into conversation with recent comparative anthropology, challenging earlier paradigms. Bazzana calls into question the popular use of a functionalist theory that spirit possession is a practice that communities and individuals use to challenge or sustain social roles and hierarchies. He sees this approach as too limiting and employs performance and ritual theory to expand our understanding of the role of the body in episodes of spirit possession. Not only is the body being taken over, but the body then reshapes its environment by performing in constructive ways.[43] Bazzana focuses primarily on the spirit, but his analysis of a distinction between being a "hostage" or a "host" of spirit possession might help us think further about how these Jewish and Christian texts conceptualize the body as a site of cosmic conflict. The body is a porous and potential host to numerous external, "foreign" elements.

Mental illness has been an especially productive site of cultural imagination. Social-historical studies of mental illness have often challenged the category as a natural one. Several humanistic studies of disease historicize the diagnosis of mental illness as embedded in and enforcing social norms. A classic example is the professional diagnosis of homosexuality as pathological. Another example includes "hysteria," a diagnosis from antiquity to the twentieth century that covered a range of symptoms and purported causes.[44] Diseases then often indicate certain cultural mythologies that either valorize or shame the sick.[45] Disease and the language around disease may be socially coded to communicate something about society or the individuals in it. Depression, eating disorders, trauma, anxiety, and others are frequently criticized as conditions produced by the social order rather than merely biological or chemical phenomena. Further, who suffers from which diseases, and how much those diseases might matter, cannot be separated from issues of class, race, gender, and other social categories. For instance, scholars have shown how pain is evaluated differently by medical professionals depending on which bodies are describing it.

43. Giovanni Bazzana, *Having the Spirit of Christ: Spirit Possession and Exorcism in the Early Christ Groups* (New Haven: Yale University Press, 2020).

44. Caroll Smith-Rosenberg, "The Hysterical Woman: Sex Roles and the Role Conflict in Nineteenth Century America," *Social Research* 39.4 (1972): 652–78; Mark Micale, *Hysterical Men: The Hidden History of Male Nervous Illness* (Cambridge: Harvard University Press, 2008).

45. Susan Sontag, *Illness as Metaphor and AIDS as Its Metaphor* (New York: Doubleday, 1990).

Considering health and healing, what are we to make of the one-handed, one-footed, one-eyed bodies that Jesus describes? Some early Christian apocalypses and depictions of hell reinforce bodily hierarchies and the disabled and feminized body as a sign of divine punishment, whether such bodies are affected by blindness, the amputation of limbs, or rot.[46] Depictions of nonnormative bodies subjected to punishment help police society. Yet these saying of Jesus have overwhelmingly been interpreted as metaphorical and therefore not real bodies worth discussing. Even in this context, these passages are read as (self-inflicted) punishment either for sin or to avoid sin. But Candida Moss has persuasively noted that these amputations are preventative, not punitive. Severing a limb to save the whole body belongs to medical, not juridical practice. In fact, these healed bodies could be signs of distinction of valiance in war. Rather than seeing them as disciplinary, what is the place of these bodies in the physiognomic landscape? Moss suggests that this promotion of mutilated bodies over whole ones "set aesthetics on its head."[47] Here, we see how the redesign of the self might intersect with questions of physiognomy and health.

Conclusion

In the Next Quest, our task is to chart some path forward out of the wreckage of previous Quests for the historical Jesus, having abandoned the positivist pretense of discovering something stable or secure about the "real Jesus." It is unclear whether the era of "post-criteria Jesus research" will yield anything that does not replicate the positivist project of its precedents. Various memory studies approaches offer greater and lesser confidence to reveal something about the Jesus of history.[48] Chris Keith has pointed out competing paradigms between those that emphasize memory as an access to the present moment in which the memory is recounted, and those that emphasize memory as a force of continuity with the past which it describes.[49] James Crossley has called scholars to consider

---

46. Meghan R. Henning, *Hell Hath No Fury: Gender, Disability, and the Invention of Damned Bodies in Early Christian Literature* (New Haven: Yale University Press, 2021).

47. Candida R. Moss, *Divine Bodies: Resurrecting Perfection in the New Testament and Early Christianity* (New Haven: Yale University Press, 2019), 61.

48. Halvor Moxnes, *Memories of Jesus: A Journey through Time* (Eugene, OR: Cascade, 2021); Dale C. Allison Jr., *Constructing Jesus: Memory, Imagination, and History* (Grand Rapids: Baker Academic, 2010); James D. G. Dunn, *Jesus Remembered*, vol. 1 in *Christianity in the Making* (Grand Rapids: Eerdmans, 2003); Jens Schröter, *Jesus of Nazareth: Jew from Galilee, Savior of the World* (Waco, TX: Baylor University Press, 2014); Anthony Le Donne, *Historical Jesus: What Can We Know and How Can We Know It?* (Grand Rapids: Eerdmans, 2011); Rafael Rodríguez, *Structuring Early Christian Memory: Jesus in Tradition, Performance, and Text* (London: T&T Clark, 2010).

49. Chris Keith, "Memory and Authenticity: Jesus Tradition and What Really Happened," *ZNW* 102.2 (2011): 155–77.

the broader socioeconomic conditions of the ancient world in the study of the historical Jesus, rather than fact-obsessed biographies that treat Jesus as a singular figure.[50] Instead, he invites us to consider the target of our research not the figure of Jesus but the earliest Palestinian tradition about Jesus. This decenters Jesus but also gets us close to the time period and the individuals who followed and remembered him.

What kinds of historical questions about the body and embodiment might we ask in the Next Quest? Prior Quests for the historical Jesus have often been in search of the "authentic" aspects of the tradition with numerous criteria for establishing different layers. When this has not been the goal, the Quest has focused on reconstructing the communities or author(s) behind the texts as expressions of their social situation. These ambitious projects have bumped up against significant limitations and questions about their possibility in recent years. Instead, future approaches might consider a new set of questions that rely less on historical imagination and hypotheses. For instance, what does the presence and functioning of the body as a feature of the narratives do? What is at stake in such narrative elements? What are the points of convergence and divergence in the record and what do those points tell us about the elasticity of the tradition? How might the relative presence and absence of discourses about the body help us to socially locate the texts?

Scholars of the historical Jesus have an incredible opportunity to connect their work to broader humanistic inquiry in the study of the body. Studies of the body and embodiment have been commonplace for decades now and have already exerted considerable influence in classics, ancient Judaism, New Testament, and early Christianity scholarship. These questions are endemic in the texts themselves and debates about the nature of bodies and the meaning of embodiment are prevalent in these sources. In some respects, there is already a rich collection of data and analysis on some of the major topics relevant to body and embodiment studies, namely health and healing, ritual, gender, race and ethnicity, embryology, and resurrection. At the same time, the biographical questions that have driven scholarship on the historical Jesus have often skipped over the body as a focused site of analysis. Learning to read these texts in new ways to reveal the broader sociopolitical contexts of such debates will help explain the somatic stakes for ancient audiences and modern historians.

---

50. James G. Crossley, *Jesus and the Chaos of History: Redirecting the Life of the Historical Jesus* (Oxford: Oxford University Press, 2015).

25

SEXUALITY

Amy-Jill Levine

If the Next Quest for the historical Jesus is to discuss Jesus and sexuality, then it needs to account for the diversity of issues concerning the topic. There is an alphabet of issues that require analysis: adultery, bridegroom, celibacy, divorce, eunuchs, fornication, gender and gender-bending (i.e., eliding a sex or gender distinction; regarding both as culturally implicated if not constructed), homosexuality (attitude, activity), illegitimacy, lactation, lust, masturbation, marriage, prostitutes, queer readings, parturition, trans identities, and the adaptation of whatever we determine to be representative of the "historical Jesus" by his followers.

Complicating the study of Jesus and sexuality is the politicization of the topic. Striving to make Jesus relevant, some commentators insist that he supports a conservative view (e.g., heterosexual, limiting intercourse to the marriage bed) that objects to divorce (except, for some, in cases of adultery), birth control and abortion, and the transgression of gender roles (taken as the natural order). Others depict him as a countercultural figure protesting a culture that mirrors current political or ecclesial systems; this Jesus is pro-queer (variously defined), pro-divorce especially in cases of domestic abuse, pro-affirmation of personal choice in various spheres, and so on.

Both approaches, especially on the popular level, tend to use Galilean and Judean Jewish practice as the negative foil, with the goal of seeing Jesus as counter to whatever political or cultural system is disliked. Such configurations, based in theology, not in history, seek the "unique" Jesus.[1]

---

1. On studies of Jesus, gender, and sexuality in relation to Jewish practice and belief, see Amy-

Studies of Jesus and sexuality complicate getting to historical arguments by attention to defining sexuality (citations to Michel Foucault, Judith Butler, etc.) coupled with tumescent technical terminology. Because theories of sexuality and even vocabularies of sexuality change frequently, whatever terms I use risk being flaccid by the time this volume goes to press.

Complicating the question as well is the turn toward the social-historical approach. Were Jesus to be eschatologically oriented, which I think he was, he may well have focused on living as if he and his followers were already within the kingdom of God, a place where procreation is neither necessary nor desirable; a place where pair-bonding or marital relations yield to a love based in community and all consumed with God; even a place where the ideal androgyne replaces bodies that code or perform "male" and "female." Alternatively, apocalyptically oriented groups can also promote a libertine lifestyle, which was likely one of the problems Paul faced in Corinth.

Therefore, rather than take the first several pages to repeat the numerous debates on the relation of apocalyptic, millenarian, and eschatological affinity to sexuality, to define sexuality and delineate its (fraught) relationship to gender, and to argue for or against what should be included in a contribution on the "historical Jesus" and sexuality (e.g., so-called Gnostic texts; labial baptismal fonts; depictions of a beardless Jesus or one lacking in muscle tone), this essay focuses on such topics as adultery, celibacy, divorce, eunuchs, homosexuality, and what general readers curious about "Jesus and sexuality" want to know and what a historical approach might reveal. I proceed alphabetically but embed other topics where appropriate.

ADULTERY

Jesus expands Exod 20:14 (cf. Lev 20:10; Deut 5:18) and its injunction against adultery by forbidding men from looking lustfully at women (Matt 5:27–28). Here he remains consistent with his scriptural antecedents that both presume a heterosexual norm and do not mention lesbian matters directly ("sex" for the anterior scripture appears to require penile involvement). The approach to Torah of ex-

Jill Levine, "Jesus, Gender, and Sexuality: A Jewish Critique," in *The Historical Jesus through Catholic and Jewish Eyes*, ed. Bryan F. Le Beau, Leonard Greenspoon, and Dennis Hamm (Harrisburg, PA: Trinity Press International, 2000), 113–30; Levine, "The Word Becomes Flesh: Jesus, Gender, and Sexuality," in *Jesus Two Thousand Years Later*, ed. J. H. Charlesworth and W. P. Weaver, Faith and Scholarship Colloquies (Harrisburg, PA: Trinity Press International, 2000), 62–83, reprinted in J. D. G. Dunn and S. McKnight, eds., *The Historical Jesus in Recent Research*, Sources for Biblical and Theological Study 10 (Winona Lake, IN: Eisenbrauns, 2005), 509–24.

tension rather than antithesis is comparable to the rabbinic idea of "building a fence around the Torah" (Pirke 'Abot 1.1), that is, making a second law to help prevent the initial commandment from being violated. Jesus similarly expands the definition of adultery to include remarriage after divorce (Matt 5:32; 19.9 // Mark 10:11–12 // Luke 16:18).

According to John 8:2–11, a text absent from the earliest manuscripts of John and sometimes appearing in Luke 21, scribes and Pharisees bring to Jesus in the temple a woman caught in adultery, cite the "law" (the appeal is to Lev 20:10) regarding stoning adulterers, and ask Jesus for his view. Were he to say "stone her," he would be violating Roman law (adultery was not a capital offense; in John 18:31 Caiaphas tells Pilate that "we" [Jews] are not allowed to execute); it also runs against the direction of rabbinic literature, which attempts to make capital punishment all but impossible. Were he to say, "do not stone her," he would appear to be in violation of Torah. The Pharisees, contrary to popular opinion, were not about to stone her. They are not carrying stones; the setting is the temple, where human bloodshed is forbidden.

Following his humiliation of his opponents by asking about their sin, Jesus does not forgive the woman; he rather tells her not to sin again. The late appearance of the narrative in the manuscript tradition; the impression that Jesus, in writing on the ground, is capable of both reading and writing; and the portrayal of the Pharisees as malevolent make historical judgments difficult.[2] However, the narrative can be seen as consistent with a memory of Jesus as being welcoming of people known for violating social welfare, typically identified as "sinners and tax collectors."

For an example of such welcome, Luke 7:36–50 repurposes the story of the woman who anoints Jesus's head (Matt 26:6–13 // Mark 14:3–9) to depict a "woman from the city, a sinner," who anoints Jesus's feet. While the "sin" goes unidentified (not all sins, even those committed by women, are sexual), the story nevertheless has Jesus support a woman known as a sinner.

Bridegroom, Marriage, and Weddings

Various gospel traditions identify Jesus as a bridegroom (e.g., John the Baptizer in John 3:29) with Jesus using the term as a self-description (Matt 9:15 // Mark

---

2. Chris Keith, *The Pericope Adulterae, the Gospel of John, and the Literacy of Jesus* (Leiden: Brill, 2009); Keith, "*Pericope Adulterae* (John 7:53–8:11)," in *The Reception of Jesus in the First Three Centuries*, ed. Chris Keith, Helen K. Bond, Christine Jacobi, and Jens Schröter (London: T&T Clark, 2019), 1:197–208.

2:19–20 // Luke 5:34–35; Matt 25:1–10, the parable of the wise and foolish virgins, addresses the delay of the parousia in terms of a delayed bridegroom). The metaphor has several functions: (1) it promotes the creation of a new family united by (metaphorical) marriage rather than by or in addition to biology; (2) it connects Jesus with earlier images of the God of Israel as Israel's groom or husband (e.g., Jer 2:2); (3) in anticipation of consummation, it utilizes sexual imagery to express ecclesial concerns; (4) by extension, the metaphor could indicate Jesus as a (sexually desirable) partner.

In the Tanak/Old Testament, allusions to God as the (male) husband and Israel as the bride or wife turn all Israelites into wives. Female Israelites in this model either get absorbed into the metaphor or disappear. However, the masculine sexuality of Jesus the bridegroom does not always feminize his followers. The bridegroom and wedding references in the Gospels maintain the masculinity of the disciples (and similarly erase women) by alluding to (male) disciples with the odd expression "sons of the bridegroom" (Matt 9:15 // Mark 2:19 // Luke 5:34). "Sons of the bridegroom" is a masculinized, potentially infantilized, and odd reference to a groom who is also a father. The masculine language in the synoptic expression is masked by English translations of "wedding guests" or "friend[s] of the bridegroom" (as in John 3:29; French, "les amis de l'époux"; German, "Hochzeitsgäste").

Andy Angel, whose study is more a christological meditation on the necessary sexuality of the human Jesus than a historical-critical analysis, extrapolates from John 3:29 that the reference to the "friend of the bridegroom" (*philos tou nymphiou*) who rejoices at the voice of the bridegroom (*chara chairei dia tēn phōnēn tou nymphiou*) is reacting to the "ecstatic moaning or shouting during sex" by reading the verse in relation to b. Ketubbot 7b–8a.[3] The reading is generous for John if not for male responses to orgasm. Jeremiah 33:11 does speak of "the voice of the bridegroom and the voice of the bride," but these voices are included among "the voices of those who sing, as they bring thank offerings to the house of the Lord." The talmudic chapters concern the who, when, where, and under what circumstances wedding benedictions are recited. Consummation may take place in a bed, even a canopied one, but *not* under the wedding canopy.

In John 4, the meeting of Jesus and the Samaritan woman at the well, Jesus takes the role of bridegroom, but as is typical for the Johannine Jesus, the convention of men and women meeting a prospective spouse at a well (Gen 24:1–27; 29:1–12; Exod 2:15–21; 1 Sam 9:11–13 shows the first break in the convention) goes unfulfilled. Similarly, in the meeting of the resurrected Jesus with Mary Magdalene in John 20, the convention of the reunited lovers from the genre of Hellenistic ro-

---

3. Andrew R. Angel, *Intimate Jesus: The Sexuality of God Incarnate* (London: SPCK, 2017).

mance (one thinks the other is dead, mistaken identity, happy reunion, marriage) goes unfulfilled.[4]

Ephesians 5:23–24 locates Jesus as the husband and the church as the wife, and although Rev 19:7–9 and 21:2 depict the marriage of the slain lamb and the heavenly Jerusalem, the tradition never indicates that Jesus married. Earlier arguments for the transitive property of Jewish marriage—all Jewish men married; Jesus was a Jewish man; Jesus must have married—miss the diversity of Jewish practice, the acceptance of celibacy among some Jews (e.g., Essenes, Philo's Therapeutae; Rabbi Azariah; Paul). The Coptic "Gospel of Jesus's Wife," a fragment of a papyrus that surfaced in 2012 that contains the words, "Jesus said to them, 'my wife . . . ,'" is a forgery. The third-century (?) Coptic Gospel of Philip from Nag Hammadi comments, "And the companion of the [. . .] Mary Magdalene [. . .] her more than [. . .] the disciples [. . .] kiss her [. . .] on her [. . .]." The term for "companion," a loan word from the Greek *koinōnos*, can but need not refer to sexual relationships.[5]

Tentative reconstructions to determine where Jesus used to kiss Mary can yield only tentative reconstructions of Jesus of Nazareth. Complicating the history is the use of sexualized images to express theological or christological themes in biblical and related literature and the use of the kiss in nonsexualized settings including ecclesial practice (Rom 16:16; 1 Cor 16:20; 2 Cor 13:12; 1 Thess 5:26). The Gospel of Philip participates in this practice: "it is by a kiss that the perfect conceive and give birth. For this reason, we also kiss one another. We receive conception from the grace which is in one another" (Gospel of Philip 59.4–5).[6]

While it is possible Jesus was remembered as being sexually appealing, and while recent readings see him appealing to both men and women, sexual appeal is not unrelated to charismatic authority, and associations of Jesus to Dionysius (e.g., John 2:1–10) and other gods and sons of gods can include sexual appeal.[7] We have no clear mechanism to separate mythic development from historical detail.

CELIBACY, VIRGINITY, CONTINENCE

Discussion of Jesus the bridegroom segues into Jesus the celibate. While nothing suggests Jesus married, numerous texts suggest a preference for virginity and

4. Adeline Fehribach, *The Women in the Life of the Bridegroom* (Collegeville, MN: Liturgical, 1998).

5. Cf. 2 Cor 2:7 on sharing in suffering and consolation; Phlm 17 on welcoming Onesimus as a partner as opposed to one enslaved.

6. Translation from Wesley W. Isenberg, "The Gospel of Philip," in *The Nag Hammadi Library in English*, ed. James M. Robinson, 3rd ed. (San Francisco: HarperSanFrancisco, 1988), 145.

7. Dale Martin, *Sex and the Single Savior: Gender and Sexuality in Biblical Interpretation* (Louisville: Westminster John Knox, 2006).

so celibacy and, if married, continence. For example, his countercultural notice that followers must "hate wife and children" as well as "father and mother . . . brothers and sisters" (Luke 14:26)—suggests a weakening of marital relations. In Matt 10:37 the same saying, in more palatable form, lacks "wife." However, Matt 19:29 // Mark 10:29 attribute to Jesus the commendation of those who have "left house or brothers or sisters or father or mother or children or fields." The term "house" can refer to the wife.[8] Complementing this nonmarital focus are sayings about reconfiguring the family to consist of "mother, brother, and sister" (Matt 12:46–50 // Mark 3:31–35; Luke 8:19–21). Since the husband-and-wife model indicates a type of pair-bonding and exclusive sexual expression for women in early Jewish polygynous practice, husband and wife drops out of this new family, where all love is equally expressed. Consequently, the movement may have had particular appeal to Jews outside of marital contexts: the widowed, deserted, divorced, and never married.

The move toward celibacy also fits within a Second Temple context. Josephus (*B.J.* 8.2) describes one group of Essenes as celibate; Philo presents celibate Therapeutae (or Therapuetrides) in *On the Contemplative Life*, and so on.[9]

The preference for celibacy need not be seen as contradicting Jesus's tendency both of generally intensifying Torah and specifically of commanding that one "honor father and mother" (Exod 20:12 // Deut 5:16 cited in Matt 19:19 // Mark 10:19 // Luke 18:20). The korban discussion in Mark 7:10–13 // Matt 15:4–6 focuses both on honoring father and mother and on not depriving them of support. On the other hand, according to Matt 8:22 // Luke 9:60, Jesus tells a potential disciple to "let the dead bury the dead," perhaps a reference to secondary burial, but nevertheless a dismissal of the ties to the biological parent in favor of the fictive kinship group.

Luke's insistence that the young Jesus remained obedient to his parents (Luke 2:51) following his separating from them to be "in his Father's house" (2:49) and the placement of Mary and the "brothers" among the followers in Jerusalem (Acts 1:14) look like attempts to control the antifamilial model found in Mark. Similarly, Johannine depictions of the "mother of Jesus" (not identified as "Mary" in the Fourth Gospel),

---

8. Amy-Jill Levine, "Women Itinerants, Jesus of Nazareth, and Historical-Critical Approaches: Reevaluating the Consensus," in *Gender and Second Temple Judaism*, ed. Kathy Ehrensperger and Shayna Sheinfield (Lanham, MD: Lexington/Fortress Academic, 2020), 45–64; Levine, "Itineràrios femininos, Jesus de Nazaré e abordagens históricos-críticas," in *Mulheres no Cristianismo primitivo: Poderosas e inspiradoras*, ed. Roberta Alexandrina da Silva, Pedro Paulo Abreu Funari, and Claudio Umpierre Carlan (São Paulo: Fonte, 2022), 191–220.

9. Pieter W. van der Horst with Silvia Castelli, "Celibacy in Early Judaism," *RB* 109.3 (2002): 390–402.

from Jesus's grudging obedience to her implied wish for wine at Cana (John 2:1–10) to his creation of the new nonbiological family of his mother and the Beloved Disciple at the cross (19:25–27), may also be attempts to control the antifamilial tradition.

Jesus apparently separated husbands and wives. Matthew 20:20 and 27:56 locate the wife of Zebedee in Jesus's entourage, but Zebedee appears to have remained in Galilee. Luke 8:3 places "Joanna, the wife of Herod's manager, Chuza," among the patrons, but not Chuza himself. Jesus heals Peter's mother-in-law, but the gospels make no mention of his wife (Matt 8:14–15 // Mark 1:29–31 // Luke 4:38–39). The only married couple, excepting Mary and Joseph (Luke 2:48), with whom Jesus is recorded to have spoken is Jairus and his wife (Mark 5:40–43 // Luke 8:51–56; the wife drops out of Matthew's version).

Paul (1 Cor 9:5) grants apostles, the "brothers of the Lord" and "Cephas," the right to be accompanied by a "sister-wife" (*adelphēn gynaika*), which may indicate the maintenance of marital ties among the disciples: the terminology is ambiguous. A "sister wife" may indicate a woman who is close as a sister but not a sexual partner. Paul himself opts for celibacy (1 Cor 7:7) as does the author of Revelation (14:4). Promotion of celibacy in apocalyptic contexts (1 Cor 7:16) also explains the disincentives to pregnancy and so, by extension, to sexual intercourse. "Woe to those who are pregnant and to those who are breast-feeding" (Matt 24:19 // Mark 13:17 // Luke 21:23; cf. Luke 23:29, where Jesus speaks of the infertile and those who are not lactating as being blessed).[10]

An apocalyptic context also provides the impetus for Mark 12:25–26 (cf. Matt 22:30), where Jesus responds to his Sadducean interlocutors by noting that resurrected bodies are like the "angels in the heavens" who neither marry (as men do) nor are given in marriage (as women are).

Sayings and parables about wedding feasts, whether from Jesus or recorded as consistent with his message, do not end well and so detract from the idea of marriage as desirable. The parable of the delayed bridegroom and the wise and foolish virgins not only lacks a bride but also leaves half of the virgins outside a bolted door (Matt 25:1–13). The parable of the wedding banquet (Matt 22:1–10), also lacking a bride, damns the original set of guests and, in what is likely Matthean expansion—Matthew tends to add violent endings to parables, and weddings in Matthew's Gospel do not go well[11]—dooms an inappropriately attired

10. Amy-Jill Levine, "The Earth Moved: Jesus, Sex, and Eschatology," in *Apocalypticism, Anti-Semitism and the Historical Jesus: Subtexts in Context*, ed. John S. Kloppenborg and John W. Marshall, JSNTSup 275 (London: T&T Clark, 2005), 83–97.

11. Marianne Blickenstaff, *"While the Bridegroom Is with Them": Marriage, Family, Gender and Violence in the Gospel of Matthew*, LNTS 292 (London: T&T Clark, 2005).

guest (22:11–14). Luke, who may have redacted Matt 22:1–10 into a "dinner party" rather than a wedding (Luke 14:16–24), also offers instruction for guests at weddings (14:8). For Luke, weddings are not a problem, but propriety at them is. On the other hand, Luke's version includes a sexual innuendo; Luke 14:20 has one of the prospective guests respond, "I have married a woman and therefore I cannot come." The lack of explicit reason ("I must go see . . . I am going to try them out") entices the reader to fill in the expected sexual behavior. This expected behavior is not, for Luke, a good excuse to decline the invitation to dinner.

Supporting this focus on celibacy is what the texts do not show. Aside from the possibility that the two on the road to Emmaus are married (Luke 24:13), Jairus and his (unnamed) wife (Mark 5:40 // Luke 8:51) and the "virgin" Mary and Joseph (when they marry remains unclear), the major married couple in the gospel tradition is Herod Antipas and Herodias: no child from this union is mentioned. Their story in the Gospels, related to Herodias's divorce, also speaks against divorce and remarriage after divorce.

Nor do the texts depict Jesus as the subject of sexual impropriety.[12] Jesus is charged with being insane (Mark 3:21), demon-possessed (John 8:48), working for Satan (Matt 12:24 // Mark 3:22 // Luke 11:15), a glutton and an alcoholic (Matt 11:19 // Luke 7:34), and a friend of tax collectors and sinners (Matt 11:19 // Luke 7:34). He is never, despite having women followers, tagged as a fornicator or an adulterer. To the contrary, he condemns not only *porneia* (see below) but also lust and even sensual desire (*aselgeia*, see Mark 7:22), granting the problems of moving from the Greek of the gospels to Jesus's Aramaic.

A negative view of child production supplements the focus on celibacy. Jesus advises his followers to become like little children (Matt 19:13–14 // Mark 10:13–14 // Luke 18:16) and according to John 13:33 addresses his disciples as "little children." This designation carried into the assemblies (Gal 4:19; 1 John 2:1, 12, 28, etc.). Children were not, contrary to some of the "Jesus as countercultural hero" approaches, "nobodies." They were highly loved (which is why parents and caregivers brought children to Jesus to heal, touch, or bless). They were also, however, dependent and physically nonreproductive beings.[13]

If the author of the Fourth Gospel had access to the Synoptics, which appears likely, then the wedding at Cana (John 2:1–11) can be seen as a Johannine move

---

12. Amy-Jill Levine, "John Meier, Women, and the Criteria of Authenticity," in *The Figure of Jesus in History and Theology: Essays in Honor of John Meier.*, ed. Vincent Skemp and Kelley Coblentz Bautch, CBQMS (Washington, DC: Catholic University of America, 2020), 90–113; and Levine, "Women Itinerants."

13. William Loader, *Enoch, Levi and Jubilees on Sexuality* (Grand Rapids: Eerdmans, 2007); Loader, *Making Sense of Sex: Attitudes towards Sexuality in Early Jewish and Christian Literature* (Grand Rapids: Eerdmans, 2013).

to affirm, indirectly, the value of marriage. This affirmation in turn raises new questions concerning the historicity of the Cana event. Finally, the tradition of Jesus's care for children (healing, raising, touching, blessing), despite this negative view of child production, may have led his followers to argue against abortion (see Did. 2.2).

The category of celibacy should not be confused with the broader categories of ascetism or discipline. Celibacy is not, for example, for those who have low libidos, a struggle. Asceticism and discipline require a deliberate abstention from doing something one wants to do. Nor should Jesus be viewed as involved in the denial of the body. The tradition finds him eating, frequently, to the point where he may well have been chubby. It also recalls his being anointed and then having to affirm the woman who anoints him (Mark 14:3–9 // Matt 26:6–13 // John 12:1–8 cf. Luke 7:36–50).

DIVORCE

Statements attributed to Jesus vary from gospel to gospel.[14] Sorting through what he said, which recognizes whatever shifts may have occurred between his Aramaic and the gospels' Greek, remains a problem. In response to the Pharisees' question regarding the permissibility of divorce, Jesus in Mark 10:2–12 forbids divorce for both men and women. Jewish women at the time of Jesus could divorce, as the case of Herodias indicates (as Josephus, *A.J.* 18.110 confirms), and in 1 Cor 7.10–16, Paul states that he has a command from "the Lord" forbidding a wife from separating from her husband and, should she do so, forbidding remarriage. Josephus indicates, with disapproval, elite Jewish women from the Herodian household who divorced their husbands (*A.J.* 15.259; 20.143–147). He also notes his first wife (of three) deserted him (*Vita* 415).

Luke 16:18 forbids remarriage after divorce but does not explicitly forbid divorce. In Matt 5:31–32 // 19:7–9, which also limits divorce to the husband's initiative, Jesus forbids divorce except in cases of *porneia*. Scholars debate whether Matthew is clarifying a teaching from Jesus that followers already understood (that is, Jesus would have approved the *porneia* exception) or whether Matthew is updating an originally clear rejection of divorce for any cause. The debate itself is imbricated with equally debated explanations for what *porneia* means.

Matthew 5:19 likely alludes to Deut 24:1–4, which speaks of the husband finding *'ervat dābār* (LXX: *aschēmon pragma*), something objectionable with his wife. The term *'ervāh* suggests (inappropriate) nakedness (e.g., Gen 9:22–23; Lev 18)

14. Jennifer Knust, *Unprotected Texts: The Bible's Surprising Contradictions about Sex and Desire* (New York: HarperOne, 2011).

leading to inappropriate sexual relations. Possible meanings of *porneia* include prostitution or pimping; incest (with varying definitions of the term; e.g., marriage forbidden by Jewish but not by Roman law); fornication (sexual intercourse outside of marriage); polygamy (permitted in Jewish contexts but not necessarily among the followers of Jesus); nonprocreative forms of sexual expression (e.g., anal, oral, or intercrural intercourse; masturbation, bestiality, same-sex relations); sexual intercourse when one partner is menstruating or immediately postpartum (or, possibly, pregnant, since there is no new possibility of conception); intercourse with supernatural beings (e.g., angels); miscegenation and exogamy; lust; and intercourse for pleasure rather than procreation.[15] In Mark 7:21–22 (cf. Matt 15:19), *porneia* appears along with "murder, adultery, theft," a standard vice list. That Jesus spoke Aramaic makes the referent less clear.

In the Roman Empire, a patrician husband or a wife could dissolve a marriage; the catch was working out the financials, including the dowry. A freedwoman required her husband's permission to divorce.

Biblical terms for "divorce" can suggest a tossing away or disposing of the spouse, but etymology need not translate into economic or social attitudes.[16] Jesus's forbidding of divorce and remarriage does not appear premised on protecting the rights of the divorced spouse. Luke 16:18 places the divorce statement in the context of avarice, which could express concern for marriage and divorce for economic reasons.[17] But this point, a Lukan concern, is not supported by other contextualizations.

Typically cited in these discussions of divorce are "the rabbis," most notably m. Giṭṭin 9.10, which quotes R. Hillel, who affirms divorce for a spoiled dinner, and R. Akiva, who permits divorce if the husband finds someone prettier than his wife on appeal to Deut 24:1: "She does not find grace in his eyes" (*lō timtzāʾ ḥen bəʿênāv*; colloquially, she does not please him). Missing from such citations is the first line of the Mishnah, where the "house of Shammai" permits divorce only on grounds of *ʿervat dābār* (Deut 24:1). The responses from Bet Hillel indicate that Bet Shammai had a narrow interpretation of Deuteronomy. The debate may connect to Matt 19:3, where the Pharisees question Jesus about divorce "for any

15. On Roman divorce legislation and practice, see Thomas A. J. McGinn, "The Law of Roman Divorce in the Time of Christ," in *The Historical Jesus in Context*, ed. Amy-Jill Levine, Dale C. Allison Jr., and John Dominic Crossan (Princeton: Princeton University Press, 2006), 309–22. Regarding *porneia*, see David Wheeler-Reed, Jennifer W. Knust, and Dale B. Martin, "Can a Man Commit πορνεία with His Wife?," *JBL* 137.2 (2018): 383–98.

16. E.g., *exapostellō* in Deut 22:19, 22 LXX; *ekballō* in Sir 7:26; *apolyō* in Matt 5:31; *aphiēmi* in 1 Cor 7:12–13).

17. Loader, *Making Sense of Sex*.

cause." Moreover, Jewish wives were protected by *ketubbot* (marriage contracts); further, no one claims that forbidding wives from divorcing husbands protects the husband from financial loss.

Jesus forbids divorce not to protect either spouse, but, treating Deuteronomy as a concession to human frailty, Jesus promotes an Edenic model of divine match-making. Since God made humans male and female (thereby reading Gen 1:26–27) as exclusive rather than as a merism (male and female and everything in between), the man leaves father and mother and cleaves to his woman. Since they are now one flesh—meaning a new family unit, not meaning permanently engaged in in-tercourse—and since they were joined by God, they are not to separate. Ephe-sians 5:31 deploys the Genesis passage in support of marital mutuality. The appeal to Gen 2, by extension, also promotes monogamy, which is the direction the follow-ers of Jesus took (e.g., 1 Tim 3:2, the bishop must be "the husband of one wife").

EUNUCHS

According to Matt 19:12, Jesus speaks of three types of eunuchs: from the mother's womb (i.e., congenital eunuchs), those made eunuchs, and those who eunuchize themselves (self-castration). The saying is typically interpreted in terms of men forgoing procreation, since the one thing a eunuch could not do was biologically reproduce. Unclear is whether the statement is a response to a taunt: since Jesus is not married and has no children (as far as we know), it is possible his opponents called him a eunuch.

The statement appears in response to the disciples' concerns over Jesus's for-bidding of divorce: if one cannot divorce, suggests Peter, then it is better not to marry. Unclear is what the statement means by "eunuch": lack or removal of tes-ticles, of penis, both? The saying would not have conveyed to earlier audiences the lack of sexual engagement: eunuchs could and did maintain both hetero- and homosexual relations, with some stereotypes implying insatiability or lewdness. The reference would have suggested a combination of slavery together with sexual availability in brothels and trusted leadership (cf. the Ethiopian officer of Acts 8). Nor would it have conveyed promotion of self-castration: connections of castra-tion with worship of the Great Mother, eunuchs in brothels, and, by extension, the association of crushed testicles with impurity (Lev 21:20; 22:24; Deut 23:1) all militate against such an interpretation. Thus, the eunuch indicated a challenge to masculine identity and so a sexual transgression.[18]

18. J. David Hester, "Eunuchs and the Postgender Jesus: Matthew 19.12 and Transgressive Sexualities," *JSNT* 28.1 (2005): 13–40.

The context of the Matthean saying defines families according to loyalty to Jesus rather than in marital or biological terms. In response to the saying, Peter affirms that he and the other (male) disciples have left all to follow him (Matt 19:27). The comment can suggest that the (male) disciples, without divorce, left their wives for the sake of Jesus and the kingdom.[19] Rhetorically, the eunuchized male promotes enslavement to God and so fits parables and statements promoting an enslaved role; the self-eunuchized forgo families and so patriarchal privilege.[20]

Another way of understanding the eunuch statement—whether it came from Jesus or is a memory of something that "sounds like" what Jesus said—is to place it into conversation with other statements, attributed to Jesus, that suggest body modification (or mutilation). For example, Matt 5:29–30 (see also Matt 18:8; Mark 9:43–45) follows the prohibition of lust and advises the excision of hands, feet, or eyes that cause stumbling (see below regarding masturbation). The tradition suggests that Jesus recognized the problematic relationship between body parts and sexuality. That Jesus recognized these biological traits can be read as not only recognition but also welcoming of intersexed individuals.[21]

HOMOSEXUALITY; SAME-SEX ATTRACTION

Jesus likely promoted celibacy, reconstructed kinship away from pair-bonding, and was never accused of homosexual practice. Like anyone else for whom there is absence of evidence, Jesus may have felt, and may have been the object of, same-sex attraction.

The jury is still out, and likely will remain so, on whether the so-called Secret Gospel of Mark, which hints at a homoerotic meeting with Mark's naked young man in Gethsemane (Mark 14:51–52), is a forgery, whether ancient or modern. The text reads: "But the youth, looking upon [Jesus], loved him and began to beseech him that he might be with him. . . . And after six days, Jesus told him what to do, and in the evening the youth comes to him, wearing a linen cloth over his naked body. And he remained with him that night, for Jesus taught him the mystery of the kingdom of God."[22] If the text is an ancient forgery, then it

19. R. Jarrett Van Tine, "Castration for the Kingdom and Avoiding the αἰτία of Adultery (Matthew 19:10–12)," *JBL* 137.2 (2018): 399–418.

20. Jennifer Alexander, "Matthew's Parable of the Eunuchs" (PhD diss., Vanderbilt University, 2021).

21. Megan K. DeFranza, *Sex Difference in Christian Theology: Male, Female, and Intersex in the Image of God* (Grand Rapids: Eerdmans, 2015).

22. Morton Smith, *Clement of Alexandria and a Secret Gospel of Mark* (Cambridge: Harvard University Press, 1973).

may reflect memories of Jesus as attracted to and by young men. Conversely, it may reflect the interest of the forger, for example, portraying an intimate but not sexual relationship between older and younger monks related to "brother-making" (*adelphopoiesis*).[23]

Related is reading John's "disciple whom Jesus loved" (John 13:23; 19:26; 21:7–20) as having a sexual component, something that the generally heteronormative scholarly approach to Jesus, until quite recently, would have left unnoted.[24] That John depicts this disciple as "lying in Jesus's bosom" (13:23) at the Last Supper suggests not only proximity but also intimacy. Complicating an erotic dimension to the verse is that the same language in John 1:18 locates the Son in the bosom of the Father (the NRSVue, whose translators cannot bring themselves to use "bosom" or even "breast," offers "father's heart"; French, "sein"; German, "Schoß"). In Luke 16:22–23, Lazarus rests in the bosom of Abraham (modern translations, also apparently uncomfortable with bosoms and breasts, have the less intimate "with" or "by his side"). Physical and emotional intimacy is not necessarily sexual.

Extended readings, whether via "gay imagination" or "a queer hermeneutics," that suggest homoerotic relationships between Jesus and various disciples, or indeed between Jesus and anyone, remain at best speculative.[25] Readers can choose to read Jesus as sexually engaged, but whether such readings provide insight into the "historical Jesus" is less clear. That Jesus is a human being makes him also a sexual being, but as a human being Jesus, like everyone else, would have a range of libidos (desires?), disciplines, attractions, and interests.

Arguments that Jesus approved of a homosexual relationship between a centurion and his sick "son" or "servant" (Matt 8:6 reads *pais*, lit. "boy"; Luke 7:2 reads *doulos*, "enslaved male") need to consider matters ranging from whether the ailing person was in a consensual relationship or his paralysis was a result of sexual abuse to (the unlikelihood of) Roman officers taking local lovers.

The same point holds for the insistence attributed to Jesus in Mark 10:44 that followers must be "a slave of all" (*estai pantōn doulos*). The footwashing scene in John 12 enacts the model, which is also consistent with several parables depicting enslaved people in the role of potential disciples. Enslaved bodies were sexually

23. Geoffrey S. Smith and Brent C. Landau, *The Secret Gospel of Mark: A Controversial Scholar, a Scandalous Gospel of Jesus, and the Fierce Debate over Its Authenticity* (New Haven and London: Cambridge University Press, 2023).

24. Martin, *Sex and the Single Savior*.

25. E.g., Lazarus, whom he "loved" (*philei*) according to John 11:3 (cf. 11.5, *ēgapa*, in relation to Lazarus and his female siblings); Thomas, whom he invited to touch his wounds (John 20:27); Judas (given the kiss); Peter (given the discussion of "love" in John 21), etc. Note also the failed disciple whom Jesus "loved" (*ēgapēsen*) according to Mark 10:21.

available to those who claimed ownership to use or distribute for their own use or for the use of others. That Jesus expected his body, or the bodies of his followers, to be sexually penetrated (as opposed to tortured to death in "nonsexual" ways) has to be extrapolated from the use of slave language; similarly, readers will need to determine if the mutilation of bodies, including crucifixion (victims were naked), should be coded as sexual.

Alternative to the view that Jesus promotes (tacitly) male same-sex attraction is the claim that his statement advocating that anyone who scandalizes a "little one" should have a millstone fastened about his neck and be drowned in the sea (Matt 18:6 // Mark 9:42 // Luke 17:2). Possibly promoting capital punishment for pederasty, the text need not have a primary (or necessary) sexual reference.[26] The "little one" (*mikros*) functions, as does the comparable "little children," to refer to members of the group gathered around Jesus. Pederastic practice was common among gentile patricians; we lack evidence for its presence, let alone its promotion, in Galilee or Judea. Then again, absence of evidence is not evidence of absence. (However, on the possibility of a sexual connotation for this expression, see below on masturbation.)

Occasionally adduced to support a negative view of male same-sex attractions is Matt 11:7–9, the reference to a man wearing "soft" clothes (*hoi ta malaka phorountes*). The term *malakos* can connote male homosexuality, but it can also mean "soft" or "fancy." The placement of men wearing such garments in "kings' houses" (Matt 11:8), in contrast to the "hard" John the Baptizer in the wilderness, need not indicate a sexual slur.

Another text adduced to suggest a view of homosexual coding is Mark 5:1–20, where Jesus permits a "legion" of demons to enter a herd of pigs, who then hurl themselves off a cliff. That there is no sea cliff in Gerasa (the setting of Mark's story), that *gerash* in Hebrew means "to expel" (a good name for the setting of an exorcism), and that the boar was the symbol of the *X Fratensis*, the legion that took Jerusalem in 70 CE, all suggest more legend than historical memory. The sexual nature enters with the notice that "pig" could signal male same-sex partners, that "entering" is another way of saying "fucking," and that destroying the pigs, or allowing them to be destroyed, is a means of characterizing Romans as effeminate, penetrated, female-organed weaklings.[27] This text is not, as far as I can tell, cited by those who see Jesus as promoting or at least not condemning

26. Will Deming, "Mark 9.42–10.12, Matthew 5.27–32, and B. Nid. 13b: A First Century Discussion of Male Sexuality," *NTS* 36 (1990): 130–41.

27. Warren Carter, "Cross-Gendered Romans and Mark's Jesus: Legion Enters the Pigs (Mark 5:1–20)," *JBL* 133.1 (2014): 139–55.

same-sex attraction. We see sexualized bodies where we want to see them. Nor is a sissifying parody pastorally helpful, other than in showing the pervasiveness of the trope.

To the (correct) comment that Jesus never said anything about homosexuality—the point that the term did not exist is also correct but tendentious; the ancient world knew of same-sex attraction and action—silence does not mean either approval or lack of concern. In cases where Jesus is silent, the historical default would be the dominant view of Second Temple Jewish life in Galilee and Judea. Nothing suggests approval of same-sex relations or attraction there at the time. Were Jesus an outlier, the case has to be made from evidence other than silence.

The tradition recalls him primarily as both celibate and as attractive to both men and women. From this we can extrapolate that Jesus was polyamorous, bisexual or polysexual, or experimental; we can also extrapolate that while he encouraged this attraction or at least did not downplay it, his focus was an apocalyptic and eschatological one in which bodies are not driven by lust, do not engage in intercourse, do not reproduce, and remain pure.

MASTURBATION

In Mark 9:43–47, Jesus recommends excision for hands, feet, and eyes that cause scandalization. The context is the scandalization of a "little one." If the saying about the "little one" refers to pederasty, then the sayings about removing bodily parts likely relate to sexualized activity, whether by action or thought. Further promoting a sexualized concern, other statements associate eyes and seeing with lust (e.g., Matt 5:8), "hand" in Hebrew is a euphemism for penis (Isa 56:5), and in Semitic languages "foot" and "feet" have the same euphemistic meaning.

The statement can be seen in the same context as the m. Niddah 2.1: "Every hand that frequently makes examinations, with women is praiseworthy, and with men, it is to be cut off." The reference to women concerns checking for vaginal or uterine bleeding, as the continuation of the Mishnah demonstrates. The reference to men probably refers to unnecessary handling of the penis (b. Nid. 13a raises the question of whether holding a penis in order to urinate is permitted; it is). Given this intertext, the hand that scandalizes or causes one to stumble, and so the hand to be excised, could be the hand that masturbates. Jesus's reputation of restoring individuals to states of ritual purity (e.g., a woman suffering vaginal or uterine hemorrhages; people suffering from skin disease; the dead) could, by extension, see him as avoiding, and helping others to avoid, unnecessary impurity such as via masturbation, (male) ejaculation, or sexual intercourse.

The eunuch statement in Matt 19:12 (see above) is consistent with the rhetorical device here: cut off what offends or what might be tempted to offend. Nothing in the tradition, however, suggests that Jesus was understood to be promoting physical mutilation.

SEX WORKERS

Despite the popular view of Jesus as a friend of sex workers (commonly designated "prostitutes") and of Mary Magdalene as a (redeemed) sex worker, no early evidence testifies to this view.[28] The group around Jesus is predominantly homosocial, and while boys and men (usually enslaved) were forced into sex work, whether in homes or in brothels, the gospels give no hint that any of the twelve were in the sex industry. The "woman from the city" (Luke 7:36–50) may have been a sex worker, but that is not a necessary reading. Mary Magdalene only became regarded as a sex worker in the fifth century with the teachings of Pope Gregory the Great. The only other reference Jesus (or the tradition) makes to sex workers is set in the imagination of the "older brother" in Luke 15:30, where he suggests to his father that the prodigal spent his inheritance on sex workers.

It is possible that the "tax collectors and sinners" (Matt 9:10–11 // Mark 2:15–16 // Luke 5:30; Matt 11:19; Luke 15:1) with whom Jesus likely associated included (male and female) sex workers. Yet even here the tradition masks the presence of sex workers; the issue is "dining with" and nothing more. Again, the lack of complaint about women followers, while an argument from silence, undercuts the presumption that Jesus was involved with sex workers.

Conversely, the tradition associates John the Baptizer with sex workers. Matthew 21:31–32 affirms that "tax collectors and sex workers" believed John whereas Pharisees did not.

ILLEGITIMACY

Matthew's genealogy includes one prostitute, Rahab (Josh 2:6), but this tells us nothing about the historical Jesus. Josephus upgrades her to an innkeeper (*A.J.* 5.8). The Matthean and Lukan birth narratives, in which Mary prior to the consummation of her marriage to Joseph is found pregnant, coupled with both John 8:41, where "the Jews" tell Jesus, "We were not conceived out of *porneia*," and Jesus's unmarried status have led to the argument that Jesus was a *mamzer*, the

---

28. Anthony Le Donne, "Did Jesus Befriend Sex Workers?," *JSHJ* 20.3 (2022): 147–55.

child of an illegitimate union.[29] The argument, based on later, prescriptive rather than descriptive rabbinic texts, conflicts with the ongoing presence of Jesus in local synagogues as well as the Jerusalem temple, the lack of taunting concerning illegitimacy, and John's concern for the "legitimate" children of God, for which the accusation in 8:41 functions to show the "Jews" own "illegitimacy."

Trans or Intersexed Identities

Images in which Jesus complicates the gender binary are frequent and run across traditions. The affirmation of eunuchs in Matt 19:12, the homosocial gathering of the disciples, and expressions of Jesus's love for particular men all take on additional nuance when viewed in relation to depictions of Jesus's body. Never described physically, the body reveals traits more likely to be associated with women. According to Mark 5:30, Jesus feels "power go out" from him or, colloquially, he leaks.[30] According to John 19:34, "blood and water" pour out of his body (parturition imagery) after it is penetrated by the soldier's sword (suggesting sexual penetration). In some early Christian art, he is depicted as beardless, having long hair, and so feminized; in art he also has breasts and in the Odes of Solomon he lactates. [31]

That Jesus speaks of himself as being like a mother hen (Matt 23:37 // Luke 13:34) is no more feminization than it is promotion of poultry.

If Jesus did promote eschatological or apocalyptic views, the *Endzeit* focus could also lead to an *Urzeit* one, and celibacy, seen as an eschatological status, could draw upon or allude to a view of a new creation with an original androgynous human.[32] This Eden to Ending model may also help explain the "metamorphosis" (*metamorphoō*, Matt 17:2 // Mark 9:2) that the disciples purport to witness: the change may reveal Jesus in Adamic garments and so possibly allude to that prelapsarian androgyny.

The disruption of the male-female binary that the eunuch evokes can also complement the view of the ideal androgyne. Complicating this reading is that the androgyne codes male but the eunuch codes not-quite-male. The following state-

29. Bruce Chilton, *Rabbi Jesus: An Intimate Biography* (New York: Doubleday, 2000).

30. Candida R. Moss, "The Man with the Flow of Power: Porous Bodies in Mark 5:25–34," *JBL* 129.3 (2010): 507–19.

31. Ally Kateusz, "The Jesus Woman and the Jesus Women" (paper presented at the Westar Institute Christianity Seminar, Spring 2019), 79–103.

32. John W. Martens, "'But from the Beginning It Was Not So': The Jewish Apocalyptic Context of Jesus's Teaching on Marriage, Divorce, and Remarriage," *Journal of Moral Theology* 10.2 (2021): 5–33.

ment from Gos. Thom. 22 fits this model: "Jesus said to them: 'When you make the two one, and when you make the inside like the outside and the outside like the inside, and the above like the below, and when you make the male and the female one and the same, so that the male not be male nor the female female . . . then you will enter the kingdom'."[33] So too Gos. Thom. 114's "let us make Mary male" saying fits as well, but at the expense of women's bodies. Whether these texts reflect what Jesus said or what he was heard to have said remains an open question.

33. See also 2 Clem. 12.2–6 and comments in Kateusz, "Jesus Woman and the Jesus Women."

26

DISABILITY, HEALINGS, MIRACLES

Meghan R. Henning

The Next Quest for the historical Jesus must account for the ways in which the gospel healing stories (and the historical Jesus himself) reflect the theo-medical impulses of early Jesus followers and the antique Christian writers who preserved these narratives. When I use the term "theo-medical" I refer to a broad range of ancient ideas about the body that can be found in diverse source material, from the Hippocratic corpus to the New Testament gospels, ideas that do not neatly fit into modern categories like science and religion, or healing and miracle. These theo-medical impulses have been read and interpreted with more literalism than many other parts of the gospel narratives, even by scholars who would resist such an interpretive outlook in most other cases. Evidence from the LXX, rabbinic literature, Greek and Roman medical texts, magical papyri, and the epigraphic and other material remains from the Asclepieia allows us to imaginatively reconstruct the bodily discourses of the cultures in which the gospels were composed and circulated. Earlier quests, as Wendy Cotter has pointed out, selectively used evidence from ancient Jewish sources to read the miracles, ignoring the ways that

---

I would like to thank James Crossley and Chris Keith for bringing together this wonderful group of colleagues for an edifying exchange around novel questions about the historical Jesus. I also owe a debt of gratitude to Isaac T. Soon and Christopher W. Skinner, who offered helpful feedback on early drafts of this chapter. As ever, I am indebted to Travis Ables for impeccable editorial assistance.

first-century Judaism and the gospels were influenced by the Roman world.[1] In doing so, the historical Jesus emerges as a far more distinctive figure rather than another divine healer amid a field of gods, divine men, priests, and doctors who all healed through divine power. In turn, the act of healing itself is elevated as the point of the story not as a culturally delimited and inflected activity, but a divine balm that cuts across time and space as a universal good. If we use all of the available evidence to reconstruct the conceptions of the body that informed Jesus and the followers who wrote and circulated the gospels, then our readings of the miracle stories radically change. These stories are no longer anomalous or strange, they cannot be divided into the tidy categories that scholarship has offered to date, nor do they speak univocally about healing as a universal "good."

To some extent, previous Quests for the historical Jesus have engaged this material—it is not as though the evidence has been completely ignored. But until now the historical Jesus hermeneutic has consistently been one that seeks to perform a differential diagnosis on the miracle stories, categorizing them in ways that mirror enlightenment consciousness rather than ancient somatic sensibilities. Much of the work on the miracle stories and the historical Jesus has been rooted in historical analysis and form-critical work that distinguishes between types of miracles, identifying forms that were tightly correlated to the modern preoccupation with the verisimilitude of the account: Adolf von Harnack imagines Luke himself making a sharp distinction between "natural and demonic diseases" and Bultmann and his followers parsed the historically implausible "wonders" from the miracles that had some factual basis.[2] In spite of a desire to apply modern scientific precision to the miracle stories, these categories are not rooted in ancient medicine or disease theory.[3]

Recent studies of the historical Jesus have emphasized a need to treat the miracles as a complex phenomenon and have tried to avoid parsing their authen-

1. Wendy Cotter, "Miracle Stories: The God Asclepius, the Pythagorean Philosophers, and the Roman Rulers," in *The Historical Jesus in Context*, ed. Amy-Jill Levine, Dale C. Allison Jr., and John Dominic Crossan (Princeton: Princeton University Press, 2006), 166–67.

2. Adolf von Harnack, *Lukas der Arzt: Der Verfasser des dritten Evangeliums und der Apostelgeschichte* (Leipzig: Hinrichs, 1906), 136; Rudolf Bultmann, *History of the Synoptic Tradition*, trans. John Marsh, 2nd rev. ed. (Oxford: Blackwell, 1968), 209–20; Martin Dibelius, *From Tradition to Gospel*, trans. Bertram Lee Woolf, 2nd rev. ed. (Cambridge: Clark and Co., 1982), 99–103; Gerd Theissen, *Miracle Stories of the Early Christian Tradition*, ed. and trans. Francis McDonagh and John Riches (Edinburgh: T&T Clark, 1983), 34.

3. Annette Weissenrieder, "Disease and Healing in a Changing World: 'Medical' Vocabulary and the Woman with the 'Issue of Blood' in the *Vetus Latina* Mark 5:25–34 and Luke 8:40–48," *Religion in the Roman Empire* 3.2 (2017): 266, has noted that recent form-critical efforts often see ancient medicine as secondary to the task at hand, a trend that, as she notes, is "unsettling."

ticity. In spite of these efforts, the diagnostic impulse lingers, especially in the guise of historicity as observable fact. Just beneath the surface of the designations for which miracles belong to the historical Jesus is an assumption that certain elements of bodily healing are universal, namely that the observable total body transformation to some normative state constitutes "healing." For example, E. P. Sanders begins with an Asclepieion inscription to drive home the point that there is no clean divide between "the natural world and the supernatural world" in antiquity, but he still continues to categorize exorcisms as distinct from healings and Jesus's miracles as distinct from magic, and offers psychosomatic explanations for the exorcisms that he thinks Jesus did perform.[4] In the end, Sanders reads Jesus's miracles through the lens of ancient apocalyptic thought. But rigorous rationality only applies to exorcistic verisimilitude; it does not apply to the bodily norms that prop up apocalyptic thought. Total body transformation is the triumphant sign of a new age, and the disabled body is vanquished along with the forces of evil.[5] The historical Jesus emerges as an apocalyptically informed *medicus*, and the historical Jesus scholar the first-year resident, learning to sift the relevant case notes from the patient's unreliable reporting. As a result of past attempts at differential diagnosis, the historical Jesus has become a powerful tool in naturalizing the ableism of post-Enlightenment medicine.

Even apart from our scholarly enterprise, the miracle stories already lend themselves to an ableist hermeneutic today. The healing stories of the gospels are narratives of dramatic and instantaneous bodily transformation that almost never center the voice or experience of the person being healed, and sometimes do not even involve their consent.[6] It is no wonder that these texts are "texts of

---

4. E. P. Sanders, *The Historical Figure of Jesus* (New York: Penguin, 1993), 141, 136, 158–59.

5. Sanders, *Historical Figure of Jesus*, 166–67. Similarly, John P. Meier arrives at a Jesus who never cursed the fig tree but affirms that Jesus's disciples saw something that made them think that he healed a blind man named Bartimaeus. Meier is extremely careful to say that he cannot truly know what happened or if the events reported would fit modern definitions of "miracle," but the historical Jesus project is still about isolating the precise line between total theological embellishment and miraculously inflected medical happenings. See John P. Meier, *Mentor, Message, and Miracles*, vol. 2 of *A Marginal Jew: Rethinking the Historical Jesus*, AYBRL (New York: Doubleday, 1994), 967–70.

6. A prime example of this is in Mark 7:31–37, where the crowds bring the deaf man to Jesus, and interpret his speech impediment (*mogilalon*) as muteness (*alalous*). We have no idea if he wished to be healed, only that the crowds and Mark see his bodily impairment as an opportunity for Jesus to experiment with his power. The trope of bringing the disabled and sick to Jesus is throughout the gospels, as in the story of the healing of the paralyzed person in Matt 9:1–8; Mark 2:1–12; Luke 5:17–26.

terror" for the disability community today.[7] The gospel authors who received and interpreted traditions about Jesus's healing activity leveraged the ancient binary thinking about the body to magnify Jesus's own bodily status. The miracles communicate his reputation as an apocalyptic healer, a fulfiller of prophecy, and an embodiment of the divine. The disabled body is a prop, an artifact of transformation, and sometimes a repository of faith.

The healing narratives use an ancient somatic lexicon to make Jesus's body intelligible, but the occasional overlaps between ancient somatic hierarchies and the ableism of our own world makes the stories nearly unintelligible today—not because they are utterly foreign, but because they are too familiar. The binary thinking about the body that we see in the Hippocratic corpus, the ancient Asclepieion, or the gospels, persists today. In this thinking the disabled body is "broken" and needs to be "fixed"—a logic present in a pre-med student who once told me that practicing medicine was like being an auto mechanic for bodies. (Thanks to some humanities courses, you will be happy to know, he is recovering well from his Cartesian trauma.)[8] This partial overlap between the ancient and modern leads readers to assume that they have a firm handle on what is happening in these stories, and to read them as triumphant healing stories akin to a one-hour medical drama.

7. Jennifer L. Koosed and Darla Schumm, "Out of the Darkness: Examining the Rhetoric of Blindness in the Gospel of John," in *Disability in Judaism, Christianity, and Islam: Sacred Texts, Historical Traditions, and Social Analysis*, ed. Darla Schumm and Michael Stoltzfus (New York: Palgrave Macmillan, 2011), 77–92; Sharon Betcher, "Disability and the Terror of the Miracle Tradition," in *Miracles Revisited: New Testament Miracle Stories and Their Concepts of Reality*, ed. Stefan Alkier and Annette Weissenrieder (Berlin: de Gruyter, 2013), 165; cf. Phyllis Trible, *Texts of Terror: Literary-Feminist Readings of Biblical Narratives* (Minneapolis: Fortress, 1984); David Mitchell and Sharon Snyder, "'Jesus Thrown Everything off Balance': Disability and Redemption in Biblical Literature," in *This Abled Body: Rethinking Disabilities in Biblical Studies*, ed. Hector Avalos, Sarah Melcher, and Jeremy Schipper (Atlanta: Society of Biblical Literature, 2007), 173–84.

8. On the way that miracles leverage the disabled body in antiquity as fundamentally weak, less desirable, and in need of transformation, see Hector Avalos, *Healthcare and the Rise of Christianity* (Peabody, MA: Hendrickson, 1999); Avalos et al., *This Abled Body*; Candida R. Moss and Jeremy Schipper, eds., *Disability Studies and Biblical Literature* (New York: Palgrave Macmillan, 2011); Meghan R. Henning, "In Sickness and in Health: 'Ancient Rituals of Truth' in the Greco-Roman World and 1 Peter," in Moss and Schipper, *Disability Studies*, 185–204; Candida R. Moss, "Mark and Matthew," in *The Bible and Disability: A Commentary*, ed. Sarah J. Melcher, Mikeal C. Parsons, and Amos Yong (Waco, TX: Baylor University Press, 2017), 275–302; D. F. Watson, "Luke-Acts," 303–32. For discussion of the interpretive perils of spaces in which contemporary and ancient bodily norms overlap, see Meghan R. Henning "Healing and Exorcisms," in *Oxford Handbook of the Synoptic Gospels*, ed. Stephen Ahearne-Kroll (Oxford: Oxford University Press, 2023), 355–71.

The Next Quest for the historical Jesus needs to join efforts that are already under way in other subfields to make the miracle stories intelligible as historically bound and culturally conditioned.[9] To historicize the miracle stories means eschewing facile similes that reinforce their violence, but also means speaking truthfully about places where the Jesus of history and his readers may have more in common with our own attitudes toward the body than we care to admit.[10] The miracle stories reinforce binaries around the life experiences of the sick and disabled that were not true in antiquity and are not true today. Those binaries are enhanced and amplified as early Christians received and interpreted the stories of Jesus healing, and early Christians increasingly used the body as a cipher for spiritual health. If we can resurface a culturally contingent Jesus, along with all of his and his followers' bodily hang-ups, we are not simply coming closer to the Jesus of history; we can also offer somatically sensitive interpretations of an ancient message for a modern world. This Next Quest has the opportunity to move from differential diagnosis and verifiability toward a Jesus whose actions may have been totally plausible in his own world but should give us pause today.

ADDING DIMENSION TO THE MIRACULOUS

To give proper interpretive attention to the Jesus of history several different areas of historical study need to come together, as is necessary for the study of the body and disability in any historical period.[11] Here the cultural model of disability offers us crucial tools for eschewing either an overidentification with the Jesus of history or alienation—it requires that we work assiduously to reconstruct the ancient bodily norms that made Jesus's miracles intelligible.[12] The agenda I set

9. I am here thinking of disability studies, medical anthropology, ancient medicine, classics, and archaeology, as well as critical theoretical work on space, the body, and gender.

10. We see this, for instance, in interpretations like Bultmann's that naturalized the idea that all attention should be on the healer and his power, and that the sick person should only be described inasmuch as it can "bring the act of the healer into its proper light." See Bultmann, *History of the Synoptic Tradition*, 219–21.

11. Dan Goodley, "Dis/entangling Critical Disability Studies," *Disability & Society* 28.5 (2013): 631–44; Katie Ellis, Mike Kent, Rachel Robertson, and Rosemarie Garland-Thomson, eds., *Interdisciplinary Approaches to Disability: Looking towards the Future* (London: Routledge, 2019).

12. On the cultural model of disability and its use in biblical studies see David T. Mitchell, *Cultural Locations of Disability* (Chicago: University of Chicago Press, 2006), 5–11; Jeremy Schipper, *Disability Studies and the Hebrew Bible: Figuring Mephibosheth in the David Story* (London: T&T Clark, 2006), 18–21; Rebecca Raphael, *Biblical Corpora: Representations of Disability in Hebrew Biblical Literature*, LHBOTS 445 (London: T&T Clark, 2008), 8–11; Moss and Schipper, *Disability Studies*, 4.

here is not exhaustive, but will initiate the inclusion of other work on bodies and the historical Jesus.

Theo-Medical Landscape and Apocalyptic Dimensions

I concur with previous quests that Jesus's healing miracles are eschatological, and likely go back (in some form) to the person of Jesus. But if that is the case then we need to more rigorously contextualize the bodily norms that are operative in the prophetic and apocalyptic outlook he employed. In Matt 11:2–6 Jesus tells the disciples of the imprisoned John the Baptist to report to him of what they see, describing his ministry in words that echo Isa 35: "Go and tell John what you hear and see: the blind receive their sight and the lame walk, lepers are cleansed and the deaf hear, and the dead are raised up, and the poor have good news preached to them. And blessed is he who takes no offense at me."[13] How and why did healing signal the prophetic or a restoration of the kingdom of God for the historical Jesus?

Medical anthropology tells us that ancient Near Eastern etiologies of disease are embedded in worldviews that emphasize community cohesion and divine communication.[14] That is, disease is a form of communication from the god and so is healing. While the individual body experiences disease and impairment, disease often represents a rupture in the community and healing its restoration. Within first-century Judaism this perspective operated in different ways for different groups. In 1 En. 7:1, apocalyptically inflected healing means that medicine is not just about harnessing "spirits" more generally (as it was in the Hebrew Bible) but about navigating between good and malevolent spirits. This is tied to a cosmological shift that is at least in part influenced by the broader culture (namely Zoroastrianism and Neoplatonism). Philo tells us that the Essenes shared the perspective that God restores health, but that they saw themselves as *therapeutai theou* who could heal body and soul.[15] But Philo also adds that the Essenes would pay for the healing of a sick person out of the shared financial resources of the community. And if the Talmud is any indication, it would seem that pragmatism toward Greco-Roman medicine may have prevailed for Pharisaic healers, especially in Palestine and Alexandria.[16]

---

13. Translation mine. Sanders, *Historical Figure of Jesus*, 168, has interpreted this passage to mean that the historical Jesus saw his healing activity as the fulfillment of prophetic hope, the beginning of a new eschatological age.

14. This section follows closely the thorough work of Laura M. Zucconi, *Ancient Medicine: From Mesopotamia to Rome* (Grand Rapids: Eerdmans, 2019), 323–55.

15. Philo, *Contempl.* 1.2. As Zucconi, *Ancient Medicine*, 325–26, notes, this depiction does not really cohere with the evidence from the Dead Sea Scrolls.

16. Stephen T. Newmyer, "Talmudic Medicine and Greco-Roman Science," *ANRW* 37.3:2895–911.

What we see from all of our sources is that the binary discourses around the body are not operating in isolation within Second Temple Judaism; they are also interspersed with ideas about anatomy and healing that are influenced by Hellenism. In the LXX we see anatomical terminology shifting to reflect Hippocratic medicine.[17] In Josephus we find retellings of stories from the Hebrew Bible that insert "physicians" or Hellenistic ideas about the body and nature.[18] Ben Sira describes the physician's abilities as a "healing gift" that "comes from the Most High" and encourages the sick to seek forgiveness and pray, to use pharmaceuticals because the pharmacist and God make them from the elements of the earth, and to seek medical care from a physician (Sir 38:1–15).[19] It appears that Ben Sira is simultaneously expressing older biblical views of healing and the body (sickness is tied to sin, healing ultimately comes from God, healing restores the community) while weaving in an affirmation of pharmacological and physician-assisted interventions that were more popular in Greek and Roman thinking about the body. In this period of history, Jewish approaches to healing, miracles, and the body were shifting, and we even see this formalized in the conceptual fluidity of early rabbinic sources, which vacillate between evaluations of the disabled body as a punishment from God and an intentional part of the created order, as is suited to a given legal or ritual context.[20]

---

17. Angela Thomas, *Anatomical Idiom and Emotional Expression: A Comparison of the Hebrew Bible and the Septuagint* (Sheffield: Sheffield Phoenix, 2014), 1.

18. Josephus, *A.J.* 2.347–348; 6.166. In his retelling of 1 Sam 16:15–16 Josephus adds "physicians" who were unable to do anything to help except try to play the spirits away with a harp. In his interpretation of Moses parting the Red Sea, the sea is intelligent and able to recognize Moses as a God-ordained leader. These shifts are subtle but reflect the tenor of first-century Judaic thought on the body and the natural world, melded with pieces of Hellenic medicine and philosophy as they were compatible.

19. As Zucconi, *Ancient Medicine*, 333–34, 352–53 notes, this passage likely reflects an attempt to combat the distrust of secular doctors who could be characterized by some as "idol worshipers" or "magicians."

20. Julia Watts Belser, "Reading Talmudic Bodies: Disability, Narrative, and the Gaze in Rabbinic Judaism," in Schumm and Stolzfus, *Disability in Judaism, Christianity and Islam*, 5–27; Julia Watts Belser and Lennart Lehmhaus, "Disability in Rabbinic Jewish Sources," in *Disability in Antiquity*, ed. Christian Laes (New York: Routledge, 2017), 434–52. Some impairments that we would categorize as a disability today, like blindness, were seen as providing special intellectual qualification within the rabbinic study house; see Belser, "Reading Talmudic Bodies"; Belser and Lehmhaus, "Disability in Rabbinic Jewish Sources." In other cases, disability precluded one from performing certain *mitzvot* (religious obligations)—the Talmud outlines deaf-mutes, those with mental disabilities, the gender indeterminate, the double sexed, women, the enslaved, the blind, the lame, the sick, and even youth as subordinate or dependent bodily existences not obligated to make pilgrimage or perform sacrifices; see m. Ḥag. 1:1 on Exod 23:17 and Belser, "Reading Talmudic Bodies." On the idea that the disabled are an important part of the created order see t. Ber. 6:3 and Belser and Lehmhaus, "Disability in Rabbinic Jewish Sources."

When we talk about the historical Jesus's apocalyptic or prophetic healings, I think we need to interrogate how the historical Jesus and his interpreters participated in a shifting theo-medical landscape within Judaism. The Next Quest must take care not to conflate first-century readings of the LXX with Bronze or Iron Age notions of the body and healing, nor assume that Jesus's participation in this already in-progress conversation represents some kind of radical reform or rupture. Jesus was a prophetic or apocalyptic healer, and the binaries of that bodily discourse overlapped with the dualistic theo-medical discourses of the Hellenistic world. Like other Jews of his time, Jesus is operating in a changing world in which both divine and deadly forces are at work on human bodies, but divine power and the coming of a new age could be mediated through a healer or physician by a number of practical means.[21]

Jesus and Asclepius

Ancient binaries of sickness and health are perhaps clearest at the Asclepieia, the healing shrines devoted to Asclepius that were active from the fourth century BCE to the fifth century CE. Inscriptions and material evidence from these shrines are voluminous, testifying to the inescapable presence of the images and bodily norms that were proliferated at the over one hundred shrines throughout the ancient Mediterranean.[22] The epigraphic evidence from these shrines makes it possible to see the specific ways medical practices and devotion to the god were intertwined.[23] The suppliant offered her devotion to the god and waited in the abaton for a dream cure, though the treatment that was offered by the god could

21. As Matthew Thiessen, *Jesus and the Forces of Death: The Gospels' Portrayal of Ritual Impurity within First Century Judaism* (Grand Rapids: Baker Academic, 2020), 21–41, argues, the framing of laws was diverse in the Judaism of this period as well. See also Liane Feldman, "Sanitized Sacrifice in Aramaic Levi's Law of the Priesthood," *JAJ* 11.3 (2020): 343–68, for a discussion of the way in which rituals and purity laws were diverse, especially at the end of the first century CE. In light of this legal and ritual diversity interpreters of the gospels need to take care not to see divergent approaches to healing and the body as "breaks" with Judaism.

22. René Josef Rüttimann, "Asklepios and Jesus: The Form, Character and Status of the Asklepios Cult in the Second Century CE and Its Influence on Early Christianity" (PhD diss., Harvard University, 1986), 11–21; Louise Cilliers and François Retief, "Dream Healing in Asclepieia in the Mediterranean," in *Dreams, Healing, and Medicine in Greece: From Antiquity to the Present*, ed. Steven M. Oberhelman (Farnham: Ashgate, 2013), 70–75; Vivian Nutton, *Ancient Medicine*, 2nd ed. (New York: Routledge, 2013), 282–83.

23. On the way that the Asclepius cult troubles distinctions between "supernatural" and "natural" healing, see Annette Weissenrieder, "Stories Just under the Skin: *Lepra* in the Gospel of Luke," in Alkier and Weissenrieder, *Miracles Revisited*, 89–92.

range from a simple healing touch and pronouncement to a prescription that mirrored those of Hippocratic medicine.[24]

One of the unique things about the epigraphic evidence from these shrines is that they purport to tell the stories of the sick in the voice of the sick person—a relatively rare occurrence. But careful study of the inscriptions quickly reveals that the stories are still very much told from the perspective of the "well," offering stories of bodily transformation that objectify the sick body and rehearse ancient binaries of sickness and health. The sick are characterized as ignorant, foolish, and bad pray-ers (they do not ask properly for what they want). In one telling inscription from Epidaurus, the healing of the sick person's body is compared to a story about Asclepius fixing a broken cup.[25] The healing encounters narrate triumphant stories of bodily transformation, ones in which the body of the sick or disabled person is a central object in the story, but the person seeking the cure is rarely elevated to subject status.[26] Even in a culture in which disability and illness were more prevalent than wellness, binary thinking about the body appears to be inescapable, on full display in a space that was supposed to be designed for the sick and disabled to encounter the divine.

EXORCISMS

Exorcisms are right at home in the theo-medical landscapes of both the ancient Asclepieia and first-century Judaism. Although previous NT scholarship has distinguished exorcisms from healings, I argue that this is another symptom of the post-Enlightenment diagnostic impulse.[27] All of our available evidence suggests

---

24. On healing via touch at the Asclepeion see *IG* 4.1.122, l. 31 (160 CE), where Asclepius touches (*haptomai*) Andromache with his hand and then she bears a son; *IG* 4.1.126, where the god touches a patient (*haptomai*) and cures Marcus Julius Apellas's hand; *IG* 4.1.122, l. 38, where the god heals by trampling over a patient to heal his knees. For examples of Hippocratic "prescriptions" like bathing or dietary regimens that show up at the shrines see *IG* 4.1.126; 4.1.122, l. 37.

25. *IG* 4.1.121, Stele A9 and A10.

26. As Belser and Lehmhaus, "Disability in Rabbinic Jewish Sources," 447, note, even in places where ancient thinkers sought to affirm the disabled body, it still occupied an object position, "set apart as a source of strangeness."

27. Henning, "Healing and Exorcisms." In one telling example, Gerd Theissen distinguishes between exorcism and healing by arguing that the healing stories bring us closer to the "dawn of medicine": "The mere absence of demonological motifs is not a distinctive feature of healings as opposed to exorcisms; what is distinctive is that the motifs of conflict are replaced by images of the transmission of healing power, images which doubtless bring us closer to the dawn of medicine than do the powerful words of exorcism." See *Miracle Stories of the Early Christian Tradition* (Edinburgh: T&T Clark, 1983), 90.

that during the time of Jesus an exorcism is one type of healing among many viable possibilities. *Daimons*, or divine agents, were not only active in contexts that were explicitly connected to a god—they were present and powerful for the ancient physician as well.[28] We see an example of Jesus mirroring the ancient physician in the exorcism in Luke 4:31–37. In Mark's version of the story the unclean spirit convulses and screams on its way out (Mark 1:26). Luke, however, changes the wording so that the exorcism "does him no harm," borrowing from the broadly held cultural idea that medical treatments should "do no harm." Although this idea is enshrined in the Hippocratic oath using different verbiage (*adikia* and *phthoria*), it is mentioned throughout ancient medical literature and in one paraphrase in the Hippocratic corpus, which uses the same phrasing of "do no harm" (*mē blaptō*) that we find in Luke.[29] Jesus as an apocalyptic doctor whose exorcisms "do no harm" may well be a Lukan creation and not a nod to the Jesus of history.

But Luke is not alone among the gospel authors in depicting exorcism as a type of healing story or in explicitly connecting Jesus's miracles to ancient medical practice. Mark groups the sick and demon-possessed together from the start of his gospel (Mark 1:32). And Matthew treats exorcism as a type of healing in his special section devoted to healing stories (Matt 8–9). It seems that the Jesus who exorcises as a matter of routine in Mark was not shocking for ancient readers or in need of revision (Matthew adds as many exorcism stories as he excises), but it could be amplified by continuing to layer the apocalyptic and medical binaries in a way that emphasized the arrival of the new age foretold by the prophets.

The short exorcistic formulae that Jesus uses in the gospels are not unique to early Christianity, nor do they transgress contemporaneous healing practices.[30]

---

28. Teun Tieleman, "Miracle and Natural Cause in Galen," in Alkier and Weissenrieder, *Miracles Revisited*, 101–14.

29. The earliest recoverable Greek of the Hippocratic Oath does not contain the precise phrasing "do no harm," and instead mentions harm avoidance twice—*adikia* and *phthoria* (Hippocratic Corpus *Oath* lines 18–19, 28). Although the exact phrase does not occur in the Oath, a closer formulation does appear in Hippocratic Corpus *Epidemics* 1.11, which, like Luke, uses *mē blaptō* ("the physician . . . must have two special objects in mind with regard to disease, namely to do good or to do no harm"). The idea that physicians should endeavor not to harm the patient was not only mentioned multiple times in the Hippocratic Oath, it appears elsewhere in the medical literature, suggesting that this was a broadly held component of ancient medical thinking which might have been known by Luke and his audience. See Henning, "Healing and Exorcisms."

30. Travis Proctor, *Demonic Bodies and the Dark Ecologies of Early Christian Culture* (Oxford: Oxford University Press, 2022), 110–14, demonstrates that short exorcistic formulae were not "unique" to early Christians. Likewise, Shaily Shashikant Patel, "Magic and Its Malcontents: Historiography as Heresiology" (paper presented at the Abrahamic Vernaculars Lecture Series,

Exorcisms, like other miracles, allowed Jesus to transform the world around him so that those who inhabited the weakest position in the binary pair could now inhabit a position of strength, a reversal of fortunes that was desired, sought after, and rare. As a result, it may be very difficult, if not impossible, to tease apart the exorcisms and healings of the historical Jesus from the interpretive tissues that surround them in the gospels.

Our task then, is to contextualize Jesus's healing activities, not naturalize them by identifying which types of ancient healing are most analogous to our own. Readers today have sought to either distance themselves from the exorcisms through modern diagnostic criteria or to read them as stories about madness. Both of these approaches are equally problematic historically and grounded in the impulse to diagnose, cordon off, and mark as grotesque any mindbody that we cannot neatly explain. This impulse is perhaps another place where our own view is too similar (rather than too far removed) from our sources.[31] My hope is that the Next Quest for the historical Jesus eschews both of these approaches, acknowledging that exorcisms as an ancient modality of healing are part of a binary thinking about the body that need not operate in concert with our own ableism in order to be comprehensible.

Ancient Economies of Cure *and* Care

While the miracle stories tell of bodies that were healed within a diffuse theo-medical landscape, the stories they tell trade upon the rarity of a cure. Most of the sick and disabled bodies in the ancient world would remain sick and disabled until death. Malnutrition, disease, intestinal parasites, and intermarriage within families were pervasive, and many people experienced progressive vision loss

---

University of Michigan, Ann Arbor, MI, November 11, 2021) has argued that magic was not necessarily "transgressive," in spite of later Christian uses of magic to delineate communal boundaries.

31. As a number of studies on the demonic in Second Temple Judaism and early Christianity have already noted, the demonic is frequently associated with whatever is marginal in a given context. Amanda Witmer, *Jesus, the Galilean Exorcist: His Exorcisms in Social and Political Context* (London: T&T Clark, 2012), 27; Jan Dochhorn, Susanne Rudnig-Zelt, and Benjamin Wold, eds., *Das Böse, der Teufel und Dämonen—Evil, the Devil, and Demons*, WUNT 2.412 (Tübingen: Mohr Siebeck, 2016); Chris Keith and Loren T. Stuckenbruck, eds., *Evil in Second Temple Judaism and Early Christianity* (Tübingen: Mohr Siebeck, 2016); Sara Ronis, "Space, Place, and the Race for Power: Rabbis, Demons, and the Construction of Babylonia," *HTR* 110.4 (2017): 588–603. On the need to read these discursive frameworks with attention to socioeconomic power and exploitation, see Candida R. Moss, "Exploitation, Exorcism, and Power: Reconfiguring Culpability for Possession in the New Testament" (paper presented at the Deliver Us from Evil Conference, Church of England online, January 20, 2022).

over the course of life. Women were compelled to have children in as rapid a succession as possible (with no nutritional supplements), leading to poorer health outcomes and a higher mortality rate than men. Though ancient medicine was impressive for its time, access to healthcare was costly and healthcare outcomes were notoriously unpredictable.[32]

In this context, people were more likely to experience long periods of medical care than they were a cure or dramatic transformation. Aelius Aristides remains a devotee to Asclepius throughout his life, living at the Asclepeion for seventeen years for easy access to ongoing treatment, and praised the god for allowing him to continue his rhetorical career with a chronic illness. Aristides receives care from the god but he is never healed in the way that so many people are in the gospels or in the inscriptions at the Asclepeia. Likewise, Paul is never able to miraculously shed his thorn in the flesh, and like Aristides he counts himself blessed by God because of his disability.[33] In Matt 25 Jesus does not commend healers to heavenly salvation, but those who visit the sick. While we only see occasional glimmers of palliative treatment in the New Testament, it seems that early Christians were not exclusively beholden to the binaries of sickness and health, and at least in some spaces living with illness and care for the sick were just as important as cure.

Though Aristides and Paul are not cured, they do, like the miracle stories, draw attention to disabled bodies in order to communicate the importance of placing trust in the divine. All of these stories of both care and cure are highly individualized—they focus intently on the body of the sick person as well as their responsibility for the condition of their body. The miracles from the Asclepeion offer stories that taut the divine power of the healer as something that is only mediated in exchange for trust.[34] Conversely, those who are not healed are characterized as ignorant or foolish because they did not trust Asclepius to heal

32. The medical literature attests that the experience of the woman with the flow of blood in Mark 5:25–26 was not anomalous—physicians were sometimes reticent to take cases that other doctors refused to treat or unsuccessfully treated because they wanted to avoid potentially harming the patient through unnecessary interventions. See Nutton, *Ancient Medicine*, 92; Hippocrates, *Morb.* 2.48; *Mul.* 1.71; *Steril.* 233; *De arte* 3.2; 8.1–7. Cf. *Epid.* 1.11.

33. Candida R. Moss, "Christly Possession and Weakened Bodies: Reconsideration of the Function of Paul's Thorn in the Flesh (2 Cor. 12:7–10)," *Journal of Religion, Disability, and Health* (2012): 319–33.

34. Some inscriptions indicate that the suppliant was healed as the result of "earnest prayer" (*IG* 2.4514) or his steadfast presence at the shrine while waiting for healing (*IC* 1.17.18). Likewise, the Hippocratic school thought that the efficacy of the medical treatment depended on the patient's trust in the physician. See for instance, Hippocrates, *De arte* 11.1–41; *Vict.* 3.71.19–23; Nutton, *Ancient Medicine*, 88, 102–3.

them.[35] Even if the total cure was an anomaly, healing was seen as communion with the divine, and illness its interruption. The disabled body was seen as weak, broken, dysfunctional, inferior, and in need of correction. The miracles offer a dramatic restoration to a strong, whole, functional body, but they also offer the restoration of relationships between the divine, the healed, and her community.[36] The intertwined binaries of faithful and unfaithful, wise and foolish, healed and sick, and whole and broken were a double-edged sword for the sick and disabled in antiquity: they placed responsibility on the disabled and chronically ill, assigning blame; but they also offered the increasingly large number of sick and disabled persons a sense of agency over something that was out of their control.[37]

Jesus's healings as we have received them are often emblematic of these ancient bodily discourses and the binaries that they reinscribe. The places in which the historical Jesus may have offered something exceptional via his healings are those traditions that offer a reversal or modification of these bodily norms, those that imagine the healed person rejoining his community, those in which the sick person has a voice or agency in her healing, or those that center on the person being healed, not only the healer.[38] It is clear that the early Jesus followers who

35. One patient at the shrine is renamed "incredulous" by the god because he did not trust in the god's power to heal (*IG* 4.1.121–122 Stele 1.3). Other patients do not receive healing because they do not do as the god says or do not ask correctly. Only after they exhibit allegiance or trust through a proper request are these suppliants healed (see for instance, *IG* 4.1.121–22 Stele 2.36; *IG* 4.1.121 Stele A2).

36. At the Pergamum Asclepeion, for instance, the abaton had windows that overlooked the city upon the hill, a design that places the suppliants to the god in close proximity to the city to which they hoped to return as they awaited healing. For some, the sights or sounds of the city would have held out the promise of being reunited with their community once healed. The shrines at Kos and Lebena also face the port city, with Lebena's abaton angled toward the beach. Vitruvius in *On Architecture* suggests that certain qualities are geographically desirable for healing temples, namely removal from the city, fresh air, fresh water, and elevation (1.2.7). I am grateful to John David Penniman for this reference and for sharing his own experiences of the layout at the surviving Greek Asclepieia.

37. In the first-century CE, increasing urbanization led to a rise in sickness, and economic barriers to health care meant that most people could not afford the best treatments. Avalos, *Healthcare and the Rise of Christianity*, 4–7, 117–19.

38. Candida R. Moss, "The Man with the Flow of Power: Porous Bodies in Mark 5:25–34," *JBL* 129.3 (2010): 507–19; Jennifer K. Koosed and Darla Schumm, "Out of the Darkness: Examining the Rhetoric of Blindness in the Gospel of John," in Schumm and Stolzfus, *Disability in Judaism, Christianity and Islam*, 77–92; Warren Carter, "'The Blind, Lame, and Paralyzed' (John 5:3): John's Gospel, Disability Studies, and Postcolonial Perspectives," in Moss and Schipper, *Disability Studies*, 129–50; Jaime Clark-Soles, "John, First–Third John, and Revelation," in *The Bible and Disability: A Commentary*, ed. S. J. Melcher, M. C. Parsons, and A. Yong (Waco, TX: Baylor University Press, 2017), 333–78; Candida R. Moss, "Mark and Matthew," in Melcher et al., *Bible and Disability*,

preserved the miracle stories were operating with both care and cure in mind, and with an eye toward including at least some miracles that disrupted the standard narratives of cure as universal or objectifying (as was also the case in contemporaneous Jewish literature).

ENFLESHING THE HISTORICAL JESUS WITH CARE

One of my honors students was enraged after reading Mitchell and Snyder's essay on Jesus's miracles and Flannery O'Connor's *A Good Man Is Hard to Find*. In this essay Mitchell and Snyder identify the challenge that narratives of redemption through bodily sacrifice and the New Testament miracle stories posed for O'Connor in a post–World War II context, namely that they could be too easily superimposed onto genocidal logics: the erasure of bodily difference is necessary for a cohesive society.[39] My student had enthusiastically participated in conversations around disability and the Bible in my seminar all semester long. He was passionate about somatically sensitive interpretations of the biblical narratives, and even saw it as an imperative within his Catholic faith. But the suggestion that the act of healing itself was culturally coded was a step too far, and he shouted: "What do they want Jesus to have done, not have healed those people!?!?!?" The historical Jesus healing makes a certain sense for his ancient culture, but if he were alive today, would healing be a sign of the miraculous? Is that the form that the apocalyptic "new age" or the prophetic reversal of hierarchies would take? We reanimate the socioeconomic violence of the ancient world if we cling to the idea that free medical care is miraculous, if that is truly the best God could do to usher in a new era. What the Next Quest for the historical Jesus can teach us is to stop looking for Doctor McDreamy in the Jesus of history.

275–302; David F. Watson, "Luke-Acts," in Melcher et al., *Bible and Disability*, 303–32; Louise A. Gosbell, "The Woman with the 'Flow of Blood' (Mark 5:25–34) and Disability in the Ancient World," *Journal of Gospels and Acts Research* 2 (2018): 22–43; Anna Rebecca Solevåg, "Zacchaeus in the Gospel of Luke: Comic Figure, Sinner, and Included 'Other'," *Journal of Literary & Cultural Disability Studies* 14.2 (2020): 225–40.

39. "Jesus as a prophet engaged in faith healing treats disability as any other socially made obstacle in that bodies may be revised into less cumbersome experiences. Whereas the removal of social barriers delimits the environment as the target of intervention, in cure/resurrection/redemption scenarios bodies are fixed to fit an unaccommodating environment." See Mitchell and Snyder, "'Jesus Thrown Everything Off Balance,'" 179, and in their final analysis: "The acceptance of disabled people can no longer be predicated on the pervasive interests that underwrite fantasies of erasure, cure, or elimination of bodily difference. Such longings for human similitude ultimately avoid rather than engage the necessity of providing provisions for our meaningful inclusion in social life" (183).

E. P. Sanders concluded his chapter on "Miracles and the Historical Jesus" with an assertion that Jesus saw himself in Isa 35, just as Matthew did, and that he shared the view that he was the fulfillment of the prophet's hopes for total body transformation for all of the sick and disabled.[40] Given the diversity of thought in first-century Judaism around healing, the body, and disability, I am not sure we can really assert this; it seems equally as likely that either the author of Matthew or Jesus is here wading into the first-century conversation about medicine and the body. As a scholar of disability studies, sure, I would love to say that the Jesus of history is the one we see siding with the Tosefta or the Talmud, affirming that disability is part of the created order and not caused by sin (as in John 9). Or from the perspective of Mad studies, it might be great to recover the Jesus who sometimes avails himself of the medical and pharmacological *techne* of the day but also sometimes distrusts it (as the audience of Ben Sira seems to have done).[41] But as a historian the best I can do is to say that all of these Jesuses (including the one who may have understood Isa 35 as a pronouncement of compulsory bodily transformation) were possible. By the same token it is equally likely that the historical Jesus operated with more than one notion of healing, the miraculous, or the body, and we err when we try to pin him down to a single rationally consistent practice of ritual or medicine. To this end, perhaps what is important for the Next Quest is not that we accurately perform a differential diagnosis of Jesus, or that we find a *cure* for our own perceptions, but that we find a way to *care* about the historical Jesus that is open to all of the possibilities and problems that a culturally contingent embodied reality entails.

---

40. Sanders, *Historical Figure of Jesus*, 168.

41. Mad studies is the branch of disability studies that is focused on mental disabilities. For a helpful introduction see Margaret Price, "Defining Mental Disability," in *The Disability Studies Reader*, ed. Lennard J. Davis, 5th ed. (New York: Routledge, 2017), 333–42. The specific comparison I am drawing here is to the way that Mad studies scholarship has acknowledged that "treatment" can sometimes be helpful and other times objectifying and violent for patients/consumers/survivors/ex-patients (p/c/s/x) of the psychiatric system. And so, as for Ben Sira, there is a tension between trust and distrust of the medical apparatus. See also Linda J. Morrison, *Talking Back to Psychiatry: The Psychiatric Consumer/Survivor/Ex-Patient Movement* (New York: Routledge, 2005); Bradley Lewis, *Moving beyond DSM, Prozac, and the New Psychiatry* (Ann Arbor: University of Michigan Press, 2006), 157.

27

Spirit World

Giovanni B. Bazzana

The Next Quest for the historical Jesus must account in a more coherent and systematic form for the role that the "spirit world" played in shaping the religious experience both of Jesus himself and of the people who collected and organized the earliest traditions about him.[1]

I will use "spirit world" here as an overarching category that embraces all the more-than-human beings that are variously designated as *pneumata*, "demons" (*daimones* or *daimonia*), or "angels" both in the documents related to the earliest Jesus movement as well as in the broader ancient Mediterranean context.[2] It is

---

1. Throughout the present contribution, I will avoid the term "demon," which is indeed widespread (as *daimonion*) in the earliest Greek traditions related to Jesus of Nazareth. That being said, due to the influence of centuries of Christian theologizing, in the West "demon" has become exclusively malignant and negative, losing that moral and ontological ambiguity that characterizes the entities encountered by Jesus and his followers. "Spirit" offers a much better alternative (and scores plenty of occurrences in the early Christian record, as *pneuma*), but it is worth noting that ancient *pneumata* should not be slotted into a stark binary between materiality and immateriality, which did not suit ancient Mediterranean conceptions of these beings at all. For the last point, see now Travis Proctor, *Demonic Bodies and the Dark Ecologies of Early Christian Culture* (Oxford: Oxford University Press, 2022).

2. As far as *angeloi* are concerned, it is worth noting (with Bogdan Bucur, who develops an original observation of Jean Daniélou) that the term is a specifically Jewish one (derived from the Scriptures in the Second Temple period), but it is basically interchangeable with *pneumata* to indicate the manifestation of more-than-human "persons." On this, see Bogdan Bucur, *Ange-*

well known that these beings were assumed as present and active in any facet of ordinary life by people inhabiting this region of the world in antiquity. But, despite this fundamental acknowledgment, for the most part modern historiographical analyses of the historical Jesus (and of other figures belonging to the Christ movement) have struggled to take seriously such a starting assumption.

In this perspective, there is little doubt then that the topic "spirit world" lends itself quite well to a renewed investigation along the guidelines sketched here for the Next Quest. Indeed, this is not only an aspect of the traditional Quest that has been largely neglected by previous scholarship, but it is also a problematic nexus that would benefit significantly from an investigation conducted in a comparative mode, as proposed by the organizers of the colloquium from which the present volume was produced.

In my brief contribution, I will try to do achieve two goals, which can only be taken as preliminary observations for a more fully developed treatment. First, I will illustrate what I consider to be the conceptual and methodological limitations that have hindered (for the most part, because exceptions do exist and are quite significant, as I will explain shortly) the study of the "spirit world" in previous iterations of the Quest for the historical Jesus. At the same time, I will also sketch what I believe could be a more suitable and productive approach to this problematic nexus. In the second section of the paper, I will examine a text—the complex exorcism story of Mark 5 and its parallels—using some facets of that narrative as a means to illustrate the gains one may derive from a renewed analysis of the relationship between the historical Jesus and the "spirit world."

Traditional Approaches

Let's start then by noting that, surprisingly enough, the significance of the above-mentioned relationship has been remarkably underappreciated in the scholarship devoted to the Quest.

This is not entirely surprising, since "spirit world" is indeed a rather tricky topic in New Testament and early Christian studies, broadly conceived. One may start from the very basic observation that, however one defines "spirit world" (and even the terminology is complex and fraught, as one will see momentarily), there can be little doubt that it played a very significant role in the religious experience (or at the very least in its literary reimagination) of early Christ groups. The narratives of gospels and acts, be they canonical or not, are full of stories in which the main

---

lomorphic Pneumatology: Clement of Alexandria and Other Early Christian Witnesses, VCSup 95 (Leiden: Brill, 2009), xxv–xxvii.

characters deal with malevolent "spirits" and exorcise them. This is already a massive amount of evidence, even without considering the ways in which "positive possession" is presented in the same writings in ways that we, as modern readers, have been habituated to overlook.[3]

To begin with, it is worth noting that the specific nature of the "spirit world" raises a series of questions that provide both challenges and opportunities also for the very methodological principles of the Next Quest. Of course, "spirit world" is a modern term, with no real counterpart in ancient documents. In them, as mentioned before, one encounters a plurality of designations (*pneumata*, demons, angels, and so on), which experienced different trajectories after the time of the historical Jesus and his earliest followers. One should definitely appreciate the well-placed challenge posed by the Next Quest's call to treat the earliest accounts of the "historical Jesus" as themselves historical artifacts. But such a starting point is exactly where one encounters knots of problems directly related to what I have called the "spirit world." The admittedly modern phrase strives to capture the fundamental datum that, for the earliest followers of Jesus (and in all likelihood for the historical Jesus himself), these more-than-human beings formed a *continuum* despite their various designations. Only later on, for instance, did demons and angels begin to be sharply separated within taxonomic structures that placed the former on the evil side and the latter on the good side with perpetual enmity and unbridgeable hostility between the two groups.[4] This is nowhere as clear as in the case of "possession," a phenomenon that, for most later Christian authors, became something exclusively negative and in need to be healed through exorcism. Thus, I believe that a beneficial task (among several others, of course) for the Next Quest may indeed be to figure out why such a transformation happened and what difference it made considering the fact that the situation was not the same for the earliest Jesus movement (and arguably for the historical Jesus).

Answering these questions may start with the historiographical problem of why, despite such a remarkable presence in the primary evidence, modern critical

3. "Positive possession" is an admittedly blunt term employed here to indicate those cases in which possession is not merely a harmful condition in need of healing but can be managed to produce beneficial effects for both the possessed individuals and their communities. This "positive" side of possession depends on the ambiguous (more than exclusively malignant or evil) nature of more-than-human beings in antiquity, and it is widely attested in ethnographic literature, as we will see below.

4. Taxonomic constructions are described by Heidi Marx-Wolf, *Spiritual Taxonomies and Ritual Authority: Platonists, Priests, and Gnostics in the Third Century C. E.* (Philadelphia: University of Pennsylvania Press, 2016). About "angels," see Ellen Muehlberger, *Angels in Late Ancient Christianity* (Oxford: Oxford University Press, 2013).

scholarship shies away almost systematically from giving any significant role to the "spirit world." The case of the "historical Jesus" provides a very telling example, in my opinion. If one glances only briefly at some of the "classics" in the subfield, such a state of affairs becomes quite evident together with its underlying causes. Perhaps the most widely appreciated and seminal volume of this kind could be considered E. P. Sanders's *Jesus and Judaism* (a truly groundbreaking book when it first appeared in 1985). In it, Sanders starts from a list of eight "indisputable facts" about the "real," "historical" Jesus.[5] Indeed, such a list includes some truly incontestable features, such as that Jesus was crucified or that he confined his activity to Israel. The rest of Sanders's hefty volume is occupied by a rigorously historical study of the figure of Jesus of Nazareth on the basis of these eight "facts." Not surprisingly, included in the list is that "Jesus was a Galilean who preached and healed," but that is the extent of what Sanders has to say about Jesus's exorcistic activity. Indeed, when readers wade into the remaining pages of the book, alongside many other observations and insights that are rightly considered seminal contributions to our historical understanding of Jesus, they do not encounter almost any other mention of the phenomenon of possession or of its healing through exorcism. Actually, Sanders makes a point that (against Morton Smith) one should not overemphasize the role of "miracles" in understanding the historical figure of Jesus.[6] It goes without saying that, given the relevance that narratives of possession have in the archive concerning Jesus, an almost complete disregard of them by the Quest weakens many of the achievements not only of Sanders's book, but also of the many others that follow similar strategies.[7]

The exceptions to this pattern of neglect are very limited in number but quite important for the advancements that they have produced. In the limited space available here, it suffices to mention Morton Smith and Pieter Craffert, two authors who would deserve a fuller discussion and who have boldly tackled the issue of the "spirit world" in a decidedly comparative key, similar to the one advocated for the Next Quest.[8]

---

5. E. P. Sanders, *Jesus and Judaism* (London: SCM, 1985), 11.

6. Sanders, *Jesus and Judaism*, 170–73. For the sake of fairness, it is also worth noting that Sanders vigorously refuses the association between exorcisms and proclamation of the kingdom, which is a staple of much historical Jesus scholarship but has no foundation in the documents at our disposal (134–35).

7. A good example is offered by J. P. Meier, who deliberately (and in contrast with Sanders) speaks about exorcisms as an appendix to his evaluation of the historicity of the kingdom saying preserved in Luke 11:20 in *Mentor, Message, and Miracles*, vol. 2 of *A Marginal Jew: Rethinking the Historical Jesus*, AYBRL (New York: Doubleday, 1994), 417–23.

8. Morton Smith, *Jesus the Magician* (San Francisco: Harper & Row, 1978), and Pieter F. Craf-

GIOVANNI B. BAZZANA

That works like these have had relatively little traction is, in my opinion, indicative of something more significant than the mere acknowledgment that treating "possession" or the "spirit world" well is a challenging task. It seems that such a state of affairs is a symptom of something methodologically problematic in the very construction of the modern historical-critical study of the Bible and of early Christianity more in general.

A New Proposal

In providing a diagnosis for such a problematic state of affairs, it is helpful to look at the phenomenon of "possession" against the broader backdrop of the study of religion, even though scholarship focused on the Bible has often been reluctant to let its subject matters be involved in such conversations (which should be considered just another symptom of the same problematic malaise). In particular, ethnographers and anthropologists have assembled an impressive archive of sophisticated scholarship on "possession" as well as "spirits."[9] A recent development in this rich body of scholarship is the observation that "possession" (as a hegemonic concept to describe a certain type of phenomena) is a relatively modern innovation deeply intertwined with colonialist and imperialist projects. As noted by Paul Christopher Johnson in a series of important contributions, "possession" became, in the hands of mostly European philosophers and intellectuals, a foil for the notion of a "buffered" individual self, a notion they were developing alongside the expansion of their nations' imperial reach. Within such a stark racial and gender binary, humans who were open to "possession" were also assumed to be ready to give up ownership of their own bodies and lands.[10] It is important to recognize that biblical criticism's methodological roots share exactly the same genealogy, and this state of affairs certainly contributes significantly to render "spirits" and "possession" such an intractable topic. Conceptual assumptions like the "buffered" self (which are foundational for the modern Western order) are troubled when one approaches these subjects seriously. In turn, such trouble

---

fert, *The Life of a Galilean Shaman: Jesus of Nazareth in Anthropological-Historical Perspective* (Eugene, OR: Cascade, 2008).

9. For a bibliographical survey (by now certainly in need of an update) see Janice Boddy, "Spirit Possession Revisited: Beyond Instrumentality," *Annual Review of Anthropology* 23 (1994): 407–34.

10. Paul Christopher Johnson, "Toward an Atlantic Genealogy of 'Spirit Possession,'" in *Spirited Things: The Work of "Spirit Possession" in Afro-Atlantic Religions*, ed. Paul Christopher Johnson (Chicago: University of Chicago Press, 2014), 23–45.

calls for a reexamination and update of the very methodological foundations of biblical criticism.[11]

These observations have two main consequences for an examination that aims at tackling the relationship between the "historical Jesus" and the "spirit world" through a different set of methodological lenses.

First, one should not treat cases of "negative" possession (meaning possession in need to be healed through exorcism, as noted above) as if "positive" possession did not exist too in the ancient Mediterranean world. A means through which New Testament criticism has been able to avoid dealing with the "spirit world" as a *continuum* has been to restrict artificially the concept of "possession" only to the influence of evil *pneumata* or to an illness that must be redressed by eliminating possession itself. Ethnographic study conducted by scholars like Michael Lambek, Janice Boddy, Frederick Smith, and Brent Crosson demonstrates instead that, in almost all cases, possession has a "positive" side as well, one that benefits both mediums and their social groups in various ways.[12] It would be strange if that were not the case also for the early Christ groups, but theological and interpretive traditions have obscured this side of the coin in a very effective way. Thus, a primary goal of the Next Quest should instead be to "rediscover" such a hidden "positive" aspect. It seems reasonable to expect that such an exercise will not only yield a more adequate historical understanding of what we designate as the early Christ movement, but will also enable us to draw different, and more productive, conclusions with respect to the early Christ movement's texts and their teaching about ontology, ethics, and anthropology.

The second overarching gain is that interactions with the "spirit world" should not be treated as extraordinary phenomena. This observation again responds to an interpretative strategy deployed by biblical criticism as a means to avoid dealing with the implications of possession as a regular (or even foundational) practice within early Christ groups (or for the experience of the historical Jesus). Exorcisms (for "negative" possession, as noted above) are often classed together with miracles and thus located in the secluded realm of the supernatural, something to which the traditional Quest has paid little or no serious attention. Once again,

11. For more on this, see Giovanni B. Bazzana, *Having the Spirit of Christ: Spirit Possession and Exorcism in the Earliest Christ Groups* (New Haven: Yale University Press, 2020), 1–23.

12. Michael Lambek, *The Weight of the Past: Living with History in Mahajanga, Madagascar* (Hampshire: Palgrave Macmillan, 2002); Janice Boddy, *Wombs and Alien Spirits: Women, Men, and the Zâr Cults in Northern Sudan* (Madison: University of Wisconsin Press, 1989); Frederick M. Smith, *The Self Possessed: Deity and Spirit Possession in South Asian Literature and Civilization* (New York: Columbia University Press, 2006); Brent J. Crosson, *Experiments with Power: Obeah and the Remaking of Religion in Trinidad* (Chicago: University of Chicago Press, 2021).

anthropological studies of the type mentioned above make quite clear that almost everywhere contact with the "spirit world" is cultivated; this is also treated and conceived as a very ordinary phenomenon. Mediums often live with their possessing spirits for a long time and develop relationships that are nourishing both for themselves and for their groups.[13] Likewise, possession should not be understood as merely the moment of flashy and often violent manifestation of a given spirit in a medium, but also as something more extended, alternating moments of presence as well as hiddenness.[14] The latter, however, have as much influence on individual and group lives as manifestations, as impressive as they may be. Once again, the relationships with the "spirit world" within early Christ groups must be analyzed as part of their ordinary life, if one wants to get a better grasp of their true significance in that context.

A SPIRIT AMONG THE TOMBS (MARK 5 AND PARALLELS)

After having discussed these methodological assumptions, let's take a brief look at the narrative preserved in Mark 5:1–20 and its Synoptic parallels to provide a more concrete exemplification. This is a very well-known story and thus I will not summarize it all, but—given the limited space at my disposal—the attention will be focused on only three features taken in the order in which they come up in the narrative.

A Man "in an Unclean Spirit" (Mark 5:2)

The first element that jumps out in the pericope has to do with the introduction of the possessed man. Mark tells readers that literally this individual "was in an unclean spirit" (*anthrōpos en pneumati akathartō*). This is a rather strange phrase that sounds very awkward in Greek and has thus created problems for translators, who often simply resort to forget about the Greek and write that the man was "with" a spirit or "had" a spirit. In purely linguistic terms though, the phrase is not as complicated as it appears at first sight. For example, we know from the papyrological record (which opens a window on the Greek as it was used in everyday interactions by common people in the early centuries CE) that the particle *en* had lost a lot of its original locative significance by the time of the composition of the

13. See, for instance, the ethnographies of Diana Espirito Santo, "Imagination, Sensation, and the Education of Attention among Cuban Spirit Mediums," *Ethnos* 77 (2012): 252–71.

14. Michael Lambek, "Rheumatic Irony: Questions of Agency and Self-Deception as Refracted through the Art of Living with Spirits," in *Illness and Irony: On the Ambiguity of Suffering in Culture*, ed. Michael Lambek and Paul Antze (New York: Berghahn, 2004), 40–59.

gospel narratives. Instead, the particle *en* had become simply the indicator of a relationship between two terms, in this case the man and the spirit.[15]

If one looks at this issue in a perspective that goes beyond the mere linguistic datum, one can easily see that early Christian documents employ a rather varied set of phrases to indicate the relationship between mediums and their possessing spirits. For instance, in some cases (as later in this very story of the Gerasene exorcism) passivity on the part of the human medium is emphasized when passive forms of the verb *daimonizō* are used (and can be translated literally as "being demonized" or more freely as "being demon-possessed").[16] But there are also other instances in which the more active "having a spirit" is used, indicating that the role played by the human medium can also be accordingly a more active one.[17] We should not conclude too hastily that such a pattern is simply the result of randomness or confusion. On the contrary, it reflects quite well the ambiguity inherent to the relationship between mediums and spirits that has been observed by several ethnographers as well. Such a relationship may begin as one of total submission of the human partner to the spirit, but it often changes through times so that one can say, to use an expression employed by Adeline Masquelier in a seminal study of possession in Niger, that the human partner becomes fully a "host" after having started off as a "hostage" of the spirit.[18] By noticing the odd phrase "being in an unclean spirit" at the beginning of this story, readers should attend carefully to the sophisticated understanding of possession that enlivens this story.

Indeed, the relationship between humans and the "spirit world" that is presupposed here (and in many other early Christian writings) is grounded in a conceptualization of the human self that is very far from the modern, "buffered" one.[19] This type of relationship presupposes that the human self is a "porous" one, open to the influences of other external agents, and in need of building its subjectivity in negotiation with (and sometime submission to) other beings. This configuration is, of course, particularly evident in Paul among other early Christ believers. At a very basic lexical level, Paul too uses the (otherwise puzzling) ex-

15. James Hope Moulton and George Milligan, *The Vocabulary of the Greek Testament Illustrated from the Papyri and Other Non-Literary Sources* (London: Hodder and Stoughton, 1930), s.v. ἐν.

16. *Pōs egeneto tō daimonizomenō* in Mark 5:16 and *parekalei auton ho daimonistheis* in v. 18.

17. For a famous passage speaking of "positive" possession as "having the spirit of Christ" one can look at Rom 8:9 (*ei de tis pneuma Christou ouk echei*).

18. Adeline Masquelier, "From Hostage to Host: Confessions of a Spirit Medium in Niger," *Ethos* 30 (2002): 49–76.

19. For this concept, see Charles Taylor, *The Sources of the Self: The Making of the Modern Identity* (Cambridge: Harvard University Press, 1989).

pression "being in Christ" (*en Christō*) exactly to indicate a foundational relation for the subjectivity of Christ believers. The foundational element here is to be possessed by Christ in a way that is obviously "positive" in Paul's mind. Of course, the human role in such relationship is described by Paul with nuances that emphasize submission, as when he says in Galatians that he does not live anymore, but Christ lives in him (2:20).[20] Or when Paul adopts systematically the language of enslavement to describe his participation in the relationship with Christ.[21] The underlying conceptualization of the self as "porous" opens up interesting venues in terms of ethics and anthropology, especially at a time like ours in which we feel a particular urgency to think about ourselves not as disconnected individuals, but as part of an interrelated whole that goes well beyond humankind.[22] At the same time, such a conceptualization raises also other problems, as, for instance, in the arresting use of the language of enslavement that I have just mentioned.

Legion

The second point under discussion here is a veritable elephant in the room with regard to the study of Mark 5:1–20 and possession in the New Testament more generally. Interestingly, Mark 5 and parallels are the only narrative of an exorcism (at least in the gospels that were later included in the canon) in which the spirit is given a proper name. Of course, "Legion" is not any other name, and for that reason it is important. Let's state clearly from the outset that, despite what has been sometime maintained, there is no doubt that any reader or hearer of this story in antiquity would have immediately associated the name "Legion" with the Roman military (see Zeichmann's essay). Even a cursory glance at the ancient literary and papyrological records shows that "legion" was not a generic term used to indicate a great quantity of something (which it has become, for instance, in English, but exactly because of the influence of this gospel story). As a Roman military term "legion" would have been well known throughout the Mediterranean and there is no doubt that, when used in this context, it introduces a clear political element in the exorcism story.[23]

20. For more on possession in Paul, see chapters 3–5 in Bazzana, *Having the Spirit of Christ*.
21. For inequality in the cultural conceptualization of possession, see J. L. Matory, "Government by Seduction: History and Tropes of 'Mounting' in the Oyo-Yoruba," in *Modernity and Its Malcontents: Ritual and Power in Post-Colonial Africa*, ed. Jean Comaroff and John F. Comaroff (Chicago: University of Chicago Press, 1993), 58–85.
22. Denise K. Buell, "The Microbes and Pneuma That Therefore I Am," in *Divinanimality: Animal Theory, Creaturely Theology*, ed. S. D. Moore (New York: Fordham University Press, 2014), 63–87.
23. On the point, see Joshua Garroway, "The Invasion of a Mustard Seed: A Reading of Mark 5.1–20," *JSNT* 32 (2009): 57–75.

But what should we do with this political and military element in understanding the exorcism?

This is an important and difficult interpretive question, because it raises a host of methodological problems. Critical interpretations of this story have often found it expedient to just avoid the exorcistic element altogether by allegorizing the entire narrative. This is what happens (to mention only a reading that has become quite popular in recent years) when one envisages everything in the story as referring in a covert way to Jesus fighting against Roman imperialism. The latter is defeated by Christ's superior power when "legion" is sent into the pigs, which then throw themselves into the lake.[24]

There is little doubt that such an interpretation is quite compelling, but it also leaves behind a number of unresolved questions. Some are apparently simplistic (and certainly a tad funny) but no less problematic. For instance, we know that pigs are excellent swimmers, and it is difficult to imagine that such a detail could have been lost on the original audiences of the story. In light of this, one may wonder what happens with "Legion." Is Jesus's victory in the confrontation definitive (with eschatological overtones, as often claimed in Christian readings of this narrative) or just temporary? Other questions have more far-reaching implications for the present discussion. If this story is designed to show how great Jesus's anti-Roman and anti-imperialist power was, the outcome is a little bit of a letdown, since it does not seem to change any actual power relationship or the situation of imperialist oppression in the region. More importantly even, what is one going to do with the exorcism? Is this feature really only there to provide a colorful allegorical cover for a political confrontation? Should we conclude (as many scholars have indeed done) that the "spirit world" did not really mean much for the religious life and experience of the early Christ groups, but was merely a convenient canvas for allegorical elaborations?

It seems that there is an alternative way to address the hermeneutical issues raised by this story, a solution that enables readers to take the spirit "Legion" seriously, while preserving the significance of the political theme in the narrative. Let's start with the observation that political and social elements are almost always present in cases of possession and often with a rather critical edge, as attested by a huge number of ethnographic accounts. One of the earliest observations of this was the first ethnographic film ever made, Jean Rouch's 1955 *Les maîtres fous*. This much-discussed documentary is the record (often quite graphic) of a Hauka pos-

24. Significant examples of this reading can be found in Mathias Klinghardt, "Legionsschweine in Gerasa: Lokalkolorit und historischer Hintergrund von Mk 5,1–20," *ZNW* 98 (2007): 28–48; or Warren Carter, "Cross-Gendered Romans and Mark's Jesus: Legion Enters the Pigs (Mark 5:1–20)," *JBL* 134 (2015): 139–55.

session ritual taking place in Ghana and provides a very intriguing comparandum for our story from Mark 5.[25] Significantly, Rouch's film has itself been the object of heated interpretive controversies, as the "masters" of the title have been sometimes taken as representing European colonial authorities or, for other viewers, as foolish "teachers" with reference to the African leaders of the Hauka movement. More recently, Paul Henley has offered a reexamination of the film, grounded in the effort of taking seriously the work performed by possession in the cultural and religious context from which the characters filmed by Rouch originated.[26] In brief, Henley concludes that the political import of the ritual cannot be taken either as a simple mockery of European colonizers or as the deranged manifestation of human suffering under the heel of imperialist oppression. Instead, the ritual is better understood as a sophisticated tool devised to attract and negotiate a relationship with the spirits that represent the power of the "other" in the eyes of African men. This powerful "other" is indeed not only the European military taking center scene in the ritual but also modern European technology, since the spirits who become manifest include, for instance, a truck driver and a train driver.

Could one see the exorcism in Mark 5:1–20 along the same lines? While true in part, conceiving this scene as either an occasion to "vent out" for an oppressed man subject to a colonial regime or as a mockery of the Roman army are reductive explanations for what is going on in a ritual of possession qua ritual of possession.[27] It seems that one can get a much more effective and richer reading of the story if instead it is conceived as something similar to the "experiments with power" that Brent Crosson has mobilized so well as a lens through which one can look at Obeah in Trinidad. The exorcism becomes then a strategy to negotiate the mighty power of the Roman army and empire for other purposes. I will explain what these purposes may be by looking at a third feature of the narrative, which has to do with the complex conclusion of the episode.

Exorcism in Gerasa

As is well known, the ending of the narrative is also longer than usual and quite strange, if compared with other exorcisms described in the gospels. On the one

25. This still very interesting document can be viewed at https://vimeo.com/522513207 (accessed on Jan. 11, 2023).

26. Paul Henley, "Spirit Possession, Power, and the Absent Presence of Islam: Re-Viewing *Les maîtres fous*," *Journal of the Royal Anthropological Institute* 12 (2006): 731–61.

27. "Venting out" as an explanation for possession phenomena is also quite a popular interpretive device in biblical studies, often supported by the functionalist anthropological analysis of Ioan M. Lewis, *Ecstatic Religion: A Study of Shamanism and Spirit Possession*, 3rd ed. (London: Routledge, 2003).

hand, there is the frightened reaction of the people of Gerasa and, on the other hand, also the denied request of the possessed man (who is curiously never given another name in the narrative) to follow Jesus. Let's start with the second half of this enigma and with the fate of the possessed man. The very fact that his designation never changes even after such an extraordinary exorcism is a remarkable indication that Jesus has in fact not completely separated him from the spirit "Legion." A long tradition of theological and christological reinterpretations of all exorcism stories has tried to present them as allegories of the eschatological defeat of evil by Christ. However, it is important to stress that all these narratives (including Mark 5:1–20) have no hint of apocalyptic or even kingdom of God language in them. Thus, it is more than warranted to suggest that the historical Jesus did not see these actions as apocalyptic or even definitive. In all likelihood, his earliest followers envisaged the conclusion of an episode like Mark 5:1–20 as much more open ended than we are habituated to think (and not only because the pigs did probably survive their dive into the waters of the lake). Indeed, elsewhere the gospel traditions state quite clearly that a return of spirits should be expected and that one should be prepared for that occurrence.[28] Likewise, ethnographies of exorcisms routinely observe that these are protracted procedures, taking even years in some cases, while the usual outcome is more often than not a coexistence between human mediums and their spirits. That is probably the case with the end of our story as well. The man remains in the region, because he has not been really completely "liberated" from Legion (and indeed that was not the aim of the exorcism to begin with). On the contrary, the spirit will return to him, but now their relationship will be more balanced, and our unnamed man will be able to use the great power of Legion for a beneficial goal, in this case the furthering of the Jesus movement in the Decapolis.

The location of this story in Gerasa can also yield some additional indication about the "positive" effects that the practice of possession may generate. The choice of exactly this city for the setting of Mark 5:1–20 puzzled readers already in antiquity (generating creative text critical solutions that cannot be discussed here). Chiefly, it seems odd to situate such a narrative in a place that is miles away from the lake of Galilee (once again our pigs would have had to run for hours before taking their famous plunge). But Gerasa is interesting in other ways too.

28. "When the unclean spirit has gone out of a person, it wanders through waterless regions looking for a resting place, but not finding any it says, 'I will return to my house from which I came.' When it returns, it finds it swept and put in order. Then it goes and brings seven other spirits more evil than itself, and they enter and live there, and the last state of that person is worse than the first" (Luke 11:24–26). This is a Q saying that could very well go back to the historical Jesus, but does not get almost any interpretive attention, since it does not fit well mainstream theological reconstructions.

As part of the Decapolis, we are almost conditioned to think about it as a totally non-Jewish city. The impressive archaeological remains associated with present-day Jerash also lead in that direction, but it must be noted that these Greco-Roman monuments were all built from the time of Hadrian on (and following the impulse of his Hellenizing policies).[29] In truth both archaeological and inscriptional evidence predating the second century CE paint a very different picture, especially with regard to the presence of a very ethnically and religiously diverse population, including a sizable percentage of Jews. We even know (if we can trust Josephus) that, at the time of the First Jewish War in 66 CE, the non-Jewish majority within the city refrained from killing all the Gerasene Jews, as happened in other centers with a mixed population.[30] In the Gerasene demoniac one should probably see a non-Jew who joins the possession cult of the Jesus movement and, on top of that, enlists the help of the powerful Roman spirit Legion. As noted above, possession is an ongoing negotiation among different identities and powers: Mark 5:1–20 (written in the aftermath of the war) sketches, through possession, a potential path for cohabitation that does not result in conflict and mutual destruction.

Conclusion

In conclusion, I would like to restate that the Next Quest for the historical Jesus must account for the role that the "spirit world" played in shaping the religious experience both of Jesus himself and of the people who collected and organized the traditions about him. This will yield a more historiographically precise representation of Jesus and his Galilean context.

This change in the orientation of the Quest should also be understood as an opportunity to reframe the study of biblical texts along some crucial axes that have to do with ontology, anthropology, and ethics. In turn, such a reorientation may enable our discipline to enter more effectively and more directly into some current conversation that has to do, for example, with the relationship between humans and the rest of the living world or with the effort to overcome the limitations of liberal individualism in political as well as intellectual action.

---

29. The development is described in Rubina Raja, *Urban Development and Regional Identities in the Eastern Roman Provinces, 50 BC–AD 250: Aphrodisias, Ephesos, Athens, Gerasa* (Copenhagen: Museum Tusculanum, 2012), 137–89.

30. See the discussion in Nathanael J. Andrade, *Syrian Identity in the Greco-Roman World* (Oxford: Oxford University Press, 2013), 160–69.

28

Ritual Impurity

Matthew Thiessen

The Next Quest for the historical Jesus must account for the near ubiquity of ancient ritual purity thinking within Judaism and the broader Mediterranean world.[1] Ancient people might have differed on the precise details about these ritual purity concerns, but almost all of them shared the belief that, if one were to enter the cultic spheres related to the gods, they must do so in a state of purity. As Paula Fredriksen has put it, ancient gods, both Jewish and non-Jewish, were particular about the "etiquette they wanted observed when humans approached them."[2] Within such a world, an ancient Jewish man who denied the importance or existence of ritual purity would indeed be a marginal Jew. In fact, such a person would not only be a marginal Jew, he would also be a marginal ancient . . . so marginal that one should probably assume that any such person is little more than the invention of someone from a modern culture that does not subscribe to ritual purity thinking.

In fact, the gospel writers, as scholars such as Thomas Kazen, Cecilia Wassén, Maurice Casey, and James Crossley have sought to show, place Jesus *within* and not

---

1. See the wide-ranging collection of essays in Christian Frevel and Christophe Nihan, eds., *Purity and the Forming of Religious Traditions in the Ancient Mediterranean World and Ancient Judaism*, Dynamics in the History of Religion 3 (Leiden: Brill, 2013).

2. Paula Fredriksen, "Compassion Is to Purity as Fish Is to Bicycle and Other Reflections on Constructions of 'Judaism' in Current Work on the Historical Jesus," in *Apocalypticism, Anti-Semitism and the Historical Jesus: Subtexts in Criticism*, ed. John S. Kloppenborg and John W. Marshall, JSNTSup 275 (London: T&T Clark, 2005), 56.

against the context of ritual purity thinking.[3] This fact will provide the foundation for several matters considered here. Jesus traditions that consistently connect the beginning of his mission to the water purifications of John the Immerser suggest that the context of purification was important for Jesus as well. Interestingly, however, the earliest traditions are silent about Jesus's own ritual purification practices. What does this silence suggest to readers? Finally, the earliest traditions depict Jesus repeatedly showing concern toward people who are experiencing long-term ritual impurities.

JOHN THE IMMERSER

As earlier historical-Jesus questers have noted, the tradition of John's ritual immersion of Jesus seems to have been a source of some embarrassment to many of Jesus's followers.[4] All the canonical gospels depict John stressing that he is not worthy to untie Jesus's sandals (Mark 1:7; Matt 3:11; Luke 3:16; John 1:27). Matthew adds to Mark's story by depicting John's initial hesitance: "I need to be baptized by you, and do you come to me?" (Matt 3:14). And in the *Gospel of the Nazarenes*, Jesus responds to his family's encouragement to go to John for immersion in the following way: "In what way have I sinned, that I would need to be immersed by him?" (frg. 2, *apud* Jerome, *Pelag.* 3.2). These various traditions all wrestle in their own way with a potentially problematic connection between John and Jesus that might suggest that Jesus is John's protégé and therefore his inferior. Consequently, despite Rafael Rodríguez's helpful efforts to complicate the criterion of embarrassment, I remain convinced that this is one of the very few points at which the criterion of embarrassment provides some degree of confidence about historical

---

3. E.g., Thomas Kazen, *Jesus and Purity Halakhah: Was Jesus Indifferent to Impurity?*, ConBNT 38 (Stockholm: Almqvist & Wiksell, 2002); Kazen, *Scripture, Interpretation, or Authority? Motives and Arguments in Jesus' Halakic Conflicts*, WUNT 320 (Tübingen: Mohr Siebeck, 2013); Cecilia Wassén, "Jesus and the Hemorrhaging Woman in Mark 5:24–34: Insights from Purity Laws from Qumran," in *Scripture in Transition: Essays on Septuagint, Hebrew Bible, and Dead Sea Scrolls in Honour of Raija Sollamo*, ed. Anssi Voitila and Jutta Jokiranta, JSJSup 126 (Leiden: Brill, 2008), 641–60; Maurice Casey, *Jesus of Nazareth: An Independent Historian's Account of His Life and Teaching* (London: Bloomsbury, 2010); James Crossley, *The Date of Mark's Gospel: Insight from the Law in Earliest Christianity*, JSNTSup 266 (London: T&T Clark, 2004); and Crossley, *Jesus and the Chaos of History: Redirecting the Life of the Historical Jesus* (Oxford: Oxford University Press, 2015), 96–133.

4. E.g., Paula Fredriksen, *From Jesus to Christ: The Origins of the New Testament Images of Christ* (New Haven: Yale University Press, 1988), 41; James D. G. Dunn, *Jesus Remembered*, vol. 1 in *Christianity in the Making* (Grand Rapids: Eerdmans, 2003), 339.

bedrock.[5] John immersed Jesus in running water (referred to as "living waters" in Hebrew), something ancient Jews perceived to be a particularly strong ritual detergent (e.g., Lev 15:13; Num 19:17; 11Q19 XLV, 16).

But even if, following Leif Vaage and William Arnal, one is not convinced that these traditions refer to a historical and embarrassing event in the life of Jesus, modern scholars must still deal with the fact that the gospel writers situated the beginning of Jesus's public mission with a story about him being immersed in water by a character named John, whose water immersions for both body and soul we know about also from Josephus (*A.J.* 18.116–119).[6] Whether John was originally a member of the Qumran community, as Joel Marcus has recently argued, or a member of a priestly family, as Luke claimed long ago (Luke 1:5), or unrelated to either group, the same sorts of purity concerns that motivated both of these ancient Jewish groups appear to have motivated John as well.[7] Consequently, the gospel writers connect the origins of Jesus's mission to the figure of John, implying that Jesus himself must be understood within a larger context of concern for purity, potentially both ritual and moral.

Silence on Jesus and Ritual Bathing

In addition to this ancient decision to contextualize Jesus's mission in relation to John's immersive practices, we must also situate the historical Jesus within our growing archaeological evidence of ancient ritual purification practices.[8] In recent

5. On the criterion of embarrassment, see Rafael Rodríguez, "The Embarrassing Truth about Jesus: The Criterion of Embarrassment and the Failure of Historical Authenticity," in *Jesus, Criteria, and the Demise of Authenticity*, ed. Chris Keith and Anthony Le Donne (London: T&T Clark, 2012), 132–51.

6. Leif Vaage, "Bird-Watching at the Baptism of Jesus: Early Christian Mythmaking in Mark 1:9–11," in *Reimagining Christian Origins: A Colloquium Honoring Burton L. Mack*, ed. Elizabeth A. Castelli and Hal Taussig (Valley Forge, PA: Trinity Press International, 1996), 280–94, and William Arnal, "Major Episodes in the Biography of Jesus: An Assessment of the Historicity of the Narrative Tradition," *TJT* 13 (1997): 201–26.

7. Joel Marcus, *John the Baptist in History and Theology* (Columbia: University of South Carolina Press, 2018). On priestly themes in Luke, see Rick Strelan, *Luke the Priest: The Authority of the Author of the Third Gospel* (Aldershot: Ashgate, 2008).

8. David Amit and Yonatan Adler, "The Observance of Ritual Purity after 70 C. E.: A Reevaluation of the Evidence in Light of Recent Archaeological Discoveries," in *"Follow the Wise"—Studies in Jewish History and Culture in Honor of Lee I. Levine*, ed. Ze'ev Weiss et al. (Winona Lake, IN: Eisenbrauns, 2010), 121–43; Yonatan Adler, "The Decline of Jewish Ritual Purity Observance in Roman Palestina: An Archaeological Perspective on Chronology and Historical Context," in *Expressions of Cult in the Southern Levant in the Greco-Roman Period: Manifestations in Text and Material Culture*, ed. Oren Tal and Ze'ev Weiss, Contextualizing the Sacred 6 (Turnhout:

decades, archaeologists have discovered a significant number of baths throughout Judea and Galilee. These baths, set apart by distinct steps, now number almost nine hundred, and many date between the first century BCE and the early second century CE.[9] Who knows how many remain to be discovered? Who knows how many have been entirely lost to us some two thousand years later? In the arid climate of the region, these baths serve as monuments to the impressive commitment many ancient Jews had to ritual purification. Individuals and communities frequently invested their time, money, and water to remove the ritual impurities that occurred both naturally and frequently. This is one of the key pieces of evidence that pulls back the curtain on what was happening outside of the texts upon which we depend so heavily. Although we may not know what percentage of ancient Jews carefully observed ritual purity, it seems that a good percentage did and that it was a widely practiced aspect of Jewish identity in the first century CE, both in Judea and Galilee. The period in which Jesus lived, then, was one in which there was a growing interest in building and, presumably, using stepped baths.

How does this help us to think more carefully about the historical Jesus? After all, the canonical gospels never once mention Jesus undergoing ritual bathing. In fact, one ancient papyrus, P.Oxy. 840, which likely dates to the fourth century CE, depicts a priest named Levi accusing Jesus of entering the temple precincts without having undergone ritual bathing.[10] This narrative reflects later Christian concerns to distance Jesus from Jewish purity concerns. But otherwise, our sources are silent. What should we do with this silence? What does the fact that our earliest gospels never mention Jesus undergoing ritual bathing signify? Thomas Kazen suggests that the fact that the gospels never depict Jesus undergoing ritual bathing reflects the historical reality that Jesus was unconcerned about ritual purity. For Kazen, this purported indifference arose from Jesus's belief that the kingdom of God was approaching and so, although he did not outright reject purity concerns, he nonetheless relativized them.[11] After all, why waste time bathing ritually if

---

Brepols, 2017), 269–84; Stuart S. Miller, *At the Intersection of Texts and Material Finds: Stepped Pools, Stone Vessels, and Ritual Purity Among the Jews of Roman Galilee*, JAJSup 16 (Göttingen: Vandenhoeck & Ruprecht, 2015).

9. See now Yonatan Adler, *The Origins of Judaism: An Archaeological-Historical Reappraisal*, AYBRL (New Haven: Yale University Press, 2022).

10. Kazen, *Jesus and Purity Halakhah*, 260, takes this to be based on a memory of Jesus's neglect of certain purification practices. More broadly, see Michael J. Kruger, *The Gospel of the Savior: An Analysis of P. Oxy. 840 and Its Place in the Gospel Traditions of Early Christianity*, TENTS 1 (Leiden: Brill, 2005).

11. Kazen, *Jesus and Purity Halakhah*, 342–53. Similarly, Tom Holmén, *Jesus and Jewish Covenant Thinking*, BIS 55 (Leiden: Brill, 2001), 236.

God's kingdom was breaking into the world? But is this the only or even the best way to read the gospels' silence around Jesus and ritual bathing?

It seems worth noting that it is exceedingly rare for ancient Jewish texts to narrate *anyone* undergoing ritual purification. To be clear, I am distinguishing here between *legal* texts like Lev 12–15 and Num 19 (and related texts) and *narrative* texts like the gospels. How many times do ancient Jewish narratives speak of a woman giving birth or a person contracting corpse impurity without mentioning any ritually bathing afterward? For instance, Moses's sister Miriam contracts *lepra*, but the author does not narrate her undergoing any purification rites after her healing (Num 12).[12] In fact, I can think of only one instance in the Hebrew Bible of what *might* be a narration of someone bathing ritually: Bathsheba bathing on her rooftop in 2 Sam 11. The narrator of this story informs readers that she was doing so in order to remove her impurity. This impurity likely arose from menstruation.[13] But the point of the narrative is not to show how careful Bathsheba was to remove ritual impurity after menstruation, as though readers were anxious to know how law observant she was. Instead, the narrator provides an explanation for why she conceived after having sex with David, since it was thought that women were particularly fertile immediately after menstruating.[14] The parenthetical remark also serves to prove that it was David and not Uriah the Hittite who impregnated Bathsheba.[15] That is, this rare instance of a narrative of ritual bathing occurs for reasons unrelated to any interest in ritual purification per se. Rather it is there to explain not only how Bathsheba came to David's attention but also how she

---

12. See, for instance, the rather odd claims of John P. Meier, *A Marginal Jew: Rethinking the Historical Jesus*, AYBRL (New Haven: Yale University Press, 1991–2016), 4:414: "A group of men traveling together for sometime while abstaining from sexual activity might be expected to raise questions about regularly recurring impurity from seminal emissions during sleep . . . yet the Jesus tradition is completely silent." Meier goes on to use this silence to conclude: "Apparently for Jesus ritual impurity is not only not a burning issue, it is not an issue at all" (4:414). Nocturnal emissions were not unique to Jesus and his unmarried followers, yet no ancient Jewish *narrative* mentions anyone bathing away such impurities. For that matter, we know with about as much certainty as is possible with regard to the ancient world that ancient Israelites and Jews were having sex, yet no Jewish narrative provides an account of anyone ritually bathing after doing so.

13. Even this interpretation is questioned, as Tikva Frymer-Kensky notes in *Reading the Women of the Bible: A New Interpretation of Their Stories* (New York: Schocken, 2002), 147.

14. On fertility immediately after menstruation, see Hippocrates, *Mul.* 1.24.2; Lev. Rab. 14.5 and Martin Krause, "II Sam 11 4 und das Konzeptionsoptimum," *ZAW* 95 (1983): 434–37.

15. For the narrator's desire to establish the certainty of Davidic paternity, see J. Cheryl Exum, *Fragmented Women: Feminist (Sub)versions of Biblical Narratives*, JSOTSup 163 (Sheffield: Sheffield Academic, 1993), 175.

came to be pregnant so quickly.[16] The only other prerabbinic narratives of ritual purification I can think of are Luke's claim that Jesus's family observed the ritual purification rites required after the birth of a male child (Luke 2:22) and the Nazirite purification rites that Paul and a few other Jewish followers of Jesus go through in Acts 21 (cf. Num 6).[17] Consequently, narrative silence around someone following the rites of ritual purification would have been entirely unsurprising. And no one takes those silences in other narratives—be they in Jewish Scriptures, Josephus, or somewhere else—to mean that an author intends to depict a ritually impure person showing indifference to the laws of ritual impurity. Rather, I imagine the cultural assumption when writing and reading these texts was that these various people underwent ritual purification and that it simply did not merit narrative space precisely because it was unexceptional behavior.

With regard to Jesus, then, this silence is historically unremarkable. But when considering the very common modern belief that Jesus generally showed indifference to, if not downright rejection of, Jewish ritual purity concerns, I think this silence has an even greater significance. If scholars as ideologically diverse as John Dominic Crossan, Marcus Borg, Scot McKnight, and Thomas Kazen are correct in believing that Jesus abandoned or showed indifference to ritual purity, is it probable that the gospel writers would have remained silent on this issue?[18] Here we need to deploy our historical imaginations.

The historical Jesus was raised in Galilee and spent most of his life there, with some brief periods in Judea and Jerusalem. Many of the inhabitants of these regions viewed Leviticus and Numbers to be authoritative and sacred and the laws pertaining to ritual impurity as binding, even as they likely argued over how exactly to observe them accurately. Virtually every settlement Jesus entered would have contained public architecture devoted to the observance of ritual purification in the form of stepped baths. While the average person's purification rituals might not have drawn the attention of others, surely the behavior of a self-proclaimed

16. Strictly speaking, Naaman's bathing in the Jordan River was not a ritual purification, although it miraculously resulted in the source of a ritual impurity (*tsāʿarat*) leaving his body.

17. Regarding the former, see Matthew Thiessen, "Luke 2:22, Leviticus 12, and Parturient Impurity," *NovT* 54 (2012): 16–29. For the latter episode, see Bart Koet, "Why Did Paul Shave His Hair (Acts 18,18)? Nazirite and Temple in the Book of Acts," in *The Centrality of Jerusalem: Historical Perspectives*, ed. Marcel Poorthuis and Chana Safrai (Kampen: Kok Pharos, 1996), 128–42.

18. John Dominic Crossan, *The Historical Jesus: The Life of a Mediterranean Jewish Peasant* (San Francisco: HarperCollins, 1991), 322–23; Marcus Borg, *Conflict, Holiness and the Politics in the Teaching of Jesus* (Harrisburg, PA: Trinity Press International, 1998), 109; and Scot McKnight, "Jesus and James on Israel and Purity," in *James the Just and Christian Origins*, ed. Bruce Chilton and Craig A. Evans, NovTSup 98 (Leiden: Brill, 1999), 91–98.

prophet and teacher would have. What if Jesus showed indifference to ritual impurity and therefore disregarded ritual purification? If his behavior fell outside the boundaries of what was generally perceived to be acceptable behavior, surely this difference would have been noticed by someone somewhere. And, again, given Jesus's burgeoning popularity, surely someone would have asked him why his behavior differed from the range of acceptable forms of behavior. Anomalous behavior would have given rise to questions, controversy, and arguments. To my mind, it seems probable that had the historical Jesus shown indifference to ritual purification, his disregard for these rituals would have left some sort of imprint on the Jesus tradition. Yet the closest thing we find in our earliest gospels is a controversy around the separate practice of the washing of hands prior to eating. To be clear, this is a distinct practice developed by the Pharisees and later adopted by the rabbis that expands and modifies ritual purity concerns in a way with which many Jews, apparently including Jesus's earliest followers, did not agree.[19]

So we have no narratives about Jesus's ritual bathing practices. The silence can and has been taken to signify that Jesus was either lax in observing such practices or disregarded them altogether, but this is a failure of the historical imagination. Rather, the silence around Jesus's ritual purification practices ought to be read as a sign that, whatever they were precisely, they were relatively uninteresting and uncontroversial, falling within the spectrum of acceptable practices observed by other first-century Jews living in Galilee and Judea. As such, his earliest followers had no reason to comment on and defend them.

THE GOSPELS ON JESUS AND RITUAL IMPURITY

In his groundbreaking book, *Constructing Jesus*, Dale Allison has observed that "the first-century traditions about Jesus are not an amorphous mess. On the contrary, certain themes, motifs, and rhetorical strategies recur again and again throughout the primary sources; and it must be in those themes and motifs and rhetorical strategies—which, taken together, leave some distinct impressions—if it is anywhere, that we will find memory."[20] Allison speaks especially of the eschatological themes in the gospels, but this important point applies to the topic

---

19. On which see Yair Furstenberg, "Defilement Penetrating the Body: A New Understanding of Contamination in Mark 7.15," *NTS* 54 (2008): 176–200; John VanMaaren, "Does Mark's Jesus Abrogate Torah? Jesus' Purity Logion and Its Illustration in Mark 7:15–23," *Journal of the Jesus Movement in Its Jewish Setting* 4 (2017): 21–41; and most recently Logan Williams, "The Stomach Purifies All Food: Jesus' Anatomical Argument in Mark 7.18–19," *NTS* (forthcoming).

20. Dale C. Allison Jr., *Constructing Jesus: Memory, Imagination, and History* (Grand Rapids: Baker Academic, 2010), 15.

of ritual impurity as well. Although the gospels never discuss Jesus's own ritual purification practices, they frequently mention Jesus interacting with ritually impure people.[21]

The Gospel of Mark, for instance, depicts one of Jesus's first deeds of power being the removal of a condition that, following the LXX translator of Leviticus, he calls *lepra* (Mark 1:40–45). Whatever the precise medical condition Mark envisages this man as having, we can be quite confident that he did not think it was what we now refer to as leprosy since Greek and Roman medical writers never used the word *lepra* to refer to leprosy (preferring terms such as *elephantiasis* or *elephas morbus*). His condition, though, makes him ritually impure. Mark's narration stresses two key things: purity (*katharizō*, 1:40, 41, 42; *katharismos*, 44) and Jesus's willingness or desire (*thelō*, 1:40, 41) to purify. Central to this story is the question not of whether Jesus is *able* to purify, but whether Jesus *desires* to purify the ritually impure. The resounding answer is *yes*.[22]

With minor variations, Matthew and Luke repeat this story (Matt 8:1–4; Luke 5:12–14). Matthew contains two additional statements that connect Jesus's mission to the purification of those with *lepra*: Jesus's command to the twelve to go to the house of Israel and, among other things, purify those with *lepra* (*leprous katharizete*, Matt 10:8), and Jesus's response to John the Immerser's question of whether Jesus was the messiah, which includes, again among other things, the claim that he purifies those with *lepra* (*leproi katharizontai*, Matt 11:5). Luke includes Jesus's response to John's question (Luke 7:22), and then contains two additional traditions about Jesus and *lepra*. The first is Jesus's reference to Elisha purifying Naaman the Syrian of *lepra*, even though there were many Israelites with *lepra* whom Elisha did not purify (Luke 4:27). The second is another purification scene, this time involving ten *leproi* (17:11–19). After being entreated for mercy, Jesus tells the men to show themselves to priests, presumably commanding them to submit to a priestly reexamination of their skin condition in accordance with Lev 14:1–3. They obey immediately, only to discover as they make their way that they have been purified (*ekatharisthēsan*). Jesus's command to the ten men in this story echoes his command to the one man with *lepra*: "Go and show yourself

21. What follows briefly surveys some of the arguments of my *Jesus and the Forces of Death: The Gospels' Portrayal of Ritual Impurity within First-Century Judaism* (Grand Rapids: Baker Academic, 2020).

22. Contrary to Joel Marcus, *Mark 8–16: A New Translation with Introduction and Commentary*, AB 27A (New Haven: Yale University Press, 2009), 933, it seems unlikely to me that the passing reference to Simon the *Lepros* in Mark 14:3 (repeated in Matt 26:6) suggests that Jesus ate in the house of a man who *currently* had *lepra*. Such an action presumably would have led to its own controversy, again something Mark is silent about!

to the priest" (*alla apelthōn deixon seauton tō hierei*, 5:14; *poreuthentes epideixate heautous tois hiereusin*, 17:14), although it lacks an explicit command to offer what Moses required for one's purification (cf. 5:14). Does this difference signify that Luke's Jesus no longer considers ritual purification important? Presumably not, since he has just *purified* the men of the underlying source of their impurity and given them instructions that affirm the priestly role in purification processes. Perhaps Luke assumes that the command in 5:14 applies broadly here as well and so does not need to be repeated. Beyond the New Testament, the Papyrus Egerton 2 gospel, which probably dates to about 200 CE, shows the continuing significance of Jesus's interactions with *lepra* in early Christian thought. And it again preserves Jesus's command to the *lepros* to go and show himself to the priests and make an offering according to the law of Moses.[23] So too the Acts of Pilate retains a memory of Jesus's healing of *lepra*, depicting a person coming forward at Jesus's trial before Pilate to proclaim that Jesus healed his *lepra* (6.2).

Another tradition related to ritual impurity can be seen in Mark's story of Jesus and the hemorrhaging woman (Mark 5:25–34). Here a woman with an abnormal genital discharge that has lasted twelve years furtively touches Jesus in the hopes that doing so will heal her. Although Mark's story does not emphasize that she is ritually impure, informed readers would have assumed this to be the case based on Lev 15:25.[24] Interpreters have taken this story to show Jesus's indifference to ritual impurity, but this is an astounding misreading of the story.[25] First, it is not sinful to contract ritual impurity and, second, Jesus is not the person who does the touching. He is touched and, without any decision on his part, the woman is healed. Jesus's intentions and actions are irrelevant to how the story unfolds. Matthew and Luke again transmit this story, albeit with minor differences. In contrast to traditions about *lepra*, though, neither Matthew nor Luke adds any new traditions regarding Jesus and genital discharges.[26]

23. While H. Idris Bell and T. C. Skeat, *Fragments of an Unknown Gospel and Other Early Christian Papyri* (Oxford: Oxford University Press, 1935), argued that the papyrus dates to 150 CE, Michael Gronewald, "Unbekanntes Evangelium oder Evangelharmonie (Fragment aus dem 'Evangelium Egerton')," in *Kölner Papyri* (*P. Köln*), ed. Michael Gronewald et al. (Opladen: Westdeutscher, 1976), 6:136–45, has convincingly shown that the papyrus dates to around 200 CE. See also Frans Neirynck, "Papyrus Egerton 2 and the Healing of the Leper," *ETL* 61 (1985): 153–60.

24. Cf. Susan Haber, "A Woman's Touch: Feminist Encounters with the Hemorrhaging Woman in Mark 5.24–34," *JSNT* 26 (2003): 171–92, and Wassén, "Jesus and the Hemorrhaging Woman."

25. E.g., Adela Yarbro Collins, *Mark: A Commentary*, Hermeneia (Minneapolis: Fortress, 2007), 284; and William Loader, *Jesus' Attitude towards the Law: A Study of the Gospels*, WUNT 2.97 (Tübingen: Mohr Siebeck, 1997), 62.

26. Unless one counts Luke's infancy narrative which depicts Jesus's family undergoing ritual purification after Jesus's birth (Luke 2:22).

Corpses are the final source of ritual impurity according to Num 19. And again the Jesus tradition contains multiple stories about Jesus and dead bodies. Mark sandwiches the story of the hemorrhaging woman and her healing with the story of a little girl who dies, only to have Jesus raise her corpse back to life (Mark 5:21–43). Matthew and Luke transmit this same story and add further stories (Matt 9:18–26; Luke 8:40–48). Luke tells the story of a dead young man, whom Jesus raises back to life as his corpse is on its way for burial (Luke 7:11–17). And at the point of Jesus's death in Matthew's Gospel, numerous people come back to life (Matt 27:50–53). Here is the one place where John's Gospel overlaps with Synoptic interests in stories about Jesus and the ritually impure since the Johannine Jesus raises a decomposing Lazarus from the dead (John 11).

Jacob Milgrom has argued that what connects these three sources of ritual impurity is the belief that the skin condition or conditions named *lepra*, genital discharges of blood and semen, and corpses are all connected to death.[27] While scholars have quibbled with this or that aspect of Milgrom's argument, many ancient Jews connected impurity more broadly to mortality and death.[28] If the gospel writers held to this same connection, as I have elsewhere argued, then one can see the theological rationale for the inclusion or creation of these stories.[29] The gospel writers, seeking to proclaim Jesus's victory over the power of death in his resurrection from the dead, might have foreshadowed that victory by telling stories about Jesus defeating death's forces in the form of various ritual impurities.[30] It is entirely conceivable that early followers of Jesus created these stories. There are theological reasons, then, that might make it attractive to invent and subsequently transmit stories of Jesus's earthly mastery over the forces of death. But it seems significant, nonetheless, that they felt free to do so, thereby depicting a Jesus who cared about ritual impurity. Again, were the historical Jesus known

27. Milgrom, "The Rationale for Biblical Impurity," *JANESCU* 22 (1993): 107–11; and Milgrom, "The Dynamics of Purity in the Priestly System," in *Purity and Holiness: The Heritage of Leviticus*, ed. Marcel J. H. M. Poorthuis and Joshua Schwartz, Jewish and Christian Perspectives Series 2 (Leiden: Brill, 2000), 29–32.

28. E.g., Tikva Frymer-Kensky, "Pollution, Purification and Purgation in Biblical Israel," in *The Word of the Lord Shall Go Forth: Essays in Honor of David Noel Freedman in Celebration of His Sixtieth Birthday*, ed. Carol L. Meyers and M. O'Connor (Winona Lake, IN: Eisenbrauns, 1983), 399–404; and Hyam Maccoby, *Ritual and Morality: The Ritual Purity System and Its Place in Judaism* (Cambridge: Cambridge University Press, 1999), 16.

29. Thiessen, *Jesus and the Forces of Death*.

30. See here Elizabeth Shively, "Purification of the Body and the Reign of God in the Gospel of Mark," *JTS* 71 (2020): 62–89. Relatedly, see Peter G. Bolt, *Jesus' Defeat of Death: Persuading Mark's Early Readers*, SNTSMS 125 (Cambridge: Cambridge University, 2003).

for relativizing or disregarding ritual impurity concerns, would they have been able to exercise such freedom?

The Halakhic Jesus

The historical figure of Jesus lived in the ancient Mediterranean world, a world in which almost everyone held to some sort of ritual purity code.[31] And he spent his life in the first-century world of Galilee and Judea, which exhibited distinctive and widespread interests in ritual purity.[32] The gospel writers situate Jesus within a mission that had its origins in a ritual immersion under John, who was, according to Luke, of priestly descent. In addition to the fact that they never mention controversies over Jesus's disregard for ritual impurity, at least as defined by Israel's priests in texts like Leviticus and Numbers, the gospel writers repeatedly depict Jesus interacting with ritually impure people and removing the sources of their respective impurities. And on one of those occasions, Jesus explicitly commands the person to observe the detailed rules around removing the residual impurity that remains after his underlying condition is removed. While one can understand why followers of Jesus would invent stories of Jesus performing miraculous healings and even raising the dead, one must still reckon with this frequently occurring theme of Jesus showing concern for ritual impurity. Why would Mark narrate stories of Jesus dealing with the ritually impure? Why would Matthew and Luke, in their own distinctive ways, add to these stories? Why does John omit stories of Jesus and *lepra*, or the hemorrhaging woman, or, for that matter, of exorcising impure *pneumata*?[33]

What all four gospels give their readers is a portrayal of Jesus who believes that ritual impurity exists, that the laws dealing with this ritual impurity matter, and that he has the power to remove ritual impurity from people, thereby restoring them to a condition where they can access the realm of the holy. If the historical Jesus did not in fact care about a theme so consistently depicted in the gospels, then we are left holding ancient texts in our hands that have so thoroughly and

31. Again, see Frevel and Nihan, *Purity*, as well as the fuller treatments of the Greek world in Robert Parker, *Miasma: Pollution and Purification in Early Greek Religion* (Oxford: Clarendon, 1983); and the Roman world in Jack L. Lennon, *Pollution and Religion in Ancient Rome* (Cambridge: Cambridge University Press, 2014).

32. Mark Chancey, *The Myth of Gentile Galilee*, SNTSMS 118 (Cambridge: Cambridge University Press, 2002).

33. Such a question assumes John's knowledge of at least one Synoptic Gospel, a case that has been made convincingly to my mind by Eve-Marie Becker, Helen K. Bond, and Catrin Williams, eds., *John's Transformation of Mark* (London: T&T Clark, 2020).

consistently misrepresented Jesus in relation to ritual impurity and the Jewish law, whether intentionally or accidentally, that we are left with very little we can confidently say about the historical Jesus and Judaism. As Helen Bond has put it, "Whether we like it or not, the story of Jesus is Mark's [and with some major and minor variations Matthew's and Luke's] story of Jesus."[34] Will we trust this story of a halakically minded Jesus who cared about ritual impurity, even if this story problematizes so many of the narratives of later Christians, which for reasons of theological anti-Judaism depict Jesus as breaking with Judaism, the Jewish law, and Jewish ritual purity and cultic concerns?[35]

34. Helen K. Bond, *The First Biography of Jesus: Genre and Meaning in Mark's Gospel* (Grand Rapids: Eerdmans, 2020), 207.

35. For an important recent effort to grapple with a law-observant Jewish Jesus in relation to contemporary Christian theology, see Barbara U. Meyer, *Jesus the Jew in Christian Memory: Theological and Philosophical Explorations* (Cambridge: Cambridge University Press, 2020).

29

Apocalypticism and Millenarianism

James Crossley

The Next Quest for the historical Jesus must account for the cross-cultural study of apocalypticism and millenarianism in premodern and peasant societies. This might seem an odd statement in favor of moving scholarship forward given that an apocalyptic Jesus is one of the defining features of the history of the Quest and promoted by some of the Quest's most famous figures. But it is equally fair to say that the debate has typically raged over questions of how literally we should take the apocalyptic or eschatological language, whether Jesus thought the kingdom was present or future, and, if future, how soon he expected it. What have tended to get sidelined are questions about cross-cultural comparison and the material interests at play in the uses of apocalyptic and millenarian language. Though scholarship has tended to focus on the resulting Jesus, one exception is Dale Allison, who has utilized an extensive range of interdisciplinary research on the recurring features of millenarianism across cultures.[1] Despite the relative age of Allison's work (in this instance, from 1998), such typological comparisons still point a way forward for historical Jesus scholarship. In this essay, I look at more precise comparisons that keep the emphasis on premodern, peasant apocalyp-

---

1. E.g., disaffection, suffering, retribution, judgment, restoration, imminent transformation, national liberation, nativism, revivalism, social deviancy, collectivism, loyalty, charismatic leadership, messianism, revision of expectations. See Dale C. Allison Jr., *Jesus of Nazareth: Millenarian Prophet* (Minneapolis: Fortress, 1998), 78–94.

ticism and millenarianism as a vehicle for expressing discontent with the world. This in turn provides us with an important approach to explain the material interests of the early Jesus movement and why it emerged when and where it did. This will further involve the comparative example of the fourteenth-century English priest, John Ball.[2]

What Are (Pre-Political) Apocalypticism and Millenarianism?

We do, of course, have important definitions of early Jewish apocalypticism at the time of Jesus that usually consist of ideas about divine disclosure, visions, dualism, wisdom, cosmology, and meteorology, and which may or may not foreground ideas about eschatology, messianism, supernatural intervention, collective salvation, and judgment on the wicked. As this implies, the potential for cross-cultural comparison is implicit even if rarely acknowledged in historical Jesus studies. To further the comparative project, we can use the definition developed by the Centre for the Critical Study of Apocalyptic and Millenarian Movements (CenSAMM). Apocalypticism involves:

> belief in the impending or possible destruction of the world itself or physical global catastrophe, and/or the destruction or radical transformation of the existing social, political, or religious order of human society—often referred to as the apocalypse . . . secular uses of the term (especially when these implicitly draw on or encode religious/supernatural themes) will also be included . . . the definition includes implicit reference to revelation and prophecy, thus the definition includes belief systems in which the idea of destruction of the world/societal order is understood to be attained by communication from divine or supernatural sources.[3]

In terms of "millenarianism," and in the tradition of Allison, we can also work with a broader cross-cultural definition (rather than in the sense of a precise Christian definition) that overlaps with this understanding of "apocalypticism." Taking the CenSAMM definition, millenarianism and comparable terms (e.g., "millennial-

2. For an earlier comparison between the two, see James Crossley, "Jesus and John Ball: Millenarian Prophets," in *"To Recover What Has Been Lost": Essays on Eschatology, Intertextuality, and Reception History in Honor of Dale C. Allison Jr*, ed. Tucker S. Ferda, Daniel Frayer-Griggs, and Nathan C. Johnson, NovTSup 183 (Leiden: Brill, 2021), 51–76.

3. CenSAMM, "Apocalypticism," in *Critical Dictionary of Apocalyptic and Millenarian Movements*, ed. James Crossley and Alastair Lockhart, January 25, 2021, www.cdamm.org/articles/apocalypticism.

ism," "millenarism") refer to "an end-times Golden Age of peace, on earth, for a long period," accompanied by ideas of a "final cataclysm and judgement." In such understandings, "collective salvation can be understood as heavenly as well as earthly, or a blend of both" and can "incorporate a diverse range of behaviours and practices, whether at odds with social norms or bolstering them, often anticipating the future transformed world." Millenarian groups have a "range of reactions to societal engagement, from violent confrontation through withdrawal from everyday life without violent confrontation, to deliberately conciliatory attitudes to the wider world."[4]

These CenSAMM definitions of "apocalypticism" and "millenarianism" were modified in light of a number of dictionary entries from a range of areas across time and place to describe a recurring phenomenon across well over two millennia. They are definitions grounded in inherited Jewish and Christian language, which is retained for convenience, but this should not be confused for the phenomena being solely Jewish and Christian (as Allison also stressed). There is, of course, much more to the wider understanding of defining apocalypticism, including the technical work currently being carried out by the Käte Hamburger Centre for Apocalyptic and Post-Apocalyptic Studies at Heidelberg University. Nevertheless, the definitions cited can provide us with a useful heuristic tool and basis for explaining the emergence and material interests of the Jesus movement.

The notion of pre-political apocalypticism can further aid such a comparative model. By "pre-political" I am alluding to Eric Hobsbawm's classic treatment of millenarianism and banditry, which has had some (but not enough) influence on historical Jesus studies, particularly in the work of Richard Horsley.[5] Hobsbawm's early work (influenced by the unfortunately now neglected A. L. Morton) looked

---

4. CenSAMM, "Millenarianism," in *Critical Dictionary of Apocalyptic and Millenarian Movements*, ed. James Crossley and Alastair Lockhart, January 15, 2021, www.cdamm.org/articles/millenarianism. For influential subcategorizations of "millennialism," see Catherine Wessinger, "Millennialism in Cross-Cultural Perspective," in *The Oxford Handbook of Millennialism*, ed. Catherine Wessinger (Oxford: Oxford University Press, 2011), 3–24.

5. See, e.g., Eric J. Hobsbawm, *Primitive Rebels: Studies in Archaic Forms of Social Movement in the 19th and 20th Centuries* (Manchester: Manchester University Press, 1959); Hobsbawm, *Bandits* (London: Weidenfeld and Nicolson, 1969); Hobsbawm, "Social Banditry: A Reply," *Comparative Studies in Society and History* 14 (1972): 503–5; Hobsbawm, "Social Banditry," in *Rural Protest: Peasant Movements and Social Change*, ed. Henry A. Landsberger (New York: Macmillan, 1973), 142–57; Hobsbawm, "Peasants and Politics," *Journal of Peasant Studies* 1 (1973): 3–22; Hobsbawm, "Peasant Land Occupations," *Past and Present* 62 (1974): 120–52. Prominent uses of Hobsbawm in historical Jesus studies include Richard A. Horsley with John S. Hanson, *Bandits, Prophets, and Messiahs: Popular Movements in the Time of Jesus* (Minneapolis: Winston, 1985); Richard A. Horsley, *Jesus and the Spiral of Violence: Popular Jewish Resistance in Roman Palestine* (San Francisco:

at bandits and millenarians in southern Europe and Latin America and how social agitation adapted, modified, or died in the face of capitalism. When Hobsbawm discussed rural banditry and peasant millenarianism as "pre-political" forms of agitation and resistance, he meant that they were pre-*capitalist* forms. Such pre-political rebels once provided a defense against unjust princes, landlords, and tax collectors while millenarians could offer a fantastical vision of a new world freed from injustice and exploitation. This hope for the transformation of the world fed into, or was rendered obsolete by, the revolutionary politics of the twentieth century and bureaucratized resistance to capitalism.

While debates rage about the ways in which Hobsbawm framed apocalypticism and millenarianism in relation to the advent of capitalism, his basic point about rural banditry and peasant millenarianism offering vehicles for expressing discontent has obvious relevance for understanding premodern, agrarian societies and the material concerns of the adherents and leaders of such groups. Hobsbawm did not focus on earlier history, but historical Jesus scholars are aware of Hobsbawm's influence (even if it is not always acknowledged) on our understanding of the social world of Jesus. Historical Jesus scholars are familiar with stories of first-century Jewish banditry, which involved kingly leadership roles, support among the rural population, anti-Roman feeling, localized disputes and vendettas, gangsterism, self-serving robbery, and hired muscle for local rulers. We know that rises in banditry could be generated by famine, heavy taxation, and bad harvests as well as changes in local rule. Banditry attracted displaced elites but was also an escape for the destitute and for ex-slaves, shepherds, soldiers, and sailors.[6] Whatever we make of the historicity of such stories, these were the known concepts associated with banditry around the time of Jesus.

Where bandits offered resistance or intimidation through the threat of physical violence in the here and now, pre-political millenarians offered a fantastical vision of supernatural transformation and divine retribution, typically in the near future. But the boundaries between millenarian, bandit, and physically violent subversive could blur, and alliances could be made for the revolutionary cause (e.g., *B.J.* 2.254–265). The Egyptian, for instance, seems to have combined prophetic ideas evoking the exodus with human-led violence, including the storming of Jerusalem (*B.J.* 2.261–263; cf. Acts 21:38). Irrespective of the personal

---

Harper & Row, 1987); John Dominic Crossan, *The Historical Jesus: The Life of a Mediterranean Jewish Peasant* (San Francisco: HarperCollins, 1991).

6. On such stories of bandits and banditry, see, e.g., *B.J.* 2.60–65, 228–235, 253, 272–276; 585–594; *A.J.* 17.270–284; 18.269–275; 20.113–121, 160–161, 232–235, 255–257; *Vita* 66, 175, 372. Cf. Luke 10:30; *B.J.* 2.125; *A.J.* 16.271–272.

views of the different leaders, that there was a blurriness in the perceptions about and conceptualization of millenarianism, apocalypticism, banditry, and violent insurrectionary is further shown in the fate of John the Baptist (*A.J.* 18.116–119) and in the earliest presentation of Jesus's death where a "whole cohort" was required for Jesus's execution (Mark 15:16) as he was crucified between two "bandits" or "insurrectionists" (Mark 15:27). From the perspective of power, there was little worry about nuance in dealing with a popular movement or fretting over whether a mass gathering was physically violent or nonviolent (cf. *A.J.* 20.97–98). Again, whatever we make of the historicity of any or all such stories, bandits and millenarians could be remembered as having shared or overlapping interests. And not without reason: whether participants acted admirably or disreputably, banditry, millenarianism, and apocalypticism were readily available options for agitation and discontent toward the existing order.

THE LANGUAGE OF DISPLACED ELITES?

This much is already known in historical Jesus studies or should be. A different sort of comparative approach to apocalypticism has been developed by Randall Reed which, if he is correct, would have significant ramifications for historical Jesus research and the argument I outlined above. Reed represents a recent trend in scholarship reacting against the idea that apocalypticism was (or is) the language of the oppressed.[7] Developing the arguments of Jonathan Z. Smith, Reed argues that apocalypticism, whether early Jewish or more broadly comparative, is the product of displaced elites.[8] Reed further claims that the social function of "the apocalyptic system" is an "ideological tool of power" that is enhanced through the threat of divine judgment, revealing that "apocalyptic is bent on exercising power to control the behaviors and beliefs of its audience . . . apocalyptic depends on a short-term solution for enforcing behavioral norms and theological beliefs."[9] On this point in relation to class location, Reed is emphatic:

7. On the anti-apocalypticism in the political trajectory of such scholarship through the Cold War to the present, see James Crossley, "The End of Apocalypticism: From Burton Mack's Jesus to North American Liberalism," *JSHJ* 19.2 (2021): 1–20.

8. Randall Reed, *A Clash of Ideologies: Marxism, Liberation Theology, and Apocalypticism in New Testament Studies* (Eugene, OR: Pickwick, 2010). Cf. Jonathan Z. Smith, "Wisdom and Apocalyptic," in *Map Is Not Territory: Studies in the History of Religions* (Leiden: Brill, 1978), 67–87; Jonathan Z. Smith, "A Pearl of Great Price and a Cargo of Yams," in *Reimagining Religion: From Babylon to Jonestown* (Chicago: Chicago University Press, 1982), 90–101. For critique, see James Crossley and Robert J. Myles, *Jesus: A Life in Class Conflict* (Winchester: Zero, 2023), 101–6.

9. Reed, *Clash of Ideologies*, 45–46, 55.

It is not the struggling under-classes who rebel against the imperial boot; rather, apocalypticism is an elite response to political displacement . . . By situating the class of the apocalypticists in the tradition of the learned scribes, we are forced to abandon notions of apocalyptic as an expression of proletarian protest. . . . Apocalyptic is a move of the powerful who have encountered a world which no longer works with the categories which have secured their power in the past.[10]

Reed's argument is not entirely without merit. There are obvious examples of apocalypticism used by displaced elites (the book of Daniel being the most famous) but if we move beyond the production of texts to the cross-cultural phenomenon of apocalypticism (as Reed himself does), then we see that his generalization fails, at least on class-based terms.[11]

Reed's explanation is too reductive and does not allow for the complexity and contradictions at work in people's lives. Indeed, a basic point about ideology is that elite ideas get modified, adopted, or even transformed among different classes and social groups. Thus, even if ancient apocalyptic *writings* were the product of a displaced elite, this still does not mean that they had a monopoly on the creative use of apocalyptic *ideas* and *beliefs*. With tongue only partly in cheek, if the reception history of the Bible has taught us anything, it is that the history of interpretation is the history of misinterpretation. Cross-culturally, we know that apocalypticism is not restricted to elites in a given society. The very existence of the recurring phenomenon of peasant myths carrying hopes of an ideal king and the hatred of evil and duplicitous royal advisors (see below) already suggests the realities are more complex. Reed's understanding of apocalypticism is an example of how academics can easily remove history from below by overemphasizing elite activities (see Meggitt's chapter).

Reed avoids, downplays, redefines, or even denies such evidence of apocalypticism from below.[12] However, a brief survey of such material shows that apoca-

10. Reed, *Clash of Ideologies*, 52–54, 56.

11. On apocalypticism "from above," see Anthony Keddie, *Revelations of Ideology: Apocalyptic Class Politics in Early Roman Palestine* (Leiden: Brill, 2018).

12. Reed, *Clash of Ideologies*, 95–98, e.g., "the kingdom of God language is not necessarily apocalyptic . . . Horsley himself gives an explanation for revolts from the time of Jesus that makes apocalyptic notions unnecessary by suggesting they were a reenactment of the Hebrew Epic, particularly the Exodus. It is perhaps no accident that some of the stories of messianic pretenders that Josephus recounts occur in the desert, the site of God leading the Hebrews to freedom." For this critique to come close to succeeding, apocalypticism would have to be strictly an issue of genre and the production of texts and, even then, would have to bypass influential Danielic ideas of a final kingdom. Otherwise, it is difficult to see how notions of kingdom of God, messianism, and expectations of a new exodus story can be removed from standard cross-

lypticism was popular outside elite circles. The movement associated with John the Baptist (Mark 1:4–11; Matt 3:1–17; Luke 3:1–22; *A.J.* 18.118; cf. Mark 11:27–32) was remembered for attracting a sizable urban and rural following. Even if the numbers were exaggerated, the point stands that apocalyptic views were taken up—or understood to have been taken up—popularly. Other descriptions of figures of leaders promising dramatic transformation include an emphasis on the significant *size* of such movements (*B.J.* 2.258–259; *A.J.* 20.97–98; cf. *B.J.* 2.261–262; Acts 21:38), including (according to Acts) Gamaliel's comparison between the Jesus movement and the movement led by Theudas (Acts 5:35–39). Certainly, leadership could have come from displaced elites and the local intelligentsia (cf. Luke 1:5–80; 3:2) but given the emphasis on size, these were not understood as exclusively elite movements. And whatever we make of the historicity of any of these presentations of popular movements, the point stands: no one thought it unusual that they were associated with millenarian apocalyptic tendencies.

We should also resist drawing a hard boundary between the producers of texts like Daniel or 4 Ezra and popular movements. Not only do they share apocalyptic themes concerning transformation and divine intervention but, as is well known, a text like Daniel held some authoritative status and was influential in the first century. Daniel itself suggests wider dissemination of its ideas in the claim that the "wise among the people shall give understanding to many" (Dan 11:33). In Reed's terms, this would be a power play (and it may well have been). But this also enhances the standard point about the spread of ideology beyond elite groups. By the time of Jesus, the use and influence of Daniel had spread and, of course, was being read in light of a context different from that of the original audience, in that a major reading was about the hope for the fall of the Roman Empire and its replacement with a new everlasting one (*A.J.* 10.209–210). If, as seems overwhelmingly likely, groups like the early Jesus movement (or at least strands within it) were expecting the kingdom or empire of God in Danielic terms, then we can hardly restrict this expectation to displaced elites in the first century.

Reed represents an understandable reaction against the romanticizing of apocalypticism as the anti-imperial language of the oppressed. In the context of the emergence of the Jesus movement, and comparable premodern agrarian societies, we should be thinking less in terms of anti-imperialism as a live concept and more about how apocalypticism helped people think about their favored sort of empire and about who *should* be in control of the world if it was not

---

cultural understandings of apocalypticism, at least when coupled with the phenomenon of millenarianism.

Rome. Apocalypticism aided thinking about a new world order and how and to whom punishment would be meted out. This sort of apocalypticism was part of an inherited language that cut across class and status and was utilized according to differing class interests. Apocalypticism was (and remains) a shared discourse that could be used, reused, appropriated, and transformed, in new and different historical and social contexts. Accordingly, the idea of apocalypticism as a fantastical language—sometimes the only available language—to express and frame pre-political discontents "from below" remains important.

JOHN BALL

John Ball provides an especially useful example of pre-political apocalypticism and millenarianism that can help us in turn think about comparable ideas at the time of Jesus. Here I summarize the detailed work done on the quest for the historical Ball.[13] Ball is now remembered for being one of the main figures and theological voices of the so-called Peasants' Revolt of 1381.[14] The revolt is most closely

13. For discussion (with bibliography) of John Ball, see James Crossley, *Spectres of John Ball: The Peasants' Revolt in English Political History, 1381–2020* (Sheffield: Equinox, 2022), 3–42.

14. While there is occasional mention of Ball in legal and ecclesiastical sources, the main sources for Ball's thinking come from the chroniclers of the revolt, especially Thomas Walsingham, Henry Knighton, and Jean Froissart as well as the *Anonimalle Chronicle* and the *Westminster Chronicle*. These sources are collected in R. B. Dobson, ed., *The Peasants' Revolt of 1381*, 2nd ed. (New York: Palgrave Macmillan, 1983). Critical editions, including the original languages, include Gaston Raynaud, ed., *Chroniques de J. Froissart: Tome Dixième 1380–1382* (Paris: Renouard, 1869); V. H. Galbraith, ed., *The Anonimalle Chronicle, 1333 to 1381* (Manchester: Manchester University Press, 1927); L. C. Hector and Barbara F. Harvey, eds., *The Westminster Chronicle, 1381–1394* (Oxford: Clarendon, 1982); G. H. Martin, ed., *Knighton's Chronicle 1337–1396* (Oxford: Clarendon, 1995); John Taylor, Wendy R. Childs, and Leslie Watkiss, eds., *The St Albans Chronicle: The Chronica Maiora of Thomas Walsingham*, vol. 1, *1376–1394* (Oxford: Oxford University Press, 2003); Peter Ainsworth and Godfried Croenen, eds., *The Online Froissart: Version 1.5* (Sheffield: HRIOnline, 2013), http://www.dhi.ac.uk/onlinefroissart. The chronicles represent much earlier source material than the gospels do for Jesus, and they are partly dependent on eyewitness tradition. Walsingham and Knighton provide us with coded letters from 1381 (Knighton, *Chronicle*, 220–25; Walsingham, *Chronica Maiora*, 548–49; Dobson, *Peasants' Revolt*, 380–83) which might have been written by Ball himself or by likeminded people in his networks. However, this does not necessarily mean easy access to the historical John Ball, as the chronicles are hostile toward him and the rebels. As historical Jesus scholars might also expect, the chronicles embellish details and accounts of the revolt and sometimes contradict one another. They do, however, provide a generally coherent account of the revolt and Ball's ideas, even if we cannot be certain about the accuracy of precise details.

associated with southeast England and, though it was far more widespread, this will remain the focus here since this was the part of the revolt with which Ball has been remembered. Moreover, the uprising was not restricted to peasants and rebels; it included local officials, artisans, escaped prisoners, and lower clergy like Ball. The uprising is one of the most obvious instances of class conflict in premodern English history. The decades of upheaval following the Black Death (1348–1349) involved labor shortages and the possibility for greater demands coming from laborers and lower orders. Parliament for its part reacted by trying to cap wages, restrict mobility, and keep serfs tied to the land. The resentments caused by such tensions were exacerbated by ongoing costly wars with France and insufficient protection from coastal raids. This was tied up with more taxes, the most infamous being the 1380 poll tax that was accompanied by intimidation and coercion and was an immediate cause of the English uprising.

Once the uprising had begun in May 1381, the southeastern rebels were soon in London. On the feast of Corpus Christi (Thursday, June 13, 1381), they entered London and the rebels' ranks were expanded with released prisoners. Though there was some rioting, the rebels were largely disciplined in their selection of political, economic, legal, and ecclesiastical targets and their written records. So significant was the rebellion that the rebels were able to negotiate with the crown, with their demands including the end of serfdom, the pardon of criminals, and the removal or execution of royal advisors. Some rebels executed justice themselves when they got into the Tower of London and beheaded leading figures of the realm, including the Archbishop of Canterbury, Simon Sudbury. While Richard II had seemingly accepted some of the rebel demands, the Kentish rebels led by Wat Tyler pushed harder in a meeting with the king, including demands for a radical restructuring of the legal system, aristocracy, and the church, all overseen by the king and one bishop. Quite what happened next is unclear, but Wat Tyler was fatally wounded while Richard pacified the rebels after the loss of their leader. In the subsequent restoration of order and authority, Ball was captured in Coventry. He was tried in St. Albans in July 1381, then hanged, drawn, and quartered, his four parts sent to four cities.

That Ball was the accepted theological voice of such discontent becomes clearer from what we know of his prerevolt life. The firmest evidence we have about Ball's early life is that he trained as a priest in York and later moved (or returned) to Colchester. From this time onward we get more precise information of his activities as an itinerant preacher. In 1364 Ball was given protection from his enemies by Edward III, which was soon revoked once the king discovered Ball "wandered from place to place preaching articles contrary to the faith of the church to the peril of his soul and the souls of others, especially of laymen."[15] Over the next two decades, Ball gained further fame and infamy for his popular preaching against the church hierarchy and the lords in fields, streets, cemeteries, and markets. This landed him in regular trouble, including excommunication and imprisonment. In one instance, from April 1381, the Archbishop of Canterbury further noted Ball's frustrating elusiveness by comparing him to a fox evading a hunter.[16] This ability to survive on the run tells us something of Ball's popular support, a general point confirmed by the presentation of Ball as the ideologue of the uprising in the summer of 1381 who was sprung from prison by rebels.[17]

The presentation of Ball's preaching from around the time of the uprising is consistent across the sources. Ball was critical of the social, economic, political, and religious order of England. The luxuries (e.g., clothing, housing, food, and drink) enjoyed by the lords were contrasted with the lot of those who worked the fields in wind and rain to maintain this state of affairs and who were rewarded with poor cloth, chaff, and water. Ball (and his sympathetic audience) was understood to have wanted a dramatic restructuring of England, including ridding the church of most of its hierarchy and putting Ball in place as the new ecclesiastical leader. As this suggests, Ball's preaching was apocalyptic in the comparative sense outlined above, namely, that he and his supporters expected imminent and dramatic social and political upheaval.[18]

While it is difficult to be certain about accuracy in its wording (and indeed location), Ball's most famous sermon associated with a mass gathering of the

15. *Calendar of the Patent Rolls: Edward III, Vol. XII, 1361–1364* (London: Hereford Times Limited, 1912), 470.

16. David Wilkins, *Concilia Magnae Britanniae et Hiberniae* (London: Gosling, 1737), 3:152.

17. It is not clear from which prison Ball was rescued. Knighton (*Chronicle*, 210–11) claimed Ball was sprung from Maidstone jail while Walsingham (*Chronica Maiora*, 544–47) claimed that rebels freed Ball from an unspecified prison. To complicate matters further, there is a record of "the traitor" John Ball being sprung from the prison at Bishop's Stortford on June 11 (TNA KB 145/3/6/1 m. 6, now made available at http://data.1381.online/projects_database/pr_sources _ro/?action=view&id=3743), which may or may not be our John Ball. See Andrew Prescott, "Judicial Records of the Rising of 1381" (PhD diss., University of London, 1984), 303–4.

18. So, e.g., Dobson, *Peasants' Revolt*, 19–20; Rodney Hilton, *Bond Men Made Free: Medieval Peasant Movements and the English Rising of 1381* (London: Routledge, 1973), 223; Alastair Dunn, *The Peasants' Revolt: England's Failed Revolution of 1381* (Stroud: Tempus, 2004), 79; Crossley, *Spectres of John Ball*, 33–34. Norman Cohn, *The Pursuit of the Millennium*, rev. ed. (Oxford: Oxford University Press, 1970), 198–204, pushed the evidence for apocalypticism too far. See, e.g., Richard Firth Green, "John Ball's Letters: Literary History and Historical Literature," in *Chaucer's England: Literature in Historical Context*, ed. Barbara A. Hanawalt (Minneapolis: University of Minnesota Press, 1992), 176–200, esp. 182, 186.

rebels at Blackheath (June 12, 1381) gives us an indication of his apocalypticism and millenarianism. Ball looked back to the beginning of human history to criticize the present social structures and anticipate their imminent transformation. As Ball was said to have opened his sermon, "Whan Adam dalf, and Eve span, Wo was þanne a gentilman?" (When Adam dug and Even span, who was then a gentleman?). For Ball, serfdom was a later imposition as was the creation of lords and their power. But, as we will see, despite leveling tendencies, this should not be mistaken for hard egalitarianism, not least given that Ball would be the new ecclesiastical ruler. Rather, this was part of a popular restructuring of the hierarchy based broadly on existing models and the hierarchical assumptions of the peasantry (rather than socialist models which emerged centuries later). Unlike the present order and most of its representatives, this idealized hierarchy would meet the political interests of the peasantry. It seems that the rebels targeted not the king but those whom they saw as corrupt advisors, believing that the youthful Richard II would take on the role of the just king in the transformed world at the head of a system of local or regional "kings" involved in the uprising. This myth of the just king belonged to, or overlapped with, a broader European tradition of an expected and idealized Christian leader who would defeat enemies and dispense justice.

This expectation of the transformation of England may be tied in with the timing of the rebels' arrival in London on the feast of Corpus Christi. The feast was a celebration of the Eucharist and the body of Christ. Margaret Aston showed in detail how contemporary understandings of Corpus Christi involved discussion of liberation and the exodus as foreshadowing Christian freedom associated with the crucifixion.[19] We can speculate how the rebels might have understood their situation in light of Corpus Christi and themes of sacrifice and liberation when they arrived on June 13, but we have some firmer indication of how Ball might have viewed these events—and strikingly this includes an instance of scribalism from below. To take one example, in a cryptic letter attributed to Ball, we see the association of breadmaking and the death of Christ. The letter refers to John Miller (likely a coded or generic name for those involved in breadmaking) who has "ground small, small, small; The King of Heaven's Son shall ransom all."[20] Aston further notes that the language of the "bread of life" and the various features of breadmaking (grain, flour, grinding, milling, etc.) were associated with Christ and

19. Margaret Aston, "Corpus Christi and Corpus Regni: Heresy and the Peasants' Revolt," *Past and Present* 143 (1994): 19–21.

20. Walsingham, *Chronica Maiora*, 548–49.

salvation in various Corpus Christi devotionals.[21] For Ball and his circle, it seems we have the construction of an idealized and unified social body and expectation of salvation with reference to labor, much in the same way as Adam and Eve were united by their respective labors.

Ball and his supporters seemed to have believed that the summer of 1381 was the expected apocalyptic moment heralding the transformation of England. Letters attributed to Ball include reference to Ball ringing a bell, which echoes the use of church bells by rebels to signal that the moment had arrived for action.[22] Echoing Johannine language (e.g., John 4:23; 5:25; 8:31–32), the letters claim that "now is tyme," which involves standing together in truth and the knowledge that truth will help the rebels' cause.[23] The belief that the apocalyptic moment was at hand is overt in the reporting of Ball's sermon at Blackheath. Ball was understood to have said that God "had now given them the time during which they could put off the yoke of their long servitude" and that "if they wished," they could "rejoice in the liberty they had long desired."[24]

As far as we can tell, the emphasis in Ball's preaching was on human activity, organization, and implementation of the divine plan rather than direct supernatural intervention. And this, unsurprisingly, involved physical violence and retribution, as the sermon at Blackheath made clear:

> He therefore urged them to be men of courage, and out of love for their virtuous fathers who had tilled their land, and pulled up and cut down the noxious weeds which usually choke the crops, to make haste themselves at that present time to do the same. They must do this first, by killing the most powerful lords of the realm, then by slaying the lawyers, justiciars, and jurors of the land, and finally, by weeding out from their land any that they knew would in the future be harmful to the commonwealth. Thus they would in the end gain peace for themselves and security for the future, if after removing the magnates, there was equal freedom between them, and they each enjoyed the same nobility, equal dignity, and similar power.[25]

There is an eschatological allusion here to the parable of the wheat and the tares (Matt 13:24–30, 36–43), a passage used to frame understandings of heresy at the

21. Aston, "Corpus Christi and Corpus Regni," 26–33.

22. Thomas Pettitt, "'Here Comes I, Jack Straw': English Folk Drama and Social Revolt," *Folklore* 95 (1984): 6–7.

23. Crossley, *Spectres of John Ball*, 33–35.

24. Walsingham, *Chronica Maiora*, 546–47.

25. Walsingham, *Chronica Maiora*, 546–47.

time, including against Ball himself.[26] Ball's sermon turns the allegation of heresy against his opponents and exploiters with the expectation of violent retaliation. This eschatology helps explain an often overlooked or misinterpreted sentiment attributed to Ball: "no one was fit for the kingdom of God who had not been born in wedlock."[27] Rather than simply promoting a moral conservatism, this sentiment was presented in the context of Ball's condemnation of exploitative clergy and teaching on socioeconomic reversal. As comparisons with the roughly contemporaneous *Piers Plowman* (B.9) and the Lollard Richard Wyche show, this saying continues Ball's anticlericalism or, at least, criticism of clergy misbehavior.[28] In this context, chaos and disorder were associated with bastardy and improper parentage exemplified by the line of Cain. This was the sort of degeneracy that was understood to have continued in the present by badly behaving priests and bishops, the "bastards" who were not fit for the kingdom.

England's transformation would involve communally shared possessions and distribution according to need with allusions to the time of the early church (Acts 2:44–45; 4:32–35). In another of the famous sayings attributed to Ball, he proclaimed that things were "not well to pass in England, nor shall do till everything be common." This would be an England without serfdom, greater lords, and exploitation of peasant labor, justified by the argument that "all come from one father and one mother, Adam and Eve."[29] Medieval ideas of everything shared in common were interpreted according to material and class interests and this was no different in Ball's circles. For them this meant liberation from serfdom and greater access to the resources of the land.[30] We find this sort of idea in one account of the rebels' demands delivered by Wat Tyler to Richard II: "all game, whether in waters or in parks and woods, should become common to all, so that everywhere in the realm, in rivers and fishponds, and woods and forests, they might take the wild beasts, and hunt the hare in the fields, and do many other such things without restraint."[31] In a transformed England with a righteous hierarchical order, the material interests of the peasantry would be properly met.

26. Aston, "Corpus Christi and Corpus Regni," 93; Crossley, *Spectres of John Ball*, 35–36; cf. Walter Waddington Shirley, ed., *Fasciculi Zizaniorum magistri Johannis Wyclif cum Tritico* (London: Longman, Brown, Green, Longmans, and Roberts, 1858), 272–74; Wilkins, *Concilia Magnae Britanniae*, 152.

27. Walsingham, *Chronica Maiora*, 544–45.

28. Steven Justice, *Writing and Rebellion: England in 1381* (Berkeley: University of California Press, 1994), 104–11; Crossley, *Spectres of John Ball*, 30–33.

29. Froissart, *Chroniques*, 10.96; cf. *Anonimalle Chronicle*, 137.

30. Crossley, *Spectres of John Ball*, 36–40.

31. Knighton, *Chronicle*, 218–19.

Jesus

The feudal society and mode of production in medieval England were obviously not the same as the economic system of first-century Galilee. Nevertheless, what they share is the premodern language of apocalypticism and millenarianism as a way of expressing dissatisfaction with the world and conceptualizing its transformation in language fitting for agrarian, artisan, and peasant contexts such as Jesus's (cf. Mark 6:3). As the background to Ball's apocalyptic and millenarian theology was agrarian class conflict, so too was that of the Jesus movement. Put crudely, a minority of urban elites dominated access to power and controlled resources produced by the overwhelmingly rural population from whom surplus was extracted. In the Levant, the town-countryside relationship helps explain class-based conflict, which included urban projects that introduced changes in traditional patterns of households, production, and demands on labor. In Galilee as Jesus was growing up, this involved the rebuilding of Sepphoris and the building of Tiberias, while in Judea this involved the expansion of the Jerusalem temple. For many Galileans and Judeans, traditional ways of life were changed. Josephus's description of the building of Tiberias (*A.J.* 18.36–38) gives further indication of the socioeconomic changes that took place. Some people were given gifts of land, some were relocated, some were forcibly removed from their land. Josephus's description reflects a basic point about such urbanization: some people benefited materially; others did not. Accordingly, some may have approved of such changes (perhaps even against their material interests); others may have not. Some may have grudgingly accepted these changes; others may have seen opportunities. Some may have materially benefited yet wanted more; others may have suffered and sought an escape. I will not rehearse the argument further, as it has been discussed in Myles's chapter, but I take this assessment of class upheavals as basically correct.

This background helps account for the tradition of fragmentation of households and creation of an alternative household, which itself can be seen as further evidence of negative perceptions about a changing Galilee and land dislocation.[32] The promises of eschatological rewards of a vastly expanded household following dislocation in Mark 10:29–31 also tell us something about the material priorities of people associated with the movement generally. The socioeconomic context of Galilee can help account for the traditions associated with Jesus about the construction of a sharp opposition between rich and poor, hostility to wealth and fine

---

32. E.g., Mark 3:20–22, 31–35; 6:1–6; 10:29–30; Matt 8:22 // Luke 9:60; Matt 10:34–36 // Luke 12:51–53 // Gos. Thom. 64; Matt 10:37 // Luke 14:26; cf. Matt 23:9.

living, concerns about a lack of sustenance and support, interest in questions of debt, and the proclaiming of eschatological blessings for the poor and punishment for the rich.[33] The tradition of Jesus calling "sinners" to change their ways partly falls into this line of thinking. Whenever the socioeconomic status of "sinners" is mentioned in Jewish texts from the Psalms through rabbinic literature, it is constantly with reference to them being rich exploiters. While this hope involved the traditional language of returning to the correct practice of the law, it should also be seen as part of the tradition of the rich being damned for being rich and needing to rectify their status—and soon.[34] It may have been foolhardy for the Jesus movement to expect sustained success in this respect, but rarely can we accuse apocalyptic and millenarian movements of lacking ambitious thinking.

Of course, such stories and sayings concerning wealth and poverty could have been created at any point in the gospel tradition or favored and transformed by a given gospel writer. Presumably, some of the ideas about wealth were inherited clichés from more elite writers. However, there is such a heavy concentration of such material across sources and forms in the gospel tradition that a case can be made that these are among the earliest ideas associated with Jesus. Moreover, inherited clichéd language still requires a context for interpretation, and if these ideas associated with Jesus emerged from the movement in a changed Galilee, then they would have different resonances than when associated with scribal elites. Here we might refer back to and compare the 1381 revolt: all things shared in common meant different things to aristocrats, monastic orders, and peasants.

Collectively, these themes of social upheaval and reversal of rich and poor were part of the earliest versions of apocalypticism and millenarianism associated with the Jesus movement. As with Ball and the rebels of 1381, this was a reimagining of the world in terms of an ideal king and idealized benign kingdom or empire that owed as much to the inherited hierarchical concepts of kingdom and kingship as it did to hierarchal peasant society and peasant myths of a golden age. As is well known, the language of the kingdom of God involved, of course, rulership over a territory, and even all peoples, under a sanctioned king.[35] It is likely that elevated language associated with the kingdom was part of the early ideas associated with the Jesus movement, including a replacement hierarchi-

33. E.g., Mark 10:17–31; Luke 6:20–26 // Matt 5:3–12; Matt 6:24 // Luke 16:13; Matt 6:25–34 // Luke 12:22–31; Matt 11:8 // Luke 7:25; Luke 12:57–59 // Matt 5:25; Luke 14:12–24 // Matt 22:1–14; Matt 5:40–42; 6:12; 18:23–35; 25:31–46; Luke 4:18; 6:20–21, 24–25, 35; 12:13–21; 16:1–8, 19–31; 16; cf. 1 En. 98:2; 102:9–11; Gos. Thom. 64).

34. See James Crossley, *Jesus and the Chaos of History: Redirecting the Quest for the Historical Jesus* (Oxford: Oxford University Press, 2015), 96–111.

35. E.g., Obad 19–21; Zech 14:9; Ps 47:2–3; Dan 7:27; cf. 1 Chr 28:5.

cal order focused on Israel (e.g., Matt 19:28 // Luke 22:29–30; Mark 10:35–45). Jesus, like Ball, would receive a significant role in the new world order. As with Ball's millenarianism, that of the early Jesus tradition likely worked with the assumption of new benign rulership and a world of plenty following the fall of the old corrupt order.[36]

If it jolts people out of a romanticized way of thinking about the kingdom of God in nonhierarchical terms, we might reword the concept as "dictatorship of God" or, better still, the "dictatorship of the peasantry," that is a hope for a benign hierarchical vanguard run in the interests of the peasantry and meeting (and exceeding) their material interests and political representation—with necessary accompanying punishments.[37] Indeed, one of the failures of the previous Quest (or at least its prominent representatives) in locating Jesus in a peasant context was not to take seriously hierarchical thinking in peasant societies.[38] But such thinking was necessary for the Jesus movement to gain sufficient support, particularly when accompanied by a culturally credible framework for public presentation of the movement (e.g., discipline, morality, values, interpretation of authoritative texts, popular authority). As with Ball the itinerant renegade lower clergyman, Jesus the itinerant preacher, exegete, and holy man represented the role of the local intelligentsia and became the figure used to unify and express wider concerns, anxieties, and discontents. Both Ball and Jesus represent the roles of the "religious organiser," a cross-cultural classification of figures assigned authority (whether officially or through popular support) who lead and mediate between people and the divine.[39] In the case of both Jesus and Ball, an uneasy relationship with the officially sanctioned channeling of the divine meant that their authority came from popular support, which was framed in terms of supernaturally sanctioned authority.

But crucially, this was not a movement restricted to Galilean agricultural workers, otherwise such localized discontent would have died out or been contained. As we saw, the early tradition also involved explicit interaction with those deemed to be oppressive and rich, and the early movement likely received some form of support from women with resources and status (e.g., Mark 15:40–41; Luke 8:1–3). As with the 1381 uprising, then, the apocalypticism that focuses on stark role reversal of rich and poor also (perhaps necessarily) obscures some

36. Cf. Pss. Sol. 17; 1QM, VI 4–6; 4Q246 II, 1–9; 4Q252 V, 1–4; 4Q521 2 II, 1–13; 11Q13 2 13; 2 Bar. 72:2–73:2.

37. Crossley and Myles, *Jesus*, 108.

38. See the criticisms raised by John H. Elliott, "Jesus Was Not an Egalitarian: A Critique of an Anachronistic and Idealist Theory," *BTB* 32.1 (2002): 75–91.

39. Crossley and Myles, *Jesus*, 47–49, 74–98.

of the more complex social realities on the grounds that were important in the widening of the localized discontent. Indeed, there would have been a range of complementary and competing interests at work in the relevant early Galilean and Judean networks (as there were in England in 1381) including heads of households, members of households, local officials, religious organizers, and different figures within peasant hierarchies. Clearly, the early Jesus movement was associated with fishers and tax collectors, thereby providing some of the most important local networks for the spread of the movement (see Kloppenborg's chapter). The survival of the Jesus movement in Galilee and beyond was also dependent on scribal or administrative "middling" roles (see Rollens's chapter), which allowed for physical, written accounts and wider dissemination of the movement's origins and ideas beyond a parochial peasantry. With this in mind, there should be no difficulty in entertaining the possibility of the coexistence of both scribalism and antiscribalism (or competing scribalisms) in either the gospel tradition or the 1381 uprising.[40] In both cases, the right kind of scribalism was what was at stake.

Conclusion

The Next Quest needs to take the cross-cultural examination of apocalyptic and millenarian movements seriously in order to further the investigation of this already heavily investigated topic. The Next Quest should move beyond the typical presentation of an apocalypticism decaffeinated in order to fulfill the scholarly promises of foregrounding an apocalypticist coming to us as one unknown.[41] One way the Next Quest can do so is with reference to premodern, agrarian-based forms of apocalypticism and millenarianism. This will sharpen our understanding of the contexts of agrarian ideas "from below," which suffer from a low level of data when compared with their apocalyptic counterparts from the scribal elites or former elites. This will also provide an important check on the romanticized view of radical liberal egalitarianism commonly attributed to Jesus. Certainly, such language still makes life difficult for the interpreter. The fantastical language of apocalypticism was obviously limited for actual changes to the order of the world, despite the spectacular promises. The binary language of stark opposition may

40. See further Chris Keith, *Jesus against the Scribal Elite: The Origins of The Conflict* (Grand Rapids: Baker Academic, 2014).

41. Deane Galbraith, "Jeremiah Never Saw That Coming: How Jesus Miscalculated the End Times," in *Jeremiah in History and Tradition*, ed. Jim West and Niels Peter Lemche (Abingdon: Routledge, 2020), 150–75.

also have simplified the complexities of class interests, but an examination of such expressions of agitation and discontent and the popular appeal of apocalyptic language remains an important part of understanding material and political concerns from below that might otherwise be inaccessible. And recognizing that such language does simplify and distort social realities on the ground can also help us understand the emergence and spread of the Jesus movement.

30

Violence and Trauma

Nathan Shedd

The Next Quest for the historical Jesus must account for the commemorative impact of violence and trauma. In asking, "Where do we go from here?" I contend that a critical understanding of how violence and trauma influence social arrangements is important. In his monograph on Christ assemblies and ancient associations, John Kloppenborg sensibly cautioned that "comparison of Christ assemblies with associations . . . does not manufacture new data that we hitherto lacked."[1] Taking our cue from Kloppenborg's prudence, we must state at the outset that scholarly discourses on violence do not create new evidence for the historical Jesus. Rather, the historian whose imagination is informed by scholarly discourses on violence and trauma is positioned to think about the existing evidence we have about Jesus in methodologically sober ways that counterbalance overly optimistic "default assumptions" about the Jesus tradition's success in offering "accurate" glimpses at Jesus.[2] But the historian whose imagination is informed by scholarly discourses on violence and trauma is also positioned to think about the task of history in relation to Jesus in more expansive ways than merely fixating on "what

I would like to thank Judy Redman for her careful reading and insightful feedback on an earlier draft of this essay.

1. John S. Kloppenborg, *Christ's Associations: Connecting and Belonging in the Ancient City* (New Haven: Yale University Press, 2019), 5.

2. See, e.g., Craig S. Keener, *Christobiography: Memory, History, and the Reliability of the Gospels* (Grand Rapids: Eerdmans, 2019).

actually happened" in the life of Jesus. A comprehensive theorizing of violence and trauma is beyond the scope of this essay. What follows instead is a snapshot of certain features of these discourses and an explanation of their potential utility. This essay thus functions as a heuristic prompt and not an enclosed demarcation of the usefulness of studying violence and trauma.

TRAUMA AND MEMORY

First, a critical understanding of violence and trauma compels us to acknowledge the complexity of the Jesus tradition as artifacts of social memory.[3] Dale Allison opened his 2010 monograph on Jesus by stressing that "the frailty of human memory should distress all who quest for the so-called historical Jesus."[4] How much more so when dealing with the memory of trauma! The concept of trauma can be described at both individual and collective levels as a "deeply felt emotional response to some occurrence" that might include violence, death, war, rape, forced migration, and so on.[5] Such catastrophic episodes, as Sarah Emmanuel rightly observes, "are not surface-level ruptures" but "cut so deep into one's sense of self that their integrity— their lucidity as a self-thinking, self-functioning human—becomes disorganized."[6] Cultural trauma, as sociologist Jeffrey Alexander has written, "occurs when members of a collectivity feel they have been subjected to a horrendous event that leaves indelible marks upon their group consciousness, marking their memories forever and changing their future identity in fundamental and irrevocable ways."[7]

---

3. With the transmission of Jesus tradition, we are dealing squarely with the gospels as artifacts of memory, regardless of whether we conceive of the Synoptic Gospels as reservoirs of eyewitness memory, the collective archives of Christ assemblies and groups, or, as Walsh has recently argued, the product of elite literate specialists interested in Judean history and culture. The gospels' textualization represents the combination of the inherited past and the present circumstances that occasioned textualization—no matter how we conceive of those present circumstances—and as such constitute the generation (or perpetuation) of social or cultural memory about Jesus. See Robyn Faith Walsh, *The Origins of Early Christian Literature: Contextualizing the New Testament within Greco-Roman Literary Culture* (Cambridge: Cambridge University Press, 2021).

4. Dale C. Allison Jr., *Constructing Jesus: Memory, Imagination, and History* (Grand Rapids: Baker Academic, 2010), 1.

5. Ron Eyerman, "The Past in the Present: Culture and the Transmission of Memory," in *The Collective Memory Reader*, ed. Jeffrey K. Olick, Vered Vinitzky-Seroussi, and Daniel Levy (Oxford: Oxford University Press, 2011), 304.

6. Sarah Emmanuel, *Trauma Theory, Trauma Story: A Narration of Biblical Studies and the World of Trauma* (Leiden: Brill, 2021), 4.

7. Jeffrey Alexander, "Toward a Cultural Theory of Trauma," in *The Collective Memory Reader*,

It is certainly true that remembering subjects are capable of remembering past trauma "with alarming accuracy."[8] Many Americans know where they were and what they were doing when President Kennedy was assassinated; likewise, many of us can recall our exact steps on September 11, 2001.[9] But it is also true that "individuals can remember sometimes in excruciating detail, memories of events that are extraordinarily unlikely to have occurred, including alien abductions and satanic rituals . . . [and] disturbing events that never happened, such as being lost in a shopping mall."[10] Some studies have shown, moreover, that psychotherapeutic techniques at retrieval (e.g., hypnosis) "can contribute to the production of false memories."[11]

When one encounters or experiences a traumatic episode, furthermore, one common survival technique is what trauma theorists label as *dissociation*. Dissociation occurs when "individuals detach . . . themselves from the ongoing experience."[12] This phenomenon complicates subsequent attempts at retrieval as recollection often resembles sensory fragments and not coherent narrative, even as trauma patients consistently claim that such fragments mirror the intense physical sensations of the originating event.[13] Van der Kolk explains that "high arousal not only changes the balance between [the rational and emotional memory systems of the brain] but also disconnects other brain areas necessary for the proper storage and integration of incoming information, such as the hippocampus and the thalamus."[14]

While repression is one survival tactic in the face of trauma, the need to overcome trauma by processing it in language of narrativized memory is also common. Trauma thus presents us with something of a paradox, for while highly emotional encounters can threaten to dissolve individual and group connectivity and survival, they are also the sites where individuals and collectives re-

---

ed. Jeffrey K. Olick, Vered Vinitzky-Seroussi, and Daniel Levy (Oxford: Oxford University Press, 2011), 307.

8. Emmanuel, *Trauma Theory, Trauma Story*, 6.

9. Robert K. McIver, *Memory, Jesus, and the Synoptic Gospels* (Atlanta: Society of Biblical Literature, 2011), 41–58.

10. Jonathan W. Schooler and Eric Eich, "Memory for Emotional Events," in *The Oxford Handbook of Memory*, ed. Endel Tulving and Fergus I. M. Craik (Oxford: Oxford University Press, 2000), 385.

11. Schooler and Eich, "Memory for Emotional Events," 385.

12. Schooler and Eich, "Memory for Emotional Events," 386.

13. Bessel van der Kolk and Rita Fisler, "Dissociation and the Fragmentary Nature of Traumatic Memories: Overview and Exploratory Study," *Journal of Traumatic Stress* 8 (1995): 513.

14. Bessel van der Kolk, *The Body Keeps the Score: Brain, Mind, and Body in the Healing of Trauma* (New York: Penguin, 2014), 178.

solve not to be overcome by sensory overload and injury. At the level of culture, Alexander contends:

> Representation of trauma depends on constructing a compelling framework of cultural classification. In one sense, this is simply telling a new story. Yet this storytelling is, at the same time, a complex and multivalent symbolic process that is *contingent, highly contested, and sometimes highly polarizing. . . .* 'Experiencing trauma' can be understood as a sociological process that *defines a painful injury to the collectivity, establishes the victim, attributes responsibility, and distributes the ideal and material consequences.* Insofar as traumas are so experienced, and thus imagined and represented, the collective identity will become significantly revised. This identity revision means that there will be *a searching re-remembering of the collective past,* for memory is not only social and fluid but deeply connected to the contemporary sense of the self. Identities are continuously constructed and secured not only by facing the present and future but also by reconstructing the collectivity's earlier life.[15]

In other words, processing trauma in terms of memory renders trauma as the locus of negotiation where culprits and victims are identified, moral evaluations of acute injury surface, and where these lines of demarcation are revisited upon subsequent commemorative practices and rituals. Trauma is also the site where competing groups offer contested evaluations of events. "Groups," as Allison avers, "do not rehearse competing memories that fail to shore up what they hold dear. Approved remembrance lives on; unapproved remembrance expires. Communities, like individuals, systematically forget."[16]

Historical Jesus scholars who wish to emphasize constructing a portrait of Jesus *before* the gospels must reckon with the fact that the Jesus tradition is thoroughly impacted by multiple traumas, including in particular the destruction of the Jerusalem temple in 70 CE, Jesus's crucifixion, and John the Baptist's beheading. Luke's Gospel, as is well known, from its ninth chapter onward portrays Jesus's itinerancy as one long journey toward Jerusalem and thus in effect filters Jesus's life through the prism of his crucifixion. The gospels themselves *acknowledge* that they have *negotiated* the meaning of Jesus's deeds and sayings after the fact of his execution and purported resurrection, indeed after Jesus's followers originally understood him in different ways. At John 2:22, the text admits that the disciples initially understood Jesus's proclamation against the temple in one way, but upon subsequent

15. Alexander, "Toward a Cultural Theory of Trauma," 309 (emphasis added).
16. Allison, *Constructing Jesus,* 7.

revisitation of this tradition in light of the crucifixion and resurrection they now understood it to refer to Jesus's physical body. We could make similar comments concerning John 12:16, which states, "His disciples did not understand these things at first; *but when Jesus was glorified, then* they remembered that these things had been written of him and had been done to him" (NRSV, italics added), and also places in the Synoptic Gospels where initial impressions of Jesus's words and deeds during his life are misapprehended by the disciples (e.g., Mark 9:32; cf. John 20:1–9).

Scholars must, furthermore, reckon with the fact that the commemorative perspectives of Jesus's adversaries are not centered but pushed to the periphery in the Jesus tradition. Even if one were to be generous and grant that the crucifixion narratives and the tale of John's beheading were based on the disciples' eyewitness memories, these traumas would still be embedded in *contested* memory because the perspectives of Pontius Pilate, Herod Antipas, Herodias, and the Jerusalem crowds are not granted. If these perspectives were approved and centered, it is reasonable for us to assume that the attributions of morality and the lines designating victim and culprit would be negotiated, and perhaps significantly so. Narrating trauma freezes a configuration of the past in time, pushing alternative conceptualizations to the margins of history. Relatedly, we cannot ignore the fact that the traumatic experiences of the actual victim of violence (Jesus himself in this case) are not *directly* represented in the Jesus tradition. We must admit that the depths of our knowledge about Jesus's crucifixion are limited without the living memory of the victim himself.

Violence Begets Violence

The second implication of studying violence and trauma is that these discourses compel us to notice how early representations of the violence applied to Jesus generate violence transgenerationally and transculturally. Under certain conditions, violence begets violence. Speaking of "what happens when individuals rally groups around themselves in a situation of conflict," Bruce Lincoln has argued that "It is when separate individuals recall their common descent from (and thus attachment to) a given ancestor that they reawaken their (latent) feelings of affinity for, and attachment to, one another. In that very moment and by that very act of memory, they (re-)define themselves as kin, that is, persons who are joined together in the same familial group. In this way the past shapes the present, *invocation* of an ancestor being simultaneously the *evocation* of a correlated social group."[17] Although Lincoln's comments focus on the resurrection of inter-

17. Bruce Lincoln, *Discourse and the Construction of Society: Comparative Studies of Myth, Ritual, and Classification* (Oxford: Oxford University Press, 1989), 20.

group bonds and affection, the converse of his assertions are also true (and his wider discussion presumes as much). Namely, that when individuals of separate groups remember their ancestral conflict, they "reawaken" dormant attitudes of hostility.

This fusion of the past and the present is akin to what the late sociologist Barry Schwartz has termed "keying":

> *Keying* transforms the meaning of activities understood in terms of one event by comparing them with activities understood in terms of another. . . . 'Keying' is more than a new word for analogical thinking, more than a way individuals mentally organize their social experience; keying transforms memory into a cultural system because it matches publicly accessible (i.e., symbolic) models of the past (written narratives, pictorial images, statues, motion pictures, music, and songs) to the experiences of the present. Keying arranges cultural symbols into a publicly visible discourse that flows through the organizations and institutions of the social world. Keying is communicative movement—talk, writing, image- and music-making—that connects otherwise separate realms of history.[18]

Recollections of violence (and its underlying conflict) reinscribe violence and conflict among "correlated social groups" in the ever-shifting horizon of the present. If narrating violence freezes configurations of the past in time—including social arrangements of morality, guilt, and designations of culprits, victims, monsters, evil, heroes, etc., as I stated previously—then *keying* such narrativized patterns of thinking to present social circumstances holds the dangerous capacity to regenerate conflict and thus reproduce violence, as Lincoln has conveyed elsewhere: "Violence is the continuation of conflict by means of physical force."[19] The potential for past antagonisms to reify into present hostility is what led many Rwandans to intentionally refuse remembering certain facets of the Rwandan genocide, in-

---

18. Barry Schwartz, *Abraham Lincoln and the Forge of National Memory* (Chicago: University of Chicago Press, 2000), 226. As an example of keying (although she does not term it as such), see Tania Oldenhage, "Walking the Way of the Cross: German Places, Church Traditions, and Holocaust Memories," in *Religion, Violence, Memory, and Place*, ed. Oren Baruch Stier and J. Shawn Landres (Bloomington: Indiana University Press, 2006), 90–99 (quote on 91), who discusses the commemorative youth ritual (i.e., "the Ecumenical Way of the Cross") that takes place throughout Germany before Easter Sunday: "Jewish experiences of suffering during the Holocaust are interpreted through the Christian story of Jesus' walk to Golgotha. Conversely, Jesus's walk to Golgotha is interpreted through the Holocaust experiences."

19. Bruce Lincoln, "Theses on Religion and Violence," *ISIM Review* 15 (2005): 12.

cluding racial tensions, as Susanna Buckley-Zistel has demonstrated.[20] "Chosen amnesia" was a cultural strategy that promoted local peace by not enflaming cultural lines of detachment.[21]

To be clear, I am not advocating for a theory of violence that attempts to overcome trauma by systematically forgetting trauma. It is relatively well known that refusing to come to terms with a violent past often benefits the violent and re-victimizes the violated.[22] Rather, my point is *that* the (uncritical) reinscription of violence holds the dangerous capacity to "inculcate ideology conducive to outbursts of violence" particularly as contemporary social groups are correlated to symbolic social groups and vice versa.[23]

This phenomenon is observable in the reception of some of the earliest conceptualizations of Jesus from antiquity. In our earliest portrayal of Jesus, the Gospel of Mark, the somatic violence of the beheading of John the Baptist and the crucifixion of Jesus are *keyed* together.[24] Both John and Jesus, for instance, are "handed over" (e.g., 1:14; 15:1, 10, 15), "grasped" (e.g., 6:17; 14:44, 46), and "bound" (e.g., 6:17; 15:1). At Mark 9:11–13, the designation of John as the prophet Elijah functions to position John's death as forerunning Jesus's demise. The recounting of John's beheading in Mark 6:14–29, moreover, comes on the heels of the Markan Jesus likening his rejection in his hometown to the rejection of the prophets (6:1–6a).

The Gospel of Matthew draws an explicit attachment between John the Baptist, Jesus, and the prophets, on the one hand, and their adversaries, on the other hand. According to Matt 14:5, Herod the tetrarch wished to kill the Baptist but was unable because the crowds viewed John as a "prophet." Likewise, according to Matt 21:46, the Pharisees and the chief priests wished to subdue Jesus but were unable because the crowds viewed Jesus as a "prophet."[25] Similarly in Matt 23, the city of Jerusalem, the Pharisees, and scribes are placed in a cultural lineage as the

20. Susanna Buckley-Zistel, "Remembering to Forget: Chosen Amnesia as a Strategy for Local Co-Existence in Post-Genocide Rwanda," *Africa* 76 (2006): 131–50; Buckley-Zistel, "Between Pragmatism, Coercion and Fear: Chosen Amnesia after the Rwandan Genocide," in *Memory and Political Change*, ed. Aleida Assmann and Linda Shortt (New York: Palgrave Macmillan, 2012), 72–88.

21. Buckley-Zistel, "Chosen Amnesia," 74–83.

22. See Aleida Assmann, "To Remember or to Forget: Which Way Out of a Shared History of Violence?," in Assmann and Shortt, *Memory and Political Change*, 53–71.

23. Nathan L. Shedd, *A Dangerous Parting: The Beheading of John the Baptist in Early Christian Memory* (Waco, TX: Baylor University Press, 2021), 48.

24. For a full discussion of how John's beheading and Jesus's crucifixion are tied together in the Gospel of Mark, see Shedd, *Dangerous Parting*, 92–99.

25. For further examples of the links between John's death and Jesus's death in Matthew, see Brian C. Dennert, *John the Baptist and the Jewish Setting of Matthew*, WUNT 403 (Tübingen: Mohr Siebeck, 2015), 238–54.

"descendants" of the killers of God's prophets. And in Matt 27 the Jewish leadership is portrayed as persuading the Jerusalem crowd into wanting Jesus crucified instead of Barabbas (27:15–23). The local Jewish crowd in turn accepts responsibility for Jesus's death and extends this responsibility to their children (27:25).[26]

For those whose conceptualization of Christian origins involves Q, these maneuvers are observable in Q as well. Sara Parks has observed, "Q also seems to take a keen interest in the topic of unjustly murdered prophets."[27] She sets forth these examples:[28]

- Q 6:22–23: "Blessed are you when they insult and [persecute] you, and [say every kind of] evil [against] you because of the son of humanity. Be glad and [exult], for vast is your reward in heaven. For this is how they [persecuted] the prophets who were before you."
- Q 11:47–48: "Woe to you, for you build the tombs of the prophets, but your forefathers killed them. Thus [you] witness [against yourselves that] you are [the sons] of your forefathers."
- Q 11:49–51: "Therefore also, Wisdom said: I will send them prophets and sages, and some of them they will kill and persecute, so that a settling of accounts for the blood of all the prophets poured out from the founding of the world may be required of this generation, from the blood of Abel to the blood of Zechariah, murdered between the sacrificial altar and the House. Yes, I tell you, an accounting will be required of this generation."
- Q 13:34: "O Jerusalem, Jerusalem, who kills the prophets and stones those sent to her! How often I wanted to gather your children together, as a hen gathers her nestlings under her wings, but you were not willing!"
- Q 16:16: "The law and the prophets were until John. From then on the kingdom of God is violated and the violent plunder it."

From these sayings in Q, we can observe the fault lines of a cultural schematic whereby (1) Jesus is aligned to the violent deaths of the prophets and to the kingdom of God; and (2) "this generation," "Jerusalem," and Jesus's adversaries are attached to the apical past—to those who shed the blood of the prophets. Alan Kirk is right to

26. Nathan Shedd, "Gospel of Matthew," in *Judeophobia in the New Testament*, ed. Sarah Rollens, Eric Vanden Eykel, and Meredith J. C. Warren (Grand Rapids: Eerdmans, 2025).

27. Sara Parks, "John the Baptist's Murder and the Vengeful Logia of Jesus: Thinking with Trauma Theory about the Stratification of Q" (paper presented at the Enoch Seminar Nangeroni Meeting on John the Baptist, Online, January 14, 2021).

28. Quotations from Q are borrowed from those in James M. Robinson, Paul Hoffman, and John S. Kloppenborg, *The Critical Edition of Q*, Hermeneia (Minneapolis: Fortress, 2000).

contend that Q 11:47–51—as a retrospective reference to the crucifixion—does not merely compare Jesus's death to the death of the prophets but incorporates Jesus's traumatic demise "into the epic memory tapestry of Israel."[29] As such, Q "passes a moral judgment on Jesus' death, and, accordingly, aggressively attacks the moral legitimacy of its opponents, the Romans and their local elite clients who were responsible for executing Jesus . . . the latter . . . are analogically mapped to those elites in Israel's sacred narrative who killed God's messengers, the prophets."[30]

The effect of this keying together in the gospels and Q of the violent crucifixion of Jesus to the violent deaths of the prophets is that the characterizations of "correlated social groups" (to employ Lincoln's language) are mutually affecting and reinforcing. Significantly, as this keying maneuver is *re*-correlated in subsequent social contexts and arrangements, the structures that enable further instances of violence are perpetuated. I have argued elsewhere that both Justin Martyr and Origen harnessed the close connection in the gospels between Jesus's crucifixion, John's beheading, and the death of the prophets to activate these figures' local adversaries as correlatives of "the Jews" writ large in the second and third centuries.[31] This anti-Jewish pattern of thinking provided the rhetorical scaffolding that upheld Justin's conviction that the suffering Jews encountered as refugees in the post–Bar Kokhba revolt years was divinely authorized (see Justin, *Dial.* 16). The concept of "the Jews" as Christ killers was reinforced ritualistically in medieval passion plays and in turn fueled and justified the maltreatment of Jews during the Spanish Inquisition.[32] Colonials in Hispaniola performed ritual dramas that conflated Judas, "the Jews," Native Americans, and Africans on the one hand, and Jesus, the apostles, and European Christians, on the other hand. As Elizabeth McAlister observes: "European Christendom dramatically performed itself as a sole civilizing force, against the barbaric and demonic forces of Jews, Native Americans, and Africans."[33]

More pertinent for the question "Where do we go from here?" confronting historical Jesus scholars today is the recognition that this cultural apparatus whereby Jesus's fatal adversaries in the gospels are conflated with "the Jews" in subsequent

29. Alan Kirk, "The Memory of Violence and the Death of Jesus in Q," in *Memory and the Jesus Tradition*, The Reception of Jesus in the First Three Centuries 2 (London: Bloomsbury, 2018), 170–71 (quote on 171).

30. Kirk, "Memory of Violence," 171–72.

31. Shedd, *Dangerous Parting*, 129–63.

32. Elizabeth McAlister, "The Jew in the Haitian Imagination: A Popular History of Anti-Judaism and Proto-Racism," in *Race, Nation, and Religion in the Americas*, ed. Henry Goldschmidt and Elizabeth McAlister (Oxford: Oxford University Press, 2004), 70.

33. McAlister, "Jew in the Haitian Imagination," 70.

times and places has continued to function in dangerous capacities in recent and current times. In an episode entitled "The Passion of the Jew," the American comedy cartoon *South Park* picks up on the potential of Mel Gibson's portrayal of Jesus's Jewish contemporaries in his film *The Passion of the Christ* to instigate racial hatred of Jews. Jonathan Gray summarizes: "After watching *Passion of the Christ* (which, satirically, is shown as a movie with nothing more than endless lashings of Jesus followed by horrific screams), [Kyle Broflovski, Cartman's Jewish friend] tells Cartman that he has been right all these years to hate Jews, an act which further inspires Cartman to rally South Park's citizens to an anti-Jew rally" aimed at exterminating Jews.[34] Later in a nightmare, Kyle sees himself in the Jewish crowd in the first century demanding Jesus's execution, and thus integrates himself into the notion of widespread Jewish culpability in Jesus's death.

Gray is right to argue that the satire advanced in the show by creators Parker and Stone functions to hold up a mirror to society "in hopes that the real-life referent to their fictionalized satire will be tainted by association, demanding reevaluation by viewers."[35] Audience members who witness the notoriously anti-Semitic character Eric Cartman—whose series reputation includes regularly hurling anti-Semitic invectives against Kyle, including blaming Jews for Jesus's death (as well as blaming Kyle for September 11 in one episode) and leading an anti-Jewish rally—are supposed to negatively evaluate Cartman and "the real-life referents" he resembles. The unfortunate irony of *South Park*, however, is that some audience members (1) are unaware of the aim of Parker and Stone's satire, and thus are susceptible to internalizing Cartman's ideological patterns of thinking, or worse (2) *are* aware of the function of *South Park*'s comedy, but do not care, and thus find in Cartman reinforcement of antisemitic ideology. Insofar as this is the case, *South Park* is complicit in advancing that which they seek to dismantle.

While Cartman's anti-Semitic words and actions in *South Park* are portrayed as extreme, they are not outlandish. Contemporary hate groups, racially motivated violent extremists, and white supremacists—indeed conceivable "real-life referents" for episodes like "Passion of the Jew"—appeal to the idea of "the Jews" as "Christ killers" to advance harmful ideology. One active white supremacist group in Arkansas activates Matt 27:25 to express their eagerness for a divinely sanctioned comprehensive extermination of the Jewish people.[36] White nationalist

---

34. Jonathan Gray, "From Whence Came Cartman: South Park's Intertextual Lineage," in *Deconstructing South Park: Critical Examinations of Animated Transgression*, ed. Brian Cogan, Critical Studies in Television (Lanham, MD: Lexington, 2012), 13.

35. Gray, "From Whence Came Cartman," 12–13.

36. For further discussion, see Shedd, "Gospel of Matthew."

and Holocaust denier John Friend runs an anti-Semitic website out of Long Beach, California, that describes anti-Semitism proudly as "stating basic facts about Jews," which apparently includes setting forth "evidence" that blames Jews for September 11.[37] Holocaust denier Carolyn Yeager argues that Jews in Germany keep trying to prosecute Nazis and, in doing so, their unsated quest for revenge replicates the Jewish demand in Matt 27: "kill him, crucify him!"[38]

RECONSTRUCTING THE HISTORICAL JESUS

Theorizing violence and trauma does not render the Jesus tradition as "accurate" or "inaccurate." These discourses rather crystallize daunting methodological obstacles that confront historical Jesus scholars. I thus want to offer a point of caution for those who seek to catch glimpses of Jesus through the prism of the evidence available to us. Future reconstructions of Jesus of Nazareth must soberly navigate the recognition that the Jesus tradition and the gospels are embedded in and testify to a variety of traumatic experiences: the beheading of John the Baptist, exploitation of the peasant class (as shown in Myles's chapter), conflict over ethnic-religious expressions of identity, Jesus's crucifixion, the destruction of the Jerusalem temple, and so on.

The commemorative transmission of individual and collective traumas like these involves configuring and buttressing an image of the past from a specific entry point. It also entails assigning and constructing blame for atrocity. As mentioned previously, we do not possess an account of Jesus's crucifixion from the ideological angle of Pontius Pilate. This does not necessarily imply that the Jesus tradition was wrong per se in configuring Jesus as an innocent victim of imperial violence. But it does underscore that historians do not possess comprehensive evidence from varied vantage points. Because our evidence is limited and rhetorically angled, the possibilities in our historiography are limited and angled. Our entry point and imaginations as writers of history are governed to an extent by the entry points of our sources.

That the Jesus tradition is embedded in traumas also illuminates the nature of our data about the historical Jesus as complex compromises between the received past and the present in terms of memory. Our analysis above on the keying of Jesus's adversaries to Jewish opposition in subsequent social horizons in the

37. For the bio of John Friend and *The Realist Report*, see https://therealistreport.com/about.

38. Carolyn Yeager, "Germany Demands 96-Year-Old Spend Four Years in Prison to Satisfy Holohoax Guilt," *Carolyn Yeager* (blog), December 1, 2017, https://carolynyeager.net/germany-demands-96-year-old-spend-four-years-prison-satisfy-holohoax-guilt.

reception history of the Jesus tradition demonstrates that the past and the present constantly negotiate with one another in acts of memory. When present social groups are made to resemble (i.e., are keyed to) past social groups, the past is simultaneously marshaled to resemble the present. In any given activation of the received past—including in our earliest portrayals of Jesus's life—the past and the present are both reconfigured by virtue of their alignment. Keying the past and the present, in other words, is a process of recontextualization, redeployment, and reconceptualization. Consequently, historians of Jesus must ask: to what extent is the received past pressuring the present and to what extent is the present distorting the past? And how do we know?

CONCLUSION

In addition to historical Jesus scholars *methodologically* accounting for the impact of trauma, future scholarship should take stock of the transgenerational effects of ancient traumas embedded in the Jesus tradition. The upshot of scholars recognizing that violence can beget trauma is that this recognition provides us the opportunity to be active in dismantling ideological patterns of thinking that structure contemporary violence. By shifting our focus to the reception of violence in the present, whether that be the anti-Jewish legacies of remembering Jesus's crucifixion or some other legacy, we can play a crucial role, even as historians of antiquity, in overcoming pressing issues that confront us today. Where do we go from here? For my part, I want to see (or increasingly see) historical Jesus scholarship that not only seeks to construct Jesus as he possibly was, but also scholarship that connects such portraits with strategies that restrain violent appropriations of Jesus.

31

Death and Martyrdom

Michael P. Barber

The Next Quest for the historical Jesus—if we are to speak of the future of Jesus studies in those terms[1]—will inevitably turn its attention to an important question about the man from Nazareth: how did he think his ministry would come to an end? For many, the passion predictions of Jesus have represented an open-and-shut case of the community's post-Easter creativity. Rudolf Bultmann wrote: "Jesus scarcely reckoned on execution at the hands of the Romans, but only on the imminent appearing of the kingdom of God."[2] Likewise, Norman Perrin saw the logia anticipating Jesus's suffering as "reaching back into the earliest days of Christian apologetic."[3]

More recently, Paula Fredriksen has argued that Jesus's death was ultimately due to the crowds' misunderstanding of his message. Jesus's arrival at Jerusalem, she maintains, triggered eschatological hopes, but in a way that he had not in-

---

1. For a critique of the "Old Quest," "New Quest," and "Third Quest" taxonomy, see Fernando Bermejo-Rubio, "The Fiction of the 'Three Quests': An Argument for Dismantling a Dubious Historiographical Paradigm," *JSHJ* 7 (2009): 211–53. However, the language of the "Next Quest" need not necessarily be tied to that specific schema.

2. Rudolf Bultmann, "The Primitive Christian Kerygma and the Historical Jesus," in *The Historical Jesus and the Kerygmatic Christ: Essays on the New Quest of the Historical Jesus*, ed. Carl E. Braaten and Roy A. Harrisville (New York: Abingdon, 1964), 23.

3. Norman Perrin, *A Modern Pilgrimage in New Testament Christology* (Philadelphia: Fortress, 1974), 75.

tended: he had preached about God's kingdom, but the crowds wanted to make *him* king. She writes: "Enthusiasm for the coming Kingdom, racing within this combustible mix of excited new hearers and faithful followers . . . would transmute quickly into enthused acclamation of Jesus as messiah. And enthusiasm infectiously spreads."[4] Jesus, then, "lost control of his audience."[5] His death was accidental to his understanding of his mission.

Others, however, have made the case that the passion predictions go back to Jesus himself. Most famous, perhaps, is Albert Schweitzer's view: Jesus attempted to "turn the wheel of the world" by, in a sense, forcing God's hand to deliver him from death.[6] Schweitzer anchored his position in apocalyptic Jewish traditions from which he believed Jesus drew. Specifically, Schweitzer argued that Jesus's outlook was shaped by Jewish traditions that expected a period of "messianic woes" to precede the dawning of the eschatological age.[7] More recent scholarship has critiqued Schweitzer's approach, observing that his terminology raises problems. First, though some sources from the Second Temple period do describe a period of eschatological suffering, they do not always feature a "messiah" figure, let alone a "suffering messiah." Second, the expression "messianic woes" is taken from later rabbinic sources.[8] Nevertheless, some have argued that Schweitzer's essential point makes good historical sense: in line with Jewish apocalyptic traditions, Jesus likely believed his own suffering would be part of the eschatological equation.[9]

When it comes to the passion predictions, then, like most debates involving the historical Jesus, arguments for various reconstructions can be made. The core issue for the historian, however, is not simply determining what is *possible* regarding Jesus but, rather, which explanation of the data is *most probable*. How should scholars in the Next Quest make that determination? Taking a page from Dale Allison, I believe the most sensible place to start is with the general impression of the sources that tell us about Jesus.[10]

4. Paula Fredriksen, *Jesus of Nazareth, King of the Jews: A Jewish Life and the Emergence of Christianity* (New York: Vintage, 1999), 245.

5. Fredriksen, *Jesus of Nazareth*, 247.

6. Albert Schweitzer, *The Quest of the Historical Jesus: A Critical Study of Its Progress from Reimarus to Wrede*, trans. William Montgomery (New York: Macmillan, 1950), 370–71.

7. Albert Schweitzer, *The Mysticism of Paul the Apostle*, trans. William Montgomery, 2nd ed. (New York: Seabury, 1968), 144.

8. For a discussion, see Dale C. Allison Jr., *The End of the Ages Has Come: An Early Interpretation of the Passion and Resurrection of Jesus* (Minneapolis: Fortress, 1985), 6 n. 6.

9. See Allison, *End of the Ages*; Brant Pitre, *Jesus, the Tribulation, and the End of the Exile: Restoration Eschatology and the Origin of the Atonement*, WUNT 2.204 (Tübingen: Mohr Siebeck, 2005).

10. Dale C. Allison Jr., *Constructing Jesus: Memory, Imagination, and History* (Grand Rapids: Baker Academic, 2010). I have offered an explanation and defense of my method elsewhere,

That Jesus anticipated dying at the hands of others is very well attested. Moreover, there is little in the way of "counterevidence." The passages that might be held up as suggesting an alternative outlook for Jesus are far from convincing. Here let us briefly survey the data.

Traditions Indicating Jesus Expected to Die a Violent Death

The notion that Jesus anticipated his own death or went to it willingly is attested in numerous sources. Here we can point to (1) Pauline texts; (2) material often identified as belonging to the Q source; (3) data found only in Mark; (4) traditions only attested in Matthew and Luke; (5) logia from the Gospel of Thomas; and (6) other early sources.[11] Consider the following.

Traditions Indicating Jesus Foresaw His Death or Died Willingly

Tradition	Reference
1. Jesus's Body Is Broken "For You"	1 Cor 11:23–26 // Matt 26:26–28 // Mark 14:22–24 // Luke 22:19–20
2. Following Jesus Entails Carrying the Cross	Matt 10:38 // Luke 14:27 [Q?]; Mark 8:34; Gos. Thom. 55
3. "Those Who Lose Their Life Will Keep It"	Matt 10:39 // Luke 17:33 [Q?]; Mark 8:35; John 12:25
4. The Son of Man . . . Will Be Killed	Mark 8:31; 9:31; cf. 10:33–34 and parr.)
5. "The Son of Man Has Come . . . to Give His Life as a Ransom for Many"	Matt 20:28 // Mark 10:45; cf. 1 Tim 2:5–6
6. Jesus Covertly Arranges the Site of the Passover Meal	Matt 26:17–19 // Mark 14:12–16 // Luke 22:7–13
7. Jesus Announces He Will Be Betrayed	Mark 14:17–21; cf. John 13:21–30
8. Jesus Prays about Drinking the "Cup"	Mark 14:32–42 and parr.

---

which I cannot fully defend here. See Michael Patrick Barber, *The Historical Jesus and the Temple: Memory, Methodology, and the Gospel of Matthew* (Cambridge: Cambridge University Press, 2023); Barber, "Did Jesus Anticipate Suffering a Violent Death? The Implications of Memory Research and Dale Allison's Methodology," *JSHJ* 18.3 (2020): 191–219.

11. I have adapted the following list from Allison, *Constructing Jesus*, 428–32.

Tradition	Reference
9. Jesus Does Not Resist Arrest	Mark 14:43–50; cf. John 18:1–9
10. Jesus Offers No Defense before Jewish Authorities	Mark 14:53–65; cf. John 18:13–24
11. Jesus Offers No Defense before Pilate	Mark 15:1–15; cf. John 18:28–19:16
12. Jesus Rebukes a Disciple Who Seeks to Rescue Jesus from Arrest	Matt 26:51–54; John 18:10
13. Jesus Exhibits No Fear upon Hearing Herod Seeks to Kill Him	Luke 13:31–33
14. Jesus Offers No Defense before Herod	Luke 23:6–12
15. The Parable of the Wicked Tenants Seems to Describe the Death of Jesus, the Son	Matt 21:33–41 // Mark 12:1–9 // Luke 20:9–16; Gos. Thom 65
16. Jesus Is the Stone "Rejected" by the Builders	Matt 21:42 // Mark 12:10 // Luke 20:17; Gos. Thom 66
17. Jesus Will Be Taken Away from His Disciples	Matt 9:15 // Mark 2:20 // Luke 5:35
18. "Destroy This Temple"	John 2:19–22
19. The Son of Man Will Be Lifted Up	John 3:14
20. "I Lay Down My Life for the Sheep"	John 10:11–18
21. "A Grain of Wheat Falls to the Earth and Dies"	John 12:23–27
22. "No One Has Greater Love Than . . . to Lay Down One's Life for One's Friends"	John 15:12–13
23. Jesus Is "Going to Him Who Sent Me"	John 16:5–10
24. Jesus Tells Peter That He Must Drink the Cup	John 18:10–12
25. James Will Be the Disciples' Leader	Gos. Thom. 12
26. "The Days Will Come When . . . You Will Not Find Me"	Gos. Thom 38
27. Jesus's Act of Obedience Makes Many Righteous	Rom 5:18–19
28. Christ Did Not Please Himself but Bore the Insults of Others	Rom 15:1–3

Tradition	Reference
29. "The Lord Jesus Christ . . . Gave Himself for Our Sins"	Gal 1:3–4
30. "The Son of God . . . Loved Me and Gave Himself for Me"	Gal 2:20
31. Jesus "Emptied Himself . . . He Humbled Himself and Became Obedient to the Point of Death"	Phil 2:7–8; cf. Rom 5:18–21
32. "Christ Loved Us and Gave Himself Up for Us"	Eph 5:2
33. Jesus's Faithfulness Is Linked to His Saving Death	Rom 3:21–26; Gal 2:15–21; Phil 3:7–11
34. Christ Jesus Gave His Testimony before Pontius Pilate	1 Tim 6:12–13
35. Jesus "Gave Himself . . . to Redeem Us from All Iniquity"	Titus 2:14
36. Jesus Suffered in Reverent Submission	Heb 5:7–9
37. Jesus Endured the Cross, "Disregarding Its Shame"	Heb 12:1–2
38. Believers Should Willingly Suffer Mistreatment as Christ Did	1 Pet 2:20–24

The catalogue above underscores the ubiquity and consistency of the notion that Jesus believed it would be necessary for himself to undergo suffering. Let me be clear: my point in assembling these is not that any one of these traditions is "authentic." The observation I would simply like to make here is that the general shape of the tradition points overwhelmingly in one direction.

Of course, one could argue that it was inevitable that, in the aftermath of his death, the followers of Jesus would have likely reflected on the significance of suffering and death and produced all of the memories that Jesus anticipated what would befall him. Yet is this the most *probable* explanation of the data? Below, I will argue that it is not. At the outset, however, we should mention that there are other aspects of the Jesus tradition that would seem to reinforce the likelihood that Jesus anticipated being rejected and suffering. One feature we can mention here is Jesus's apparent association with John.

That Jesus was baptized by John is typically regarded as a reflecting history.[12] It is also widely accepted that Jesus's relationship with John likely involved more than a one-time interaction. Their messages seem to have had some overlap.[13] What is more, from Mark, Matthew, and Josephus we learn that John was arrested and killed due to his preaching (Matt 14:3–12 // Mark 6:17–29; A.J. 18.116–119). Though the gospel and Josephan accounts diverge on the details, that John's death was in some way attributable to his ministry is therefore broadly accepted.[14] Would Jesus have been unaware that his activities could bring him to a similar end? That seems highly unlikely.

Furthermore, Jesus is remembered as contrasting John the Baptist with a "reed shaken in the wind," an expression that is linked to an affirmation of John's identity as a prophet (Matt 11:7–9 // Luke 7:24–26 [Q?]). The saying highlights John's resolve to proclaim a dangerous message. The saying comports well with a Jewish tradition that observed that prophets were often rejected and killed by their contemporaries.[15] John's death, then, would easily have been seen as consistent with a prophetic identity. In fact, Jesus is said to have known and applied the notion that prophets are typically rejected to himself (Matt 13:57 // Mark 6:4; Luke 4:24 // John 4:44 // Gos. Thom. 31; cf. Luke 13:33). That Jesus saw himself as having some sort of prophetic role is generally accepted.[16] Regardless of what we make of the historical value of any particular tradition, if he had seen himself as taking up a role akin to John's or other prophetic figures, he would have had good reason to think he would suffer a violent end.

---

12. See, e.g., Maurice Casey, *Jesus of Nazareth: An Independent Historian's Account of His Life and Teaching* (London: T&T Clark, 2010), 176–77; E. P. Sanders, *Jesus and Judaism* (Philadelphia: Fortress, 1985), 11; Bart Ehrman, *Jesus: Apocalyptic Prophet of the New Millennium* (Oxford: Oxford University Press, 1999), 137–39.

13. See, e.g., Helen K. Bond, *The Historical Jesus: A Guide for the Perplexed* (London: T&T Clark, 2012), 82–88; Fredriksen, *Jesus of Nazareth*, 191–97; John P. Meier, *A Marginal Jew: Rethinking the Historical Jesus*, AYBRL (New Haven: Yale University Press, 1991–2016), 2:100–233.

14. See, e.g., Joan Taylor, *The Immerser: John the Baptist within Second Temple Judaism* (Grand Rapids: Eerdmans, 1997), 213–59.

15. See, e.g., 2 Chr 36:15–16; Jer 11:21; 12:6; 26:20–23; Josephus, A.J. 10.38; cf. Liv. Pro. 1:1.

16. See Tobias Hägerland, *Jesus and the Forgiveness of Sins: An Aspect of His Prophetic Mission*, SNTSMS 150 (Cambridge: Cambridge University Press, 2011), 202, "The characterization of the historical Jesus as a prophet is, in fact, almost unanimously affirmed by scholarship." In particular, the idea that Jesus made predictions about the coming destruction of the temple is supported by its recurrent attestation, its plausibility within a Second Temple Jewish context, and the effects of Jesus. It is widely accepted as reflecting aspects of Jesus's historical message. See the discussion in Barber, *Historical Jesus and the Temple*, 89–97.

Possible Counterevidence

There are traditions that have been viewed as indicating that Jesus did not anticipate coming to an untimely demise: (1) Jesus's prayer in Gethsemane (Matt 26:36–
46 // Mark 14:32–42 // Luke 22:39–46); (2) Jesus's quotation of Psalm 22 from the
cross (Matt 27:46 // Mark 15:34); and (3) the disciples' desertion of Jesus at his
arrest (Matt 26:56 // Mark 14:50).[17] None of these, however, can be construed
as counterevidence that weighs significantly against the traditions cited above.
First, the scene in Gethsemane "does not suggest failure of nerve, but rather firm
determination, even in the face of disappointment."[18]

Second, we should recognize that Psalm 22 tells a story, the point of which is
that God does not abandon the righteous in their suffering but vindicates them
(cf. Ps 22:19–31). Though Jesus is not remembered as quoting the entire psalm, it
seems unlikely that its fuller context would have been irrelevant to him. At the
very least, it seems relevant for Mark.[19] Either way, here we do not find unambiguous counterevidence.

Finally, one need not posit that the disciples had never heard Jesus speak
about being to put death to explain why none of them died with Jesus. Another
more natural explanation exists: fear. In Gethsemane, Jesus himself is portrayed
as dreading death. That the disciples flee emphasizes that they lack Jesus's fortitude. Moreover, the gospel tradition reveals that the Jesus's disciples often misunderstood his words.[20] It is entirely plausible, then, that they did not fully ap-
prehend Jesus's forecasts. Or perhaps they thought that when the moment came,
they would be granted a miraculous victory in defending Jesus (cf. Mark 8:32).
This might explain the gospel narrative where one disciple boldly attacks one of
those who had come to arrest Jesus but flees when Jesus condemns his action (cf.
Matt 26:51–56 // Mark 14:47–50 // Luke 22:49–53 // John 18:10–11).

In the end, there simply seems to be no significant counterevidence that
weighs against the notion that Jesus anticipated being put to death. Various re-

17. For the first two, see Hermann Samuel Reimarus, *Reimarus: Fragments*, ed. Charles Talbert, trans. Ralph S. Fraser, Lives of Jesus Series (Philadelphia: Fortress, 1970), 150; C. K. Barrett,
Jesus and the Gospel Tradition (Philadelphia: Fortress, 1968), 60. I owe the first reference to
Allison (*Constructing Jesus*, 432 n. 160). I thank Paula Fredriksen for alerting me to Barrett's
discussion about the desertion of the disciples.

18. Barrett, *Jesus and the Gospel Tradition*, 49. See also Allison, *Constructing Jesus*, 419.

19. See the discussion in Joel Marcus, *The Way of the Lord: Christological Exegesis of the Old
Testament in the Gospel of Mark* (London: T&T Clark, 1992), 180–86. While Marcus's claim about
the appearance of Psalm 22 in the Dead Sea Scrolls is unpersuasive, his overall argument about
the wider use of the psalm in Mark remains difficult to contest.

20. See Mark 4:13; 6:52; Matt 15:16 // Mark 7:17; Matt 16:11 // Mark 8:17, 21; Mark 9:32 // Luke
9:45; Luke 22:45; John 12:16; 13:7; 20:9.

constructions can always be offered. The question is: do we have good reason to go beyond the data at hand? I think not.

Beyond Broad Impressions

It should also be noted that many of the traditions that indicate Jesus expected to suffer are difficult to dismiss. Special attention might be given to Paul's account of the Last Supper, which constitutes the only report of an episode from Jesus's life found in the apostle's letters. Paul explains that he received the account "from the Lord" (*apo tou kyriou*), using the technical language of the transmission of tradition (1 Cor 11:23: *paralambanō, paradidōmi*; cf. 11:2; 15:3). The point then is not that Paul received the story from some sort of visionary experience but, rather, as E. P. Sanders says, "that he is passing on material that he believes goes back to Jesus."[21] Significantly, Jesus here speaks of his body being given "for you." Moreover, the combination of Jesus's blood with the language of "covenant" evokes the sacrificial scene of Exod 24. In other words, Jesus's death is here described in sacrificial terms.[22] Recognizing the strength of the Last Supper tradition, even Fredriksen acknowledges that these traditions may indicate that, in the end, Jesus understood he would not escape Jerusalem with his life.[23]

We might also mention the parable of the wicked tenants, which is attested in all three Synoptic Gospels and Thomas (Matt 21:33–41 // Mark 12:1–9 // Luke 20:9–16; Gos. Thom. 65). John P. Meier has made a strong case that the line about the owner's son's death refers to Jesus's fate and that it should be seen as reflecting his own teaching.[24]

JESUS'S ANTICIPATION OF SUFFERING WITHIN A JEWISH CONTEXT

All this being said, compiling lists of traditions does not constitute a sufficient historical argument. As Allison says, "espying a pattern is not enough; we need to account for it sensibly."[25] He writes: "I believe that once recurrent attestation highlights a theme or motif, we should seek to interpret that theme or motif in the light of early Judaism, and in such a way that helps us make sense of what we

---

21. E. P. Sanders, *Paul: The Apostle's Life, Letters, and Thought* (Minneapolis: Fortress, 2015), 210.

22. See Brant Pitre, Michael P. Barber, and John A. Kincaid, *Paul, a New Covenant Jew: Rethinking Pauline Theology* (Grand Rapids: Eerdmans, 2019), 229–40.

23. Fredriksen, *Jesus of Nazareth*, 252.

24. Meier, *Marginal Jew*, 5:240–53.

25. Allison, *Constructing Jesus*, 21.

otherwise know about Christian origins."[26] Here, then, we will consider the plausibility of the general impression that Jesus anticipated suffering within his Second
Temple Jewish context. We will then consider this portrait in light of his effects.

Eschatological Suffering within a Jewish Context

It is entirely believable that Jesus would have anticipated suffering for his beliefs
and that such suffering would play a part in God's plan for Israel. In somewhat
recent memory, righteous Jews had suffered for their faith at the hands of gentile persecutors, namely the Greeks. In 2 Maccabees, written sometime in the
second century BCE, this affliction is understood to have helped effect Israel's
vindication:

> *For we are suffering because of our own sins.* And if our living Lord is angry for
> a little while, to rebuke and discipline us, *he will again be reconciled with his
> own servants.* . . . I, like my brothers, give up body and life for the laws of our
> fathers, appealing to God to show mercy soon to our nation and by afflictions
> and plagues to make you confess that he alone is God, and *through me and my
> brothers to bring to an end the wrath of the Almighty* which has justly fallen on
> our whole nation. (2 Macc 7:32–38 NRSV)

The martyr explicitly explains that it is "through me and my brothers" that "the
wrath of the Almighty" will come to an end.

The Jewish work known as 4 Maccabees, a source that is difficult to date
(ca. 18–55 CE), expands on what is found in 2 Maccabees.

> [the martyrs] became *responsible for the downfall of the tyranny* which beset
> our nation, overcoming the tyrant by their fortitude so that *through them their
> own land was purified.* (4 Macc 1:11 NRSV)

> Through the blood of these righteous ones and through the propitiation [*hilas-
> tērion*] of their death the divine providence rescued Israel. (4 Macc 17:22)[27]

---

26. Allison, *Constructing Jesus*, 21.

27. Translation from H. Anderson, "4 Maccabees: A New Translation and Introduction," in
*Expansions of the "Old Testament" and Legends, Wisdom and Philosophical Literature, Prayers,
Psalms and Odes, Fragments of Lost Judeo-Hellenistic Works*, vol. 2 of *The Old Testament Pseude-
pigrapha*, ed. James H. Charlesworth (New Haven: Yale University Press, 1983), 563.

It is worth noting that the last passage from 4 Maccabees 17 interprets the death of the martyrs as a *hilastērion*, a term derived from the world cultic atonement (cf. Exod 25:16; Ezek 43:14, 17, 20).[28] In all of this, the path to Israel's "rescue" runs through a period of suffering.

The Suffering of the Righteous in Apocalyptic Traditions

Would Jesus have had reason to think suffering lay ahead for him personally? If, as seems likely, Jesus's message was shaped by Jewish eschatology, this seems probable. Notwithstanding the need for some nuance, Schweitzer's essential point that eschatological traditions often involved the belief in a coming period of tribulation was on target. The general idea can be located in works like Daniel and the Dead Sea Scrolls:

There shall be a time of anguish, such as has never occurred since nations first came into existence. But at that time your people shall be delivered. . . . Many of those who sleep in the dust of the earth shall awake, some to everlasting life, and some to shame and everlasting contempt. (Dan 12:1–2, NRSV)

It will be *a time of suffering fo[r al]l the nation redeemed by God. Of all their sufferings, none will be like this*, hastening till eternal redemption is fulfilled. (1Q33 I, 11–12)[29]

Its [Ps 37:11] interpretation concerns the congregation of the poor who will take upon themselves *the period of affliction* and will be rescued from all the snares of Belial. Afterwards, all who shall po[sse]ss the land will enjoy and grow fat with everything enjoy[able to] the flesh. (4Q171 II, 9–12)[30]

In each of these texts we find that the "deliverance," "redemption," or divine "rescue" of Israel follows a calamitous period involving suffering. Many other passages could be spotlighted.[31]

---

28. For a discussion, see Stephen Finlan, *The Background and Content of Paul's Cultic Atonement Metaphors* (Atlanta: Society of Biblical Literature, 2004), 29–44.

29. Translation from Florentino García Martínez and Eibert J. C. Tigchelaar, eds., *The Dead Sea Scrolls Study Edition* (Leiden: Brill, 1997–1998), 1:115.

30. Translation by Pitre, *Jesus*, 97.

31. Zech 13.8–9; 4Q174 1 I, 18–19; II, 1–7; 1 En. 46:8–47:2; 56:5–57:3; 91:5–74; 93:1–10; 103:15; Jub. 23:11–31; Sib. Or. 3:182–195; Pss. Sol. 17:11–32; T. Mos. 9:1–7.

The Danielic Son of Man and the Eschatological Suffering of the Righteous

There is one final passage that is especially worth mentioning, namely, Daniel 7. The prophet first describes the coming of four beasts, which represent four kings or kingdoms (cf. Dan 7:17, 23). The last of these persecutes God's people until the eschatological kingdom is given to the saints.

> [The Fourth Beast] will speak words against the Most High,
> and *will wear out the saints of the Most High* . . .
> and *they will be handed over into his hand*
> for a time, two times, and half a time . . .
> And the kingdom and the dominion . . .
> will be given to the people of the saints of the Most High;
> their kingdom will be an everlasting kingdom. (Dan 7:25, 27)

Once again, the notion that the eschatological age—the coming "everlasting kingdom"— will only arrive after a period of tribulation and suffering.

What is especially noticeable in all of this is that the vision also includes the account of the famous "Son of Man" figure. After the appearance of the fourth beast, Daniel relates:

> I saw one like a human being [lit., son of man]
>   coming with the clouds of heaven.
> And he came to the Ancient One
>   and was presented before him.
> To him was given dominion
>   and glory and kingship,
> that all peoples, nations, and languages
>   should serve him.
> His dominion is an everlasting dominion
>   that shall not pass away,
> and his kingship is one
>   that shall never be destroyed. (Dan 7:13–14 NRSV)

The passage is open to different readings, but it seems probable that the "Son of Man" figure serves as a kind of representative for the people. After all, the fourth beast is simultaneously both a "king" (Dan 7:17) and a "kingdom" (7:23). Since the "one like a son of man" is also given "kingship" (7:14), it makes sense that he functions in the same way as representative of a people, namely, the "saints."

It is no surprise, then, that the meaning of the vision is said to be: "the kingdom . . . will be given to the saints" (7:27). The Son of Man figure thus likely serves as a representative of the saints who suffer. Indeed, Maurice Casey has shown that this interpretation survived in the writings of early church writers.[32] All of this may help us better understand memories of Jesus.

Jesus and the Suffering Son of Man

We do not have room here for a detailed analysis of Jesus's use of the phrase "the Son of Man." Suffice it to say, our sources identify the referent of the "Son of Man" sayings as Jesus.[33] That Jesus is sometimes remembered as speaking about the Son of Man in the third person has caused some to dispute that the historical Jesus identified himself as this figure. What is often neglected, however, is that "illeism"—speaking of oneself in the third person—was not as unusual in the ancient world as it is in ours. Paul, for example, is known for using the convention (e.g., 1 Cor 3:5; 2 Cor 12:1–4).[34] Indeed, many have made the case that Jesus used the expression inspired by Danielic traditions.[35]

It is, therefore, striking that our sources repeatedly indicate that Jesus spoke of his coming suffering with "the Son of Man" language:

> The *Son of Man* must undergo great suffering, and be rejected by the elders, the chief priests, and the scribes, and be killed, and after three days rise again. (Mark 8:31 NRSV)

> For the *Son of Man* came not to be served but to serve, and to give his life a ransom for many. (Mark 10:45 NRSV)

> For the *Son of Man* goes as it is written of him, but woe to that one by whom *the Son of Man* is *betrayed* [or: *given over*]! (Mark 14:21 NRSV; cf. Matt 26:24 // Luke 22:22; cf. John 13:21–30)

32. See Maurice Casey, *The Solution to the 'Son of Man' Problem*, LNTS 343 (London: T&T Clark, 2007), 82–91. I thank James Crossley for suggesting this reference.

33. E.g., Matt 8:20 // Luke 9:58 [Q?]; Matt 9:6 // Mark 2:10 // Luke 5:24; Matt 11:19; Matt 12:40 // Luke 11:30 [Q?]; Matt 16:13; Matt 17:22–23 // Mark 9:31 // Luke 9:34.

34. See the treatment of the practice in ancient sources by Roderick Elledge, *Use of the Third Person for Self-Reference by Jesus and YHWH: A Study of Illeism in the Bible and Ancient Near Eastern Texts and Its Implications for Christology*, LNTS 575 (London: T&T Clark, 2017), 25–117.

35. See, e.g., Adela Yarbro Collins, "The Apocalyptic Son of Man Sayings," in *The Future of Early Christianity*, ed. Birger A. Pearson (Minneapolis: Fortress, 1991), 220–28.

And just as Moses lifted up the serpent in the wilderness, so must the *Son of Man* be lifted up. (John 3:14 NRSV)[36]

The hour has come for the *Son of Man* to be glorified. (John 12:23 NRSV)[37]

Following T. W. Manson, Dale Allison has pointed out that such sayings are likely influenced by Daniel 7.[38] Manson takes the view that the Son of Man figure seems to serve as a representative of the saints who suffer at the hands of the fourth beast during the latter days (cf. Dan 7:18).[39] Jesus probably included himself among such a group. Regardless of whether or not Jesus used the title to refer to himself alone as an exalted figure, a strong case can be made that he likely used it in reference to his own eschatological suffering.

The saying in Mark 9:31 (parr. in Matt 17:22–23 // Luke 9:44) especially seems indebted to the Danielic passage:

The *Son of Man* will be *handed over into the hands of men*, and they will kill him. Once he is killed, after three days he will rise. (Mark 9:31)

Consider the following parallels:

Daniel 7:25	**Mark 9:31**
"the saints" (represented by the Son of Man figure)	"The Son of Man"
"will be handed over" (Old Greek: *paradothēsetai*; Theodotion: *dothēsetai*)	"will be handed over" (*paradidotai*)

36. That this passage relates to Jesus's crucifixion is widely accepted among scholars. See, e.g., Rudolf Bultmann, *The Gospel of John: A Commentary*, trans. G. R. Beasley-Murray et al. (Philadelphia: Westminster, 1971), 152–53; Raymond E. Brown, *The Gospel according to John*, AB 29–29A (New York: Doubleday, 1966), 1:146.

37. That this passage relates to Jesus's death is made clear from the following verse (cf. John 12:24).

38. See Allison, *End of the Ages*, 136–40; Allison, *Jesus of Nazareth: Millenarian Prophet* (Minneapolis: Fortress Press, 1998), 65–66, especially n. 242; Allison, "Q 12:51–53 and Mark 9:11–13 and the Messianic Woes," in *Authenticating the Words of Jesus*, ed. B. D. Chilton and C. A. Evans (Leiden: Brill, 1999), 307–9; T. W. Manson, "The Son of Man in Daniel, Enoch, and the Gospels," *BJRL* 32 (1950): 171–95; Manson, *The Teaching of Jesus* (Cambridge: Cambridge University, 1967), 229–31.

39. In Daniel 12, those who suffer are later depicted as glorified, raising the question of whether the heavenly "son of man" figure in Daniel 7 somehow contains an allusion to the glorified people of God.

"in the hand" (Old Greek: *en cheiri*; Theodotion: *eis tas cheiras*)	"into the hands [*eis cheiras*] of men"
"for a time, two times, and half a time"	"*after three days* he will rise"

I am not arguing that Mark 9:31 should be construed as the *ipsissima verba Jesu*. Here we simply see that Jesus's passion predictions seemed to be remembered in Danielic terms. One could argue that this feature was merely due to the influence of the early community. Yet why this tendency should not be traced back to impressions made by Jesus himself is difficult to understand. [40]

JESUS'S ANTICIPATION OF SUFFERING IN LIGHT OF HIS EFFECTS

The memory of Jesus expecting to suffer is deeply implanted in our sources. It is also consistent with his Jewish context, especially Jewish apocalyptic eschatology. It should also be observed that the connection between suffering and Jewish eschatological tribulation traditions appears in the writings of Jesus's early followers.

Use of Eschatological Tribulation Traditions by Early Jesus Believers

It seems apparent that the outlook of the early followers of Jesus was informed by Jewish apocalyptic traditions that anticipated a coming period of tribulation before the arrival of the kingdom.[41] This can be found as early as Paul's Letters.[42] For example, Paul views Christ's death as the hinge on which deliverance from "the present evil age" turns (Gal 1:4). The language here is steeped in that of Jewish apocalyptic eschatology.[43] As others have shown, then, for Paul, Jesus's death is likely related to Jewish expectations involving a time of eschatological tribulation.[44]

40. For further discussion, see Thomas Kazen, "The Coming of the Son of Man Revisited," *JSHJ* 5.2 (2007): 155–74; Scot McKnight, *Jesus and His Death* (Waco, TX: Baylor University Press, 2005), 234–39.

41. See, e.g., the studies in Allison, *End of the Ages*; Harry A. Hahne, *The Corruption and Redemption of Creation: Nature in Romans 8:19–22 and Jewish Apocalyptic Literature*, LNTS 336 (London: T&T Clark, 2006); Pitre, *Jesus*; C. Marvin Pate and Douglas C. Kennard, *Deliverance Now and Not Yet: The New Testament and the Great Tribulation*, StBibLit 54 (New York: Lang, 2003).

42. See Allison, *End of the Ages*, 62–69, for a treatment of eschatological tribulation traditions in Paul.

43. See Pitre, Barber, and Kincaid, *Paul, a New Covenant Jew*, 57–58, 64–94.

44. Pate and Kennard, *Deliverance Now and Not Yet*, 224.

Furthermore, it is not simply Jesus's sufferings that are viewed within this eschatological matrix. In Romans 8 the apostle declares that the believer's afflictions are incomparable to the "glory to be revealed in us" (Rom 8:18), drawing on eschatological hopes. He goes on to say: "the whole creation has been groaning in *birth pangs* together until now" (8:22). In some Jewish texts, the arrival of the age to come is linked not only to eschatological tribulation, but the afflictions of this period are explicitly depicted as *birth pangs*.[45] Therefore, by speaking of eschatological hope for the coming glory "to be revealed" in combination with an account of sufferings as birth pangs, the apostle can be seen as drawing from Jewish eschatological tribulation traditions.[46]

Indeed, Paul is not alone here. Numerous other passages from the New Testament period could be mentioned.[47] If such a perspective was known to ancient Jews and can be located within the early community, why must we insist it was unimportant to Jesus?

Paul's Expectation of Suffering and the Scandal of the Kingdom

Finally, Paul himself anticipated experiencing suffering. He writes, "we told you beforehand that we were to suffer affliction" (1 Thess 3:4). Similarly, in his letter to the Philippians, the apostle talks about how he is "poured as a libation," using sacrificial terminology typically understood as a martyrological reference (Phil 2:17).[48] The best explanation of this dimension of Paul's message would seem to be that his outlook was shaped by memories of Jesus's teaching regarding his own fate.[49]

We might also add another observation here: Paul seems to have understood that his message would likely have fatal consequences for him. He was proclaiming a message that the rulers of this world would be subject to Christ whose kingdom was dawning.[50] He also tells us that he came into conflict with at least one king, Aretas of Damascus (2 Cor 11:32). Though we do not know why exactly Aretas went after Paul, the detail at least offers some food for thought about how Paul's teaching could rankle authorities. The same could be said for Jesus.

45. 1QHᵃ XI, 7–10; 1 En. 62:1–4.

46. Pitre, Barber, and Kincaid, *Paul, a New Covenant Jew*, 216–21.

47. See, e.g., Acts 14:22; Col 1:24–27; 1 Pet 3:13–22; 4:7–19; Rev 2:9–11; 7:14. See also Mark Dubis, *Messianic Woes in First Peter: Suffering and Eschatology in 1 Peter 4:12–19*, StBibLit 33 (New York: Lang, 2002); Allison, *End of the Ages*, 63–64.

48. See, e.g., Paul A. Holloway, *Philippians*, Hermeneia (Minneapolis: Fortress, 2017), 136–37.

49. See Allison, *End of the Ages*, 62–69, for a treatment of eschatological tribulation traditions in Paul. In addition, see Allison, *Constructing Jesus*, 63.

50. Cf. 1 Cor 2:6; 15:24–28; Rom 14:17; 1 Cor 4:20; 6:9–10; 15:50; Gal 5:21; 1 Thess 2:12.

That the kingdom was a key aspect of Jesus's teaching is usually accepted by scholars.[51] It was a theme echoed by the early Jesus movement.[52] It is also broadly attested across our sources and fits comfortably within Jesus's Jewish context.[53] It especially fits well with the notion that Jesus's message was shaped by Jewish apocalyptic hopes.

If Jesus proclaimed a kingdom, it is hard to believe he never thought about what role he saw himself having in it, or that his disciples would not have asked him about it. Indeed, Allison offers a long list of traditions—mostly but not solely derived from the Synoptics (and Q?)—that indicate Jesus believed he would play "a starring role in the eschatological drama."[54] Some of these are especially difficult to dismiss as later innovations. Take, for instance, Jesus's appointment of a group of twelve disciples. That Jesus had such a group and that they were in some way related to eschatological hopes for the twelve tribes of Israel (cf. Matt 19:28 // Luke 22:30) is accepted by Jesus scholars from a wide array of perspectives.[55] Our earliest writer, Paul, attests to the twelve being known to early believers (1 Cor 15:5). It also seems unlikely that the twelve emerged as a group only after Jesus's ministry.[56] That Jesus likely appointed such a group, then, is suggestive of his own self-understanding. There is no evidence that he counted himself among the twelve. Rather, it seems that he chose them and led them.[57] This suggests he saw himself as having a leadership role of the eschatological Israel.

Also worthy of special attention is the tradition that Jesus was crucified as "the King of the Jews."[58] Crucifixion was the penalty suffered by thieves, murderers,

51. See, e.g., the comments on the state of the question in Bond, *Historical Jesus*, 89.

52. In addition to the Pauline passages cited above, see also Acts 1:6; 8:12; 14:22; 19:8; 20:25; 28:23, 31; Eph 5:5; Col 1:13; 4:11; 2 Thess 1:5; 2 Tim 4:1, 18; Heb 1:8; 12:28; Jas 2:5; 2 Pet 1:11; Rev 1:6, 9; Did. 9:4; Papias in Eusebius, *Hist. eccl.* 3.39.12.

53. For a list of passages from Mark, the Q material, and the Synoptics, see Allison, *Constructing Jesus*, 165–68. See also John 3:5, 18:36; Gos. Thom. 22, 27, 46, 49, 54, 57, 76, 82, 96–99, 107, 109, 113–114. Concerning Jesus's Jewish context, see, e.g., Exod 15:18; Isa 24:23; 52:7; 2 Chr 13:8; Obad 21; Zech 4:9; Dan 2:44; 4:3, 34; 6:26; 7:14, 18; Wis 10.10; 1 En. 91:12–13; 4Q400 1 II, 14; 4Q405 23 II, 11.

54. See Allison, *Constructing Jesus*, 226, 231.

55. See, e.g., Bond, *Historical Jesus*, 96–97; Ehrman, *Apocalyptic Prophet*, 186; Meier, *Marginal Jew*, 3:138; Sanders, *Jesus and Judaism*, 98–106.

56. See the extensive treatment in Meier, *Marginal Jew*, 3:125–97.

57. Allison, *Constructing Jesus*, 233, citing Étienne Trocmé, *The Childhood of Christianity*, trans. John Bowden (London: SCM, 1977), 10.

58. Matt 27:11 // Mark 15:2 // Luke 23:3 // John 18:33; Mark 15:9, 12 // John 18:39; Matt 27:29 // Mark 15:18 // John 18:33; Luke 23:3; Matt 27:37 // Mark 15:26 // Luke 23:38 // John 19:19; John 19:20–21.

and political insurrectionists, but there is no evidence that Jesus was accused of the first two crimes. The most probable explanation of Jesus dying on a cross, then, is that, as John Collins puts it, he "was viewed as a messianic pretender."[59] Furthermore, the wording of the titulus, "King of the Jews," is unlikely to have its origin in Jesus's disciples.[60] The title reflects non-Jewish tendencies; Jews more probably would have used the expression "King of Israel" (Matt 27:42; cf. also 1 Sam 24:14; Prov 1:1; John 1:49).[61] Finally, that Jesus was derided as "King of the Jews" at his crucifixion is congruent with the parodic features of Roman crucifixion.[62] The titulus, then, is widely thought to be significant for historical reconstructions of Jesus.[63] Paula Fredriksen acknowledges, "Whether at any time in his ministry Jesus claimed for himself the title messiah—the evidence on this point is extremely ambiguous—he certainly died as if he had."[64]

Yet, although I find great value in Fredriksen's work, her proposal that Jesus died as a result of losing his audience is unnecessary. Whatever we conclude about whether Jesus spoke of himself explicitly as the messiah, he most probably preached about the kingdom, and it seems unlikely that he thought he would play a marginal role in it. More likely than not that, like Paul, he would have understood that this message was dangerous. Moreover, Jesus's message likely included echoes to Jewish apocalyptic traditions. It seems the Next Quest's exploration of Jesus's outlook will bring us full circle back to Schweitzer. Informed by Jewish eschatological tribulation traditions, Jesus most probably anticipated his death.

Martyrdom and Comparable Figures

Allison points out that figures like Justin Martyr, Martin Luther King Jr., and Óscar Romero knew that their activities would end with their deaths; why should we conclude Jesus was significantly less self-aware?[65] Here a brief word about these individuals is necessary since they provide concrete examples of others

59. John J. Collins, *The Apocalyptic Imagination: An Introduction to Jewish Apocalyptic Literature*, 2nd ed. (Grand Rapids: Eerdmans, 1998), 259.

60. Joseph A. Fitzmyer, *The Gospel according to Luke*, AB 28–28A (Garden City, NY: Doubleday, 1981, 1985), 1:773.

61. See Allison, *Constructing Jesus*, 235.

62. Allison, *Constructing Jesus*, 234–35, drawing on Nils Alstrup Dahl, "The Crucified Messiah," in *Jesus the Christ: The Historical Origins of Christology Doctrine*, ed. Donald H. Juel (Minneapolis: Fortress, 1991), 36–37. See also Meier, *Marginal Jew*, 3:24.

63. See, e.g., Sanders, *Jesus and Judaism*, 294.

64. Fredriksen, *From Jesus to Christ*, 123.

65. Allison, *Constructing Jesus*, 433.

who recognized that their commitments would have fatal consequences for themselves. That these three realized that their convictions would lead to their doom is well attested.

First in his *Second Apology* Justin writes: "I also expect to be the victim of a plot and to be affixed to the stake."[66] The authenticity of this work is not contested. Moreover, we have strong evidence that Justin was in fact put to death. The earliest account of his death is reported in the *Acts of Justin and His Companions*, an account that dates to his own period.[67] Although it exists in three different recensions, all of them agree on the fundamental point that Justin died as a martyr. Also, given that Justin says he expects to die at the "stake" in the *Second Apology*, it is notable that all three recensions of the *Acts of Justin and His Companions* suggest that Justin and his companions were beheaded (5.1). In short, it does not seem that either the *Second Apology* or the *Acts of Justin and His Companions* was redacted to harmonize with a tradition about Justin's death.[68] Justin most likely knew he would die, even if he was wrong about the precise method of his execution.

Second, the story of Martin Luther King Jr. is very well known, and for the purposes of this discussion what is worth underscoring is his awareness that his activism would likely have fatal consequences. The danger was ever present. In 1956, he was stabbed in a department store in Harlem. After receiving one death threat while in Florida in 1964, King said: "If physical death is the price that I must pay to free my white brothers and sisters from a permanent death of the spirit, then nothing can be more redemptive."[69] In an interview recorded in December of 1968, King told BBC interviewer Gerald Priestland: "I live every day under the threat of death, and I have no illusions about it."[70] Coretta Scott King remembered, "Throughout 1967, and during the planning of the Poor People's Campaign early in 1968, we had, beyond everything, a sense of fate closing in."[71] She also said: "He

66. *2 Apol.* 3.1; quoted from Thomas B. Falls, trans., *Saint Justin Martyr: The First Apology, The Second Apology, Dialogue with Trypho, Exhortation to the Greeks, Discourse to the Greeks, The Monarchy or The Rule of God*, FC 6 (Washington, DC: Catholic University of America Press, 1948), 122.

67. See Wolfram Kinzig, *Christian Persecution in Antiquity*, trans. Markus Bockmuehl (Waco, TX: Baylor University Press, 2021), 54. For further discussion on the textual issues and related literature, see Herbert Musurillo, *Acts of the Christian Martyrs* (Oxford: Oxford University Press, 1972), 2:xvii–xx.

68. The argument that different Justins are in view has not won approval. See Musurillo, *Acts of the Christian Martyrs*, 2:xviii.

69. Jason Sokol, *The Heavens Might Crack: The Death and Legacy of Martin Luther King Jr.* (New York: Basic, 2018), 12–13.

70. Sokol, *Heavens Might Crack*, 12.

71. Sokol, *Heavens Might Crack*, 19.

knew that at any moment his physical life could be cut short and we faced this possibility squarely and honestly. He knew that this was a sick society . . . which would ultimately lead to his death."[72] King was assassinated on April 4, 1969.

Third, Óscar Romero's elevation to the office of archbishop coincided with a time of repressive violence and oppressive poverty. His transformation from quiet, cautious churchman to outspoken critic of social injustice is often traced to the brutal killing of his dear friend Fr. Rutilio Grande in March 1977. Grande was killed with an elderly man and a young boy. He was specifically targeted because of his pastoral work. Romero knew that his own words and actions as bishop would lead him to a similar fate. The militants had a well-known slogan: "Be a patriot, kill a priest."[73] Romero recalled the realization that came over him when Grande was murdered: "I thought 'if they killed him for doing what he was doing, it's my job to go down that same road.'"[74] When the President offered him certain protections, Romero refused, later saying of his decision: "I wanted to run the same risks that the people are running; it would be a pastoral anti-testimony if I were very secure, while my people are so insecure."[75] Elsewhere, he explained: "if God accepts the sacrifice of my life, let my blood be a seed of freedom and the sign that hope will soon be reality. Let my death, if it is accepted by God, be for my people's liberation and as a witness of hope in the future. . . . A bishop will die, but God's church, which is the people, will never perish."[76] On March 24, 1980, Romero gave a homily on John 12:24: "I tell you, unless a grain of wheat falls into the earth and dies, it remains just a single grain; but if it dies, it bears much fruit." He explained, "whoever out of love for Christ give themselves to the service of others will live, like the grain of wheat that dies, but only apparently."[77] Moments after walking away from the pulpit, he was shot by a gunman.

While it is true that Justin, King, and Romero each lived in vastly different historical contexts than the first-century Jewish world of Jesus, there is no reason to insist their stories are completely irrelevant to the question of Jesus's own outlook.

72. Sokol, *Heavens Might Crack*, 26.

73. Matthew Philipp Whelan, *Blood in the Fields: Óscar Romero, Catholic Social Teaching, and Land Reform* (Washington, DC: Catholic University of America Press, 2020), 3.

74. Maria Lopez Vigil, *Oscar Romero: Memories in Mosaic*, trans. Kathy Ogle (Washington, DC: EPICA, 2000), 159.

75. Óscar Romero, *Su diario: del 31 de marzo 1978 al 20 de marzo de 1980* (San Salvador: Archdiocese of San Salvador, 1990), 75–76. English translation taken from Anna L. Peterson and Manuel A. Vásquez, "Oscar Romero and the Politics of Sainthood," *Postscripts* 5.3 (2009): 270.

76. English translation from James R. Brockman, *Romero: A Life* (Maryknoll: Orbis, 1989), 248.

77. English translation from Brockman, *Romero*, 224.

Their stories witness to the plausibility of individuals holding convictions greater than fear of death. That Jesus anticipated his own death is recurrently attested, coherent within Second Temple Jewish beliefs, and makes sense in light of his effects. The best explanation of the historical data we possess, then, is that the memory of Jesus predicting his own demise likely reflects impressions he himself made on others during his public ministry.

32

THE RESURRECTION AND
COMPARATIVE MICROHISTORY

Justin J. Meggitt

The Next Quest for the historical Jesus must account for the fact that we are examining a subject that is small in historical scale though not in consequence. At its center is a figure who, although briefly obtaining some local prominence during his life, is mostly known to us through records that detail his interactions with a handful of followers and critics. We should therefore use *microhistory*, a historiographical approach particularly developed to scrutinize such cases, where the focus of attention is of necessity narrow, even if the implications are not. More specifically, a microhistorical approach that embraces a *comparative* method is especially needed. In what follows, I shall demonstrate how comparative microhistory has the potential to transform future work in the field, generating new ways of thinking about subjects that are all too familiar to those engaged in the Quest by looking again at the resurrection, perhaps the most challenging subject in the study of the historical Jesus but also one about which there seems little new that can be usefully said.

The claim that those studying the historical Jesus should turn to microhistory will probably provoke a number of responses. Some might think my recommendation is strangely old-fashioned. Surely microhistory had its heyday around fifty years ago, with classic works such as Carlo Ginzburg's 1976 *Il formaggio e i vermi*?[1]

---

1. Carlo Ginzburg, *Il formaggio e i vermi* (Turin: Einaudi, 1976).

If it had possessed any potential to contribute to the study of the historical Jesus, would it not have already done so by now, and found its way into the introductory textbooks and syllabi that deal with the subject?[2] Others might sigh at the development of another supposedly indispensable method or theoretical perspective that will produce—as so many approaches in the study of the New Testament have done—answers to questions no one had previously bothered asking, and even less wished answered; promising much but delivering the abstruse, the anodyne, and the obvious. Such responses, though understandable, are unjustified, as a *comparative microhistorical* approach to the historical Jesus has the potential to open up new ways of understanding and a new impetus to the Quest.

And the Next Quest does matter. Among many reasons that can be given, I would like to single out two that are closely related and particularly significant. First, even if denial of the historicity of Jesus is rarely found among scholars within the field, the increasing popularity of this position in wider culture is unavoidable. While I won't rehearse arguments I have made elsewhere about this phenomenon, unless those working in New Testament and Christian origins continue to think critically and publicly about what can be said about Jesus, it is likely that the denial of the historicity of Jesus will very soon become the de facto position in wider popular and academic discourse.[3] This might not appear to matter to some in the field, who have no theological investment in whether Jesus the man existed or not, but—and this is the second reason for pursuing the Quest I would like to emphasize—the Quest for the historical Jesus matters because the nonelite in history matter. They matter not just as faceless aggregates but as specific individuals with lived, if constrained, agency. To deny the historical reality of a figure such as Jesus, either directly by denying his historicity or indirectly by deciding that there is nothing that can reasonably be said about him, is to collude with "the enormous condescension of posterity" and to contribute, however unintentionally, to the functional erasure of those without power from history.[4] It is all the more grotesque in the case of Jesus because we possess so much, relatively speaking, that claims to tell us about his life. Compare our sources about him with those that we have for similar contemporaries such as the Egyptian prophet or Theudas.[5] Despite the challenges posed by the earliest

2. The approach has been ignored by those in the field. For an unpublished exception, see Richard J. Bauckham, "Gospels as Micro-History & Perspectival History" (lecture, Southern Baptist Theological Seminary, Louisville, KY, February 16, 2011), https://repository.sbts.edu/handle/10392/2744. I would like to thank Professor Bauckham for making the text of his lecture available to me.

3. Justin J. Meggitt, "'More Ingenious Than Learned'? Examining the Quest for the Non-Historical Jesus," *NTS* 65.4 (2019): 443–60.

4. E. P. Thompson, *The Making of the English Working Class* (London: Penguin, 1963), 12.

5. For the Egyptian prophet, see Josephus, *B.J.* 2.261–263; *A.J.* 20.169–170; Acts 21:38. For Theudas, see Josephus, *A.J.* 20.97–98; Acts 5:36.

508

sources we have for Jesus, especially the difficulties that arise from both the fecund imagination of the early Christians and their lack of discrimination when deciding what traditions they should pass on, this wider ethical imperative, not to perpetuate the silencing of the poor in history, makes the Quest a *necessary* undertaking.[6]

The historical study of the resurrection of Jesus also matters. It is unavoidable or, rather, *should be*, for anyone studying the historical Jesus. As Gerd Lüdemann rightly says, "The story of Jesus after his death is also part of his life, since it is only because of this history that we still know anything about him."[7] Studies of the historical Jesus should not end at his death, though most do.[8] It is disingenuous to place the resurrection in a different category from all the other events associated with the life of Jesus and say that it is not capable of historical analysis.[9] It is a potentially *provable* historical event, even if the nature of the sources we have, and the distance in time between the first century and now, makes it highly unlikely that it can ever be historically *proven*.[10] Indeed, in its historical context, it is not as exceptional as many New Testament scholars assume. In the early Roman Empire it was not unusual to believe that the dead—not just those who *appeared* to be dead[11]—could be restored to life, leave an empty tomb behind, and engage in everyday activities such as walking, eating, drinking, and sex.[12]

6. For the creativity of early Christian traditions about Jesus, see Justin J. Meggitt, "Popular Mythology in the Early Empire and the Multiplicity of Jesus Traditions," in *Sources of the Jesus Tradition: Separating History from Myth*, ed. R. Joseph Hoffmann (Amherst, NY: Prometheus, 2010), 53–80.

7. Gerd Lüdemann, *Jesus after Two Thousand Years: What He Really Said and Did* (London: SCM, 2000), 692.

8. Markus N. A. Bockmuehl, "Resurrection," in *The Cambridge Companion to Jesus*, ed. Markus Bockmuehl (Cambridge: Cambridge University Press, 2001), 102.

9. E.g., John P. Meier, *Roots of the Problem and the Person*, vol. 1 of *A Marginal Jew: Rethinking the Historical Jesus*, AYBRL (New York: Doubleday, 1991), 13.

10. Contrary to the position of Peter Carnley, *Resurrection in Retrospect: A Critical Examination of the Theology of N. T. Wright* (Eugene, OR: Cascade, 2019). For notable recent attempts, see Michael R. Licona, *The Resurrection of Jesus: A New Historiographical Approach* (Downers Grove, IL: InterVarsity Press, 2010); Andrew Loke, *Investigating the Resurrection of Jesus Christ: A New Transdisciplinary Approach* (London: Routledge, 2020); Matthew Levering, *Did Jesus Rise from the Dead? Historical and Theological Reflections* (Oxford: Oxford University Press, 2019).

11. See Glen Warren Bowersock, *Fiction as History: Nero to Julian* (Berkeley: University of California Press, 1994), 99–119; Jan Bremmer, "Ghosts, Resurrections, and Empty Tombs in the Gospels, the Greek Novel, and the Second Sophistic," in *The Gospels and Their Stories in Anthropological Perspective*, ed. Joseph Verheyden and John S. Kloppenborg, WUNT 409 (Tübingen: Mohr Siebeck, 2018), 233–52; Judith Perkins, "Fictive Scheintod and Christian Resurrection," *R&T* 13.3 (2006): 396–418.

12. For example, Philinnion in Phlegon of Tralles, *Mir.* 1. See William Hansen, ed., *Phlegon of Tralles' Book of Marvels* (Exeter: Exeter University Press, 1996), 25–28, 65–85; D. Felton, *Haunted Greece and Rome: Ghost Stories from Classical Antiquity* (Austin: University of Texas Press, 1999),

However, while the resurrection of Jesus is a legitimate subject of historical inquiry, this paper is not about its *historicity*, the analysis of which has reached a methodological impasse.[13] The question of *historicity* should not be the only, or even the primary, matter of historical concern when those studying the historical Jesus turn their attention to the resurrection. Rather, this essay is intended to demonstrate that the application of comparative microhistory can open up fresh ways of understanding how the resurrection may have been understood by his closest associates.

THE NATURE OF MICROHISTORY

Although there is considerable variation in what can be labeled a "microhistory," and it has undergone substantial changes since the inception of Italian *microstoria* in the 1970s in the works of Edoardo Grendi, Carlo Ginzburg, and Giovanni Levi, according to a leading, current exponent, István Szijártó, there are three formal characteristics common to most microhistorical works.[14] First, microhistory is history that engages in "the intensive historical investigation of a relatively well-defined smaller object, most often a single event, or 'a village community, a group of families, even an individual person.'"[15] Second, it "has an objective that is much more far-reaching than that of a case study: micro-historians always look for the answers for 'great historical questions' ... when studying small objects. As Charles Joyner said, they 'search for answers to large questions in small places.'"[16] Third,

---

26–29. For other revenants, see Phlegon of Tralles, *Mir.* 3.4–5; Heliodorus, *Aeth.* 6.14–15; Apuleius, *Metam.* 1.5–19; 2.21–30; Lucan, *Phar.* 6.588–830; Matt 27:52–53; Eusebius, *Hist. eccl.* 4.3.2. See also John Granger Cook, "Resurrection in Paganism and the Question of an Empty Tomb in 1 Corinthians 15," *NTS* 63.1 (2017): 56–75.

13. Simon J. Joseph, "Redescribing the Resurrection: Beyond the Methodological Impasse?," *BTB* 45.3 (2015): 155–73.

14. István M. Szijártó, introduction to *What Is Microhistory? Theory and Practice*, by Sigurður Gylfi Magnússon and István M. Szijártó (London: Routledge, 2013), 4–5.

15. Szijártó, introduction to *What Is Microhistory?*, 4. Quoting Carlo Ginzburg and Carlo Poni, "The Name and the Game: Unequal Exchange and the Historiographic Marketplace," in *Microhistory and the Lost Peoples of Europe*, ed. E. Muir and G. Ruggiero (Baltimore: Johns Hopkins University Press, 1991), 3.

16. Szijártó, introduction to *What Is Microhistory?*, 5. Quoting Charles W. Joyner, *Shared Traditions: Southern History and Folk Culture* (Champaign: University of Illinois Press, 1999), 1. This is the most contentious of the characteristics identified by Szijártó. See also Sigurður Gylfi Magnússon, "Far-Reaching Microhistory: The Use of Microhistorical Perspective in a Globalized World," *Rethinking History* 21.3 (2017): 312–41.

microhistory puts a stress upon agency: "For microhistorians, people who lived in the past are not merely puppets on the hands of great underlying forces of history, but they are regarded as active individuals, conscious actors."[17]

Microhistory is not a field, as it is delineated by neither a subject of inquiry nor a specific method. Rather, microhistory is best understood as a historical *practice*.[18] And it is a practice that is distinguished by its evidentiary paradigm, one that it shares with some social sciences that Ginzburg calls the "the method of clues."[19] It attends to the seemingly insignificant and marginal, "starting an investigation from something that does not quite fit, something odd that needs to be explained."[20]

Contrary to the assumptions of some, microhistory did *not* reach the height of its historiographical influence in the 1970s and 1980s. It has continued to flourish and, in recent years, has developed rapidly. It has been transformed by wider historiographical currents, finding its place within such significant historiographical developments as the emergence of global and connected histories.[21] It has also provided useful ways of understanding how wider change is experienced within "small spaces," as evident in recent studies of, for example, slavery, migration, gender and religious transformation.[22]

Microhistory as a practice has significant potential for our purposes. It is, for instance, comfortable with the unknown. The closer the magnification of a subject, the more questions arise; "the more we know, and the more we see, the better we discern the gaps in knowledge."[23] Although most of those studying the *historical* Jesus have long acknowledged this, we need to embrace the fact that our work can only take place in a "realm of surmise and supposition," an admission common

17. Szijártó, introduction to *What Is Microhistory?*, 5. Although, at this scale of analysis, the structures that constrain agency are barely visible, that does not make them any less real.

18. See Thomas V. Cohen, "The Macrohistory of Microhistory," *Journal of Medieval and Early Modern Studies* 47.1 (2017): 54.

19. For Ginzburg's discussion of this method, see Carlo Ginzburg, "Clues: Roots of an Evidential Paradigm," in *Clues, Myths, and the Historical Method*, trans. John Tedeschi and Anne C. Tedeschi (Baltimore: Johns Hopkins University Press, 2013), 87–113.

20. Matti Peltonen, "Clues, Margins, and Monads: The Micro-Macro Link in Historical Research," *HistTh* 40.3 (2001): 349.

21. E.g., Magnússon, "Far-Reaching Microhistory"; Guillaume Calafat and Romain Bertrand, "La microhistoire globale: affaire(s) à suivre," *Annales. Histoire, Sciences Sociales* 73.1 (2018): 3–18.

22. For indicative examples, see Nikki M. Taylor, *Driven toward Madness* (Athens: Ohio University Press, 2017); Natalie Zemon Davis, *Trickster Travels: A Sixteenth-Century Muslim between Worlds* (New York: Hill and Wang, 2006); Julia Roos, "An Afro-German Microhistory: Gender, Religion, and the Challenges of Diasporic Dwelling," *Central European History* 49.2 (2016): 240–60.

23. Cohen, "Macrohistory of Microhistory," 55.

to microhistory.[24] Microhistory also offers a way forward for the challenges of the amnesia and fragmentation that plague the field. All branches of knowledge suffer from what Francis Bacon called "decays, depressions, oblivions, [and] removes."[25] But the capacious character of microhistory as a *practice* may provide a means of alleviating this within the Quest, as it encompasses a myriad of perspectives and methods and recognizes the value of studies that appear, at face value, to be peripheral in either approach or focus to those that dominate within a field.

The subject of our study is, in many ways, typical of this form of historical inquiry. Microhistory "swarms with underlings and outsiders, history's lost men and women and forgotten children."[26] And while Jesus has certainly not been "lost" from historical view, by any reading of the surviving data he clearly did not occupy an established position of social, political, or religious power.[27] Microhistory also has a love of the deviant event, something that "in its strangeness, challenges values, institutions and principles, and jostles narrative habits of those who perceive it and respond . . . the odd, testing the normal, shows us something of its contours."[28] And it is hard to get a more deviant event than a resurrection.

COMPARATIVE MICROHISTORY

Comparative microhistory is especially helpful for our purposes. At first sight, it seems almost an oxymoron. After all, microhistory typically focuses on particular processes and personal experiences—the rigorous examination of one specific case—and is concerned with what has been called the "exceptional normal," characteristics that seem to make it incompatible with the business of comparison.[29] However, comparison does, in fact, have a place in microhistory, and many of its leading advocates, including Ginzburg and Levi, have noted its potential.[30]

24. E.g., see Henry Joel Cadbury, *The Peril of Modernizing Jesus* (New York: Macmillan, 1937). Quote from Thomas V. Cohen, *Roman Tales: A Reader's Guide to the Art of Microhistory* (London: Routledge, 2019), 4.

25. Francis Bacon, *Of the Proficience and Advancement of Learning* (London: Tomes, 1605), ii, 1–2.

26. Cohen, *Roman Tales*, 5.

27. Although there are indications that he may have benefited from the largesse of some who did; e.g., Luke 8:1–3.

28. Cohen, *Roman Tales*, 7.

29. Risto Alapuro, "Revisiting Microhistory from the Perspective of Comparisons," in *Historical Knowledge: In Quest of Theory, Method and Evidence*, ed. Susanna Fellman and Marjatta Rahikainen (Newcastle-upon-Tyne: Cambridge Scholars Publishing, 2011), 133.

30. Alapuro, "Revisiting Microhistory," 133. It is also a familiar, if underscrutinized, feature of much New Testament scholarship. See John M. G. Barclay and Benjamin G. White, eds., *The*

Comparison can be undertaken for all kinds of reasons. Given the significance of the comparative method in the natural and social sciences, it can be employed in order to make historical analysis more "scientific," providing a means of formulating and testing hypotheses where experimentation is impossible.[31] It can also help overcome the parochialism that arises as a consequence of doing all our thinking within a narrow field, something that plagues the study of the historical Jesus or at least many of the contributions that carry the most weight among New Testament scholars.[32] In addition, at its best it can produce "unexpected juxtapositions that fire the imagination," generating new interpretative possibilities and the consideration of previously overlooked factors.[33] For scholars of the historical Jesus it also helps the vital process of *enstrangement*, of making the familiar unfamiliar once again, so it can be examined afresh. I use the antiquated term *enstrangement* here deliberately in preference to the more common *estrangement*. Although the notion of *estrangement* can be analytically helpful for our purposes—for example, in the form of *cognitive estrangement* presented in the seminal work of Darko Suvin[34]—*estrangement* tends to connote a state of alienation and hostility, and often assumes a specific, ideological position on the part of the interpreter (for example, Suvin's Marxism). *Enstrangement* allows for a relationship between the interpreter and the thing made strange that is not necessarily predicated upon conflict.[35]

Employing comparisons is not as daunting as it might appear. It is not, for instance, necessary to have a similar level of expertise in two or more distinct fields.

New Testament in Comparison: Validity, Method and Purpose in Comparing Traditions, LNTS 600 (London: T&T Clark, 2020).

31. In the natural and social sciences, see e.g., Charles C. Ragin, *The Comparative Method: Moving beyond Qualitative and Quantitative Strategies* (Oakland: University of California Press, 2014); Paul H. Harvey and Mark Pagel, *The Comparative Method in Evolutionary Biology* (Oxford: Oxford University Press, 1991). As a means of formulating and testing hypotheses, see William H. Sewell, "Marc Bloch and the Logic of Comparative History," *HistTh* 6.2 (1967): 208–18.

32. An observation made by a number of critics; e.g., James Crossley, "The Next Quest for the Historical Jesus," *JSHJ* 19.3 (2021): 261–64.

33. Michael Hanagan, "'Shall I Compare Thee . . . ?' Problems of Comparative Historical Analysis," *International Review of Social History* 56.1 (2011): 138.

34. Darko Suvin, *Metamorphoses of Science Fiction: On the Poetics and History of a Literary Genre* (New Haven: Yale University Press, 1979). Suvin's concept could be usefully applied to ostensibly utopian and parabolic material within the Jesus traditions.

35. The term has become more widely used since the 1990 translation of the work of Viktor Shklvosky by Benjamin Sher, where the Russian neologism "ostranenie" (остранение) is translated as "enstrangement." See Victor Shklovsky, *Theory of Prose*, trans. Benjamin Sher (London: Dalkey Archive, 2015), xix.

That is rarely the case wherever comparison is employed in historical writing.[36] There is value in what Jürgen Kocka has called "asymmetrical" comparisons.[37] Of course there are challenges with comparison. It may be difficult to discern the criteria for deciding what can be productively compared, and choices may appear arbitrary or idiosyncratic. Any comparison also, of necessity, involves a degree of abstraction in the analysis that flattens out the particularities of the subjects compared. It may also prove difficult to give the degree of contextual data one would expect if we restricted ourselves to the primary object of our analysis. As Heinz-Gerhard Haput and Jürgen Kocka rightly note, "The comparative approach is thus always partly at odds with these basic principles of historical scholarship. The more cases we employ for a comparison, the less possible it is to work closely with primary sources, and hence the greater our dependence upon the secondary literature."[38] And, of course, comparative work also makes greater demands on the consumers of the scholarship, including those who may be required to peer review such material. They are even less likely to be equipped with the detailed specialist knowledge necessary to evaluate what is being presented and may need to take much of the analysis and data that it purports to be based upon trust. The unfortunate history of the use of comparison more broadly within the study of religion should also mean that we are cautious when we deploy it.[39] Although Michael Stausberg is right to say that it is not comparison that is the problem but its inadequate use, a problem that besets any scholarly operation.[40] In one sense, what I am advocating is hardly new: comparison has always been a tool in the study of the historical Jesus and the emergence of Christianity.[41] Indeed, it was employed by the earliest critics and defenders of the resurrection of Jesus, and it remains a staple of many recent contributions to critical debates about

36. For an exception, see Allan Mitchell, *The Great Train Race: Railways and the Franco-German Rivalry, 1815–1914* (New York: Berghahn, 2000).

37. Jürgen Kocka, "Asymmetrical Historical Comparison: The Case of the German Sonderweg," *HistTh* 38.1 (1999): 40–50.

38. Heinz-Gerhard Haupt and Jürgen Kocka, "Comparative History: Methods, Aims and Problems," in *Comparison and History: Europe in Cross-National Perspective*, ed. Deborah Cohen and Maura O'Connor (London: Routledge, 2004), 25.

39. See Arvind Sharma, "Orientalism and the Comparison of Religions," in *Comparing Religions: Possibilities and Perils?*, ed. Thomas A. Idinopulos, Brian C. Wilson, and James C. Hanges (Leiden: Brill, 2006), 221–33.

40. Michael Stausberg, "Comparison," in *The Routledge Handbook of Research Methods in the Study of Religion*, ed. Michael Stausberg and Steven Engler (London: Taylor & Francis, 2011), 22.

41. See Jonathan Z. Smith, *Drudgery Divine: On the Comparison of Early Christianities and the Religions of Late Antiquity* (Chicago: University of Chicago Press, 1990).

the topic.[42] However, it has been resisted by some who treat the accounts of the resurrection of Jesus as sui generis, quarantining them from such analysis.[43]

What follows is not really an example of microhistory *proper* but rather an attempt to show, in a compressed form, its possibilities for studying the historical Jesus. I shall begin with a brief description of two claims of resurrection drawn from the period of the English Revolution: Dorcas Erbury in 1656 and John Robins in 1651. It is helpful to know, for those unfamiliar with the wider context, that the English Revolution was a period of dramatic political, social, and religious upheaval that took place during the 1640s and 1650s, and which famously included the beheading of Charles I in 1649. As a popular ballad of the time declared: "The world is turned upside down."[44] The revolution was part of a series of wider revolutions and interconnected wars that occurred in Britain and Ireland in the mid-seventeenth century. I have not chosen Erbury and Robins because they provide us with analogues that closely resemble the resurrection of Jesus. Rather, I have selected them, in part, because of the opposite: the differences enhance the potential for *enstrangement*. If the stories had closely resembled accounts of the resurrection of Jesus, it would be hard not to constantly note apparent similarities (or differences), a process that militates against Jesus's resurrection being viewed afresh (and might result in the scholar contracting a bad case of parallelomania).[45] By examining these singular, contrasting stories and *then* returning to the resurrection of Jesus, the intention is to *make the resurrection strange again* and reap the interpretative benefits this will bring.

DORCAS ERBURY

Jailed in Exeter sometime between July and August 1656, Dorcas Erbury (also spelled Erbery or Erberie) was raised from the dead. She was fortunate. Jane Ingram, a fellow Quaker prisoner, had died a few days earlier and not come back to

42. For an ancient example, see Origen, *Cels.* 2.55–58. Such parallels were also used to argue for the reasonableness of belief in Jesus's resurrection by the apologist Justin (*1 Apol.* 21–22). More recently, see Gary R. Habermas, "Resurrection Claims in Non-Christian Religions," *Religious Studies* 25.2 (1989): 167–77; Dale C. Allison Jr., *The Resurrection of Jesus: Apologetics, Polemics, History* (London: T&T Clark, 2021), 210–302.

43. Richard C. Miller, *Resurrection and Reception in Early Christianity* (New York: Routledge, 2015), 161.

44. Anonymous, *The World Is Turned Upside Down* (London: s.n., 1646). The title was used by Christopher Hill in his still influential—though much critiqued—study of the radical ideas that emerged in this period. See Christopher Hill, *The World Turned Upside Down: Radical Ideas during the English Revolution* (Harmondsworth: Penguin, 1972).

45. Samuel Sandmel, "Parallelomania," *JBL* 81 (1962): 1–13.

life, a permanent victim of the poor conditions in which they, and a number of other early Friends, were held. In Erbury's case, she was convinced that she had survived because James Nayler (also spelled Naylor and Nailor), a Quaker leader incarcerated with her, had intervened and resurrected her in front of witnesses.[46] To Erbury, Nayler was, in her own words, "the onley [sic] begotten Son of God" and "the Holy Lord of Israel," and she had "no other Saviour but him."[47]

On October 27, soon after her release, she found herself before Bristol magistrates being interrogated about her part in another unusual event, one that scandalized the city and would soon become infamous throughout England and beyond.[48] They wanted to know why she had joined a small group of other Quakers in proclaiming "Hosanna, holy, holy, King of Israel" as Nayler rode into that city in clear imitation of Jesus's entry into Jerusalem.[49] It was during the magistrates' questioning that she first publicly declared what had happened a few weeks earlier in her Exeter cell.[50] Erbury repeated the claim that she had been resurrected a few weeks later when she, Nayler, and some other Quakers involved in the Bristol spectacle found themselves answering for their actions before a parliamentary committee in London.[51] Nayler was judged guilty of blasphemy by the House of Commons after an unprecedented trial that extended over ten days of the legislature's time.[52] He subsequently suffered a series of brutal punishments that included, in addition to being whipped and pilloried, having his tongue bored through with a hot iron and the letter B for blasphemer burned onto his fore-

---

46. They were among about twenty Quakers who had been imprisoned for vagrancy. See Joseph Besse, *A Collection of the Sufferings of the People Called Quakers*, 2 vols. (London: Hinde, 1753), 149. Regarding the resurrection, see Ralph Farmer, *Sathan Inthron'd in His Chair of Pestilence* (London: Thomas, 1657), 19; John Deacon, *The Grand Impostor Examined* (London: Brome, 1656), 34.

47. Anonymous, *A True Narrative of the Examination, Tryall, and Sufferings of James Nayler* (London: s.n., 1657), 8; John Deacon, *An Exact History of the Life of James Naylor* (London: Thomas, 1657), 25; Farmer, *Sathan Inthron'd*, 18; William Grigge, *The Quaker's Jesus* (London: Simmonds, 1658), 10.

48. For evidence of its significance outside of England, see Brandon Marriott, *Transnational Networks and Cross-Religious Exchange in the Seventeenth-Century Mediterranean and Atlantic Worlds: Sabbatai Sevi and the Lost Tribes of Israel* (London: Routledge, 2015), 37–62. Nayler's resurrection of Erbury is a central feature in subsequent textual and pictorial retellings of his life.

49. London, Library of the Society of Friends, Swarthmore MSS 1.188.

50. Deacon, *Life of James Naylor*, 11; Richard Blome, *The Fanatick History* (London: Sims, 1660), 101.

51. Deacon, *Grand Impostor Examined*, 34.

52. John Coffey, *Persecution and Toleration in Protestant England, 1558–1689* (Harlow: Longman, 2000), 154. For the trial see William G. Bittle, *James Nayler: 1618–1660: The Quaker Indicted by Parliament* (York: Sessions, 1987), 113–67.

head.[53] He served three years in prison and, perhaps unsurprisingly, died within a year of his release.[54]

In the months after her resurrection, Erbury appears to have maintained her belief that she had been raised from the dead by Nayler, standing beside her savior as he endured his corporal punishment.[55] Although the documentary evidence is limited, as it is for most women in early modern England, it is probable that she continued to believe that she had been raised from the dead for the rest of her life. Unlike others involved in the Bristol affair who subsequently repented (including Nayler himself), when she died her life was not commemorated by the movement, despite her remaining an active Quaker and suffering further imprisonments as a consequence of her forthright Quaker preaching.[56] Erbury's belief in her own resurrection would have been increasingly difficult to reconcile with the more sober form of Quakerism that emerged after the events of 1656.[57] While the initial years of the movement were accompanied by supernatural claims of various kinds—whether judged to be divine or demonic in origin[58]—such as raisings from the dead, these became less common after the Nayler incident and a source of embarrassment to the increasingly respectable sect.[59]

53. Anonymous, *True Narrative*, 34–35.

54. See Bittle, *James Nayler*, 168–75. Although the proximate cause of Nayler's death was a vicious mugging.

55. Deacon, *Life of James Naylor*, 35, 44.

56. Lloyd Bowen, "The Seeds and Fruits of Revolution: The Erbery Family and Religious Radicalism in Seventeenth-Century Glamorgan," *Welsh History Review* 25.3 (2011): 362, 366; Besse, *People Called Quakers*, 365, 740; Edward Burrough, *A Declaration of the Present Sufferings of above 140. Persons of the People of God (Who Are Now in Prison,) Called Quakers* (London: Simmons, 1659), 4; Christine Trevett, "William Erbery and His Daughter Dorcas: Dissenter and Resurrected Radical," *Journal of Welsh Religious History* 4 (1996): 35–36. Erbury was also one of the seven thousand Quaker women who petitioned Parliament against tithes. See Mary Forster, *These Several Papers Was Sent to the Parliament the Twentieth Day of the Fifth Moneth, 1659*, ed. Mary Forster (London: Westwood, 1659), 57. Regarding Nayler, see Erin Bell, "Eighteenth-Century Quakerism and the Rehabilitation of James Nayler, Seventeenth-Century Radical," *JEH* 59.3 (2008): 426–46.

57. For the significance of 1656, see Leo Damrosch, *The Sorrows of the Quaker Jesus: James Nayler and the Puritan Crackdown on the Free Spirit* (Cambridge: Harvard University Press, 1996).

58. George Fox, writing in the mid-1670s, says of this earlier period: "Many great and wonderful things were produced by the heavenly power in those days . . . beyond what this unbelieving age is able to receive or bear." George Fox, *A Journal*, ed. Thomas Ellwood (London: Northcott, 1694), 28. Quakers accused of being in league with the devil stood trial in Cambridge in 1659 for having turned a woman into a horse. See Anonymous, *Strange and Terrible Newes from Cambridge* (London: Brooks, 1659).

59. Most famously the failed resurrection of William Pool in 1657. See Henry Joel Cadbury, ed., *George Fox's 'Book of Miracles'* (Philadelphia: Friends General Conference, 2000),

Of course, Erbury's understanding of her resurrection may have changed over time. Quakers and others in this period often used the language of resurrection to describe a decisive, embodied spiritual event that might involve being *close* to physical death, but it was rarely employed to convey the belief that the person had actually died.[60] Even Nayler himself appears to have experienced something like this, falling into a trance for three days a little while before Erbury's resurrection, and reemerging with a new sense of his own spiritual significance.[61] Nonetheless, given how adamant and public Erbury was about what had happened in Exeter prison, and her willingness to suffer for her witness to it, it seems unlikely she would have abandoned her original, literal belief in her physical resurrection, even if others may have done so.

Needless to say, although Nayler initially confirmed that Erbury had been bodily resurrected, after his release from his sentence for blasphemy he denied it occurred.[62] Nayler instead complained that he had been "led by others" during this whole period.[63] This shift reflected his readmission to the wider Quaker movement, most of which had been shocked by his behaviour at Bristol.[64] At least for a brief period, however, Nayler seems to have shared his followers' exalted estimation of himself, including his power to resurrect the dead.[65]

There are indications that at least initially others shared Erbury's understanding of what had occurred. An anonymous Quaker work published soon after Nayler's punishment, largely supportive of him, included the striking question: "Is it blasphemy to raise from the dead?"[66] But there are indications that some, from

---

11–13. Claims about the miraculous did persist. Many of the over 150 miracles recorded in Fox's unpublished *Book of Miracles* date from the years after the Bristol incident.

60. E.g., see Henry Jessey, *The Exceeding Riches of Grace Advanced by the Spirit of Grace, in an Empty Creature (Viz) Mrs. Sarah Wight* (London: Mortlock, 1658), 27; Anna Trapnel, *A Legacy for Saints; Being Several Experiences of the Dealings of God with Anna Trapnel* (London: Brewster, 1654), 40.

61. Farmer, *Sathan Inthron'd*, 22–23.

62. Deacon, *Grand Impostor Examined*, 18; Anonymous, *True Narrative*, 15; James Nayler, *Glory to God Almighty Who Ruleth in the Heavens, and in Whose Hands Are All the Kingdoms of the Earth* (London: Simmons, 1659), 3. See also James Nayler, *A Collection of Sundry Books, Epistles and Papers Written by James Nayler*, ed. George Whitehead (London: Sowle, 1716), liv.

63. Nayler, *Glory to God Almighty*, 3.

64. Bittle, *James Nayler*, 170; Fox, *Journal*, 171, 220.

65. A point persuasively made in Euan MacArthur, *James Nayler and the Quest for Historic Quaker Identity* (Leiden: Brill, 2024).

66. Anonymous, *True Narrative*, 8. It is impossible to determine who authored this document. See Kate Peters, *Print Culture and the Early Quakers*, Cambridge Studies in Early Modern British History (Cambridge: Cambridge University Press, 2005), 241 n. 32.

the outset, were less convinced. Samuel Cater and Robert Crab had both been with Erbury and Nayler in Exeter prison and accompanied them on Nayler's infamous entry to Bristol. But they were discharged after the first interrogation by that city's magistrates with no indication that they held to Erbury's interpretation of what had happened to her.[67] Even Robert Rich, an ardent supporter of Nayler who was very close to the events and continued to publicly champion Nayler long after the latter's death—famously kissing Nayler's wounds after he was branded—made no mention of Erbury's resurrection in his writings.[68]

JOHN ROBINS

A few years before Erbury came back to life in Exeter, John Robins was in London proclaiming that he was the "first Adam" who, after about 5,600 years, "was risen again from the dead."[69] In addition, he was "God Almighty . . . the Judge of the Quick and of the Dead," he would soon gather 144,000 Jews and lead them to the Mount of Olives, and his wife was about to give birth to Christ.[70] At least a dozen close followers shared his distinctive beliefs, as well as being convinced that Robins had not only been resurrected but had resurrected them and others too.[71] These unusual convictions seem to have emerged in 1650 as a result of a vision of one of Robins's key followers, Joshua Garment.[72] By mid-1651, after many of its members had been imprisoned for blasphemy and a number recanted, the group and their god disappeared from the historical record.[73]

67. Grigge, *Quaker's Jesus*, 11; Trevett, "William Erbery," 37.

68. E.g., Robert Rich, *Hidden Things Brought to Light* (London: Smith, 1678), 38; Deacon, *Grand Impostor Examined*, 23.

69. Lodowick Muggleton, *The Acts of the Witnesses of the Spirit in Five Parts* (London: s.n., 1699), 21.

70. Muggleton, *Acts of the Witnesses*, 21; John Taylor, *Ranters of Both Sexes, Male and Female* (London: John Hammon, 1651), 2; John Reeve and Lodowick Muggleton, *A Transcendent Spiritu-all Treatise upon Several Heavenly Doctrines* (London: s.n., 1653), 7–8; E. H., *All the Proceedings at the Sessions of the Peace Holden at Westminster, on the 20. Day of June, 1651* (London: Harper, 1651), 8. For Robins's claim to divinity, see also Anonymous, *A List of Some of the Grand Blasphemers and Blasphemies* (London: Ibbitson, 1654), 7.

71. Muggleton, *Acts of the Witnesses*, 21; E. H., *All the Proceedings*, 4.

72. Joshua Garment, *The Hebrews Deliverance at Hand* (London: s.n., 1651), 4.

73. The first group of seven was detained on May 12, 1651, and imprisoned in Westminster Gatehouse before six of them signed a confession and were released on June 20. On May 18 another group of ten, including Robins himself, was imprisoned in Clerkenwell. See Ariel Hessayon, ed., *The Refiner's Fire: The Collected Works of Theaurau John Tany* (London: Breviary Stuff, 2018), 538–39; Ariel Hessayon, "Robins, John (fl. 1641–1652)," in *Oxford Dictionary of National Biography*,

Despite the sparse sources, we can sketch something of the ways in which these multiple resurrections were understood within the Robins group by the leader, the devout followers, and some apostates. Although initially quite certain about the truth of his claims, Robins underwent a rapid change soon after he and nine of his worshipers were incarcerated in New Prison Clerkenwell for blasphemy a few months after his mission to London began.[74] Despite his acolytes still loyally professing their faith in his divinity, he now denied it, even declaring that a woman who continued to believe that he was God ought to be hanged.[75] When asked about his fundamental beliefs, he quoted the Apostles' Creed, including its clause about the (future) resurrection of the dead.[76] By so doing Robins demonstrated his Christian orthodoxy and apparently disavowed one of the foundational beliefs of his movement, boldly proclaimed by his followers, that "John Robins had power to raise the dead."[77] He would go on to issue a statement from prison explicitly rejecting his divinity, though confirming that he had a special calling to convert Jews.[78] He also wrote a formal recantation addressed to Oliver Cromwell, something that seems to have gained him his freedom relatively quickly. From what we can tell, he then fled London, giving his followers the slip, and apparently returned to his old life in southwest England.[79] Although he claimed, shortly before he vanished, that "he should come forth with a greater Power" in the future, no more was heard of him.[80] Of course, it is hard to know whether his professed change of heart was as sincere as it was convenient. While he clearly remained certain that he had a divinely appointed role of some kind, there are good grounds to think that Robins's belief in both his own resurrection from the dead and his ability to resurrect others was probably short-lived.

It is difficult to ascertain what happened to the resurrection beliefs of Robins's followers once their god deserted them. Not only are the sources limited, but most were illiterate and, except for Joshua Garment, produced no writings of their own.[81] However, it seems likely that there was considerable variation between them, with a few proving more steadfast in their convictions than Robins himself.

May 28, 2015, https://www.oxforddnb.com/display/10.1093/ref:odnb/9780198614128.001.0001/odnb-9780198614128-e-23826.

74. G. H., *The Declaration of John Robins, the False Prophet* (London: Wood, 1651), 6.

75. G. H., *Declaration of John Robins*, 3.

76. G. H., *Declaration of John Robins*, 4–5.

77. E. H., *All the Proceedings*, 3, 6; Taylor, *Ranters of Both Sexes*, 2.

78. G. H., *Declaration of John Robins*, 6.

79. Reeve and Muggleton, *Transcendent Spirituall Treatise*, 10; Hessayon, "Robins, John."

80. Muggleton, *Acts of the Witnesses*, 47.

81. See E. H., *All the Proceedings*, 3–4.

When apprehended, they did not all respond in the same way. One group, after initially confessing their belief in Robins and his ability to bring the dead back to life, subsequently denounced him as someone who gained his miraculous powers from the devil.[82] That being said, one of their number, Thomas Kerby, remained faithful to their unusual creed.[83] His obduracy led to him being sentenced to six months imprisonment with hard labor and corporal punishment, the maximum sentence under the 1650 Blasphemy Act for a first offense, enduring prison longer than Robins himself.[84]

The beliefs of the apostates that had parted company before the movement began to be persecuted can be seen in the writings of John Reeve and Ludowick Muggleton. Reeve and Muggleton are best known for establishing the Muggletonian sect, a movement that would prove surprisingly resilient, only dying out in the late 1970s, and was predicated on the belief that they were the two witnesses of Rev 11.[85] However, before taking on their prophetic roles, both were clearly closely associated with Robins and his followers and believed the miraculous claims made about him.[86] Muggleton, for example, was certain not only that Robins had raised a number of biblical figures from the past, but that he "had Nine or Tenn of them at my House at a time, of those that were said to be raised from the Dead," and he did "not speak this from Hearsay from others, but from a perfect Knowledge."[87] Subsequently, however, they would declare Robins the "man of sin" and the "Antichrist" and a "false Christ."[88] They still believed in his ability to work miracles but now viewed these as "great lying signs and wonders" (2 Thess 2:9) done by the power of "the very prince of devils in this last Age."[89]

REREADING THE RESURRECTION

As we noted earlier, microhistory is characterized by its evidentiary paradigm, Ginzburg's "method of clues." It customarily starts its investigation by identifying

82. E. H., *All the Proceedings*, 4–5.

83. E. H., *All the Proceedings*, 8.

84. See Coffey, *Persecution and Toleration*, 149–50. He served three months. Hessayon, *Refiner's Fire*, 538.

85. For Muggletonians, see William Lamont, *Last Witnesses: The Muggletonian History, 1652–1979* (Aldershot: Ashgate, 2006); Christopher Hill, William M. Lamont, and Barry Reay, *The World of the Muggletonians* (London: Temple Smith, 1983).

86. Muggleton, *Acts of the Witnesses*, 23.

87. Muggleton, *Acts of the Witnesses*, 21.

88. Reeve and Muggleton, *Transcendent Spirituall Treatise*, 8–9; Matt 24:24; Mark 13:22.

89. Reeve and Muggleton, *Transcendent Spirituall Treatise*, 8; Lodowick Muggleton, *A True Interpretation of the Eleventh Chapter of the Revelation of St. John* (London: s.n., 1662), 155, 157–58.

"something that does not quite fit, something odd that needs to be explained."[90] Of course, what exactly "does not fit" in the accounts of the resurrection in the New Testament is not self-evident. At one level, it would seem almost perverse to single out anything in particular as anomalous, given that the event, in toto, is hardly an everyday occurrence in any culture. Nonetheless, rereading the material again after the brief immersion in the early modern comparative material and experiencing the resulting *enstrangement* while also keeping in mind the micro-historical concentration on the agency of all the social actors, does throw up what Ginzburg would call a "clue": Matt 28:17—*kai idontes auton prosekunēsan, hoi de edistasan*—"When they saw him, they worshiped him; but some doubted" (NRSV). There is, by any reading, something decidedly "odd" about this verse, which occurs immediately before the Great Commission, and it is not a strangeness that can be dismissed by appeals to problems with the manuscript tradition, as there are none. Unlike the narratives in Luke and John and the longer ending of Mark, in which the doubts of some disciples about the resurrection are subsequently resolved, there is no indication in the remaining few lines of Matthew that this ever occurred.[91] This feature of Matthew's resurrection narrative is all the more surprising given the vital importance of believing witnesses in other early Christian accounts of the resurrection and also in the roughly analogous Greco-Roman apotheosis traditions that may have shaped the expectations of readers.[92]

It is, therefore, surprising that Matt 28:17 has been passed over with little comment in most discussions of the resurrection. For example, N. T. Wright only expends one paragraph on this verse in the 817 pages that constitute his magnum opus claiming to demonstrate its historicity.[93] Normally it is the grammatical rather than historical difficulties raised by Matt 28:17 that have attracted attention, in particular whether *hoi de edistasan* should be understood as partitive.[94] Where

90. Peltonen, "Clues, Margins, and Monads," 349.

91. Luke 24:13–35 (Cleopas and one unnamed companion); 24:36–43 (the Eleven and their companions); John 20:24–29 (Thomas); Mark 16:14–18 (the eleven) and 16:20, which are both part of all manuscripts that include the longer ending (except Codex Washingtonianus) and indicate that the author believed that the eleven's doubts had been overcome. Nor, unlike the other gospels, are the eleven depicted as doing anything more; cf. Mark 16:20; Luke 24:52–53; John 20:28. See J. David Woodington, *The Dubious Disciples: Doubt and Disbelief in the Post-Resurrection Scenes of the Four Gospels*, BZNW 241 (Berlin: de Gruyter, 2020), 85.

92. E.g., Luke 24; John 20–21; Acts 1:1–11, 22; 1 Cor 15:5–8. See Wendy Cotter, "Greco-Roman Apotheosis Traditions and the Resurrection Appearances in Matthew," in *The Gospel of Matthew in Current Study*, ed. David E. Aune (Grand Rapids: Eerdmans, 2001), 127–53.

93. N. T. Wright, *The Resurrection of the Son of God*, vol. 3 of *Christian Origins and the Question of God* (Minneapolis: Fortress, 2003), 643.

94. For the partitive interpretation, see P. W. van der Horst, "Once More: The Translation

its historical implications have been in view, various exegetical maneuvers have often been deployed to diminish the obvious problems raised by the verse.[95] For instance, it is regularly claimed that the verse's meaning should be governed by the only other appearance of the verb *distazō* "to doubt" in the New Testament, which is found a number of chapters earlier in Jesus's response to Peter's failure to walk on water (Matt 14:31).[96] In this vein, *distazō* should be taken as conveying the idea that the disciples did have some faith, albeit only a little, when faced with the risen Jesus.[97] A few try to avoid the difficulty by interpreting *hoi de edistasan* as a reference to the doubt of others, rather than the eleven.[98] This saves the disciples from the accusation of disbelief, a reading that is found in most patristic interpretations.[99] But such interpretations are strained—for example, nobody other than the apostles is described as being present at this point in Matthew's narrative (28:16)[100]—and appear predicated upon the belief that Matthew cannot *really* have meant to conclude his narrative with the eleven, or some of them, unconvinced of Jesus's resurrection. But that is what he did.

So, the "clue" clearly cannot be ignored and invites further critical reflection. Although it is possible that Matthew's inability to provide a resolution to the disciples' doubt is a literary failing on his part, a judgment that would be in tension with the prevailing assessment of his compositional skill, it seems more likely that it reflects a memory present in Matthew's community.[101] Given that *edistasan* is intransitive, clearly Matthew was uninterested in the object of their doubt and tells us nothing about its cause. However, we can speculate, and speculation is not a dirty word but an activity that underlies most disciplines, even if unac-

---

of Δέ in Matthew 28.17," *JSNT* 8.27 (1986): 27–30. Against, see Keith Howard Reeves, "They Worshipped Him, and They Doubted: Matthew 28.17," *Bible Translator* 49.3 (1998): 344–49; Keith Howard Reeves, *The Resurrection Narrative in Matthew: A Literary-Critical Examination* (Lampeter: Mellen, 1993), 69–74.

95. For a useful discussion of the issues, see Woodington, *Dubious Disciples*, 84–96. See also J. D. Atkins, *The Doubt of the Apostles and the Resurrection Faith of the Early Church: The Post-Resurrection Appearance Stories of the Gospels in Ancient Reception and Modern Debate*, WUNT 495 (Tübingen: Mohr Siebeck, 2019), 169–71, 190–94, 198–99, 213–14, 224–26.

96. For the wider narrative, see Matt 14:22–33; Mark 6:45–52.

97. E.g., Charles H. Talbert, *Matthew* (Grand Rapids: Baker Academic, 2010), 312.

98. E.g., Leon Morris, *The Gospel according to Matthew* (Grand Rapids: Eerdmans, 1992), 745; Erich Klostermann, *Das Matthäusevangelium*, 4th ed. (Tübingen: Mohr, 1971), 231.

99. Reeves, "They Worshipped Him," 345.

100. Matthew's positive redactional portrayal of the disciples has led some to argue for this position. See Alan Hugh McNeile, *The Gospel according to St. Matthew: The Greek Text with Introduction, Notes, and Indices* (London: Macmillan, 1915), 434.

101. For a survey of potential suggestions, see Woodington, *Dubious Disciples*, 88.

knowledged.[102] Indeed, the microhistorical perspective encourages us to do so, because it does not operate with the assumption that historical knowledge is solely a choice between what can be definitively established about the past and what cannot, but is also concerned with historical understanding generated by the disciplined interplay between historical imagination and evidence; it is an exploration of what plausibly might have been, and not purely concerned with determining what unarguably was.[103] In our case, we can speculate about the possible reasons for the unresolved doubt found in Matt 28:17 in a way informed not just by knowledge of the religious and cultural context within which the events occurred but also the repertoire of possibilities raised by the comparative material we have just examined.

If we begin with our knowledge of the religious and cultural context, a few suggestions immediately spring to mind, some familiar, some less so. It is possible some apostles viewed the resurrected Jesus—or, rather, what others may have claimed was the resurrected Jesus—as not deserving of worship because they thought he was a ghost or spirit of some kind, the sort of reaction we find in Luke's Gospel (24:37, 39).[104] Or possibly they thought that it *was* Jesus physically back from the dead, but as a result of nefarious, prohibited means, of the kind used by the witch of Endor to summon up Samuel, an influential biblical narrative during this period.[105] Necromancy was also well known across the cultures in the Roman Empire, so the belief that some could conjure up the spirits of the dead, and even reanimate corpses of the recently deceased, was familiar to many.[106] Or maybe they thought what they saw was Jesus's guardian angel, a figure believed to be the double of the person to whom it was assigned, a being that was either evil or good,

102. For "speculation" as an unacknowledged method in the sciences, see Richard Swedberg, "Does Speculation Belong in Social Science Research?," *Sociological Methods & Research* 50.1 (2021): 45–74.

103. Cohen, *Roman Tales*, 8.

104. Something that they and others had given Jesus during his lifetime, see Matt 2:2, 8, 11; 8:2; 9:18; 14:33; 15:25; 20:20; 28:9. See also Matt 14:26, Mark 6:49. For examples of belief in visible, postmortem spirits resembling angels within Judaism of the period, see 1 En. 39:5; 45:4–5; 51.4, 54:1–2; 104:4; 2 Bar. 51:1–12; Matt 22:30; Mark 12:25; Luke 20:36.

105. 1 Sam 28:3–25; Sir 46:19–20. See Gideon Bohak, *Ancient Jewish Magic: A History* (Cambridge: Cambridge University Press, 2008), 38.

106. Daniel Ogden, *Greek and Roman Necromancy* (Princeton: Princeton University Press, 2004). The most famous, paradigmatic example is the raising of Tiresias by Odysseus in Homer, *Od.* 10.488–540, 11.13–149. For further examples, see Daniel Ogden, *Magic, Witchcraft, and Ghosts in the Greek and Roman Worlds: A Sourcebook*, 2nd ed. (Oxford: Oxford University Press, 2009), 179–205. Other examples include the witch Erictho in Lucan, *Phar.* 6.588–830 and the Isis priest Zatchlas in Apuleius, *Metam.* 2.28–30.

but certainty not one that merited worship.[107] Perhaps the disciples thought that what they saw just *appeared* to be Jesus but had no connection to him, a demon impersonating their dead leader, perhaps out of revenge for the suffering Jesus had caused other demons when he was alive.[108]

However, armed with our comparative knowledge of the cases of Erbury and Robins, we might go further, and raise other reasonable possibilities that have not been considered in the critical literature. Given that many of Robins's followers, including the apostates Reeve and Muggleton, continued to believe in the supernatural powers of their erstwhile god but became convinced that these were diabolical in origin, it is possible that when faced with the risen Jesus some disciples thought something similar. Perhaps they believed that what they now saw before them was a result of Jesus's own magical skill and evidence that his opponents were correct in their assessment of him as someone who carried out miracles by the power of Beelzebul (Matt 12:24; Mark 3:22; Luke 11:15; cf. John 8:48). Or possibly, like Cater and Crab when faced with Erbury's resurrection, some just did not believe that whatever they saw was evidence that a resurrection had taken place. Perhaps, as Robins would eventually come to believe of his own resurrection, they did not think that they had witnessed a resurrection but remained committed to one in the future (just as some Christians associated with Cerinthus would later hold that "Christ is not risen yet, but will rise together with everyone").[109] Or perhaps, just as Nayler and many of Robins's followers rejected their initial understanding of the resurrections with which they were associated as a result of persecution and a desire to return to the lives that they had previously led, Matt 28:17 might point toward a memory not that some apostles doubted when initially faced with what they believed was the risen Jesus, but rather that some subsequently abandoned this interpretation of whatever they saw. Perhaps "persecution," or the "cares of the world," or the "lure of wealth," (Matt 13:18–23; 24:10; Mark 4:13–20; Luke 8:11–15) or any of the other factors that led early Christians to leave the movement also took their toll on the apostles too.

The notion that at least some of Jesus's apostles remained unconvinced that he had risen from the dead seems, at first sight, unlikely. Aside from Matt 28:17, there

---

107. E.g., Acts 12:15; Philo, *QE* 1, 23; Herm. Mand. 6.2; Gen. Rab. 78.3. See also b. Šabb. 119b. For guardian angels, see Ps 91:11; Jub. 35:16–17; 3 Bar. 11–16; LAB 11:12, 15:5; Matt 18:10 (Luke 22:43; Acts 27:23–24); Heb 1:14; Herm. Vis. 5.1–4; Clement of Alexandria, *Strom.* 6.17.157. See also Darrell Hannah, "Guardian Angels and Angelic National Patrons in Second Temple Judaism and Early Christianity," in *Angels: The Concept of Celestial Beings: Origins, Development and Reception*, ed. Friedrich V. Reiterer, Tobias Nicklas, and Karin Schöpflin (Berlin: de Gruyter, 2007), 423–32.

108. The notion that demons could pretend to be the dead is found in Tertullian, *An.* 57.

109. Epiphanius, *Pan.* 28.6.6.

is no tradition in early Christian writings, or those of their critics, that directly supports such a claim. But such a suggestion is not as fanciful as it might seem. The "twelve" are clearly important in traditions about the life of the historical Jesus but considerably less so after his death, even if they retained, as a group, limited symbolic significance (1 Cor 15:5; Rev 21:14).[110] There is, admittedly, some interest in them at the outset of Acts of the Apostles (Acts 1:1–26), but aside from references to Peter, John, and James the brother of John, no apostle is mentioned by name for the rest of the book, and others, notably Paul, take center stage for most of it.[111] Outside of Acts and the Gospels, only Peter and John are mentioned by name in the New Testament (excluding the pseudonymous claims of apostolic authorship of a number of epistles).[112] For all the subsequent veneration that the apostles received, and the development of extensive legendary traditions about them in literature and art, there is not even a stable list of exactly who they were.[113] Although some have recently been more optimistic about the "quest for the historical apostles," there is little that can be established historically about any of them, as virtually all the sources, including the accounts of their martyrdoms, were written at least 150 years after their deaths.[114] It is therefore possible that, aside from the apostles Peter, John and James, others may have left the movement or, if they remained within it, propagated a form of Christianity in which Jesus's resurrection was not significant, as we can see in the epistles of James and Jude, or in the so-called Two Ways tradition behind a cluster of early Christian texts

110. Matt 10:1, 5; 11:1; 19:28; 20:17; 26:14; Mark 3:14; 4:10; 6:7; 9:35; 10:32; 11:11; 14:10, 17, 20, 43; Luke 6:13; 8:1; 9:1, 12; 18:31; 22:3, 30, 47; John 6:67, 70, 71; 20:24. The reference to the "twelve" in 1 Cor 15:5 implies an appearance *after* Matthias had been chosen as Judas's replacement (Acts 1:26) and is in conflict with the appearances to the "eleven" found in Matt 28:16–18; Luke 24:33–50 (Mark 16:14) and implied in John.

111. Peter: Acts 1:15; 2:14, 37, 38; 3:6, 12; 4:8; 5:3, 8–9, 15, 29; 8:20; 9:32, 34, 38–40; 10:5, 9, 13–14, 17–19, 21, 23, 25–26, 32, 34, 44–46; 11:2, 4, 7, 13; 12:3, 5–7, 9, 11, 14, 16, 18; 15:7. Peter and John: Acts 3:1, 4, 11; 4:1, 13, 19; 8:14, 17, 25; John: Acts 12:2; James (the brother of John): Acts 12:2. These three are also singled out in the gospels, see Matt 17:1; Mark 9:2; Luke 9:28 (cf. Luke 8:51).

112. Peter (Cephas): Gal 2:7, 8, 11, 14; Peter (Cephas) and John: Gal 2:9.

113. E.g., see Roald Dijkstra, *The Apostles in Early Christian Art and Poetry* (Leiden: Brill, 2016). Compare the lists found in Matt 10:2–4; Mark 3:16–19; Luke 6:13–16 (Acts 1:13). The author of Luke-Acts corrects the list provided by Mark, replacing Thaddeus with Judas, son of James (Luke 6:16; Acts 1:13). John contains no list and of the seven disciples he names (Peter: 1:42; Andrew: 1:40; Philip: 1:43; Nathanael: 1:45; Judas Iscariot: 6:71; Thomas: 11:16; Judas: 14:22), he diverges from Mark by including not just Judas the son of James, but another figure, Nathanael, as well as giving prominence to one that is not named, the so-called "beloved disciple" (John 13:23; 20:2; 21:7, 20).

114. See W. Brian Shelton, *Quest for the Historical Apostles: Tracing Their Lives and Legacies* (Grand Rapids: Baker Academic, 2018). See also Sean McDowell, *The Fate of the Apostles: Examining the Martyrdom Accounts of the Closest Followers of Jesus* (Farnham: Ashgate, 2015).

such as the Didache, Epistle of Barnabas, and the *Doctrina Apostolorum*.[115] The idea that forms of Christianity might, at least prior to Marcion, be uninterested in the resurrection has certainly become less unimaginable than it once was as a result of the work of Markus Vinzent.[116]

However plausible these speculations are judged to be, we clearly need to be wary of the kind of claim about the apostles that typifies many treatments of the resurrection of Jesus. We cannot simply state, as Brian Shelton has recently done, that "These men were confident in the resurrection and focused on transforming unbelievers into Christians."[117] Nor should we uncritically agree with Pheme Perkins when she says, "That early Christians believed Jesus of Nazareth to have been raised up or exalted by God is not an issue."[118] We just do not know that to be the case and Matt 28:17 may indicate otherwise.

CONCLUSION

This has only been a brief attempt to demonstrate the potential value of microhistory and, in particular, comparative microhistory for the study of the historical Jesus. It has shown that approaching the resurrection of Jesus with a microhistorical lens can identify new or neglected historical questions and possibilities, and there are good reasons to think that this would be true of any issue that is of interest to those undertaking the Quest for the historical Jesus. In fact, I would reiterate my initial point: our sources for the life of Jesus, concerned as they are with a subject that is small in scale though not in consequence, demand such an approach. And *comparative* microhistory, and the *enstrangement* it encourages, is especially effective for our purposes as it serves to widen our historical imagination, a necessary activity as we try to identify what we can reasonably infer from the data we have before us. Comparative microhistory has the potential to revitalize a Quest that is in need of a resurrection of its own.

115. Edwin K. Broadhead, *Jewish Ways of Following Jesus: Redrawing the Religious Map of Antiquity* (Tübingen: Mohr Siebeck, 2011), 128–31; Kurt Niederwimmer, *The Didache: A Commentary* (Minneapolis: Fortress, 1998), 30–52. Markus Vinzent, *Christ's Resurrection in Early Christianity and the Making of the New Testament* (Farnham: Ashgate, 2011).

116. Vinzent, *Christ's Resurrection in Early Christianity*.

117. Shelton, *Quest for the Historical Apostles*, 5.

118. Pheme Perkins, "The Resurrection of Jesus of Nazareth," in *Studying the Historical Jesus*, ed. Bruce Chilton and Craig Evans (Leiden: Brill, 1994), 424–25.

33

Whakapapa and Genealogy

Wayne Te Kaawa

"Ko te whakapapa te taumata tiketike o te mātauranga Māori" (genealogy is the pinnacle of Māori knowledge).[1] This statement by Sir James Henare outlines the connection between *mātauranga māori* and *whakapapa*. *Mātauranga māori* is Māori knowledge and ways of knowing, a critical part of academic theological studies in Aotearoa New Zealand. You cannot do theology in this country without engaging with *mātauranga māori*. Knowledge and ways of knowing from a Māori worldview begins with understanding connections and relationships between the physical, spiritual, human, and nonhuman worlds. These connections are called *whakapapa*, which is likened to genealogy. *Whakapapa* in its fullest expression and understanding is the layering of generations upon generations that show connections and relationships. Using a Māori worldview, the initial research question is "who or what is this thing I am encountering, and what is my relationship to it?" In this chapter I will apply a *whakapapa* analysis to the genealogy of Jesus contained in Matt 1:1–17. Motivating this approach is the need for the Next Quest for the historical Jesus to adopt a broader, cross-cultural understanding of why the gospels provide genealogies of Jesus and how they might be interpreted.

1. Pierre Lyndon, personal conversations, Queenstown, August 29, 2018.

WHAKAPAPA AND THE GENEALOGY OF JESUS

At the heart of the Māori world is *whakapapa*; it is the anchor that remains planted in the earth while the world around it is characterized by constant change. *Whakapapa* records, preserves, transmits, and maps relationships between people and the world that they live in physically and spiritually. Matthew makes a number of claims in its genealogy. First, Jesus has a human genealogy. Second, Jesus is the messiah. Third, Jesus is the son of David, the son of Abraham. Fourth, there are significant women in his genealogy. Finally, while the genealogy is that of Joseph's family, he is introduced as the husband of Mary. These facts stated can only be fully understood in the context of genealogy. A *whakapapa* methodology will be helpful in providing new insights into these claims.

Sir Apirana Ngata, perhaps the most well known and respected Māori leader in history, defines *whakapapa* as the process of laying one thing upon another. He says that if you visualize the founding ancestors as the first generation, the next and succeeding ancestors are placed on them in layers.[2] This methodology of layering creates a foundation that locates a person in relation to your ancestors, to each other, to the environment, and to God.

Examining the genealogy of Jesus in Matthew's Gospel, New Zealand Pākehā theologian Warren Carter uses the same methodology of layering that Ngata articulates. According to Carter, genealogy locates Jesus within the biblical story by associating him with some of the prestigious ancestors of biblical history. This defines the relationship of Jesus to his ancestors where every name evokes a layer of stories.[3] The genealogy of Jesus in the Gospel of Matthew is a layering of generations and narratives that provides an interpretative framework clothed in names, stories, places, and events that shape the biblical narrative, placing the origins of Jesus in a specific time and place.

Pei Te Hurinui Jones of Tainui, who was mentored by Sir Apirana Ngata, says that great emphasis was placed on the genealogical method of fixing the sequence of events, and therefore *whakapapa* lines should be examined in conjunction with the history.[4] *Whakapapa* and history have to be studied in conjunction with each other as one flows from the other rationally explaining and interpreting the

---

2. Apirana T. Ngata, *Rauru nui a Toi lectures and Ngati Kahungunu Origin* (Wellington: Victoria University Press, 1972), 6.

3. Warren Carter, *Matthew and the Margins: A Socio-Political and Religious Reading* (Maryknoll, NY: Orbis, 2000), 53.

4. Pei Te Hurinui Jones, "Māori Genealogies," *Journal of the Polynesian Society* 62.2 (1958): 162–65.

other. To study them in isolation would seriously compromise the greater picture. Studying the genealogies in Genesis, Claus Westermann proposes a similar view to that of Jones that genealogies reflect a view of history and provide a context and timeframe.[5] The genealogy of Jesus presents history in the form of lists of successive generations intentionally preserving the memory of the ancestors while providing a context and a timeframe for the human life of Jesus of Nazareth.

A contemporary of A. T. Ngata, Te Rangihīroa (Sir Peter Buck) believed *whakapapa* to be a living tradition. According to Buck, *whakapapa* contained the knowledge of the ancestors and was handed on from generation to generation by word of mouth in order that it might live.[6] Esther Marie Menn from the Lutheran School of Theology in Chicago describes genealogy in similar terms describing it as a method of transmitting knowledge intergenerationally. This type of transmission is a fundamental structure in biblical literature that undergirds both the extended birth narratives and the skeletal genealogies.[7]

Professor Whatarangi Winiata, the founder of Te Wānanga o Ngāti Raukawa, a Māori indigenous university, provides a succinct definition of *whakapapa* as "having the ability to ground oneself."[8] He explains that *whaka* means "to make" and *papa* means the "earth or ground." Grounding oneself is fully expressed in the word *tūrangawaewae*, meaning a place to stand in the world. According to David Garland, genealogy sketches the contour of salvation history and highlights the fact that the time of Israel inaugurated by Abraham has reached its fulfillment with the birth of Jesus, the one called Christ in the genealogy.[9] The genealogy attributed to Jesus has the similar effect of grounding him in the physical land of Israel, in his ancestors and in history that has salvation at its core.

A core value of Māori belief is that every living being has a *whakapapa*. It is the basis for the organization of knowledge in all aspects of creation and the subsequent development of all things animate and inanimate, from *Atua* (divine) to humans to every aspect of nature including time. As Dr. Ranginui Walker says: *Kia whakatōmuri te haere whakamua* "I walk backwards into the future with my

---

5. Claus Westermann, *Genesis 1–11, A Commentary* (Minneapolis: Augsburg, 1990), 325.

6. Te Rangihīroa, *The Coming of the Māori* (Wellington: Whitcombe and Tombs, 1949), 408.

7. Esther Marie Menn, *Judah and Tamar (Genesis 38) in Ancient Jewish Exegesis: Studies in Literary and Hermeneutics* (Leiden: Brill, 1997), 15.

8. Shane Edwards, "Nā te Mātauranga Māori ka Ora Tonu te Ao Māori: Through Māori Knowledge Te Ao Māori Will Resonate," in *Conversation in Mātauranga Māori*, ed. Taiarhia Black et al. (Wellington: New Zealand Qualifications Authority, 2012), 37–58.

9. David E. Garland, *Reading Matthew: A Literary and Theological Commentary on the First Gospel* (New York: Crossroads, 1993), 13.

eye fixed on the past."[10] In this statement Walker is seeing genealogy as traveling backward in time to the future as it unfolds in the present as a continuum into the past. The past, present, and future are held in creative tension. Genealogy is constantly evolving. Friis Plum says that the fluidity of genealogies leads to alterations concurrent with changes in points of view and ideology.[11] Matthew presents its genealogy in descending order that begins in the past and works back in time and history to the ancestor, Abraham. The genealogy contains matriarchs as well as patriachs. The fluidity of the genealogy warrants careful examination.

Those who have been charged with the responsibility of teaching *whakapapa* to future generations also define how intergenerational knowledge will be transferred to the next generation and what parts of the *whakapapa* will be passed on. Karyn Paringatai of the University of Otago, who was raised outside her tribal boundaries, poses the question: what criteria are used when deciding how to prioritize *whakapapa*?[12] The transmission of *whakapapa* is defined by the person who possesses that knowledge. Elaine Wainwright says that this also says something about the person who holds and retells that knowledge.[13] The authors and editors of the Gospel of Matthew chose to include their versions of the genealogy of Jesus with specific names written in a specific way for a specific reason. In analyzing the genealogy of Jesus, a *whakapapa* methodology will consider the politics behind the creation of the genealogy of Jesus.

According to Dr. Te Ahukaramu Royal of Ngāti Raukawa, *whakapapa* is regarded as an analytical tool that has been employed as a means to understand the world and relationships.[14] A feature of Matthew's genealogy of Jesus is the inclusion of four women. Scholars such as Raymond E. Brown and Elaine Wainwright have surveyed various theories on why they have been included. One theory is the women were included as notable sinners or as departing from the purity of the Jewish race. The women are reputed, so this theory goes, to have backgrounds as seductresses, prostitutes, or adulteresses or as gentile foreign women. This last category fits with the gentile-friendly theology of Matthew. A *whakapapa* meth-

10. Ranginui Walker, *Ngā Pepa a Ranginui: The Walker Papers* (Auckland: Penguin, 1996), 14.
11. Karin Friis Plum, "Genealogy as Theology," *SJT* 3.1 (1989): 66–92.
12. Karyn Paringatai, "Māori Identity Development Outside of Tribal Environments," *Aotearoa New Zealand Social Work* 26.1 (2014): 49.
13. Elaine Wainwright, *Towards a Feminist Critical Reading of the Gospel according to Matthew* (New York: de Gruyter, 1991), 67.
14. Te Ahukaramu Royal, "Te Ao Mārama: A Research Paradigm in Te Pūmanawa Hauora," in *Proceedings of Te Oru Rangahau: Māori Research and Development Conference* (Palmerston North: School of Māori Studies, 1998), 78–86.

odology offers plenty of scope to examine further the network of relationships in the genealogy of Jesus.

The application of a *whakapapa* methodology points to the humanness of Jesus. The plot of a good novel is usually sketched in the opening chapter, which provides the framework for the remainder of the novel. The location of the genealogy as the opening chapter in Matthew and the identification of Jesus as a descendant of David, who is called the messiah, reveal the plot for the remainder of the gospels. The genealogies establish the structure and intent of the remaining sections of Matthew (and Luke) to reveal how Jesus, a human person who had a human birth, is the messiah, the heir to the throne of David. Any Quest for the historical Jesus must include the significance of his genealogy, as it is so prominent in the opening of the Gospel of Matthew. Once we assess the importance of genealogy we can make further suggestions about its importance for understanding the historical Jesus.

WHAKAPAPA AND LAND

Identity is an important concept for Māori that is tied to the land. The New Zealand Land Wars, more than any other event in the history of the country, strained the identity of the people of the land. Their status changed from being a people who exercised ownership over the land to being a dependent vulnerable landless minority people. When the identity of people is tied to the land, changes in the ownership status of the land will evidently affect the identity of the people, which results in people having to renegotiate their identity and place in the world.

Land in the Māori world is described as *whenua*, which has a double meaning of the physical land and the placenta during pregnancy. One is physically tied to the land as a baby is tied to the mother in the womb. In Māori society a customary practice is to bury the baby's placenta in their tribal lands, tying the child to the land and giving them inalienable birth rights to the land. Other important words associated with land are: *whenua tuku iho* (land inherited), *whenua raupatu* (confiscated land), *whenua tautohetohe* (land disputed), *riro whenua atu, hoki whenua mai* (land confiscated must be returned), and *tangata whenua* (people of the land). The land is a physical entity with a historical element, layered in human customs and is underpinned with a spiritual dimension.

Dr. Joseph Te Rito of Ngāti Kahungunu says that *whakapapa* is more than simple genealogy; it is a framework for understanding one's identity.[15] Māori self-identify as *tangata whenua*, people of the land. This is best expressed in a Māori

15. See: J. Te Rito, "Whakapapa: A Framework for Understanding Identity," *MAI Review* 2

proverb: *ko au te whenua, ko te whenua ko au* "I am the land, the land is me." There is no distinction between land and people; the person is what the land looks like in physical human form. Other *iwi* (people) feel more of an affinity with a river and have a similar expression: *ko au ko te awa, ko te awa ko au* "I am the river, the river is me." The river and people are one; the people is what the river looks like in human form. When we pollute the land, waterways, and oceans, what effect does this have on the identity of people who take their identity from the land and water?

Professor Wiremu Doherty of Ngāi Tūhoe and current CEO of tertiary provider Te Whare Wānanga o Awanuiarangi provides another definition of *whakapapa* based on his interpretation of the word that helps to understand the connection between the land and people. The key concept in the word *whakapapa*, according to Doherty, is *raupapa*,which means to lay out or to map the stages of development.[16] The land is layered in stories that act as a map. Understanding the stories hidden in the landscape can add another dimension to understanding the connection between land and people. There is a wondeful Māori proverb that says *kei raro i te tarutaru ngā tuhi tīpuna* "under the leaves are the footprints of our ancestors." When you walk on the land you are walking on history. This proverb is shown in the narrative of Jesus and the Samaritan woman (John 4:4–42). Echoes of the ancestors' footprints can be seen clearly. The encounter takes place not far from where their common ancestor Jacob had given his son Joseph some land. The well is associated with Jacob and from where he, his family and flocks of animals drank. The Samaritan woman's ancestors also worshiped on the mountain where their encounter takes place. The connections between Jesus and the Samaritan woman is mapped into the landscape through stories.

This mapping of the land can also be applied to the wider story of Jesus by mapping the principal geographic locations of his ministry in sequential order to give greater insight into his ministry and identity. His early life is spent in the Galilean town of Nazareth where he is often identified in the gospels as Jesus of Nazareth (e.g., Mark 10:47; John 1:45). Other geographic features include Galilee as the region where he practiced his itinerant ministry. Jesus is also referred to on occasions as the Galilean. Another geographic feature that he is identified with is the road as he spent much of his time traveling. Postresurrection, Matthew relocates Jesus and his disciple back in Galilee in the commissioning of the disciples.

(2007): Article 2; Te Rito, "Whakapapa and Whenua: An Insider's View," *MAI Review* 3 (2007): Article 1.

16. Wiremu Doherty, "Mātauranga ā Iwi as It Applies to Tūhoe, Te Mātauranga a Tūhoe," in *Enhancing Mātauranga Māori and Global Indigenous Knowledge* (Wellington: New Zealand Qualifications Authority, 2014), 35.

Taking in the physical features of name, place, and space that are associated with Jesus in the gospels can provide further insights into his identity. Indeed, this also complements the argument about the importance of understanding Galilee and homeplace as influential contexts and ideas in the development of the earliest ideas about the historical Jesus.

WOMEN OF THE LAND IN THE GENEALOGY OF JESUS

As the Old Testament story unfolds, what emerges is a land-locked theology where the struggles over land take precedence. Walter Brueggemann says that land is a central, if not the central theme of biblical faith. Biblical faith is a pursuit of historical belonging that includes a sense of destiny derived from such belonging.[17] Brueggemann goes on to suggest that the theme of land might be a way of organizing biblical theology. This, of course, provides a major system of theological thought inherited and assumed by the historical Jesus. And, moreover, if you place land at the center of Jesus's genealogy, what new insights would this provide to understanding the historical Jesus?

As a symbol, land demonstrates an intimate link between a person and their environment. The Quest is to understand Jesus Christ in his historical context and his natural environment. Hans Conzelmann claimed that the land and its features provide christological facts that are not often noticed. Typical locations in the canonical gospels include mountains, lakes, the plain, a desert, and the Jordan River, which are used in particular ways to highlight the christological significance of Jesus.[18] These poetics of land demand that geography, topology, and the aesthetic relationship between people and the land be taken into serious consideration when forming an opinion of who Jesus Christ is and his significance. But we should also take seriously that these ideas are based on ideas that predated the gospel writers.

Understanding the Jesus of history means understanding the Jesus of a particular land. Jesus was a descendant of illustrious ancestors who were promised a particular piece of land. In biblical and contemporary modern-day Israel, land is an emotive and a contested subject. In the Old Testament, the Israelites take possession of a land promised to them, but the land in question belonged to another people. After the Israelites take possession of the land, they defend it fiercely and at times lose control of the land. Jesus belonged to this land, identified with the

---

17. Walter Brueggemann, *The Land: Place as Gift, Promise and Challenge in Biblical Faith* (Philadelphia: Fortress, 1977), 3.

18. Hans Conzelmann, *The Theology of St. Luke* (London: Faber and Faber, 1960), 70–71.

Israelite tradition and actively practiced Judaism, the religion of his people which contains the seeds of Christianity.[19]

Like land in the context of Aotearoa New Zealand, land in the Old Testament is a contested commodity. Land brings with it the memory of trauma between Māori and European settlers and between Israelites and Canaanites in the biblical context. The story of land in the Old Testament moves from the original declaration by God in the Genesis creation stories that "it is good" and brings forth life. As the story progresses land becomes a struggle between different groups of people over sovereignty of the land. The right of possession, occupation of the land, and survival in the land become central issues for Israelites and Canaanites, Māori and Pākehā. Land and the memory associated with the land are contested.

Whenever we conceptualize land we are engaging in a social construct; we are expressing our values and our theology of land and its associated concepts of ownership. According to Geoffrey Lilburne, a theology of the land must include the wisdom of indigenous people.[20] The Canaanite people are the indigenous people of the land of Canaan and the Old Testament shows interest in this land. As the story progresses, the Canaanites become dispossessed of the land and disenfranchised as a people. The presence of Canaanite women in the genealogy of Jesus sees a disenfranchised people become visible again. It is for good reason that whenever Native American scholar Robert Allen Warrior reads the Bible, he reads the text through Canaanite eyes and argues that "the Canaanites should be at the centre of Christian theological reflection and political action."[21] The experiences of Native Americans, Māori, and First Nations Australians mirror that of the Canaanites and have much to teach theology in relation to faith and indigenous peoples.

The visibility of Canaanites in the gospel texts is significant for four reasons. First, the inclusion of the encounter between a (Canaanite) Syrophoenician woman and Jesus cannot be ignored (Matt 15:21–28; Mark 7:24–30). Second, at some stage Jesus must address his own identity as a descendant of Canaanite people. Third, Jesus must realign his field of mission to include the Canaanite people. Fourth and most critically, as an advocate of justice and reconciliation, Jesus must address the suffering and oppression of Canaanite people. These particular issues are quite critical

19. W. D. Davis, *The Gospel and the Land: Early Christian and Jewish Territorial Doctrine* (Berkeley: University of California Press, 1974), 366.

20. Geoffrey Lilburne, *A Sense of Place: A Christian Theology of the Land* (Nashville: Abingdon, 1989), 92.

21. Robert Allen Warrior, "Canaanites, Cowboys, and Indians: Deliverance, Conquest, and Liberation Theology Today," in *Native and Christian, Indigenous Voices on Religious Identity in the United States and Canada*, ed. James Treat (New York: Routledge, 1996), 100.

in light of the Israeli-Palestinian conflict today and other areas of the world where land, identity, belonging, and ownership are in conflict. The inclusion of Canaanite women in the genealogy of Jesus becomes a voice of justice and peace. But it is also an ancient issue, and assessing Jesus in relation to the Canaanite claims is present in the gospels (at least Matthew's) and therefore it must at least have potentially been an issue in the pre-gospel understandings of Jesus or the historical Jesus himself.

Land does not exist in a vacuum; it has a history to it that involves interaction with people. Sacred places are identified; shrines, monuments, and altars are built that signify some activity that the people have experienced in that particular place. The gospels present another layer in the history of the land with their focus on the presence and activity of Jesus Christ. In an article written in *Heartlands*, Dean Graetz reflects on Aboriginal Australian land practices and beliefs, saying that the land itself is active, having its own being and its own memory.[22] He goes on to quote an Aboriginal proverb: "we have forgotten but the land never forgets." This multilayered understanding of the land and the living world may not have been so alien to first-century apocalpytic thinking either (Rom 8:19–23).

We can develop such ideas about the land in relation to the role of women. Critical exegesis of biblical texts confronts the reader of the text with the question: what is the reader's role in the narrative? When the reader engages with the question, he or she enters into the text from their own unique situation, thereby bringing the narrative to life and uncovering parts of the story that may have been relegated either to the margins or even to the dark underside of history. Māori have a self-descriptive two-word phrase *tangata whenua* "people of the land." These two words allow me to enter into the text as *tangata whenua*, exploring a whole world of indigeneity that has been previously overlooked and ignored. An example of this in the text is the indigeneity of three of the women in the genealogy of Jesus and how this opens up a whole new hermeneutical world of indigeneity.

The words "people of the land" are mentioned in the narative of Sarah's death when the Canaanites arrive to pay their respects. Discussions take place concerning identity, status, land to bury Sarah, and ownership of land. Abraham acknowledges the Canaanite leaders as the "people of the land" not once but twice and even bows in their presence. In another narrative, Rebecca, daughter-in-law of Abraham, refers to the Hittite women as "women of the land." Tamar, Ruth, and Rahab are decendants of Canaanite women of the land who marry into the Abraham line. Their inclusion in the genealogy of Jesus as his ancestresses means that they should be viewed first and foremost as women of the land. This adds a further dimension to the indigeneity of Jesus as a descendant of women of the land.

22. Lilburne, *Sense of Place*, 34.

Where references to indigenous peoples are utilized, this inevitably has political connotations as indigenous people the world over have suffered the fate of imperialism and colonization. In this inhumane process the identity of the indigenes is reworked and reshaped by the colonizer to fit their propaganda. Where narratives of indigenous people have survived, there is an element of resistance and renegotiation of their identity in the narrative. This is a common thread in the inclusion of the women in Jesus's genealogy; they become sites of indigenous struggle in a world not of their making but constructed by someone else.

The inclusion of Tamar, Rahab, and Ruth (an Aramean, Canaanite, and Moabite respectively) along with the naming of Uriah (a Canaanite) in the genealogy of Jesus makes the genealogy a site of struggle over the identity and indigeneity of Jesus as distinct from his racial or ethnic purity as an Israelite. Matthew shows Jesus to be the descendant of patriarchs and kings. The inclusion of Tamar, Rahab, Ruth, and Uriah recalls the internal struggle within the Israelite nation not to compromise their racial or ethnic purity as the chosen race of God. Their history begins with their foundering ancestor Abraham, who arrives in the land known as Canaan where he bows twice to the Hittites, thus acknowledging them as the "people of the land." The Canaanites acknowledge Abraham as a prince among them, allowing the Abraham family to live peacefully among the Canaanites for four generations as landowners. In spite of that acknowledgment, Abraham's preference is for his son Isaac to marry from within his own extended family. He dispatches one of his servants to find a wife from Abraham's own lands, and he returns with Rebecca, the granddaughter of Abraham's brother Nahor. When Rebecca's son Jacob is of age to marry, Rebecca instructs her husband not to allow their son to marry a woman of the land. Her grandson Judah ignores the family tradition of opposing mixed marriage in order to maintain their racial or ethnic purity. Judah marries a woman of the land and also finds a woman of the land, Tamar, for his son. This introduces the people of the land into the genealogy of Jesus, and this is further extended, deepened, and broadened by Rahab and Ruth.

Successive commentators have argued that the reason for the inclusion of Tamar, Rahab, and Ruth in the genealogy is that they represent irregularities that include being sinners, sexual promiscuity, seductresses, prostitutes, adulteresses who had scandalous relationships with Jewish men, gentiles, or foreigners. This is a selected interpretation of history with many overtones that ignore the indigeneity of the women (and Uriah). These women exist in a world and narratives constructed by men of a culture different from their own.

The narrative of Tamar takes place in the land of Canaan, which is her hereditary land. Her father owns his own house, which shows that he was a person of status. As the narrative develops, Tamar becomes a wife, sister-in-law, daughter-in-law, widow, widowed daughter, prostitute, the woman, the consecrated woman, the condemned, and finally a mother. Tamar is never acknowledged as a woman of the land living in her own land, but instead becomes the other, the outsider. Going from a woman of the land to the other disenfranchises her and severely compromises her rights, privileges, and options. Tamar is *tangata whenua*, a person, a woman of the land with an unacknowledged history and *whakapapa*. This disenfranchisement of women of the land to being the other flows into the narrative of the second woman named Rahab in the genealogy of Jesus.

Rahab is introduced into the biblical story as a prostitute living in the walls of Jericho. The story of Rahab is the story of indigenous people who consistently throughout history have had to fight for their survival using the limited options available to them against more powerful forces who use brutal tactics, including genocide, without conscience to exterminate entire populations and take possession of the land. Rahab is an indigenous Canaanite woman of the land living in her ancestral land that carries the name of her ancestor, Canaan. In the biblical narrative Rahab is a prostitute with no mention of her ethnicity, which signifies that this narrative is shaped and written with a political ideology that recasts indigenous people in a stereotypical negative frame of being a weak, heathen, and pagan people. This is a legacy of colonization and imperialism that dominates, controls, and exploits people and their lands. As an indigenous woman of the land, Rahab, according to information in the text, has her own business and her own house, provides and cares for her family, and has acknowledged status in the community evidenced by the king's officials coming to visit her. In written material indigenous people are recast as the voiceless, spoken for, or the binary other as opposed to the normalized people and world of the text. This is consistent in the narratives of the three women named in the genealogy of Jesus. Both Tamar and Rahab have a pre-Israelite history in the land of their ancestor.

The Moabites were part of the wider Canaanite nation. Interracial marriage with the Moabites was discouraged due to the rules surrounding racial purity. In Māori society, showing your connections to other tribes is important for maintaining peace and prosperity. Many of the genealogies recorded in the Old Testament also show their links to their neighboring nations. Genesis contains the narrative of Moab, the ancestor of the Moabites who was the grandson of Haran, brother of Abraham. There are genealogical links and shared history between Israel and the Moabites.

Whakapapa is more than the recording of names; it also conveys information concerning power structures and relationships in the time of the people who are named. The story of Ruth is a valuable source to examine the power structures that held Ruth in tension with Israelite laws and customs. Indigenous people who have suffered colonization are highly marginalized people who cannot use the normal channels of society to claim their rights. Arriving in Bethlehem, Ruth is acknowledged as a foreigner, a Moabite woman, and at best as the daughter-in-law of Naomi, a constant reminder of her "otherness" that critiques Jewish particularism, racial purity, and interracial marriage.

The issue is, who has legal responsibility for Ruth? One way that indigenous peoples have sought justice is to pitch the law against the law. Ruth responds by pitching the law against the law by holding her late father-in-law's relation to account. The issue of land is central in the story of Ruth. In the marriage transactions her husband has to buy the land that belonged to his late relation Elimelech. In the purchase Boaz also purchases all the property that belonged to Chilion and Mahlon, the late sons of Elimelech. In the transaction Boaz takes legal responsibility for the widows, Naomi and Ruth, in order to maintain the names of their late husbands in the property. Thereafter, Boaz takes Ruth as his wife.

The women of Bethlehem tell the story of Ruth. They talk about her but do not use her name. She is compared to Rachel, Leah, and Tamar who also married into the family and are celebrated as matriarchal figures. Often Ruth is not acknowledged by name but as the Moabite, a Moabite widow, and daughter-in-law. Her role after marriage, defined in relation to Jewish men, is to continue the male lineage. When she produces a son, the women of Bethlehem name him Obed and they acknowledge him not as the son of Ruth but as the son of Naomi, her former mother-in-law. As a Moabite woman, Ruth is also a woman of the land. At no point in the narrative does Ruth deny her identity as a Moabite. She became an Israelite by choice, thus accepting the God and people of her mother-in-law. Including the name of Ruth in the genealogy of Jesus stresses the need for an inclusive attitude toward those who are descendants of the people of the land.

Conclusion

Robert Allen Warrior, a First Nations theologian, says that the task is to move the Canaanites to the center of Christian theological reflection and political action.[23] The women in the genealogy of Jesus are the ignored voice of the people of the land, perhaps even of the land itself. Keeping the indigeneity of the women at the center of the genealogy ensures that the struggles of indigenous people worldwide become the hereditary mission of justice for the followers of Jesus yesterday, today, and tomorrow. To ignore their position in the genealogy of Jesus is to condemn the voices of indigenous people to silence and invisibility. Indigeneity is an important

---

23. Warrior, "Canaanites, Cowboys, and Indians," 93–104.

factor for the inclusion of Tamar, Rahab, Ruth, and Uriah in the genealogy of Jesus. Their inclusion makes the genealogy of Jesus a site of struggle for the indigenous voice of the "people of the land" to be heard. And what has been shown by such theologians should also apply to the first-century world of Jesus and the gospels. All these issues were likewise part of the national story inherited by Jesus and his fellow Jews and, clearly, genealogies were deemed important enough to be included in two gospels. Whatever we make of Matthew's genealogy in relation to the historical Jesus, the existence of such a genealogy itself is important. This genealogy is first-century evidence of a crucial medium that encompasses the story of the land and questions of indigeneity that were inherited by Jesus, his family, and his first followers. We can start to see, then, genealogy and the cross-cultural study of genealogy must be taken seriously in the Next Quest for the historical Jesus. Indeed, there is so much more to be written and will be written by indigenous scholars concerning the genealogy of Jesus that is beneficial to understanding the historical Jesus of a certain time, place, land, and environment and with a specific human genealogy.

34

Survival of Popular Movements

Nathan C. Johnson

The Next Quest for the historical Jesus must take greater account of the memory of other popular messianic and prophetic movements in antiquity. Previous scholarship on messianism has rightly attended to literary material from the time of Jesus, including the beliefs, ideologies, and practices enshrined in the Dead Sea Scrolls, the so-called Pseudepigrapha, and the writings of Josephus and Philo. Indeed, scholarship has focused on this literature to such a degree that Paula Fredriksen even quips that some scholars apparently assume that "ancient [Jewish] actors walk[ed] around with both volumes of Charlesworth in their heads."[1] Textual analysis is necessary and important, but overemphasizing its importance has led to a puzzling inattention to other relevant material. While most volumes on the historical Jesus will have some discussion of what "messiah" meant in the ancient world and its attestation in various ancient texts, few examine actual, flesh-and-blood messiah figures from antiquity. This essay will briefly explore why this neglect occurs, and also how inclusion of messianic (and prophetic) movements promises to shift our thinking about the Jesus movement and its remembrance. To give traction to the topic of Jesus and other messiahs and prophets, I will primarily be

---

1. Paula Fredriksen, "*Al Tirah* ('Fear Not!'): Jewish Apocalyptic Eschatology, from Schweitzer to Allison, and After," in *To Recover What Has Been Lost: Essays on Eschatology, Intertextuality, and Reception History in Honor of Dale C. Allison Jr.*, ed. Tucker S. Ferda, Daniel Frayer-Griggs, and Nathan C. Johnson, NovTSup 183 (Leiden: Brill, 2021), 24.

considering a figure that has not received attention even among those scholars who do include social movements in their work on Jesus. Surprisingly, this neglected sect persisted for centuries and held to the deathlessness of their messiah, who was a rough contemporary of Jesus of Nazareth. But first, we move to consider why other messiahs and prophets are often sidelined in Jesus research.

JOSEPHUS AND THE OTHERS

Our primary source for other figures who were likely acclaimed as messiahs is Josephus. However, Josephus is notoriously reticent about calling these figures *christoi*, instead labeling them "deceivers," "charlatans," and "bandits." Since virtually our sole source on these figures does not call them "messiahs," many have excluded them from the discussion of Jesus or, when they do appear, have used them as a revolutionary foil to Jesus's pacifism. In other words, for some the Josephan shoe fits—these were mere "pretenders" and "would-bes." But Matthew Novenson has recently provided a convincing solution to the problem of why Josephus does not deem these figures to be messiahs, namely, that a "well-known Josephan tendency, the translation of Jewish idioms into Greek and Roman ones, is quite sufficient to explain why he does not call the insurgents 'messiahs.' It is not that he fears being perceived as anti-Roman; it is simply that he is carrying out his literary project of cultural translation."[2] For Novenson, Josephus avoids calling these popular leaders "messiahs" because this would be unintelligible to his Roman target audience. One recalls here Suetonius's gaffe saying that the Roman Jews were "continually making disturbances at the instigation of *Chrestus*" (*Claud.* 25). To the Roman mind, "Christ" is a foreign category. Thus, "Josephus is constrained by literary convention, by his own chosen project of cultural translation from a Jewish idiom to a Roman one. He calls the insurgents 'diadem-wearers' for the same reason that he calls the Pharisees 'Stoics': because that is the term by which his audience will understand what he means."[3]

If Novenson is right, as I believe him to be, then the various leaders of Jewish social movements in Josephus are admissible to the conversation on ancient messianism and prophecy and are of further relevance to Jesus research.

These movements span from 4 BCE and the "Robber War" in the power vacuum created by the death of Herod the Great to at least Bar Kokhba's demise in 135 CE. The leaders of these movements can be characterized according to several

---

2. Matthew V. Novenson, *The Grammar of Messianism: An Ancient Jewish Political Idiom and Its Users* (Oxford: Oxford University Press, 2017), 146.

3. Novenson, *Grammar of Messianism*, 148.

different types, as Richard Horsley observes: prophets, messiahs, and bandits, with some overlap between these categories.[4]

THE PROBLEM OF PERSISTENCE

A thorough exploration of these movements is not required here—that has been done elsewhere.[5] Rather, it is the *use* to which these movements are put in Jesus research, when they are mentioned at all, that must be reckoned. When scholars invoke the names "Theudas" or "Athronges" or "Simon bar Kokhba," it is often for the purpose of noting distance rather than proximity between Jesus and them.[6] When they are likened to one another, it is frequently for apologetic purposes: Jesus and the "others" all led popular social movements but, so the logic goes, only one of these movements was "successful." As some have observed, we do not see "Theudasians" or "Anthrongesians" or "Bar Kokhbaites" today, so what was unique about the Jesus movement? Why did it persist while the other movements faltered

4. Richard A. Horsley and John S. Hanson, *Bandits, Prophets, and Messiahs: Popular Movements in the Time of Jesus* (Harrisburg, PA: Trinity Press International, 1999). For instance, in the case of the infamous prophet from Egypt (i.e., the Egyptian, ca. 55 CE), the charismatic leader of the movement "said that he wanted to demonstrate [to his followers] that at his command from the Mount of Olives the walls of Jerusalem would fall, through which he promised to give them entrance into the city" (*A.J.* 20.170) so that he could establish himself as king (*B.J.* 2.261). Thus, the figure acts as both a sign prophet and a figure seeking to be king—the categories are flexible and can be fused together.

5. On the sign prophets, see further P. W. Barnett, "The Jewish Sign Prophets A.D. 40–70: Their Intentions and Origin," *NTS* 27 (1981): 679–97; Rebecca Gray, *Prophetic Figures in Late Second Temple Jewish Palestine: The Evidence from Josephus* (Oxford: Oxford University Press, 1993); Peter Höffken, *Josephus Flavius und das prophetische Erbe Israels*, Lüneburger theologische Beiträge 4 (Berlin: Lit, 2006); Nathan C. Johnson, "Early Jewish Sign Prophets," in *Critical Dictionary of Apocalyptic and Millenarian Movements*, ed. James Crossley and Alastair Lockhart, December 8, 2021, https://www.cdamm.org/articles/early-jewish-sign-prophets. On the messiah and bandit figures, see Morton Smith, "Messiahs: Robbers, Jurists, Prophets, and Magicians," *Proceedings of the American Academy for Jewish Research* 44 (1977): 185–95; Richard A. Horsley, "Popular Messianic Movements around the Time of Jesus," *CBQ* 46 (1984): 471–95; Richard A. Horsley, "'Messianic' Figures and Movements in First-Century Palestine," in *The Messiah: Developments in Earliest Judaism and Christianity*, ed. James H. Charlesworth (Minneapolis: Fortress, 1990), 276–95; Nathan C. Johnson, "Early Jewish Messiahs," in *Critical Dictionary of Apocalyptic and Millenarian Movements*, ed. James Crossley and Alastair Lockhart (forthcoming).

6. E.g., N. T. Wright conducts a thought experiment around the shameful deaths of Simon bar Giora and Simon bar Kokhba in contrast with Jesus's messianic claim: *The Resurrection of the Son of God*, vol. 3 of *Christian Origins and the Question of God* (Minneapolis: Fortress, 2003), 558–59. See also N. T. Wright, *The New Testament and the People of God*, vol. 1 of *Christian Origins and the Question of God* (Minneapolis: Fortress, 1992), 170–81.

and disappeared? The persistence of what later became Christianity finds its apologetic foil in the disappearance of other messianic and prophetic movements.

This is sometimes then rephrased in essentialist terms: what was it about the Jesus movement that allowed it to persist and grow *that was not true of these other movements*?[7] The question is asked in such a way to point out differences between Jesus's program and other movements: something greater than these was purportedly here.

What then is said to be "unique" about the Jesus movement? One approach, going back at least as far as Martin Luther, is to draw a contrast between the "political" aspirations of "Jewish" messianic figures on the one hand, and Jesus's spiritual movement on the other. The Jesus movement was successful, so it is asserted, because the Christian messiah focused on inward spirituality rather than external political aspirations. The Gospel of John's words—"My kingdom is not of this world"—here become programmatic (John 18:36). Luther's troubling invective is characteristic: the Christian messiah would "not rule in a worldly manner, as the mad Kokhbaites, these bloodthirsty Jews, rave." Rather, he would rule the domain of the individual heart as a mild shepherd.[8] Such a supersessionist approach sees Judaism as territorial and nationalistic, whereas the Christianized Jesus movement is universalist, nonterritorial, and so primarily spiritual.[9] Of course, this approach is hard pressed to explain Jesus's near singular focus on Israel and injunction to "go nowhere among the gentiles" (Matt 10:5). But even more significantly, such an approach reinscribes larger conversations, which Novenson has helpfully mapped out and rebutted, about the "political" Jewish messiah and the detached "spiritual" Christian messiah.[10] Overcoming the Jewish-Christian messianic binary, Novenson argues that "Jewish messianism—of which Christian messianism can be thought of as just an extraordinarily well-documented example—always and everywhere involves the interplay of biblical tradition and empirical circumstance. In this crucial respect, there is no difference whatsoever

---

7. N. T. Wright, for example, appeals to the category of "anomaly": "A messianic movement without a physically present Messiah posed something of an anomaly. . . . What was it that made ['early Christians'] launch the claim, scandalous to Jews, incomprehensible to Gentiles, that Jesus was indeed the Messiah?" N. T. Wright, *Jesus and the Victory of God*, vol. 2 of *Christian Origins and the Question of God* (Minneapolis: Fortress, 1996), 487.

8. Luther, "On the Jews and Their Lies," in *The Annotated Luther,* Volume 5: *Christian Life in the World*, ed. Hans Joachim Hillerbrand (Minneapolis: Fortress, 2017), 282.

9. E.g., according to N. T. Wright, Christian messianism "lost its ethnic specificity: the Messiah did not belong only to the Jews. The 'messianic battle' changed its character: the Messiah would not fight a military campaign." *Resurrection of the Son of God*, 562–63.

10. See further Novenson, *Grammar of Messianism*, 187–216.

between the Jewish messiah and the Christian messiah."[11] The Jewish-Christian messiah distinction, Novenson wryly observes, "does not recognize a distinction; it creates one. It inscribes a convenient notional boundary where there is otherwise uncomfortable contested territory."[12] Seeking the "uniqueness" of Christian messianism through the political-spiritual binary has a long, untenable history. And, as the example of Luther hints, it stems from ironically *political* motives— the privileged differentiation of one religious group over and against another.

Beyond the political-spiritual distinction lies a more common endpoint to the search for Christian uniqueness. When one asks "Why are there no Athrongesians and Theudasians today? Why are there still Christians? What made this movement successful?" a one-word answer inevitably comes forth: resurrection. On this reading, the Jesus movement is the only one to claim the resurrection of their leader, thus rolling away the stony obstacle to the movement's persistence and its being deemed a failure.[13] In this response, the belief in the founder's resurrection is the ingredient that unlocks the potential for continuance and flourishing. And only the Jesus movement, it is claimed, had this belief in the deathlessness of its founder.

Except, as we shall see, it wasn't alone. Another parallel movement that has received scant attention in previous quests had similar beliefs and persisted. Before examining this other movement, I will grant three things to those who claim that the persistence of the Jesus movement is unprecedented.

1.   It is true that we lack evidence for the continuance of the messianic social movements described in Josephus. When Athronges, Theudas, Simon of Perea *et alii* died, so too, it would seem, did their movements. Even the so-called fourth philosophy associated with Judas the Galilean, which had the greatest claim to longevity, seems to have dissipated. His movement began in 6 CE and continued with his sons after him decades later. However, their crucifixions could scarcely be deemed a "success," and the movement appears to have morphed into what fueled the First Revolt and then died with it.

2.   It is also true that the popular prophetic movements in Josephus apparently

11. Novenson, *Grammar of Messianism*, 196.

12. Novenson, *Grammar of Messianism*, 216.

13. N. T. Wright notes, "Without the resurrection . . . it is simply inconceivable that anyone would have regarded the Jesus as Messiah, especially if they had not regarded him thus beforehand" (*Jesus and the Victory of God*, 488). E. P. Sanders inquires, "Without the resurrection, would [Jesus's] disciples have endured longer than did John the Baptist's? We can only guess, but I would guess not." *Jesus and Judaism* (Philadelphia: Fortress, 1985), 240.

disappeared with their prophetic leaders (i.e., the Samaritan, Jonathan the Weaver, and others).[14]

3.   It is lastly true that the *Testimonium Flavianum* expresses some astonishment at the fact that "the tribe of the Christians, so named from him, are still not extinct to this day" (*A.J.* 18.64). If this is original and not part of Christian interpolation, then this group was the exception to Josephus's rule of obsolescence following the death or disappearance of the charismatic leader.

If the claim is that the Jesus Movement was successful and persisted because it proclaimed the deathlessness of its messiah, then the popular Jewish movements narrated by Josephus do little to undermine this argument. Josephus's *Testimonium Flavianum* may even admit surprise at the continuance of the Jesus movement.

However, Josephus is not our sole source for popular Jewish movements in the first century. Other movements left traces in history, even if they don't pepper the pages of Josephus's *Jewish Antiquities* or *Jewish War*. One movement that seems to have escaped Josephus's attention—perhaps because it did not fit his narrative of national social decline—merits attention after one final caveat. If you have guessed that the movement discussed in this chapter stems from John the Baptist, I am sorry to disappoint. With John we do have some evidence of the continuance of his movement after his execution.[15] Indeed, with the Mandaeans we witness John's ongoing religious influence from late antiquity to today in Iraq and the Mandaean diaspora.[16] Further, Mark 6 tantalizingly mentions Herod's belief that Jesus was John *redivivus*, with the tetrarch worrying: "The one I beheaded, John, is risen" (6:16). Likewise, a mysterious "they" reports to Herod: "John the Immerser has been raised from the dead, and his powers are thus at work in [Jesus]" (6:14). Much could be and has been said about this passage, but for now it is sufficient

---

14. The sole exception may be "the Egyptian," who was apparently still at large, if Luke is to be trusted, in the 40s (Acts 21:38). But again, this is insufficient evidence of "success" in terms of creating a durable movement.

15. As Joel Marcus argues, "the Baptist movement did not die out just because the Jesus movement had appeared on the scene." *John the Baptist in History and Theology* (Columbia: University of South Carolina Press, 2018), 14. As the Pseudo-Clementine *Recognitions* has it, "some also of the disciples of John, who imagined they were great, separated themselves from the people and proclaimed their master as the Christ [messiah]" (Ps.-Clem. *Rec.* 1.54.8 [trans. Marcus]).

16. See further Charles G. Häberl and James F. McGrath, eds., *The Mandaean Book of John: Critical Edition, Translation, and Commentary* (Berlin: de Gruyter, 2020). I am grateful to Robyn Faith Walsh and James F. McGrath for emphasizing the ongoing importance of the Mandaeans.

to note that resurrection is not tied to the continuance of *John's* movement, but to theories about the success of *Jesus's* miracle-working activity.[17]

Rather, a contemporaneous messianic movement that persisted for centuries and held to the deathlessness of their messiah stems from a different source—the messianic figure variously known as "Dositheus" or "Dusis."[18] This shadowy figure, as we shall see, undercuts the claim to uniqueness in the persistence of the Jesus movement, all the while providing a helpful comparandum in our study of Jesus.

THE NEGLECTED DOSITHEANS

I have just made three claims about Dositheus: he was a rough contemporary of Jesus, his movement persisted after his disappearance, and his followers believed he did not die. We will explore each in turn.

What we know of Dositheus is cobbled together from various patristic and Samaritan sources. Significantly, all are hostile. Thus, what he and his followers actually did and believed is difficult to discern, a bit like reconstructing Jesus on the basis of antagonistic Roman and rabbinic sources or solely from the words of Celsus.[19] Nevertheless, Stanley Isser in the 1970s attempted a mirror reading of these unfriendly accounts and summarized "what Dositheus' supporters were probably saying about him": "Dositheus, (a native Samaritan?) unjustly accused or persecuted by tyranny, taught as a prophet like Moses. He performed miracles and refuted the Samaritan scholars.... His death, like that of Moses, was in a cave; his body was never found, an indication that he had ascended to heaven. Either he never died or he rose immediately from the dead."[20] To this we may add that he was also active in the first century, being linked to the reestablishment of the

17. See, *inter alios*, Adela Yarbro Collins, *Mark: A Commentary*, Hermeneia (Minneapolis: Fortress, 2007), 304; Joel Marcus, *Mark 1–8: A New Translation with Introduction and Commentary*, AB 27 (New York: Doubleday, 2000), 393; Nathan L. Shedd, *A Dangerous Parting: The Beheading of John the Baptist in Early Christian Memory* (Waco, TX: Baylor University Press, 2021), 116–26.

18. Throughout I use the former, Dositheus, unless quoting sources with "Dusis" or "Dustan." On the different names, as well as other figures known by these names, see Stanley Jerome Isser, *The Dositheans: A Samaritan Sect in Late Antiquity* (Leiden: Brill, 1976), 5–111. Isser concludes that "The sects of Dustan and Dusis are similar in belief and practice; and if we were to argue that both bear similarity to Epiphanius' Dositheans, the two might appear to be the same sect (if A=B and B=C, then A=C)" and that "there existed only one primitive Dosithean sect (though it later gave rise to subsects)" (109).

19. See further Chris Keith and Larry W. Hurtado, eds., *Jesus among Friends and Enemies: A Historical and Literary Introduction to Jesus in the Gospels* (Grand Rapids: Baker Academic, 2011).

20. Isser, *Dositheans*, 158. See also Stanley Jerome Isser, "Dositheus, Jesus, and a Moses Are-

cult on Mount Gerizim, and a rough contemporary of Jesus, likely flourishing in the 30s or 40s of the Common Era.[21]

ANOTHER PERSISTENT MESSIANIC MOVEMENT

The second key claim here is that, unlike the oft-repeated apologetic about other messianic movements, Dositheus's movement persisted. Again, the common use to which popular social movements are put in the study of Jesus is to show that they unraveled. To invoke Gamaliel's famous judgment from the Acts of the Apostles, "if [a] plan or undertaking is of human origin, it will fail" (5:38). As early as Acts, the failure of other messianic (Judas the Galilean) and prophetic (Theudas) movements was used to show the superiority of the Jesus movement, which over time flourished. But Dositheus's movement also persisted, and though its origins in first-century Samaria are obscured, there is sufficient evidence to confirm its continuance for centuries. This perseverance is seen in four ways: geographical spread, diversity, longevity, and institutionalization.

Regarding geographical spread, our hostile sources all agree on one particular: that the movement with Dositheus originally began in Samaria.[22] But it did not stay there. Origen evidently had contact with the Dositheans in Palestine and Alexandria in the third century. Eulogius, as reported by Photius (before 858), knows of the existence of the group in sixth-century Alexandria.[23] Subsequent movements are attested in Bashan and the Transjordan with affirmations of its continuance in Alexandria.[24] In short, it was a surprisingly widespread movement in the late antique Mediterranean world.

Second, in addition to geographical spread the movement sparked a number of diverse offshoots. From the vantage point of the fourteenth century, the Samaritan chronicler Abu l-Fath was able to survey the outgrowth of the Dositheans. He reckoned at least seven (and up to nine) distinct groups who claimed Dositheus ("Dusis" in Abu'l-Fath) as their founder: the Ba'unay (with subgroup Ansami), Qila-

---

talugy," in *Christianity, Judaism and Other Greco-Roman Cults, Part 4*, ed. Jacob Neusner (Leiden: Brill, 1975), 188.

21. Isser concludes of the Dosithean sect "that its origin is to be sought in the first half of the first century A.D." (*Dositheans*, 109).

22. Some sources claim he was a rejected and dissatisfied Judean who moved to Samaria to find new dupes, others say he had connections to Egypt, but most affirm him to be of Samaritan origin. Whatever his own ethnonational identity, the sect associated with him began in Samaria and had revivalist connections to Mount Gerazim.

23. Isser, *Dositheans*, 69.

24. Isser, *Dositheans*, 103–4.

tay, the sects of Abiyyah and Dosah, followers of Shalīh (with subgroup Yaṣdaq), Aulianah, and Fasqutay.[25] As Isser summarizes, "Samaritan traditions clearly saw Dositheanism not as monolithic, but as a movement that developed and diversified. Several 'Dosithean' sects emerged, based on sometimes contradictory versions of the teachings of Dositheus."[26] Thus the movement was diverse.

Third, these geographically diverse sects hint at the longevity of the movement. From Hegesippus in the second century to Eulogius in the sixth, we see religious subgroups extending the influence of Dositheus at least five hundred years after his disappearance.[27] Beyond this, we have evidence of Dosithean communities in the ninth century. According to the *Continuatio of the Samaritan Chronicle of Abū l-Fath*, Muslim rebels on the Mediterranean coast of Samaria "plundered and killed, burned villages, looted the synagogues and burned the meeting place of the Dositheans in Arsūf [because] they could not enter into it."[28] As a result, the leader of the Samaritan community Asasabī cut ties with the Dositheans in the 840s: he "pledged the Samaritans on oath in front of Mt Gerizim and made it known that they would not eat with the Dositheans, drink with them, marry them or give [their children] in marriage to them."[29] The Samaritan high priest likewise excommunicated the Dositheans in the time of the caliphate of al-Mutawakkil (847–861 CE): the Samaritans "should not give or take [anything] from them ever and . . . no one should eat with them or drink with them."[30] This

---

25. Abu l-Fath, *Annales Samaritani*, ed. E. Vilmar (Paris: Gotha, 1865). Translation from Isser, *Dositheans*, 80–82. "The sects derive from the followers and writings of Dusis, some in agreement with the original teaching and some opposed to it. Each apparently had its own interpretation of the life of Dusis and his teachings" (103). The list of seven is also found in *Chronicle Adler*.

26. Isser, *Dositheans*, 68.

27. Indeed, the witness of Abu l-Fath in the fourteenth century intimates that "many of the customs of either Dustan or Dusis may have been recent additions (where not attested by Epiphanius), whose milieu was not the first century but the eighth century sectarian activity of eastern medieval Jewry." See Isser, *Dositheans*, 105.

28. Translation from Milka Levy-Rubin, *The Continuatio of the Samaritan Chronicle of Abū l-Fath al-Sāmirī al-Danafī*, Studies in Late Antiquity and Early Islam 10 (Princeton: Darwin, 2002), 69–70.

29. Translation from Levy-Rubin, *Continuatio*, 87. Reinhard Pummer dates this during the rule of Ibrahim al-Mu'taṣim (833–842 CE). See Reinhard Pummer, *The Samaritans: A Profile* (Grand Rapids: Eerdmans, 2016), 123.

30. Indeed, the Dositheans were barred from participating in the Feast of Tabernacles on Mount Gerizim: "The Dositheans were prevented from [joining in] the prayer until they were excluded even from the recitation of the book (i.e., the Torah)." Translation from Levy-Rubin, *Continuatio*, 94. As Pummer summarizes, "What emerges from these narratives is that [the Dositheans] had synagogues, that Muslim rebels attacked them at times of unrest, and that

is the last historical trace left of the Dositheans, but it is noteworthy that the sect persisted at least eight centuries.

Fourth, and building upon the previous point, the Dositheans achieved religiously institutional status. As John Collins notes of the messianic and prophetic millenarian figures of first-century Judaism (Theudas et al.), their movements died and disappeared with these charismatic leaders, failing to coalesce into the institutionalized forms that some other millenarian movements attain.[31] Such, however, was not the case with Dositheus. His movement appears to have achieved what Max Weber called the "routinization [*Veralltäglichung*] of the charisma" of its leader that eventuated in stable religious communities.[32] Epiphanius reports that "the Dositheans differ from them (other Samaritan sects) in many ways: for they admit resurrection, and they have (their own) communities" (*Pan.* 13.9).[33] Significantly, Epiphanius writes in the present tense: they *currently* believe in the resurrection (*anastasin homologousi*); they *have* their own communities in his day (*politeiai par autois eisin*). Much later, according to Abu l-Fatḥ, the seven to nine Dosithean sects apparently formed religiously regulated settings and "instituted their own synagogues and priests."[34] Further, we recall that what the Muslim rebels looted and burned in the ninth century were "the synagogues and . . . the meeting place of the Dositheans."[35] The presence of Dosithean synagogues and meeting places approximately eight hundred years after the disappearance of the founding figure is remarkable. Likewise, the Dositheans had their own scriptures, a further mark of institutional stability. Dositheus himself was rumored to have written or

---

the mainstream Samaritans distanced themselves from them in no uncertain terms." Pummer, *Samaritans*, 123.

31. John J. Collins, "Millenarianism in Ancient Judaism," in *Critical Dictionary of Apocalyptic and Millenarian Movements*, ed. James Crossley and Alastair Lockhart, January 15, 2021, https://www.cdamm.org/articles/ancient-judaism.

32. "A religious community arises in connection with a prophetic movement as a result of routinization, i.e., as a result of the process whereby either the prophet himself or his disciples secure the permanence of his preaching and the congregations' distribution of grace, hence insuring the economic existence of the enterprise." Max Weber, *The Sociology of Religion*, trans. Ephraim Fischoff (Boston: Beacon, 1963), 60–61.

33. Translation from Isser, "Dositheus, Jesus, and a Moses Aretalogy," 168. Cf. Frank Williams, trans., *The Panarion of Epiphanius of Salamis: Book I (Sects 1–46)*, 2nd ed. (Leiden: Brill, 2009), 38–39.

34. Isser, *Dositheans*, 76. One priest was named "Zar'ah" (76). Pummer comments similarly: "it is certain that the Samaritans in antiquity were not a monolithic community but comprised of several factions. The Dositheans were one of them, but there probably were also subgroups that differed in various practices from each other." Pummer, *Samaritans*, 127.

35. Pummer, *Samaritans*, 122. This occurred during the caliphates of Muhammad al-Amin (809–813 CE) and again Ibrahim al-Mu'taṣim (833–842 CE).

edited several books, and he also apparently redacted the Samaritan Pentateuch for his followers, creating a durable institutional touchpoint for future sects.[36]

Adding these four points together, we are in a position to see that Dositheus, a messianic and prophetic figure, was a formidable and durable presence on the late antique Samaritan religious scene. He was a divisive figure, who was both rejected and accepted. His movement coalesced into authoritative texts, routinized worship, and stable religious institutions. Though his memory, as we shall see next, was maligned in our only sources, his adherents were numerous, widespread, diverse, institutionalizing, and enduring.

The final fate of the sect is a mystery; we do not know how long it persisted after persecution in Arsūf and excommunication in Samaria. As Reinhard Pummer notes, the fourteenth-century Samaritan chronicles speak of the sect only "in the past tense."[37] When nineteenth-century Western scholars asked native Samaritans about the existence of the sect, in a letter dated January 1, 1811 the Samaritans of Nablus answered that "they are mentioned in their old books, but presently not one person of this sect is found among them," finally closing the chapter on the Dositheans.[38]

Memory and Apologetics

Having dealt with their geographical spread, diversity, and longevity, the number of Dositheans still must be discussed. Our purpose here is not, of course, to concern ourselves with the actual number of Dositheans in the diverse eras and areas of Mediterranean antiquity—that is unknowable. Rather, it is to discern how such numerical reckoning is being used.

In memory studies, it is often noted how the past is conceived of in terms of the present, even as the past puts pressure on and constrains present renditions. In the case of the Dositheans, Christian apologists used the movement as a foil for the numerical superiority of Christianity as a way to discount and discredit this rival sect.

For instance, Origen notes how the Dositheans constituted only a pathetic following: "The Dositheans also did not flourish even in their early days; at the present

---

36. In one legend, one of his followers is called upon to read the Haftarah in a nonsectarian synagogue. After he slips in the wording of Dositheus's version, he is dragged outside and stoned to death. The episode, though legendary, points to the tension around divergent versions of the Pentateuch and its deployment in sectarian Samaritan controversies and also intimates the stable institutional form the sect was taking.

37. Pummer, *Samaritans*, 127.

38. Pummer, *Samaritans*, 127.

time their numbers have become exceedingly few, so that their whole number is said not to amount to thirty" (*Cels.* 6.11).[39] Origen leverages this reckoning in his counterargument against Celsus, who accuses Christians of proclaiming Jesus even though there were numerous others who said they were the messiah or Son of God. As Celsus sarcastically asks, "Are they to throw dice in order to divine where they may turn, and whom they are to follow?" (*Cels.* 6.11). If many claim to be the messiah, why follow Jesus? Origen's counterargument is that these movements all "proved to be of no significance" (6.11). Only the Jesus movement endured, and hence only its founder is the true messiah. Elsewhere he informs Celsus of Gamaliel's aforementioned dictum that if a movement "be of human origin, it will fail" (1.57). Thus, for Origen, Dositheus was a failure because his movement had all but vanished.

However, as we have witnessed, there is plenty of evidence to counter Origen's counterargument—the Dositheans did not disappear. Rather it was his contemporary circumstances that constrained and guided Origen's telling of the past and present, not simple historical reportage. In fact, we can see that Origen is not even accurate in reporting a number short of thirty. In the Pseudo-Clementine literature, Dositheus is described as one of the disciples of John the Baptist, and takes over his movement of "Day Baptists" (*hēmerobaptistai*) after the death of the prophet.[40] Significantly for our purposes, the *Clementina* describe John's sect as having "thirty" inner members, one for each phase of the moon: "there was a certain John, a hemerobaptist, . . . the forerunner of our Lord Jesus; and as the Lord had twelve apostles, bearing the number of the twelve months of the sun, so also John had thirty chief men, according to the monthly reckoning of the moon."[41] The association of Dositheus and John (and Simon Magus!) is undoubtedly spurious, but it shows how Origen retrieves the number thirty to demonstrate the inferiority and invalidity of the Dositheans.[42] As Isser notes, "the numerical superiority of the

---

39. Translations from Henry Chadwick, *Origen: Contra Celsum* (Cambridge: Cambridge University Press, 1980).

40. All this occurs while Simon Magus is away studying magic in Egypt. Upon his return, he retakes charge of the movement (Dositheus attempts to strike him with a staff, but it passes through Simon). Dositheus orders the other members to obey Simon, and dies shortly thereafter (Ps.-Clem. *Hom.* 2.22–24; Ps.-Clem. *Rec.* 2.8–12). On the issue of John and the "Day Baptists," see further Edmondo Lupieri, "John the Gnostic: The Figure of the Baptist in Origen and Heterodox Gnosticism," StPatr 17 (1989): 322–27; Marcus, *John the Baptist*, 15–18, 139–41. For a brief guide on John in Josephus and the Gospels, see Nathan Shedd, "John the Baptist," *Critical Dictionary of Apocalyptic and Millenarian Movements*, ed. James Crossley and Alastair Lockhart, January 15, 2021, www.cdamm.org/articles/john-the-baptist.

41. Ps.-Clem. *Hom.* 2.23; translation modified from *ANF* 8:233; cf. Ps.-Clem. *Rec.* 2.8 (*ANF* 8:99).

42. Significantly, Origen claims Simon Magus's following also dwindled to thirty, showing another possible connection to the *Clementina*; so Marcel Borret's note in SC 147:206 n. 1.

'catholic' Christians was beginning to be an important point in their propaganda against other sects."[43] If another group had a messianic prophetic founder and a persistent following, how else could one counter their validity than by casting doubt on their success? Thus Origen—whether purposely or not—grossly underestimates the number of the Dositheans to show the comparative validity and superiority of Jesus as the true Son of God. The apologetic needs of the present shape how the past—and in this case even the relative present—are represented, even as the past puts some pressure on this present formulation in the form of the number thirty.[44]

Contesting the Nondeath of a Messiah

In addition to the issues of the persistence of the sect, the third key element in comparing the Dositheans and the Jesus movement involves the ultimate fate of their heroes. For both, the whereabouts of their bodies is heavily contested. A recital of the different accounts for the empty tomb and the polemics surrounding it is unnecessary here. Rather, it is significant to note that there was a similar battle over the death and body of Dositheus. On the one hand, his followers purportedly held to the nondeath of their messiah. Origen notes:

> From the Samaritans one Dositheus arose and asserted that he was the prophesied messiah, there are Dositheans to this day who originate from him; they both preserve books by Dositheus and certain myths about him to the effect that he did not taste death, but is still alive somewhere. (*Comm. Jo.* 18.27.162 on John 4:25, my translation)

So, where was Dositheus according to his followers? We don't know. Nor do we know if they thought he simply never died, as Origen intimates, or that he died and was resurrected. The latter appears to be the case in Abu l-Fatḥ: "They said that the dead would rise soon, or else Dusis was not a prophet, because he died (prematurely) at the age of twenty-eight years."[45] Here, his followers believe in

---

43. Isser, *Dositheans*, 30.

44. Indeed, in this case it is uncertain if "thirty" is truly from the past—it is rather a past memory in the *Clementina* that Origen retrieves for apologetic purposes. Origen's use of "thirty" is thus a good example of the "continuity" perspective in social memory theory—the past and the present together shape how the past is retrieved and conceived. See Chris Keith, "Social Memory Theory and Gospels Research: The First Decade (Part One)," *EC* 6.3 (2015): 363.

45. Isser, *Dositheans*, 79.

resurrection *because of* his death.[46] Indeed, one sect (the Ba'unay) purportedly believed that "people will be resurrected because Dusis had died a disgraceful death."[47] And elsewhere it is said that burial practices testified to their belief in the resurrection: "When one of them died, they girdled him with a sturdy belt, and put a staff in his hand and sandals on his feet, for they said, 'When we arise from the tomb, we will arise in haste.' And it is said that they believed that as soon as a dead man is buried, he arises from the grave and goes to Paradise."[48] As always, we lack a friendly account of Dositheus's fate, so it is uncertain what his followers truly believed, though there may have been disagreement even among them.

The later "hostile" accounts naturally deny that he did not die or was resurrected. Indeed, in some tellings, not only did he in fact die, but he did so due to his own incompetence. As one strand of the tradition has it, Dositheus retreated to a cave to fast and seek wisdom. But he fasted too much, not wisely but "foolishly" starving himself to death. So, while his followers claimed he did not taste death, his detractors claimed that he died because he did not taste *anything*.

As with Jesus, death was a key issue for the claim to messianic status. We have already noted how Origen (among others) attests that Dositheus's followers believed him to be the "prophet like Moses." According to Deut 18, this prophet was to be followed unquestioningly. By contrast, false prophets must be rejected, and they can be recognized in two ways: their predictions prove false or they "die." We do not know if Dositheus made any prophetic predictions à la the Jewish sign prophets in Josephus. But we do know that his demise was hotly contested, and that a false claimant to Moses's prophetic office would "die." Indeed, the Samaritan Pentateuch inserts and repeats the "prophet like Moses" material from Deut 18 in the lead-up to the giving of the Torah on Sinai in Exod 20. This serves to seal the "prophet like Moses" as the divinely authorized giver and interpreter of the law—something that Dositheus apparently claimed to be in his redaction of the Pentateuch, and which his detractors naturally denied. Thus, accounts of Dositheus's death serve as a point of contestation for his messianic status—he died shamefully and thus cannot be the messiah—a clear parallel with the polemics over Jesus's death.

Lastly, as with Jesus, Dositheus's body is another locus of polemics. As I've alluded to, apparently Dositheus's body was never found. For some of his followers, this signified that he was elsewhere—perhaps alive somewhere waiting

46. Isser, "Dositheus, Jesus, and a Moses Aretalogy," 188.
47. Translation of Abu l-Fath, *Chronicle*, from Isser, *Dositheans*, 80.
48. Translation of Abu l-Fath, *Chronicle*, from Isser, *Dositheans*, 79. The garb imitates Moses's Passover regulations for eating in haste (Exod 12:11).

to join the faithful at the opportune time, or perhaps translated to heaven à la Moses in the Samaritan tradition.⁴⁹ Others apparently believed he did die but was immediately raised to heaven, thus justifying their belief in the resurrection. To echo Paul, the logic appears to have been: "If the dead are not raised, how then is Dositheus risen?"

Disputing accounts of the body's disappearance, later detractors of the sect argue that his followers actually did find his body, or more accurately his corpse. In one telling, they came upon it rotting in a cave, "with worms creeping out and a cloud of flies settled on it."⁵⁰ Another claims, differently, that "dogs devoured his corpse," hinting that perhaps it was missing after all.⁵¹ Whatever the details, these differing accounts show that Dositheus's body was a site of contestation in the memory of his followers and detractors. As Nathan Shedd notes, quoting Doug Henry: "In commemorative activity, the symbolic frameworks of bodily violence are subject to contestation, 'as those with competing claims over meaning try to inscribe their own version of reality onto individuals.'"⁵² As with Jesus, contestation over the whereabouts of the body and its state—as a rotting and consumed corpse? A risen human body? A heavenly astral body?—is at the heart of disagreements between different religious groups.

CONCLUSION

I began by urging that the Next Quest for the historical Jesus take seriously flesh-and-blood messianic and prophetic figures in the ancient world. Far from an accoutrement to literary sources, these actors and the movements they spurred help us better understand the Jesus movement and are also fields of inquiry in their own right. I highlighted a lesser known figure and his durable following to undercut a number of recurring claims in former Quests. When asking why the Jesus movement survived and others did not, past scholarship has often looked to the category of uniqueness⁵³—the unique persistence of the Jesus movement

49. Isser discusses this tradition in the *Memar Marqah*, though notably Moses does eventually die after visiting heaven. Isser, "Dositheus, Jesus, and a Moses Aretalogy," 179.

50. Epiphanius, *Pan.* 2.13. Translation from Isser, *Dositheans*, 41. Cf. Williams, *Panarion*, 39.

51. Translation of Abu l-Fatḥ, *Chronicle* from Isser, *Dositheans*, 78.

52. Shedd, *Dangerous Parting*, 53. Quoting Doug Henry, "Violence and the Body: Somatic Expressions of Trauma and Vulnerability during War," *Medical Anthropology Quarterly* 20 (2006): 385.

53. In addition to providing counterexamples, another approach to problematizing the history of Christian difference is to dispense with the category of uniqueness altogether, à la Jonathan Z. Smith: "The 'unique' is an attribute that must be disposed of, especially when linked

as explained by the resurrection.[54] But the question itself is incorrectly framed. Other movements did survive.[55] And one of these movements spread and gained institutional status for at least nine centuries and also held to the deathlessness of its founding figure. So, while we may not have "Theudasians" or "Athrongesians" or "Bar Kokhbaites," and we do have "Christians," we should not forget that for nearly a millennium there were also "Dositheans."

Thus, if Christianity is not unique in this regard, perhaps the better question than "why did Christianity uniquely persist?" is what is to be gained by setting the Jesus movement alongside other popular Jewish and Samaritan social movements in antiquity? The answer for the Next Quest is, I hope, quite a lot.

---

to some notion of incomparable value, if progress in thinking through the enterprise of comparison is to be made." Jonathan Z. Smith, *Drudgery Divine: On the Comparison of Early Christianities and the Religions of Late Antiquity* (Chicago: University of Chicago Press, 1990), 36.

54. Similarly, E. P. Sanders on Jesus among other messiah and prophet figures: "I worry a bit about the word 'unique.' Others also thought that they spoke for God and were appointed directly by him to lead his people into the kingdom." Sanders, *Jesus and Judaism*, 240.

55. In addition to the Dositheans, one notes the Mandaeans, the Manichaeans (thanks to Paula Fredriksen for this insight), and even the messiah movement of Shukr Kuḥayl II, who claimed to be the risen embodiment of Shukr Kuḥayl I. See further Bat-Zion Eraqi Klorman, "The Messiah Shukr Kuḥayl II (1868–75) and His Tithe (*Ma'aśer*): Ideology and Practice as a Means to Hasten Redemption," in *Essential Papers on Messianic Movements and Personalities in Jewish History*, ed. Marc Saperstein (New York: New York University Press, 1992), 457–69.

Bibliography

Abbasi, Rushain. "Islam and the Invention of Religion: A Study of Medieval Muslim Discourses on *Dīn*." *Studia Islamica* 116 (2021): 1–106.

Achtemeier, Paul J. "Omne Verbum Sonat: The New Testament and the Oral Environment of Late Western Antiquity." *JBL* 109 (1990): 3–27.

Achtemeier, Paul J., Joel B. Green, and Marianne Meye Thompson, eds. *Introducing the New Testament: Its Literature and Theology.* 2nd ed. Grand Rapids: Eerdmans, 2001.

Adams, Edward. *The Earliest Christian Meeting Places: Almost Exclusively Houses?* Rev. ed. LNTS 450. London: Bloomsbury, 2016.

Adams, Samuel L. *Social and Economic Life in Second Temple Judea.* Louisville: Westminster John Knox, 2014.

Adler, Yonatan. "The Decline of Jewish Ritual Purity Observance in Roman Palestina: An Archaeological Perspective on Chronology and Historical Context." Pages 269–84 in *Expressions of Cult in the Southern Levant in the Greco-Roman Period: Manifestations in Text and Material Culture.* Edited by Oren Tal and Ze'ev Weiss. Contextualizing the Sacred 6. Turnhout: Brepols, 2017.

———. *The Origins of Judaism: An Archaeological-Historical Reappraisal.* AYBRL. New Haven: Yale University Press, 2022.

Adorno, Theodor. *Aesthetic Theory.* Edited by Gretel Adorno and Rolf Tiedemann. Translated by Robert Hullot-Kentor. Theory and History of Literature 88. Minneapolis: University of Minnesota Press, 1997.

Agamben, Giorgio. *Profanations*. Translated by Jeff Fort. New York: Zone, 2015.

Ainsworth, Peter, and Godfried Croenen, eds. *The Online Froissart: Version 1.5*. Sheffield: HRIOnline, 2013. http://www.dhi.ac.uk/onlinefroissart.

Alapuro, Risto. "Revisiting Microhistory from the Perspective of Comparisons." Pages 133–54 in *Historical Knowledge: In Quest of Theory, Method, and Evidence*. Edited by Susanna Fellman and Marjatta Rahikainen. Newcastle-upon-Tyne: Cambridge Scholars, 2011.

Albertz, Martin. "Zur Formgeschichte der Auferstehungsberichte." *ZAW* 21 (1922): 259–69.

Alexander, Jeffrey. "Toward a Cultural Theory of Trauma." Pages 307–10 in *The Collective Memory Reader*. Edited by Jeffrey K. Olick, Vered Vinitzky-Seroussi, and Daniel Levy. Oxford: Oxford University Press, 2011.

Alexander, Jennifer. "Matthew's Parable of the Eunuchs." PhD diss., Vanderbilt University, 2021.

Alexander, Loveday. *The Preface to Luke's Gospel: Literary Convention and Social Context in Luke 1.1–4 and Acts 1.1*. SNTSMS 78. Cambridge: Cambridge University Press, 1993.

Allison, Dale C., Jr. *Constructing Jesus: Memory, Imagination, and History*. Grand Rapids: Baker Academic, 2010.

———. *The End of the Ages Has Come: An Early Interpretation of the Passion and Resurrection of Jesus*. Minneapolis: Fortress, 1985.

———. "It Don't Come Easy: A History of Disillusionment." Pages 186–99 in *Jesus, Criteria, and the Demise of Authenticity*. Edited by Chris Keith and Anthony Le Donne. London: T&T Clark, 2012.

———. *Jesus of Nazareth: Millenarian Prophet*. Minneapolis: Fortress, 1998.

———. "Q 12:51–53 and Mark 9:11–13 and the Messianic Woes." Pages 289–310 in *Authenticating the Words of Jesus*. Edited by Bruce D. Chilton and Craig A. Evans. Leiden: Brill, 2002.

———. *Resurrecting Jesus: The Earliest Christian Tradition and Its Interpreters*. London: T&T Clark, 2005.

———. *The Resurrection of Jesus: Apologetics, Polemics, History*. London: T&T Clark, 2021.

Alston, Richard. *Soldier and Society in Roman Egypt: A Social History*. London: Routledge, 1995.

Amit, David, and Yonatan Adler. "The Observance of Ritual Purity after 70 C. E.: A Reevaluation of the Evidence in Light of Recent Archaeological Discoveries." Pages 121–43 in *"Follow the Wise": Studies in Jewish History and Culture in Honor of Lee I. Levine*. Edited by Zeev Weiss, Oded Irshai, Jodi Magness, and Seth Schwartz. Winona Lake, IN: Eisenbrauns, 2010.

Andersen, Marc, Uffe Schjoedt, Kristoffer L. Nielbo, and Jesper Sørensen. "Mystical Experience in the Lab." *MTSR* 26.3 (2014): 217–45.

Anderson, H. "4 Maccabees: A New Translation and Introduction." Pages 531–64 in *Expansions of the "Old Testament" and Legends, Wisdom and Philosophical Literature, Prayers, Psalms and Odes, Fragments of Lost Judeo-Hellenistic Works.* Vol. 2 of *The Old Testament Pseudepigrapha.* Edited by James H. Charlesworth. New Haven: Yale University Press, 1983.

Andrade, Nathanael J. *Syrian Identity in the Greco-Roman World.* Oxford: Oxford University Press, 2013.

Angel, Andrew R. *Intimate Jesus: The Sexuality of God Incarnate.* London: SPCK, 2017.

Anonymous. *Calendar of the Patent Rolls: Edward III, Vol. XII, 1361–1364.* London: Hereford Times Limited, 1912.

———. *A List of Some of the Grand Blasphemers and Blasphemies.* London: Ibbitson, 1654.

———. *Strange and Terrible Newes from Cambridge.* London: Brooks, 1659.

———. *A True Narrative of the Examination, Tryall, and Sufferings of James Nayler.* London: s.n., 1657.

———. *The World Is Turned Upside Down.* London: s.n., 1646.

Appleby, Joyce, Lynn Hunt, and Margaret Jacob. *Telling the Truth about History.* New York: Norton, 1994.

Ariel, Donald T. "Identifying the Mints, Minters and Meanings of the First Jewish Revolt Coins." Pages 373–97 in *The Jewish Revolt against Rome: Interdisciplinary Perspectives.* Edited by Mladen Popović. JSJSup 154. Leiden: Brill, 2011.

Arnal, William E. "The Collection and Synthesis of 'Tradition' and the Second-Century Invention of Christianity." *MTSR* 23 (2011): 193–215.

———. "Gendered Couplets in Q and Legal Formulations: From the Rhetoric to Social History." *JBL* 116.1 (1997): 75–94.

———. "The Gospel of Mark as Reflection on Exile and Identity." Pages 57–67 in *Introducing Religion: Essays in Honor of Jonathan Z. Smith.* Edited by Willi Braun and Russell T. McCutcheon. London: Equinox, 2008.

———. *Jesus and the Village Scribes: Galilean Conflicts and the Setting of Q.* Minneapolis: Fortress, 2001.

———. "Major Episodes in the Biography of Jesus: An Assessment of the Historicity of the Narrative Tradition." *TJT* 13 (1997): 201–26.

———. *The Symbolic Jesus: Historical Scholarship, Judaism and the Construction of Contemporary Identity.* London: Equinox, 2005.

———. "The Trouble with Q." *Foundations & Facets Forum* 2.1 (2013): 7–77.

———. "What Branches Grow Out of This Stony Rubbish? Christian Origins and the Study of Religion." *SR* 39.4 (2010): 549–72.

Asad, Talal. *Genealogies of Religion: Discipline and Reasons of Power in Christianity and Islam.* Baltimore: Johns Hopkins University Press, 1993.

Ash, Rhiannon, Judith Mossman, and Francis B. Titchener, eds. *Fame and Infamy: Essays for Christopher Pelling on Characterization in Greek and Roman Biography.* Oxford: Oxford University Press, 2015.

Ashworth, William. "The Iguanodon 'Horn,' 1840." *Paper Dinosaurs 1824–1969.* Linda Hall Library, January 2009. https://dino.lindahall.org/man1840a.shtml.

Assmann, Aleida. "To Remember or to Forget: Which Way Out of a Shared History of Violence?" Pages 53–71 in *Memory and Political Change.* Edited by Aleida Assmann and Linda Shortt. New York: Palgrave Macmillan, 2012.

Aston, Margaret. "Corpus Christi and Corpus Regni: Heresy and the Peasants' Revolt." *Past and Present* 143 (1994): 3–47.

Atkins, J. D. *The Doubt of the Apostles and the Resurrection Faith of the Early Church: The Post-Resurrection Appearance Stories of the Gospels in Ancient Reception and Modern Debate.* WUNT 495. Tübingen: Mohr Siebeck, 2019.

Aune, David. *The New Testament in Its Literary Environment.* Philadelphia: Westminster, 1987.

Avalos, Hector. *Healthcare and the Rise of Christianity.* Peabody, MA: Hendrickson, 1999.

Aviam, Mordechai. "People, Land, Economy, and Belief in First-Century Galilee and Its Origins: A Comprehensive Archaeological Synthesis." Pages 5–48 in *The Galilean Economy in the Time of Jesus.* Edited by David A. Fiensy and Ralph K. Hawkins. Atlanta: SBL Press, 2013.

Avrin, Leila. *Scribes, Script, and Books: The Book Arts from Antiquity to the Renaissance.* New York: American Library Association, 1991.

Bacon, Francis. *Of the Proficience and Advancement of Learning.* London: Tomes, 1605.

Bakhos, Carol. "Orality and Writing." Pages 482–99 in *The Oxford Handbook of Jewish Daily Life in Roman Palestine.* Edited by Catherine Hezser. Oxford: Oxford University Press, 2010.

Ballentine, Debra Scoggins. *The Conflict Myth and the Biblical Tradition.* Oxford: Oxford University Press, 2015.

Bammel, Ernst. "The Revolution Theory from Reimarus to Brandon." Pages 11–68 in *Jesus and the Politics of His Day.* Edited by C. F. D. Moule and Ernst Bammel. Cambridge: Cambridge University Press, 1983.

Barber, Michael Patrick. "Did Jesus Anticipate Suffering a Violent Death? The Implications of Memory Research and Dale Allison's Methodology." *JSHJ* 18.3 (2020): 191–219.

———. *The Historical Jesus and the Temple: Memory, Methodology, and the Gospel of Matthew.* Cambridge: Cambridge University Press, 2023.

Barclay, John M. G., and Benjamin G. White, eds. *The New Testament in Comparison: Validity, Method, and Purpose in Comparing Traditions*. LNTS 600. London: T&T Clark, 2020.

Barnett, P. W. "The Jewish Sign Prophets A.D. 40–70: Their Intentions and Origin." *NTS* 27 (1981): 679–97.

Barrett, C. K. *Jesus and the Gospel Tradition*. Philadelphia: Fortress, 1968.

Barrett, Justin L. "Cognitive Constraints on Hindu Concepts of the Divine." *JSSR* 37 (1998): 608–19.

———. "Theological Correctness: Cognitive Constraint and the Study of Religion." *MTSR* 11 (1999): 325–39.

Barrett, Justin L., and Frank C. Keil. "Conceptualizing a Nonnatural Entity: Anthropomorphism in God Concepts." *Cognitive Psychology* 31.3 (1996): 219–47.

Bauckham, Richard J. "The Bethany Family in John 11–12: History or Fiction?" Pages 185–202 in *Aspects of Historicity in the Fourth Gospel*. Vol. 2 of *John, Jesus, and History*. Edited by Paul N. Anderson, Felix Just, and Tom Thatcher. Atlanta: SBL Press, 2009.

———. "Gospels as Micro-History & Perspectival History." Lecture. Southern Baptist Theological Seminary, Louisville, Kentucky, February 16, 2011. https://repository.sbts.edu/handle/10392/2744.

———. *Jesus and the Eyewitnesses: The Gospels as Eyewitness Testimony*. 2nd ed. Grand Rapids: Eerdmans, 2017.

———, ed. *Magdala of Galilee: A Jewish City in the Hellenistic and Roman Period*. Waco, TX: Baylor University Press, 2018.

Bauckham, Richard J., and Stefano de Luca. "Magdala as We Now Know It." *Early Christianity* 6 (2015): 91–118.

Baudrillard, Jean. *Simulacra and Simulation*. Translated by Sheila Faria Glaser. Ann Arbor: University of Michigan Press, 1994.

Bazzana, Giovanni B. "*Basileia* and Debt Relief: The Forgiveness of Debts in the Lord's Prayer in the Light of Documentary Papyri." *CBQ* 73 (2011): 511–25.

———. "Galilean Village Scribes as the Author of the Sayings Gospel Q." Pages 133–48 in *Q in Context II: Social Setting and Archaeological Background of the Sayings Source*. Edited by Markus Tiwald. BBB 173. Bonn: Bonn University Press, 2015.

———. *Having the Spirit of Christ: Spirit Possession and Exorcism in the Early Christ Groups*. New Haven: Yale University Press, 2020.

———. *Kingdom of Bureaucracy: The Political Theology of Village Scribes in the Sayings Gospel Q: The Ideological Project in the Sayings Gospel Q*. BETL 274. Leuven: Peeters, 2015.

———. "'You Will Write Two Booklets and Send One to Clement and One to Grapte': Formal Features, Circulation, and Social Function of Ancient Apocalyptic Literature." Pages 43–70 in *Scribal Practices and Social Structures Among Jesus Adherents: Essays in Honour of John S. Kloppenborg*. Edited by William E. Arnal, Richard S. Ascough, Robert A. Derrenbacker, and Philip A. Harland. BETL 285. Leuven: Peeters, 2016.

Beard, J. R. Preface to *Voices of the Church in Reply to Dr D. F. Strauss, Author of "Das Leben Jesu."* Edited by J. R. Beard. London: Simpkin, Marshall, and Co., 1845.

Becker, Eve-Marie, Helen K. Bond, and Catrin Williams, eds. *John's Transformation of Mark*. London: T&T Clark, 2020.

Becker, Eve-Marie, Troels Engberg-Pedersen, and Mogens Müller, eds. *Mark and Paul: Comparative Essays Part II, For and Against Pauline Influence on Mark*. BZNW 199. Berlin: de Gruyter, 2014.

Becker, Jürgen. *Jesus of Nazareth*. Translated by James E. Crouch. Berlin: de Gruyter, 1998.

Beckwith, Roger T. *Calendar and Chronology, Jewish and Christian: Biblical, Intertestamental and Patristic Studies*. Leiden: Brill, 2001.

BeDuhn, Jason. "Augustine, Faustus, and the Jews." Pages 295–316 in *Manichaeism and Early Christianity*. Edited by Johannes van Oort. NHMS 99. Leiden: Brill, 2021.

———. "Biblical Antitheses, Adda, and the *Acts of Archelaus*." Pages 131–47 in *Frontiers of Faith: The Christian Encounter with Manichaeism in the Acta of Archelaus*. Edited by Jason BeDuhn and Paul Mirecki. NHMS 6. Leiden: Brill, 2007.

Belchem, John. "Republicanism, Popular Constitutionalism and the Radical Platform in Early Nineteenth-Century England." *Social History* 6 (1981): 1–32.

Bell, Erin. "Eighteenth-Century Quakerism and the Rehabilitation of James Nayler, Seventeenth-Century Radical." *JEH* 59.3 (2008): 426–46.

Bell, Idris, and T. C. Skeat. *Fragments of an Unknown Gospel and Other Early Christian Papyri*. Oxford: Oxford University Press, 1935.

Belser, Julia Watts. "Reading Talmudic Bodies: Disability, Narrative, and the Gaze in Rabbinic Judaism." Pages 5–27 in *Disability in Judaism, Christianity and Islam: Sacred Texts, Historical Traditions and Social Analysis*. Edited by Darla Schumm and Michael Stolzfus. New York: Palgrave Macmillan, 2011.

Belser, Julia Watts, and Lennart Lehmhaus. "Disability in Rabbinic Jewish Sources." Pages 434–52 in *Disability in Antiquity*. Edited by Christian Laes. New York: Routledge, 2017.

Ben-Arieh, Yehoshua. *The Rediscovery of the Holy Land in the Nineteenth Century*. Jerusalem: Magnes, 1979.

Benfatto, Miriam. "The Work of Isaac Ben Abraham Troki (16th Century): On the Place of the Sefer Hizzuq Emunah in the Quest for the Historical Jesus." *JSHJ* 17.1–2 (2019): 102–20.

Bengtsson, Per Å. *Passover in the Targum Pseudo-Jonathan Genesis: The Connection of*

Early Biblical Events with Passover in Targum Pseudo-Jonathan in a Synagogue Setting. Stockholm: Almqvist & Wiksell, 2001.

Benjamin, Walter. "Little History of Photography." Pages 2:508–30 in *Selected Writings*.

———. "On Some Motifs in Baudelaire." Pages 4:313–55 in *Selected Writings*.

———. "The Religious Position of the New Youth." Pages 168–70 in *Walter Benjamin: Early Writings, 1910–1917*. Edited by Howard Eiland. Translated by Howard Eiland et al. Cambridge: Belknap, 2011.

———. *Selected Writings*. Edited by Michael W. Jennings et al. Translated by Rodney Livingston et al. 4 vols. Cambridge: Belknap, 1991–1999.

———. "The Work of Art in the Age of Technological Reproducibility (Third Version)." Pages 4:251–83 in *Selected Writings*.

Ben-Yehuda, Nachman. *Masada Myth: Collective Memory and Mythmaking in Israel*. Madison: University of Wisconsin Press, 1995.

Berger, Klaus. *Die Auferstehung des Propheten und die Erhöhung des Menschensohnes: Traditionsgeschichtliche Untersuchungen zur Deutung des Geschickes Jesu in frühchristlichen Texten*. SUNT 13. Göttingen: Vandenhoeck & Ruprecht, 1976.

Bermejo-Rubio, Fernando. "The Fiction of the 'Three Quests': An Argument for Dismantling a Dubious Historical Paradigm." *JSHJ* 7 (2009): 211–53.

———. "Theses on the Nature of Leben-Jesu-Forschung: A Proposal for a Paradigm Shift in Understanding the Quest." *JSHJ* 17 (2009): 1–34.

Bernabé, Alberto. "La toile de Pénélope: A-t-il existé un mythe orphique sur Dionysos et les Titans?" *RHR* 219 (2002): 401–33.

Bernhardt, Christoph, and Elsa Vonau. "Zwischen Fordismus und Sozialreform: Rationalisierungsstrategien im deutschen und französischen Wohnungsbau 1900–1933." *Zeithistorische Forschungen* 6.2 (2009): 230–54.

Bernier, Jonathan. *Aposynagōgos and the Historical Jesus in John: Rethinking the Historicity of the Johannine Expulsion Passages*. BIS 122. Leiden: Brill, 2013.

Besse, Joseph. *A Collection of the Sufferings of the People Called Quakers*. 2 vols. London: Hinde, 1753.

Betcher, Sharon. "Disability and the Terror of the Miracle Tradition." Pages 161–81 in *Miracles Revisited: New Testament Miracle Stories and Their Concepts of Reality*. Edited by Stefan Alkier and Annette Weissenrieder. Berlin: de Gruyter, 2013.

Binder, Donald D. *Into the Temple Courts: The Place of the Synagogues in the Second Temple Period*. SBLDS 169. Atlanta: Society of Biblical Literature, 1999.

Birch, Jonathan C. P. *Jesus in an Age of Enlightenment: Radical Gospels from Thomas Hobbes to Thomas Jefferson*. New York: Palgrave Macmillan, 2019.

———. "Revolutionary Contexts for the Quest: Jesus in the Rhetoric and Methods of Early Modern Intellectual History." *JSHJ* 17.1–2 (2019): 35–80.

———. "The Road to Reimarus: Origins of the Quest for the Historical Jesus." Pages

19–47 in *Holy Land as Homeland? Models for Constructing the Historic Landscapes of Jesus.* Edited by Keith Whitelam. Sheffield: Phoenix, 2011.

Bittle, William G. *James Nayler: 1618–1660: The Quaker Indicted by Parliament.* York: Sessions, 1987.

Black, C. Clifton. *Mark's Gospel: History, Theology, Interpretation.* Grand Rapids: Eerdmans, 2023.

Black, Matthew. "The Use of Rhetorical Terminology in Papias on Mark and Matthew." *JSNT* 37 (1989): 31–41.

Black, Ngatapa, producer. *Wairua.* Series 1, episode 4. Aired August 29, 2010, on Māori Television. https://www.maoritelevision.com/shows/wairua/S01E004/wairua -series-1-episode-4.

Blanton, Ward. *Displacing Christian Origins: Philosophy, Secularity, and the New Testament.* Chicago: Chicago University Press, 2007.

Blickenstaff, Marianne. *"While the Bridegroom Is with Them": Marriage, Family, Gender and Violence in the Gospel of Matthew.* LNTS 292. London: T&T Clark, 2005.

Blome, Richard. *The Fanatick History.* London: Sims, 1660.

Bock, Darrell. *Studying the Historical Jesus: A Guide to Sources and Methods.* Grand Rapids: Baker, 2002.

Bockmuehl, Markus N. A. "Resurrection." Pages 102–18 in *The Cambridge Companion to Jesus.* Edited by Markus Bockmuehl. Cambridge: Cambridge University Press, 2001.

Boddy, Janice P. "Spirit Possession Revisited: Beyond Instrumentality." *Annual Review of Anthropology* 23 (1994): 407–34.

———. *Wombs and Alien Spirits: Women, Men, and the Zār Cult in Northern Sudan.* New Directions in Anthropological Writing. Madison: University of Wisconsin Press, 1989.

Boer, Roland, and Christina Petterson. "Hand of the Master: Of Slaveholders and the Slave-Relation." Pages 139–52 in *Class Struggle in the New Testament.* Edited by Robert J. Myles. Lanham, MD: Lexington/Fortress Academic, 2019.

———. *Time of Troubles: A New Economic Framework for Early Christianity.* Minneapolis: Fortress, 2017.

Bohak, Gideon. *Ancient Jewish Magic: A History.* Cambridge: Cambridge University Press, 2008.

Bolt, Peter. *Jesus' Defeat of Death: Persuading Mark's Early Readers.* SNTSMS 125. Cambridge: Cambridge University Press, 2003.

Bond, Helen K. "Dating the Death of Jesus: Memory and the Religious Imagination." *NTS* 59 (2013): 461–75.

———. *The First Biography of Jesus: Genre and Meaning in Mark's Gospel.* Grand Rapids: Eerdmans, 2020.

———. *The Historical Jesus: A Guide for the Perplexed.* London: Bloomsbury, 2012.

Bonz, Marianne. *The Past as Legacy: Luke-Acts and Ancient Epic*. Minneapolis: Fortress, 2000.

Borg, Marcus. *Conflict, Holiness, and Politics in the Teachings of Jesus*. Harrisburg, PA: Trinity Press International, 1998.

Borgen, Peder. *Bread from Heaven: An Exegetical Study of the Concept of Manna in the Gospel of John and the Writings of Philo*. Leiden: Brill, 1965.

———. *The Gospel of John: More Light from Philo, Paul and Archaeology: The Scriptures, Tradition, Exposition, Settings, Meaning*. NTSup 154. Leiden: Brill, 2014.

Bornkamm, Günther. "Die Bedeutung des historischen Jesus für den Glauben." Pages 57–71 in *Die Frage nach dem historischen Jesus* by Ferdinand Hahn, Wenzel Lohff, and Günther Bornkamm. 2nd ed. Göttingen: Vandenhoeck & Ruprecht, 1966.

———. *Jesus of Nazareth*. Translated by Irene and Fraser McLuskey with James M. Robinson. New York: Harper & Row, 1960.

———. "The Significance of the Historical Jesus for Faith." Pages 69–86 in *What Can We Know about Jesus?* by Ferdinand Hahn, Wenzel Lohff, and Günther Bornkamm. Translated by Grover Foley. Edinburgh: Saint Andrew Press, 1969.

Botha, Pieter J. J. "Historical Jesus Research and Relevance in South Africa." *HvTSt* 65.1 (2009): art. 154.

Boulakia, Jean David C. "Lead in the Roman World." *American Journal of Archaeology* 76.2 (1972): 139–44.

Bourdieu, Pierre. *The Field of Cultural Production: Essays on Art and Literature*. Edited by Randal Johnson. New York: Columbia University Press, 1993.

———. *The Logic of Practice*. Translated by Richard Nice. Stanford: Stanford University Press, 1990.

———. *Masculine Domination*. Translated by Richard Nice. Stanford: Stanford University Press, 1998.

———. *Outline of a Theory of Practice*. Translated by Richard Nice. Cambridge: Cambridge University Press, 1977.

Bovon, François. *Luke 1: A Commentary on the Gospel of Luke 1:1–9:50*. Hermeneia. Minneapolis: Fortress, 2002.

Bowen, Lloyd. "The Seeds and Fruits of Revolution: The Erbery Family and Religious Radicalism in Seventeenth-Century Glamorgan." *Welsh History Review* 25.3 (2011): 346–73.

Bowersock, Glen Warren. *Fiction as History: Nero to Julian*. Berkeley: University of California Press, 1994.

Boyd, Barbara. "Virgil's Camilla and the Traditions of Catalogue and Ecphrasis (Aeneid 7.803–17)." *AJP* 113.2 (1992): 213–34.

Boyer, Pascal. "Religious Thought and Behavior as By-Products of Brain Function." *Trends in Cognitive Sciences* 7.3 (2003): 119–24.

Bradbury, Richard. "Frederick Douglass and the Chartists." Pages 169–86 in *Liberating Sojourn: Frederick Douglass and Transnational Reform*. Edited by Alan Rice and Martin Crawford. Athens: University of Georgia Press, 1999.

Brand, Mattias. *Religion and the Everyday Life of Manichaeans in Kellis: Beyond Light and Darkness*. NHMS 102. Leiden: Brill, 2022.

Brandon, S. G. F. "Jesus and the Zealots: The Aftermath." *BJRL* 54.1 (1971): 47–66.

———. *Jesus and the Zealots: A Study of the Political Factor in Primitive Christianity*. New York: Scribner's Sons, 1967.

Braudy, Leo. *The Frenzy of the Renown: Fame and Its History*. New York: Vintage, 1980.

Braun, Willi. *Jesus and Addiction to Origins: Toward an Anthropocentric Study of Religion*. Edited by Russell McCutcheon. Sheffield: Equinox, 2020.

———. "The Past as Simulacrum in the Canonical Narratives of Christian Origins." *R&T* 8 (2001): 213–28.

Bremmer, Jan. "Ghosts, Resurrections, and Empty Tombs in the Gospels, the Greek Novel, and the Second Sophistic." Pages 233–52 in *The Gospels and Their Stories in Anthropological Perspective*. Edited by Joseph Verheyden and John S. Kloppenborg. WUNT 409. Tübingen: Mohr Siebeck, 2018.

Breuilly, John. "Nationalism and the History of Ideas." Pages 187–223 in *Proceedings of the British Academy* 105. Oxford: Oxford University Press, 2000.

Brierley, Benjamin. *Home Memories and Recollections of a Life*. Manchester: Heywood & Son, 1886.

Broadhead, Edwin K. *Jewish Ways of Following Jesus: Redrawing the Religious Map of Antiquity*. Tübingen: Mohr Siebeck, 2011.

Brockman, James R. *Romero: A Life*. Maryknoll, NY: Orbis, 1989.

Brooke, George J. *Reading the Dead Sea Scrolls: Essays in Method*. EJL 39. Atlanta: Society of Biblical Literature, 2013.

Brown, Colin. *A History of the Quests for the Historical Jesus*. Edited by Craig A. Evans. 2 vols. Grand Rapids: Zondervan Academic, 2022.

Brown, Raymond Edward. *The Community of the Beloved Disciple*. New York: Paulist Press, 1979.

———. *The Critical Meaning of the Bible: How a Modern Reading of the Bible Challenges Christians, the Church, and the Churches*. New York: Paulist, 1981.

———. *The Gospel according to John*. 2 vols. AB 29–29A. New York: Doubleday, 1966.

Brubaker, Rogers. *Ethnicity without Groups*. Cambridge: Harvard University Press, 2004.

Brueggemann, Walter. *The Land: Place as Gift, Promise and Challenge in Biblical Faith*. Philadelphia: Fortress, 1977.

Buckley-Zistel, Susanne. "Between Pragmatism, Coercion and Fear: Chosen Amnesia after the Rwandan Genocide." Pages 72–88 in *Memory and Political Change*. Edited by Aleida Assmann and Linda Shortt. New York: Palgrave Macmillan, 2012.

————. "Remembering to Forget: Chosen Amnesia as a Strategy for Local Co-Existence in Post-Genocide Rwanda." *Africa* 76 (2006): 131–50.

Buck-Morss, Susan. "Aesthetics and Anaesthetics: Walter Benjamin's Artwork Essay Reconsidered." *October* 62 (1992): 3–41.

Bucur, Bogdan. *Angelomorphic Pneumatology: Clement of Alexandria and Other Early Christian Witnesses.* VCSup 95. Leiden: Brill, 2009.

Buell, Denise K. "The Microbes and Pneuma That Therefore I Am." Pages 63–87 in *Divinanimality: Animal Theory, Creaturely Theology.* Edited by Stephen D. Moore. New York: Fordham University Press, 2014.

Bulbulia, Joseph. "Are There Any Religions? An Evolutionary Exploration." *MTSR* 17.2 (2005): 71–100.

Bultmann, Rudolf. *The Gospel of John: A Commentary.* Translated by George R. Beasley-Murray, Rupert W. N. Hoare, and John K. Riches. Philadelphia: Westminster, 1971.

————. *History of the Synoptic Tradition.* Translated by John Marsh. 2nd rev. ed. Oxford: Blackwell, 1968.

————. *Jesus and the Word.* Translated by Louise Pettibone Smith and Erminie Huntress. New York: Scribner's Sons, 1934.

————. *New Testament and Mythology and Other Basic Writings.* Translated and edited Schubert M. Ogden. Philadelphia: Fortress, 1984.

————. "The Primitive Christian Kerygma and the Historical Jesus." Pages 15–42 in *The Historical Jesus and the Kerygmatic Christ: Essays on the New Quest of the Historical Jesus.* Edited and translated by Carl E. Braaten and Roy A. Harrisville. New York: Abingdon, 1964.

Burns, David. *The Life and Death of the Radical Historical Jesus.* Oxford: Oxford University Press, 2013.

Burridge, Richard A. *What Are the Gospels? A Comparison with Graeco-Roman Biography.* Cambridge: Cambridge University Press, 1992.

Burrough, Edward. *A Declaration of the Present Sufferings of Above 140. Persons of the People of God (Who Are Now in Prison,) Called Quakers.* London: Simmons, 1659.

Burrus, Virginia. "The Gospel of Luke and the Acts of the Apostles." Pages 133–55 in *A Postcolonial Commentary on the New Testament Writings.* Edited by Fernando F. Segovia and R. S. Sugirtharajah. New York: T&T Clark, 2007.

Byrne, Ryan, and Bernadette McNary-Zak, eds. *Resurrecting the Brother of Jesus.* Chapel Hill: University of North Carolina Press, 2009.

Byrskog, Samuel. "A Century with the *Sitz im Leben*: From Form-Critical Setting to Gospel Community and Beyond." *ZNW* 98 (2007): 1–27.

————. *Jesus the Only Teacher: Didactic Authority and Transmission in Ancient Israel, Ancient Judaism and the Matthean Community.* ConBNT 24. Stockholm: Almqvist & Wiksell, 1994.

———. *Story as History—History as Story: The Gospel Tradition in the Context of Ancient Oral History*. WUNT 123. Tübingen: Mohr Siebeck, 2000.

Cadbury, Henry Joel, ed. *George Fox's Book of Miracles*. Philadelphia: Friends General Conference, 2000.

———. *The Peril of Modernizing Jesus*. New York: Macmillan, 1937.

Calafat, Guillaume, and Romain Bertrand. "La microhistoire globale: affaire(s) à suivre." *Annales. Histoire, Sciences Sociales* 73.1 (2018): 3–18.

Callahan, Allen Dwight. "God's Only Begotten Thug." Pages 39–52 in *Bitter the Chastening Rod: Africana Biblical Interpretation after Stony the Road We Trod in the Age of Black Lives Matter, SayHerName and MeToo*. Edited by Mitzi J. Smith, Angela Parker, and Ericka Dunbar. Lanham, MD: Lexington/Fortress Academic, 2022.

Callon, Callie. *Reading Bodies: Physiognomy as a Strategy of Persuasion in Early Christian Discourse*. London: T&T Clark, 2019.

———. "The Unibrow That Never Was: Paul's Appearance in the Acts of Paul and Thecla." Pages 99–116 in *Dressing Jews and Christians in Antiquity*. Edited by Alicia Batten, Carly Daniel-Hughes, and Kristi Upson-Saia. Surrey: Ashgate, 2014.

Calpino, Teresa J. "The Magdalene of Contemporary Biblical Scholarship." Pages 297–317 in *Mary Magdalene from the New Testament to the New Age and Beyond*. Edited by Edmondo F. Lupieri. TBN 24. Leiden: Brill, 2019.

Campany, Robert Ford. "'Religious' as a Category: A Comparative Case Study." *Numen* 65 (2018): 333–76.

Carey, Holly J. *Jesus' Cry from the Cross: Towards a First-Century Understanding of the Intertextual Relationship between Psalm 22 and the Narrative of Mark's Gospel*. LNTS 398. London: T&T Clark, 2009.

Carlyle, Thomas. *On Heroes, Hero-Worship, and the Heroic in History*. Edited by Carl Niemeyer. 1841. Repr., Lincoln. University of Nebraska Press, 1966.

———. *The Life of John Sterling*. London: Chapman and Hall, 1851.

Carnley, Peter. *Resurrection in Retrospect: A Critical Examination of the Theology of N. T. Wright*. Eugene, OR: Cascade, 2019.

Carter, Warren. "'The Blind, Lame, and Paralyzed' (John 5:3): John's Gospel, Disability Studies, and Postcolonial Perspectives." Pages 129–50 in *Disability Studies and Biblical Literature*. Edited by Candida Moss and Jeremy Schipper. New York: Palgrave Macmillan, 2011.

———. "Cross-Gendered Romans and Mark's Jesus: Legion Enters the Pigs (Mark 5:1–20)." *JBL* 133 (2015): 139–55.

———. *Matthew and the Margins: A Socio-Political and Religious Reading*. Maryknoll, NY: Orbis, 2000.

Casey, Maurice. *Jesus of Nazareth: An Independent Historian's Account of His Life and Teaching*. London: Bloomsbury, 2010.

———. *The Solution to the 'Son of Man' Problem*. LNTS 343. London: T&T Clark, 2007.

Catchpole, David. "The Fearful Silence of the Women at the Tomb: A Study in Markan Theology." *Journal of Theology for Southern Africa* 18 (1977): 3–10.

Cavallo, Gugliermo. "Discorsi sul libro." Pages 613–47 in *La produzione e la circolazione del testo. 3. I Greci e Roma*. Vol. 1 of *Lo Spazio letterario della Grecia antica*. Edited by Giuseppe Cambiano, Luciano Canfora, and Diego Lanza. Rome: Salerno, 1994.

CenSAMM. "Apocalypticism." In *Critical Dictionary of Apocalyptic and Millenarian Movements*. Edited by James Crossley and Alastair Lockhart. January 15, 2021. www.cdamm.org/articles/apocalypticism.

———. "Millenarianism." In *Critical Dictionary of Apocalyptic and Millenarian Movements*. Edited by James Crossley and Alastair Lockhart. January 15, 2021. www.cdamm.org/articles/millenarianism.

Chadwick, Owen. *The Victorian Church: Part I, 1829–1859*. Oxford: Oxford University Press, 1966.

Chance, J. Bradley. "Fiction in Ancient Biography: An Approach to a Sensitive Issue in Gospel Interpretation." *PRSt* 18 (1991): 125–42.

Chancey, Mark. *The Myth of Gentile Galilee*. SNTSMS 118. Cambridge: Cambridge University Press, 2002.

Charles, Ronald. *The Silencing of Slaves in Early Jewish and Christian Texts*. London: Routledge, 2020.

Charlesworth, James H., ed. *The Historical Jesus: An Essential Guide*. Nashville: Abingdon, 2008.

———. *Jesus and Archaeology*. Grand Rapids: Eerdmans, 2006.

Charlton, William H. "Building a Model of the Kinneret Boat." *INA Quarterly* 19.3 (1992): 3–7.

Chase, Malcolm. *Chartism: A New History*. Manchester: Manchester University Press, 2007.

———. "Evans, Thomas (b. 1763, d. in or before 1831)." In *Oxford Dictionary of National Biography*. January 3, 2008. https://www.oxforddnb.com/display/10.1093/ref:odnb/9780198614128.001.0001/odnb-9780198614128-e-47140.

———. *"The People's Farm": English Radical Agrarianism, 1775–1840*. Oxford: Clarendon, 1988.

Chiai, Gian Franco. "Good Emperors, Bad Emperors: The Fiction of Physiognomic Representation in Suetonius' *De vita Caesarum* and Common Sense Physiognomics." Pages 203–26 in *Visualizing the Invisible with the Human Body: Physiognomy and Ekphrasis in the Ancient World*. Edited by J. Johnson and A. Stavru. Berlin: de Gruyter, 2019.

Chilesa, Bagele. *Indigenous Research Methodologies*. 2nd ed. Los Angeles: SAGE, 2020.

Chilton, Bruce. *Rabbi Jesus: An Intimate Biography*. New York: Doubleday, 2000.

Chiu, Angeline. *Ovid's Women of the Year: Narratives of Roman Identity in the Fasti*. Ann Arbor: University of Michigan Press, 2016.

Cilliers, Louise, and François Retie. "Dream Healing in Asclepieia in the Mediterranean." Pages 69–92 in *Dreams, Healing, and Medicine in Greece: From Antiquity to the Present*. Edited by Steven M. Oberhelman. Farnham: Ashgate, 2013.

Claeys, Gregory. "Thomas Evans and the Development of Spenceanism, 1815–16." *Bulletin of the Society for the Study of Labour History* 48 (1984): 24–30.

Clark-Soles, Jaime. "John, First–Third John, and Revelation." Pages 333–78 in *The Bible and Disability: A Commentary*. Edited by S. J. Melcher, M. C. Parsons, and A. Yong. Waco, TX: Baylor University Press, 2017.

Clarke, Simon. "What in F---'s Name is Fordism?" Pages 13–30 in *Fordism and Flexibility: Division and Change*. Edited by Nigel Gilbert, Roger Burrows, and Anna Pollert. London: Macmillan, 1994.

Clarysse, Willy. "Nemesion Son of Zolios." In *Leuven Homepage of Papyrus Collections*. ArchID 149. 2012. https://www.trismegistos.org/arch/archives/pdf/149.pdf.

Clay, Diskin. "Lucian of Samosata: Four Philosophical Lives (Nigrinus, Demonax, Peregrinus, Alexander Pseudomantis)." *ANRW* 36.5:3406–50.

Clermont-Ganneau, Charles. *Archaeological Researches in Palestine during the Years 1873–1874*. London: Palestine Exploration Fund, 1896.

———. "Discovery of a Tablet from Herod's Temple." *Palestinian Exploration Fund Quarterly Statement* 3.3 (1871): 132–34.

Clifford, Jo. *The Gospel according to Jesus, Queen of Heaven*. Edited by James T. Harding, Annabel Cooper, and Duncan Lockerbie. 10th anniversary ed. Edinburgh: Stewed Rhubarb, 2019.

Coakley, Sarah, ed. *Religion and the Body*. Cambridge: Cambridge University Press, 1997.

Cobb, John B. "The Post-Bultmannian Trend." *JBR* 30.1 (1962): 3–11.

Cobb, L. Stephanie. *Dying to Be Men: Gender and Language in Early Christian Martyr Texts*. New York: Columbia University Press, 2008.

Coffey, John. *Persecution and Toleration in Protestant England, 1558–1689*. Harlow: Longman, 2000.

Cohen, Daniel. "The Gerasene Demoniac: A Jewish Approach to Liberation before 70 CE." Pages 152–73 in *Judaism, Jewish Identities and the Gospel Tradition: Essays in Honour of Maurice Casey*. Edited by James G. Crossley. London: Equinox, 2010.

Cohen, Emma. *The Mind Possessed: The Cognition of Spirit Possession in an Afro-Brazilian Religious Tradition*. Oxford: Oxford University Press, 2007.

Cohen, Shaye J. D. "Crossing the Boundary and Becoming a Jew." *HTR* 82.1 (1989): 13–33.

———. *From the Maccabees to the Mishnah*. 3rd ed. Louisville: Westminster John Knox, 2014.

———. "Judaism without Circumcision and 'Judaism' without 'Circumcision' in Ignatius." *HTR* 95.4 (2002): 395–415.

———. "The Origins of the Matrilineal Principle in Rabbinic Law." *AJSR* 10.1 (1985): 19–53.

———. "'Those Who Say They Are Jews and Are Not': How Do You Know a Jew in Antiquity When You See One?" Pages 1–45 in *The Diasporas in Antiquity*. Edited by Shaye J. D. Cohen and Ernest S. Frerich. BJS 288. Atlanta: Scholars Press, 1993.

———. "Were Pharisees and Rabbis the Leaders of Communal Prayer and Torah Study in Antiquity? The Evidence of the New Testament, Josephus, and the Early Church Fathers." Pages 89–105 in *Evolution of the Synagogue: Problems and Progress*. Edited by Howard Clark Kee and Lynn H. Cohick. Harrisburg, PA: Trinity Press International, 1999.

Cohen, Thomas V. "The Macrohistory of Microhistory." *Journal of Medieval and Early Modern Studies* 47.1 (2017): 53–73.

———. *Roman Tales: A Reader's Guide to the Art of Microhistory.* London: Routledge, 2019.

Cohn, Norman. *The Pursuit of the Millennium.* Rev. ed. Oxford: Oxford University Press, 1970.

Colebrook, Claire. *Gilles Deleuze.* Routledge Critical Thinkers. Abingdon: Routledge, 2002.

Collingwood, R. G. *The Idea of History.* Oxford: Clarendon, 1946.

Collins, Adela Yarbro. "The Apocalyptic Son of Man Sayings." Pages 220–28 in *The Future of Early Christianity*. Edited by Birger A. Pearson. Minneapolis: Fortress, 1991.

———. *Is Mark's Gospel a Life of Jesus? The Question of Genre.* Milwaukee: Marquette University Press, 1992.

———. *Mark: A Commentary.* Hermeneia. Minneapolis: Fortress, 2007.

Collins, John J. *The Apocalyptic Imagination: An Introduction to Jewish Apocalyptic Literature.* 2nd ed. Grand Rapids: Eerdmans, 1998.

———. "Millenarianism in Ancient Judaism." In *Critical Dictionary of Apocalyptic and Millenarian Movements*. Edited by James Crossley and Alastair Lockhart. January 15, 2021. https://www.cdamm.org/articles/ancient-judaism.

Coloe, Mary L. "Gentiles in the Gospel of John: Narrative Possibilities—John 12:12–43." Pages 209–23 in *Attitudes to Gentiles in Ancient Judaism and Early Christianity*. Edited by David C. Sim and James S. McLaren. London: Bloomsbury, 2013.

Colson, F. H. "Τάξει in Papias (The Gospels and Rhetorical Schools)." *JTS* 14 (1912): 62–69.

Concannon, Cavan W. *Profaning Paul.* Class 200: New Studies in Religion. Chicago: University of Chicago Press, 2021.

Cone, James. *Black Theology and Black Power.* Maryknoll, NY: Orbis, 1997.

Connell, R. W., and J. W. Messerschmidt. "Hegemonic Masculinity. Rethinking the Concept." *Gender and Society* 19 (2005): 829–59.

Conway, Colleen. *Behold the Man: Jesus and Greco-Roman Masculinities.* Oxford: Oxford University Press, 2008.

Conzelmann, Hans. *The Theology of St. Luke.* London: Faber and Faber, 1960.

Cook, John Granger. "Resurrection in Paganism and the Question of an Empty Tomb in 1 Corinthians 15." *NTS* 63.1 (2017): 56–75.

Corley, Kathleen E. *Women and the Historical Jesus: Feminist Myths of Christian Origins.* Santa Rosa, CA: Polebridge, 2002.

Cotter, Wendy. "Greco-Roman Apotheosis Traditions and the Resurrection Appearances in Matthew." Pages 127–53 in *The Gospel of Matthew in Current Study.* Edited by David E. Aune. Grand Rapids: Eerdmans, 2001.

———. "Miracle Stories: The God Asclepius, the Pythagorean Philosophers, and the Roman Rulers." Pages 166–78 in *The Historical Jesus in Context.* Edited by Amy-Jill Levine, Dale C. Allison Jr., and John Dominic Crossan. Princeton: Princeton University Press, 2006.

Craffert, Pieter F. *The Life of a Galilean Shaman: Jesus of Nazareth in Anthropological-Historical Perspective.* Eugene, OR: Cascade, 2008.

Crawford, Sidnie White. *Rewriting Scripture in Second Temple Times.* Grand Rapids: Eerdmans, 2008.

———. *Scribes and Scrolls at Qumran.* Grand Rapids: Eerdmans, 2019.

Cribiore, Raffaella. *Gymnastics of the Mind: Greek Education in Hellenistic and Roman Egypt.* Princeton: Princeton University Press, 2001.

Cross, Charles R. *Heavier Than Heaven: A Biography of Kurt Cobain.* New York: Hachette, 2019.

Crosson, Brent J. *Experiments with Power: Obeah and the Remaking of Religion in Trinidad.* Chicago: University of Chicago Press, 2021.

Crossan, John Dominic. *The Historical Jesus: The Life of a Mediterranean Jewish Peasant.* San Francisco: HarperSanFrancisco, 1991.

Crossan, John Dominic, and Jonathan L. Reed. *Excavating Jesus: Beneath the Stones, Behind the Texts.* Rev. ed. San Francisco: HarperSanFrancisco, 2002.

Crossley, James. "Against the Historical Plausibility of the Empty Tomb Story and the Bodily Resurrection of Jesus: A Response to N. T. Wright." *JSHJ* 3.2 (2005): 171–86.

———. "Class Conflict and Galilee at the Time of Jesus." Pages 163–85 in *The Struggle over Class: Socioeconomic Analysis of Ancient Christian Texts.* Edited by G. Anthony Keddie, Michael Flexsenhar III, and Steven J. Friesen. Atlanta: SBL Press, 2021.

———. *The Date of Mark's Gospel: Insight from the Law in Earliest Christianity.* JSNTSup 266. London: T&T Clark, 2004.

————. "The End of Apocalypticism: From Burton Mack's Jesus to North American Liberalism." *JSHJ* 19.2 (2021): 1–20.

————. "Jesus and John Ball: Millenarian Prophets." Pages 51–76 in *"To Recover What Has Been Lost": Essays on Eschatology, Intertextuality, and Reception History in Honor of Dale C. Allison Jr.* Edited by Tucker S. Ferda, Daniel Frayer-Griggs, and Nathan C. Johnson. Leiden: Brill, 2021.

————. *Jesus and the Chaos of History: Redirecting the Life of the Historical Jesus.* Oxford: Oxford University Press, 2015.

————. *Jesus in an Age of Neoliberalism: Quests, Scholarship and Ideology.* New York: Routledge, 2012.

————. *Jesus in an Age of Terror: Scholarly Projects for a New American Century.* London: Routledge, 2008.

————. "The Next Quest for the Historical Jesus." *JSHJ* 19 (2021): 261–64.

————. *Spectres of John Ball: The Peasants' Revolt in English Political History, 1381–2020.* Sheffield: Equinox, 2022.

————. "A 'Very Jewish' Jesus: Perpetuating the Myth of Superiority." *JSHJ* 11.2 (2013): 109–29.

————. *Why Christianity Happened: A Sociohistorical Account of Christian Origins (26–50CE).* Louisville: Westminster John Knox, 2006.

Crossley, James, and Robert J. Myles. *Jesus: A Life in Class Conflict.* Winchester: Zero Books, 2023.

Crossley, Nick. "Phenomenology and the Body." Pages 130–43 in *Routledge Handbook of Body Studies.* Edited by Bryan S. Turner. London: Routledge, 2012.

Crowther, Margaret Anne. *Church Embattled.* Newton Abbot: David & Charles, 1970.

Curry, Kenneth, ed. *New Letters of Robert Southey.* Vol. 1. New York: Columbia University Press, 1965.

Czachesz, István, and Risto Uro, eds. *Mind, Morality and Magic: Cognitive Science Approaches in Biblical Studies.* London: Routledge, 2014.

Dahl, Nils Alstrup. "The Crucified Messiah." Pages 27–47 in *Jesus the Christ: The Historical Origins of Christology Doctrine.* Edited by Donald H. Juel. Minneapolis: Fortress Press, 1991.

Daise, Michael Allen. "Jesus and the Jewish Festivals: Methodological Reflections." Pages 283–304 in *Jesus Research: New Methodologies and Perceptions.* Edited by James H. Charlesworth. Grand Rapids: Eerdmans, 2007.

Dalman, Gustaf. *Arbeit und Sitte in Palästina.* 7 vols. Gütersloh: Bertelsmann, 1928–1942.

————. *Jesus-Jeshua: Studies in the Gospels.* Translated by Paul Levertoff. London: SPCK, 1929.

————. *Sacred Sites and Ways: Studies in the Topography of the Gospels.* Translated by Paul Levertoff. London: SPCK, 1935.

Damm, Alexander. *Ancient Rhetoric and the Synoptic Problem: Clarifying Markan Priority*. BETL 252. Leuven: Peeters, 2013.

Damrosch, Leo. *The Sorrows of the Quaker Jesus: James Nayler and the Puritan Crackdown on the Free Spirit*. Cambridge: Harvard University Press, 1996.

Dapaah, Daniel S. *The Relationship between John the Baptist and Jesus of Nazareth: A Critical Study*. Lanham, MD: University Press of America, 2005.

Davies, W. D. *The Gospel and the Land: Early Christian and Jewish Territorial Doctrine*. Berkeley: University of California Press, 1974.

Davis, Natalie Zemon. *Trickster Travels: A Sixteenth-Century Muslim between Worlds*. New York: Hill and Wang, 2006.

Davis, Stephen T. "'Seeing' the Risen Jesus." Pages 126–47 in *The Resurrection: An Interdisciplinary Symposium on the Resurrection of Jesus*. Edited by Stephen T. Davis, Daniel Kendall, and Gerald O'Collins. Oxford: Oxford University Press, 1997.

Deacon, John. *An Exact History of the Life of James Naylor*. London: Edward Thomas, 1657.

———. *The Grand Impostor Examined*. London: Henry Brome, 1656.

DeFranza, Megan K. *Sex Difference in Christian Theology: Male, Female, and Intersex in the Image of God*. Grand Rapids: Eerdmans, 2015.

DeLillo, Don. *White Noise*. New York: Penguin, 1986.

Deming, Will. "Mark 9.42–10.12, Matthew 5.27–32, and B. Nid. 13b: A First Century Discussion of Male Sexuality." *NTS* 36 (1990): 130–41.

Dennert, Brian C. *John the Baptist and the Jewish Setting of Matthew*. WUNT 403. Tübingen: Mohr Siebeck, 2015.

Derico, Travis M. *Oral Tradition and Synoptic Verbal Agreement: Evaluating the Empirical Evidence for Literary Dependence*. Eugene, OR: Pickwick, 2016.

De Temmerman, Koen, ed. *The Oxford Handbook of Ancient Biography*. Oxford: Oxford University Press, 2020.

De Temmerman, Koen, and Kristoffel Demoen, eds. *Writing Biography in Greece and Rome: Narrative Technique and Fictionalization*. Cambridge: Cambridge University Press, 2016.

Dibelius, Martin. *Britisches Christentum und britische Weltmacht*. Schriften des deutschen Instituts für außenpolitische Forschung 36. Berlin: Junker und Dünnhaupt, 1940.

———. *From Tradition to Gospel*. Translated by Bertram Lee Woolf. New York: Scribner's Sons, 1934.

———. "Jesus in Contemporary German Theology." *JR* 11.2 (1931): 179–211.

Dickey, Eleanor. "Teaching Latin to Greek Speakers in Antiquity." Pages 30–51 in *Learning Latin and Greek From Antiquity to the Present*. Edited by Elizabeth Archibald, William Brockliss, and Jonathan Gnoza. Cambridge: Cambridge University Press, 2015.

Dijkstra, Roald. *The Apostles in Early Christian Art and Poetry.* Leiden: Brill, 2016.

Dochhorn, Jan, Susanne Rudnig-Zelt, and Benjamin Wold, eds. *Das Böse, der Teufel und Dämonen—Evil, the Devil, and Demons.* WUNT 2.412. Tübingen: Mohr Siebeck, 2016.

Dobson, R. B., ed. *The Peasants' Revolt of 1381.* 2nd ed. New York: Macmillan, 1983.

Dodd, C. H. *The Apostolic Preaching and Its Developments.* New York: Harper & Row, 1962.

———. "The Framework of the Gospel Narrative." *ExpT* 43 (1931–32): 396–400.

Dodd, Valerie A. "Strauss's English Propagandists and the Politics of Unitarianism, 1841–1845." *Church History* 50.4 (1981): 415–35.

Dodson, Derek S. *Reading Dreams: An Audience-Critical Approach to the Dreams in the Gospel of Matthew.* LNTS 397. London: T&T Clark, 2009.

Doherty, Wiremu. "Mātauranga ā Iwi as It Applies to Tūhoe, Te Mātauranga a Tūhoe." Pages 29–46 in *Enhancing Mātauranga Māori and Global Indigenous Knowledge.* Wellington: New Zealand Qualifications Authority, 2014.

Donahue, John R. "Tax Collectors and Sinners: An Attempt at an Identification." *CBQ* 33 (1971): 39–61.

Douglas, Mary. *Purity and Danger: An Analysis of Concepts of Pollution and Taboo.* London: Routledge, 1966.

Dray, William H. *History as Re-Enactment: R. G. Collingwood's Idea of History.* Oxford: Oxford University Press, 1995.

Driesch, Angela von den, and Joachim Boessneck. "Final Report on the Zooarchaeological Investigation of Animal Bone Finds from Tell Hesban." Pages 65–108 in *Faunal Remains: Taphonomical and Zooarchaeological Studies of the Animal Remains from Tell Hesban and Vicinity.* Edited by Øystein S. LaBianca and Angela von den Driesch. Hesban 13. Berrien Springs, MI: Andrews University Press, 1995.

Dube, Musa. *Postcolonial Feminist Interpretation of the Bible.* St. Louis: Chalice, 2000.

Dubis, Mark. *Messianic Woes in First Peter: Suffering and Eschatology in 1 Peter 4:12–19.* StBibLit 33. New York: Lang, 2002.

Duden, Barbara. *The Woman beneath the Skin: A Doctor's Patients in Eighteenth-Century Germany.* Cambridge: Harvard University Press, 1991.

Dungan, David Laird. *A History of the Synoptic Problem: The Canon, the Text, the Composition, and the Interpretation of the Gospels.* New York: Doubleday, 1999.

Dunn, Alastair. *The Peasants' Revolt: England's Failed Revolution of 1381.* Stroud: Tempus, 2004.

Dunn, James D. G. *Jesus Remembered.* Vol. 1 of *Christianity in the Making.* Grand Rapids: Eerdmans, 2003.

———. *Romans 9–16.* WBC 38B. Nashville: Thomas Nelson, 1988.

Edmonds, Radcliffe G. "Extra-Ordinary People: Mystai and Magoi, Magicians and Or- phics in the Derveni Papyrus." *CP* 103 (2008): 16–39.

———. "Tearing Apart the Zagreus Myth: A Few Disparaging Remarks on Orphism and Original Sin." *ClAnt* 18 (1999): 35–73.

Edwards, Mark J., and Simon Swain, eds. *Portraits: Biographical Representation in the Greek and Latin Literature of the Roman Empire.* Oxford: Clarendon, 1997.

Edwards, Michael S. *Purge This Realm: A Life of Joseph Rayner Stephens.* London: Ep- worth, 1994.

Edwards, Shane. "Nā te Mātauranga Māori ka Ora Tonu te Ao Māori: Through Māori Knowledge Te Ao Māori Will Resonate." Pages 37–58 in *Conversation in Mātau- ranga Māori.* Edited by Taiarahia Black et al. Wellington: New Zealand Quali- fications Authority, 2012.

Egan, Pierce. *Wat Tyler; Or, the Rebellion of 1381.* London: Peirce, 1847.

E. H. *All the Proceedings at the Sessions of the Peace Holden at Westminster, on the 20. Day of June, 1651.* London: Harper, 1651.

Ehrman, Bart. *Jesus: Apocalyptic Prophet of the New Millennium.* Oxford: Oxford Uni- versity Press, 1999.

Eiland, Howard. "Reception in Distraction." *Boundary* 2 (2003): 51–66.

Eilberg-Schwartz, Howard. *People of the Body: Jews and Judaism from an Embodied Perspective.* New York: SUNY Press, 1992.

Elledge, Roderick. *Use of the Third Person for Self-Reference by Jesus and YHWH: A Study of Illeism in the Bible and Ancient Near Eastern Texts and Its Implications for Christology,* LNTS 575. London: T&T Clark, 2017.

Elliott, Ebenezer. *The Poetical Works of Ebenezer Elliott, the Corn-Law Rhymer.* Edin- burgh: Tait, 1840.

Elliott, John H. "Jesus Was Not an Egalitarian: A Critique of an Anachronistic and Idealist Theory." *BTB* 32.1 (2002): 75–91.

Elliott, Neil. "Diagnosing an Allergic Reaction: The Avoidance of Marx in Pauline Scholarship." *BCT* 8.2 (2012): 3–15.

Ellis, Katie, Mike Kent, Rachel Robertson, and Rosemarie Garland-Thomson, eds. *In- terdisciplinary Approaches to Disability: Looking towards the Future.* London: Routledge, 2019.

El-Maghrabi, Mohamed Gaber, and Cornelia Römer, eds. *More Texts from the Archive of Socrates. Papyri from House 17, Level B, in Karanis (P. Cair. Mich. III).* Archiv für Papyrusforschung und verwandte Gebiete – Beihefte 45. Berlin: de Gruy- ter, 2021.

———. *Texts from the "Archive" of Socrates, the Tax Collector, and Other Contexts at Karanis (P. Cair. Mich. II).* Archiv für Papyrusforschung und verwandte Gebiete – Beihefte 35. Berlin: de Gruyter, 2015.

El Mansy, Aliyah. "Τελῶναι im Neuen Testament—Zwischen sozialer Realität und literarischem Stereotyp." Habilitationsschrift, Philipps-Universität Marburg, 2021.

Emmanuel, Sarah. *Trauma Theory, Trauma Story: A Narration of Biblical Studies and the World of Trauma*. Leiden: Brill, 2021.

Endsjø, Dag Øistein. *Greek Resurrection Beliefs and the Success of Christianity*. New York: Palgrave Macmillan, 2009.

Engels, Friedrich. *The Condition of the Working Class in England*. Translated by Florence Kelley Wischnewetzky. London: Sonnenschein & Co., 1892.

Englebrecht, Johan. "In Memory of Her: The Life and Times of Winsome Munro." *R&T* 3.2 (1996): 86–92.

Enslin, Morton Scott. "An Additional Step toward the Understanding of Jesus." *JR* 9 (1929): 419–35.

———. "John and Jesus." *ZNW* 66 (1975): 1–18.

Epiphanius. *The Panarion of Epiphanius of Salamis: Book I (Sects 1–46)*. Translated by Frank Williams. 2nd ed. Leiden: Brill, 2009.

Epstein, James. "'Our Real Constitution': Trial Defence and Radical Memory in the Age of Revolution." Pages 22–51 in *Re-reading the Constitution: New Narratives in the Political History of England's Long Nineteenth Century*. Edited by James Vernon. Cambridge: Cambridge University Press, 1996.

———. *Radical Expression: Political Language, Ritual, and Symbol in England, 1790–1850*. Oxford: Oxford University Press, 1994.

Eraqi Klorman, Bat-Zion. "The Messiah Shukr Kuḥayl II (1868–75) and His Tithe (*Ma'aśer*): Ideology and Practice as a Means to Hasten Redemption." Pages 457–69 in *Essential Papers on Messianic Movements and Personalities in Jewish History*. Edited by Marc Saperstein. New York: New York University Press, 1992.

Erdkamp, Paul. *The Grain Market in the Roman Empire: A Social, Political and Economic Study*. Cambridge: Cambridge University Press, 2005.

Eshel, Hanan. "Publius Quinctilius Varus in Jewish Sources." *JJS* 59 (2008): 112–19.

Espirito Santo, Diana. "Imagination, Sensation, and the Education of Attention among Cuban Spirit Mediums." *Ethnos* 77 (2012): 252–71.

Evans, Craig A. "From Gospel to Gospel: The Function of Isaiah in the New Testament." Pages 651–91 in W*riting and Reading the Scroll of Isaiah: Studies of an Interpretive Tradition*. Edited by Craig C. Broyles and Craig A. Evans. Leiden: Brill, 1997.

———. *Jesus and His World: The Archaeological Evidence*. Louisville: Westminster John Knox, 2012.

———. *Jesus and the Ossuaries: What Jewish Burial Practices Reveal about the Beginning of Christianity*. Waco, TX: Baylor University Press, 2003.

———. *Jesus and the Remains of His Day: Studies in Jesus and the Evidence of Material Culture*. Peabody, MA: Hendrickson, 2015.

Evans, C. Stephen. *The Historical Christ and the Jesus of Faith: The Incarnational Narrative as History.* Oxford: Oxford University Press, 1996.

Evans, Elizabeth C. "Physiognomics in the Ancient World." TAPS 59.5 (1969): 1–101.

Evans, Thomas. *Christian Policy, the Salvation of the Empire.* London: Seale and Bates, 1816.

Eve, Eric. *The Jewish Context of Jesus's Miracles.* Sheffield: Sheffield Academic, 2002.

———. "Spit in Your Eye: The Blind Man of Bethsaida and the Blind Man of Alexandria." *NTS* 54 (2008): 1–17.

Exum, J. Cheryl. *Fragmented Women: Feminist (Sub)versions of Biblical Narratives.* JSOTSup 163. Sheffield: Sheffield Academic, 1993.

Eyerman, Ron. "The Past in the Present: Culture and the Transmission of Memory." Pages 304–6 in *The Collective Memory Reader.* Edited by Jeffrey K. Olick, Vered Vinitzky-Seroussi, and Daniel Levy. Oxford: Oxford University Press, 2011.

Eyl, Jennifer. *Signs, Wonders, and Gifts: Divination in the Letters of Paul.* Oxford: Oxford University Press, 2019.

Facchini, Cristiana. "Jesus the Pharisee: Leon Modena, the Historical Jesus, and Renaissance Venice." *JSHJ* 17.1–2 (2019): 81–101.

Falk, Harvey. *Jesus the Pharisee: A New Look at the Jewishness of Jesus.* New York: Paulist, 1985.

Farmer, Ralph. *Sathan Inthron'd in His Chair of Pestilence.* London: Thomas, 1657.

Farmer, William R. "State *Interesse* and Markan Primacy: 1870–1914." Pages 15–49 in *Biblical Studies and the Shifting of Paradigms, 1850–1914.* Edited by Henning Graf Reventlow and William Farmer. Sheffield: Sheffield Academic, 1995.

Fehribach, Adeline. *The Women in the Life of the Bridegroom.* Collegeville, MN: Liturgical, 1998.

Felder, Cain Hope. Introduction to *Stony the Road We Trod: African American Biblical Interpretation.* Edited by Cain Hope Felder. Minneapolis: Fortress, 1991.

Feldman, Liane. "Sanitized Sacrifice in Aramaic Levi's Law of the Priesthood." *JAJ* 11.3 (2020): 343–68.

Felton, Debbie. *Haunted Greece and Rome: Ghost Stories from Classical Antiquity.* Austin: University of Texas Press, 1999.

Ferda, Tucker S. *Jesus, the Gospels, and the Galilean Crisis.* LNTS 601. London: Bloomsbury T&T Clark, 2019.

———. "John the Baptist, Isaiah 40, and the Ingathering of the Exiles." *JSHJ* 10 (2012): 154–88.

Fine, Steven. *This Holy Place: On the Sanctity of the Synagogue during the Greco-Roman Period.* Notre Dame: University of Notre Dame Press, 1997.

Finegan, Jack. *The Archaeology of the New Testament: The Life of Jesus and the Beginning of the Early Church.* Rev. ed. Princeton: Princeton University Press, 1993.

Finkelstein, Israel, and Neil Silberman. *The Bible Unearthed: Archaeology's New Vision of Ancient Israel and the Origin of Its Sacred Texts.* New York: Free Press, 2000.

Finlan, Stephen. *The Background and Content of Paul's Cultic Atonement Metaphors.* Atlanta: Society of Biblical Literature, 2004.

Fischer, Moshe, Benjamin Isaac, and Israel Roll. *Roman Roads in Judaea II: The Jaffa-Jerusalem Roads.* Oxford: Tempvs Reparatvm, 1996.

Fitzgerald, Timothy. *The Ideology of Religious Studies.* Oxford: Oxford University Press, 2000.

Fitzmyer, Joseph A. *The Gospel according to Luke.* 2 vols. AB 28–28A. Garden City, NY: Doubleday, 1981, 1985.

———. *Tobit.* CEJL. Berlin: de Gruyter, 2003.

Flannery-Dailey, Frances. *Dreamers, Scribes, and Priests: Jewish Dreams in the Hellenistic and Roman Eras.* JSJSup 90. Leiden: Brill, 2004.

Foley, John Miles. *How to Read an Oral Poem.* Urbana: University of Illinois Press, 2002.

———. *Oral Tradition and the Internet: Pathways of the Mind.* Urbana: University of Illinois Press, 2012.

———. "The Riddle of Q: Oral Ancestor, Textual Precedent, or Ideological Creation?" Pages 123–40 in *Oral Performance, Popular Tradition, and Hidden Transcript in Q.* Edited by Richard A. Horsley. SemeiaSt 60. Atlanta: SBL Press, 2006.

———. *The Singer of Tales in Performance.* Voices in Performance and Text. Bloomington: Indiana University Press, 1995.

———. "Traditional Signs and Homeric Art." Pages 56–82 in *Written Voices, Spoken Signs: Tradition, Performance, and the Epic Text.* Edited by Egbert J. Bakker and Ahuvia Kahane. Cambridge: Harvard University Press, 1997.

Forgas, Joseph P. "She Just Doesn't Look Like a Philosopher . . . ? Affective Influences on the Halo Effect in Impression Formation." *European Journal of Social Psychology* 41 (2011): 812–17.

Forgas, Joseph P., and Simon M. Lahan. "Halo Effects." Pages 276–90 in *Cognitive Illusions: Intriguing Phenomena in Thinking, Judgment and Memory.* Edited by Rüdiger F. Pohl. London: Routledge, 2017.

Forster, Mary. *These Several Papers Was Sent to the Parliament the Twentieth Day of the Fifth Moneth, 1659.* Edited by Mary Forster. London: Westwood, 1659.

Foster, Paul. "Memory, Orality, and the Fourth Gospel: Three Dead-Ends in Historical Jesus Research." *JSHJ* 10 (2012): 191–227.

Foucault, Michel. *Discipline and Punish: The Birth of the Prison.* Translated by Alan Sheridan. New York: Vintage, 1977.

Fox, George. *A Journal.* Edited by Thomas Ellwood. London: Northcott, 1694.

Fradkin, Arlene. "Long-Distance Trade in the Lower Galilee: New Evidence from Sepphoris." Pages 107–16 in *Archaeology and the Galilee: Texts and Contexts in* the Graeco-Roman and Byzantine Periods. Edited by Douglas R. Edwards and C. Thomas McCollough. Atlanta: Scholars Press, 1997.

Frampton, Stephanie Ann. "What to Do with Books in the 'De Finibus'." *TAPA* 146.1 (2016): 117–47.

Fredriksen, Paula. *"Al Tirah* ('Fear Not!'): Jewish Apocalyptic Eschatology, from Schweitzer to Allison, and After." Pages 15–38 in *To Recover What Has Been Lost: Essays on Eschatology, Intertextuality, and Reception History in Honor of Dale C. Allison Jr.* Edited by Tucker S. Ferda, Daniel Frayer-Griggs, and Nathan C. Johnson. NovTSup 183. Leiden: Brill, 2021.

———. "Compassion Is to Purity as Fish Is to Bicycle and Other Reflections on Constructions of 'Judaism' in Current Work on the Historical Jesus." Pages 55–67 in *Apocalypticism, Anti-Semitism and the Historical Jesus: Subtexts in Criticism.* Edited by John S. Kloppenborg and John W. Marshall. JSNTSup 275. London: T&T Clark, 2005.

———. *From Jesus to Christ: The Origins of the New Testament Images of Christ.* 2nd ed. New Haven: Yale University Press, 2000.

———. "The Historical Jesus, the Scene in the Temple, and the Gospel of John." Pages 249–76 in *Critical Appraisals of Critical Views.* Vol. 1 of *John, Jesus, and History.* Edited by Paul N. Anderson, Felix Just, and Tom Thatcher. Atlanta: SBL Press, 2007.

———. *Jesus of Nazareth: King of the Jews.* New York: Vintage, 1999.

———. "What Does It Mean to See Paul 'within Judaism'?" *JBL* 141.2 (2022): 359–80.

———. *When Christians Were Jews: The First Generation.* New Haven: Yale University Press, 2018.

Frendo, Anthony. *Pre-Exilic Israel, the Hebrew Bible, and Archaeology: Integrating Text and Artefact.* London: T&T Clark, 2011.

Frevel, Christian, and Christophe Nihan, eds. *Purity and the Forming of Religious Traditions in the Ancient Mediterranean World and Ancient Judaism.* Dynamics in the History of Religion 3. Leiden: Brill, 2013.

Freyne, Sean. *Augustine and the Jews.* New Haven: Yale University Press, 2010.

———. *Jesus: A Jewish Galilean.* London: T&T Clark, 2004.

Friesen, Steven J. "The Blessings of Hegemony: Poverty, Paul's Assemblies, and the Class Interests of the Professorate." Pages 117–28 in *The Bible in the Public Square.* Edited by Cynthia Briggs Kitteredge, Ellen Bradshaw Aitken, and Jonathan A. Draper. Minneapolis: Fortress, 2008.

———. "Poverty in Pauline Studies: Beyond the So-Called New Consensus." *JSNT* 23.3 (2004): 323–61.

Frymer-Kensky, Tikva. "Pollution, Purification and Purgation in Biblical Israel." Pages 399–404 in *The Word of the Lord Shall Go Forth: Essays in Honor of David Noel*

Freedman in Celebration of His Sixtieth Birthday. Edited by Carol L. Meyers and M. O'Connor. Winona Lake, IN: Eisenbrauns, 1983.

———. *Reading the Women of the Bible: A New Interpretation of Their Stories*. New York: Schocken, 2002.

Fuller, Reginald H. "The Criterion of Dissimilarity: The Wrong Tool?" Pages 42–48 in *Christological Perspectives: Essays in Honor of Harvey K. McArthur*. Edited by Robert F. Berkey and Sarah A. Edwards. New York: Pilgrim, 1982.

———. *The Mission and Achievement of Jesus: An Examination of the Presuppositions of New Testament Theology*. SBT 12. London: SCM, 1954.

Funk, Robert W., and Roy W. Hoover. *The Five Gospels: What Did Jesus Really Say? The Search for the Authentic Words of Jesus*. San Francisco: HarperCollins, 1993.

Furstenberg, Yair. "Defilement Penetrating the Body: A New Understanding of Contamination in Mark 7.15." *NTS* 54 (2008): 176–200.

Gadamer, Hans-Georg. *Wahrheit und Methode: Grundzüge einer philosophischen Hermeneutik*. Tübingen: Mohr, 1960.

Gainsford, Peter. "Formal Analysis of Recognition Scenes in the 'Odyssey'." *JHS* 123 (2003): 41–59.

Galbraith, Deane. "Jeremiah Never Saw That Coming: How Jesus Miscalculated the End Times." Pages 150–75 in *Jeremiah in History and Tradition*. Edited by Jim West and Niels Peter Lemche. Abingdon: Routledge, 2020.

———. "The Origin of Archangels: Ideological Mystification of Nobility." Pages 209–40 in *Class Struggle in the New Testament*. Edited by Robert J. Myles. Lanham, MD: Lexington/Fortress Academic, 2019.

———. "The Perpetuation of Racial Assumptions in Biblical Studies." Pages 116–34 in *History, Politics and the Bible from the Iron Age to the Media Age: Essays in Honour of Keith W. Whitelam*. Edited by James G. Crossley and Jim West. London: Bloomsbury, 2016.

———. "Religion without Scare Quotes: Cognitive Science of Religion and the Humanities." *Religion, Brain and Behavior* (2023): https://doi.org/10.1080/21535 99X.2023.2234441.

Galbraith, V. H., ed. *The Anonimalle Chronicle, 1333 to 1381*. Manchester: Manchester University Press, 1927.

Galili, Ehud, Avshalom Zemer, and Baruch Rosen. "Ancient Fishing Gear and Associated Artifacts from Underwater Explorations in Israel—A Comparative Study." *Archaeofauna* 22 (2013): 145–66.

García Martínez, Florentino, and Eibert J. C. Tigchelaar. *The Dead Sea Scrolls Study Edition*. 2 vols. Leiden: Brill, 1997–1998.

Gardner, Iain, and Samuel Lieu. *Manichaean Texts from the Roman Empire*. Cambridge: Cambridge University Press, 2004.

Garland, David E. *Reading Matthew: A Literary and Theological Commentary on the First Gospel.* New York: Crossroads, 1993.

Garland, Robert. *Celebrity in Antiquity: From Media Tarts to Tabloid Queens.* Classical Inter/Faces. London: Bristol Classical Press, 2012.

Garment, Joshua. *The Hebrews Deliverance at Hand.* London: s.n., 1651.

Garroway, Joshua. "The Invasion of a Mustard Seed: A Reading of Mark 5.1–20." *JSNT* 32 (2009): 57–75.

Gartman, David. *From Autos to Architecture: Fordism and Architectural Aesthetics in the Twentieth Century.* New York: Princeton Architectural Press, 2009.

Gasparini, Valentino, Maik Patzelt, and Rubina Raja, eds. *Lived Religion in the Ancient Mediterranean World: Approaching Religious Transformations from Archaeology, History and Classics.* Berlin: de Gruyter, 2020.

Gathercole, Simon. *The Composition of the Gospel of Thomas: Original Language and Influences.* SNTSMS 151. Cambridge: Cambridge University Press, 2012.

———. *The Gospel of Thomas: Introduction and Commentary.* TENTS 11. Leiden: Brill, 2014.

Gattrall, Jefferson J. A. *The Real and the Sacred: Picturing Jesus in Nineteenth-Century Fiction.* Ann Arbor: University of Michigan Press, 2014.

Geertz, Armin W. "How Did Ignorance Become Fact in American Religious Studies? A Reluctant Reply to Ivan Strenski." *SMSR* 86.1 (2020): 365–403.

Georgi, Dieter. "The Interest in the Life of Jesus Theology as a Paradigm for the Social History of Biblical Criticism." *HTR* 85.1 (1992): 52–83.

Gerber, Albrecht. *Deissmann the Philologist.* BZNW 171. Berlin: de Gruyter, 2010.

Gerhardsson, Birger. *Memory and Manuscript: Oral Tradition and Written Transmission in Rabbinic Judaism and Early Christianity with Tradition and Transmission in Early Christianity.* Grand Rapids: Eerdmans, 1998.

Gerolemou, Maria. "Representing the Insane." Pages 271–82 in *Visualizing the Invisible with the Human Body: Physiognomy and Ekphrasis in the Ancient World.* Edited by J. Johnson and A. Stavru. Berlin: de Gruyter, 2019.

G. H. *The Declaration of John Robins, the False Prophet.* London: Wood, 1651.

Giannini, Alexander, ed. *Paradoxographorum Graecorum reliquiae.* Milan: Istituto Editoriale Italiano, 1966.

Gibson, Josh. "The Chartists and the Constitution: Revisiting British Popular Constitutionalism." *Journal of British Studies* 56 (2017): 70–90.

———. "Natural Right and the Intellectual Context of Early Chartist Thought." *History Workshop Journal* 84 (2017): 194–213.

Gibson, Shimon. "British Archaeological Institutions in Mandatory Palestine, 1917–1948." *PEQ* 131 (1999): 15–143.

———. *The Final Days of Jesus: The Archaeological Evidence.* New York: HarperOne, 2009.

Gideon, Siegfried. *Mechanization Takes Command: A Contribution to Anonymous History.* New York: Norton, 1948.

Gill, Victoria. "Giant Dinosaurs 'Held Heads High'." *BBC News*, May 29, 2009. http://news.bbc.co.uk/2/hi/science/nature/8068789.stm.

Ginzburg, Carlo. "Clues: Roots of an Evidential Paradigm." Pages 87–113 in *Clues, Myths, and the Historical Method.* Translated by John Tedeschi and Anne C. Tedeschi. Baltimore: Johns Hopkins University Press, 2013.

———. *Il formaggio e i vermi.* Turin: Einaudi, 1976.

Ginzburg, Carlo, and Carlo Poni. "The Name and the Game: Unequal Exchange and the Historiographic Marketplace." Pages 2–10 in *Microhistory and the Lost Peoples of Europe.* Edited by E. Muir and G. Ruggiero. Baltimore: Johns Hopkins University Press, 1991.

Glancy, Jennifer A. *Corporal Knowledge: Early Christian Bodies.* Oxford: Oxford University Press, 2010.

———. *Slavery in Early Christianity.* Oxford: Oxford University Press, 2002.

Glendinning, Victoria. "Lies and Silences." Pages 49–62 in *The Troubled Face of Biography.* Edited by Eric Homberger and John Charmley. London: Macmillan, 1988.

Gnilka, Joachim. "Wie urteilte Jesus über seinen Tod?" Pages 13–50 in *Der Tod Jesu.* Edited by Karl Kertelge. Freiburg: Herder, 1976.

Gnuse, Robert Karl. *Dreams and Dream Reports in the Writings of Josephus: A Traditio-Historical Analysis.* AGJU 36. Leiden: Brill, 1996.

Goodacre, Mark. "How Empty Was the Tomb." *JSNT* 44.1 (2021): 134–48.

———. "A World without Mark: An Experiment in Erasure History." *BibInt* 31 (2023): 120–34.

Goodley, Dan. "Dis/entangling Critical Disability Studies." *Disability & Society* 28.5 (2013): 631–44.

Gophen, Moshe. "Fisheries Management in Lake Kinneret (Israel)." *Lake and Reservoir Management* 2.1 (1986): 327–32.

Gosbell, Louise A. "The Woman with the 'Flow of Blood' (Mark 5:25–34) and Disability in the Ancient World." *Journal of Gospels and Acts Research* 2 (2018): 22–43.

Goss, Robert. *Jesus Acted Up: A Gay and Lesbian Manifesto.* San Francisco: Harper, 1993.

Gousopoulos, Christina. "Sub-Elite Readers and the Transmission of Christian Literary Texts." *ETL* 97.1 (2021): 37–59.

Graf, Fritz, and Sarah Iles Johnston. *Ritual Texts for the Afterlife: Orpheus and the Bacchic Gold Tablets.* 2nd ed. New York: Routledge, 2013.

Gramsci, Antonio. *Selections from the Prison Notebooks.* Edited and translated by Quintin Hoare and Geoffrey Nowell Smith. New York: International Publishers, 1971.

Gray, Jonathan. "From Whence Came Cartman: South Park's Intertextual Lineage." Pages 3–16 in *Deconstructing South Park: Critical Examinations of Animated*

Transgression. Edited by Brian Cogan. Critical Studies in Television. Lanham, MD: Lexington/Fortress Academic, 2012.

Gray, Rebecca. *Prophetic Figures in Late Second Temple Jewish Palestine: The Evidence from Josephus*. Oxford: Oxford University Press, 1993.

Grazia, Victoria de. *Irresistible Empire: America's Advance through 20th-Century Europe*. Cambridge: Belknap, 2004.

Graziosi, Barbara. *Inventing Homer: The Early Reception of Epic*. Cambridge: Cambridge University Press, 2002.

Green, Richard Firth. "John Ball's Letters: Literary History and Historical Literature." Pages 176–200 in *Chaucer's England: Literature in Historical Context*. Edited by Barbara A. Hanawalt. Minneapolis: University of Minnesota Press, 1992.

Grey, Matthew. "Priests, Judean Community Assemblies, and Synagogue Development in the Second Temple Period." Pages 97–131 in *The Synagogue in Ancient Palestine: Current Issues and Emerging Trends*. Edited by Rick Bonnie, Raimo Hakola, and Ulla Tervahauta. FRLANT 279. Göttingen: Vandenhoeck & Ruprecht, 2020.

Griffith, R. Marie. *God's Daughters: Evangelical Women and the Power of Submission*. Berkeley: University of California Press, 1997.

Grigge, William. *The Quaker's Jesus*. London: Simmonds, 1658.

Grimes, William. "The Man Who Rendered Jesus for the Age of Duplication." *New York Times*, October 12, 1994.

Gronewald, Michael. "Unbekanntes Evangelium oder Evangelharmonie (Fragment aus dem 'Evangelium Egerton')." Pages 6:136–45 in *Kölner Papyri (P. Köln)*. Edited by Michael Gronewald et al. Opladen: Westdeutscher, 1976.

Gunkel, Hermann. *The Stories of Genesis: A Translation of the Third Edition of the Introduction to Hermann Gunkel's Commentary on the Book of Genesis*. Translated by John J. Scullion. Edited by William R. Scott. Vallejo, CA: BIBAL, 1994.

Guttgemans, Erhard T. *Candid Questions concerning Gospel Form Criticism: A Methodological Sketch of the Fundamental Problematics of Form and Redaction Criticism*. Translated by William G. Doty. Pittsburgh: Wipf & Stock, 1979.

Haber, Susan. *They Shall Purify Themselves: Essays on Purity in Early Judaism*. Atlanta: Society of Biblical Literature, 2008.

———. "A Woman's Touch: Feminist Encounters with the Hemorrhaging Woman in Mark 5.24–34." *JSNT* 26 (2003): 171–92.

Häberl, Charles G., and James F. McGrath, eds. *The Mandaean Book of John: Critical Edition, Translation, and Commentary*. Berlin: de Gruyter, 2020.

Habermas, Gary R. "Resurrection Claims in Non-Christian Religions." *RelS* 25.2 (1989): 167–77.

Hägerland, Tobias. *Jesus and the Forgiveness of Sins: An Aspect of His Prophetic Mission*. SNTSMS 150. Cambridge: Cambridge University Press, 2011.

Hägg, Tomas. *The Art of Biography in Antiquity.* Cambridge: Cambridge University Press, 2012.

Hahn, Ferdinand. "Methodological Reflections on the Historical Investigation of Jesus." Pages 35–105 in *Historical Investigation and New Testament Faith.* Translated by Robert Maddox. Edited by Edgard Krentz. Philadephia: Fortress, 1983.

———. "The Quest of the Historical Jesus and the Special Character of the Sources Available to Us." Pages 9–48 in *What Can We Know about Jesus?* by Ferdinand Hahn, Wenzel Lohff, and Günther Bornkamm. Translated by Grover Foley. Edinburgh: Saint Andrew Press, 1969.

Hahne, Harry A. *The Corruption and Redemption of Creation: Nature in Romans 8:19–22 and Jewish Apocalyptic Literature.* LNTS 336. London: T&T Clark, 2006.

Haines-Eitzen, Kim. *Guardians of Letters: Literacy, Power, and the Transmitters of Early Christian Literature.* Oxford: Oxford University Press, 2000.

Halbwachs, Maurice. *On Collective Memory.* Edited and translated by Lewis A. Coser. Chicago: University of Chicago Press, 1992.

Hanagan, Michael. "'Shall I Compare Thee . . . ?' Problems of Comparative Historical Analysis." *International Review of Social History* 56.1 (2011): 133–46.

Hannah, Darrell. "Guardian Angels and Angelic National Patrons in Second Temple Judaism and Early Christianity." Pages 413–35 in *Angels: The Concept of Celestial Beings: Origins, Development and Reception.* Edited by Friedrich V. Reiterer, Tobias Nicklas, and Karin Schöpflin. Berlin: de Gruyter, 2007.

Hansen, Miriam Bratu. "Benjamin's Aura." *Critical Inquiry* 34.2 (2008): 336–75.

Harding, James Edward. "Understanding in All Things: The Revelation and Transmission of Divine Insight in the Qumran Scrolls and the New Testament." PhD diss., University of Sheffield, 2001.

Harkins, Angela Kim. "Looking at the *Shepherd of Hermas* through the Experience of Lived Religion." Pages 49–70 in *Lived Religion in the Ancient Mediterranean World: Approaching Religious Transformations from Archaeology, History and Classics.* Edited by Valentino Gasparani, Maik Patzelt, and Rubina Raja. Berlin: de Gruyter 2020.

Harland, Philip A. *Dynamics of Identity in the World of the Early Christians.* London: T&T Clark, 2009.

Harnack, Adolf von. *Lukas der Arzt: Der Verfasser des dritten Evangeliums und der Apostelgeschichte.* Leipzig: Hinrichs, 1906.

Harrill, J. Albert. *Slaves in the New Testament: Literary, Social, and Moral Dimensions.* Minneapolis: Fortress, 2006.

Hart, Gary Warren. *Right from the Start: A Chronicle of the McGovern Campaign.* New York: Quadrangle, 1973.

Hartman, Saidiya. *Lose Your Mother: A Journey along the Atlantic Slave Route*. New York: Farrar, Straus and Giroux, 2008.

———. "Venus in Two Acts." *Small Axe* 26 (2008): 1–14.

Hartmann, Tilo, and Charlotte Goldhoorn. "Horton and Wohl Revisited: Exploring Viewers' Experience of Parasocial Interaction." *Journal of Communication* 61 (2011): 1104–112.

Harvey, David. *The Condition of Postmodernity: An Inquiry into the Origins of Cultural Change*. Oxford: Blackwell, 1989.

Harvey, Paul. *Howard Thurman and the Disinherited: A Religious Biography*. Grand Rapids: Eerdmans, 2020.

Harvey, Paul H., and Mark Pagel. *The Comparative Method in Evolutionary Biology*. Oxford: Oxford University Press, 1991.

Harvey, Susan Ashbrook. *Scenting Salvation: Ancient Christianity and the Olfactory Imagination*. Berkeley: University of California Press, 2006.

Harvey, Van A. *The Historian and the Believer: The Morality of Historical Knowledge and Christian Belief, with a New Introduction by the Author*. Urbana: University of Illinois Press, 1996.

Harvey, Van A., and Schubert M. Ogden. "How New Is the 'New Quest of the Historical Jesus'?" Pages 197–242 in *The Historical Jesus and the Kerygmatic Christ: Essays on the New Quest of the Historical Jesus*. Edited and translated by Carl W. Braaten and Roy A. Harrisville. New York: Abingdon, 1964.

Haupt, Heinz-Gerhard, and Jürgen Kocka. "Comparative History: Methods, Aims and Problems." Pages 23–39 in *Comparison and History: Europe in Cross-National Perspective*. Edited by Deborah Cohen and Maura O'Connor. London: Routledge, 2004.

Hay, David M. "Politics and Exegesis in Philo's Treatise on Dreams." Pages 429–38 in *Society of Biblical Literature 1987 Seminar Papers*. Edited by Kent H. Richards. SBLSP 26. Atlanta: Scholars Press, 1987.

Head, Peter. "The Nazi Quest for an Aryan Jesus." *JSHJ* 2 (2004): 55–89.

Hearon, Holly E. *The Mary Magdalene Tradition: Witness and Counter-Witness in Early Christian Communities*. Collegeville, MN: Liturgical, 2004.

Hector, L. C., and Barbara F. Harvey, eds. *The Westminster Chronicle, 1381–1394*. Oxford: Clarendon, 1982.

Henare, Amiria, Martin Holbraad, and Sari Wastell. "Introduction: Thinking through Things." Pages 1–31 in *Thinking through Things: Theorising Artefacts Ethnographically*. Edited by Amiria Henare, Martin Holbraad, and Sari Wastell. London: Routledge, 2007.

Hengel, Martin. *Was Jesus a Revolutionist?* Translated by William Klassen. Philadelphia: Fortress, 1971.

———. *Victory over Violence and Was Jesus a Revolutionist?* Translated by David E. Green. Minneapolis: Augsburg Fortress, 2003.

Hengel, Martin, and Anna Maria Schwemer. *Der messianische Anspruch Jesu und die Anfänge der Christologie.* WUNT 138. Tübingen: Mohr Siebeck, 2001.

Henley, Paul. "Spirit Possession, Power, and the Absent Presence of Islam: Re-Viewing *Les maîtres fous.*" *Journal of the Royal Anthropological Institute* 12 (2006): 731–61.

Hennell, Charles C. *Inquiry concerning the Origin of Christianity.* London: Smallfield and Son, 1838.

Hennell, Sara S. *A Memoir of Charles Christian Hennell.* Privately published, 1899.

Henning, Meghan R. "Healing and Exorcisms." Pages 355–71 in *Oxford Handbook of the Synoptic Gospels.* Edited by Stephen Ahearne-Kroll. Oxford: Oxford University Press, 2023.

———. *Hell Hath No Fury: Gender, Disability, and the Invention of Damned Bodies in Early Christian Literature.* New Haven: Yale University Press, 2021.

———. "In Sickness and in Health: 'Ancient Rituals of Truth' in the Greco-Roman World and 1 Peter." Pages 185–204 in *Disability Studies and Biblical Literature.* Edited by Candida R. Moss and Jeremy Schipper. New York: Palgrave Macmillan, 2011.

Heschel, Susannah. *Abraham Geiger and the Jewish Jesus.* Chicago: University of Chicago Press, 1998.

———. *The Aryan Jesus: Christian Theologians and the Bible in Nazi Germany.* Princeton: Princeton University Press, 2008.

Hesemann, Michael. *Jesus of Nazareth: Archaeologists Retracing the Footsteps of Christ.* San Francisco: Ignatius, 2021.

Hessayon, Ariel. "Robins, John (fl. 1641–1652)." In *Oxford Dictionary of National Biography.* May 28, 2015. https://www.oxforddnb.com/display/10.1093/ref:odnb/9780198614128.001.0001/odnb-9780198614128-e-23826.

———, ed. *The Refiner's Fire: The Collected Works of Theaurau John Tany.* London: Breviary Stuff, 2018.

Hester, J. David. "Eunuchs and the Postgender Jesus: Matthew 19.12 and Transgressive Sexualities." *JSNT* 28.1 (2005): 13–40.

Heussi, Karl. *Die Krisis des Historismus.* Tübingen: Mohr, 1932.

Hezser, Catherine. *Jewish Literacy in Roman Palestine.* TSAJ 81. Tübingen: Mohr Siebeck, 2001.

Hidalgo, Jacqueline M. "The Politics of Reading: US Latinas, Biblical Studies, and Retrofitted Memory in Demetria Martínez's Mother Tongue." *Journal of Feminist Studies of Religion* 29 (2013): 120–31.

Hill, Christopher. "The Norman Yoke." Pages 11–66 in *Democracy and the Labour Movement: Essays in Honour of Dona Torr*. Edited by John Saville. London: Lawrence and Wishart, 1954.

——. *The World Turned Upside Down: Radical Ideas during the English Revolution*. Harmondsworth: Penguin, 1972.

Hill, Christopher, William M. Lamont, and Barry Reay. *The World of the Muggletonians*. London: Temple Smith, 1983.

Hillerbrand, Hans Joachim, ed. *Christian Life in the World*. Vol. 5 of *The Annotated Luther*. Minneapolis: Fortress, 2017.

Hilton, Rodney. *Bond Men Made Free: Medieval Peasant Movements and the English Rising of 1381*. London: Routledge, 1973.

Hoadley, Frank Taliaferro. "The Controversy over Southey's *Wat Tyler*." *Studies in Philology* 38 (1941): 81–96.

Hobsbawm, Eric J. *The Age of Extremes: A History of the World, 1914–1991*. New York: Vintage, 1994.

——. *Bandits*. London: Weidenfeld and Nicolson, 1969.

——. "Peasant Land Occupations." *Past and Present* 62 (1974): 120–52.

——. "Peasants and Politics." *Journal of Peasant Studies* 1 (1973): 3–22.

——. *Primitive Rebels: Studies in Archaic Forms of Social Movement in the 19th and 20th Centuries*. Manchester: Manchester University Press, 1959.

——. "Social Banditry." Pages 142–57 in *Rural Protest: Peasant Movements and Social Change*. Edited by Henry A. Landsberger. New York: Macmillan, 1973.

——. "Social Banditry: A Reply." *Comparative Studies in Society and History* 14 (1972): 503–5.

Hock, Ronald F., and Edward N. O'Neil. *The Chreia and Ancient Rhetoric: The Progymnasmata*. Atlanta: Scholars Press, 1986.

Höffken, Peter. *Josephus Flavius und das prophetische Erbe Israels*. Lüneburger theologische Beiträge 4. Berlin: Lit, 2006.

Hoffmann, Paul. *Studien zur Frühgeschichte der Jesus-Bewegung*. SBAB 17. Stuttgart: Katholisches Bibelwerk, 1994.

——. *Studien zur Theologie der Logienquelle*. NTAbh 8. Münster: Aschendorff, 1972.

Hoklotubbe, T. Christopher. "(En)Visioning Creator's Revelation on Turtle Island: On Dreams, Visions and Decolonizing Biblicism." In *Multiracial Biblical Studies*. Edited by Wongi Park. SemeiaSt. Atlanta: SBL Press, forthcoming.

Holbraad, Martin. "The Power of Powder: Multiplicity and Motion in the Divinatory Cosmology of Cuban Ifá (or Mana, Again)." Pages 189–225 in *Thinking through*

Things: Theorising Artefacts Ethnographically. Edited by Amiria Henare, Martin Holbraad, and Sari Wastell. London: Routledge, 2007.

Holbraad, Martin, and Morten Axel Pedersen. *The Ontological Turn: An Anthropological Exposition.* New Departures in Anthropology. Cambridge: Cambridge University Press, 2017.

Holloway, Paul A. *Philippians.* Hermeneia. Minneapolis: Fortress, 2017.

Holmén, Tom. *Jesus and Jewish Covenant Thinking.* BIS 55. Leiden: Brill, 2001.

Hooker, Morna D. "Christology and Method." *NTS* 17.4 (1971): 480–87.

———. "Foreword: Forty Years On." Pages xiii–xvii in *Jesus, Criteria, and the Demise of Authenticity.* Edited by Chris Keith and Anthony Le Donne. London: T&T Clark, 2012.

———. "On Using the Wrong Tool." *Theology* 75 (1972): 570–81.

Horrell, David G. *Ethnicity and Inclusion: Religion, Race, and Whiteness in Constructions of Jewish and Christian Identities.* Grand Rapids: Eerdmans, 2020.

Horsfield, Peter. *From Jesus to the Internet: A History of Christianity and Media.* West Sussex: Wiley-Blackwell, 2015.

Horsley, Richard A. "'By the Finger of God': Jesus and Imperial Violence." Pages 51–80 in *Violence in the New Testament.* Edited by Shelly Matthews and E. Leigh Gibson. London: T&T Clark, 2005.

———. *Christian Origins.* Minneapolis: Fortress, 2010.

———. *Galilee: History, Politics, People.* Valley Forge, PA: Trinity Press International, 1995.

———. "The Historical Context of Q." Pages 46–60 in *Whoever Hears You Hears Me? Prophets, Performance, and Tradition in Q.* Edited by Richard A. Horsley. Harrisburg, PA: Trinity Press International, 1999.

———. *Jesus and the Spiral of Violence: Popular Jewish Resistance in Roman Palestine.* San Francisco: Harper & Row, 1987.

———. "'Messianic' Figures and Movements in First-Century Palestine." Pages 276–95 in *The Messiah: Developments in Earliest Judaism and Christianity.* Edited by James H. Charlesworth. Minneapolis: Fortress, 1990.

———. "Popular Messianic Movements around the Time of Jesus." *CBQ* 46 (1984): 471–95.

———. *Sociology and the Jesus Movement.* New York: Crossroad, 1989.

Horsley, Richard A., with John S. Hanson. *Bandits, Prophets, and Messiahs: Popular Movements in the Time of Jesus.* Minneapolis: Winston, 1985.

Horst, Pieter W. van der. "Once More: The Translation of Δέ in Matthew 28.17." *JSNT* 8.27 (1986): 27–30.

Horst, Pieter W. van der, with Silvia Castelli. "Celibacy in Early Judaism." *RB* 109.3 (2002): 390–402.

Horton, D., and R. Wohl. "Mass Communication and Para-Social Interaction: Observations on Intimacy at a Distance." *Psychiatry* 19 (1956): 215–29.

Howley, Joseph. *Aulus Gellius and Roman Reading Culture: Text, Presence, and Imperial Knowledge in the Noctes Atticae.* Cambridge: Cambridge University Press, 2018.

Hoyles, Martin. *William Cuffay: The Life and Times of a Chartist Leader.* Hertford: Hansib, 2013.

Huebner, Sabine R. *Papyri and the Social World of the New Testament.* Cambridge: Cambridge University Press, 2019.

Hughes, Patrick W. "Irreligion Made Easy: The Reaction to Thomas Paine's *The Age of Reason*." Pages 109–31 in *New Directions in Thomas Paine Studies.* Edited by Scott Cleary and Ivy Linton Stabell. New York: Palgrave Macmillan, 2016.

Hultgren, Arland J. "Form Criticism and Jesus Research." Pages 1:649–71 in *Handbook for the Study of the Historical Jesus.* Edited by Tom Holmén and Stanley E. Porter. 4 vols. Leiden: Brill, 2011.

Hultgren, Stephen. *Narrative Elements in the Double Tradition: A Study of Their Place within the Framework of the Gospel Narrative.* BZNW 113. Berlin: de Gruyter, 2002.

Humphrey, Edith M. *And I Turned to See the Voice: The Rhetoric of Vision in the New Testament.* Grand Rapids: Baker Academic, 2007.

Hunter, Richard. *The Measure of Homer: The Ancient Reception of the Iliad and the Odyssey.* Cambridge: Cambridge University Press, 2018.

Huzzey, Richard. *Freedom Burning: Anti-Slavery and Empire in Victorian Britain.* Ithaca: Cornell University Press, 2012.

Iggers, Georg G. *The German Conception of History: The National Tradition of Historical Thought from Herder to the Present.* Rev. ed. Middletown: Wesleyan University Press, 1983.

Ilan, Tal. "The Women of the Q Community within Early Judaism." Pages 195–212 in *Q in Context II: Social Setting and Archaeological Background of the Sayings Source.* Bonn: Bonn University Press, 2015.

Isaac, Benjamin. "The Decapolis in Syria: A Neglected Inscription." *ZPE* 44 (1981): 67–74.

———. *The Limits of Empire: The Roman Army in the East.* Rev. ed. Oxford: Clarendon, 1992.

Isenberg, Wesley W. "The Gospel of Philip." Pages 139–60 in *The Nag Hammadi Library in English.* Edited by James M. Robinson. 3rd ed. San Francisco: HarperSanFrancisco, 1988.

Isser, Stanley Jerome. *The Dositheans: A Samaritan Sect in Late Antiquity.* Leiden: Brill, 1976.

———. "Dositheus, Jesus, and a Moses Aretalogy." Pages 167–89 in *Christianity, Ju-*

daism and Other Greco-Roman Cults, Part 4. Edited by Jacob Neusner. Leiden: Brill, 1975.

Iverson, Kelly R. "Orality and the Gospels: A Survey of Recent Research." *CBR* 8 (2009): 71–106.

Jablonka, Ivan. *History Is a Contemporary Literature: Manifesto for the Social Sciences.* Ithaca: Cornell University Press, 2018.

Jackson, Zakiyyah Iman. *Becoming Human: Matter and Meaning in an Anti-Black World.* New York: New York University Press, 2020.

Jacobovici, Simcha, and Charles Pellegrino. *The Jesus Family Tomb: The Discovery, the Investigation, and the Evidence That Could Change History.* San Francisco: HarperCollins, 2007.

Jacobs, Andrew S. *Christ Circumcised: A Study in Early Christian History and Difference.* Philadelphia: University of Pennsylvania Press, 2012.

Jacobson, Arland. "The Literary Unity of Q." *JBL* 101.3 (1982): 365–89.

James, Simon. "The Community of the Soldiers: A Major Identity and Centre of Power in the Roman Empire." Pages 14–25 in *Proceedings of the Eighth Theoretical Roman Archaeology Conference.* Edited by Patricia Baker, Colin Forcey, Sophia Jundi, and Robert Witcher. Oxford: Oxbow, 1999.

———. "Soldiers and Civilians: Identity and Interaction in Roman Britain." Pages 77–89 in *Britons and Romans: Advancing an Archaeological Agenda.* Edited by Simon James and Martin Millett. Council for British Archaeology Research Report 125. York: Council for British Archaeology, 2001.

Jameson, Fredric. *The Political Unconscious: Narrative as a Socially Symbolic Act.* Ithaca: Cornell University Press, 1981.

Jauss, H. R. *Toward an Aesthetic of Reception.* Translated by T. Bahti. Minneapolis: University of Minnesota Press, 1982.

Jensen, Morten Hørning. "Climate, Droughts, Wars, and Famines in Galilee as a Background for Understanding the Historical Jesus." *JBL* 131.2 (2012): 307–24.

———. "Herod Antipas in Galilee: Friend or Foe of the Historical Jesus?" *JSHJ* 5.1 (2007): 7–32.

———. *Herod Antipas in Galilee: The Literary and Archaeological Sources on the Reign of Herod Antipas and Its Socio-Economic Impact on Galilee.* WUNT 2.215. Tübingen: Mohr Siebeck, 2006.

———. "The Political History in Galilee from the First Century BCE to the End of the Second Century CE." Pages 1:51–77 in *Galilee: In the Late Second Temple and Mishnaic Periods.* Edited by David A. Fiensy and James Riley Strange. Minneapolis: Fortress, 2014.

———. "Rural Galilee and Rapid Changes: An Investigation of the Socio-Economic Dynamics and Developments in Roman Galilee." *Biblica* 93.1 (2012): 43–67.

Jeremias, Joachim. *New Testament Theology: The Proclamation of Jesus*. Translated by John Bowden. New York: Scribner's Sons, 1971.

———. *The Parables of Jesus*. Translated by S. H. Hooke. 2nd ed. New York: Scribner's Sons, 1972.

Jessey, Henry. *The Exceeding Riches of Grace Advanced by the Spirit of Grace, in an Empty Creature (Viz) Mris. [sic] Sarah Wight*. London: Mortlock, 1658.

Johnson, Brian D. "The Jewish Feasts and Questions of Historicity in John 5–12." Pages 117–30 in *Aspects of Historicity in the Fourth Gospel*. Vol. 2 of *John, Jesus, and History*. Edited by Paul N. Anderson, Felix Just, and Tom Thatcher. Atlanta: SBL Press, 2009.

Johnson, Luke Timothy. *The Real Jesus: The Misguided Quest for the Historical Jesus and the Truth of the Traditional Gospels*. San Francisco: HarperSanFrancisco, 1996.

Johnson, Matthew V., James A. Noel, and Demetrius K. Williams, eds. *Onesimus Our Brother: Reading Religion, Race, and Culture in Philemon*. Minneapolis: Fortress, 2012.

Johnson, Nathan C. "Early Jewish Messiahs." In *Critical Dictionary of Apocalyptic and Millenarian Movements*. Edited by James Crossley and Alastair Lockhart. Forthcoming.

———. "Early Jewish Sign Prophets." In *Critical Dictionary of Apocalyptic and Millenarian Movements*. Edited by James Crossley and Alastair Lockhart. December 8, 2021. https://www.cdamm.org/articles/early-jewish-sign-prophets.

Johnson, Paul Christopher. "Toward an Atlantic Genealogy of 'Spirit Possession.'" Pages 23–45 in *Spirited Things: The Work of "Spirit Possession" in Afro-Atlantic Religions*. Edited by Paul Christopher Johnson. Chicago: University of Chicago Press, 2014.

Johnson-DeBaufre, Melanie. *Jesus among Her Children: Q, Eschatology, and the Construction of Christian Origins*. HTS 55. Cambridge: Harvard University Press, 2005.

Johnston, Sarah Iles. *The Story of Myth*. Cambridge: Harvard University Press, 2018.

Jones, Pei Te Hurinui. "Māori Genealogies." *Journal of the Polynesian Society* 62.2 (1958): 162–65.

Jongkind, Dirk. "'The Lilies of the Field' Reconsidered: 'Codex Sinaiticus' and the Gospel of Thomas." *NovT* 48 (2006): 209–16.

Joseph, Simon J. "Redescribing the Resurrection: Beyond the Methodological Impasse?" *BTB* 45.3 (2015): 155–73.

Josephus. *Jewish Antiquities*. Vol. 9, *Book 20*. Translated by Louis H. Feldman. LCL. Cambridge: Harvard University Press, 1965.

Joshel, Sandra, and Lauren Hackworth Petersen. "Slaves in the Workshop." Pages

118–61 in *The Material Life of Roman Slaves*. Cambridge: Cambridge University Press, 2014.

Joyner, Charles W. *Shared Traditions: Southern History and Folk Culture*. Champaign: University of Illinois Press, 1999.

Joynes, Christine E. "Changing Horizons: Reflections on a Decade at Oxford University's Centre for Reception History of the Bible." *JBR* 1.1 (2014): 161–71.

Justice, Steven. *Writing and Rebellion: England in 1381*. Berkeley: University of California Press, 1994.

Justin Martyr. *The First Apology, The Second Apology, Dialogue with Trypho, Exhortation to the Greeks, Discourse to the Greeks, The Monarchy or The Rule of God*. Translated by Thomas B. Falls. Fathers of the Church 6. Washington, DC: Catholic University of America Press, 1948.

Kark, Ruth, and Haim Goren. "Pioneering British Exploration and Scriptural Geography: The Syrian Society/The Palestine Association." *The Geographical Journal* 177 (2011): 264–74.

Kartzow, Marianne Bjelland. *The Slave Metaphor and Gendered Enslavement in Early Christian Discourse: Double Trouble Embodied*. London: Routledge, 2018.

Käsemann, Ernst. "The Problem of the Historical Jesus." Pages 15–47 in *Essays on New Testament Themes*. Translated by W. J. Montague. SBT 41. London: SCM, 1964.

———. *On Being a Disciple of the Crucified Nazarene: Unpublished Lectures and Sermons*. Edited by Rudolf Landau. Translated by Roy A. Harrisville. Grand Rapids: Eerdmans, 2010.

Kateusz, Ally. "The Jesus Woman and the Jesus Women." Paper presented at the Westar Institute Christianity Seminar. Spring 2019.

Kautsky, John. *The Political Consequences of Modernization*. New York: Wiley, 1971.

Kay, Aaron C., et al. "God and the Government: Testing a Compensatory Control Mechanism for the Support of External Systems." *Journal of Personality and Social Psychology* 95.1 (2008): 18–35.

Kazen, Thomas. "The Coming of the Son of Man Revisited." *JSHJ* 5.2 (2007): 155–74.

———. *Issues of Impurity in Early Judaism*. ConBNT 45. Winona Lake, IN: Eisenbrauns, 2010.

———. *Jesus and Purity Halakhah: Was Jesus Indifferent to Impurity?* ConBNT 38. Stockholm: Almqvist & Wiksell, 2002.

———. *Scripture, Interpretation, or Authority? Motives and Arguments in Jesus' Halakic Conflicts*. WUNT 320. Tübingen: Mohr Siebeck, 2013.

Keane, John. *Tom Paine: A Political Life*. London: Bloomsbury, 1995.

Keddie, Anthony. *Class and Power in Roman Palestine: The Socioeconomic Setting of Judaism and Christian Origins*. Cambridge: Cambridge University Press, 2019.

———. *Revelations of Ideology: Apocalyptic Class Politics in Early Roman Palestine.* Leiden: Brill, 2018.

Keener, Craig S. *Christobiography: Memories, History, and the Reliability of the Gospels.* Grand Rapids: Eerdmans, 2019.

———. *The Historical Jesus of the Gospels.* Grand Rapids: Eerdmans, 2009.

Keith, Chris. "Die Evangelien als 'kerygmatische Erzählungen' über Jesus und die 'Kriterien' in der Jesusforschung." Pages 86–98 in *Jesus Handbuch.* Edited by Jens Schröter and Christine Jacobi. Translated by Matthias Müller. Tübingen: Mohr Siebeck, 2017.

———. *The Gospel as Manuscript: An Early History of the Jesus Tradition as Material Artifact.* Oxford: Oxford University Press, 2020.

———. "The Indebtedness of the Criteria Approach to Form Criticism and Recent Attempts to Rehabilitate the Search for an Authentic Jesus." Pages 25–48 in *Jesus, Criteria, and the Demise of Authenticity.* Edited by Chris Keith and Anthony Le Donne. London: T&T Clark, 2012.

———. *Jesus against the Scribal Elite: The Origins of the Conflict.* 2nd ed. London: T&T Clark, 2020. First published 2014 by Baker Academic.

———. *Jesus' Literacy: Scribal Culture and the Teacher from Galilee.* LNTS 413. London: T&T Clark, 2011.

———. "Memory and Authenticity: Jesus Tradition and What Really Happened." *ZNW* 102 (2011): 155–77.

———. "The Narratives of the Gospels and the Historical Jesus: Current Debates, Prior Debates, and the Goal of Historical Jesus Research." *JSNT* 38.4 (2016): 426–55.

———. "*Pericope Adulterae* (John 7:53–8:11)." Pages 1:197–208 in *The Reception of Jesus in the First Three Centuries.* Edited by Chris Keith, Helen K. Bond, Christine Jacobi, and Jens Schröter. London: T&T Clark, 2019.

———. *The Pericope Adulterae, the Gospel of John, and the Literacy of Jesus.* Leiden: Brill, 2009.

———. "Social Memory Theory and Gospels Research: The First Decade (Part One)." *EC* 6.3 (2015): 354–76.

Keith, Chris, and Anthony Le Donne, eds. *Jesus, Criteria, and the Demise of Authenticity.* London: T&T Clark, 2012.

Keith, Chris, Helen K. Bond, Christine Jacobi, and Jens Schröter, eds. *The Reception of Jesus in the First Three Centuries.* 3 vols. London: T&T Clark, 2019.

Keith, Chris, and Larry W. Hurtado, eds. *Jesus among Friends and Enemies: A Historical and Literary Introduction to Jesus in the Gospels.* Grand Rapids: Baker Academic, 2011.

Keith, Chris, and Loren T. Stuckenbruck. *Evil in Second Temple Judaism and Early Christianity.* Tübingen: Mohr Siebeck, 2016.

Kelber, Werner H. "Apostolic Tradition and the Form of the Gospel." Pages 24–46 in *Discipleship in the New Testament.* Edited by Fernando F. Segovia. Philadelphia: Fortress, 1985.

———. *Imprints, Voiceprints, and Footprints of Memory: Collected Essays of Werner H. Kelber.* RBS 74. Atlanta: SBL Press, 2013.

———. "Jesus and Tradition: Words in Time, Words in Space." *Semeia* 65 (1995): 139–67.

———. *The Oral and the Written Gospel: The Hermeneutics of Speaking and Writing in the Synoptic Tradition, Mark, Paul, and Q.* Philadelphia: Fortress, 1983.

Keller, Catherine. "'She Talks Too Much': Magdalene Meditations." Pages 234–54 in *Toward a Theology of Eros: Transfiguring Passion at the Limits of Discipline.* Edited by Virginia Burrus and Catherine Keller. New York: Fordham University Press, 2006.

Kelley, Anna C. "Searching for Professional Women in the Mid to Late Roman Textile Industry." *Past & Present* (2023): 3–43.

Kelley, Shawn. *Racializing Jesus: Race, Ideology and the Formation of Modern Biblical Scholarship.* London: Routledge, 2002.

Keulen, Wytse. *Gellius the Satirist: Roman Cultural Authority in Attic Nights.* Leiden: Brill, 2009.

King, Rebekka. "The Author, the Atheist, and the Academic Study of Religion: Bourdieu and the Reception of Biblical Criticism by Progressive Christians." *BSR* 41 (2012): 14–20.

Kinney, Robert S. *Hellenistic Dimensions of the Gospel of Matthew: Background and Rhetoric.* Tübingen: Mohr Siebeck, 2016.

Kinzig, Wolfram. *Christian Persecution in Antiquity.* Translated by Markus Bockmuehl. Waco, TX: Baylor University Press, 2021.

Kirk, Alan. "Administrative Writing, Oral Tradition, and Q." Paper presented at the Annual Meeting of the Society of Biblical Literature, Q Section. San Antonio, TX, 2004.

———. *The Composition of the Sayings Source: Genre, Synchrony, and Wisdom Redaction in Q.* NovTSup 91. Leiden: Brill, 2014.

———. "The Memory of Violence and the Death of Jesus in Q." Pages 163–78 in *Memory and the Jesus Tradition.* The Reception of Jesus in the First Three Centuries 2. London: Bloomsbury, 2018.

———. *Q in Matthew: Ancient Media, Memory, and Early Scribal Transmission of the Jesus Tradition.* LNTS 564. London: T&T Clark, 2016.

———. "The Scribe as Tradent." Pages 97–115 in *Scribal Practices and Social Structures among Jesus' Adherents: Essays in Honour of John S. Kloppenborg.* Edited by William E. Arnal, Richard A. Ascough, Robert A. Derrenbacker, and Philip A. Harland. BETL 285. Leuven: Peeters, 2016.

Kirk, J. R. Daniel, and Stephen L. Young. "'I Will Set His Hand to the Sea': Psalm 88:26 LXX and Christology in Mark." *JBL* 133 (2014): 333–40.

Klinghardt, Matthias. "Legionsschweine in Gerasa: Lokalkolorit und Historischer Hintergrund von Mk 5,1–20." *ZNW* 98 (2007): 28–48.

Kloppenborg, John S. "Agrarian Discourse in the Sayings of Jesus." Pages 104–28 in *Engaging Economics: New Testament Scenarios and Early Christian Interpretation.* Edited by Bruce Longenecker and Kelly Liebengood. Grand Rapids: Eerdmans, 2009.

———. "As One Unknown, Without a Name? Co-Opting the Apocalyptic Jesus." Pages 1–23 in *Apocalypticism, Anti-Semitism and the Historical Jesus: Subtexts in Criticism.* Edited by John S. Kloppenborg and John W. Marshall. London: T&T Clark, 2005.

———. *Christ's Associations: Connecting and Belonging in the Ancient City.* New Haven: Yale University Press, 2019.

———. *Excavating Q: The History and Setting of the Sayings Gospel.* Minneapolis: Fortress Press, 2000.

———. *The Formation of Q: Trajectories in Ancient Wisdom Collections.* Minneapolis: Fortress, 1987.

———. "Jesus, Fishermen and Tax Collectors: Papyrology and the Construction of the Ancient Economy of Roman Palestine." *ETL* 94.4 (2018): 571–99.

———. "Literary Convention, Self-Evidence and the Social History of the Q People." *Semeia* 55 (1991): 77–102.

———. "Q, Bethsaida, Khorazin, and Capernaum." Pages 60–90 in *Q in Context II: Social Setting and Archaeological Background of the Sayings Source.* Edited by Markus Tiwald. BBB 173. Bonn: Bonn University Press, 2015.

———. "The Sayings Gospel Q and the Quest of the Historical Jesus." *HTR* 89.4 (1996): 307–44.

———. *The Tenants in the Vineyard: Ideology, Economics, and Agrarian Conflict in Jewish Palestine.* Tübingen: Mohr Siebeck, 2006.

Klostermann, Erich. *Das matthäusevangelium.* 4th ed. Tübingen: Mohr, 1971.

Knapp, Robert C. *Invisible Romans.* London: Profile, 2011.

Knock, Thomas J. *The Rise of a Prairie Statesman: The Life and Times of George McGovern.* Princeton: Princeton University Press, 2016.

Knust, Jennifer. *Unprotected Texts: The Bible's Surprising Contradictions about Sex and Desire.* New York: HarperOne, 2011.

Kocka, Jürgen. "Asymmetrical Historical Comparison: The Case of the German Sonderweg." *HistTh* 38.1 (1999): 40–50.

Koet, Bart. "Why Did Paul Shave His Hair (Acts 18,18)? Nazirite and Temple in the Book of Acts." Pages 128–42 in *The Centrality of Jerusalem: Historical Perspectives*. Edited by Marcel Poorthuis and Chana Safrai. Kampen: Kok Pharos, 1996.

Kolk, Bessel van der. *The Body Keeps the Score: Brain, Mind, and Body in the Healing of Trauma*. New York: Penguin, 2014.

Kolk, Bessel van der, and Rita Fisler. "Dissociation and the Fragmentary Nature of Traumatic Memories: Overview and Exploratory Study." *Journal of Traumatic Stress* 8 (1995): 505–25.

Koosed, Jennifer L., and Darla Schumm. "Out of the Darkness: Examining the Rhetoric of Blindness in the Gospel of John." Pages 77–92 in *Disability in Judaism, Christianity, and Islam: Sacred Texts, Historical Traditions, and Social Analysis*. Edited by Darla Schumm and Michael Stoltzfus. New York: Palgrave Macmillan, 2011.

Konstan, David, and Robyn Faith Walsh. "Civic and Subversive Biography in Antiquity." Pages 26–43 in *Writing Biography in Greece and Rome: Narrative Technique and Fictionalization*. Edited by Koen De Temmerman and Kristoffel Demoen. Cambridge: Cambridge University Press, 2016.

Korner, Ralph J. *The Origin and Meaning of Ekklēsia in the Early Jesus Movement*. AJEC 98. Leiden: Brill, 2017.

Kovach, Margaret. *Indigenous Methodologies: Characteristics, Conversations, and Contexts*. 2nd ed. Toronto: University of Toronto Press, 2021.

Kraus, Thomas J. "The Lending of Books in the Fourth Century C. E. P. Oxy. LXIII 4365—A Letter on Papyrus and the Reciprocal Lending of Literature Having Become Apocryphal." Pages 185–206 in *Ad Fontes: Original Manuscripts and Their Significance for Studying Early Christianity, Selected Essays*. Leiden: Brill, 2007.

Krause, Andrew R. *Synagogues in the Works of Flavius Josephus: Rhetoric, Spatiality, and First-Century Institutions*. AJEC 97. Leiden: Brill, 2017.

Krause, Martin. "II Sam 11 4 und das Konzeptionsoptimum." *ZAW* 95 (1983): 434–37.

Kretschmar, Gottfried. *Der Evangelisch-Soziale Kongreß: Der deutsche Protestantismus und die soziale Frage*. Stuttgart: Evangelisches Verlagswerk, 1972.

Kruger, Michael J. *The Gospel of the Savior: An Analysis of P. Oxy. 840 and Its Place in the Gospel Traditions of Early Christianity*. Leiden: Brill, 2005.

Kunkel, Fritz. *Creation Continues: A Psychological Interpretation of Matthew*. Mahwah, NJ: Paulist, 1989.

LaFleur, William R. "Body." Pages 36–54 in *Critical Terms in Religious Studies*. Edited by Mark Taylor. Chicago: University of Chicago Press, 1998.

Laird, Doris Marley. "Colin Morris: Modern Missionary." PhD diss., Florida State University, 1980.

Lambek, Michael. *Knowledge and Practice in Mayotte: Local Discourses of Islam, Sorcery and Spirit Possession*. Anthropological Horizons. Toronto: University of Toronto Press, 1993.

———. "Rheumatic Irony: Questions of Agency and Self-Deception as Refracted through the Art of Living with Spirits." Pages 40–59 in *Illness and Irony: On the Ambiguity of Suffering in Culture*. Edited by Michael Lambek and Paul Antze. New York: Berghahn, 2004.

———. "On Being Present to History: Historicity and Brigand Spirits in Madagascar." *Hau: Journal of Ethnographic Theory* 6.1 (2016): 317–41.

———. *The Weight of the Past: Living with History in Mahajanga, Madagascar*. Hampshire: Palgrave Macmillan, 2002.

Lamont, William. *Last Witnesses: The Muggletonian History, 1652–1979*. Aldershot: Ashgate, 2006.

Langerwerf, Lydia. "'Many Are the Wonders in Greece': Pausanias the Wandering Philosopher." Pages 305–26 in *Recognizing Miracles in Antiquity and Beyond*. Edited by Maria Gerolemou. Berlin: de Gruyter, 2018.

Last, Richard, and Philip A. Harland. *Group Survival in the Ancient Mediterranean: Rethinking Material Conditions in the Landscape of Jews and Christians*. London: T&T Clark, 2020.

Le Donne, Anthony. "The Criterion of Coherence: Its Development, Inevitability, and Historiographical Limitations." Pages 95–114 in *Jesus, Criteria, and the Demise of Authenticity*. Edited by Chris Keith and Anthony Le Donne. London: T&T Clark, 2012.

———. "Did Jesus Befriend Sex Workers?" *JSHJ* 20.3 (2022): 147–55.

———. *Historical Jesus: What Can We Know and How Can We Know It?* Grand Rapids: Eerdmans, 2011.

———. *The Historiographical Jesus: Memory, Typology, and the Son of David*. Waco, TX: Baylor University Press, 2009.

———. "The Rise of the Quest for an Authentic Jesus: An Introduction to the Crumbling Foundations of Jesus Research." Pages 3–21 in *Jesus, Criteria, and the Demise of Authenticity*. Edited by Chris Keith and Anthony Le Donne. London: T&T Clark, 2012.

Lehtipuu, Outi. *Debates over the Resurrection of the Dead: Constructing Early Christian Identity*. Oxford: Oxford University Press, 2015.

Lenin, Vladimir. *What Is to Be Done?* Translated by Joe Fineberg and George Hanna. London: Penguin, 1988.

Lennon, Jack J. *Pollution and Religion in Ancient Rome*. Cambridge: Cambridge University Press, 2014.

Lettsome, Raquel St. Claire. "Mary's Slave Song: The Tensions and Turnarounds of Faithfully Reading Doulē in the Magnificat." *Int* 75.1 (2021): 6–18.

Levering, Matthew. *Did Jesus Rise from the Dead? Historical and Theological Reflections*. Oxford: Oxford University Press, 2019.

Levine, Amy-Jill. "The Earth Moved: Jesus, Sex, and Eschatology." Pages 83–97 in *Apoc-

alypticism, Anti-Semitism and the Historical Jesus: Subtexts in Context. Edited by John S. Kloppenborg and John W. Marshall. JSNTSup 275. London: T&T Clark, 2005.

———. "The Gospel and Acts." Pages 295–314 in *The Oxford Handbook of New Testament, Gender, and Sexuality.* Edited by Benjamin H. Dunning. Oxford: Oxford University Press, 2019.

———. "Itineràrios femininos, Jesus de Nazaré e abordagens históricos-críticas." Pages 191–220 in *Mulheres no Cristianismo primitivo: Poderosas e inspiradoras.* Edited by Roberta Alexandrina da Silva, Pedro Paulo Abreu Funari, and Claudio Umpierre Carlan. São Paulo: Fonte, 2022.

———. "Jesus, Gender, and Sexuality: A Jewish Critique." Pages 113–30 in *The Historical Jesus through Catholic and Jewish Eyes.* Edited by Bryan F. Le Beau, Leonard Greenspoon, and Dennis Hamm. Harrisburg, PA: Trinity Press International, 2000.

———. "John Meier, Women, and the Criteria of Authenticity." Pages 90–113 in *The Figure of Jesus in History and Theology: Essays in Honor of John Meier.* Edited by Vincent Skemp and Kelley Coblentz Bautch. CBQMS. Washington, DC: Catholic University of America, 2020.

———. *The Misunderstood Jew: The Church and the Scandal of the Jewish Jesus.* San Francisco: HarperCollins, 2006.

———. "Who's Catering the Q Affair? Feminist Observations on Q Paraenesis." *Semeia* 50 (1990): 145–61.

———. "Women in the Q Communities and Traditions." Pages 150–70 in *Women and Christian Origins.* Edited by Ross S. Kraemer and Mary Rose D'Angelo. Oxford: Oxford University Press, 1999.

———. "Women Itinerants, Jesus of Nazareth, and Historical-Critical Approaches: Reevaluating the Consensus." Pages 45–64 in *Gender and Second Temple Judaism.* Edited by Kathy Ehrensperger and Shayna Sheinfeld. Lanham, MD: Lexington/Fortress Academic, 2020.

———. "The Word Becomes Flesh: Jesus, Gender, and Sexuality." Pages 62–83 in *Jesus Two Thousand Years Later.* Edited by J. H. Charlesworth and W. P. Weaver. Harrisburg, PA: Trinity Press International, 2000.

Levine, Lee I. *The Ancient Synagogue: The First Thousand Years.* 2nd ed. New Haven: Yale University Press, 2005.

Levy-Rubin, Milka. *The Continuatio of the Samaritan Chronicle of Abū l-Fatḥ al-Sāmirī al-Danafī.* Studies in Late Antiquity and Early Islam 10. Princeton, NJ: Darwin, 2002.

Lewis, Bradley. *Moving beyond DSM, Prozac, and the New Psychiatry.* Ann Arbor: University of Michigan Press, 2006.

Licona, Michael R. *The Resurrection of Jesus: A New Historiographical Approach.* Downers Grove, IL: InterVarsity Press, 2010.

Liebersohn, Harry. *Religion and Industrial Society: The Protestant Social Congress in Wilhelmine Germany.* TAPS 76.6. Philadelphia: American Philosophical Society, 1986.

Lietzmann, Hans. *Messe und Herrenmahl: Eine Studie zur Geschichte der Liturgie.* Bonn: Marcus and Weber, 1926.

Lieu, Judith. "The Synagogue and the Separation of the Christians." Pages 189–207 in *The Ancient Synagogue from Its Origins until 200 CE: Papers Presented at an International Conference at Lund University, October 14–17, 2001.* Edited by Birger Olsson and Magnus Zetterholm. ConBNT 39. Stockholm: Almqvist & Wiksell, 2003.

Lilburne, Geoffrey. *A Sense of Place: A Christian Theology of the Land.* Nashville: Abingdon, 1989.

Lincoln, Bruce. *Discourse and the Construction of Society: Comparative Studies of Myth, Ritual, and Classification.* Oxford: Oxford University Press, 1989.

———. *Theorizing Myth: Narrative, Ideology, and Scholarship.* Chicago: University of Chicago Press, 1999.

———. "Theses on Method." *MTSR* 8 (1996): 225–27.

———. "Theses on Religion and Violence." *ISIM Review* 15 (2005): 12.

Lipdius, R. A., ed. *Acta Pauli et Theclae.* Vol. 1 of *Acta Apostolorum Apocrypha.* Leipzig: Mendelssohn, 1891.

Litwa, M. David. *How the Gospels Became History: Jesus and Mediterranean Myths.* New Haven: Yale University Press, 2019.

———. *Iesus Deus: The Early Christian Depiction of Jesus as a Mediterranean God.* Minneapolis: Fortress, 2014.

Livy. *History of Rome.* Vol. 8, *Books 28–30.* Translated by Frank Gardner Moore. LCL. Cambridge: Harvard University Press, 1949.

Loader, William. *Enoch, Levi and Jubilees on Sexuality.* Grand Rapids: Eerdmans, 2007.

———. "The Historical Jesus Puzzle." *Colloquium* 29.2 (1997): 131–50.

———. *Jesus' Attitude towards the Law: A Study of the Gospels.* WUNT 2.97. Tübingen: Mohr Siebeck, 1997.

———. *Making Sense of Sex: Attitudes towards Sexuality in Early Jewish and Christian Literature.* Grand Rapids: Eerdmans, 2013.

Löfstedt, Torsten. "Myths, Visions, and Related Literary Forms in the Gospels." *SEÅ* 80 (2015): 99–123.

Lohfink, Norbert. *Die Väter Israels im Deuteronomium: Mit einer Stellungnahme von Thomas Römer.* OBO 111. Göttingen: Vandenhoeck & Ruprecht, 1991.

Loke, Andrew. *Investigating the Resurrection of Jesus Christ: A New Transdisciplinary Approach.* London: Routledge, 2020.

Lord, Albert B. *The Singer of Tales.* Cambridge: Harvard University Press, 1960.

Lorentzen, J., and C. Ekenstam, eds. *Män i Norden: Manlighet och modernitet 1840–1940.* Hedemora: Gidlund, 2006.

Lucian. *Phalaris. Hippias or the Bath. Dionysus. Heracles. Amber or the Swans. The Fly. Nigrinus. Demonax. The Hall. My Native Land. Octogenarians. A True Story. Slander. The Consonants at Law. The Carousal (Symposium) or the Lapiths.* Translated by A. M. Harmon. LCL. Cambridge: Harvard University Press, 1913.

Lüdemann, Gerd. *Jesus after Two Thousand Years: What He Really Said and Did.* London: SCM, 2000.

———. *The Resurrection of Jesus: History, Experience, Theology.* London: SCM, 1994.

Luff, Rosemary Margaret. *The Impact of Jesus in First-Century Palestine.* Cambridge: Cambridge University Press, 2019.

Luijendijk, AnneMarie. "A New Testament Papyrus and Its Documentary Context: An Early Christian Writing Exercise from the Archive of Leonides (P.Oxy. II 209/ p^{10})." *JBL* 129.3 (2011): 575–96.

Lukács, Georg. "What Is Orthodox Marxism?" In *History and Class Consciousness.* Translated by Rodney Livingstone. Cambridge: MIT Press, 1971.

Lund, N. W. *Chiasmus in the New Testament: A Study in Formgeschichte.* Chapel Hill: University of North Carolina Press, 1942.

Lupieri, Edmondo. "John the Gnostic: The Figure of the Baptist in Origen and Heterodox Gnosticism." StPatr 17 (1989): 322–27.

Luttwak, Edward N. *The Grand Strategy of the Roman Empire from the First Century A.D. to the Third.* Baltimore: Johns Hopkins University Press, 1976.

Luz, Ulrich. *Exegetische Aufsätze.* WUNT 357. Tübingen: Mohr Siebeck, 2016.

———. *Matthew: A Commentary.* 3 vols. Hermeneia. Minneapolis: Fortress, 2007–2016.

MacArthur, Euan. *James Nayler and the Quest for Historic Quaker Identity.* Leiden: Brill, 2024.

Maccoby, Hyam. *Jesus the Pharisee.* London: SCM, 2003.

———. *Ritual and Morality: The Ritual Purity System and Its Place in Judaism.* Cambridge: Cambridge University Press, 1999.

MacDonald, Dennis R. *The Homeric Epics and the Gospel of Mark.* New Haven: Yale University Press, 2000.

Macquarrie, John. *The Scope of Demythologizing: Bultmann and His Critics.* London: SCM, 1960.

Magnússon, Sigurður Gylfi. "Far-Reaching Microhistory: The Use of Microhistorical Perspective in a Globalized World." *Rethinking History* 21.3 (2017): 312–41.

Mahmood, Saba. *Politics of Piety: The Islamic Revival and the Feminist Subject.* Princeton: Princeton University Press, 2005.

Māhuika, Rangimarie. "Kaupapa Māori Theory Is Critical and Anti-Colonial." *MAI Review* 3.4 (2008): 1–16.

Malina, Bruce J., and Jerome H. Neyrey. *Portraits of Paul: An Archaeology of Ancient Personality.* Louisville: Westminster John Knox, 1996.

Manogue, Ralph Anthony. "Southey and William Wordsworth: New Light on an Old Quarrel." *Charles Lamb Bulletin* 38 (1982): 105–14.

Manson, T. W. "The Son of Man in Daniel, Enoch, and the Gospels." *BJRL* 32 (1950): 171–95.

———. *The Teaching of Jesus.* Cambridge: Cambridge University, 1967.

Mantel, Hilary. "Resurrection: The Art and Craft." *BBC Radio 4.* Radio 4 Reith Lectures, 2017. https://www.bbc.co.uk/programmes/b08vkm52.

Marchal, Joseph, ed. *Bodies on the Verge: Queering Pauline Studies.* Atlanta: SBL Press, 2019.

Marcucci, Laetitia. "Physiognomic Roots in the Rhetoric of Cicero and Quintilian." Pages 183–201 in *Visualizing the Invisible with the Human Body: Physiognomy and Ekphrasis in the Ancient World.* Edited by J. Johnson and A. Stavru. Berlin: de Gruyter, 2019.

Marcus, Joel. *John the Baptist in History and Theology.* Columbia: University of South Carolina Press, 2018.

———. *Mark 1–8: A New Translation with Introduction and Commentary.* AB 27. New York: Doubleday, 2000.

———. *Mark 8–16: A New Translation with Introduction and Commentary.* AB 27A. New Haven: Yale University Press, 2009.

———. *The Way of the Lord: Christological Exegesis of the Old Testament in the Gospel of Mark.* London: T&T Clark, 1992.

Marin, Alexandra, and Barry Wellman. "Social Network Analysis: An Introduction." Pages 11–26 in *The SAGE Handbook of Social Network Analysis.* Edited by John Scott and Peter J. Carrington. London: SAGE, 2014.

Marriott, Brandon. *Transnational Networks and Cross-Religious Exchange in the Seventeenth-Century Mediterranean and Atlantic Worlds: Sabbatai Sevi and the Lost Tribes of Israel.* London: Routledge, 2015.

Marsh, Clive. "Quests of the Historical Jesus in New Historicist Perspective." *BibInt* 5 (1997): 403–37.

Martens, John W. "'But from the Beginning It Was Not So': The Jewish Apocalyptic Context of Jesus's Teaching on Marriage, Divorce, and Remarriage." *Journal of Moral Theology* 10.2 (2021): 5–33.

Martin, Clarice J. "Womanist Interpretations of the New Testament: The Quest for

Holistic and Inclusive Translation and Interpretation." Pages 19–41 in *I Found God in Me: A Womanist Biblical Hermeneutics Reader*. Edited by Mitzi J. Smith. Eugene, OR: Cascade, 2015.

Martin, Craig. *A Critical Introduction to the Study of Religion*. 2nd ed. New York: Routledge, 2017.

Martin, Dale. *The Corinthian Body*. New Haven: Yale University Press, 1999.

———. *Sex and the Single Savior: Gender and Sexuality in Biblical Interpretation*. Louisville: Westminster John Knox, 2006.

Martin, G. H., ed. *Knighton's Chronicle 1337–1396*. Oxford: Clarendon, 1995.

Marx, Karl, and Friedrich Engels. *The Marx-Engels Reader*. Edited by Robert C. Tucker. New York: Norton, 1978.

Marx-Wolf, Heidi. *Spiritual Taxonomies and Ritual Authority: Platonists, Priests, and Gnostics in the Third Century C. E.* Philadelphia: University of Pennsylvania Press, 2016.

Marxsen, Willi. *Der Evangelist Markus: Studien zur Redaktions-geschichte des Evangeliums*. 2nd ed. Göttingen: Vandenhoeck & Ruprecht, 1959.

Marzano, Annalisa. *Harvesting the Sea: The Exploitation of Marine Resources in the Roman Mediterranean*. Oxford Studies on the Roman Economy. Oxford: Oxford University Press, 2013.

Masquelier, Adeline. "From Hostage to Host: Confessions of a Spirit Medium in Niger." *Ethos* 30 (2002): 49–76.

Massumi, Brian. "Realer Than Real: The Simulacrum according to Deleuze and Guattari." *Copyright* 1 (1987): 90–97.

Masuzawa, Tomoko. *The Invention of World Religions*. Chicago: University of Chicago Press, 2005.

Matory, J. L. "Government by Seduction: History and Tropes of 'Mounting' in the Oyo-Yoruba." Pages 58–85 in *Modernity and Its Malcontents: Ritual and Power in Post-Colonial Africa*. Edited by Jean Comaroff and John F. Comaroff. Chicago: University of Chicago Press, 1993.

Mattila, Sharon Lea. "Jesus and the 'Middle Peasants'? Problematizing a Social-Scientific Concept." *CBQ* 72.2 (2010): 291–313.

———. "Revisiting Jesus' Capernaum: A Village of Only Subsistence-Level Fishers and Farmers?" Pages 75–138 in *The Galilean Economy in the Time of Jesus*. Edited by David A. Fiensy and Ralph K. Hawkins. Atlanta: SBL Press, 2013.

Mays, Kelly J. "Slaves in Heaven, Laborers in Hell: Chartist Poets' Ambivalent Identification with the (Black) Slave." *Victorian Poetry* 39 (2001): 137–63.

Maza, Sarah. *Thinking about History*. Chicago: University of Chicago Press, 2017.

McAlister, Elizabeth. "The Jew in the Haitian Imagination: A Popular History of Anti-Judaism and Proto-Racism." Pages 61–81 in *Race, Nation, and Religion in the*

Americas. Edited by Henry Goldschmidt and Elizabeth McAlister. Oxford: Oxford University Press, 2004.

McCalman, Iain. *Radical Underworld: Prophets, Revolutionaries, and Pornographers in London, 1795–1840*. Cambridge: Cambridge University Press, 1988.

McCauley, Esau. "Guest Editor's Foreword." *JSHJ* 17.3 (2019): 173–75.

McCollough, Tom. "The Synagogue at Khirbet Qana in Its Village Context." Pages 81–95 in *The Synagogue in Ancient Palestine: Current Issues and Emerging Trends*. Edited by Rick Bonnie, Raimo Hakola, and Ulla Tervahauta. FRLANT 279. Göttingen: Vandenhoeck & Ruprecht, 2020.

McCutcheon, Russell. *Critics Not Caretakers: Redescribing the Public Study of Religion*. Albany: SUNY Press, 2001.

———. "Myth." Pages 190–208 in *Guide to the Study of Religion*. Edited by Willi Braun and Russell T. McCutcheon. New York: Cassell, 2000.

McDowell, Sean. *The Fate of the Apostles: Examining the Martyrdom Accounts of the Closest Followers of Jesus*. Farnham: Ashgate, 2015.

McGinn, Thomas A. J. "The Law of Roman Divorce in the Time of Christ." Pages 309–22 in *The Historical Jesus in Context*. Edited by Amy-Jill Levine, Dale C. Allison Jr., and John Dominic Crossan. Princeton: Princeton University Press, 2006.

McGrath, James F. "Obedient unto Death: Philippians 2:8, Gethsemane, and the Historical Jesus." *JSHJ* 14 (2016): 223–40.

McGuire, Meredith B. *Lived Religion: Faith and Practice in Everyday Life*. Oxford: Oxford University Press, 2008.

McIver, Robert K. *Memory, Jesus, and the Synoptic Gospels*. Atlanta: Society of Biblical Literature, 2011.

McKnight, Scot. *Jesus and His Death: Historiography, the Historical Jesus, and Atonement Theory*. Waco, TX: Baylor University Press, 2005.

———. "Jesus and James on Israel and Purity." Pages 91–98 in *James the Just and Christian Origins*. Edited by Bruce Chilton and Craig A. Evans. NovTSup 98. Leiden: Brill, 1999.

McNeile, Alan Hugh. *The Gospel according to St. Matthew: The Greek Text with Introduction, Notes, and Indices*. London: Macmillan, 1915.

Meggitt, Justin J. "'More Ingenious Than Learned'? Examining the Quest for the Non-Historical Jesus." *NTS* 65.4 (2019): 443–60.

———. "Popular Mythology in the Early Empire and the Multiplicity of Jesus Traditions." Pages 53–80 in *Sources of the Jesus Tradition: Separating History from Myth*. Edited by R. Joseph Hoffmann. Amherst, NY: Prometheus, 2010.

Meier, John P. "The Debate on the Resurrection of the Dead: An Incident from the Ministry of the Historical Jesus?" *JSNT* 77 (2000): 3–24.

———. *A Marginal Jew: Rethinking the Historical Jesus*. 5 vols. AYBRL. New Haven: Yale University Press, 1991–2016.

———. "The Present State of the 'Third Quest' for the Historical Jesus." *Biblica* 80 (1999): 459–87.

Meinhardt, Molly Dewsnap, ed. *Jesus: The Last Day*. Washington, DC: Biblical Archaeology Society, 2003.

Melman, Billie. "Claiming the Nation's Past: The Invention of an Anglo-Saxon Tradition." *Journal of Contemporary History* 26 (1991): 575–95.

Menn, Esther Marie. *Judah and Tamar (Genesis 38) in Ancient Jewish Exegesis: Studies in Literary and Hermeneutics*. Leiden: Brill, 1997.

Meyer, Barbara. *Jesus the Jew in Christian Memory: Theological and Philosophical Explorations*. Cambridge: Cambridge University Press, 2020.

Micale, Mark. *Hysterical Men: The Hidden History of Male Nervous Illness*. Cambridge: Harvard University Press, 2008.

Middleton, Paul, ed. *The Wiley Blackwell Companion to Christian Martyrdom*. Hoboken, NJ: Wiley & Sons, 2020.

Milgrom, Jacob. "The Dynamics of Purity in the Priestly System." Pages 29–32 in *Purity and Holiness: The Heritage of Leviticus*. Edited by Marcel J. H. M. Poorthuis and Joshua Schwartz. Jewish and Christian Perspectives Series 2. Leiden: Brill, 2000.

———. "The Rationale for Biblical Impurity." *JANES* 22 (1993): 107–11.

Miller, Patricia Cox. *The Corporeal Imagination: Signifying the Holy in Late Ancient Christianity*. Philadelphia: University of Pennsylvania Press, 2009.

Miller, Richard C. "Mark's Empty Tomb and Other Translation Fables in Classical Antiquity." *JBL* 129.4 (2010): 759–76.

———. *Resurrection and Reception in Early Christianity*. New York: Routledge, 2015.

Miller, Robert J. "The Domain and Function of Epistemological Humility in Historical Jesus Studies." *JSHJ* 12 (2014): 130–42.

———. "When It's Futile to Argue about the Historical Jesus." *JSHJ* 9 (2011): 85–95.

Miller, Stuart S. *At the Intersection of Texts and Material Finds: Stepped Pools, Stone Vessels, and Ritual Purity among the Jews of Roman Galilee*. JAJSup 16. Göttingen: Vandenhoeck & Ruprecht, 2015.

Minnen, Peter van. "House-to-House Enquiries: An Interdisciplinary Approach to Roman Karanis." *ZPE* 100 (1994): 227–51.

Mitchell, Allan. *The Great Train Race: Railways and the Franco-German Rivalry, 1815–1914*. New York: Berghahn, 2000.

Mitchell, David T. *Cultural Locations of Disability*. Chicago: University of Chicago Press, 2006.

Mitchell, David T., and Sharon Snyder. "'Jesus Thrown Everything off Balance': Disability and Redemption in Biblical Literature." Pages 173–84 in *This Abled Body: Re-*

thinking Disabilities in Biblical Studies. Edited by Hector Avalos, Sarah Melcher, and Jeremy Schipper. Atlanta: Society of Biblical Literature, 2007.

Møller, Hilde Brekke. *The Vermes Quest: The Significance of Geza Vermes for Jesus Research*. London and New York: T&T Clark, 2017.

Momigliano, Arnaldo. *The Development of Greek Biography*. Cambridge: Harvard University Press, 1971.

Moore, Stephen. *God's Beauty Parlor: And Other Queer Spaces in and around the Bible*. Stanford: Stanford University Press, 2001.

———. *God's Gym: Divine Male Bodies of the Bible*. New York: Routledge, 1996.

Moore, Stephen D., and Janice Capel Anderson, eds. *New Testament Masculinities*. SemeiaSt 45. Atlanta: Society of Biblical Literature, 2003.

———, "Taking It like a Man: Masculinity in 4 Maccabees." *JBL* 117 (1998): 249–73.

Moore, Stephen D., and Yvonne Sherwood. *The Invention of the Biblical Scholar: A Critical Manifesto*. Minneapolis: Fortress, 2011.

Moreland, Milton. "The Jesus Movement in the Villages of Roman Galilee: Archaeology, Q, and Modern Anthropological Theory." Pages 159–80 in *Oral Performance, Popular Tradition, and Hidden Transcript in Q*. Edited by Richard A. Horsley. Atlanta: SBL Press, 2006.

Morgan, David. *Icons of American Protestantism: The Art of Warner Sallman*. New Haven: Yale University Press, 1996.

Morris, Colin. *Unyoung, Uncoloured, Unpoor*. London: Epworth, 1969.

Morris, Leon. *The Gospel according to Matthew*. Grand Rapids: Eerdmans, 1992.

Morrison, Linda J. *Talking Back to Psychiatry: The Psychiatric Consumer/Survivor/Ex-Patient Movement*. New York: Routledge, 2005.

Morrison, Toni. *The Source of Self-Regard*. New York: Vintage, 2019.

Moscrop, John J. *Measuring Jerusalem: The Palestine Exploration Fund and British Interests in the Holy Land*. Leicester: Leicester University Press, 1999.

Moss, Candida R. "Between the Lines: Looking for the Contributions of Enslaved Literate Laborers in a Second-Century Text (P. Berol. 11632)." *Studies in Late Antiquity* 5.3 (2021): 432–52.

———. "Christly Possession and Weakened Bodies: Reconsideration of the Function of Paul's Thorn in the Flesh (2 Cor. 12:7–10)." *Journal of Religion, Disability, and Health* (2012): 319–33.

———. *Divine Bodies: Resurrecting Perfection in the New Testament and Early Christianity*. New Haven: Yale University Press, 2019.

———. "Exploitation, Exorcism, and Power: Reconfiguring Culpability for Possession in the New Testament." Paper presented at the Deliver Us from Evil Conference, Church of England, online, January 20, 2022.

———. "Fashioning Mark: Early Christian Discussions about the Scribe and Status of the Second Gospel." *NTS* 67 (2021): 181–204.

———. "The Man with the Flow of Power: Porous Bodies in Mark 5:25–34." *JBL* 129 (2010): 507–19.

———. "Mark and Matthew." Pages 275–302 in *The Bible and Disability: A Commentary.* Edited by Sarah J. Melcher, Mikeal C. Parsons, and Amos Yong. Waco, TX: Baylor University Press, 2017.

———. *The Myth of Persecution: How Early Christians Invented a Story of Martyrdom.* New York: HarperOne, 2013.

———. "The Secretary: Enslaved Workers, Stenography, and the Production of Early Christian Literature." *JTS* 74.1 (2023): 20–56.

Moss, Candida R., and Jeremy Schipper, eds. *Disability Studies and Biblical Literature.* New York: Palgrave Macmillan, 2011.

Mosser, Carl. "Torah Instruction, Discussion, and Prophecy in First-Century Synagogues." Pages 523–51 in *Christian Origins and Hellenistic Judaism: Social and Literary Contexts for the New Testament.* Edited by Stanley E. Porter and Andrew Pitts. TENTS 10. Leiden: Brill, 2013.

Moule, C. F. D., and Ernst Bammel, eds. *Jesus and the Politics of His Day.* Cambridge: Cambridge University Press, 1983.

Moulton, James H., and George Milligan. *The Vocabulary of the Greek Testament Illustrated from the Papyri and Other Non-Literary Sources.* London: Hodder and Stoughton, 1930.

Mournet, Terence C. *Oral Tradition and Literary Dependency: Variability and Stability in the Synoptic Tradition and Q.* WUNT 195. Tübingen: Mohr Siebeck, 2005.

Moxnes, Halvor. "The Contextuality of Constructing Histories of Jesus: Modern and Ancient Masculinities." Pages 93–114 in *Jesus, Quo Vadis? Entwicklungen und Perspektiven der aktuellen Jesusforschung.* Edited by Eckhart David Schmidt. Biblisch-Theologische Studien 177. Göttingen: Vandenhoeck & Ruprecht, 2018.

———. "From Unique Personality to Charismatic Movement: 100 Years of Shifting Paradigms in Historical Jesus Research." Pages 187–200 in *Religion in Late Modernity: Essays in Honor of Pål Repstad.* Edited by Inger Furseth and Paul Leer-Salvesen. Trondheim: Tapir, 2007.

———. "The Historical Jesus: From Master Narrative to Cultural Context." *BTB* 28.4 (1998): 135–49.

———. *Jesus and the Rise of Nationalism: A New Quest for the Nineteenth-Century Historical Jesus.* London: I. B. Tauris, 2012.

———. *Memories of Jesus: A Journey through Time.* Eugene, OR: Wipf & Stock, 2021.

———. *Putting Jesus in His Place: A Radical Vision of Household and Kingdom.* Louisville: Westminster John Knox, 2003.

———. "Was Jesus a Charismatic Leader? The Use of Social Models in the History of the Jesus Movement." Pages 51–72 in *"Lampada per i miei passi è la tua parola, luce sul mio cammino" (Sal 119,105): Studi offerti a Marcello Del Verme in occasione del suo 75° compleanno.* Edited by P. Giustiniani and F. del Pizzo. Bornato in Franciacorta: Sardini, 2017.

Mroczek, Eva. *The Literary Imagination in Jewish Antiquity.* Oxford: Oxford University Press, 2016.

Muehlberger, Ellen. *Angels in Late Ancient Christianity.* Oxford: Oxford University Press, 2013.

Muggleton, Lodowick. *The Acts of the Witnesses of the Spirit in Five Parts.* London: s.n., 1699.

———. *A True Interpretation of the Eleventh Chapter of the Revelation of St. John.* London: s.n., 1662.

Munro, Winsome. *Jesus Born a Slave: The Social and Economic Origins of Jesus' Message.* Lewiston, NY: Mellen, 1998.

Musurillo, Herbert. *Acts of the Christian Martyrs.* Vol. 2. Oxford: Oxford University Press, 1972.

Myles, Robert J., ed. *Class Struggle in the New Testament.* Lanham, MD: Lexington/Fortress Academic, 2019.

———. "The Fetish for a Subversive Jesus." *JSHJ* 14.1 (2016): 52–70.

———. "Fishing for Entrepreneurs in the Sea of Galilee? Unmasking Neoliberal Ideology in Biblical Interpretation." Pages 115–38 in *Class Struggle in the New Testament.* Edited by Robert J. Myles. Lanham, MD: Lexington/Fortress Academic, 2019.

Myllykoski, Matti. "The Social History of Q and the Jewish War." Pages 143–99 in *Symbols and Strata: Essays on the Sayings Gospel Q.* Edited by Risto Uro. Helsinki: The Finnish Exegetical Society, 1996.

Naish, Darren. *Dinopedia: A Brief Compendium of Dinosaur Lore.* Princeton: Princeton University Press, 2021.

Nash, Geoffrey. "Death and Resurrection: The Renans in Syria (1860–61)." Pages 69–77 in *Knowledge Is Light: Travellers in the Near East.* Edited by Katherine Salahi. Oxford: Oxbow, 2011.

Nayler, James. *A Collection of Sundry Books, Epistles and Papers Written by James Nayler.* Edited by George Whitehead. London: Sowle, 1716.

———. *Glory to God Almighty Who Ruleth in the Heavens, and in Whose Hands Are All the Kingdoms of the Earth.* London: Simmons, 1659.

Neirynck, Frans. "Papyrus Egerton 2 and the Healing of the Leper." *ETL* 61 (1985): 153–60.

Neisser, Ulric. "John Dean's Memory: A Case Study." Pages 102–15 in *Introductory Readings for Cognitive Psychology*. Edited by Richard P. Honeck. Guilford, CT: Duskin, 1994.

Newmyer, Stephen T. "Talmudic Medicine and Greco-Roman Science: Crosscurrents and Resistance." *ANRW* 37.3:2895–911.

Ngata, Apirana T. *Rauru nui a Toi Lectures and Ngati Kahungunu Origin*. Wellington: Victoria University Press, 1972.

Niditch, Susan. *The Symbolic Vision in Biblical Tradition*. HSM 30. Cambridge: Scholars Press, 1980.

Niederwimmer, Kurt. *The Didache: A Commentary*. Hermeneia. Minneapolis: Fortress, 1998.

Nineham, Dennis. "Epilogue." Pages 186–204 in *The Myth of God Incarnate*. Edited by John Hick. London: SCM, 1977.

Novakovic, Lidija. "The Scriptures and Scriptural Interpretation." Pages 85–104 in *The World of the New Testament: Cultural, Social, and Historical Contexts*. Edited by Joel B. Green and Lee Martin McDonald. Grand Rapids: Baker Academic, 2013.

Novenson, Matthew V. *The Grammar of Messianism: An Ancient Jewish Political Idiom and Its Users*. New York: Oxford University Press, 2017.

Nutton, Vivian. *Ancient Medicine*. 2nd ed. New York: Routledge, 2013.

Oakman, Douglas E. *Jesus and the Peasants*. Matrix: The Bible in Mediterranean Context 4. Eugene, OR: Wipf & Stock, 2008.

——. *The Radical Jesus, the Bible, and the Great Transformation*. Matrix: The Bible in Mediterranean Context 12. Eugene, OR: Cascade, 2021.

Ogden, Daniel. *Greek and Roman Necromancy*. Princeton: Princeton University Press, 2004.

——. *Magic, Witchcraft, and Ghosts in the Greek and Roman Worlds: A Sourcebook*. 2nd ed. Oxford: Oxford University Press, 2009.

Ogden, Schubert M. *Christ without Myth: A Study Based on the Theology of Rudolf Bultmann*. New York: Harper & Bros., 1961.

Ohman, Richard. *Politics of Knowledge: The Commercialization of the University, the Professions, and Print Culture*. Middletown: Wesleyan University Press, 2003.

Oldenhage, Tania. "Walking the Way of the Cross: German Places, Church Traditions, and Holocaust Memories." Pages 89–99 in *Religion, Violence, Memory, and Place*. Edited by Oren Baruch Stier and J. Shawn Landres. Bloomington: Indiana University Press, 2006.

O'Neill, Mrs. *The Bondman: A Story of the Days of Wat Tyler*. London: Smith, Elder, and Co., 1833.

Oppenheim, A. Leo. *The Interpretation of Dreams in the Ancient Near East: With a*

Translation of an Assyrian Dream-Book. TAPS 46/3. Philadelphia: American Philosophical Society, 1956.

Orsi, Robert A. *Between Heaven and Earth: The Religious Worlds People Make and the Scholars Who Study Them.* Princeton: Princeton University Press, 2005.

———. "When 2+2=5." *The American Scholar*, March 1, 2007. https://theamericanscho lar.org/when-2-2-5/.

Osborne, Grant R. "Tradition Criticism and Jesus Research." Page 1:673–93 in *Handbook for the Study of the Historical Jesus.* Edited by Tom Holmén and Stanley E. Porter. 4 vols. Leiden: Brill, 2011.

Osiek, Carolyn. "The Women at the Tomb: What Are They Doing There?" *Ex Auditu* 9 (1993): 97–107.

Ott, Heinrich. "Rudolf Bultmann's Philosophy of History." Pages 51–64 in *The Theology of Rudolf Bultmann.* Edited by Charles W. Kegley. New York: Harper & Row, 1966.

Outka, Elizabeth. "Buying Time: *Howards End* and Commodified Nostaglia." *Modernisms* 36.3 (2003): 330–50.

Packer, Ian, Tim Fulford, and Lynda Pratt, eds. *The Collected Letters of Robert Southey: Part Five, 1816–1818.* Romantic Circles, 2016. https://romantic-circles.org/edi tions/southey_letters/Part_Five/HTML/letterEEd.26.2882.html.

Pagán, Victoria E. "Beyond Teutoburg: Transgression and Transformation in Tacitus *Annales* 1.61–62." *CP* 94 (1999): 302–20.

Paine, Thomas. *The Age of Reason: Being an Investigation of True and of Fabulous Theology.* Boston: Hall, 1794.

———. *The Age of Reason: Being an Investigation of True and of Fabulous Theology. Part the Second.* London: Symonds, 1795.

———. *Examination of the Passages in the New Testament, Quoted from the Old and Called Prophecies concerning Jesus Christ.* New York: Paine, 1807.

———. *The Theological Works.* London: Carlile, 1819.

Palacek, Martin. "The Ontological Turn Revisited: Theoretical Decline; Why Cannot Ontologists Fulfil Their Promise?" *Anthropological Theory* 22.2 (2022): 154–75.

Palmié, Stephan. *Wizards and Scientists: Explorations in Afro-Cuban Modernity and Tradition.* Durham: Duke University Press, 2002.

Paringatai, Karyn. "Māori Identity Development outside of Tribal Environments." *Aotearoa New Zealand Social Work* 26.1 (2014): 49.

Park, Wongi. "Multiracial Biblical Studies." *JBL* 140.3 (2021): 425–59.

———. *The Politics of Race and Ethnicity in Matthew's Passion Narrative.* New York: Palgrave Macmillan, 2019.

Parker, Angela N. *If God Still Breathes, Why Can't I? Black Lives Matter and Biblical Authority.* Grand Rapids: Eerdmans, 2021.

———. "Invoking Paul's μὴ γένοιτο and Sofia's 'Hell No' against the Stubborn Whiteness of Biblical Scholarship." *Political Theology Network*, November 26, 2020. https://politicaltheology.com/invoking-pauls-μὴ-γένοιτο-and-sofias-hell-no-against-the-stubborn-whiteness-of-biblical-scholarship/.

Parker, D. C. *The Living Text of the Gospels*. Cambridge: Cambridge University Press, 1997.

Parker, Robert. *Miasma: Pollution and Purification in Early Greek Religion*. Oxford: Clarendon, 1983.

Parks, Sara. "'The Brooten Phenomenon': Moving Women from the Margins in Second-Temple and New Testament Scholarship." *BCT* 15 (2019): 46–64.

———. "John the Baptist's Murder and the Vengeful Logia of Jesus: Thinking with Trauma Theory about the Stratification of Q." Paper presented at the Enoch Seminar Nangeroni Meeting on John the Baptist. Online, January 14, 2021.

———. *Women in Q: Gender in the Rhetoric of Jesus*. Minneapolis: Fortress, 2019.

Parsons, Mikeal C. *Body and Character in Luke and Acts: The Subversion of Physiognomy in Early Christianity*. Grand Rapids: Baker Academic, 2006.

Pate, C. Marvin, and Douglas C. Kennard. *Deliverance Now and Not Yet: The New Testament and the Great Tribulation*. StBibLit 54. New York: Lang, 2003.

Patel, Shaily Shashikant. "Magic and Its Malcontents: Historiography as Heresiology." Paper presented at the Abrahamic Vernaculars Lecture Series, University of Michigan. Ann Arbor, MI, November 11, 2021.

———. *Smoke and Mirrors: Discourses of Magic in Early Petrine Traditions*. New York: Oxford University Press, forthcoming.

Patterson, Orlando. *Slavery and Social Death: A Comparative Study*. Cambridge: Harvard University Press, 2018.

Patterson, Stephen J. "The Historical Jesus and the Search for God." *HTS* 54 (1998): 476–503.

Patton, Laurie, and Wendy Doniger, eds. *Myth and Method*. Charlottesville: University of Virginia Press, 1996.

Patzelt, Maik. "Introduction to Section 1." Pages 11–22 in *Lived Religion in the Ancient Mediterranean World: Approaching Religious Transformations from Archaeology, History and Classics*. Edited by Valentino Gasparani, Maik Patzelt, and Rubina Raja. Berlin: de Gruyter 2020.

Peabody, David Barrett. "H. J. Holtzmann and His European Colleagues: Aspects of the Nineteenth-Century Discussion of Gospel Origins." Pages 50–131 in *Biblical Studies and the Shifting of Paradigms, 1850–1914*. Edited by Henning Graf Reventlow and William Farmer. Sheffield: Sheffield Academic, 1995.

Peirce, Charles S. *Collected Papers I–VIII*. Edited by Charles Hartshome, Paul Weiss, and Arthur W. Burks. Cambridge: Harvard University Press, 1931–1958.

Pelling, C. B. R. "Childhood and Personality in Greek Biography." Pages 213–44 in *Char-*

acterization and Individuality in Greek Literature. Edited by C. B. R. Pelling. Oxford: Clarendon, 1990.

—————. *Life of Antony*. Cambridge: Cambridge University Press, 1988.

—————. "Truth and Fiction in Plutarch's *Lives*." Pages 19–52 in *Antonine Literature*. Edited by D. A. Russell. Oxford: Oxford University Press, 1990.

Peltonen, Matti. "Clues, Margins, and Monads: The Micro-Macro Link in Historical Research." *HistTh* 40.3 (2001): 347–59.

Pendleton-Jullian, Ann, and John Seely Brown. *Design Unbound: Designing for Emergence in a White Water World*. 2 vols. Cambridge: MIT Press, 2018.

Pérez i Díaz, Mar. *Mark, A Pauline Theologian: A Re-Reading of the Traditions of Jesus in the Light of Paul's Theology*. Tübingen: Mohr Siebeck, 2020.

Perkins, Judith. "Fictive Scheintod and Christian Resurrection." *R&T* 13.3 (2006): 396–418.

Perkins, Pheme. "The Resurrection of Jesus of Nazareth." Pages 423–42 in *Studying the Historical Jesus*. Edited by Bruce Chilton and Craig Evans. Leiden: Brill, 1994.

Perrin, Andrew B. *The Dynamics of Dream-Vision Revelation in the Aramaic Dead Sea Scrolls*. JAJSup 19. Göttingen: Vandenhoeck & Ruprecht, 2017.

Perrin, Norman. *A Modern Pilgrimage in New Testament Christology*. Philadelphia: Fortress, 1974.

—————. *What Is Redaction Criticism?* London: SPCK, 1970.

Pesch, Rudolf. "Zur Entstehung des Glaubens an die Auferstehung Jesu: Ein Vorschlag zur Diskussion." *Theologische Quartalschrift* 153.3 (1973): 201–28.

Peters, Janelle. "Gendered Activity and Jesus's Saying Not to Worry." *Neot* 50 (2016): 35–52.

—————. "Robes of Transfiguration and Salvation in Early Christian Texts." Pages 279–88 in *Dress in Mediterranean Antiquity: Greeks, Romans, Jews, Christians*. Edited by Alicia Batten and Kelly Olson. London: Bloomsbury, 2021.

Peters, Kate. *Print Culture and the Early Quakers*. Cambridge Studies in Early Modern British History. Cambridge: Cambridge University Press, 2005.

Petersen, Lauren Hackworth. "The Baker His Tomb His Wife and Her Breadbasket: The Monument of Eurysaces in Rome." *Art Bulletin* (2003): 230–57.

Peterson, Anna L., and Manuel A. Vásquez. "Oscar Romero and the Politics of Sainthood." *Postscripts* 5.3 (2009): 265–91.

Petsalis-Diomidis, Alexia. *Truly beyond Wonders: Aelius Aristides and the Cult of Asklepios*. Oxford: Oxford University Press, 2010.

Pettitt. Thomas. "'Here Comes I, Jack Straw': English Folk Drama and Social Revolt." *Folklore* 95 (1984): 3–20.

Phlegon of Tralles' Book of Marvels. Edited and translated by William Hansen. Exeter: University of Exeter Press, 1996.

Pinheiro, Ester. "Brazil Continues to Be the Country with the Largest Number of Trans

People Killed." *Brasil de Fato*, January 24, 2022. https://www.brasildefato.com
.br/2022/01/23/brazil-continues-to-be-the-country-with-the-largest-number-of
-trans-people-killed.

Pitre, Brant. *Jesus, the Tribulation, and the End of the Exile: Restoration Eschatology
and the Origin of the Atonement.* WUNT 204. Tübingen: Mohr Siebeck, 2005.

Pitre, Brant, Michael P. Barber, and John A. Kincaid. *Paul, a New Covenant Jew: Rethinking Pauline Theology.* Grand Rapids: Eerdmans, 2019.

Pizzolato, Nicola. *Challenging Global Capitalism: Labor, Migration, Radical Struggle
and Urban Change in Detroit and Turin.* New York: Palgrave Macmillan, 2013.

Plum, Karin Friis. "Genealogy as Theology." *SJT* 3.1 (1989): 66–92.

Plumer, Eric. *Augustine's Commentary on Galatians.* Oxford: Oxford University Press,
2003.

Plutarch. *Lives.* Vol. 6, *Dion and Brutus. Timoleon and Aemilius Paulus.* Translated by
Bernadotte Perrin. LCL. Cambridge: Harvard University Press, 1918.

Porter, James. *Homer: The Very Idea.* Chicago: University of Chicago Press, 2021.

Porter, Stanley E. *The Criteria for Authenticity in Historical Jesus Research: Previous
Discussions and New Proposals.* LNTS 191. London: T&T Clark, 2000.

Porter, Stanley E., and Andrew W. Pitts. "The Pre-Citation Fallacy in New Testament
Scholarship and Sanders's Tendencies of the Synoptic Tradition." Pages 89–107
in *Christian Origins and the Establishment of the Early Jesus Movement.* Edited
by Stanley E. Porter and Andrew W. Pitts. TENTS 12. Leiden: Brill, 2018.

Prescott, Andrew. "Judicial Records of the Rising of 1381." PhD diss., University of London, 1984.

Price, Margaret. "Defining Mental Disability." Pages 333–42 in *The Disability Studies
Reader.* Edited by Lennard J. Davis. 5th ed. New York: Routledge, 2017.

Priest, Robert D. *The Gospel according to Renan: Reading, Writing, and Religion in
Nineteenth-Century France.* Oxford Historical Monographs. Oxford: Oxford
University Press, 2015.

Priestley, Jessica. *Herodotus and Hellenistic Culture: Literary Studies in the Reception of
the Histories.* Oxford: Oxford University Press, 2014.

Proctor, Travis. *Demonic Bodies and the Dark Ecologies of Early Christian Culture.* Oxford: Oxford University Press, 2022.

Prosser, Jay. *Second Skins: The Body Narratives of Transsexuality.* New York: Columbia
University Press, 1998.

Pryzwansky, Molly M. "Cornelius Nepos: Key Issues and Critical Approaches." *CJ* 105
(2009): 97–108.

Pummer, Reinhard. *The Samaritans: A Profile.* Grand Rapids: Eerdmans, 2016.

———. "Samaritan Synagogues and Jewish Synagogues: Similarities and Differences."
Pages 105–42 in *Jews, Christians, and Polytheists in the Ancient Synagogue: Cul-*

tural Interaction during the Greco-Roman Period. Edited by Steve Fine. New York: Routledge, 1999.

Purzycki, Benjamin G., and Richard Sosis. *Religion Evolving: Cultural, Cognitive, and Ecological Dynamics.* Sheffield: Equinox, 2022.

Ragin, Charles C. *The Comparative Method: Moving beyond Qualitative and Quantitative Strategies.* Oakland: University of California Press, 2014.

Raja, Rubina. *Urban Development and Regional Identities in the Eastern Roman Provinces, 50 BC–AD 250: Aphrodisias, Ephesos, Athens, Gerasa.* Copenhagen: Museum Tusculanum, 2012.

Ramelli, Ilaria, and David Konstan. "The Use of *XAPA* in the New Testament and Its Background in Hellenistic Moral Philosophy." *Exemplaria Classica* 14 (2010): 185–204.

Randall, Thomas, trans. *S. John 9–21.* Vol. 2 of *Commentary on the Gospel according to S. John.* Library of the Fathers of the Holy Catholic Church 48. London: Smith, 1885.

Raphael, Rebecca. *Biblical Corpora: Representations of Disability in Hebrew Biblical Literature.* LHBOTS 445. London: T&T Clark, 2008.

Rasimus, Tuomas, Troels Engberg-Pedersen, and Ismo Dunderberg, eds. *Stoicism in Early Christianity.* Grand Rapids: Baker Academic, 2010.

Rau, Eckhard, and Silke Petersen. *Perspektiven des Lebens Jesu: Plädoyer für die Anknüpfung an eine schwierige Forschungstradition.* Stuttgart: Kohlhammer, 2013.

Rawson, Elizabeth. *Intellectual Life in the Late Roman Republic.* London: Duckworth, 2002.

Raynaud, Gaston. *Chroniques de J. Froissart: Tome Dixième 1380–1382.* Paris: Renouard, 1869.

Redden, Jason. "Social Formation in the Study of Religion." *RC* 9 (2015): 501–11.

Reed, Annette Yoshiko. "Writing Jewish Astronomy in the Early Hellenistic Age: The Enochic *Astronomical Book* as Aramaic Wisdom and Archival Impulse." *DSD* 24 (2017): 1–37.

Reed, Jonathan L. "The Archaeological Contributions to the Study of Jesus and the Gospels." Pages 40–54 in *The Historical Jesus in Context.* Edited by Amy-Jill Levine, Dale C. Allison Jr., and John Dominic Crossan. Princeton: Princeton University Press, 2007.

———. *Archaeology and the Galilean Jesus: A Re-Examination of the Evidence.* Harrisburg, PA: Trinity Press International, 2000.

———. *The HarperCollins Visual Guide to the New Testament: What Archaeology Reveals about the First Christians.* New York: HarperCollins, 2007.

———. "Overcoming the James Ossuary and the Legacy of Biblical Archaeology." Pages

187–206 in *Resurrecting the Brother of Jesus*. Edited by Ryan Byrne and Bernadette McNary-Zak. Chapel Hill: University of North Carolina Press, 2009.

———. Review of *Herod Antipas in Galilee: The Literary and Archaeological Sources on
the Reign of Herod Antipas and Its Socio-Economic Impact on Galilee*, by Morton H. Jensen. *JSJ* 38.3 (2007): 402–5.

———. "The Social Map of Q." Pages 17–36 in *Conflict and Invention: Literary, Rhetorical, and Social Studies on the Sayings Gospel Q*. Edited by John S. Kloppenborg.
Valley Forge, PA: Trinity Press International, 1995.

Reed, Randall. *A Clash of Ideologies: Marxism, Liberation Theology, and Apocalypticism
in New Testament Studies*. Eugene, OR: Pickwick, 2010.

Reeve, John, and Lodowick Muggleton. *A Transcendent Spirituall Treatise upon Several
Heavenly Doctrines*. London: s.n., 1653.

Reeves, Keith H. *The Resurrection Narrative in Matthew: A Literary-Critical Examination*. Lampeter: Mellen, 1993.

———. "They Worshipped Him, and They Doubted: Matthew 28.17." *Bible Translator* 49.3 (1998): 344–49.

Reimarus, Hermann Samuel. *Reimarus: Fragments*. Edited by Charles Talbert. Translated by Ralph S. Fraser. Lives of Jesus Series. Philadelphia: Fortress, 1970.

Reinhartz, Adele. *Caiaphas the High Priest*. Columbia: University of South Carolina
Press, 2011.

———. *Cast out of the Covenant: Jews and Anti-Judaism in the Gospel of John*. Lanham,
MD: Lexington/Fortress Academic, 2018.

———. "The Vanishing Jews of Antiquity." *Marginalia Review of Books*, June 24,
2014. http://marginalia.lareviewofbooks.org/vanishing-jews-antiquity-adele-
reinhartz/.

Renan, Joseph Ernest. *The History of the Origins of Christianity. Book I. Life of Jesus*.
London: Matthieson and Co., 1896.

———. *Mission de Phénicie*. Paris: Imprimerie impériale, 1864.

Rhani, Zakaria. "Le chérif et la possédée: Sainteté, rituel et pouvoir au Maroc."
L'homme 190 (2009): 27–50.

Rich, Robert. *Hidden Things Brought to Light*. London: Smith, 1678.

Richardson, Megan. *The Right to Privacy: Origins and Influence of a Nineteenth-Century
Idea*. Cambridge: Cambridge University Press, 2017.

Richardson, Peter. *Building Jewish in the Roman East*. Waco, TX: Baylor University Press,
2004.

Riemer, Ulrike. "Miracle Stories and Their Narrative Intent in the Context of the Ruler
Cult of Classical Antiquity." Pages 32–47 in *Wonders Never Cease: The Purpose
of Narrating Miracle Stories in the New Testament and Its Religious Environment*.

Edited by Michael Labahn and B. Jan Lietaert Peerbolte. LNTS 288. London: T&T Clark, 2006.

Robbins, Michael. *The Primordial Mind in Health and Illness: A Cross-Cultural Perspective.* London: Routledge, 2011.

Roberts, Erin. "Myth, Our Bloodless Battleground." Pages 9–17 in *Christian Tourist Attractions, Mythmaking, and Identity Formation.* Edited by Erin Roberts and Jennifer Eyl. London: Bloomsbury, 2019.

Robinson, Edward. *Biblical Researches in Palestine and Adjacent Countries.* 3 vols. London: Murray, 1841.

Robinson, James M. *The Gospel of Jesus: In Search of the Original Good News.* San Francisco: HarperOne, 2005.

———. *A New Quest for the Historical Jesus.* SBT 25. London: SCM, 1959.

———. *The Problem of History in Mark.* SBT 21. London: SCM, 1957.

———. "The Recent Debate on the 'New Quest.'" *JBR* 30.3 (1962): 198–208.

Robinson, James M., and Christoph Heil. "The Lilies of the Field: Saying 36 of the Gospel of Thomas and Secondary Accretions in Q 12.22b–31." *NTS* 47 (2001): 1–25.

Robinson, James M., Paul Hoffmann, and John S. Kloppenborg. *The Critical Edition of Q.* Hermeneia. Minneapolis: Fortress, 2000.

Rocca, Samuel. *Herod's Judaea: A Mediterranean State in the Classical World.* TSAJ 122. Tübingen: Mohr Siebeck, 2008.

Rodríguez, Rafael. "Authenticating Criteria: The Use and Misuse of a Critical Method." *JSHJ* 7 (2009): 152–67.

———. "The Embarrassing Truth about Jesus: The Criterion of Embarrassment and the Failure of Historical Authenticity." Pages 132–51 in *Jesus, Criteria, and the Demise of Authenticity.* Edited by Chris Keith and Anthony Le Donne. London: T&T Clark, 2012.

———. "Great Divide." Pages 163–64 in *The Dictionary of the Bible and Ancient Media.* Edited by Tom Thatcher, Chris Keith, Raymond F. Person Jr., and Elsie R. Stern. London: Bloomsbury, 2017.

———. *Jesus Darkly: Remembering Jesus with the New Testament.* Nashville: Abingdon, 2018.

———. *Oral Tradition and the New Testament: A Guide for the Perplexed.* London: T&T Clark, 2014.

———. *Structuring Early Christian Memory: Jesus in Tradition, Performance, and Text.* LNTS 407. London: T&T Clark, 2010.

———. "What Is History? Reading John 1 as Historical Representation." *JSHJ* 16 (2018): 31–51.

———. "Your Will Be Done: Remembering Jesus' Submission to the Father." Pages 294–318 in *"To Recover What Has Been Lost": Essays on Eschatology, Intertextual-*

ity, and Reception History in Honor of Dale C. Allison Jr. Edited by Tucker S. Ferda, Daniel Frayer-Griggs, and Nathan C. Johnson. NovTSup 183. Leiden: Brill, 2021.

———. "Zeal That Consumed: Memory of Jerusalem's Temple and Jesus's Body in the Gospel of John." Pages 201–18 in *The Gospel of John*. Edited by Thomas R. Hatina. Vol. 4 of *Biblical Interpretation in Early Christian Gospels*. LNTS 613. London: T&T Clark, 2020.

Rollens, Sarah E. *Framing Social Criticism in the Jesus Movement: The Ideological Project in the Sayings Gospel Q.* Tübingen: Mohr Siebeck, 2014.

———. "Why We Have Failed to Theorize Scribes in Antiquity." Pages 117–33 in *Scribal Practices and Social Structures among Jesus' Adherents: Essays in Honour of John S. Kloppenborg*. Edited by William E. Arnal, Richard A. Ascough, Robert A. Derrenbacker, and Philip A. Harland. BETL 285. Leuven: Peeters, 2016.

Rollens, Sarah E., and Anthony Le Donne. "The Historical Jesus." Pages 50–72 in *The Cambridge Companion to the New Testament*. Edited by Patrick Gray. Cambridge: Cambridge University Press, 2021.

Romero, Óscar. *Su diario: del 31 de marzo 1978 al 20 de marzo de 1980*. San Salvador: Archdiocese of San Salvador, 1990.

Ronis, Sara. "Space, Place, and the Race for Power: Rabbis, Demons, and the Construction of Babylonia." *HTR* 110.4 (2017): 588–603.

Roos, Julia. "An Afro-German Microhistory: Gender, Religion, and the Challenges of Diasporic Dwelling." *Central European History* 49.2 (2016): 240–60.

Roth, Jonathan P. "The Army and the Economy in Judaea and Palaestina." Pages 375–97 in *The Roman Army and the Economy*. Edited by Paul Erdkamp. Amsterdam: Gieben, 2002.

———. "Jewish Military Forces in the Roman Service." Pages 79–94 in *Essential Essays for the Study of the Military in New Testament Palestine*. Edited by Christopher B. Zeichmann. Eugene, OR: Wipf & Stock, 2019.

Rothschild, Clare K. *Baptist Traditions and Q*. WUNT 190. Tübingen: Mohr Siebeck, 2005.

Rousseau, John J., and Rami Arav. *Jesus and His World: An Archaeological and Cultural Dictionary*. Minneapolis: Fortress, 1995.

Rowe, C. Kavin. *One True Life: The Stoics and Early Christians as Rival Traditions*. New Haven: Yale University Press, 2016.

Rowland, Christopher. *The Open Heaven: A Study of Apocalyptic in Judaism and Early Christianity*. London: SPCK, 1982.

Royal, Te Ahukaramu. "Te Ao Mārama: A Research Paradigm in Te Pūmanawa Hauora." Pages 78–87 in *Proceedings of Te Oru Rangahau: Māori Research and Development Conference*. Palmerston North: School of Māori Studies, 1998.

Royle, Edward. *Revolutionary Britannia? Reflections on the Threat of Revolution in Britain, 1789–1848*. Manchester: Manchester University Press, 2000.

Ruberg, Willemijn. *History of the Body.* London: Red Globe, 2020.

Ruether, Rosemary Radford. "Anti-Semitism in Christian Theology." *Theology Today* 30.4 (1974): 365–81.

———. "Can Christology Be Liberated from Patriarchy?" Pages 7–29 in *Reconstructing the Christ Symbol.* Edited by M. Stevens. New York: Paulist, 1993.

———. *Faith and Fratricide.* New York: Seabury, 1974.

Runesson, Anders. "The Historical Jesus, the Gospels, and First-Century Jewish Society: The Importance of the Synagogue for Understanding the New Testament." Pages 265–97 in *A City Set on a Hill: Essays in Honor of James F. Strange.* Edited by Daniel Warner and Donald D. Binder. Mountain Home, AR: BorderStone, 2014.

———. *The Origins of the Synagogue: A Socio-Historical Study.* Stockholm: Almqvist & Wiksell, 2001.

———. "Placing Paul: Institutional Structures and Theological Strategy in the World of the Early Christ-Believers." *SEÅ* 80 (2015): 43–67.

———. "Synagogue." Pages 2:766–72 in *T&T Clark Companion to Second Temple Judaism.* Edited by Daniel M. Gurtner and Loren T. Stuckenbruck. London: T&T Clark, 2019.

———. "Synagogues at the Intersection of Text and Archaeology: The Genesis and Framework of Second Temple Judaism." In *Second Temple Judaism in Scholarly Perspective: Integration of Recent Developments.* Edited by Dan M. Gurtner and Loren T. Stuckenbruck. London: T&T Clark, 2024.

Runesson, Anders, Donald D. Binder, and Birger Olsson. *The Ancient Synagogue: From Its Origins to 200 CE. A Source Book.* AJEC 72. Leiden: Brill, 2008.

Runesson, Anders, and Wally V. Cirafesi. "Reassessing the Impact of 70 CE on the Origins and Development of Palestinian Synagogues." Pages 37–57 in *The Synagogue in Ancient Palestine: Current Issues and Emerging Trends.* Edited by Rick Bonnie, Raimo Hakola and Ulla Tervahauta. FRLANT 279. Göttingen: Vandenhoeck & Ruprecht, 2020.

Runesson, Anders, and Rebecca Runesson. *Judaism for Gentiles: Reading Paul beyond the Parting of the Ways Paradigm.* WUNT 494. Tübingen: Mohr Siebeck, 2022.

Rüttimann, René Josef. "Asklepios and Jesus: The Form, Character and Status of the Asklepios Cult in the Second Century CE and Its Influence on Early Christianity." PhD diss., Harvard University, 1986.

Ryan, Jordan J. *The Role of the Synagogue in the Aims of Jesus.* Minneapolis: Fortress, 2017.

———. "The Socio-Political Context of Public Synagogue Debates in the Second Temple Period." Pages 133–52 in *The Synagogue in Ancient Palestine: Current Issues and Emerging Trends.* Edited by Rick Bonnie, Raimo Hakola, and Ulla Tervahauta. FRLANT 279. Göttingen: Vandenhoeck & Ruprecht, 2020.

Sailor, Dylan. "The Agricola." Pages 23–44 in *A Companion to Tacitus*. Edited by Victoria E. Pagán. Chichester: Wiley-Blackwell, 2012.

Salamon, Gayle. *Assuming a Body: Transgender and the Rhetorics of Materiality*. New York: Columbia University Press, 2010.

Saldarini, Anthony J. *Pharisees, Scribes, and Sadducees in Palestinian Society: A Sociological Approach*. Grand Rapids: Eerdmans, 2001.

Saller, Richard. "Anecdotes as Historical Evidence for the Principate." *GR* 27 (1980): 69–83.

Sanders, E. P. *The Historical Figure of Jesus*. London: Penguin, 1993.

———. *Jesus and Judaism*. Philadelphia: Fortress; London: SCM, 1985.

———. "Jesus' Galilee." Pages 3–41 in *Fair Play: Diversity and Conflicts in Early Christianity; Essays in Honour of Heikki Räisänen*. Edited by Ismo Dunderberg, Christopher M. Tuckett, and Kari Syreeni. NovTSup 103. Leiden: Brill, 2002.

———. *Judaism: Practice and Belief, 63 BCE–66 CE*. Rev. ed. London: SCM, 1992.

———. *Paul: The Apostle's Life, Letters, and Thought*. Minneapolis: Fortress, 2015.

———. *The Tendencies of the Synoptic Tradition*. SNTSMS 9. Cambridge: Cambridge University Press, 1969.

Sanders, Henry A. "Two Fragmentary Birth-Certificates from the Michigan Collection." *Memoirs of the American Academy in Rome* 9 (1931): 61–80.

Sanders, Mike. *The Poetry of Chartism: Aesthetics, Politics, History*. Cambridge: Cambridge University Press, 2009.

Sandmel, Samuel. "Parallelomania." *JBL* 81 (1962): 1–13.

Sandnes, Karl Olav. *The Gospel "according to Homer and Virgil": Cento and Canon*. Leiden: Brill, 2011.

Sawicki, Marianne. *Crossing Galilee: Architectures of Contact in the Occupied Land of Jesus*. London: Bloomsbury, 2000.

———. "Who Wouldn't Marry Jesus?" Pages 301–20 in *A Wandering Galilean: Essays in Honour of Seán Freyne*. Edited by Zuleika Rodgers, Margaret Daly-Denton, and Anne Fitzpatrick-McKinley. Leiden: Brill, 2009.

Schaberg, Jane. *The Illegitimacy of Jesus: A Feminist Theological Interpretation of the Infancy Narratives*. Sheffield: Sheffield Academic, 1995.

———. *The Resurrection of Mary Magdalene: Legends, Apocrypha, and the Christian Testament*. New York: Continuum, 2003.

Scheffler, Eben. "Caring for the Needy in the Acts of the Apostles." *Neot* 50 (2016): 131–66.

Schilbrack, Kevin, ed. "A Realist Social Ontology of Religion." *Religion* 47.2 (2017): 161–78.

———. *Thinking through Myths: Philosophical Perspectives*. New York: Routledge, 2002.

Schipper, Jeremy. *Disability Studies and the Hebrew Bible: Figuring Mephibosheth in the David Story.* London: T&T Clark, 2006.

Schleiermacher, Friedrich. *The Life of Jesus.* Edited by J. C. Verheyden. Philadelphia: Fortress, 1975.

———. "Über den Begriff des grossen Manne. Am 24 Januar 1826." Pages 1:520–31 in *Werke: Auswahl in vier Bänden.* Leipzig: Eckhardt, 1910.

Schlosser, Jacques. "Scholarly Rigor and Intuition in Historical Research into Jesus." Translated by Brian McNeil. Pages 1:475–507 in *Handbook for the Study of the Historical Jesus.* Edited by Tom Holmén and Stanley E. Porter. 4 vols. Leiden: Brill, 2011.

Schooler, Jonathan W., and Eric Eich. "Memory for Emotional Events." Pages 379–92 in *The Oxford Handbook of Memory.* Edited by Endel Tulving and Fergus I. M. Craik. Oxford: Oxford University Press, 2000.

Schröter, Jens. "The Criteria of Authenticity in Jesus Research and Historiographical Method." Pages 49–70 in *Jesus, Criteria, and the Demise of Authenticity.* Edited by Chris Keith and Anthony Le Donne. London: T&T Clark, 2012.

———. *Erinnerung an Jesu Worte: Studien zur Rezeption der Logienüberlieferung in Markus, Q und Thomas.* WMANT 76. Neukirchen-Vluyn: Neukirchener, 1997.

———. *From Jesus to the New Testament: Early Christian Theology and the Origin of the New Testament Canon.* Translated by Wayne Coppins. BMSEC. Waco, TX: Baylor University Press, 2013.

———. "How Close Were Jesus and the Pharisees?" Pages 220–39 in *The Pharisees.* Edited by Joseph Sievers and Amy-Jill Levine. Grand Rapids: Eerdmans, 2021.

———. *Jesus of Nazareth: Jew from Galilee, Savior of the World.* Translated by Wayne Coppins and S. Brian Pounds. Waco, TX: Baylor University Press, 2014.

———. *Von Jesus zum Neuen Testament.* WUNT 204. Tübingen: Mohr Siebeck, 2007.

Schudson, Michael. "The Present in the Past versus the Past in the Present." *Communication* 11 (1989): 105–13.

Schumer, Nathan. "The Population of Sepphoris: Rethinking Urbanization in Early and Middle Roman Galilee." *JAJ* 8.1 (2017): 90–111.

Schüssler Fiorenza, Elisabeth. *Democratizing Biblical Studies: Toward an Emancipatory Educational Space.* Minneapolis: Fortress, 2009.

———. "The Ethics of Biblical Interpretation: Decentering Biblical Scholarship." *JBL* 107 (1988): 3–17.

———. *Jesus and the Politics of Interpretation.* New York: Continuum, 2000.

Schwartz, Barry. *Abraham Lincoln and the Forge of National Memory.* Chicago: University of Chicago Press, 2000.

———. "Social Change and Collective Memory: The Democratization of George Washington." *American Sociological Review* 56 (1991): 221–36.

Schwartz, Seth. "Conversion to Judaism in the Second Temple Period: A Functionalist Approach." Pages 223–36 in *Studies in Josephus and the Varieties of Ancient Judaism: Louis H. Feldman Jubilee Volume*. Edited by Shaye J. D. Cohen and Joshua J. Schwartz. AJEC 67. Leiden: Brill, 2007.

Schweitzer, Albert. *The Mystery of the Kingdom of God*. Translated by Walter Lowrie. Eugene: Wipf & Stock, 1970.

———. *The Mysticism of Paul the Apostle*. Translated by William Montgomery. 2nd ed. New York: Seabury, 1968.

———. *Out of My Life and Thought: An Autobiography*. Translated by C. T. Campion. New York: Mentor, 1953.

———. *The Quest of the Historical Jesus: A Critical Study of Its Progress from Reimarus to Wrede*. Translated by William Montgomery. New York: Macmillan, 1950.

Schwendner, Gregg. "Greek Writ Plain: Village Scribes, Q, and the Palaeography of the Earliest Christian Papyri." Pages 88–119 in *Scribes and Their Remains*. Edited by Craig A. Evans and Jeremiah J. Johnston. London: Bloomsbury, 2020.

Scott, Joan W. "The Evidence of Experience." *Critical Inquiry* 17.4 (1991): 773–97.

Secord, Jared. *Christian Intellectuals and the Roman Empire: From Justin Martyr to Origen*. University Park: Pennsylvania State University Press, 2020.

Seed, John. "Unitarianism, Political Economy and the Antinomies of Liberal Culture in Manchester, 1830–50." *Social History* 7.1 (1982): 1–25.

Segal, Michael. "Between Bible and Rewritten Bible." Pages 10–28 in *Biblical Interpretation at Qumran*. Edited by Matthias Henze. Grand Rapids: Eerdmans, 2005.

Segal, Robert. *Myth: A Very Short Introduction*. Oxford: Oxford University Press, 2004.

Sellers, Ian. "Hennell, Charles Christian (1809–1850)." In *Oxford Dictionary of National Biography*, September 23, 2004. https://www.oxforddnb.com/display/10.1093/ref:odnb/9780198614128.001.0001/odnb-9780198614128-e-12939.

Sessa, Kristina. *Daily Life in Late Antiquity*. Cambridge: Cambridge University Press, 2018.

Sewell, William H. "Marc Bloch and the Logic of Comparative History." *HistTh* 6.2 (1967): 208–18.

Seybold, Klaus. "Der Traum in der Bibel." Pages 32–54 in *Traum und Träumen: Traumanalysen in Wissenschaft, Religion und Kunst*. Edited by Therese Wagner-Simon and Gaetano Benedetti. Göttingen: Vandenhoeck & Ruprecht, 1984.

Shanks, Hershel, ed. *Where Christianity Was Born*. Washington, DC: Biblical Archaeological Society, 2006.

Shanks, Hershel, and Dan B. Cole, eds. *Archaeology in the World of Herod, Jesus and Paul*, vol. 2 of *Archaeology and the Bible*. Washington, DC: Biblical Archaeology Society, 1990.

Shanks, Hershel, and Ben Witherington. *The Brother of Jesus: The Dramatic Story and*

Meaning of the First Archaeological Link to Jesus and His Family. San Francisco: HarperCollins, 2003.

Sharma, Arvind. "Orientalism and the Comparison of Religions." Pages 221–33 in *Comparing Religions: Possibilities and Perils?* Edited by Thomas A. Idinopulos, Brian C. Wilson, and James C. Hanges. Leiden: Brill, 2006.

Shatzman, Israel. *The Armies of the Hasmonaeans and Herod: From Hellenistic to Roman Frameworks*. TSAJ 25. Tübingen: Mohr Siebeck, 1991.

Shaver, John H., et al. "News Exposure Predicts Anti-Muslim Prejudice." *PLoS ONE* 12.3 (2017): 1–19.

Shedd, Nathan L. *A Dangerous Parting: The Beheading of John the Baptist in Early Christian Memory*. Waco, TX: Baylor University Press, 2021.

———. "Gospel of Matthew." In *Judeophobia in the New Testament*. Edited by Sarah Rollens, Eric Vanden Eykel, and Meredith J. C. Warren. Grand Rapids: Eerdmans, 2025.

———. "John the Baptist." In *Critical Dictionary of Apocalyptic and Millenarian Movements*. Edited by James Crossley and Alastair Lockhart. January 16, 2021. https://www.cdamm.org/assets/articlePDFs/18527-john-the-baptist.pdf.

Sheldon, Rose Mary. *Intelligence Activities in Ancient Rome: Trust in the Gods, but Verify*. London: Routledge, 2005.

Shelton, W. Brian. *Quest for the Historical Apostles: Tracing Their Lives and Legacies*. Grand Rapids: Baker Academic, 2018.

Shirley, Walter Waddington, ed. *Fasciculi Zizaniorum magistri Johannis Wyclif cum Tritico*. Rolls Series. London: Longman, Brown, Green, Longmans, and Roberts, 1858.

Shively, Elizabeth. "Purification of the Body and the Reign of God in the Gospel of Mark." *JTS* 71 (2020): 62–89.

Shklovsky, Victor. *Theory of Prose*. Translated by Benjamin Sher. London: Dalkey Archive, 2015.

Siker, Jeffrey S. "First to the Gentiles': A Literary Analysis of Luke 4:16–30." *JBL* 111.1 (1992): 73–90.

Sim, David. "Matthew 7.21–23: Further Evidence of Its Anti-Pauline Perspective." *NTS* 53 (2007): 325–43.

———. "Matthew's Use of Mark: Did Matthew Intend to Supplement or to Replace His Primary Source?" *NTS* 57 (2011): 176–92.

Slater, Thomas B. "Thurman, Johnson, Hendricks and the Third Quest." Pages 37–55 in *Afrocentric Interpretations of Jesus and the Gospel Traditions: Things Black Scholars See That White Scholars Overlook*. Edited by Thomas B. Slater. Lewiston: Mellen, 2015.

Smit, Peter-Ben, Ovidiu Creangă, and Adriaan van Klinken. "The Reception of the

Bible in the Construction of Masculinities in Jewish and Christian Con/Texts." *JBR* 2 (2015): 135–43.

Smith, Abraham. "'Low in the Well': A Mystic's Creative Message of Hope in *Jesus and the Disinherited.*" *JSHJ* 17.3 (2019): 185–200.

Smith, Barry D. *The Meaning of Jesus' Death: Reviewing the New Testament's Interpretations.* London: Bloomsbury, 2017.

Smith, D. Moody. "Jesus Tradition in the Gospel of John." Pages 3:1997–2040 in *Handbook for the Study of the Historical Jesus.* Edited by Tom Holmén and Stanley E. Porter. 4 vols. Leiden; Boston: Brill, 2011.

Smith, Frederick M. *The Self Possessed: Deity and Spirit Possession in South Asian Literature and Civilization.* New York: Columbia University Press, 2006.

Smith, Geoffrey S., and Brent C. Landau. *The Secret Gospel of Mark: A Controversial Scholar, a Scandalous Gospel of Jesus, and the Fierce Debate over Its Authenticity.* New Haven: Yale University Press, 2023.

Smith, Jonathan Z. *Drudgery Divine: On the Comparison of Early Christianities and the Religions of Late Antiquity.* Chicago: University of Chicago Press, 1990.

———. *Map Is Not Territory: Studies in the History of Religions.* Leiden: Brill, 1978.

———. *Reimagining Religion: From Babylon to Jonestown.* Chicago: Chicago University Press, 1982.

Smith, Linda Tuhiwai. *Decolonizing Methodologies: Research and Indigenous Peoples.* 2nd ed. London: Zed, 2012.

Smith, Mitzi J. "Abolitionist Messiah: A Man Named Jesus Born of a Doule." Pages 53–70 in *Bitter the Chastening Rod: Africana Biblical Interpretation after Stony the Road We Trod in the Age of BLM, SayHerName, and MeToo.* Edited by Mitzi Smith, Angela Parker, and Ericka Dunbar. Lanham, MD: Lexington/Fortress Academic, 2022.

———. "'He Never Said a Mumbalin Word': A Womanist Perspective of Crucifixion, Sexual Violence, and Sacralized Silence." Pages 46–66 in *When Did We See You Naked? Jesus as a Victim of Sexual Violence.* Edited by Jayme Reaves and David Tombs. London: SCM, 2021.

———. "Howard Thurman and the Religion of Jesus: Survival of the Disinherited and Womanist Wisdom." *JSHJ* 17 (2019): 271–91.

Smith, Mitzi J., and Yung Suk Kim. *Toward Decentering the New Testament.* Eugene, OR: Cascade, 2018.

Smith, Morton. *Clement of Alexandria and a Secret Gospel of Mark.* Cambridge: Harvard University Press, 1973.

———. *Jesus the Magician.* San Francisco: Harper & Row, 1978.

———. "Messiahs: Robbers, Jurists, Prophets, and Magicians." *Proceedings of the American Academy for Jewish Research* 44 (1977): 185–95.

Smith-Rosenberg, Caroll. "The Hysterical Woman: Sex Roles and the Role Conflict in Nineteenth Century America." *Social Research* 39.4 (1972): 652–78.

Sokol, Jason. *The Heavens Might Crack: The Death and Legacy of Martin Luther King Jr.* New York: Basic, 2018.

Soler, Renaud. *Edward Robinson (1794–1863) et l'émergence de l'archéologie biblique.* Paris: Geuthner, 2014.

Solevåg, Anna Rebecca. "Zacchaeus in the Gospel of Luke: Comic Figure, Sinner, and Included 'Other'." *Journal of Literary & Cultural Disability Studies* 14.2 (2020): 225–40.

Sontag, Susan. *Illness as Metaphor and AIDS as Its Metaphor.* New York: Doubleday, 1990.

Sosis, Richard. "The Building Blocks of Religious Systems: Approaching Religion as a Complex Adaptive System." Pages 421–49 in *Evolution, Development and Complexity: Multiscale Evolutionary Models of Complex Adaptive Systems.* Edited by Georgi Yordanov Georgiev et al. New York: Springer, 2018.

Southey, Robert. *Wat Tyler.* London: Hone, 1817.

Speck, W. A. *Robert Southey: Entire Man of Letters.* New Haven: Yale University Press, 2006.

Sperber, Daniel. "Objects of Trade between Palestine and Egypt in Roman Times." *JESHO* 19.2 (1976): 113–47.

Spigel, Chad S. *Ancient Synagogue Seating Capacities: Methodology, Analysis and Limits.* TSAJ 149. Tübingen: Mohr Siebeck, 2012.

Spode, Hasso. "Fordism, Mass Tourism and the Third Reich: The 'Strength through Joy' Seaside Resort as an Index Fossil." *Journal of Social History* 38.1 (2004): 127–55.

Spurling, Hilary. "Neither Morbid nor Ordinary." Pages 113–22 in *The Troubled Face of Biography.* Edited by Eric Homberger and John Charmley. London: Macmillan, 1988.

Staley, David J. *Historical Imagination.* London: Routledge, 2021.

Stausberg, Michael. "Comparison." Pages 21–39 in *The Routledge Handbook of Research Methods in the Study of Religion.* Edited by Michael Stausberg and Steven Engler. London: Taylor & Francis, 2011.

Stavru, Alessandro. "Pathos, Physiognomy, and Ekphrasis from Aristotle to the Second Sophistic." Pages 143–60 in *Visualizing the Invisible with the Human Body: Physiognomy and Ekphrasis in the Ancient World.* Edited by J. Johnson and A. Stavru. Berlin: de Gruyter, 2019.

Ste. Croix, G. E. M. de. *The Class Struggle in the Ancient Greek World.* Ithaca: Cornell University Press, 1981.

Stefaniw, Blossom. "Feminist Historiography and Uses of the Past." *Studies in Late Antiquity* 4 (2020): 260–83.

Steffy, J. Richard. "The Boat: A Preliminary Study of Its Construction." In *The Excavations of an Ancient Boat in the Sea of Galilee (Lake Kinneret)*, edited by Shelley Wachsmann. Atiqot, vol. 19, 29–47. Jerusalem: Israel Antiquities Authority, 1990.

Stegemann, Ekkehard W., and Wolfgang Stegemann. *The Jesus Movement: A Social History of Its First Century*. Translated by O. C. Dean. Minneapolis: Fortress, 1999.

Stein, Robert H. *Mark*. BECNT. Grand Rapids: Baker Academic, 2008.

Steinmetz, George. "Scientific Authority and the Transition to Post-Fordism: The Plausibility of Positivism in U.S. Sociology since 1945." Pages 275–322 in *The Politics of Method in the Human Sciences: Positivism and Its Epistemological Other*. Edited by George Steinmetz. Durham: Duke University Press, 2005.

Stewart, Charles. *Dreaming and Historical Consciousness in Island Greece*. Chicago: University of Chicago Press, 2017.

Stock, Brian. *Augustine the Reader: Meditation, Self-Knowledge and the Ethics of Interpretation*. Cambridge: Harvard University Press, 1996.

Stowers, Stanley K. "The Concept of 'Community' and the History of Early Christianity." *MTSR* 23 (2011): 238–56.

———. "The Religion of Plant and Animal Offerings versus the Religion of Meanings, Essences, and Textual Mysteries." Pages 35–56 in *Ancient Mediterranean Sacrifice*. Edited by J. W. Knust and Z. Várhelyi. Oxford: Oxford University Press, 2011.

Strauss, David Friedrich. *The Life of Jesus, Critically Examined by Dr David Friedrich Strauss. Translated from the Fourth German Edition*. Vol. 1. Translated by George Eliot. London: Chapman Brothers, 1846.

———. *The Life of Jesus, or, A Critical Examination of His History*. 4 vols. London: Hetherington, 1842–1844.

———. "Vorwort von Dr Strauss." Pages iii–viii in Charles C. Hennell, *Untersuchung über den Ursprung des Christentums: Aus dem Englischen*. Stuttgart: Hallberger, 1840.

Strelan, Rick. *Luke the Priest: The Authority of the Author of the Third Gospel*. Aldershot: Ashgate, 2008.

Stuckenbruck, Loren. "What Is Second Temple Judaism?" Pages 1:1–19 in *T&T Clark Encyclopedia of Second Temple Judaism*. Edited by Daniel M. Gurtner and Loren Stuckenbruck. 2 vols. London: T&T Clark, 2020.

Stuhlmacher, Peter. "Die Stellung Jesu und des Paulus zu Jerusalem: Versuch einer Erinnerung." *ZNW* 86 (1989): 140–56.

Sugirtharajah, R. S. *Asian Biblical Hermeneutics and Postcolonialism: Contesting the Interpretations*. Sheffield: Sheffield Academic Press, 1998.

Suvin, Darko. *Metamorphoses of Science Fiction: On the Poetics and History of a Literary Genre*. New Haven: Yale University Press, 1979.

Swedberg, Richard. "Does Speculation Belong in Social Science Research?" *Sociological Methods & Research* 50.1 (2021): 45–74.

Sweetman, Will. *Mapping Hinduism: 'Hinduism' and the Study of Indian Religions, 1600–1776*. Neue Hallesche Berichte 4. Halle: Verlag der Franckeschen Stiftungen, 2003.

Szijártó, István M. Introduction to *What Is Microhistory? Theory and Practice*. By Sigurður Gylfi Magnússon and István M. Szijártó. London: Routledge, 2013.

Tacitus. *Annals: Books 4–6, 11–12*. Translated by John Jackson. LCL. Cambridge: Harvard University Press, 1937.

Taira, Teemu. *Taking "Religion" Seriously: Essays on the Discursive Study of Religion*. Leiden: Brill, 2022.

Talbert, Charles H. *Matthew*. Grand Rapids: Baker Academic, 2010.

Tan, Kim Huat. *The Zion Traditions and the Aims of Jesus*. SNTMS 91. Cambridge: Cambridge University Press, 1997.

Tardieu, Michel. "Exégèse Manichéenne du Nouveau Testament." Pages 123–46 in *Les règles de l'interprétation*. Edited by Michel Tardieu. Paris: Cerf, 1987.

Taylor, Catherine Gines. *Late Antique Images of the Virgin Annunciate Spinning: Allotting the Scarlet and the Purple*. Leiden: Brill, 2018.

Taylor, Charles. *The Sources of the Self: The Making of the Modern Identity*. Cambridge: Harvard University Press, 1989.

Taylor, Joan E. *Christians and the Holy Places: The Myth of Jewish-Christian Origins*. Rev. ed. Oxford: Clarendon, 2003.

———. *The Englishman, the Moor and the Holy City: The True Adventures of an Elizabethan Traveller*. Stroud: Tempus, 2006.

———. "The Garden of Gethsemane—Not the Place of Jesus' Arrest." *BAR* 21.4 (1995): 26–35.

———. "Golgotha: A Reconsideration of the Evidence for the Sites of Jesus' Crucifixion and Burial." *NTS* 44 (1998): 180–203.

———. "The Historical Brian: Reception Exegesis in Practice." Pages in 93–106 in *Jesus and Brian*. Edited by Joan E. Taylor. London: Bloomsbury, 2015.

———. *The Immerser: John the Baptist within Second Temple Judaism*. Grand Rapids: Eerdmans, 1997.

———. "Jesus as News: Crises of Health and Overpopulation in Galilee." *JSNT* 44.1 (2021): 8–30.

———. "John Speed's 'Canaan' and British Travel to Palestine: A Journey with Maps." Pages 103–23 in *The King James Version at 400: Assessing Its Genius as Bible Translation and Its Literary Influence*. Edited by David G. Burke, John F. Kutsko, and Philip H. Towner. Atlanta: SBL Press, 2013.

———. "Magdala's Mistaken Identity." *BAR* 48.3 (2022): 55–58.

———. "Missing Magdala and the Name of Mary 'Magdalene'." *PEQ* 146.3 (2014): 205–23.

———. "Pontius Pilate and the Imperial Cult in Roman Judaea." *NTS* 52 (2006): 555–82.

———. *What Did Jesus Look Like?* London: Bloomsbury T&T Clark, 2018.

Taylor, Joan E., and Federico Adinolfi. "John the Baptist and Jesus the Baptist: A Narrative Critical Approach." *JSHJ* 10 (2012): 247–84.

Taylor, Joan E., and Shimon Gibson. *Beneath the Church of the Holy Sepulchre: The Archaeology and Early History of Traditional Golgotha.* London: Palestine Exploration Fund, 1994.

Taylor, John. *Ranters of Both Sexes, Male and Female.* London: Hammon, 1651.

Taylor, John, Wendy R. Childs, and Leslie Watkiss, eds. *The St Albans Chronicle: The Chronica Maiora of Thomas Walsingham.* Vol. 1, *1376–1394.* Oxford: Oxford University Press, 2003.

Taylor, Justin. "Bread That Is Broken—And Unbroken." Pages 525–37 in *A Wandering Galilean: Essays in Honour of Seán Freyne.* Edited by Zuleika Rodgers, Margaret Daly-Denton, and Anne Fitzpatrick-McKinley. Leiden: Brill, 2009.

Taylor, Marion A. *Women in the Story of Jesus: The Gospels through the Eyes of Nineteenth-Century Female Biblical Interpreters.* Grand Rapids: Eerdmans, 2016.

Taylor, Michael P., Mathew J. Wedel, and Darren Naish. "Head and Neck Posture in Sauropod Dinosaurs Inferred from Extant Animals." *Acta Palaeontologica Polonica* 54.2 (2009): 213–20.

Taylor, Nikki M. *Driven toward Madness.* Athens: Ohio University Press, 2017.

Taylor, Richard. *Te Ika a Maui.* London: Wertheim and Macintosh, 1855.

Tedlock, Barbara. "Dreaming and Dream Research." Pages 1–30 in *Dreaming: Anthropological and Psychological Interpretations.* Edited by Barbara Tedlock. Santa Fe: School of American Research Press, 1992.

Te Rangihīroa. *The Coming of the Māori.* Wellington: Whitcombe and Tombs, 1949.

Te Rito, J. "Whakapapa: A Framework for Understanding Identity." *MAI Review* 2 (2007): Article 2.

———. "Whakapapa and Whenua: An Insider's View." *MAI Review* 3 (2007): Article 1.

Thate, Michael J. *The Godman and the Sea: The Empty Tomb, the Trauma of the Jews, and the Gospel of Mark.* Philadelphia: University of Pennsylvania Press, 2019.

Theissen, Gerd. *Miracle Stories of the Early Christian Tradition.* Edited and translated by Francis McDonagh and John Riches. Edinburgh: T&T Clark, 1983.

———. *Soziologie der Jesusbewegung: Ein Beitrag zur Entstehungsgeschichte des Urchristentums.* Theologische Existenz Heute 194. Munich: Kaiser, 1977.

Theissen, Gerd, and Annette Merz. *The Historical Jesus: A Comprehensive Guide.* Translated by John Bowden. Minneapolis: Fortress, 1998.

Theissen, Gerd, and Dagmar Winter. *The Quest for the Plausible Jesus: The Question of Criteria.* Translated by M. Eugene Boring. Louisville: Westminster John Knox, 2002.

Thiering, B. E. *Jesus and the Riddle of the Dead Sea Scrolls: Unlocking the Secrets of His Life Story.* Toronto: Doubleday Canada, 1992.

Thiessen, Matthew. *Contesting Conversion: Genealogy, Circumcision, and Identity in Ancient Judaism and Christianity.* Oxford: Oxford University Press, 2011.

———. *Jesus and the Forces of Death: The Gospels' Portrayal of Ritual Impurity within First-Century Judaism.* Grand Rapids: Baker Academic, 2020.

———. "Luke 2:22, Leviticus 12, and Parturient Impurity." *NovT* 54 (2012): 16–29.

Thom, Johan. "Cleanthes' Hymn to Zeus and Early Christian Literature." Pages 477–99 in *Antiquity and Humanity: Essays on Ancient Religion and Philosophy.* Edited by Adela Yarbro Collins and Margaret M. Mitchell. Tübingen: Mohr Siebeck, 2001.

Thomas, Angela. *Anatomical Idiom and Emotional Expression: A Comparison of the Hebrew Bible and the Septuagint.* Sheffield: Sheffield Phoenix, 2014.

Thompson, Dorothy. *The Chartists: Popular Politics in the Industrial Revolution.* New York: Pantheon, 1984.

Thompson, E. P. *The Making of the English Working Class.* London: Penguin, 1963.

Thorsteinsson, Runar. *Roman Christianity and Roman Stoicism: A Comparative Study of Ancient Morality.* Oxford: Oxford University Press, 2010.

Thurman, Howard. *Jesus and the Disinherited.* New York: Abingdon-Cokesbury, 1949.

Thwaite, Ann. "Writing Lives." Pages 17–32 in *The Troubled Face of Biography.* Edited by Eric Homberger and John Charmley. London: Macmillan, 1988.

Tieleman, Teun. "Miracle and Natural Cause in Galen." Pages 101–14 in *Miracles Revisited: New Testament Miracle Stories and Their Concepts of Reality.* Edited by Stefan Alkier and Annette Weissenrieder. Boston: de Gruyter, 2013.

Tosh, John. *Manliness and Masculinities in Nineteenth-Century Britain.* Harlow: Longman, 2005.

Townshend, James R. "Camilla and Virgil's Aesthetic of the Grotesque." Paper presented at the Antiquities Interdisciplinary Research Group (AIRG) at the University of Miami, 2020.

Trapnel, Anna. *A Legacy for Saints; Being Several Experiences of the Dealings of God with Anna Trapnel.* London: Brewster, 1654.

Trevett, Christine. "William Erbery and His Daughter Dorcas: Dissenter and Resurrected Radical." *Journal of Welsh Religious History* 4 (1996): 23–50.

Trible, Phyllis. *Texts of Terror: Literary-Feminist Readings of Biblical Narratives.* Minneapolis: Fortress, 1984.

Troche, Facundo Daniel. "Fishing in the Lake of Galilee and the Socio-Economic Context of Jesus' Movement." Pages 81–107 in *Texts, Practices, and Groups: Multidisciplinary Approaches to the History of Jesus' Followers in the First Two Centuries;*

First Annual Meeting of Bertinoro (2–5 October 2014). Edited by Adriana Destro and Mauro Pesce. Judaïsme ancien et origines du christianisme 10. Turnhout: Brepols, 2017.

———. "Il sistema della pesca nel lago di Galilea al tempo di Gesù. Indagine sulla base dei papiri documentari e dei dati archeologici e letterari." PhD diss., Università di Bologna, 2015.

Trocmé, Étienne. *The Childhood of Christianity*. Translated by John Bowden. London: SCM, 1977.

Tuckett, Christopher. "Form Criticism." Pages 21–38 in *Jesus in Memory: Traditions in Oral and Scribal Perspectives*. Edited by Werner H. Kelber and Samuel Byrskog. Waco, TX: Baylor University Press, 2009.

Tupamahu, Ekaputra. "The Stubborn Invisibility of Whiteness in Biblical Scholarship." *Political Theology Network*, November 12, 2020. https://politicaltheology.com/the-stubborn-invisibility-of-whiteness-in-biblical-scholarship/.

Turchin, Peter, et al. "Seshat: The Global History Databank." *Cliodynamics* 6.1 (2015): 77–107.

Turner, Katie. *Costuming Christ: Re-Dressing First-Century 'Christians' and 'Jews' in Passion Drama*. Library of New Testament Studies. London: T&T Clark, forthcoming.

Ulrich, Eugene. "The Jewish Scriptures: Texts, Versions, Canons." Pages 121–50 in *Early Judaism: A Comprehensive Overview*. Edited by John J. Collins and Daniel C. Harlow. Grand Rapids: Eerdmans, 2012.

Vaage, Leif. "Bird-Watching at the Baptism of Jesus: Early Christian Mythmaking in Mark 1:9–11." Pages 280–94 in *Reimagining Christian Origins: A Colloquium Honoring Burton L. Mack*. Edited by Elizabeth A. Castelli and Hal Taussig. Valley Forge, PA: Trinity Press International, 1996.

Vanden Bossche, Chris R. *Reform Acts: Chartism, Social Agency and the Victorian Novel, 1832–1867*. Baltimore: Johns Hopkins University Press, 2014.

Vandorpe, Katelijn, Willy Clarysse, and H. Verreth. *Graeco-Roman Archives from the Fayum*. Collectanea Hellenistica – KVAB 6. Leuven: Peeters, 2015.

VanMaaren, John. "Does Mark's Jesus Abrogate Torah? Jesus' Purity Logion and Its Illustration in Mark 7:15–23." *Journal of the Jesus Movement in Its Jewish Setting* 4 (2017): 21–41.

Van Tine, R. Jarrett. "Castration for the Kingdom and Avoiding the αἰτία of Adultery (Matthew 19:10–12)." *JBL* 137.2 (2018): 399–418.

Vardi, Amiel. "Gellius against the Professors." *ZPE* 137 (2001): 41–54.

Vellius Paterculus. *Compendium of Roman History. Res Gestae Divi Augusti*. Translated by Frederick W. Shipley. LCL. Cambridge: Harvard University Press, 1924.

Vermes, Geza. *The Religion of Jesus the Jew*. London: SCM, 1993.

———. *Searching for the Real Jesus: Jesus, the Dead Sea Scrolls and Other Religious Themes.* London: SCM, 2009.

Vigil, Maria Lopez. *Oscar Romero: Memories in Mosaic.* Translated by Kathy Ogle. Washington, DC: EPICA, 2000.

Vinzent, Markus. *Christ's Resurrection in Early Christianity and the Making of the New Testament.* Farnham: Ashgate, 2011.

Vogüé, Melchior de. *Le Temple de Jerusalem: Monographie du Haram-ech-Chérif. Suivie d'un essai sur la topographie de la Ville-Sainte.* Paris: Noblet & Baudry, 1864.

Wainwright, Elaine. *Towards a Feminist Critical Reading of the Gospel according to Matthew.* Berlin: de Gruyter, 1991.

Walker, Ranginui. *Ngā Pepa a Ranginui, The Walker Papers.* Auckland: Penguin, 1996.

Wallis, Ian. *The Galilean Wonderworker: Reassessing Jesus's Reputation for Healing and Exorcism.* Eugene, OR: Cascade, 2020.

Walsh, Robyn Faith. "*Argumentum ad lunam*: Pauline Discourse, 'Double Death,' and Competition on the Moon." *HTR*, forthcoming.

———. "IVDAEA DEVICTA: The Gospels as Imperial 'Captive Literature.'" Pages 89–114 in *Class Struggle in the New Testament.* Edited by Robert J. Myles. Lanham, MD: Lexington/Fortress Academic, 2019.

———. *The Origins of Early Christian Literature: Contextualizing the New Testament within Greco-Roman Literary Culture.* Cambridge: Cambridge University Press, 2021.

———. "Q and the 'Big Bang' Theory of Christian Origins." Pages 483–534 in *Redescribing the Gospel of Mark.* Edited by Barry S. Crawford and Merrill P. Miller. ECL 22. Atlanta: SBL Press, 2017.

———. "The *Satyrica* and the Gospels in the Second Century." *ClQ* 70.1 (2020): 356–67.

Walters, Amy M. "Elisabeth Schüssler Fiorenza and the Quest for the Historical Jesus." *Open Theology* 6 (2020): 468–74.

Warrior, Robert Allen. "Canaanites, Cowboys, and Indians: Deliverance, Conquest, and Liberation Theology Today." Pages 93–104 in *Native and Christian: Indigenous Voices on Religious Identity in the United States and Canada.* Edited by James Treat. New York: Routledge, 1996.

Wassén, Cecilia. "Jesus and the Hemorrhaging Woman in Mark 5:24–34: Insights from Purity Laws from Qumran." Pages 641–60 in *Scripture in Transition: Essays on Septuagint, Hebrew Bible, and Dead Sea Scrolls in Honour of Raija Sollamo.* Edited by Anssi Voitila and Jutta Jokiranta. JSJSup 126. Leiden: Brill, 2008.

Watson, David F. "Luke-Acts." Pages 303–32 in *The Bible and Disability: A Commentary.* Edited by Sarah J. Melcher, Mikeal C. Parsons, and Amos Yong. Waco, TX: Baylor University Press, 2017.

Watts, Joseph, et al. "Pulotu: Database of Austronesian Supernatural Beliefs and Practices." *PLoS ONE* 10.9 (2015): e0136783.

Webb, Robert L. "The Rules of the Game: History and Historical Method in the Context of Faith: The Via Media of Methodological Naturalism." *JSHJ* 9 (2011): 59–84.

Wedderburn, Alexander J. M. *The Death of Jesus: Some Reflections on Jesus-Traditions and Paul.* WUNT 299. Tübingen: Mohr Siebeck, 2013.

———. *Jesus and the Historians.* WUNT 269. Tübingen: Mohr Siebeck, 2010.

Weinberg, Darin. "Social Constructionism and the Body." Pages 144–56 in *Routledge Handbook of Body Studies.* Edited by Bryan S. Turner. London: Routledge, 2012.

Weinstein, Benjamin. "Popular Constitutionalism and the London Corresponding Society." *Albion* 34 (2002): 37–57.

Weissenrieder, Annette. "Disease and Healing in a Changing World: 'Medical' Vocabulary and the Woman with the 'Issue of Blood' in the *Vetus Latina* Mark 5:25–34 and Luke 8:40–48." *Religion in the Roman Empire* 3.2 (2017): 265–85.

———. "Stories Just under the Skin: *Lepra* in the Gospel of Luke." Pages 73–100 in *Miracles Revisited: New Testament Miracle Stories and Their Concepts of Reality.* Edited by Stefan Alkier and Annette Weissenrieder. Berlin: de Gruyter, 2013.

Wendt, Heidi. *At the Temple Gates: The Religion of Freelance Experts in the Roman Empire.* Oxford: Oxford University Press, 2016.

———. "Secrecy as Pauline Influence on the Gospel of Mark." *JBL* 140 (2021): 579–600.

Werker, Ella. "Identification of the Wood." Pages 65–75 in *The Excavations of an Ancient Boat in the Sea of Galilee (Lake Kinneret).* Edited by Shelley Wachsmann. Atiqot 19. Jerusalem: Israel Antiquities Authority, 1990.

Wessinger, Catherine. "Millennialism in Cross-Cultural Perspective." Pages 3–24 in *The Oxford Handbook of Millennialism.* Edited by Catherine Wessinger. Oxford: Oxford University Press, 2011.

West, M. L. "The Invention of Homer." *ClQ* 49 (1999): 364–82.

Westermann, Claus. *Genesis 1–11, A Commentary.* Minneapolis: Augsburg, 1990.

Wheeler-Reed, David, Jennifer W. Knust, and Dale B. Martin. "Can a Man Commit πορνεία with His Wife?" *JBL* 137.2 (2018): 383–98.

Whelan, Matthew Philipp. *Blood in the Fields: Óscar Romero, Catholic Social Teaching, and Land Reform.* Washington, DC: The Catholic University of America Press, 2020.

White, Cindel J. M., et al. "Cognitive Pathways to Belief in Karma and Belief in God." *Cognitive Science* 45.1 (2021): e12935.

White, Cindel J. M., Michael Muthukrishna, and Ara Norenzayan. "Cultural Similarity among Coreligionists within and between Countries." *Proceedings of the National Academy of the Sciences* 118.37 (2021): 1–9.

White, Claire. *An Introduction to the Cognitive Science of Religion: Connecting Evolution, Brain, Cognition, and Culture.* Abingdon: Routledge, 2021.

White, Jonathan. *Making Our Own History: A User's Guide to Marx's Historical Materialism.* Glasgow: Praxis, 2021.

Whitlock, Matthew G., ed. *Critical Theory and Early Christianity.* Sheffield: Equinox, 2022.

———. "Introduction: Making Early Christian Texts Strange (Again)." Pages 1–32 in *Critical Theory and Early Christianity.* Edited by Matthew G. Whitlock. Sheffield: Equinox, 2022.

Whitmarsh, Tim. *Beyond the Second Sophistic: Adventures in Greek Postclassicism.* Berkeley: University of California Press, 2013.

Wickham, Chris. *Framing the Early Middle Ages: Europe and the Mediterranean 400–800.* Oxford: Oxford University Press, 2006.

Wilkins, David. *Concilia Magnae Britanniae et Hiberniae.* Vol. 3. London: Gosling, 1737.

Wilkinson, John Donald. *Jerusalem as Jesus Knew It: Archaeology as Evidence.* London: Thames and Hudson, 1978.

Williams, Logan. "The Stomach Purifies All Food: Jesus' Anatomical Argument in Mark 7.18–19." *NTS,* forthcoming.

Williams, R. D. "The Function and Structure of Virgil's Catalogue in *Aeneid* 7." *ClQ* 11 (1961): 146–53.

Wilson, R. McL., trans. "Acts of Paul and Thecla." Pages 2:239–46 in *New Testament Apocrypha.* Edited by Wilhelm Schneemelcher. Rev. ed. Louisville: Westminster John Knox, 1992.

Wilson, Shawn. *Research Is Ceremony: Indigenous Research Methods.* Black Point: Fernwood, 2008.

Wimbush, Vincent L. "Interpreters Enslaving/Enslaved/Runagate." *JBL* 130 (2011): 5–24.

Winter, Dagmar. "Saving the Quest for Authenticity from the Criterion of Dissimilarity: History and Plausibility." Pages 115–31 in *Jesus, Criteria, and the Demise of Authenticity.* Edited by Chris Keith and Anthony Le Donne. London: T&T Clark, 2012.

Witmer, Amanda. *Jesus, the Galilean Exorcist: His Exorcisms in Social and Political Context.* London: T&T Clark, 2012.

Woodington, J. David. *The Dubious Disciples: Doubt and Disbelief in the Post-Resurrection Scenes of the Four Gospels.* BZNW 241. Berlin: de Gruyter, 2020.

Wootten, David. *The Illustrators: The British Art of Illustration, 1780–1993.* London: Beetles, 1993.

Wrede, William. *Das Messiasgeheimnis in den Evangelien: Zugleich ein Beitrag zum Verständnis des Markusevangeliums.* Göttingen: Vandenhoeck & Ruprecht, 1901.

Wright, N. T. *Jesus and the Victory of God*. Vol. 2 of *Christian Origins and the Question of God*. Minneapolis: Fortress, 1996.

———. *The New Testament and the People of God*. Vol. 1 of *Christian Origins and the Question of God*. Minneapolis: Fortress, 1992.

———. *The Resurrection of the Son of God*. Vol. 3 of *Christian Origins and the Question of God*. Minneapolis: Fortress, 2003.

Young, Stephen. "'Let's Take the Text Seriously': The Protectionist Doxa of Mainstream New Testament Studies." *MTSR* 32 (2020): 345–54.

———. "The Marcosian Redemption: Mythmaking, the Afterlife, and Early Christian Religiosity." *JECH* 6 (2016): 77–110.

———. *Paul among the Mythmakers: Sins, Gods, and Scriptures*. Edinburgh: Edinburgh University Press, forthcoming.

Zealoushead, Zachary. *Plots and Placemen, or Green Bag Glory, an Historical Melo Drama, in Two Acts. As Performed at the Boroughmonger's Private Theatre*. London: Seale, 1817.

Zeichmann, Christopher B. *Database of Military Inscriptions and Papyri of Early Roman Palestine*. https://armyofromanpalestine.com/.

———, ed. *Database of Military Inscriptions and Papyri of Early Roman Palestine with Map and Gazetteer of Military Sites*. Revised and updated ed. Aquila Legionis 24–25. Madrid: Signifer, 2022.

———. "Military Forces in Judaea 6–130 CE: The *Status Quaestionis* and Relevance for New Testament Studies." *CBR* 17 (2018): 86–120.

———. *The Roman Army and the New Testament*. Lanham, MD: Lexington/Fortress Academic, 2018.

———. "Romans Go Home? The Military as a Site of Class Struggle in the Roman East and the New Testament." Pages 53–65 in *Class Struggle in the New Testament*. Edited by Robert J. Myles. Lanham, MD: Lexington/Fortress Academic, 2019.

Zimmermann, Ruben. *Puzzling the Parables of Jesus: Methods and Interpretation*. Minneapolis: Fortress, 2015.

Zola, Nicholas J. "Evangelizing Tatian: The Diatessaron's Place in the Emergence of the Fourfold Gospel Canon." *PRSt* 43 (2016): 399–414.

Zucconi, Laura M. *Ancient Medicine: From Mesopotamia to Rome*. Grand Rapids: Eerdmans, 2019.

Zumstein, Jean. *Das Johannesevangelium*. Göttingen: Vandenhoeck & Ruprecht, 2016.

Zumthor, Paul. *Essai de Poétique Médiévale*. Paris: Seuil, 1972.

Contributors

Michael P. Barber, Augustine Institute Graduate School of Theology, United States of America

Giovanni B. Bazzana, Harvard Divinity School, United States of America

Helen K. Bond, University of Edinburgh, United Kingdom

James Crossley, MF Norwegian School of Theology, Religion, and Society, Norway, and Centre for the Critical Study of Apocalyptic and Millenarian Movements, United Kingdom

Tucker S. Ferda, Pittsburgh Theological Seminary, United States of America

Paula Fredriksen, Boston University, United States of America, and the Hebrew University of Jerusalem, Israel

Deane Galbraith, University of Otago, Aotearoa New Zealand

Mark Goodacre, Duke University, United States of America

Meghan R. Henning, University of Dayton, United States of America

Nathan C. Johnson, University of Indianapolis, United States of America

Chris Keith, MF Norwegian School of Theology, Religion, and Society, Norway

John S. Kloppenborg, University of Toronto, Canada

Amy-Jill Levine, Hartford International University for Religion and Peace, United States of America, and Vanderbilt University, United States of America

Brandon Massey, University of Münster, Germany

Justin J. Meggitt, University of Cambridge, United Kingdom

Halvor Moxnes, University of Oslo, Norway

Robert J. Myles, Wollaston Theological College, University of Divinity, Australia

Wongi Park, Belmont University, United States of America

Janelle Peters, Loyola Marymount University, United States of America

Taylor G. Petrey, Kalamazoo College, United States of America

Adele Reinhartz, University of Ottawa, Canada, and University of the Free State, South Africa

Rafael Rodríguez, Johnson University, United States of America

Sarah E. Rollens, Rhodes College, United States of America

Anders Runesson, University of Oslo, Norway

Nathan Shedd, William Jessup University, United States of America, and Johnson University, United States of America

Mitzi J. Smith, Columbia Theological Seminary, United States of America, and University of South Africa, South Africa

Joan Taylor, King's College London, United Kingdom

Wayne Te Kaawa, University of Otago, Aotearoa New Zealand

Matthew Thiessen, McMaster University, Canada

Robyn Faith Walsh, University of Miami, United States of America

Matthew G. Whitlock, Seattle University, United States of America

Stephen Young, Appalachian State University, United States of America

Christopher B. Zeichmann, Toronto Metropolitan University, Canada

INDEX OF AUTHORS

778

Webb, Robert L., 118
Weber, Max, 550
Wedderburn, Alexander J. M., 40n34, 87n42, 353n31
Wedel, Mathew J., 120n20
Weinstein, Benjamin, 215n28
Weiss, Johannes, 37
Weiss, P., 152n17
Weiss, Ze'ev, 447n8
Weissenrieder, Annette, 418n3, 420n7, 424n23, 426n28
Wellhausen, Julius, 362
Wellman, Barry, 241n6
Wendt, Heidi, 179n31, 183n46, 186n54
Werker, Ella, 242n10, 242n12
Wessinger, Catherine, 459n4
West, Jim, 164n87, 359n4, 473n41
West, M. L., 172n4
Westermann, A., 331n22
Westermann, Claus, 530
Wheeler-Reed, David, 408n15
Whelan, Matthew Philipp, 505n73
White, Benjamin G., 512n30
White, Cindel J. M., 149, 150n11
White, Claire, 149
White, Jonathan, 221n47
Whitelam, Keith, 202n1
Whitlock, Matthew G., 233n37
Whitmarsh, Tim, 332
Wickham, Chris, 301n7
Wilkins, David, 466n16, 469n26
Wilkinson, John David, 128–29n2
Williams, Catrin H., 71n20, 346n8, 455n33
Williams, Demetrius K., 7n10
Williams, Frank, 550n33, 555n50
Williams, Logan, 451n19

Williams, R. D., 335n40
Wilson, Brian C., 514n39
Wilson, R. McL., 380n27, 380n28
Wilson, Shawn, 155
Wimbush, Vincent L., 359
Winiata, Whatarangi, 530
Winter, Dagmar, 104n25
Wischnewetzky, Florence Kelley, 202–3n2
Witherington, Ben, 129n5
Witmer, Amanda, 427n31
Wohl, R., 230n26
Wold, Benjamin, 427n31
Wolff, B., 37–38n23
Woodington, J. David, 522n91, 523n95, 523n101
Woolf, B. L., 75n30, 162n74, 418n2
Wootten, David, 137n26
Wrede, William, 330
Wright, N. T., 10–11n18, 157, 358, 522n93, 543n6, 544n7, 544n9, 545n13

Yeager, Carolyn, 485
Yong, Amos, 420n8, 429n38
Young, Stephen L., 175n15, 178n27, 179n31, 180n36, 184n47, 188n58

Zealoushead, Zachary, 219n41
Zeichmann, Christopher B., 9, 286n4, 287n6, 287n8, 289n12, 294n16
Zemer, Avshalom, 243n15
Zetterholm, Magnus, 272n9
Zimmermann, Ruben, 77–78n2, 94n68, 101n18
Zola, Nicholas, 90n56
Zucconi, Laura M., 422n14, 422n15, 423n19
Zumstein, Jean, 345–46n5
Zumthor, Paul, 86

Index of Subjects

adultery, 400–401

anti-Semitism/anti-Judaism, 60–61, 358, 367–69, 456; and the ethical aims of historical Jesus scholarship, 367–69; German Protestant, 359–63; hate crimes and violence, 367–69, 483–85

apocalypticism, 12–13, 457–74; CenSAMM definition, 458–59; definitions, 458–61; eschatological suffering in Jewish apocalyptic eschatology traditions, 488, 494–500; Hobsbawm on peasant millenarianism and rural banditry, 459–61; the Jesus movement and apocalyptic eschatological tribulation traditions, 352–55, 500–501; the Jesus movement and social upheavals in first-century Galilee, 470–73; Jesus's healing miracles in the Hellenistic theo-medical landscape, 422–24; John Ball and the 1381 English peasants' uprising, 218–20, 464–69, 471–73; and millenarianism, 457–74; pre-political, 12–13, 457–74; Reed's comparative approach (as product of displaced elites), 461–64; the suffering of the righteous, 496

archaeology, biblical: evidence for military personnel and sites in prewar Judea,

290–91, 292–97; and "New Testament background," 128–30; problematic notion of "proof" language and, 142–43; and the so-called Third Quest, 130, 133–34. *See also* material and visual culture

armies and soldiers. *See* militarism in early Roman Palestine

Asclepius cult, 417, 419, 424–25, 428–29

aura. *See* fame and aura

Ball, John (fourteenth-century English priest), 218–20, 464–69, 471–73

baptism of Jesus, 53, 99–100n13, 121–23, 162–63, 344, 446–47, 455, 492

Bar Kokhba Revolt, 483, 542–43, 556

biography and reconstruction of the historical Jesus, 23–25, 62–76; ancient Greco-Roman genre of biography (*bioi*), 64–70, 73, 74, 329, 332, 391; chronological ordering of events in the Gospels, 74–75; and "fictionalization" in ancient biography, 66–70; and form criticism, 63; the Gospels and *chreiai* (anecdotes), 71–73, 74; the Gospels and historical material, 70–73; the Gospels and oral transmission, 63; the Gospels'

teachings and Jewish tradition, 194–95; the Gospels and Paul on the universal Jesus and gentile mission, 55–58; the Gospels' Jewish Jesus in Galilean Jewish milieu, 50–53, 60–61; the Gospels' unique Jesus, 53–55, 58, 60–61; the Gospels' un-Jewish Jesus, 53, 60–61; Hennell and English dissenting tradition, 204–6; how the narrative genre shaped Gospel depictions of Jesus, 59–60; and Jesus's anticipation of suffering in a Jewish apocalyptic eschatological context, 488, 494–500; John's use of the identity label *Ioudaioi* ("Jew"), 56–57, 363–67; and observance of Jewish law, 186–87, 194–95, 395, 455–56; and ritual purity laws, 395, 455–56; Thurman on, 43–44. *See also* race, ethnicity, and whiteness; Second Temple Judaism; synagogues and civic institutions
John the Baptist, 114, 119, 121–23, 166–67, 175, 239, 314, 422, 492; baptism of Jesus, 53, 99–100n13, 121–23, 344, 446–47, 455, 492; continuance of the Baptist movement after his death, 546–47; and the Dositheans, 166, 552; as independent Jewish mythmaker, 180; and Jesus's expectation of suffering, 491–92; and the Mandaeans, 546–47; and pre-political apocalypticism and millenarianism, 461, 463; prophetic role and death, 492; and ritual purity in the ancient world, 446–47, 455; and sex workers, 414; violence/trauma and beheading of, 478–79, 481, 485
Judas the Galilean, 204, 206, 281, 545, 548
Justin Martyr, 483, 503–6

"keying," 480–83, 485–86. *See also* violence and trauma
King, Coretta Scott, 504–5
King, Martin Luther, Jr., 42–43, 44, 503–6
Kleinliteratur, 63, 79

Last Supper, 160, 165, 411; artistic depictions, 223–24; Paul's account and language of transmission of tradition, 494; visionary origin, 165
late Latin quest for the "historical Jesus" (late Roman North Africa), 191–200; antecedents, 191–93; Augustine as historical thinker, 196–200; Augustine's polemic

against Faustus, 191–93, 196–200; Faustus's arguments about historical Jesus, 192–95, 199–200; Manichaean Christology, 192–200
Les maîtres fous (1955 film), 441–42
lived religion paradigm, 152–53, 165–68
Lord's Prayer, 247, 258, 260, 315

Mandaeans, 166, 546, 556n55
Manichaeans: application of lived religion paradigm to, 152n20; Augustine's polemic against Faustus, 191–93, 196–200; Christology and the late Latin quest in Roman North Africa, 192–200; Faustus's arguments about historical Jesus, 192–95, 199–200; persistence of the movement, 556n55
Māori of Aotearoa New Zealand: concept of *raupapa*, 533; *moemoeā* (visions/dreams), 157–59, 168; ontologies and mountains as ancestors, 154; self-identity as *tangata whenua* (people of the land), 532–33, 536, 538; studying *whakapapa* in conjunction with history, 529–30; *whakapapa* and *whenua* (land), 532–34; *whakapapa* methodology applied to Matthew's genealogy of Jesus, 12, 528–40. *See also* genealogy of Jesus
Marcionite Christians, 193n5
Markan priority, theory of, 360–63, 369
Mary. *See* slavery/enslavement
masculinities, theory of, 26–27, 402
masturbation, 413–14
material and visual culture, 128–46; archaeology and "New Testament background," 128–30; artistic depictions of a "Palestinian" Jesus and biblical scenes, 136–38, 145–46; biblical sites and the Christian tourism industry, 140–42; Dalman and Palestinian context, 134–35, 138; de Vogüé and Clermont-Ganneau's studies ancient relics of Ottoman Palestine, 132–33; observations of contemporary Palestinian culture, 133–36, 145–46; packaging and presenting material culture, 139–42; problematic notion of "biblical archaeology" and "proof" language, 142–43; Renan's *Vie de Jésus* and contemporary Palestine, 133; Robinson's geographical studies of the Bible, 132; search for reliable material culture

Matthew, 56–57, 363–67; the ethnic terms *ethnos* and *ethnikos* in Matthew, 364–67; the ethnic term *xenos* in Matthew, 366–67; the ethnocentric framework of Matthew's Gospel, 363–67; Eurocentrism, 47–48, 155–56, 359, 369; German Protestant anti-Semitism and anti-Catholicism, 359–63; racist context of the theory of Markan priority and the Two Source Hypothesis, 360–63; redefining the ethical aims of scholarship, 367–69; responses to Jesus as militant revolutionary, 44–48; responses to Thurman and the civil rights movement, 42–44; rethinking ethnic terminology, 56–57, 363–67; the way forward (future research), 369–70. *See also* Jewishness of Jesus; slavery/enslavement

reception history, 3–5, 17–31; accounting for the inaccessibility of the past, 108–11; the challenge of a transgender Jesus, 28–30, 31, 415–16; as creative imagination, 30–31; and historical imagination, 19–21, 30–31; Jesus and masculinity, 26–27, 402; and memory studies, 21–23; in the Next Quest, 3–5, 18–19; question of Jesus as a unique individual, 25–26; relationship between the "history of scholarship" and, 3–5, 21–23; rhetoric of distance and aura, 224, 230, 236; the study of, 17–18; two kinds of reception-historical approaches, 108–11; writing a biography of Jesus, 23–25

redaction criticism, 33, 63, 173, 237, 347

resurrection: Bornkamm and the passion-resurrection predictions in Mark, 99–101; comparative microhistory approach to, 507–27; comparing two claims from the English Revolution, 515–21, 525; Dorcas Erbury and the Nayler incident at Exeter prison, 515–19, 525; Dositheus's nondeath and, 547, 553–55; John Robins and his followers, 519–21, 525; lived religion paradigm applied to beliefs of the early Jesus movement, 165–68; Matthew's narrative and *hoi de edistasan* (the disciples' doubt), 522–27; question of Jesus's uniqueness, 25–26, 545, 555–56; rereading the Gospel accounts and

the disciples' belief or doubt, 521–27; why historical study matters, 509–10

ritual impurity in the ancient world, 395, 445–56; the gospel writers' silence on Jesus and ritual bathing, 447–51, 455; the gospel writers' stories of Jesus's interactions with ritually impure people, 451–55; and the halakhic Jesus (the law-observant Jewish Jesus), 395, 455–56; and Jesus's healing miracles, 395; and John's ritual immersion of Jesus, 446–47, 455; stories of Jesus and corpses, 454; stories of people with *lepra*, 449, 452–53, 454; story of Jesus and the hemorrhaging woman, 312, 321, 340, 413, 453–54. *See also* bodies and embodiment; sexuality

Robins, John, 519–21, 525

Robinson, Edward, 132

Romero, Óscar, 503–6

Rouch, Jean, 441–42

Sabbath controversies, so-called, 53

Sandys, Edwina, 28

scribal Galilee, 247–52, 253–68, 473; archive of Sokrates son of Sarapion from mid-second-century Karanis, 248–51; challenges of talking about scribes in New Testament studies, 254–55, 264; and the early Jesus movement, 251–52, 263–66; implications for the study of the historical Jesus, 266–68; "public synagogues" and scribes' work, 280; Q scribes, 247–48, 251, 255–68; Q scribes' compositional technique and form, 259–63; scribal networks, 247–52, 263–68, 473. *See also* networks

Second Temple Judaism: Jesus's anticipation of suffering within apocalyptic eschatological context of, 488, 494–500; synagogues and Jewish civic institutions, 269–83. *See also* Jewishness of Jesus; synagogues and civic institutions

sexuality, 8–9, 26–27, 399–416; adultery, 400–401; ancient constructions of gender and, 8–9, 26–30; bridegroom metaphor, marriage, and weddings, 401–7; celibacy, virginity, and continence, 403–7, 410, 413, 415; divorce and remarriage, 399, 401, 406,

INDEX OF SCRIPTURE

Index of Other Ancient Sources